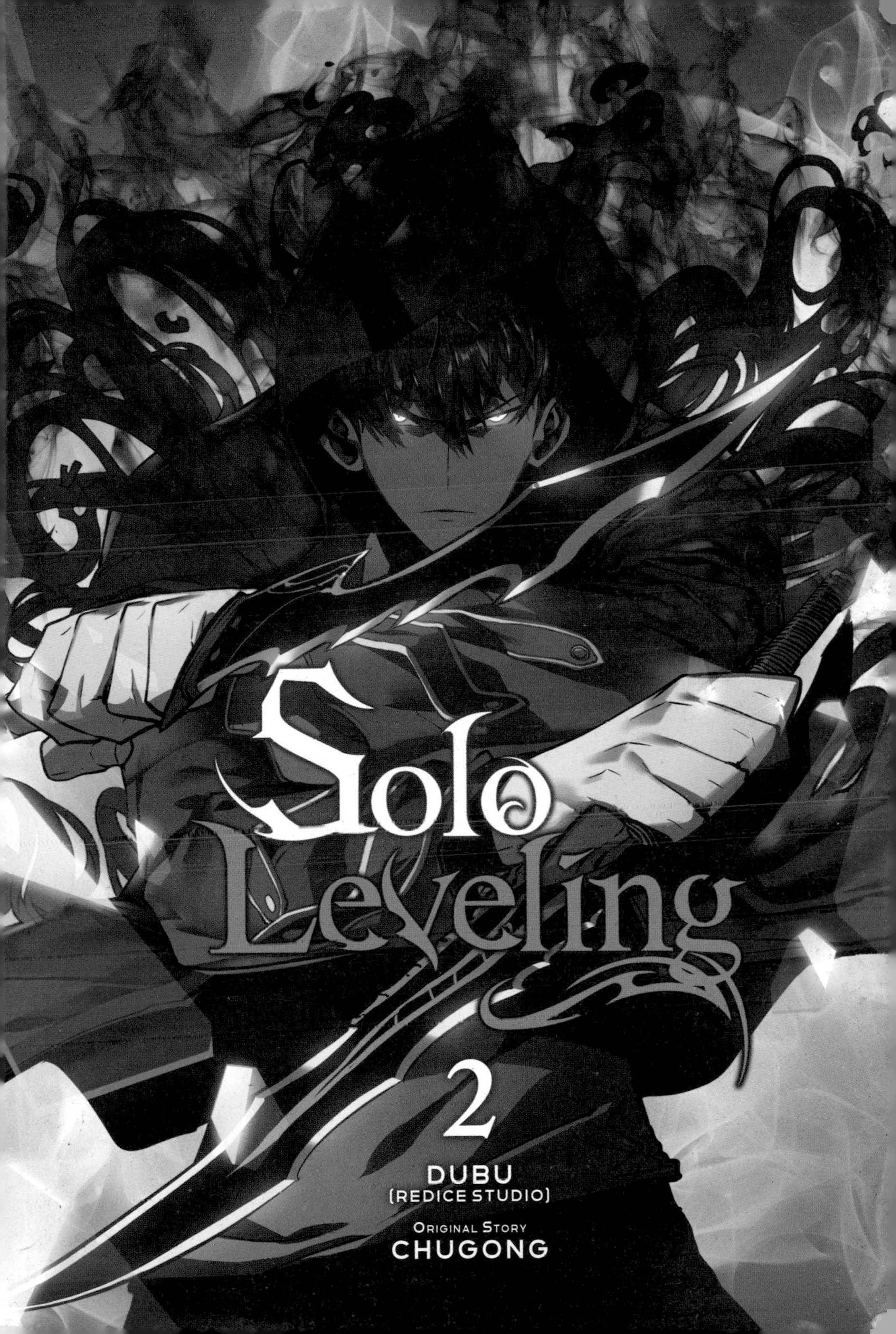
Solo Leveling
2
DUBU
(REDICE STUDIO)
Original Story
CHUGONG

CHARACTERS

Jinwoo Sung

E-rank Hunter

Joohee Lee

B-rank Hunter / Healer

Jinho Yoo

D-rank Hunter

Dongsuk Hwang

C-rank Hunter

CONTENTS

Solo
Leveling

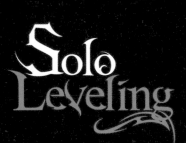

CHAPTER 3 Quest

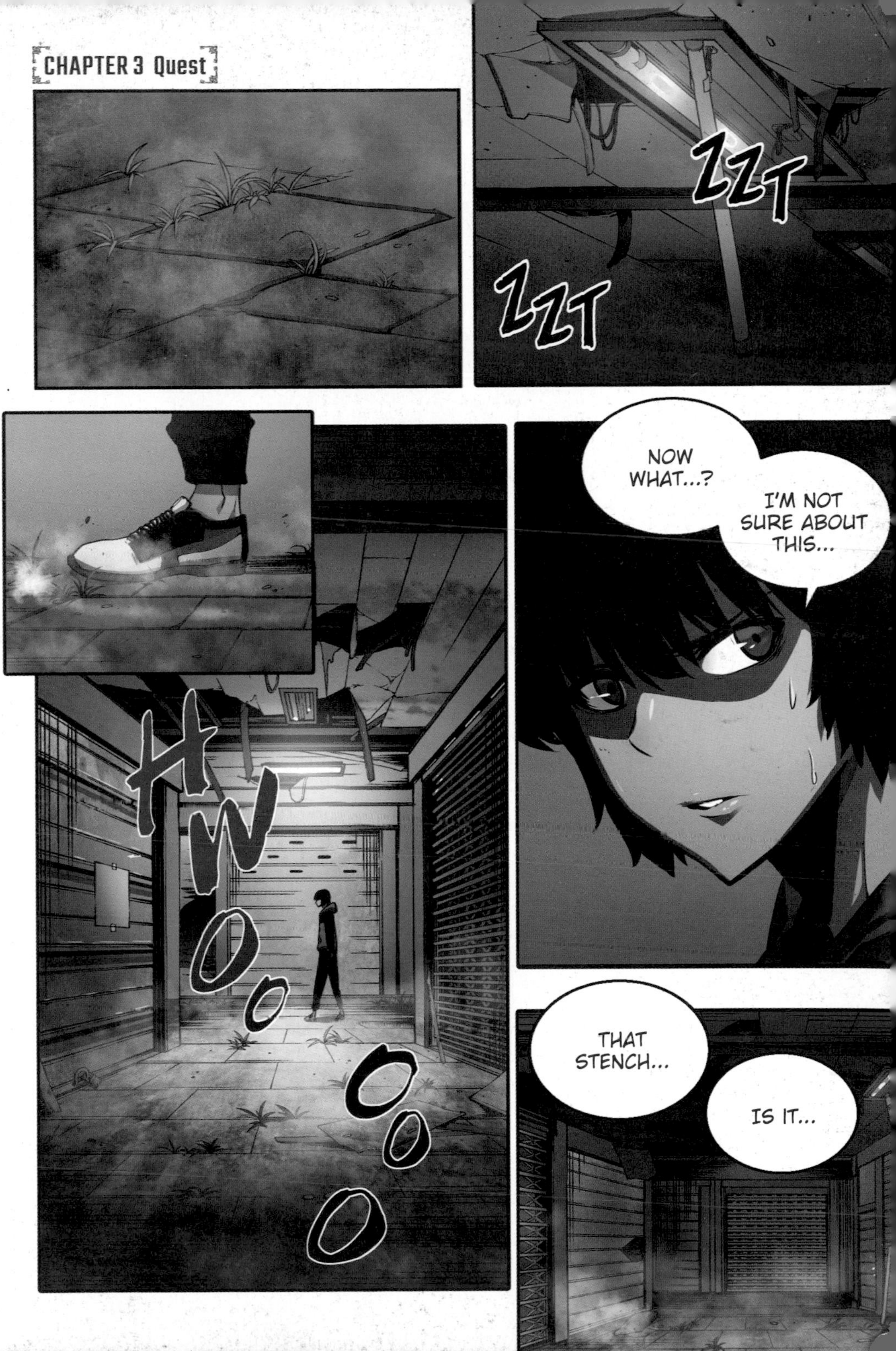

ZZT
ZZT
HWOOOOO
NOW WHAT...?
I'M NOT SURE ABOUT THIS...
THAT STENCH...
IS IT...

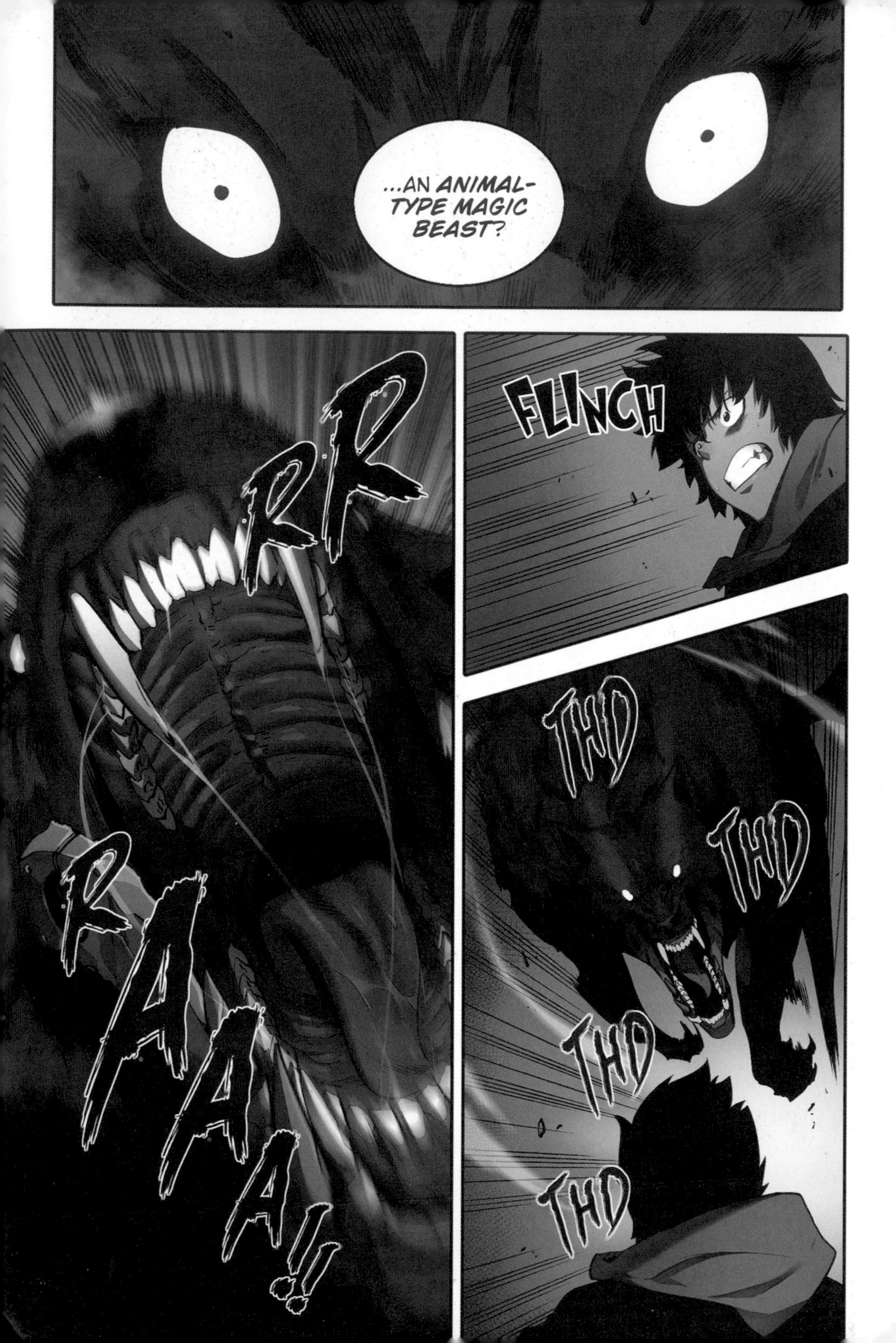

...AN ANIMAL-TYPE MAGIC BEAST?
RRRAAA!!
FLINCH
THD
THD
THD
THD

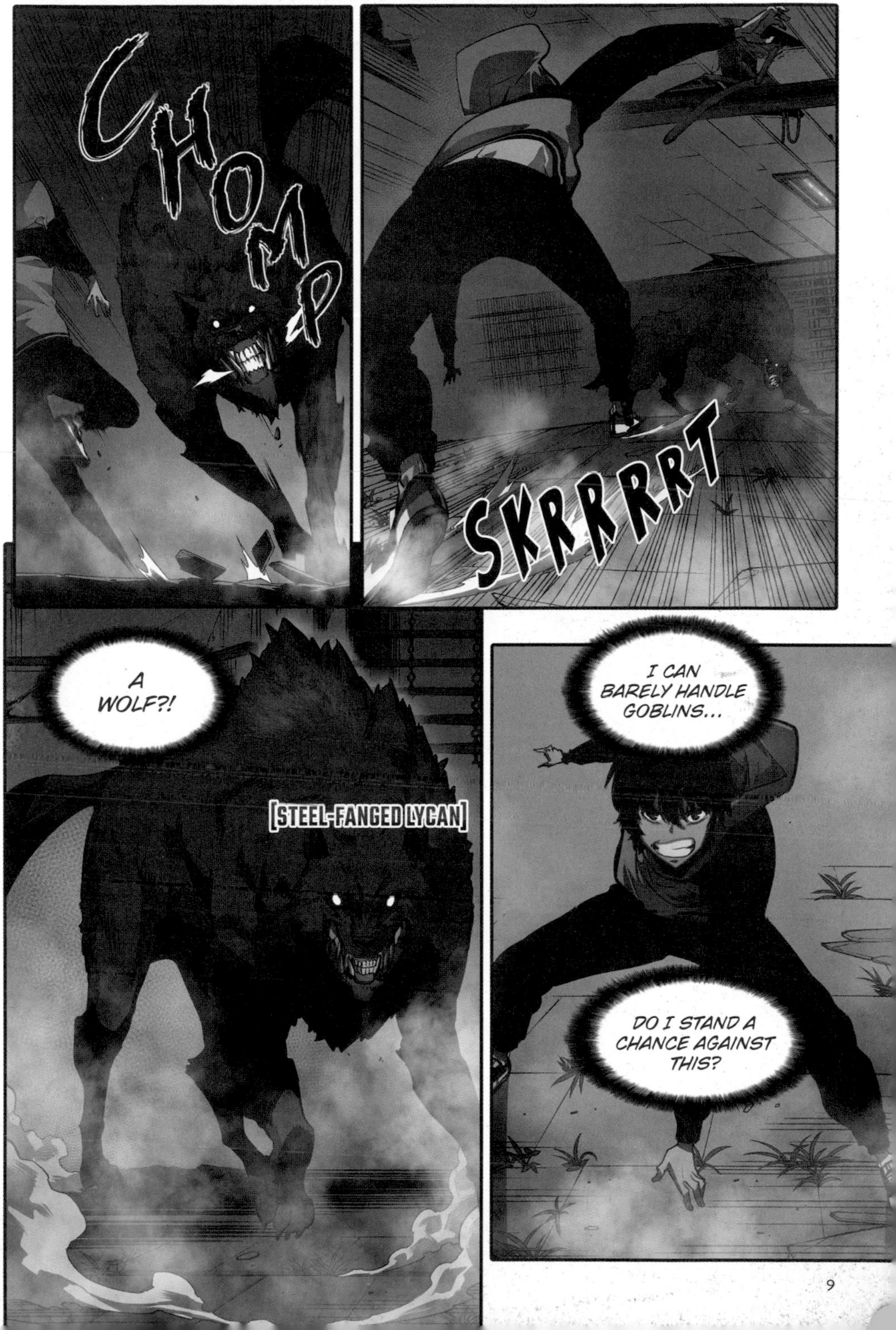
CHOMP
SKRRRRT
A WOLF?!
[STEEL-FANGED LYCAN]
I CAN BARELY HANDLE GOBLINS...
DO I STAND A CHANCE AGAINST THIS?

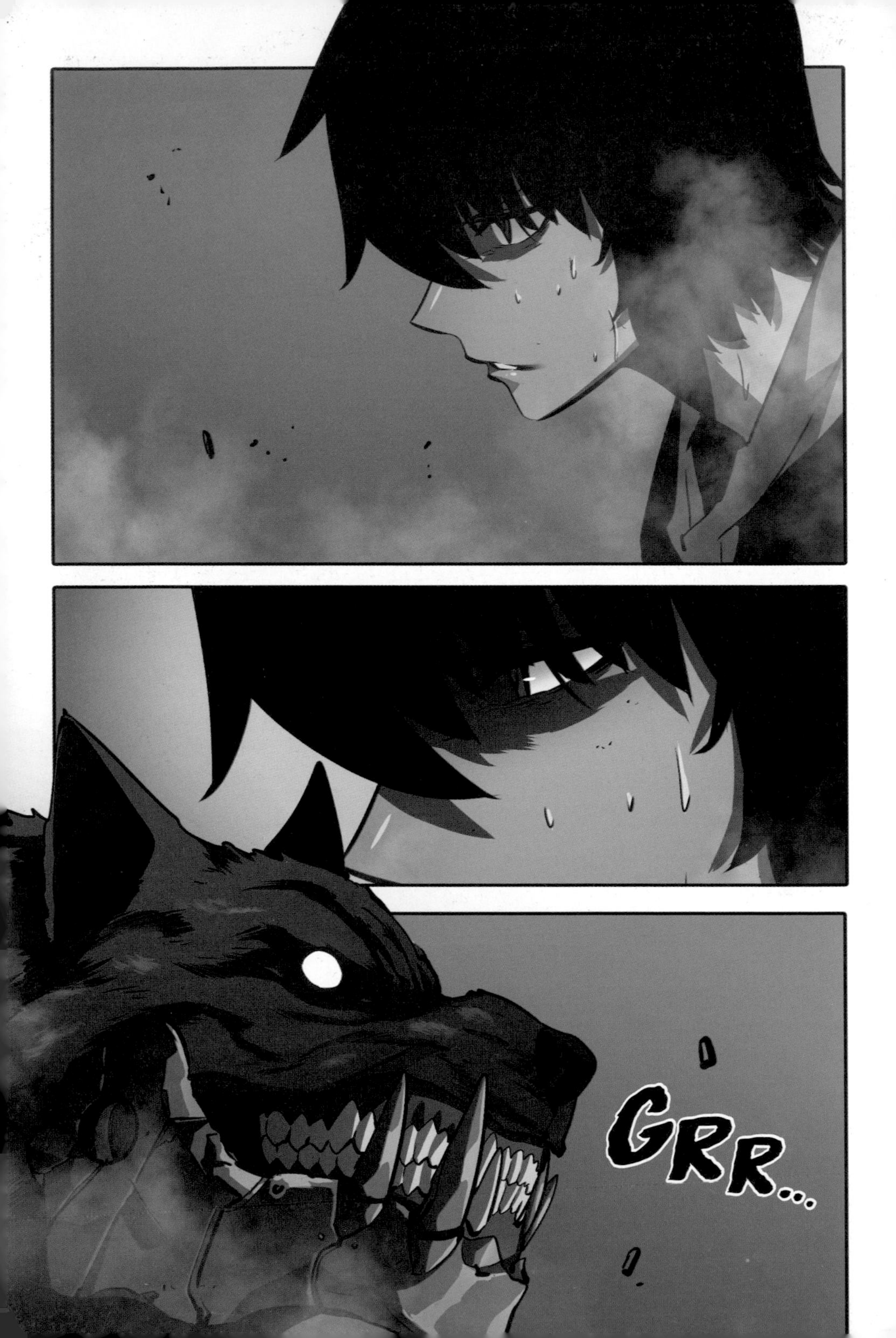
GRR...

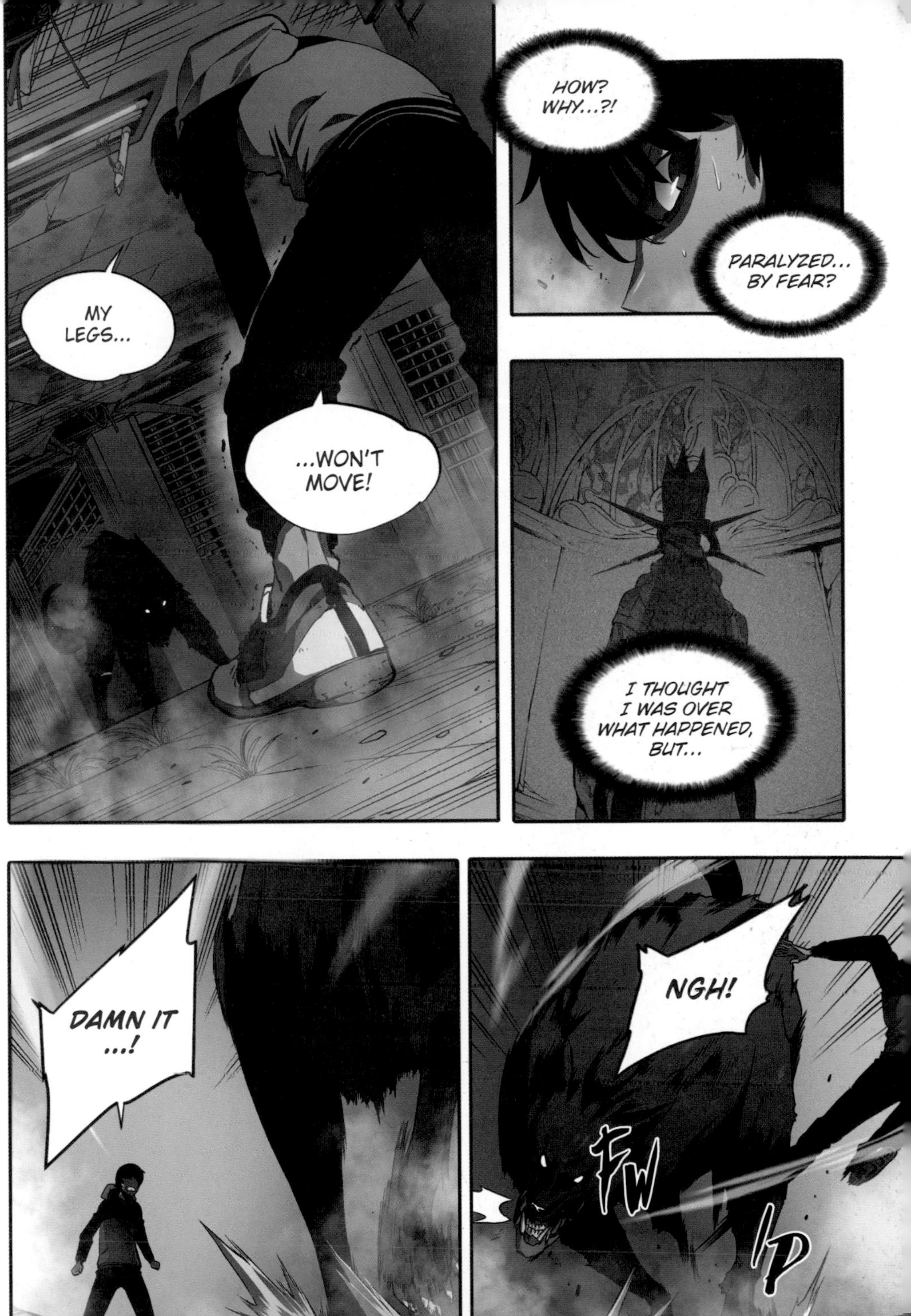
MY LEGS...
...WON'T MOVE!
HOW? WHY...?!
PARALYZED... BY FEAR?
I THOUGHT I WAS OVER WHAT HAPPENED, BUT...
DAMN IT ...!
NGH!
FWIP

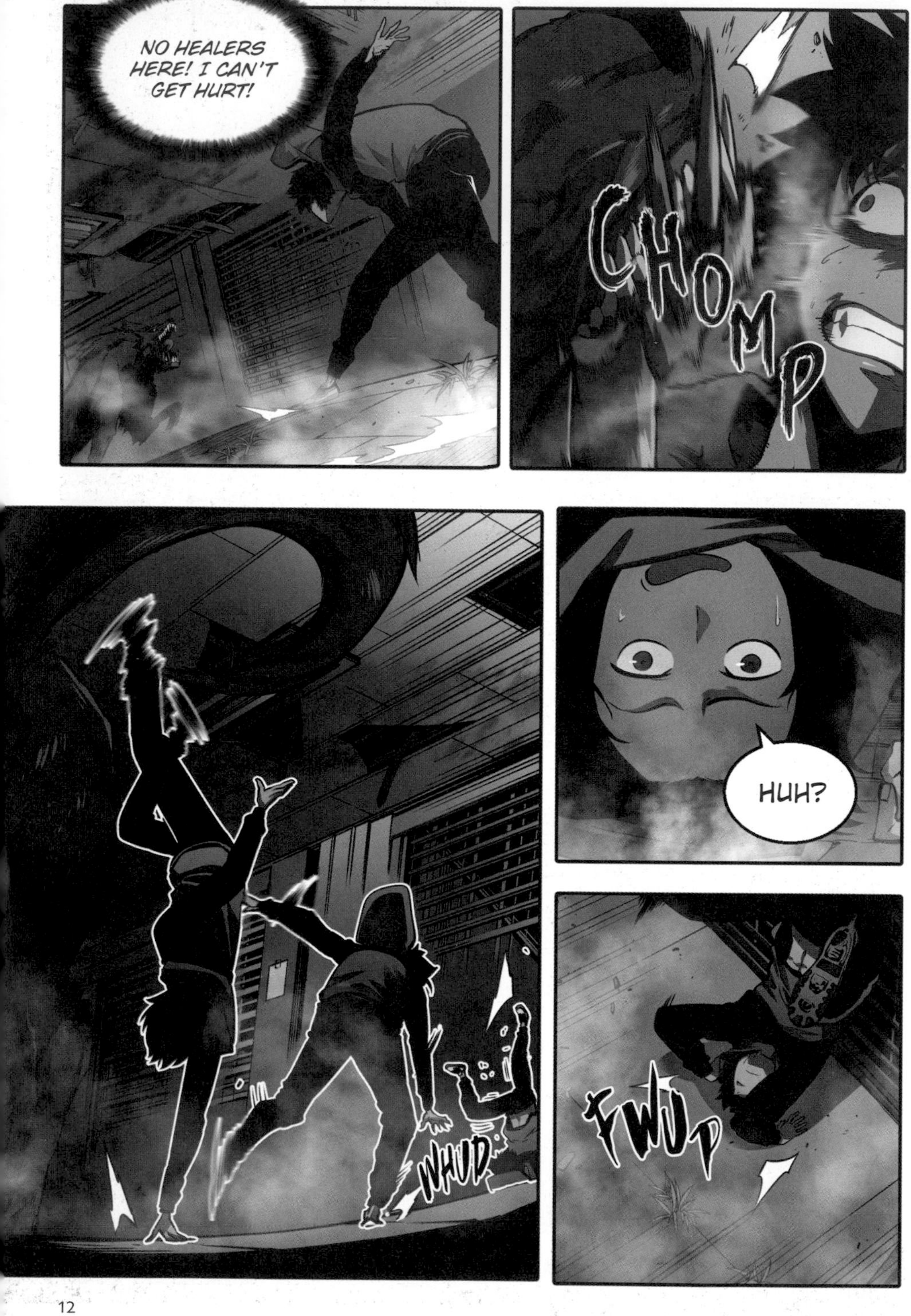
NO HEALERS HERE! I CAN'T GET HURT!
CHOMP
HUH?
WHUD
FWUP

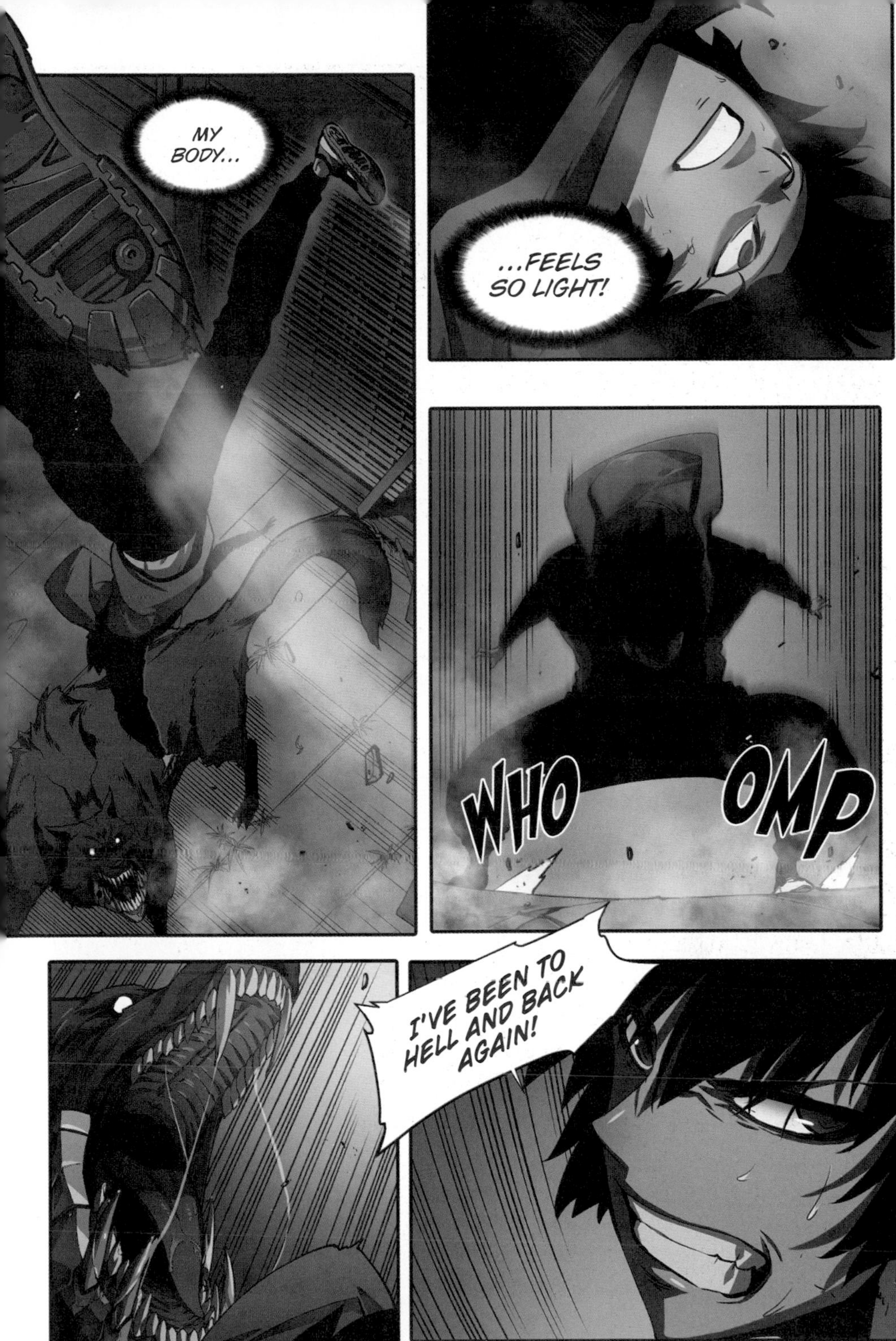
MY BODY...
...FEELS SO LIGHT!
WHO OMP
I'VE BEEN TO HELL AND BACK AGAIN!

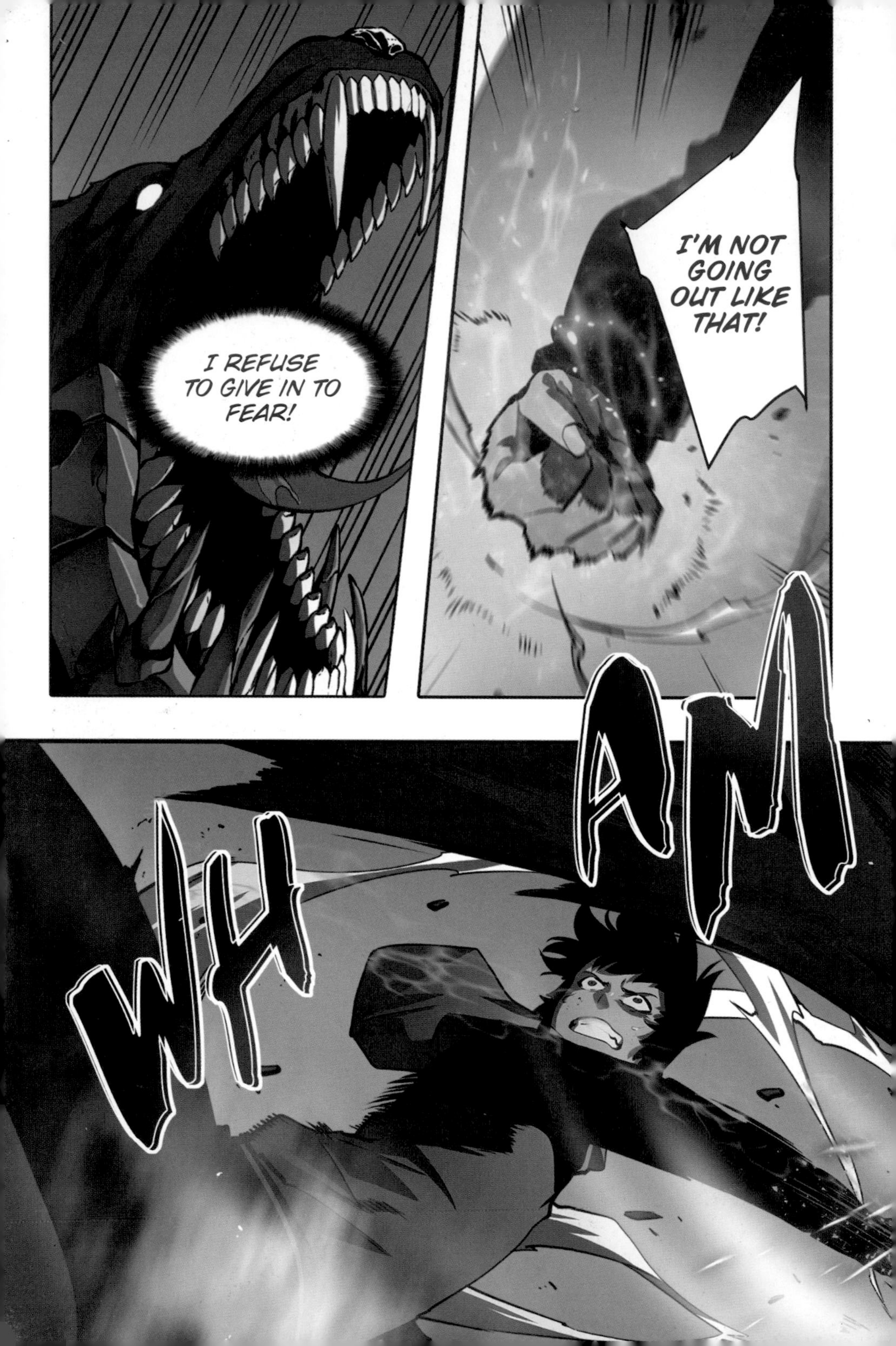
I REFUSE TO GIVE IN TO FEAR!
I'M NOT GOING OUT LIKE THAT!
WHAM

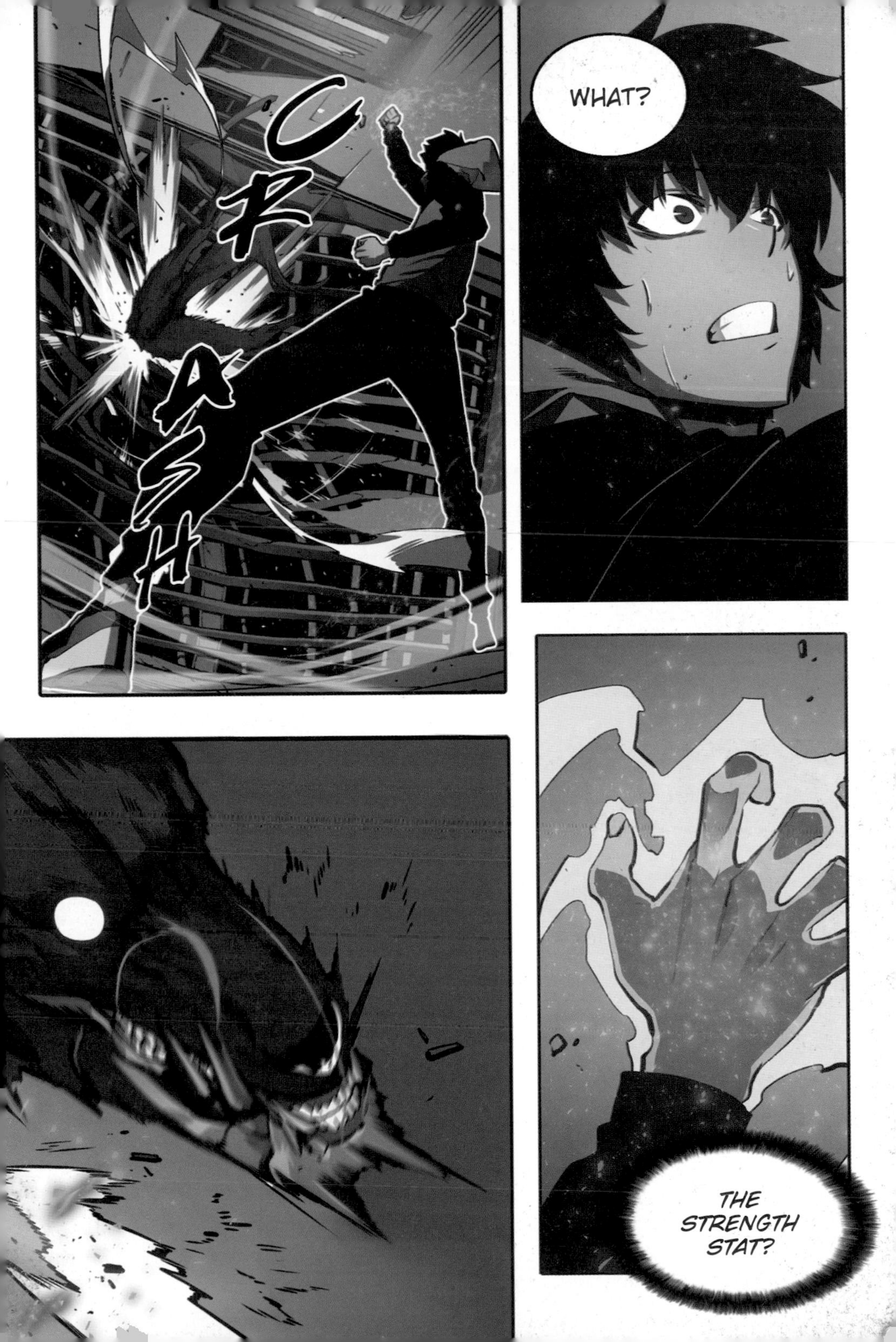
CRASH
WHAT?
THE STRENGTH STAT?

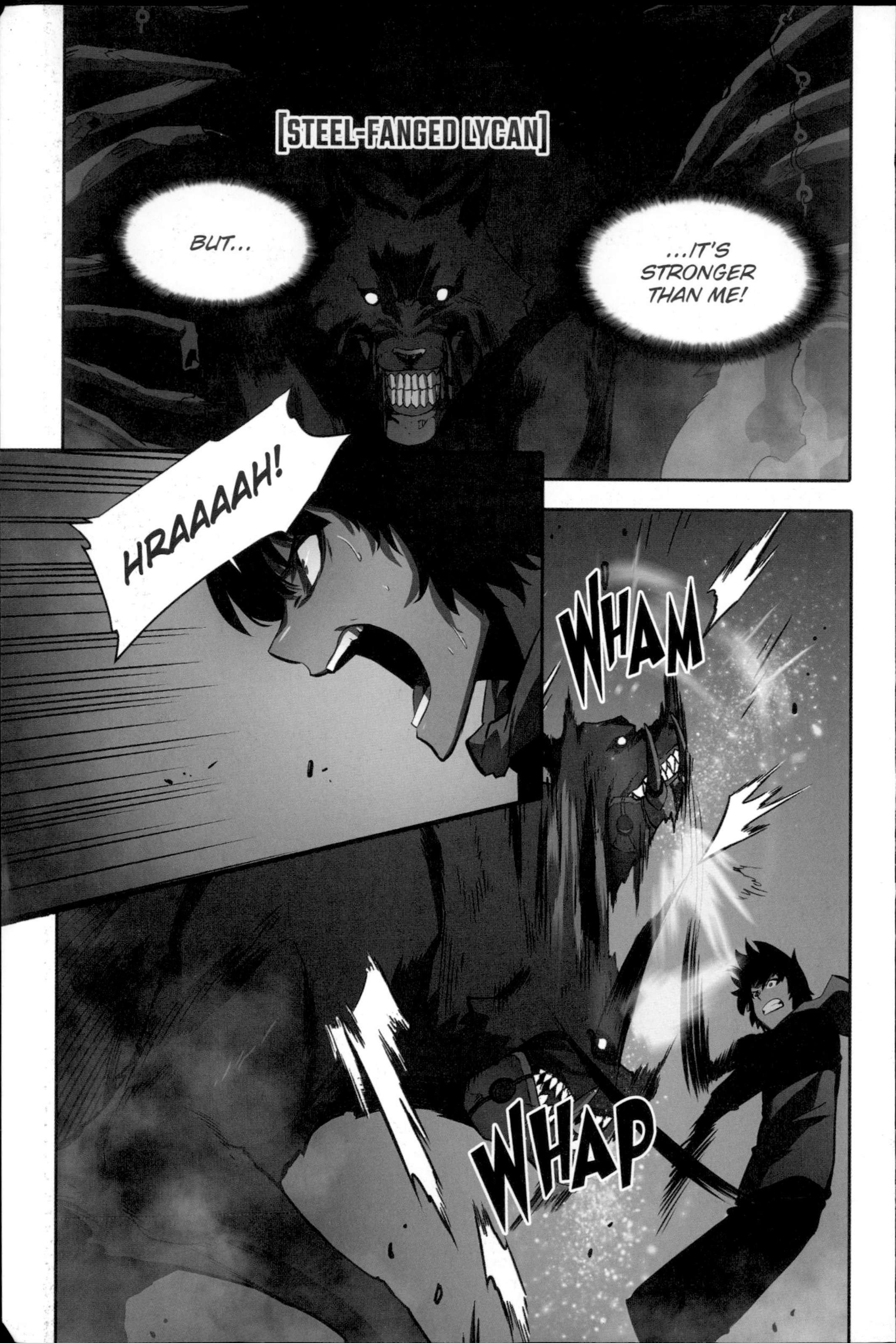
[STEEL-FANGED LYCAN]
BUT...
...IT'S STRONGER THAN ME!
HRAAAAH!
WHAM
WHAP

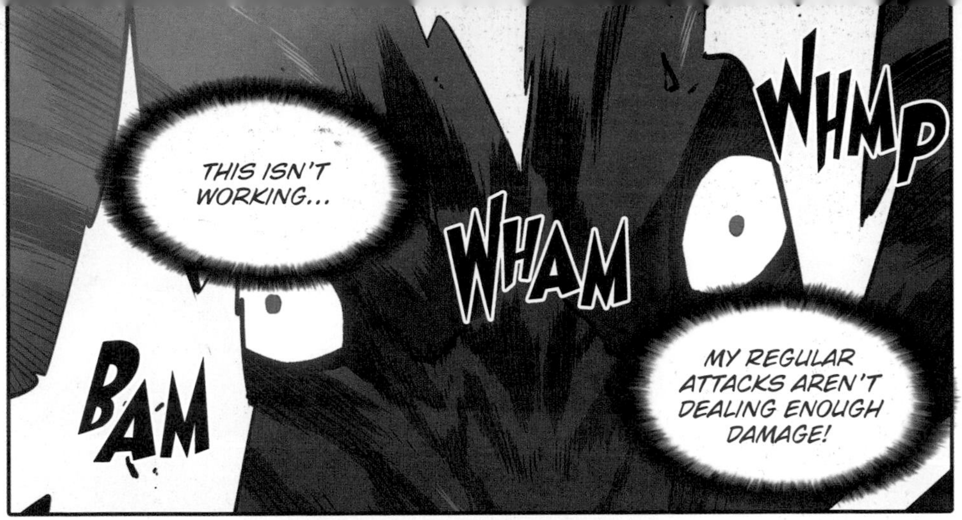
THIS ISN'T WORKING...
BAM
WHAM
WHMP
MY REGULAR ATTACKS AREN'T DEALING ENOUGH DAMAGE!

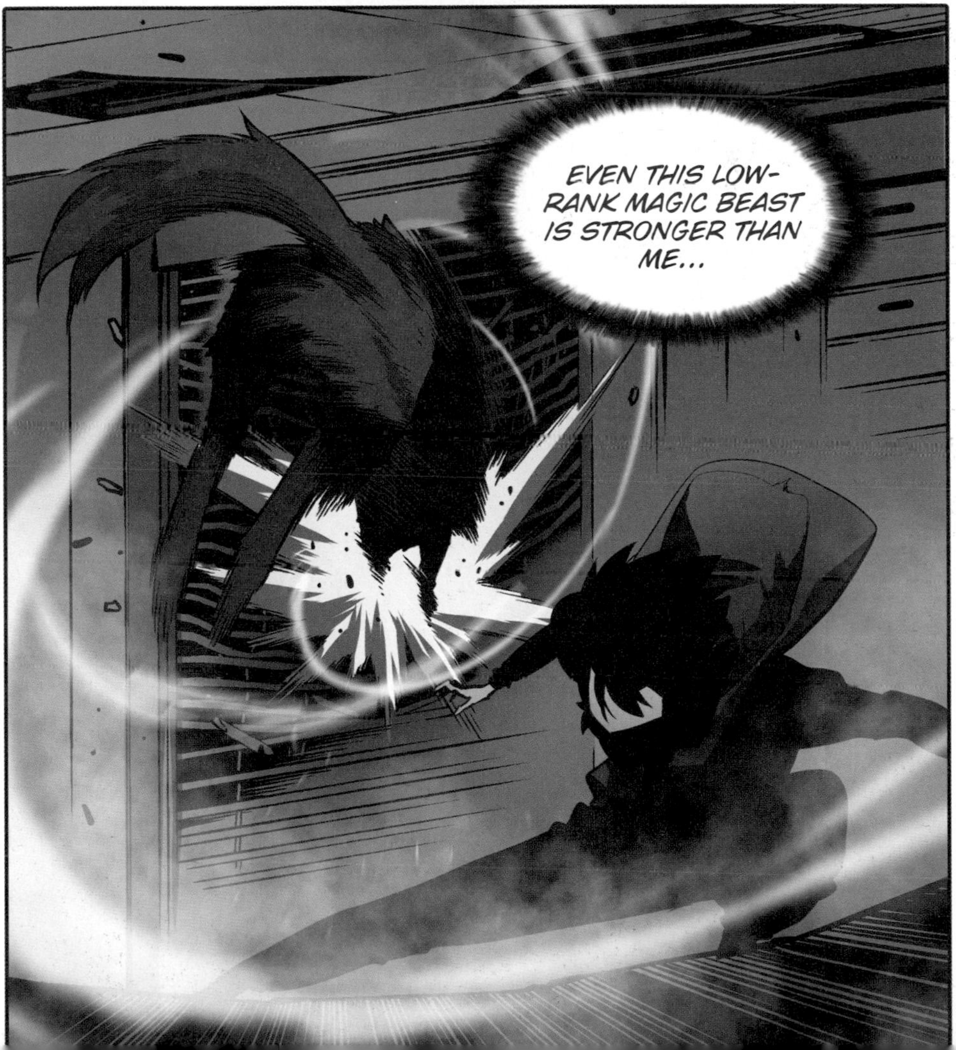
EVEN THIS LOW-RANK MAGIC BEAST IS STRONGER THAN ME...

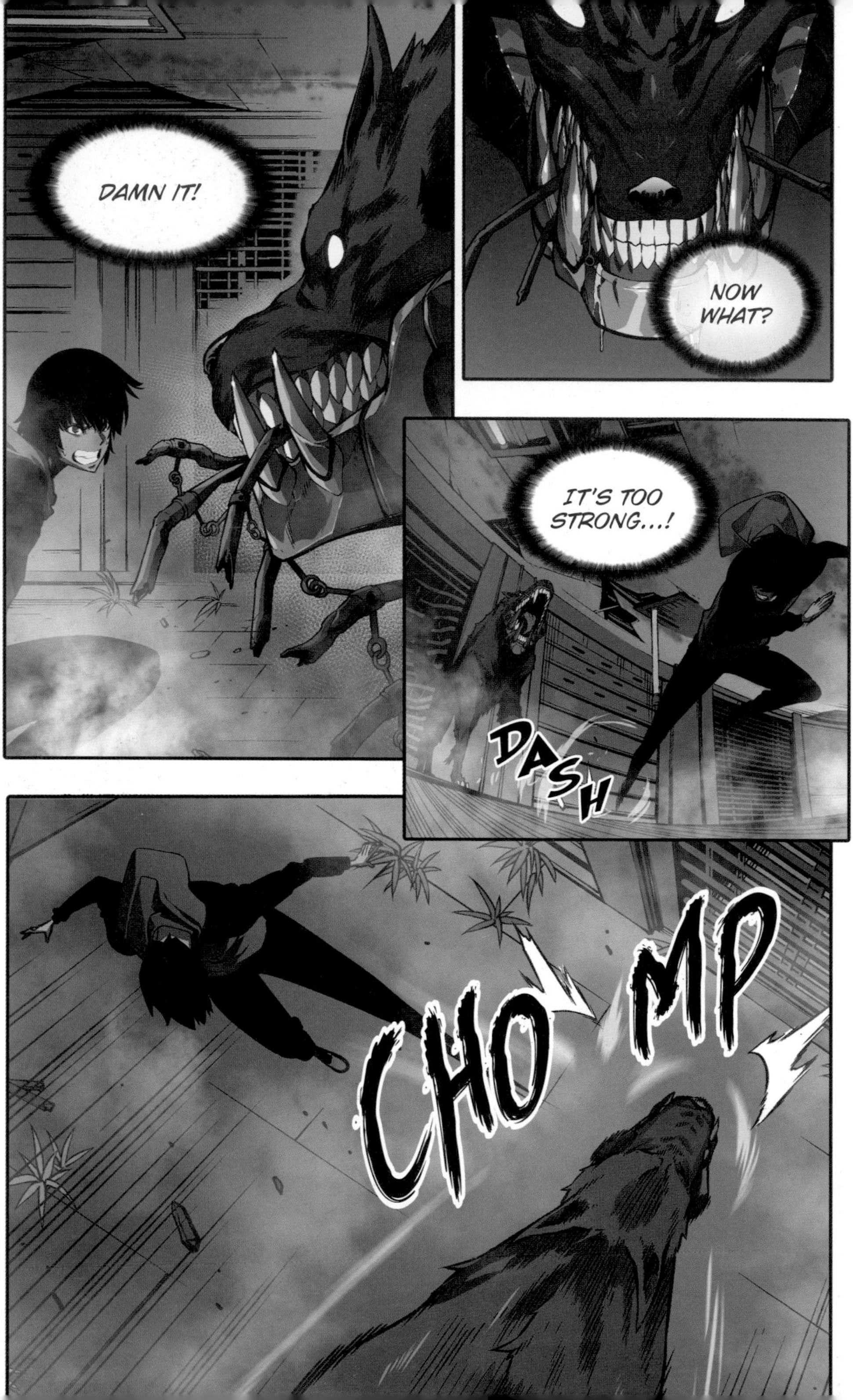
DAMN IT!
NOW WHAT?
IT'S TOO STRONG...!
DASH
CHOMP

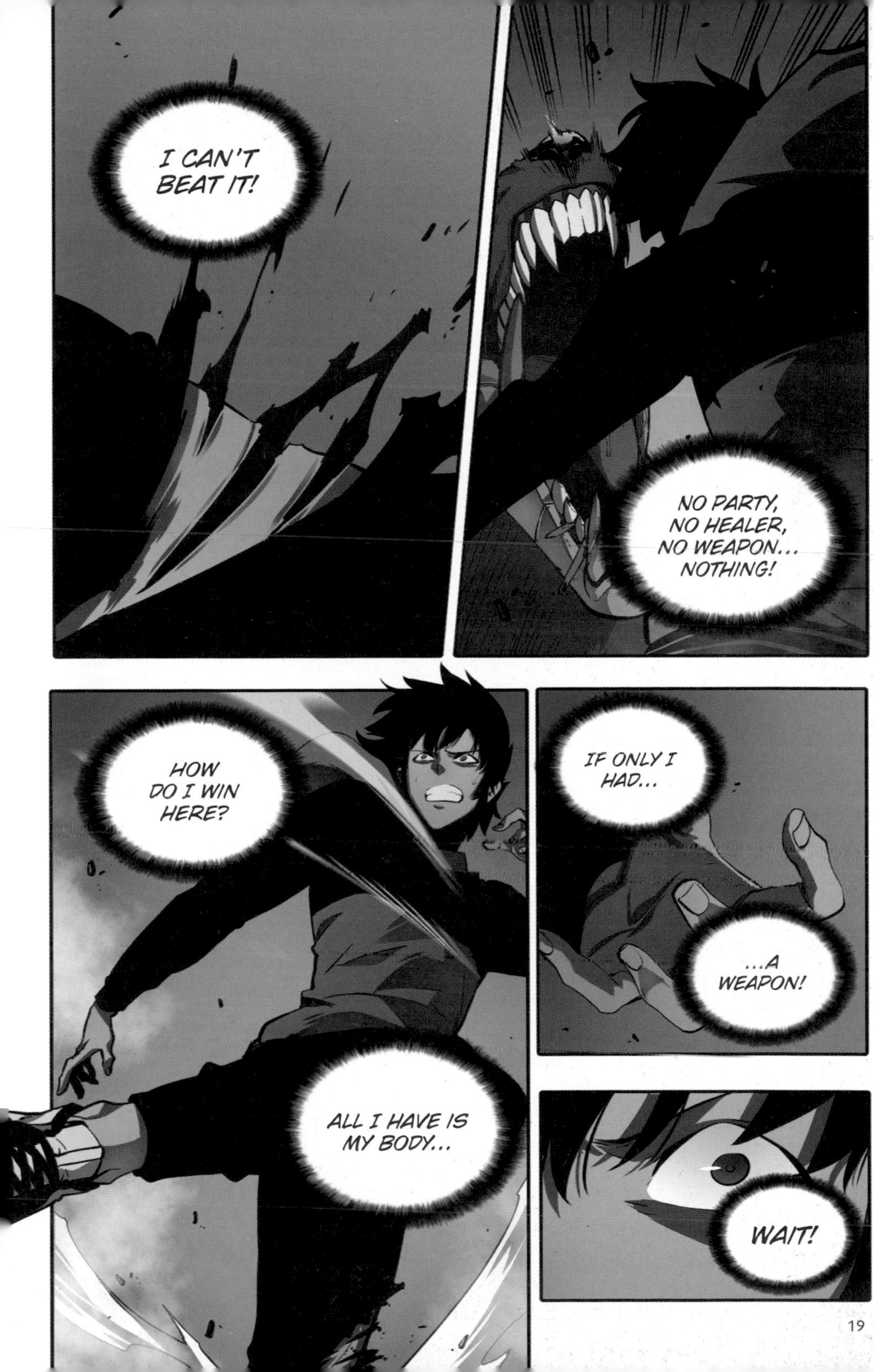
I CAN'T BEAT IT!
NO PARTY, NO HEALER, NO WEAPON... NOTHING!
HOW DO I WIN HERE?
ALL I HAVE IS MY BODY...
IF ONLY I HAD...
...A WEAPON!
WAIT!

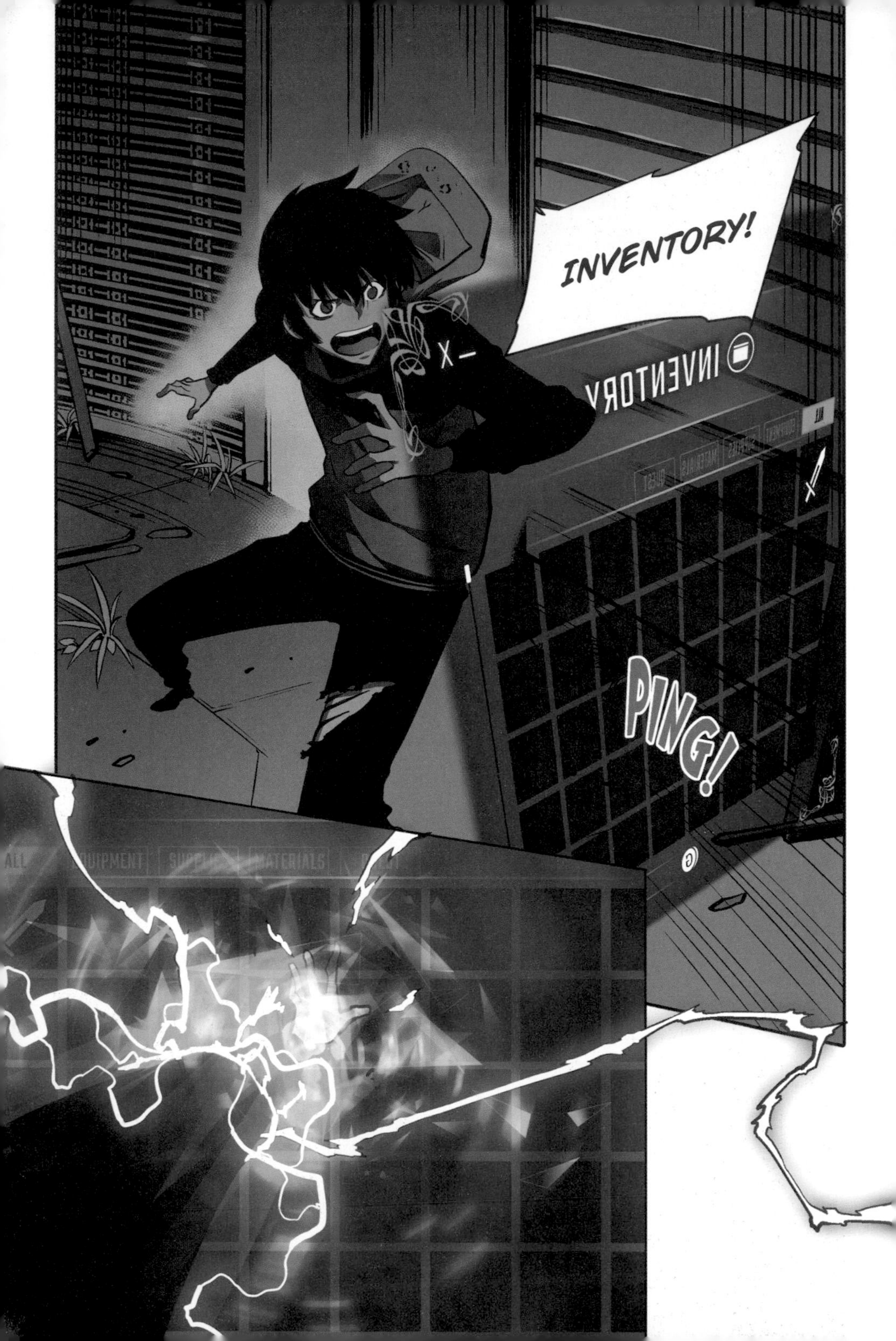
INVENTORY!
PING!

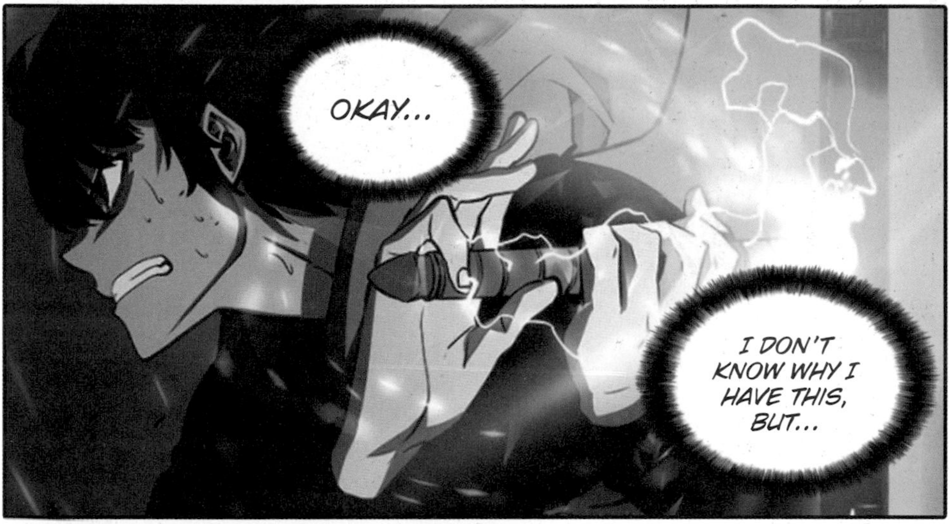
OKAY...
I DON'T KNOW WHY I HAVE THIS, BUT...
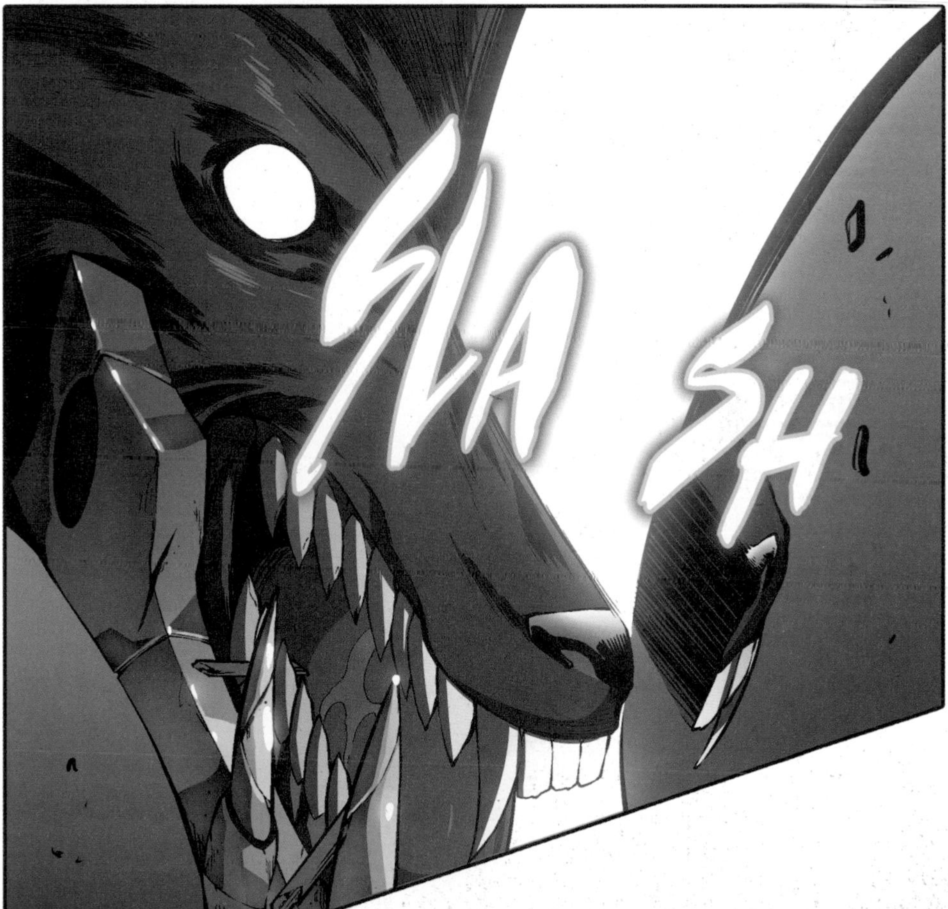
SLASH

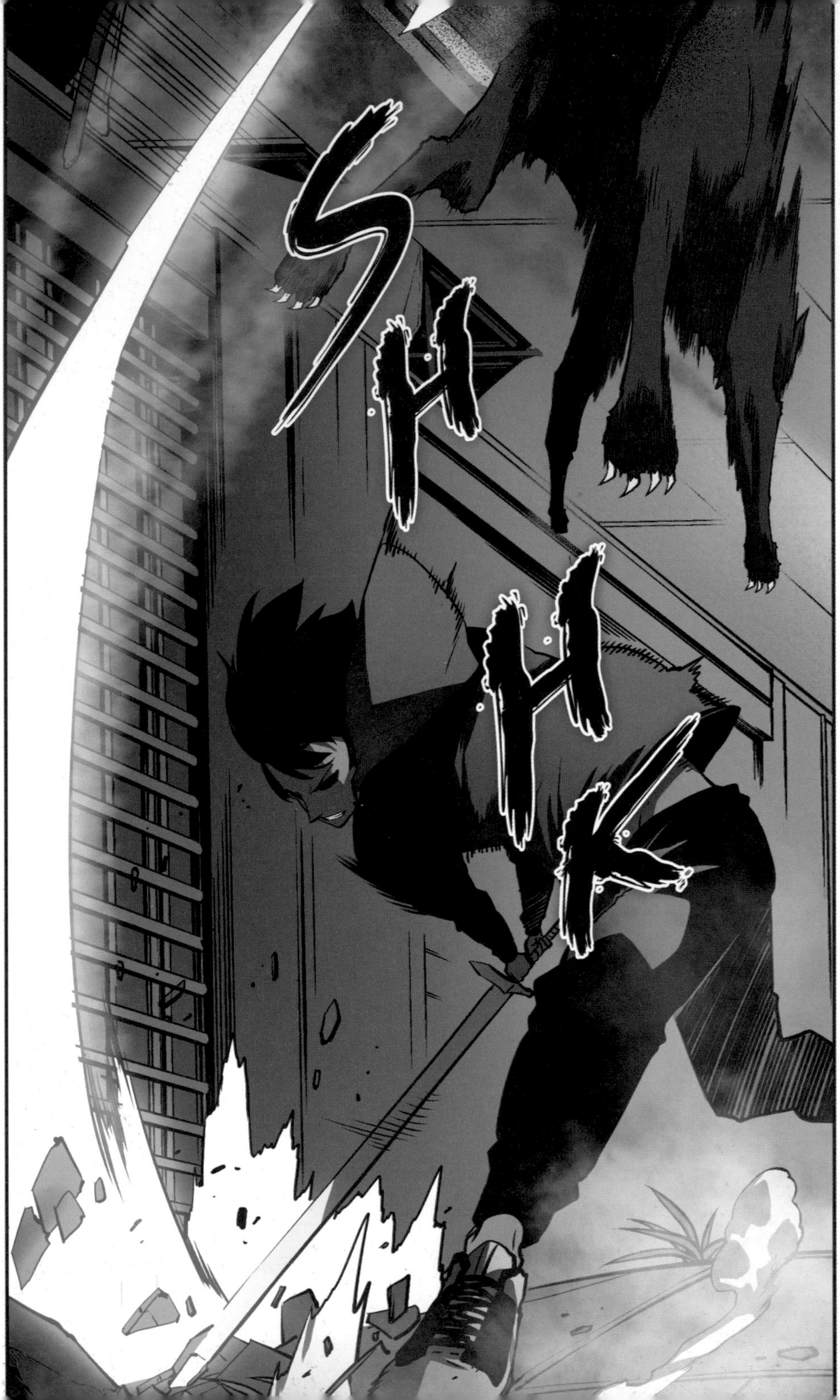
SHHK

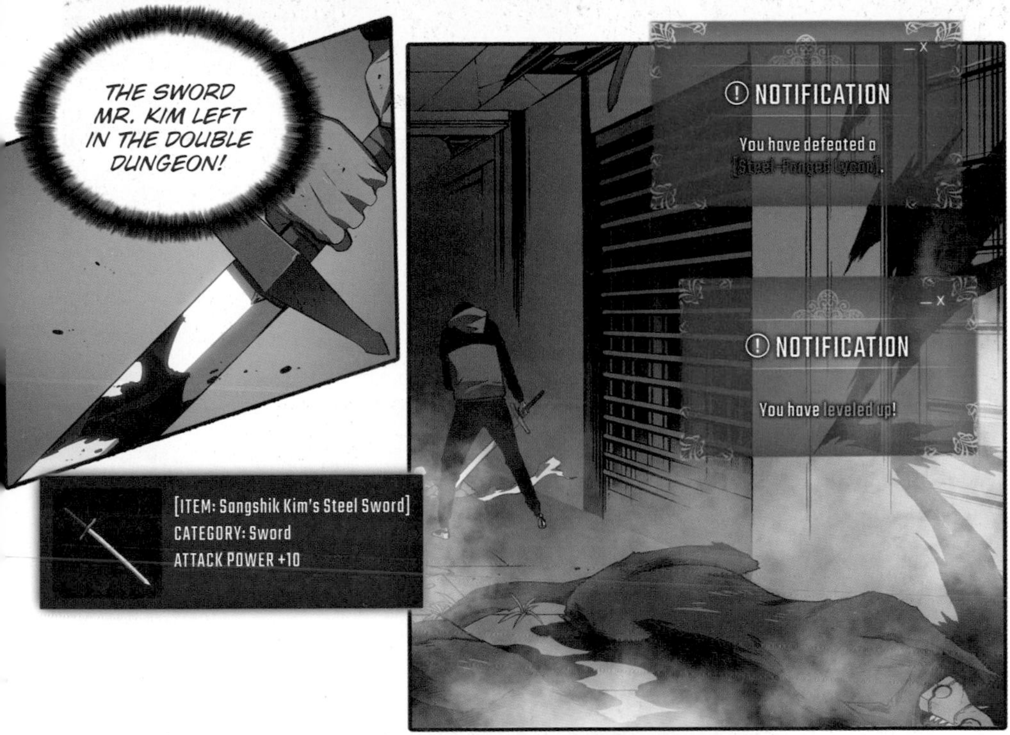
THE SWORD MR. KIM LEFT IN THE DOUBLE DUNGEON!
[ITEM: Sangshik Kim's Steel Sword]
CATEGORY: Sword
ATTACK POWER +10
NOTIFICATION
You have defeated a [Steel-Fanged Lycan].
NOTIFICATION
You have leveled up!

While exchange rates fluctuate daily, an easy conversion estimate is about 1,000 KRW to 1 USD.

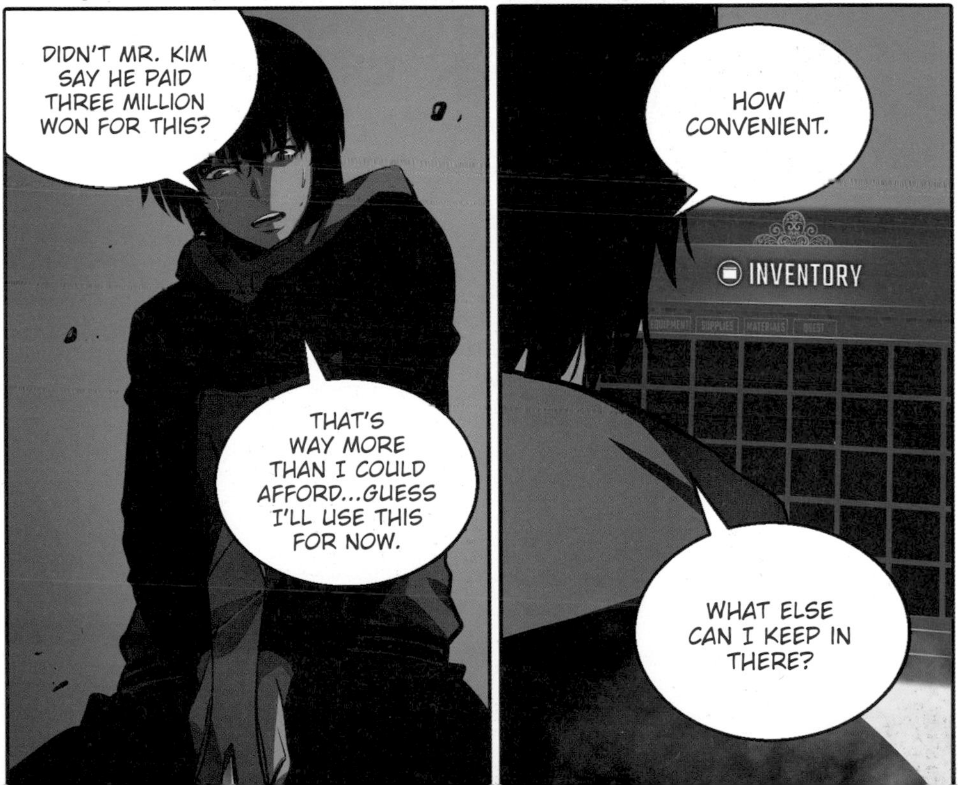
DIDN'T MR. KIM SAY HE PAID THREE MILLION WON FOR THIS?
THAT'S WAY MORE THAN I COULD AFFORD...GUESS I'LL USE THIS FOR NOW.
HOW CONVENIENT.
INVENTORY
EQUIPMENT SUPPLIES MATERIALS QUEST
WHAT ELSE CAN I KEEP IN THERE?

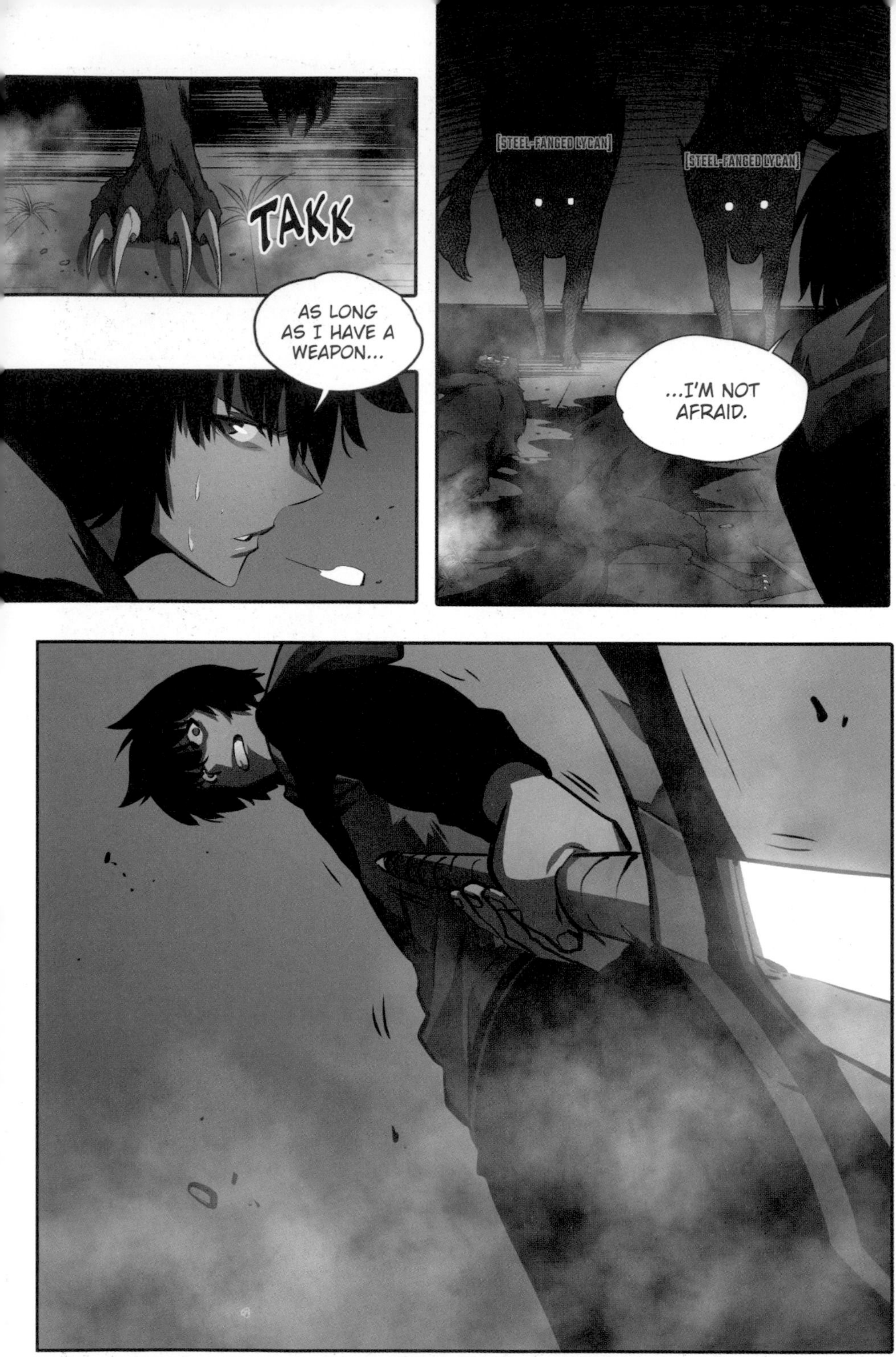
TAKK
AS LONG AS I HAVE A WEAPON...
[STEEL-FANGED LYCAN]
[STEEL-FANGED LYCAN]
...I'M NOT AFRAID.

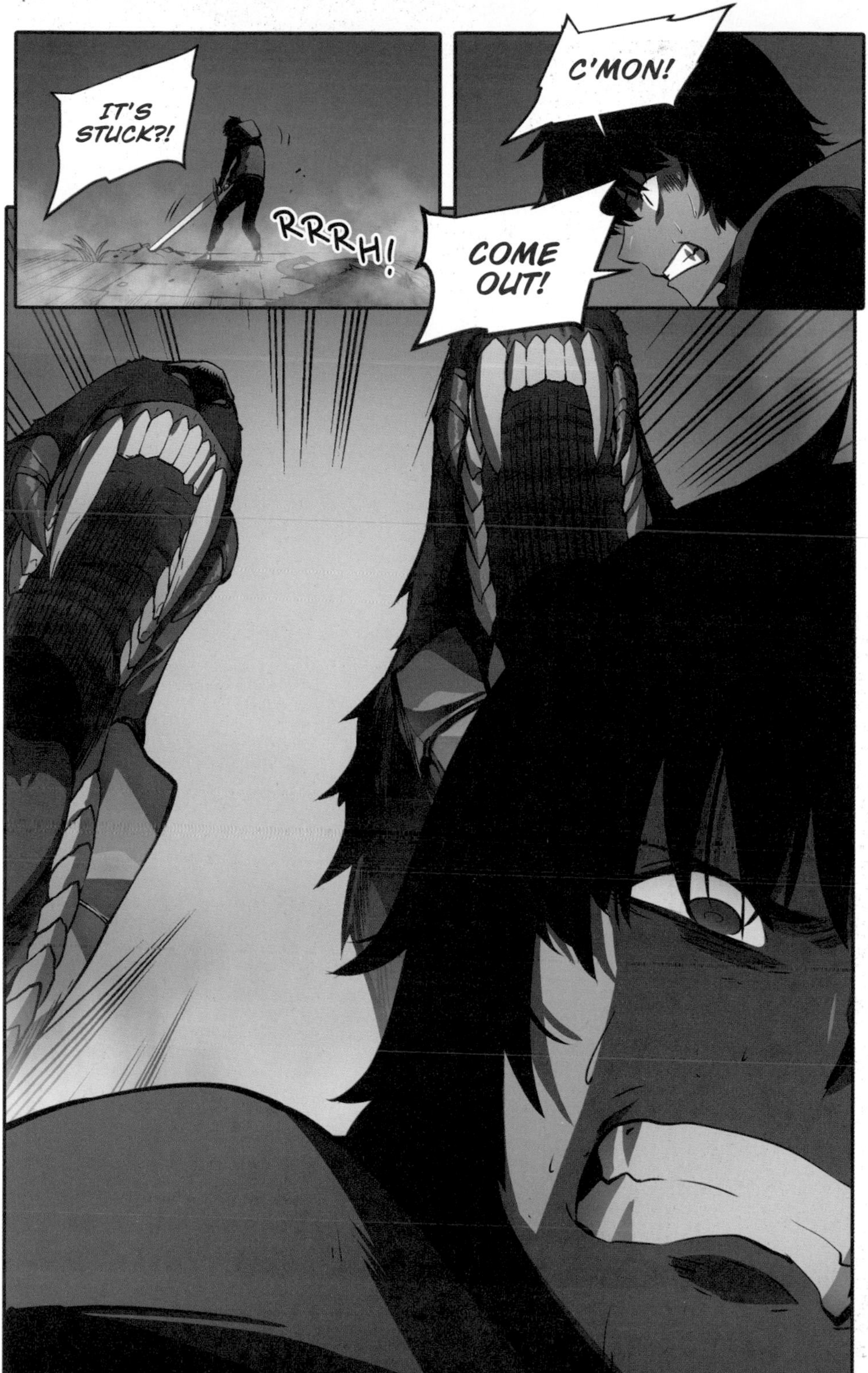
IT'S STUCK?!
RRRH!
C'MON!
COME OUT!

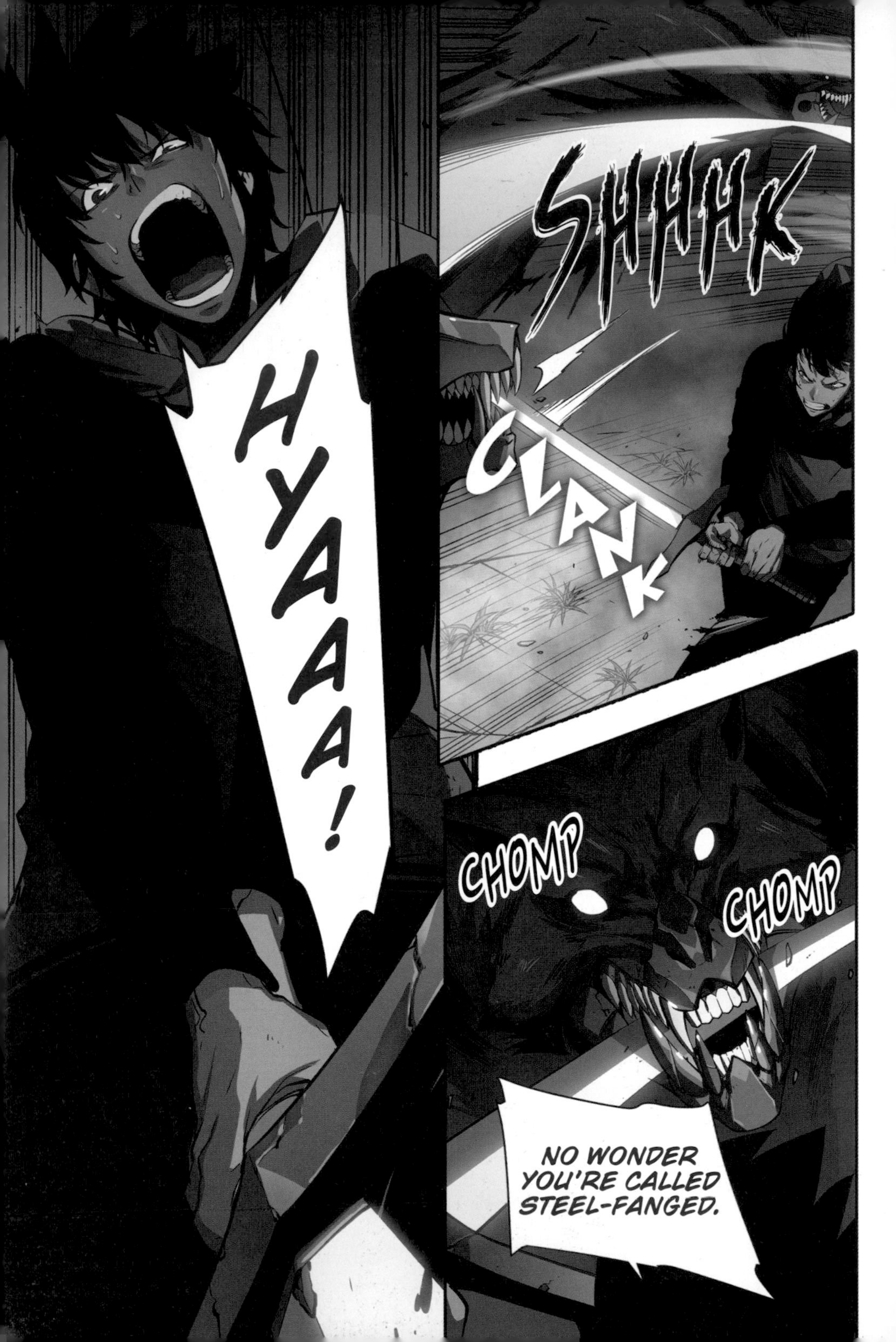
HYAAA!
SHHHK
CLANK
CHOMP
CHOMP
NO WONDER YOU'RE CALLED STEEL-FANGED.

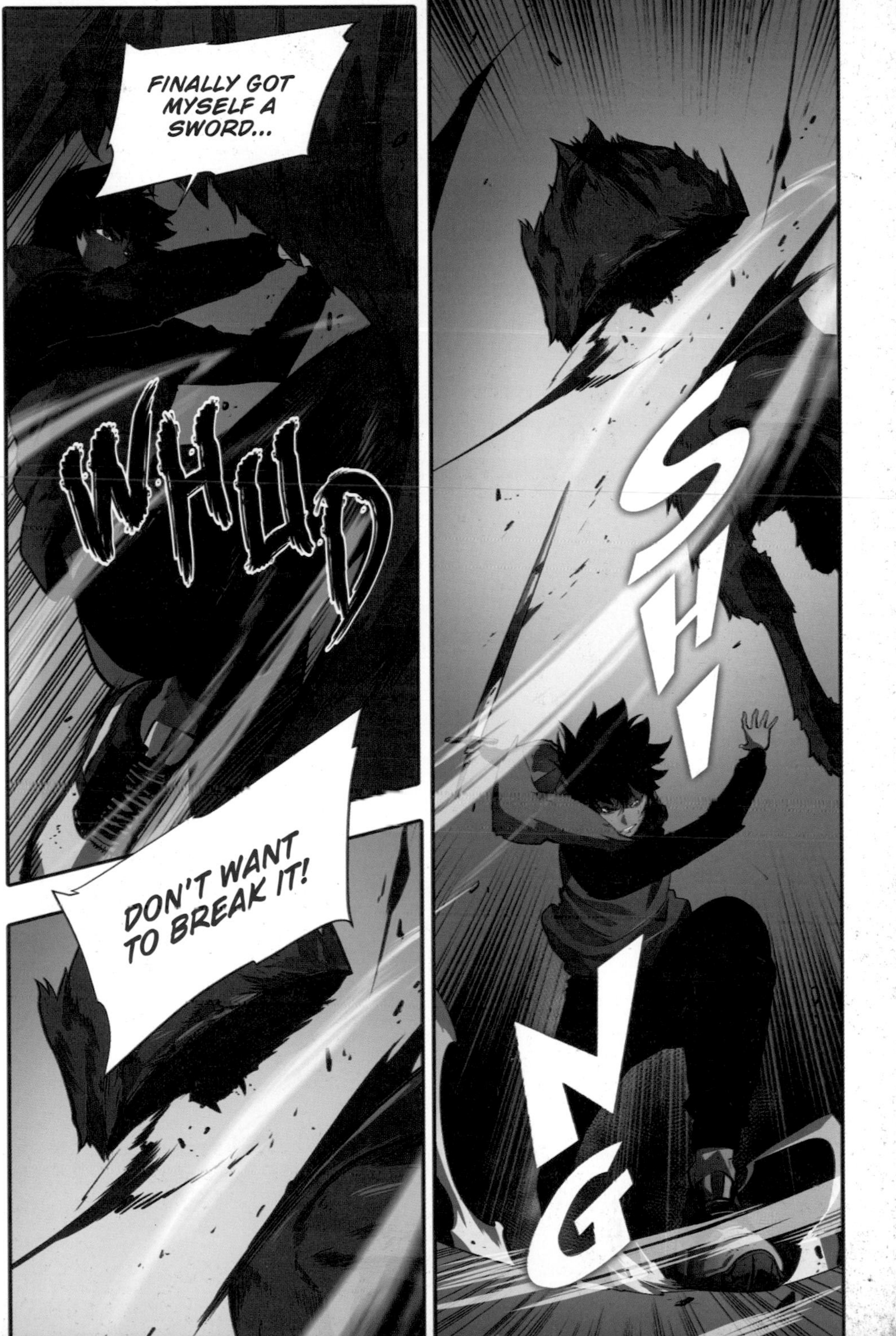
FINALLY GOT MYSELF A SWORD...
WHUD
DON'T WANT TO BREAK IT!
SHING

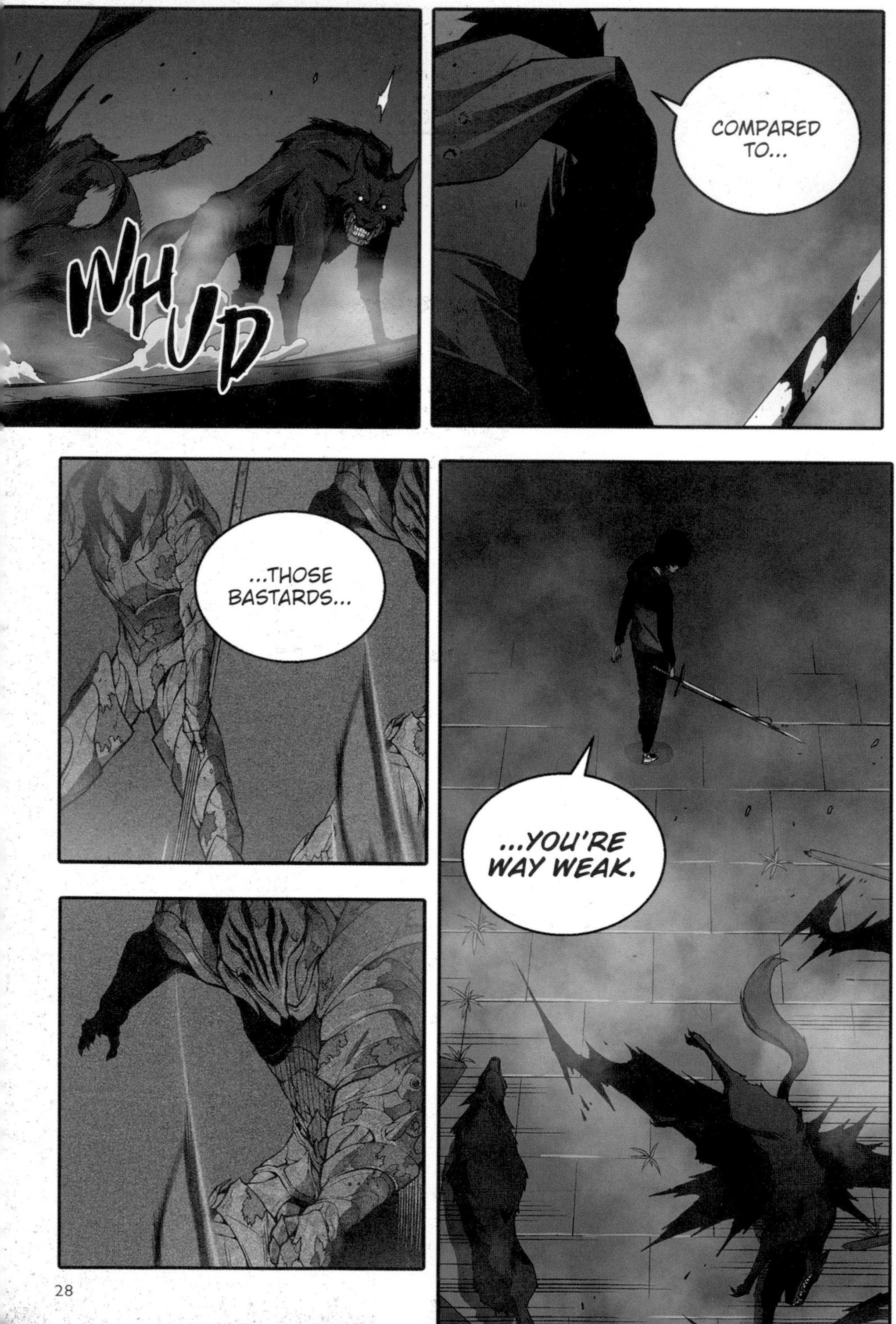
WHUD
COMPARED TO...
...THOSE BASTARDS...
...YOU'RE WAY WEAK.

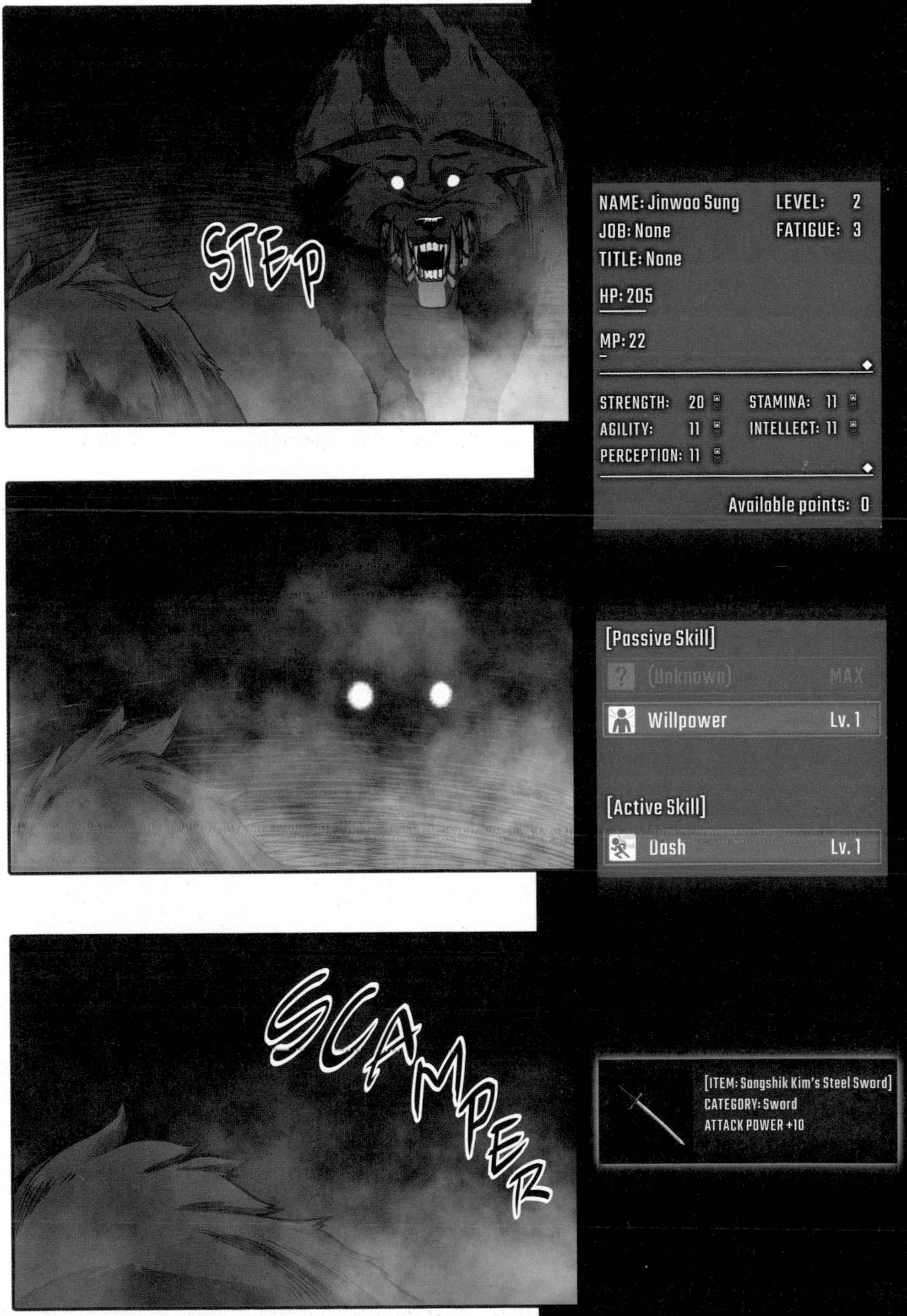

STEP
NAME: Jinwoo Sung LEVEL: 2
JOB: None FATIGUE: 3
TITLE: None
HP: 205
MP: 22
STRENGTH: 20 STAMINA: 11
AGILITY: 11 INTELLECT: 11
PERCEPTION: 11
Available points: 0
[Passive Skill]
? (Unknown) MAX
Willpower Lv. 1
[Active Skill]
Dash Lv. 1
SCAMPER
[ITEM: Sangshik Kim's Steel Sword]
CATEGORY: Sword
ATTACK POWER +10

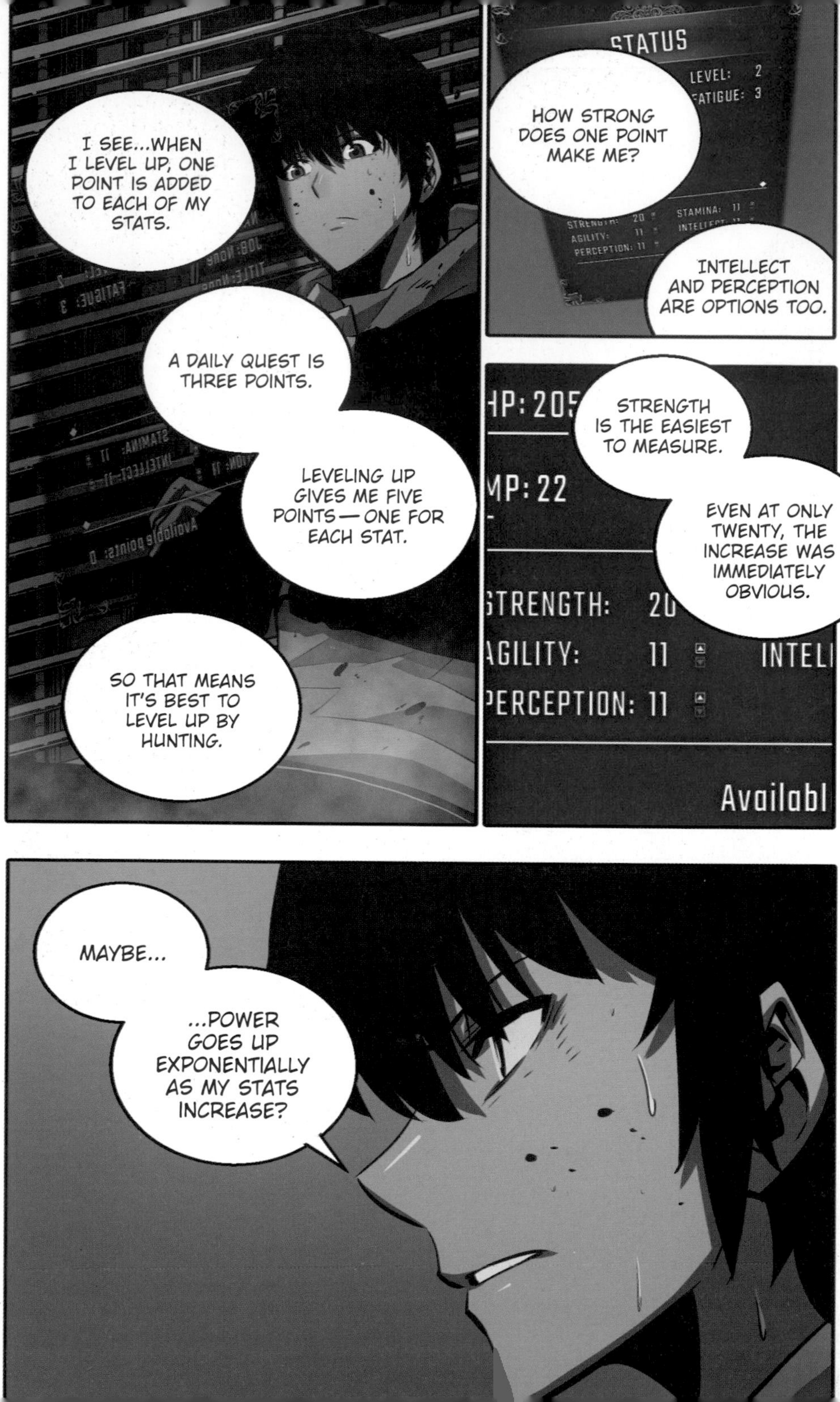
I SEE...WHEN I LEVEL UP, ONE POINT IS ADDED TO EACH OF MY STATS.
A DAILY QUEST IS THREE POINTS.
LEVELING UP GIVES ME FIVE POINTS—ONE FOR EACH STAT.
SO THAT MEANS IT'S BEST TO LEVEL UP BY HUNTING.
STATUS
LEVEL: 2
HOW STRONG DOES ONE POINT MAKE ME?
INTELLECT AND PERCEPTION ARE OPTIONS TOO.
STRENGTH IS THE EASIEST TO MEASURE.
MP: 22
EVEN AT ONLY TWENTY, THE INCREASE WAS IMMEDIATELY OBVIOUS.
MAYBE...
...POWER GOES UP EXPONENTIALLY AS MY STATS INCREASE?

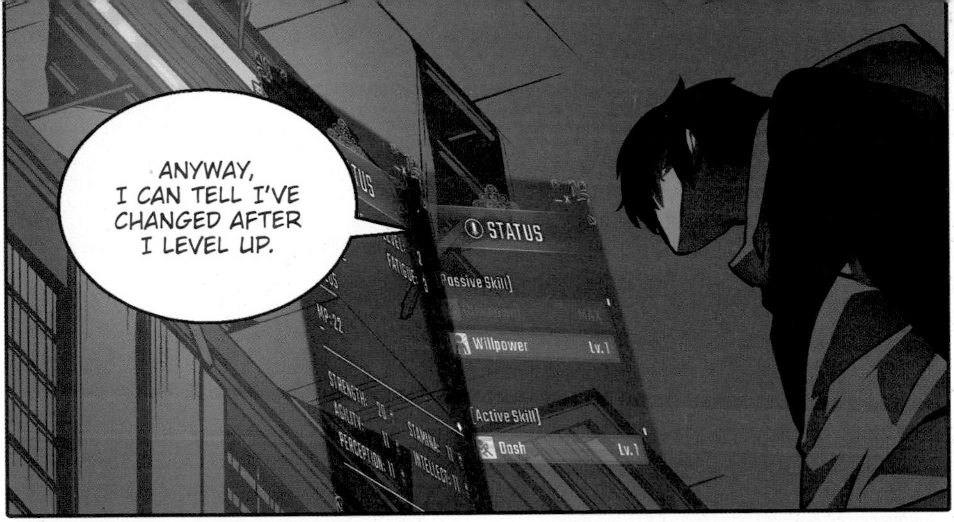
ANYWAY, I CAN TELL I'VE CHANGED AFTER I LEVEL UP.
STATUS
[Passive Skill]
Willpower Lv. 1
[Active Skill]
Dash Lv. 1

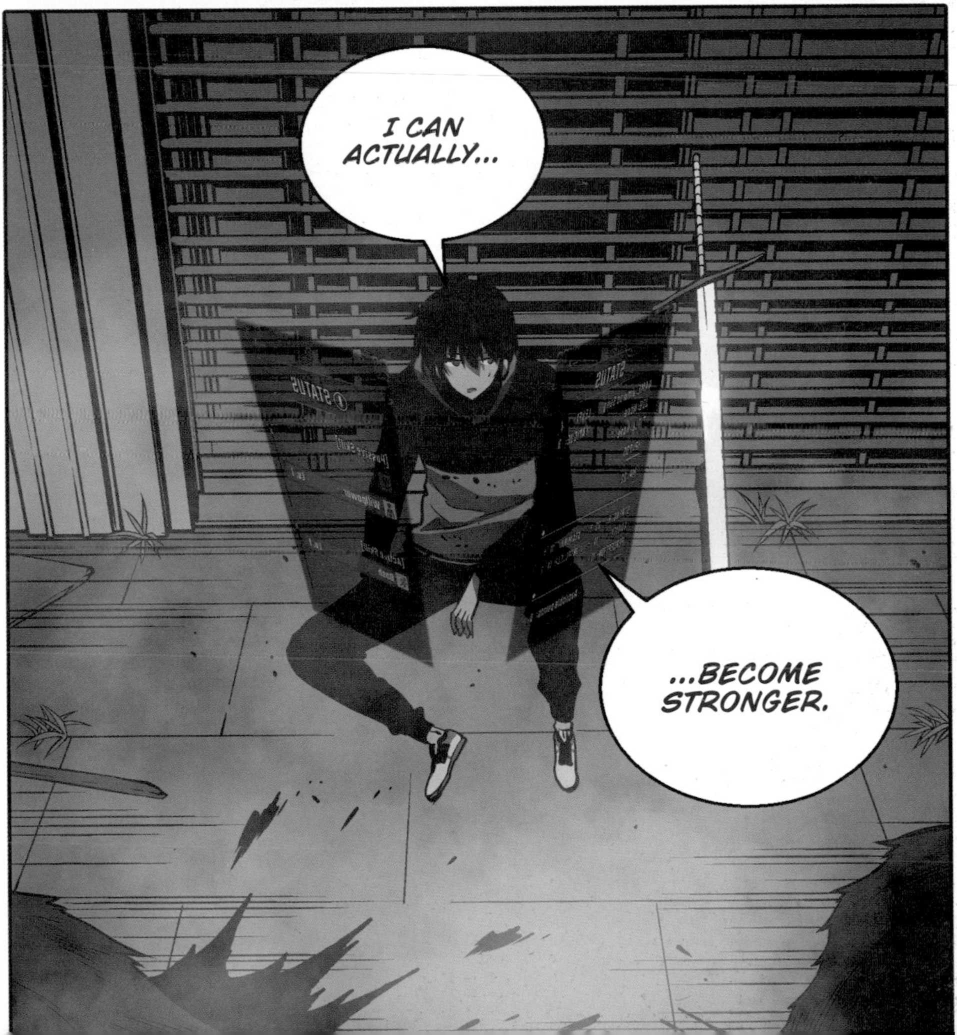
I CAN ACTUALLY...
...BECOME STRONGER.

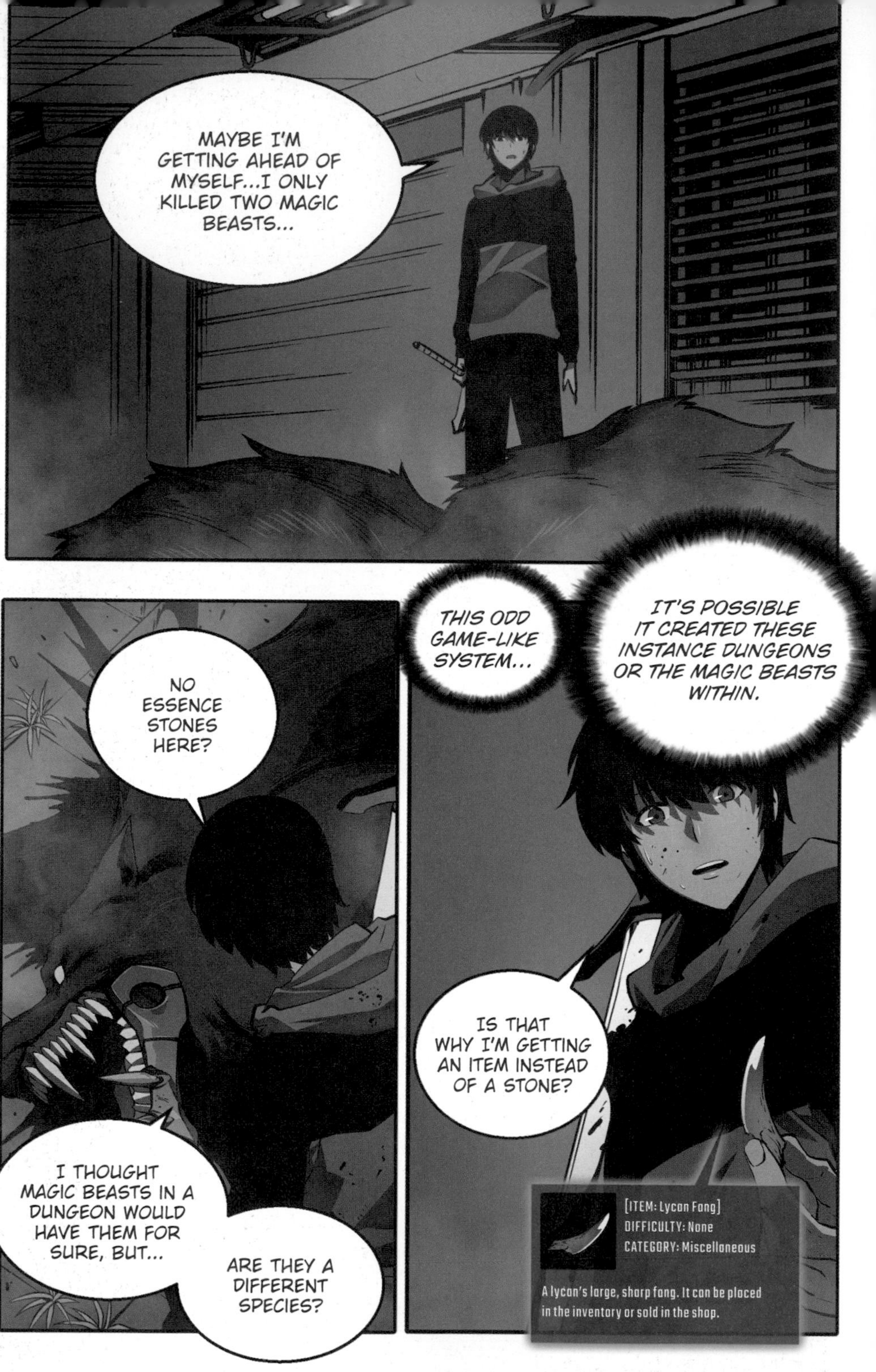
MAYBE I'M GETTING AHEAD OF MYSELF...I ONLY KILLED TWO MAGIC BEASTS...
NO ESSENCE STONES HERE?
I THOUGHT MAGIC BEASTS IN A DUNGEON WOULD HAVE THEM FOR SURE, BUT...
ARE THEY A DIFFERENT SPECIES?
THIS ODD GAME-LIKE SYSTEM...
IT'S POSSIBLE IT CREATED THESE INSTANCE DUNGEONS OR THE MAGIC BEASTS WITHIN.
IS THAT WHY I'M GETTING AN ITEM INSTEAD OF A STONE?
[ITEM: Lycan Fang]
DIFFICULTY: None
CATEGORY: Miscellaneous
A lycan's large, sharp fang. It can be placed in the inventory or sold in the shop.

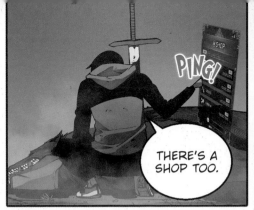

PING!
THERE'S A SHOP TOO.
BUY
SELL
NOTIFICATION
You cannot buy anything at your level.
Would you like to sell [Item: Lycan Fang]?
SURE.
SELL
CANCEL
SELL
20
TING LING!
TWENTY GOLD? IT'S NOT REAL MONEY, SO I DON'T KNOW HOW MUCH THIS IS ACTUALLY WORTH.

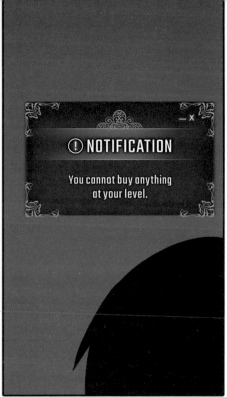

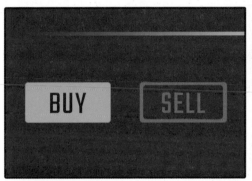

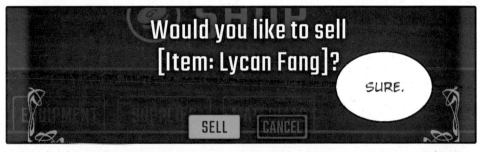

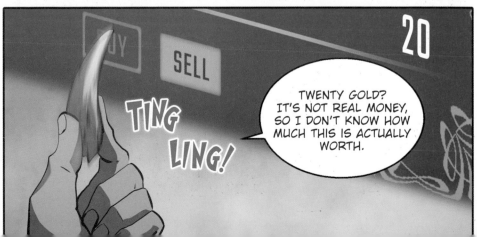

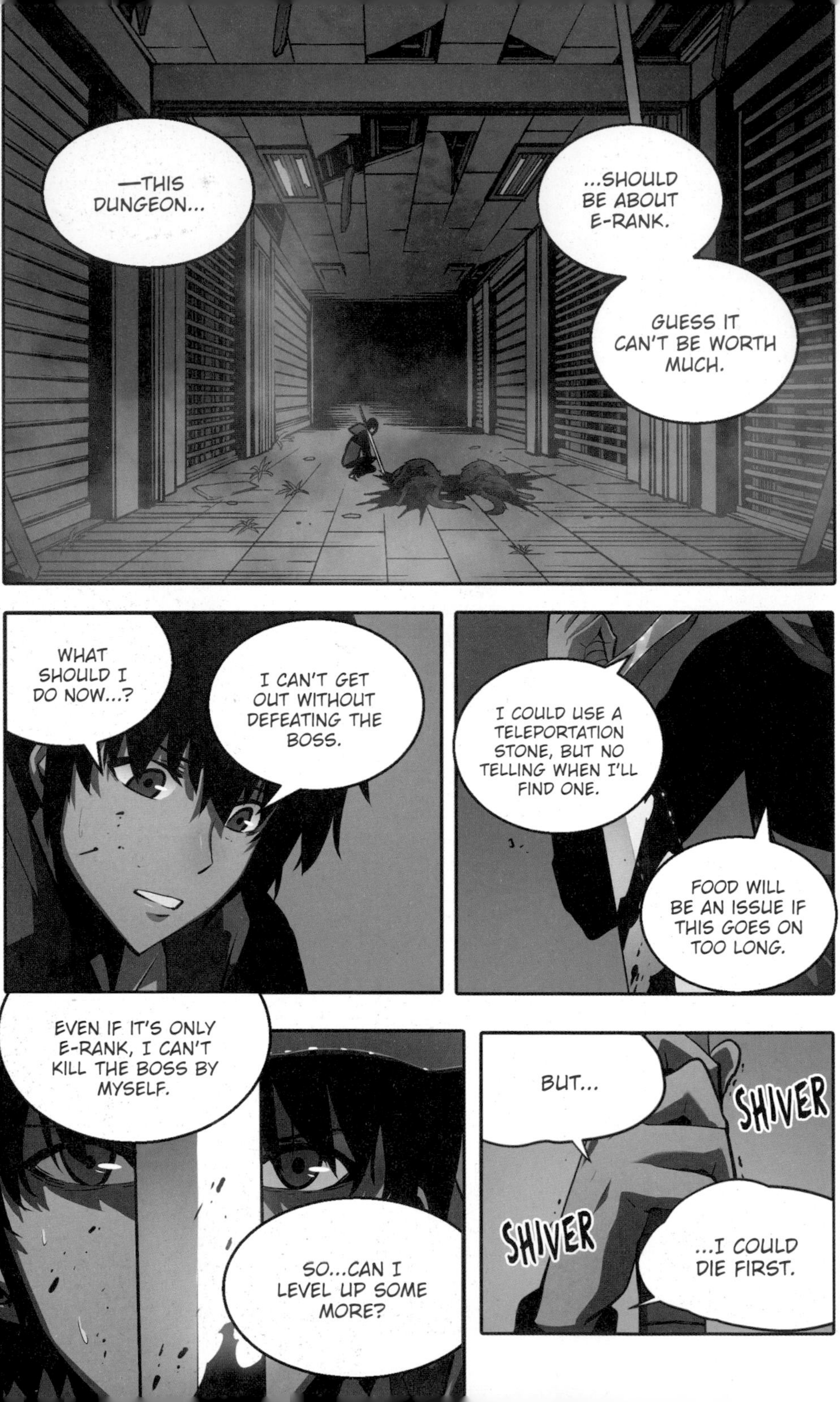
—THIS DUNGEON...
...SHOULD BE ABOUT E-RANK.
GUESS IT CAN'T BE WORTH MUCH.
WHAT SHOULD I DO NOW...?
I CAN'T GET OUT WITHOUT DEFEATING THE BOSS.
I COULD USE A TELEPORTATION STONE, BUT NO TELLING WHEN I'LL FIND ONE.
FOOD WILL BE AN ISSUE IF THIS GOES ON TOO LONG.
EVEN IF IT'S ONLY E-RANK, I CAN'T KILL THE BOSS BY MYSELF.
SO...CAN I LEVEL UP SOME MORE?
BUT...
SHIVER
SHIVER
...I COULD DIE FIRST.

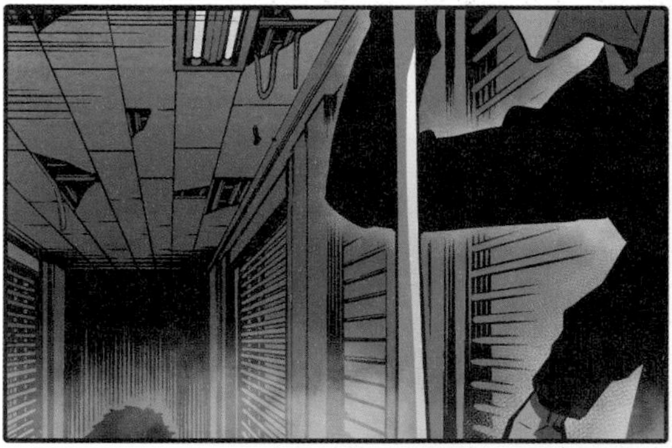
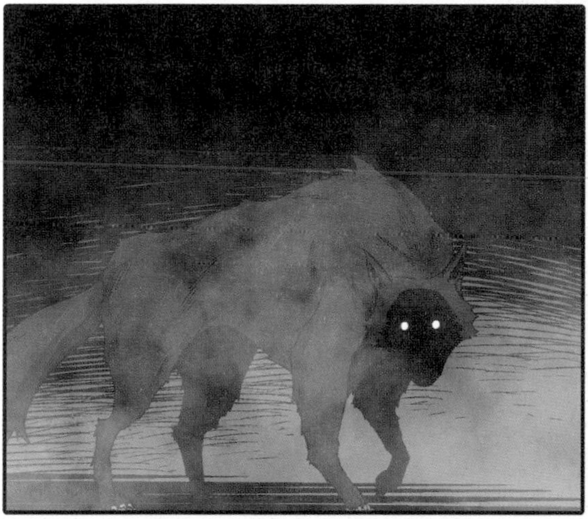
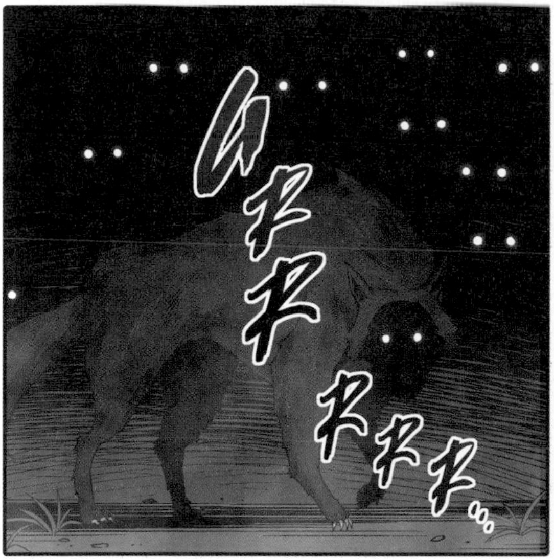
Grrrrr...
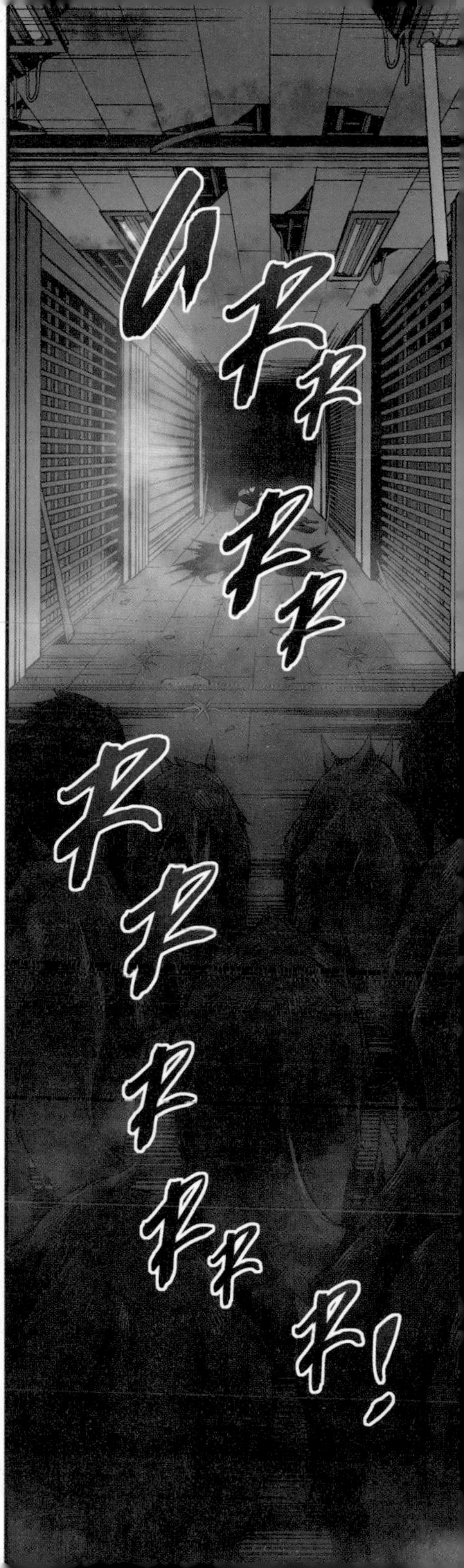
Grrrrrrrrrr!

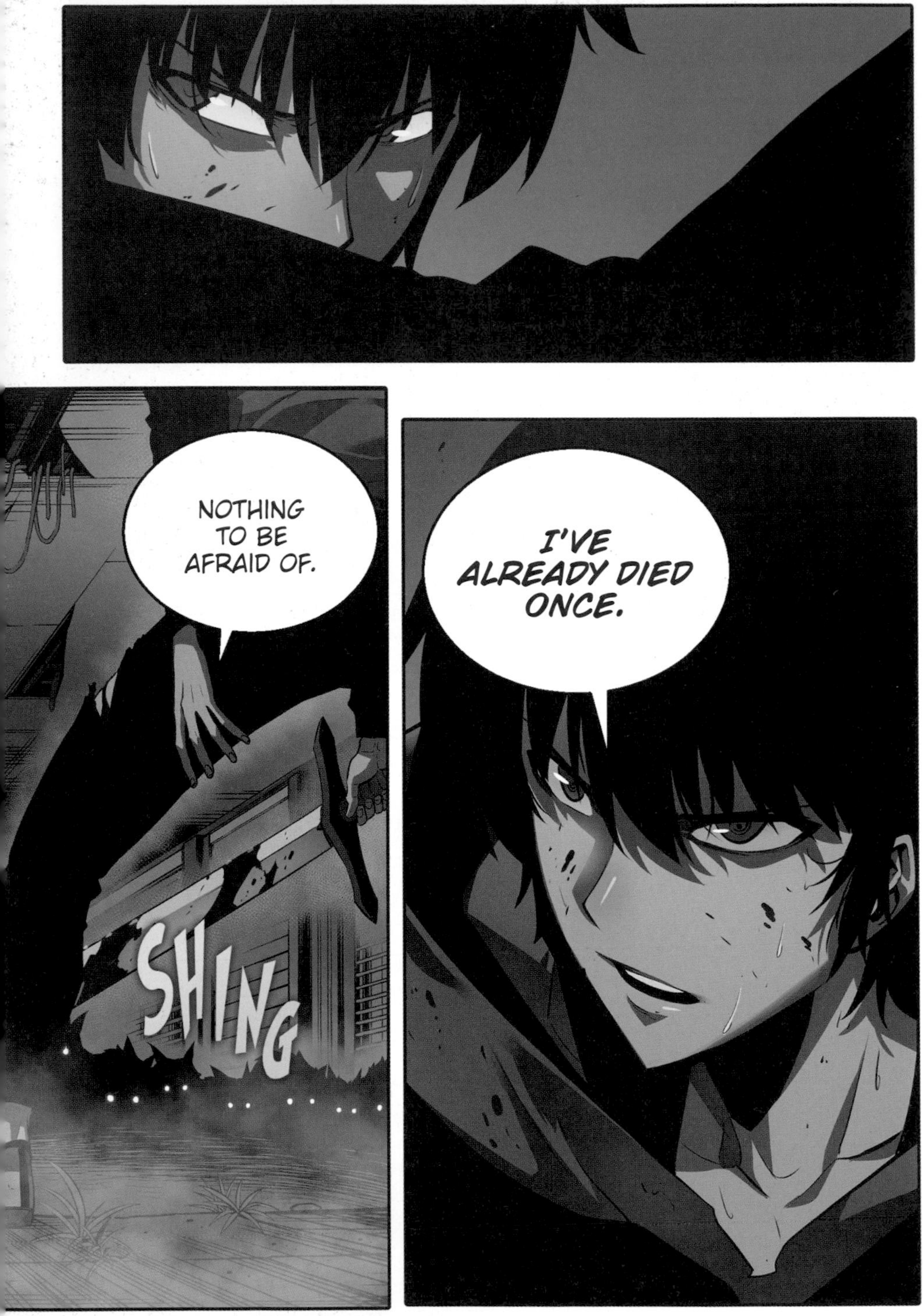
NOTHING TO BE AFRAID OF.
SHING
I'VE ALREADY DIED ONCE.

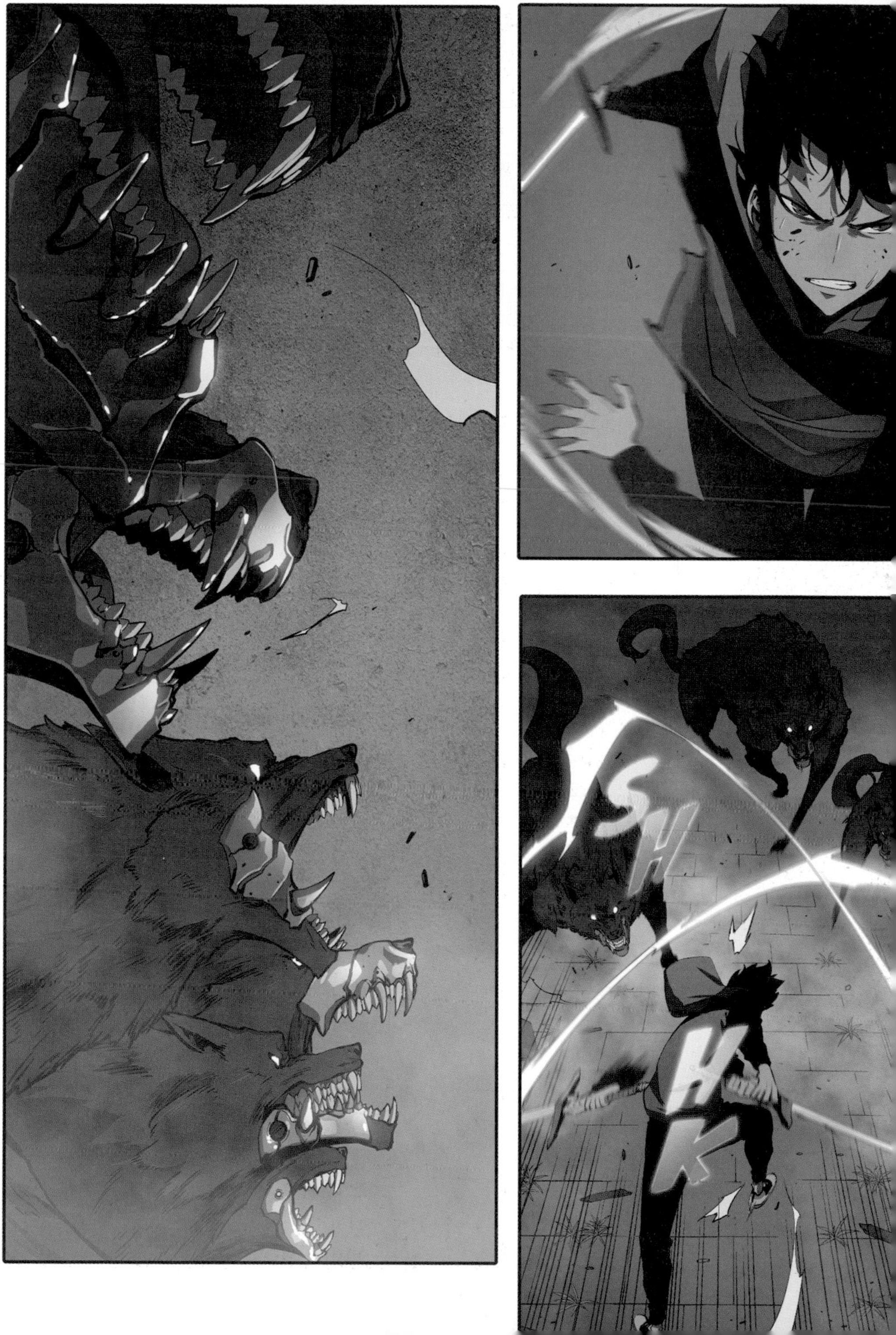
SHHK

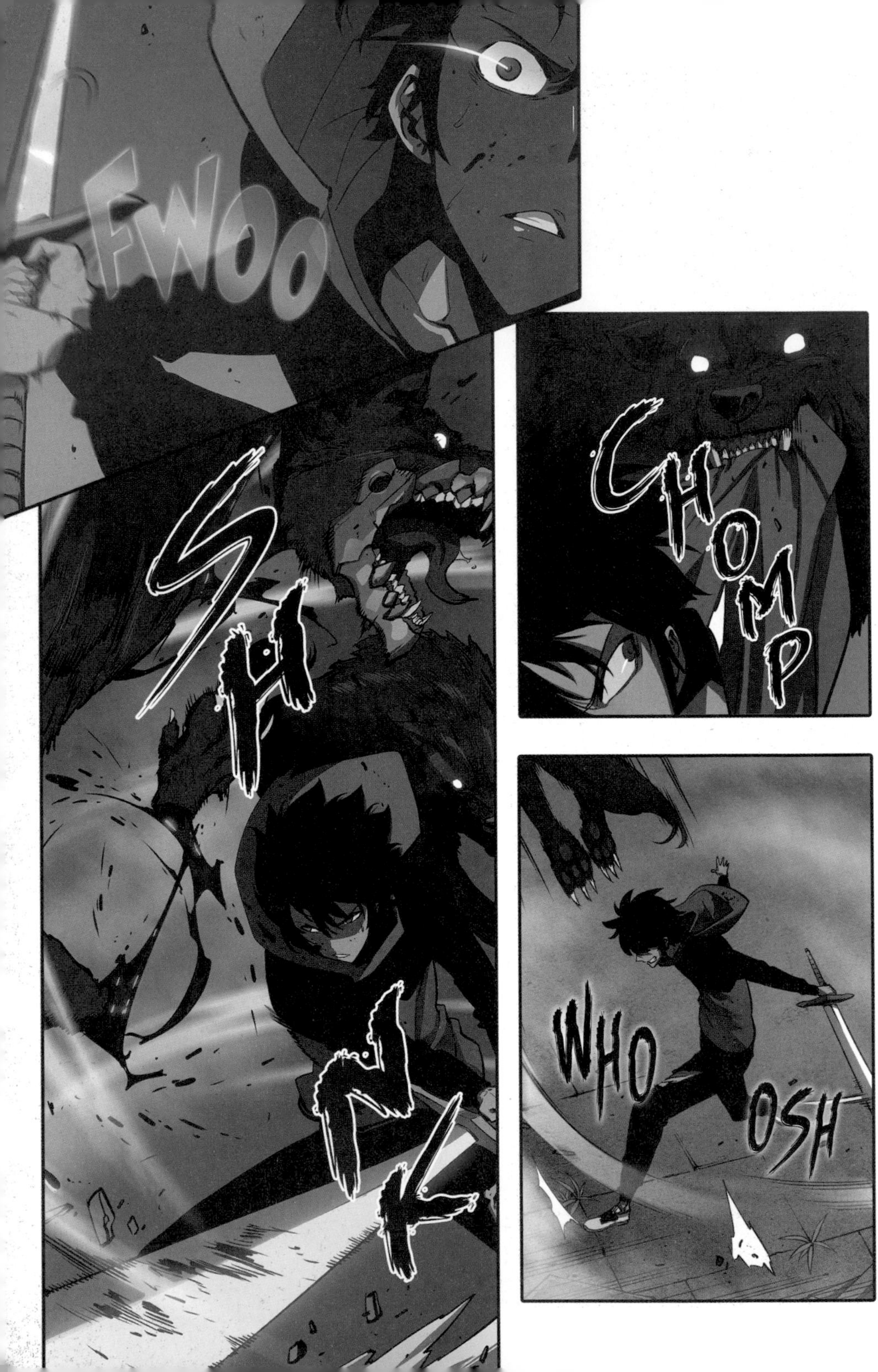
FWOO
SHUNK
CHOMP
WHOOSH

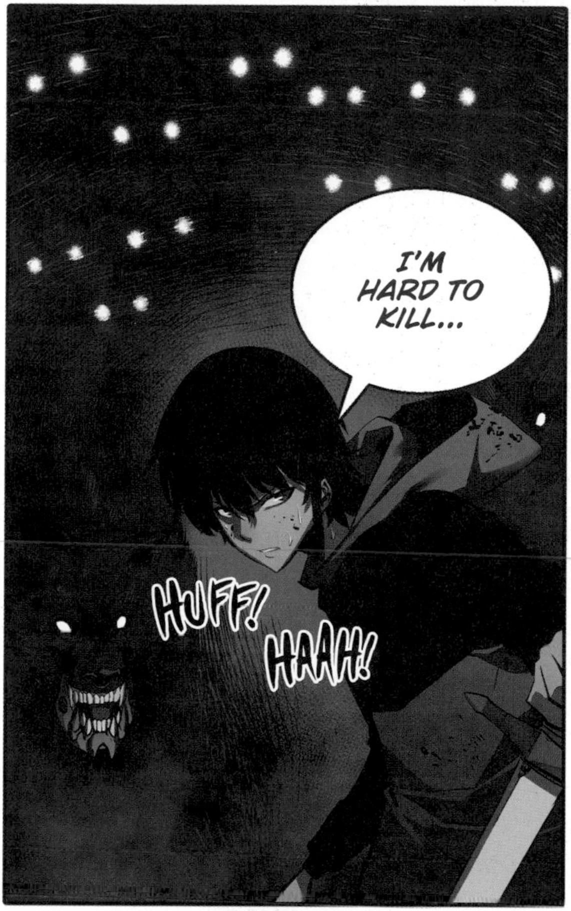
I'M HARD TO KILL...
HUFF!
HAAH!
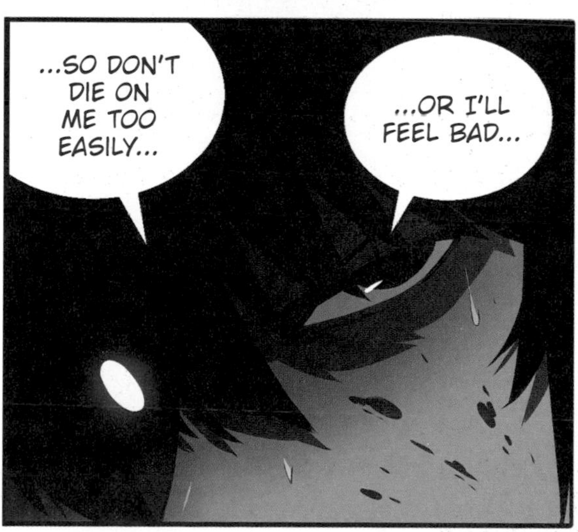
...SO DON'T DIE ON ME TOO EASILY...
...OR I'LL FEEL BAD...
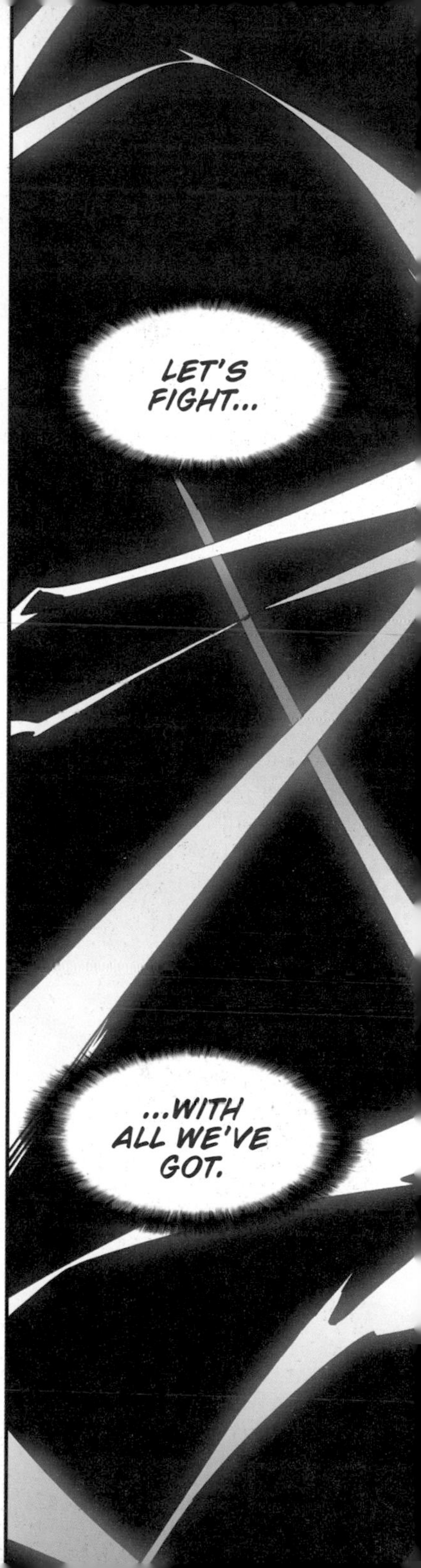
LET'S FIGHT...
...WITH ALL WE'VE GOT.

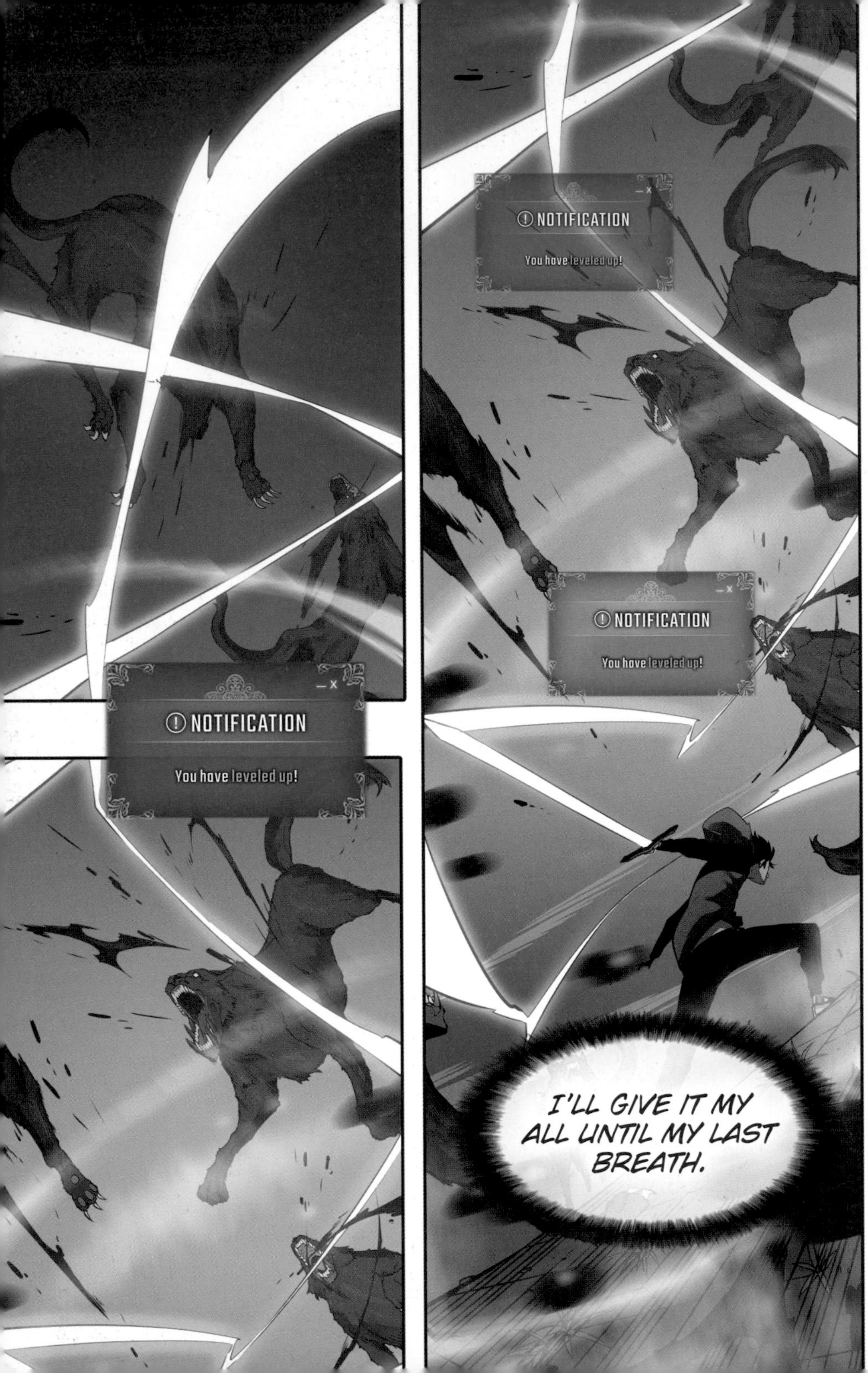
NOTIFICATION
You have leveled up!
NOTIFICATION
You have leveled up!
NOTIFICATION
You have leveled up!
I'LL GIVE IT MY ALL UNTIL MY LAST BREATH.

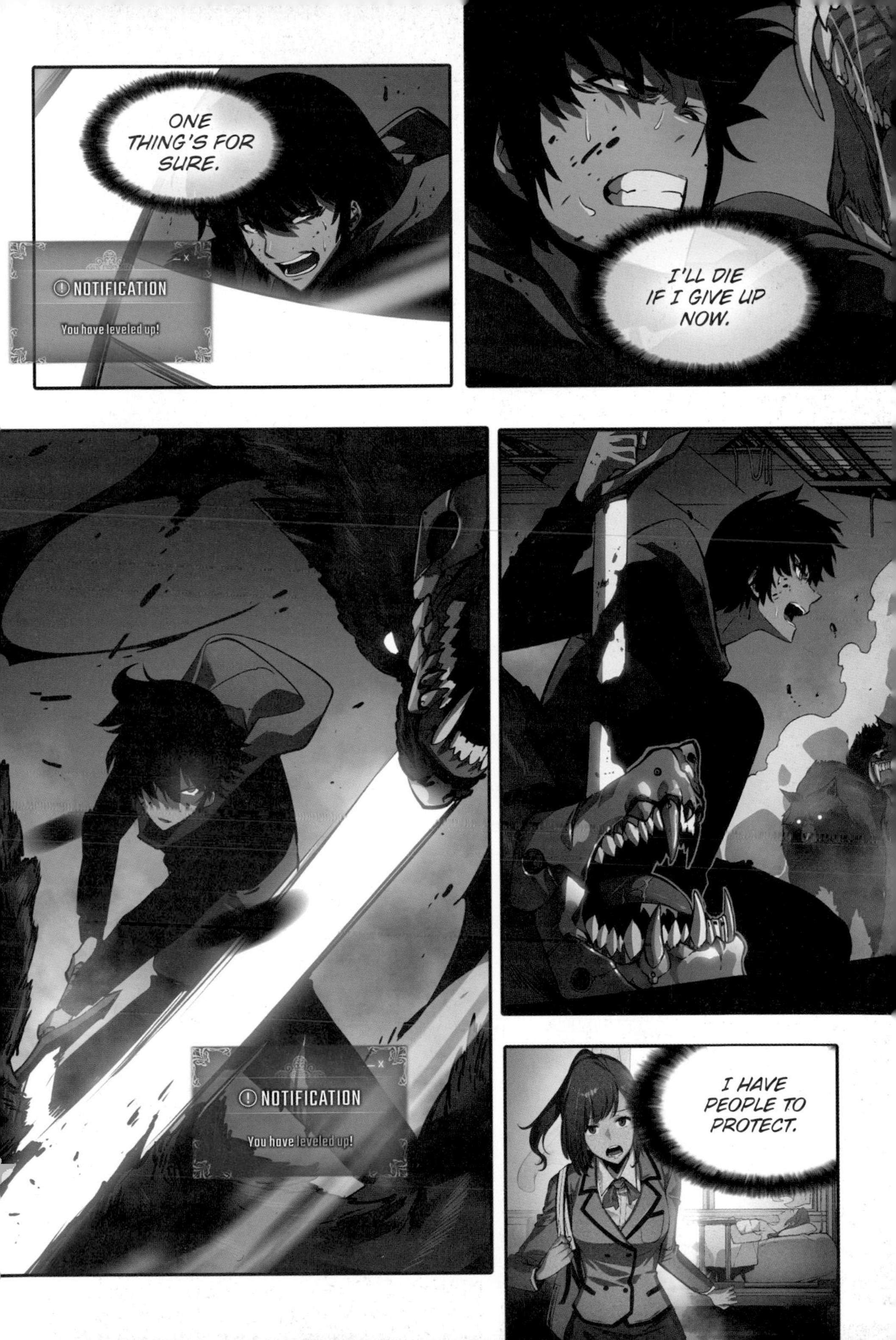
ONE THING'S FOR SURE.
NOTIFICATION
You have leveled up!
I'LL DIE IF I GIVE UP NOW.
NOTIFICATION
You have leveled up!
I HAVE PEOPLE TO PROTECT.

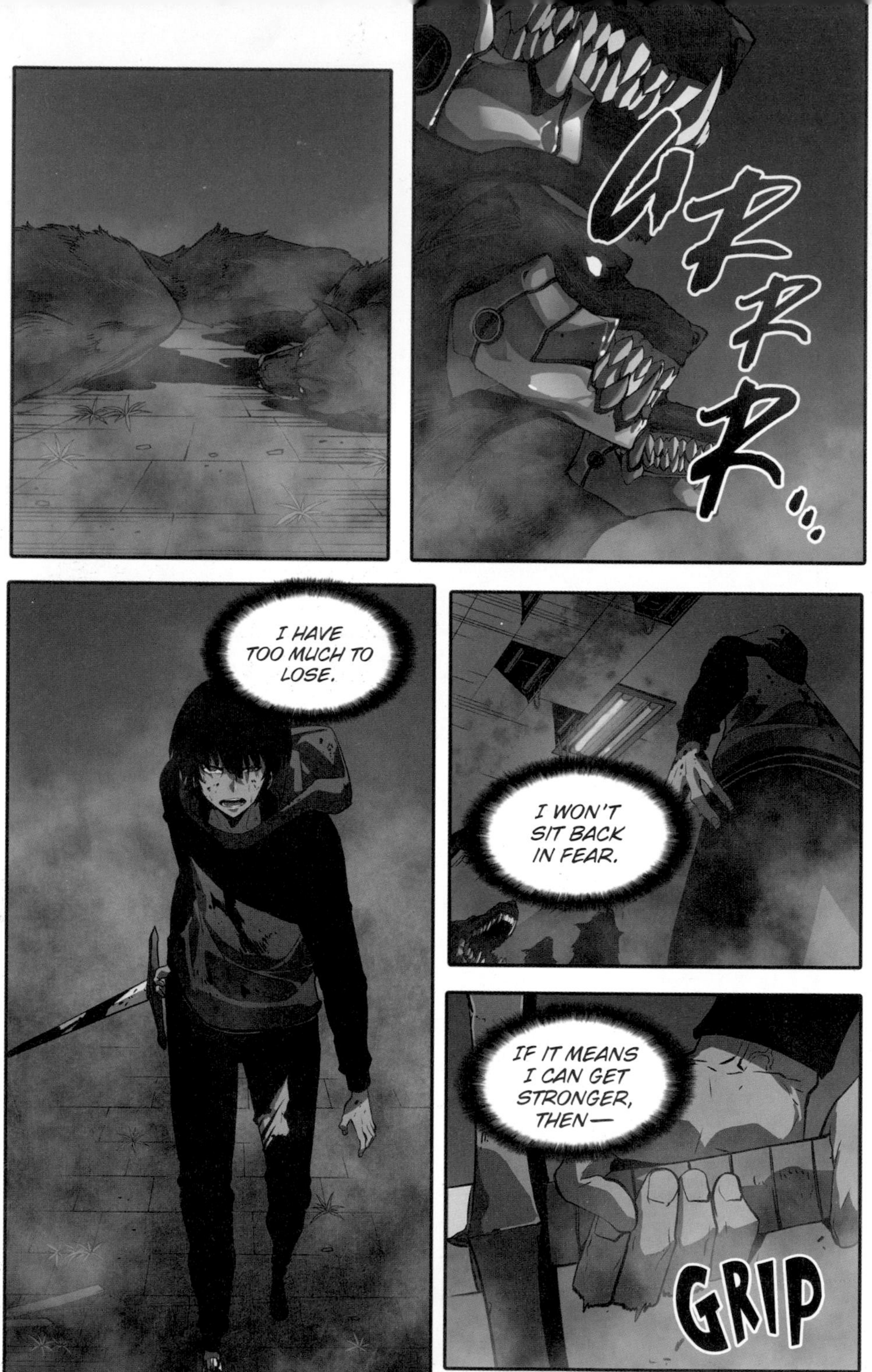
GRRRR...
I HAVE TOO MUCH TO LOSE.
I WON'T SIT BACK IN FEAR.
IF IT MEANS I CAN GET STRONGER, THEN—
GRIP

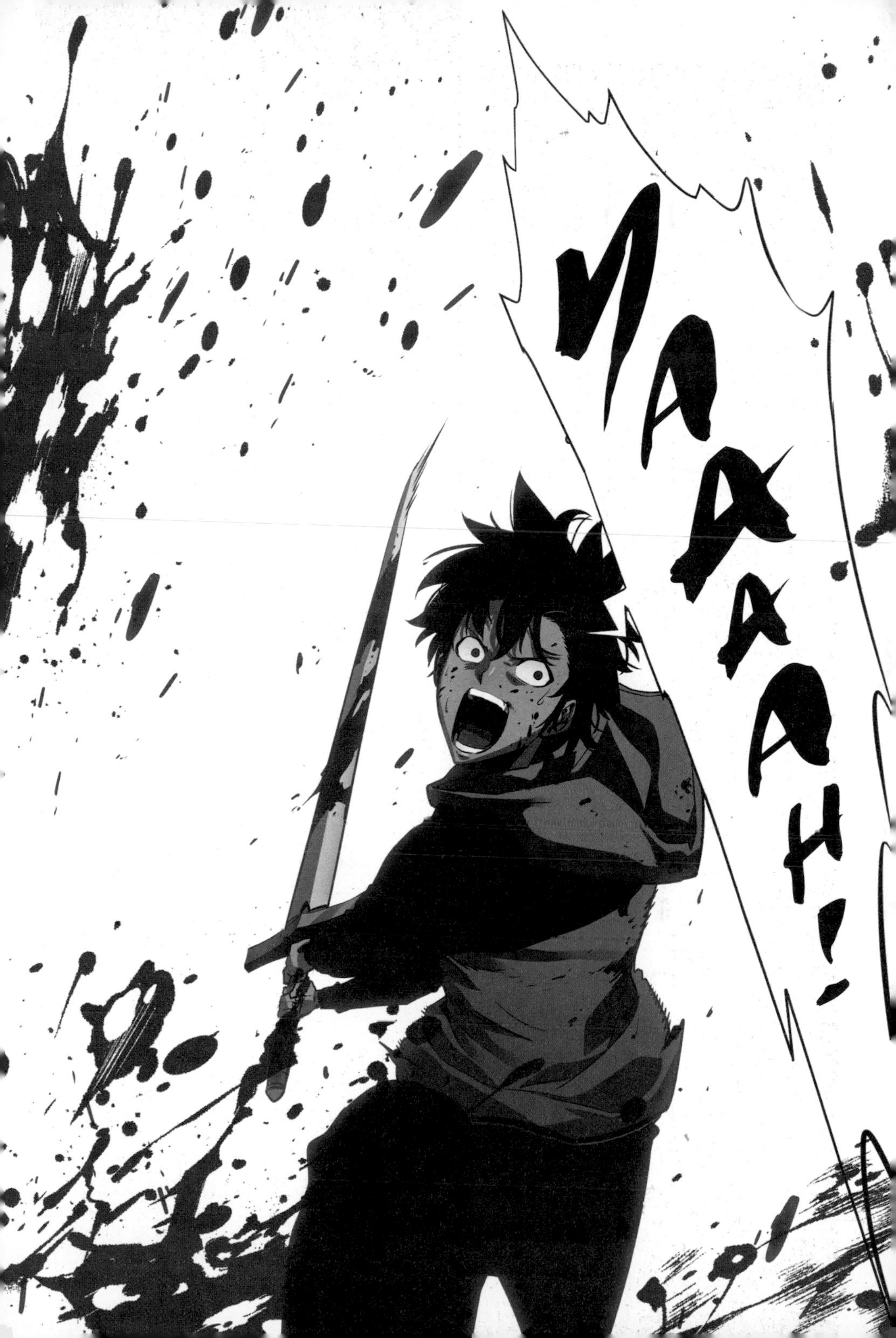
NAAAAAH!!

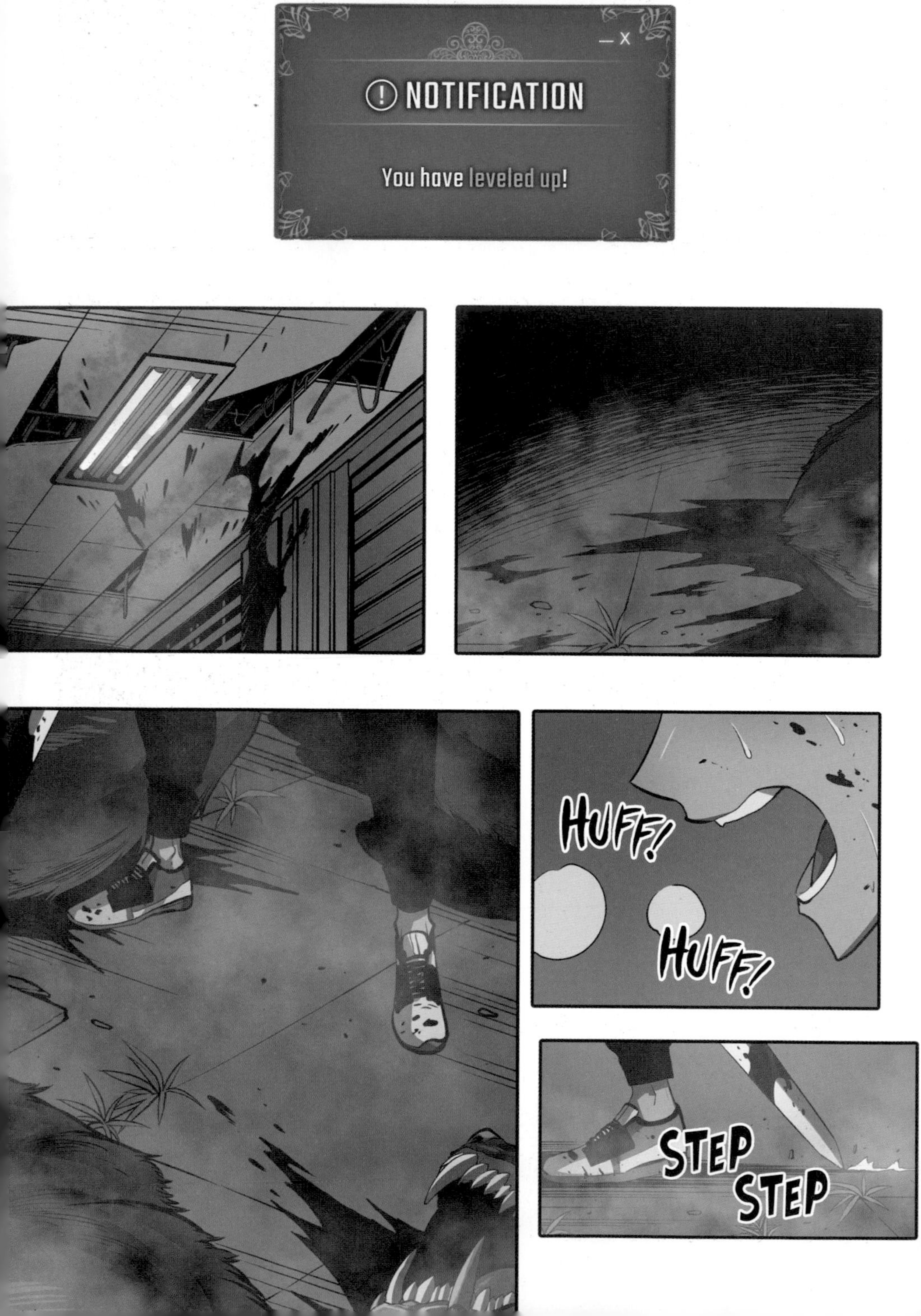

NOTIFICATION
You have leveled up!
HUFF!
HUFF!
STEP
STEP

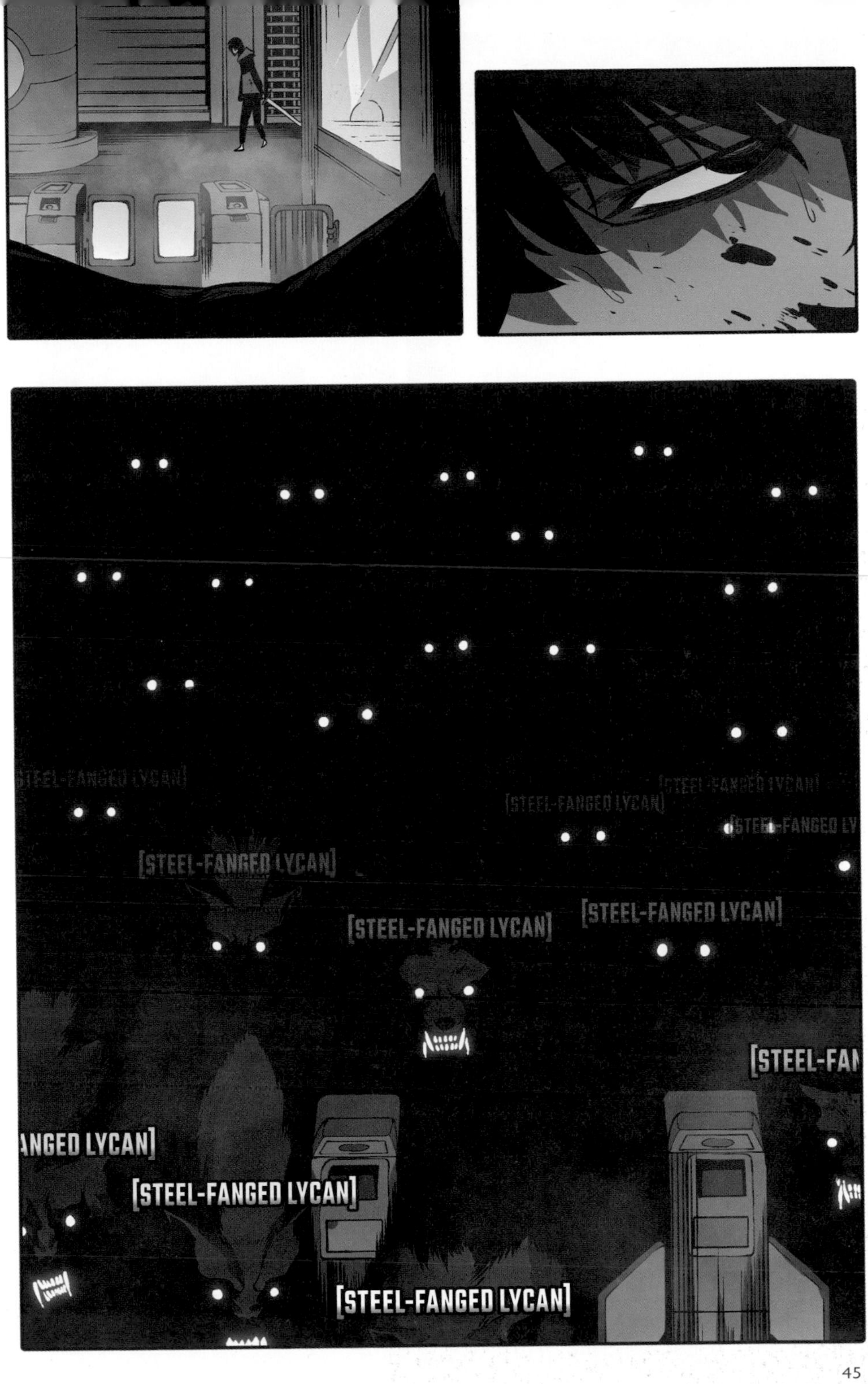

STEEL-FANGED LYCAN]
[STEEL-FANGED LYCAN]
[STEEL-FANGED LYCAN]
[STEEL-FANGED LY
[STEEL-FANGED LYCAN]
[STEEL-FANGED LYCAN]
[STEEL-FANGED LYCAN]
[STEEL-FAN
ANGED LYCAN]
[STEEL-FANGED LYCAN]
[STEEL-FANGED LYCAN]

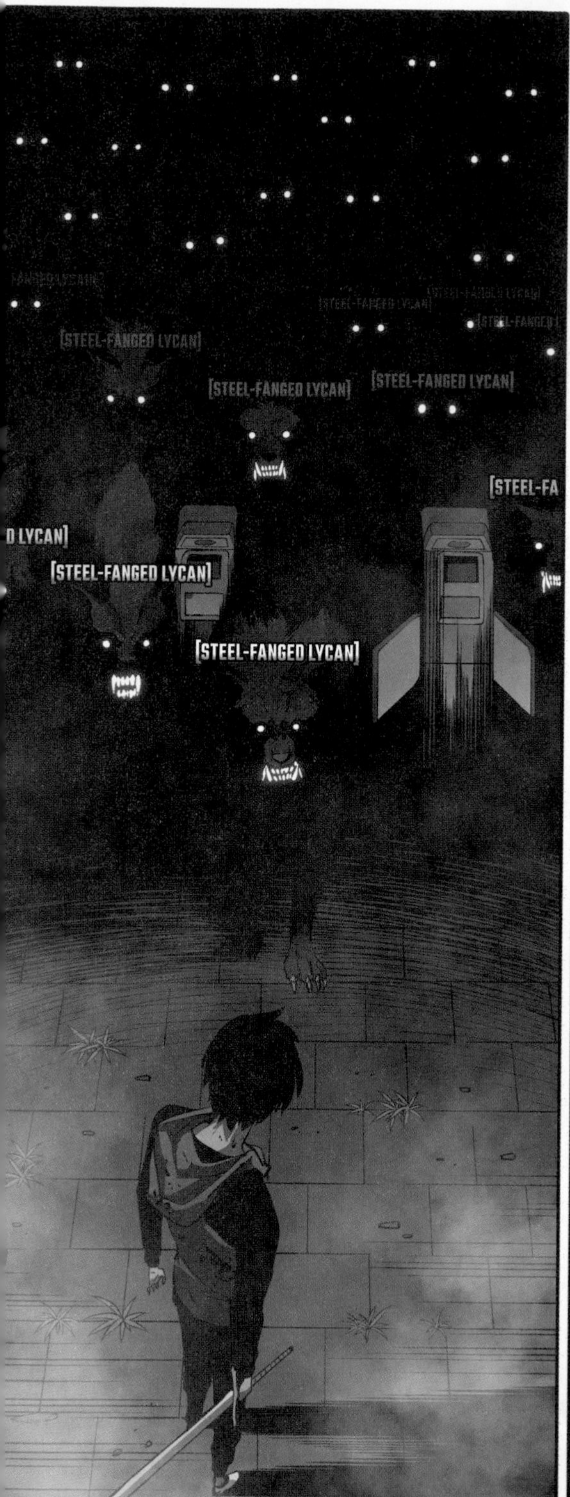
[STEEL-FANGED LYCAN]
[STEEL-FANGED LYCAN]
[STEEL-FANGED LYCAN]
[STEEL-FA
D LYCAN]
[STEEL-FANGED LYCAN]
[STEEL-FANGED LYCAN]
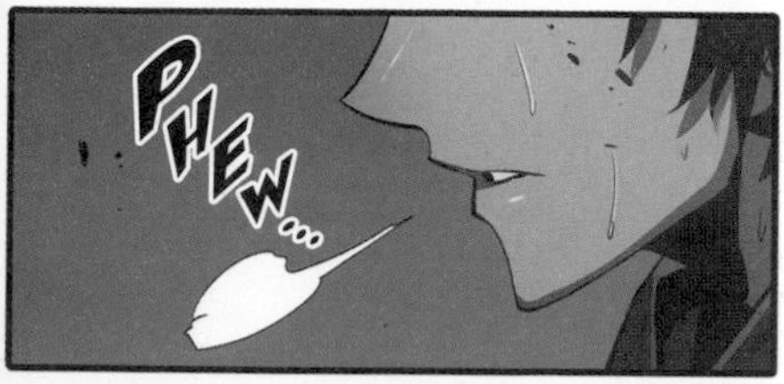
PHEW...
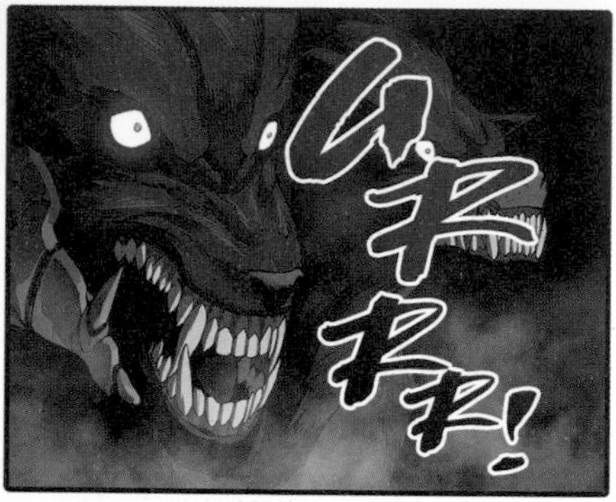
GRRR!
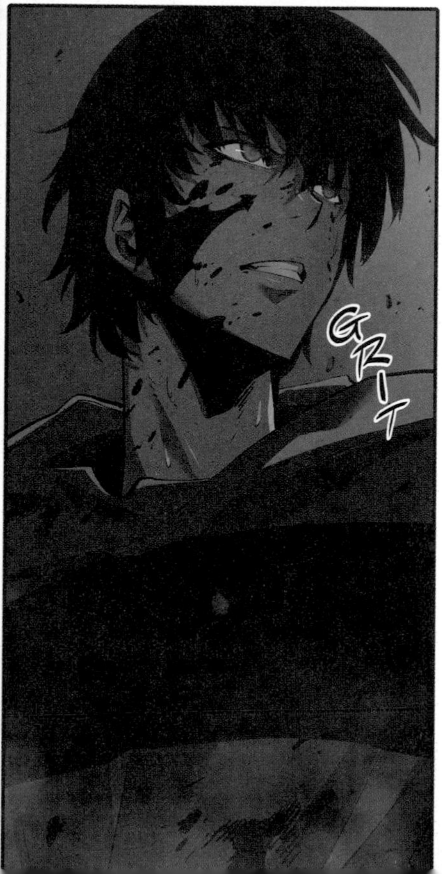
GRIT

① NOTIFICATION

You have acquired [Title: Wolf Assassin].

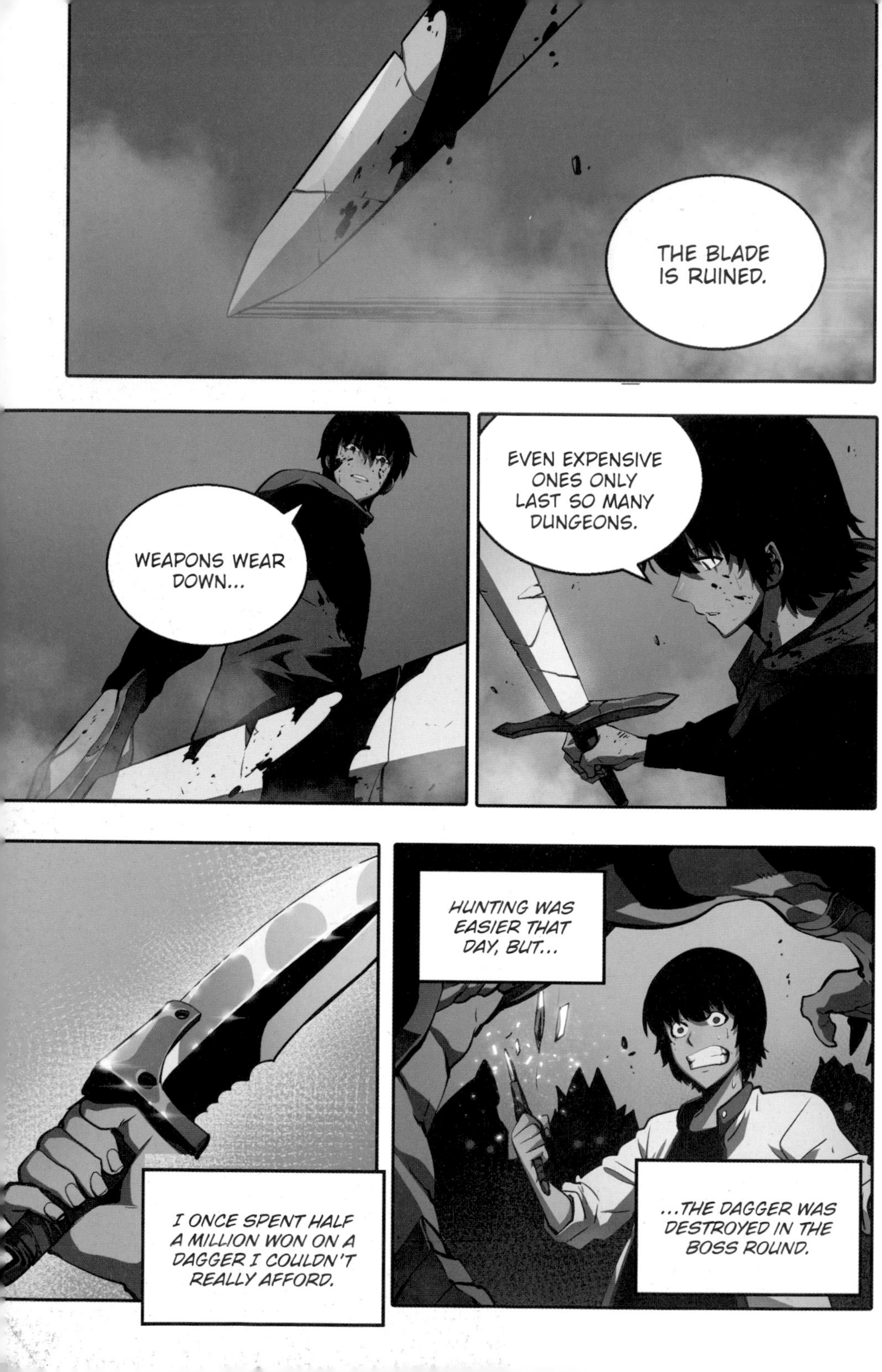
THE BLADE IS RUINED.
WEAPONS WEAR DOWN...
EVEN EXPENSIVE ONES ONLY LAST SO MANY DUNGEONS.
I ONCE SPENT HALF A MILLION WON ON A DAGGER I COULDN'T REALLY AFFORD.
HUNTING WAS EASIER THAT DAY, BUT...
...THE DAGGER WAS DESTROYED IN THE BOSS ROUND.

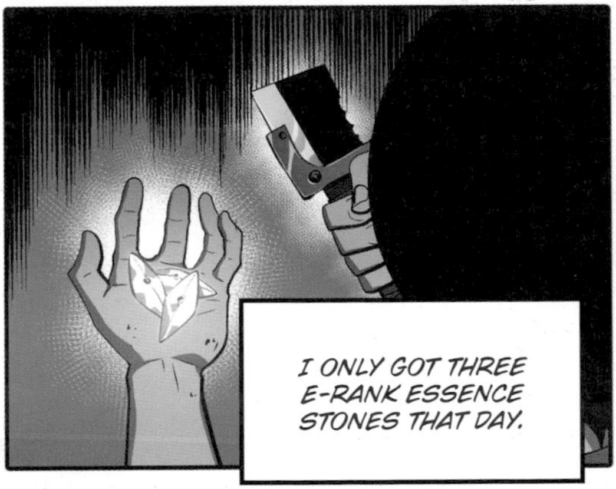
I ONLY GOT THREE E-RANK ESSENCE STONES THAT DAY.
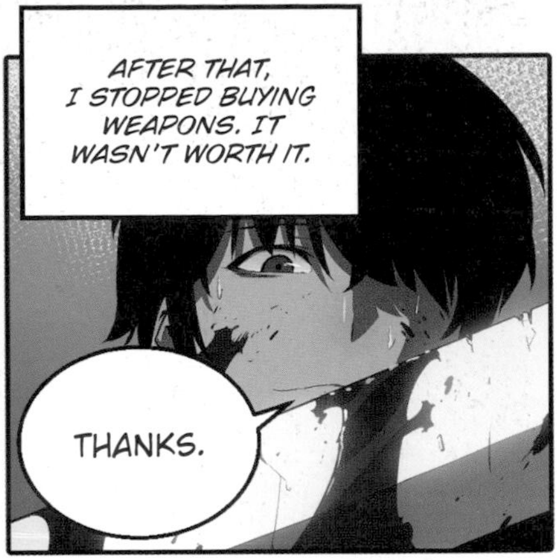
AFTER THAT, I STOPPED BUYING WEAPONS. IT WASN'T WORTH IT.
THANKS.
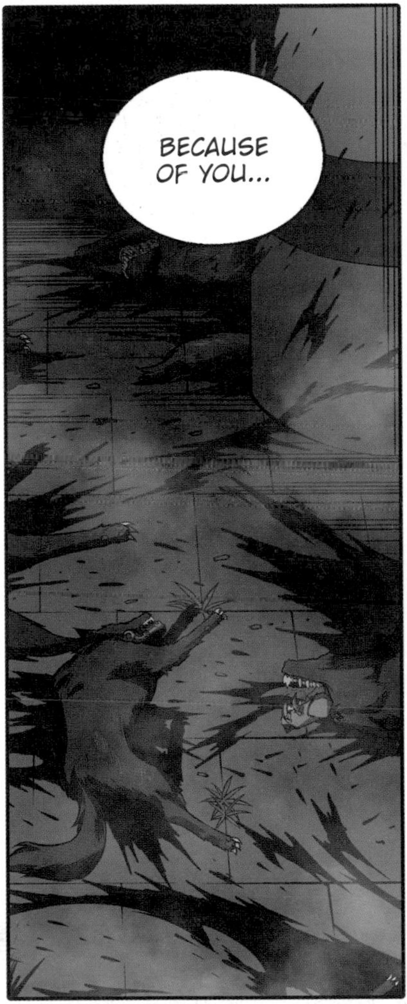
BECAUSE OF YOU...
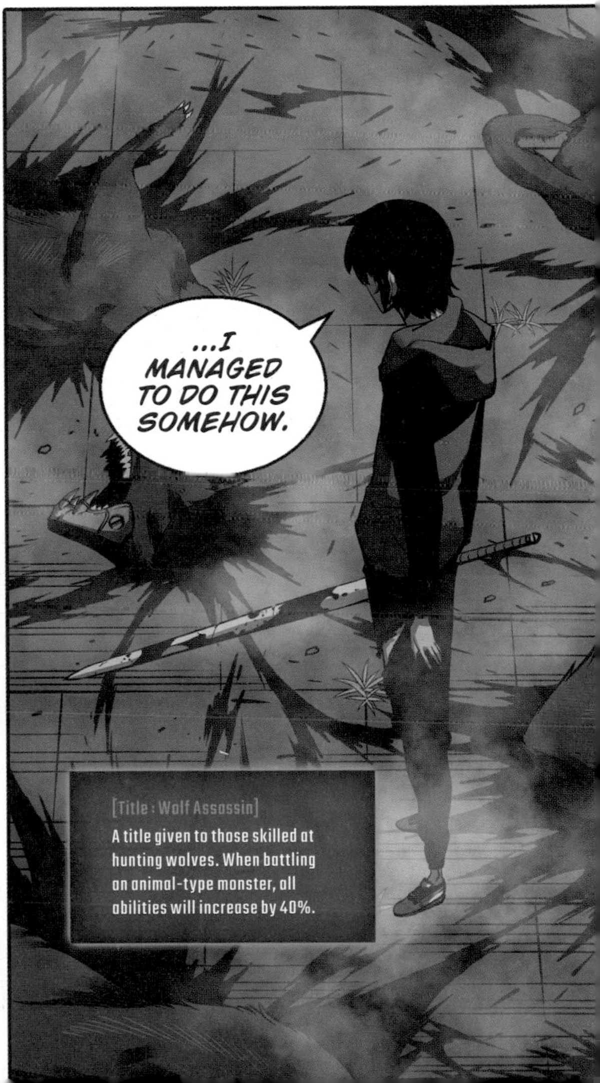
...I MANAGED TO DO THIS SOMEHOW.
[Title : Wolf Assassin]
A title given to those skilled at hunting wolves. When battling an animal-type monster, all abilities will increase by 40%.

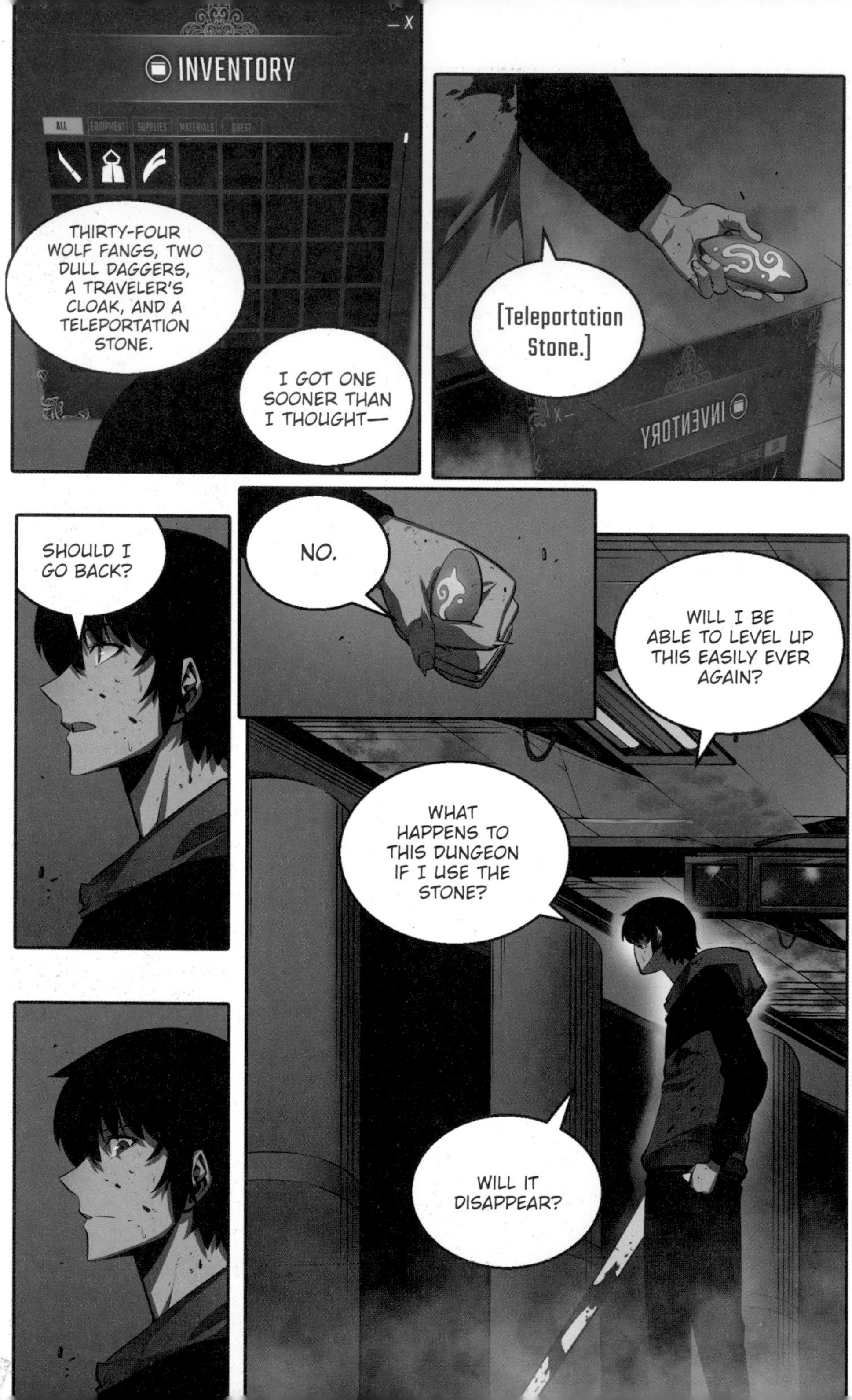
INVENTORY
ALL EQUIPMENT SUPPLIES MATERIALS QUEST
THIRTY-FOUR WOLF FANGS, TWO DULL DAGGERS, A TRAVELER'S CLOAK, AND A TELEPORTATION STONE.
I GOT ONE SOONER THAN I THOUGHT—
[Teleportation Stone.]
SHOULD I GO BACK?
NO.
WILL I BE ABLE TO LEVEL UP THIS EASILY EVER AGAIN?
WHAT HAPPENS TO THIS DUNGEON IF I USE THE STONE?
WILL IT DISAPPEAR?

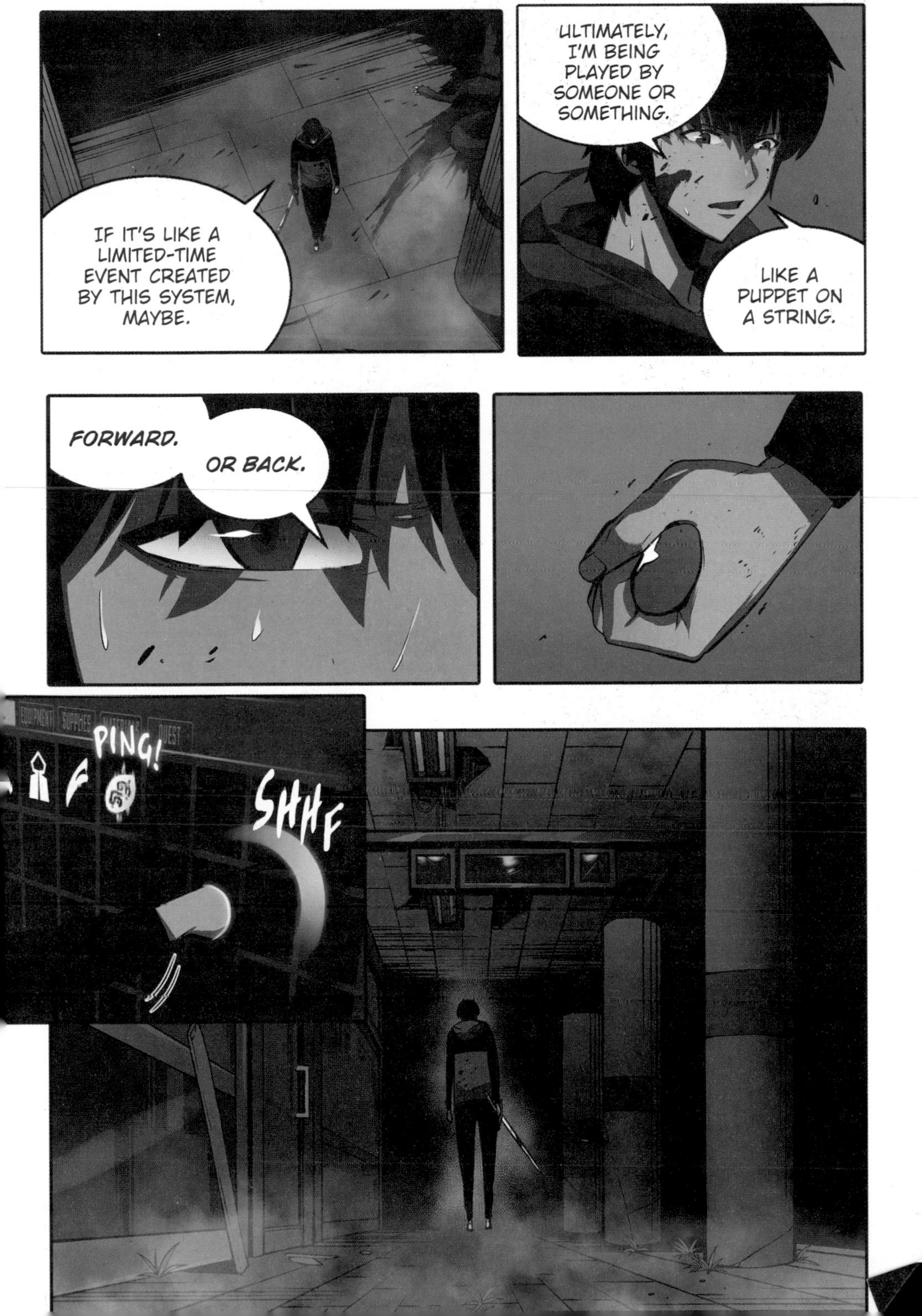
IF IT'S LIKE A LIMITED-TIME EVENT CREATED BY THIS SYSTEM, MAYBE.
ULTIMATELY, I'M BEING PLAYED BY SOMEONE OR SOMETHING.
LIKE A PUPPET ON A STRING.
FORWARD.
OR BACK.
EQUIPMENT
SUPPLIES
QUEST
PING!
SHHF

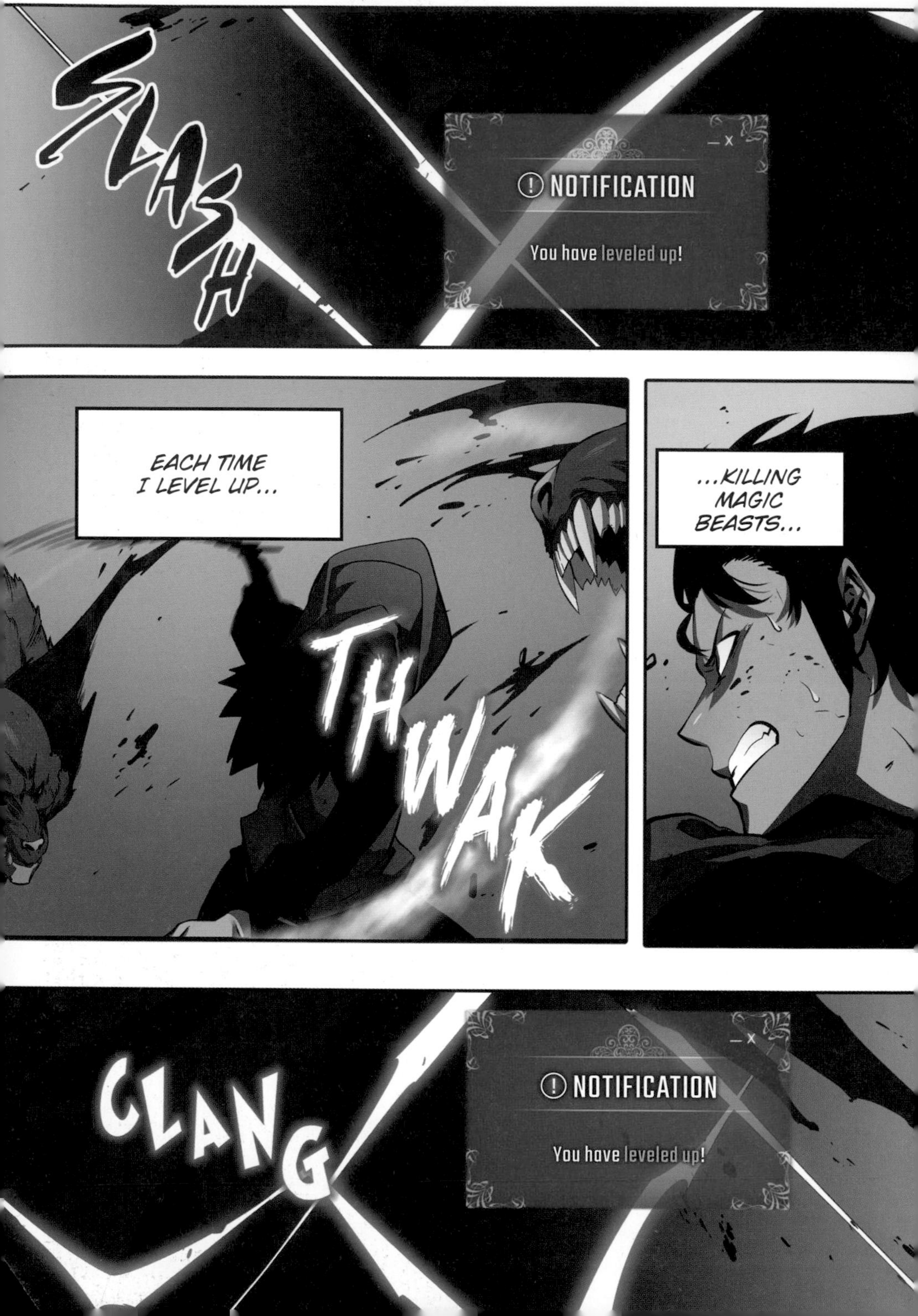
SLASH
NOTIFICATION
You have leveled up!
EACH TIME I LEVEL UP...
THWAK
...KILLING MAGIC BEASTS...
CLANG
NOTIFICATION
You have leveled up!

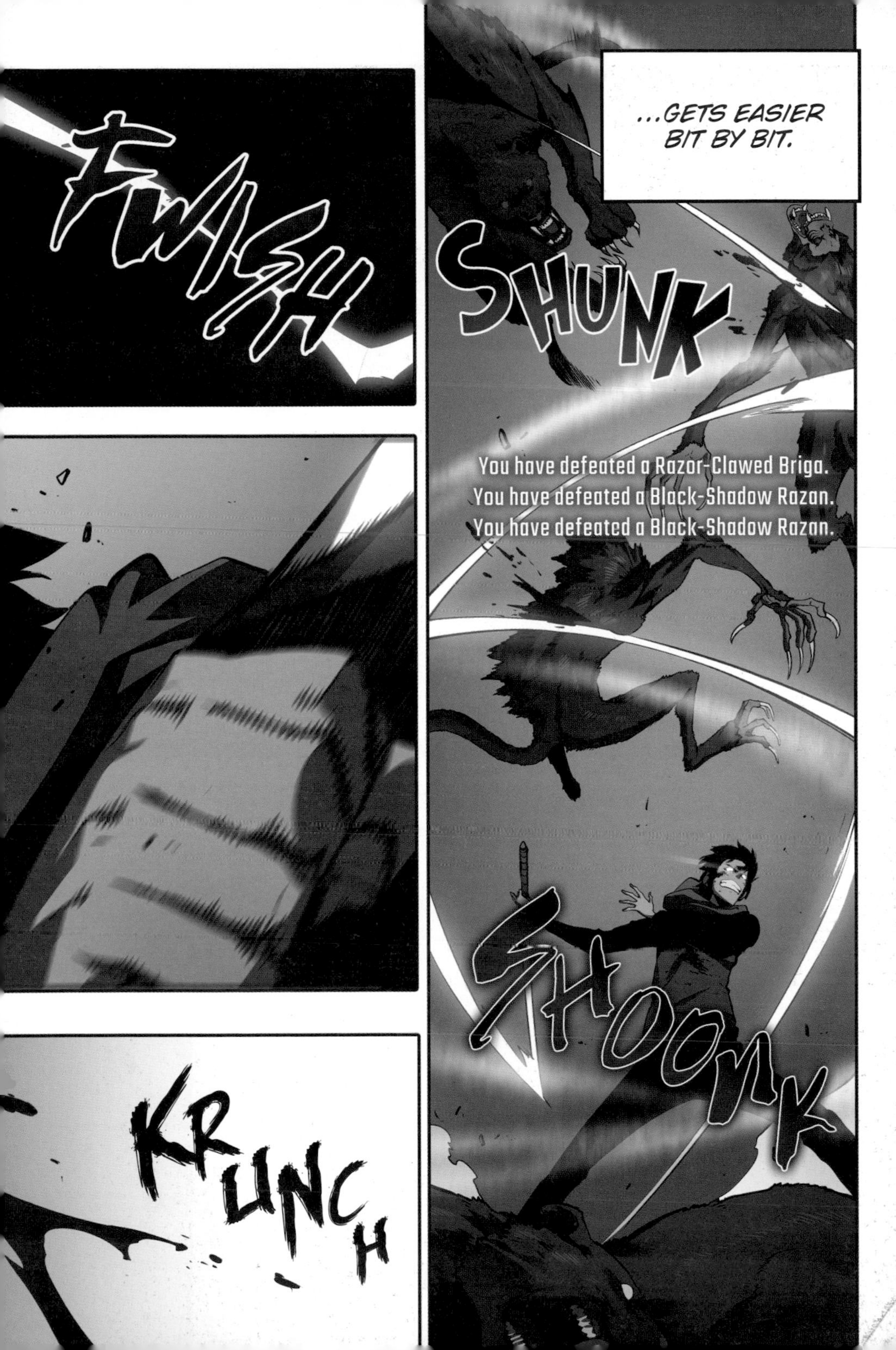
FWASH
KRUNCH
...GETS EASIER BIT BY BIT.
SHUNK
You have defeated a Razor-Clawed Briga.
You have defeated a Black-Shadow Razan.
You have defeated a Black-Shadow Razan.
SHOOONK

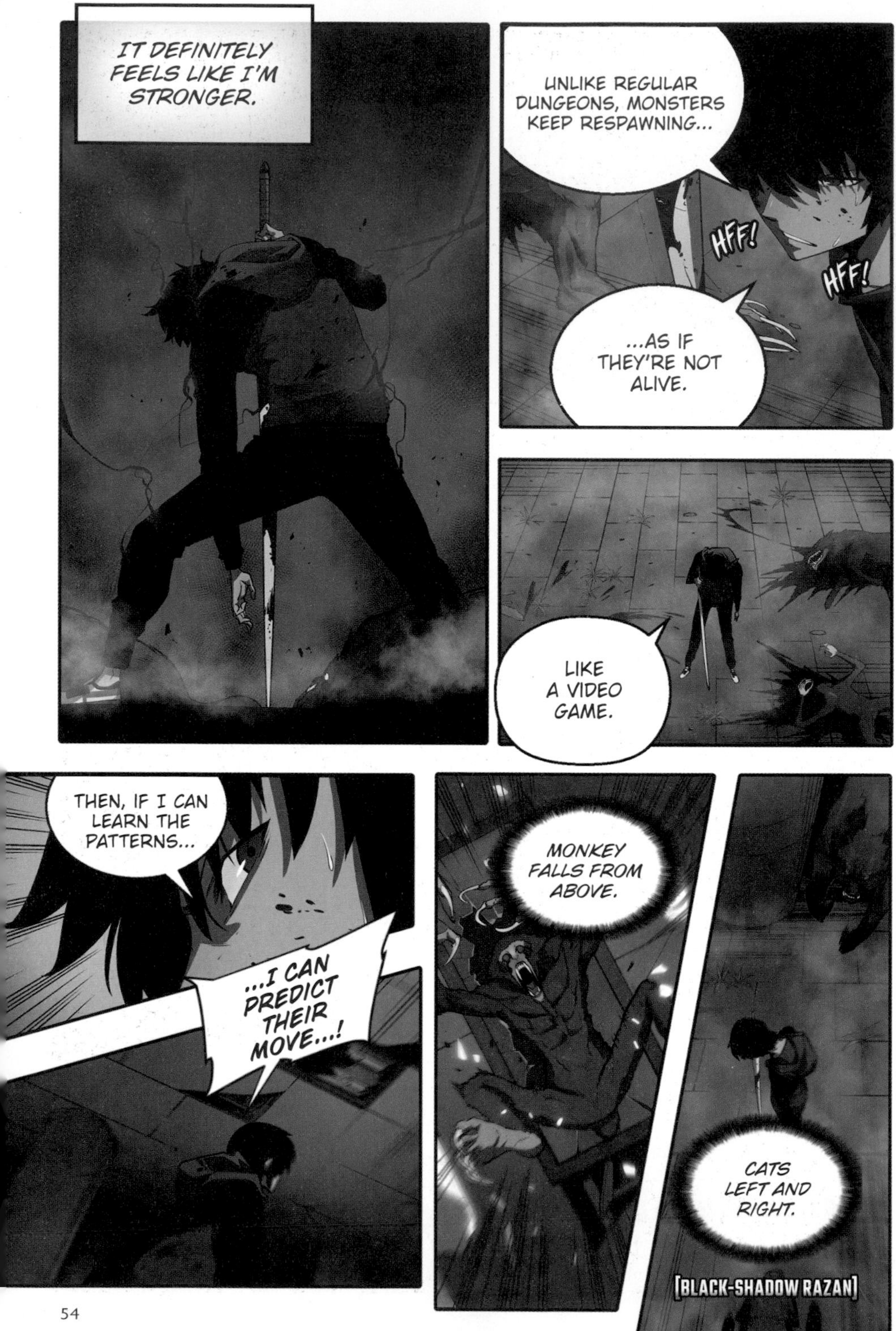
IT DEFINITELY FEELS LIKE I'M STRONGER.
UNLIKE REGULAR DUNGEONS, MONSTERS KEEP RESPAWNING...
HFF!
HFF!
...AS IF THEY'RE NOT ALIVE.
LIKE A VIDEO GAME.
THEN, IF I CAN LEARN THE PATTERNS...
...I CAN PREDICT THEIR MOVE...!
MONKEY FALLS FROM ABOVE.
CATS LEFT AND RIGHT.
[BLACK-SHADOW RAZAN]

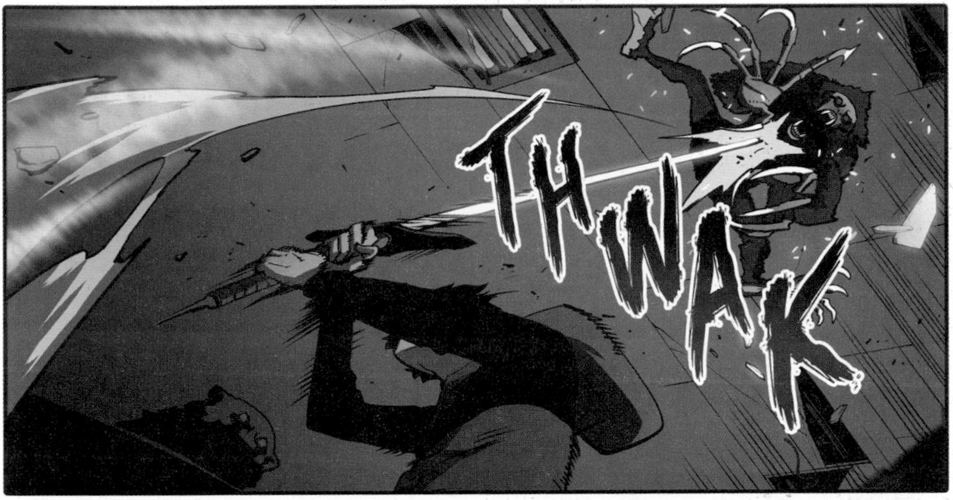
THWAK
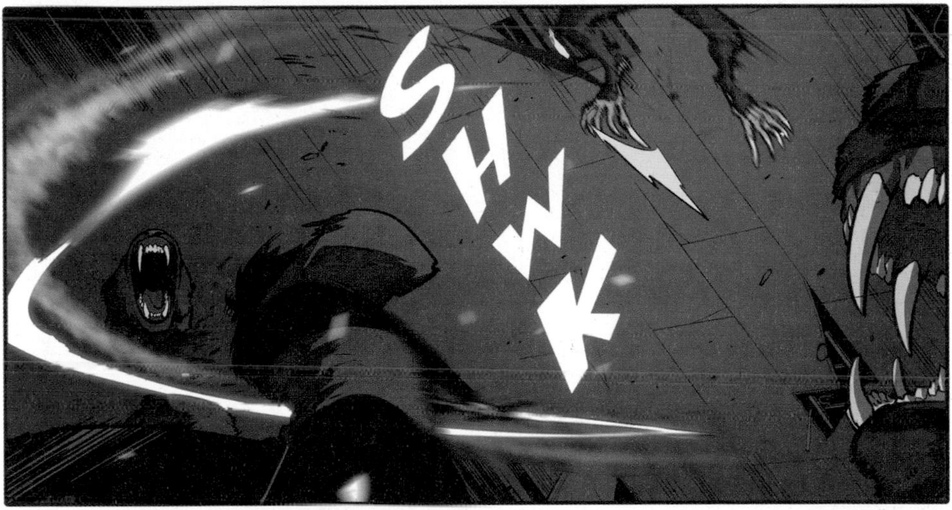
SHWK
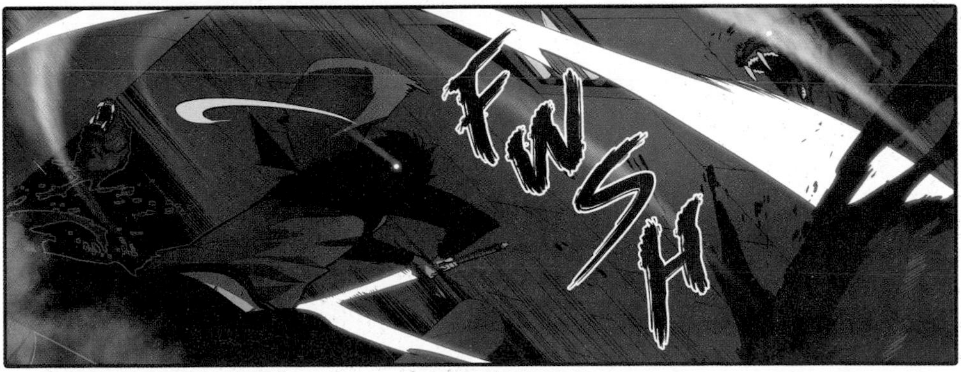
FWSH

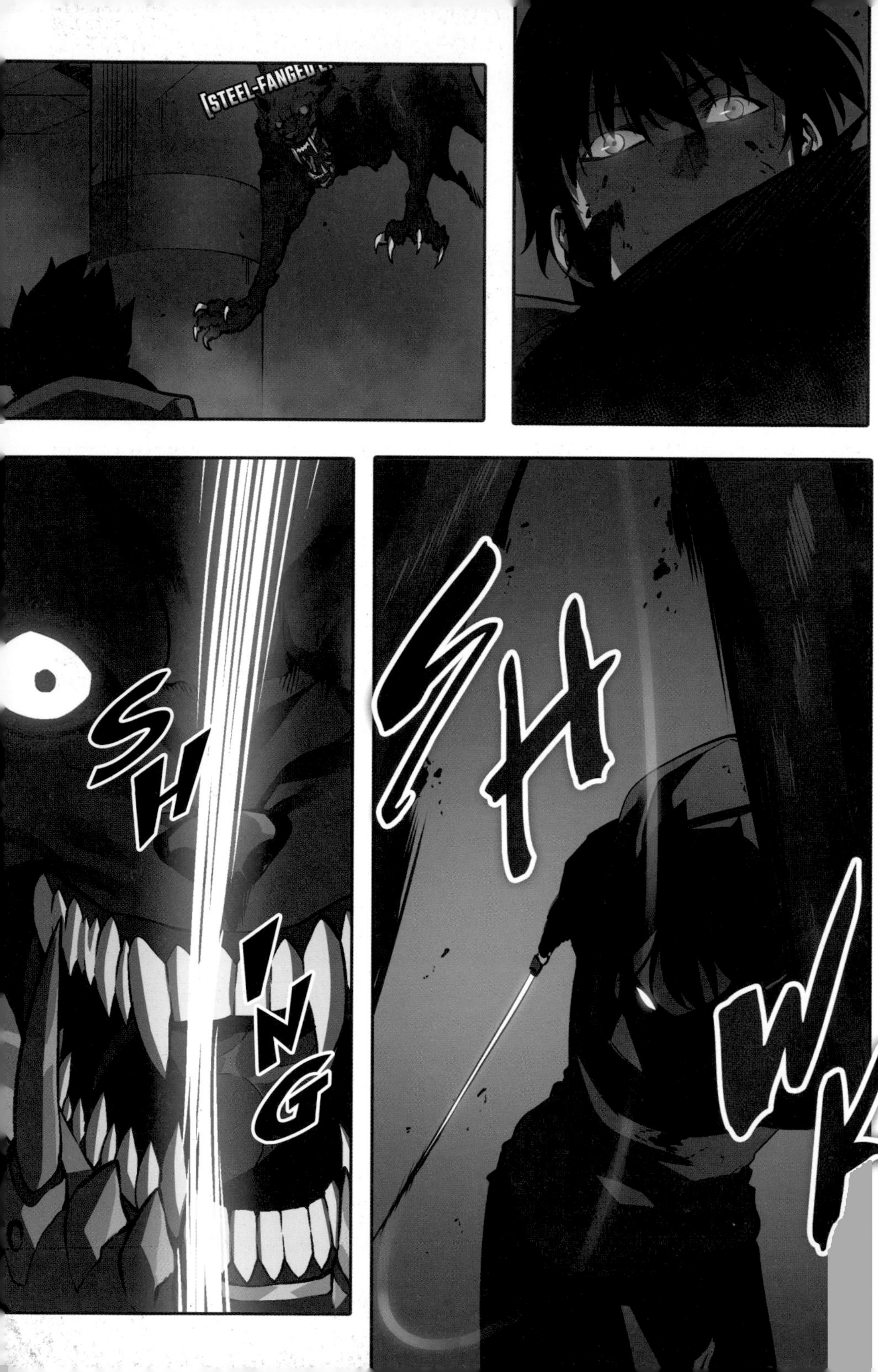
[STEEL-FANGED
SHING
SHWK

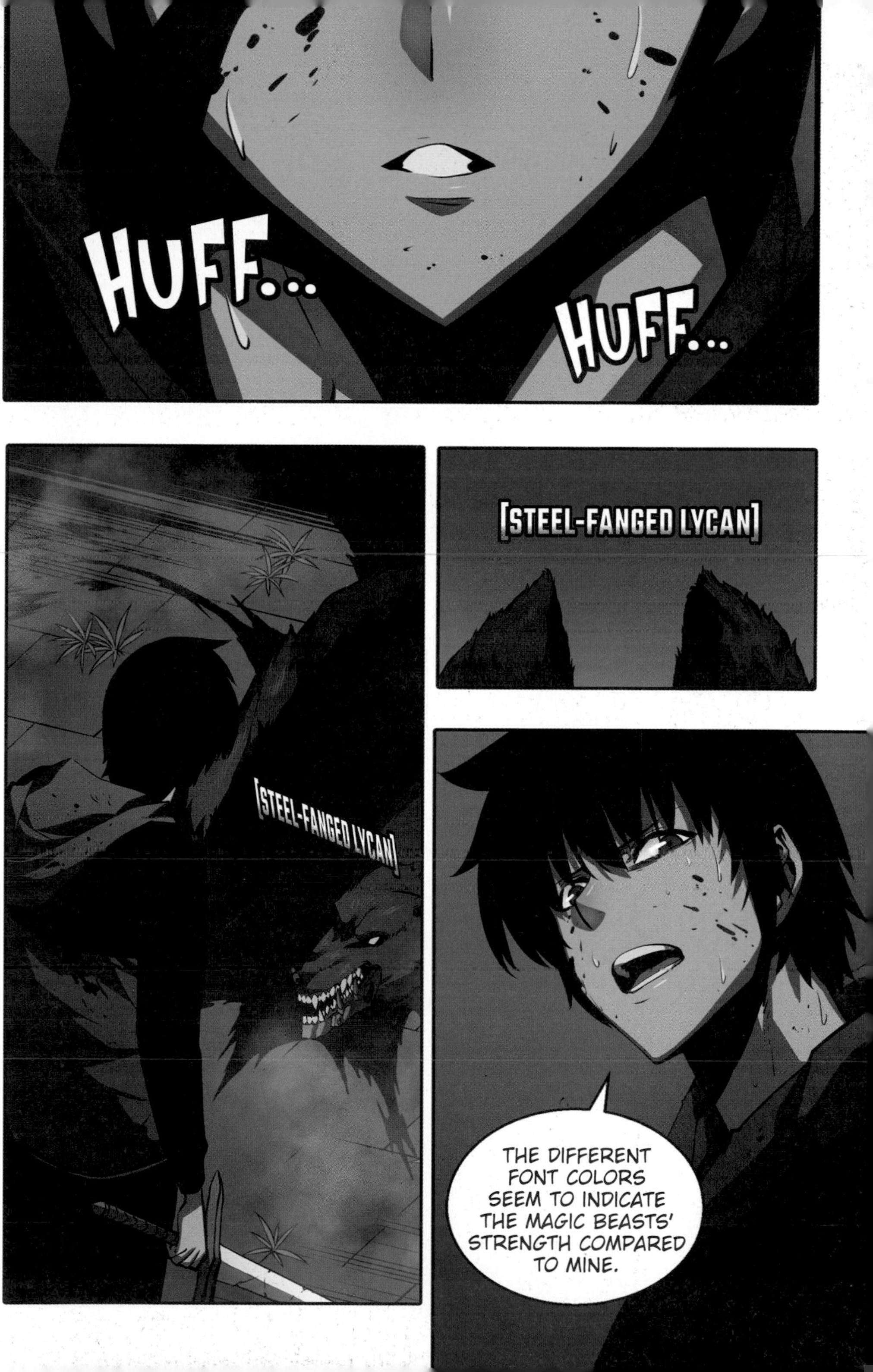
HUFF...
HUFF...
[STEEL-FANGED LYCAN]
[STEEL-FANGED LYCAN]
THE DIFFERENT FONT COLORS SEEM TO INDICATE THE MAGIC BEASTS' STRENGTH COMPARED TO MINE.

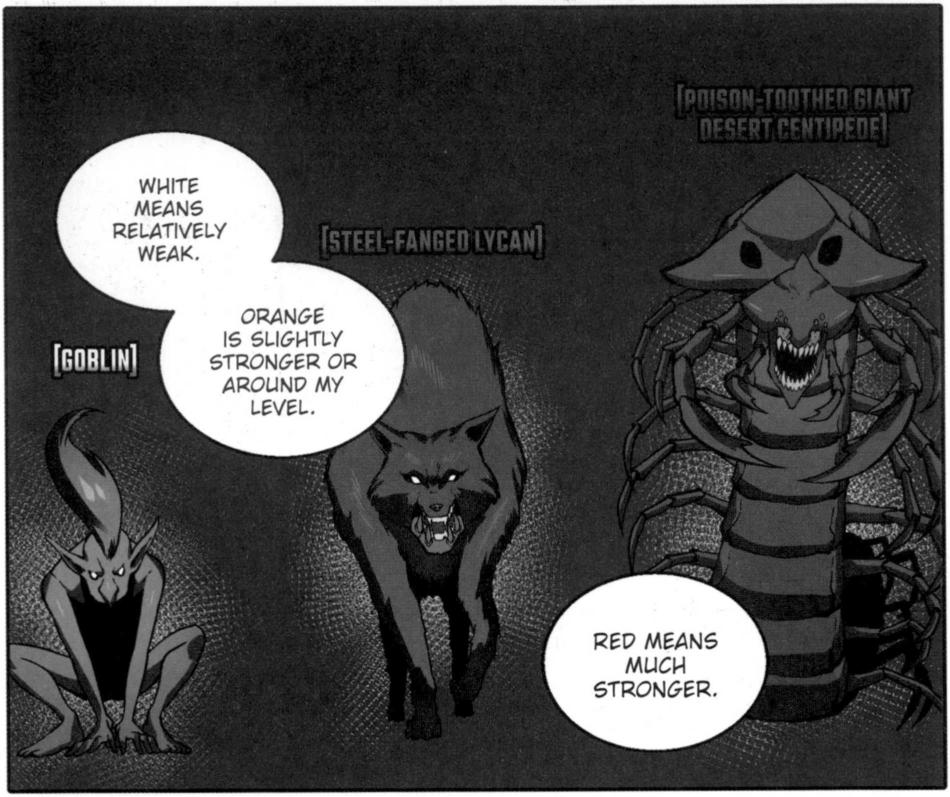
WHITE MEANS RELATIVELY WEAK.
[GOBLIN]
[STEEL-FANGED LYCAN]
ORANGE IS SLIGHTLY STRONGER OR AROUND MY LEVEL.
[POISON-TOOTHED GIANT DESERT CENTIPEDE]
RED MEANS MUCH STRONGER.

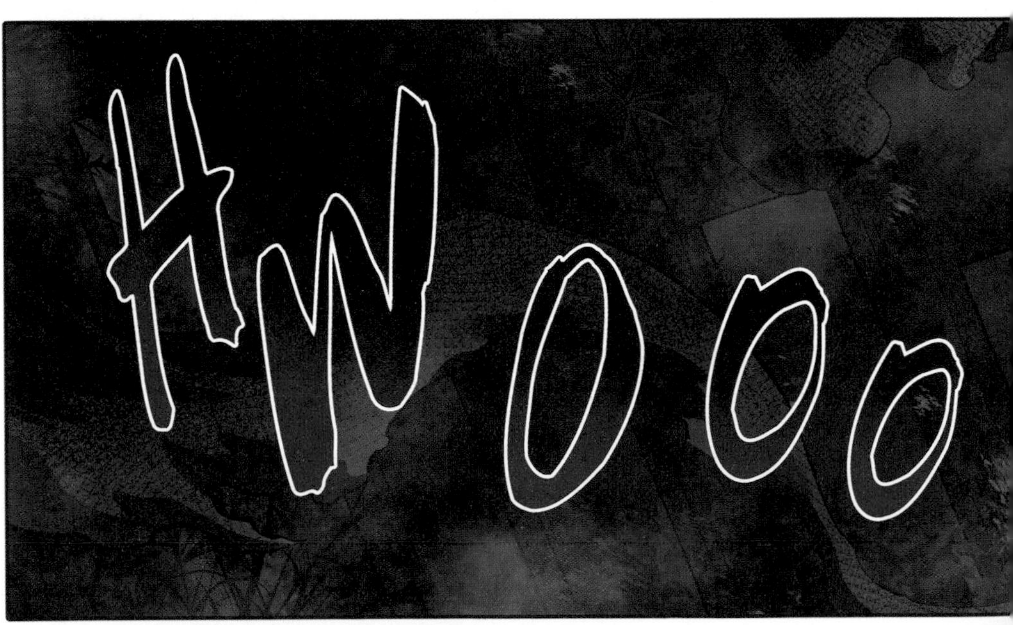
HWOOO

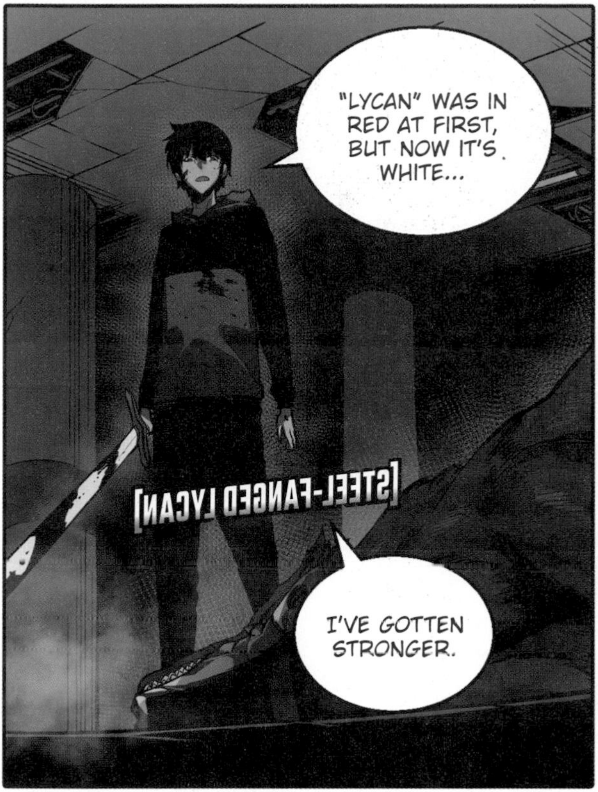
"LYCAN" WAS IN RED AT FIRST, BUT NOW IT'S WHITE...
[STEEL-FANGED LYCAN]
I'VE GOTTEN STRONGER.
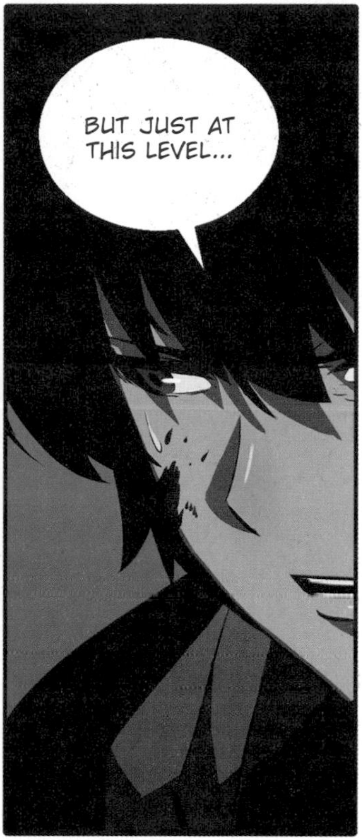
BUT JUST AT THIS LEVEL...
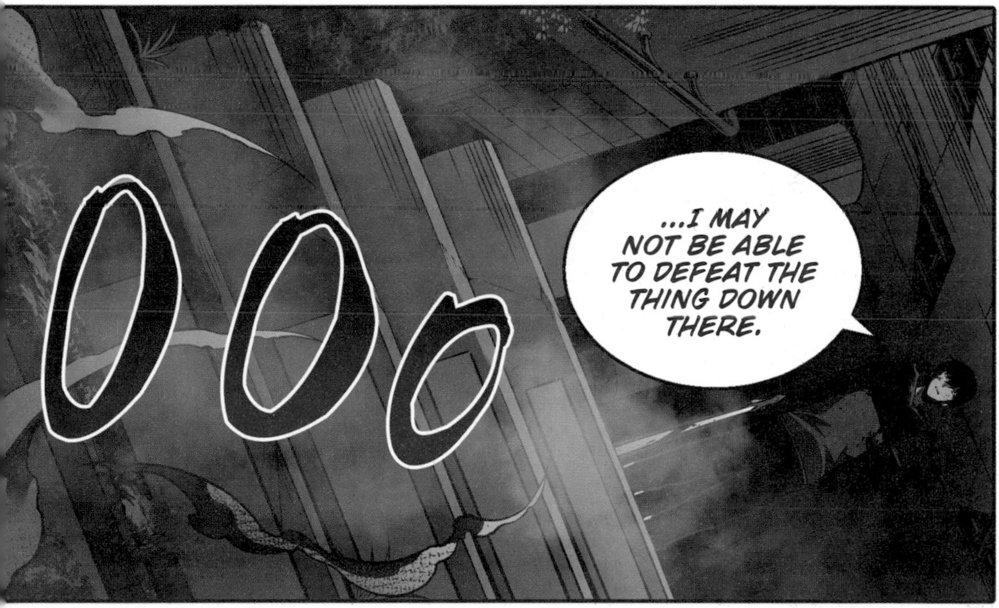
OOo
...I MAY NOT BE ABLE TO DEFEAT THE THING DOWN THERE.

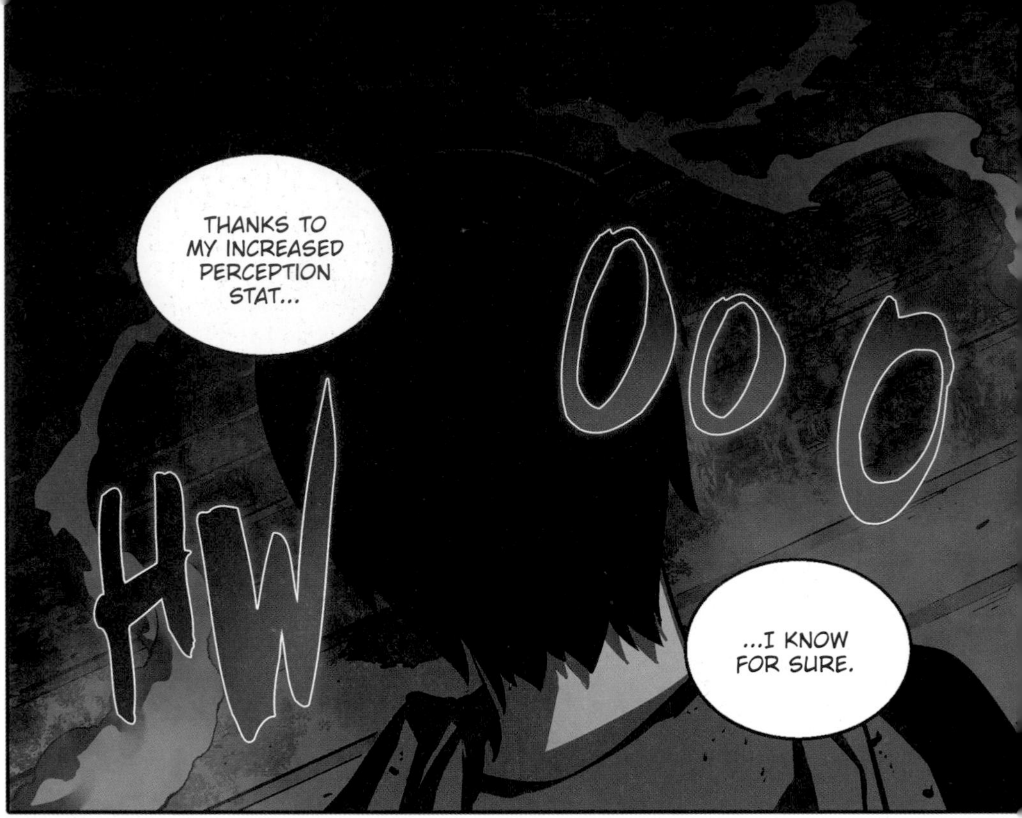
THANKS TO MY INCREASED PERCEPTION STAT...
HWOOO
...I KNOW FOR SURE.

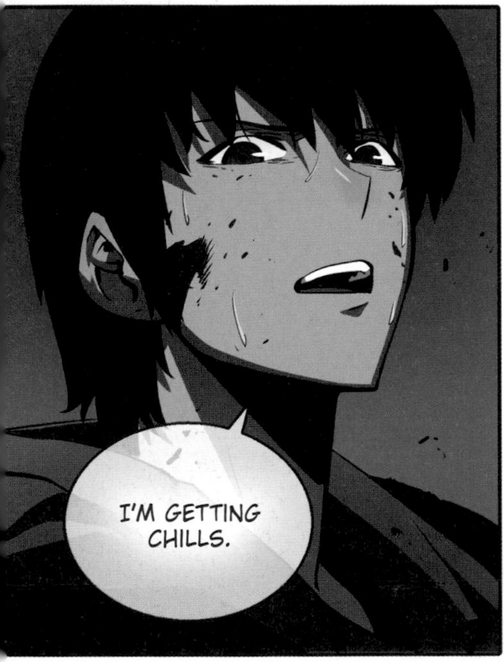
I'M GETTING CHILLS.

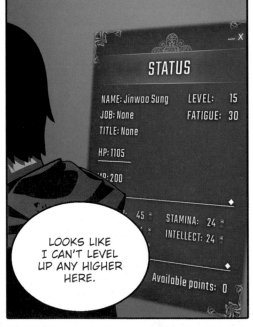

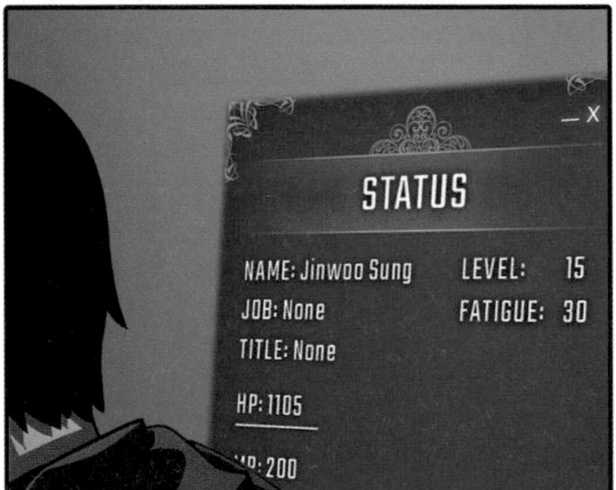
STATUS
NAME: Jinwoo Sung
LEVEL: 15
JOB: None
FATIGUE: 30
TITLE: None
HP: 1105
STAMINA: 24
INTELLECT: 24
Available points: 0
LOOKS LIKE I CAN'T LEVEL UP ANY HIGHER HERE.

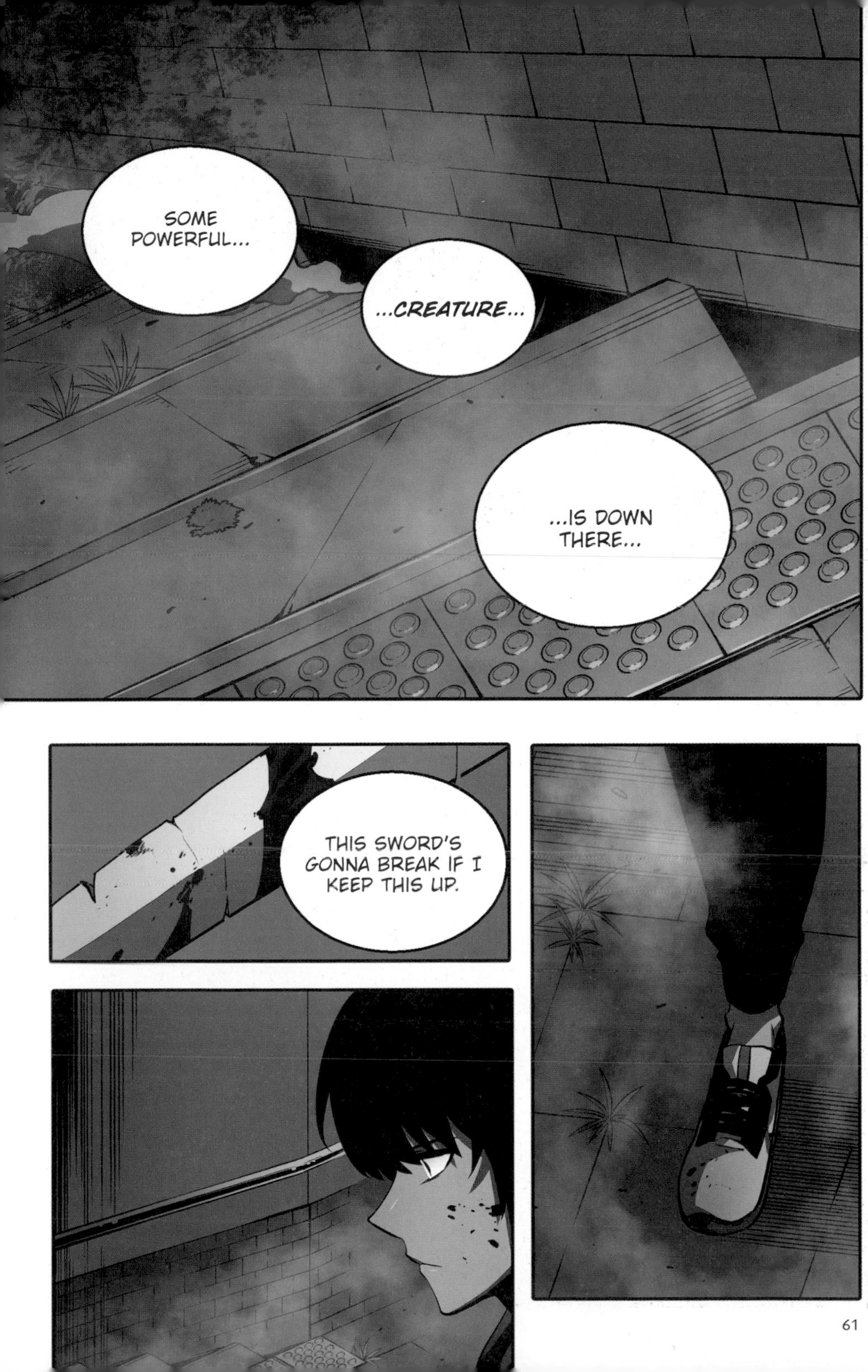
SOME POWERFUL...
...CREATURE...
...IS DOWN THERE...
THIS SWORD'S GONNA BREAK IF I KEEP THIS UP.

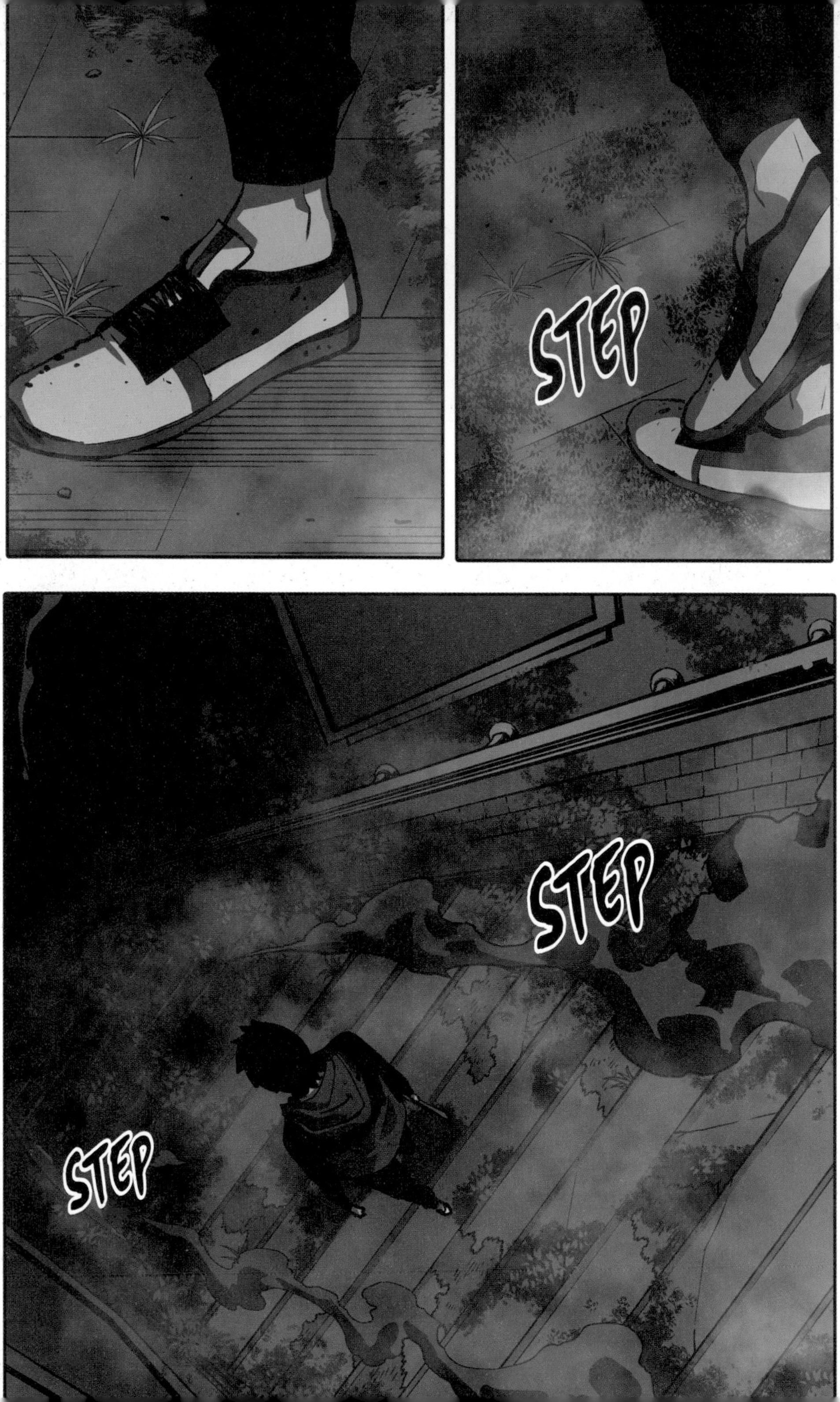
STEP
STEP
STEP

CHAPTER 4

Boss Round

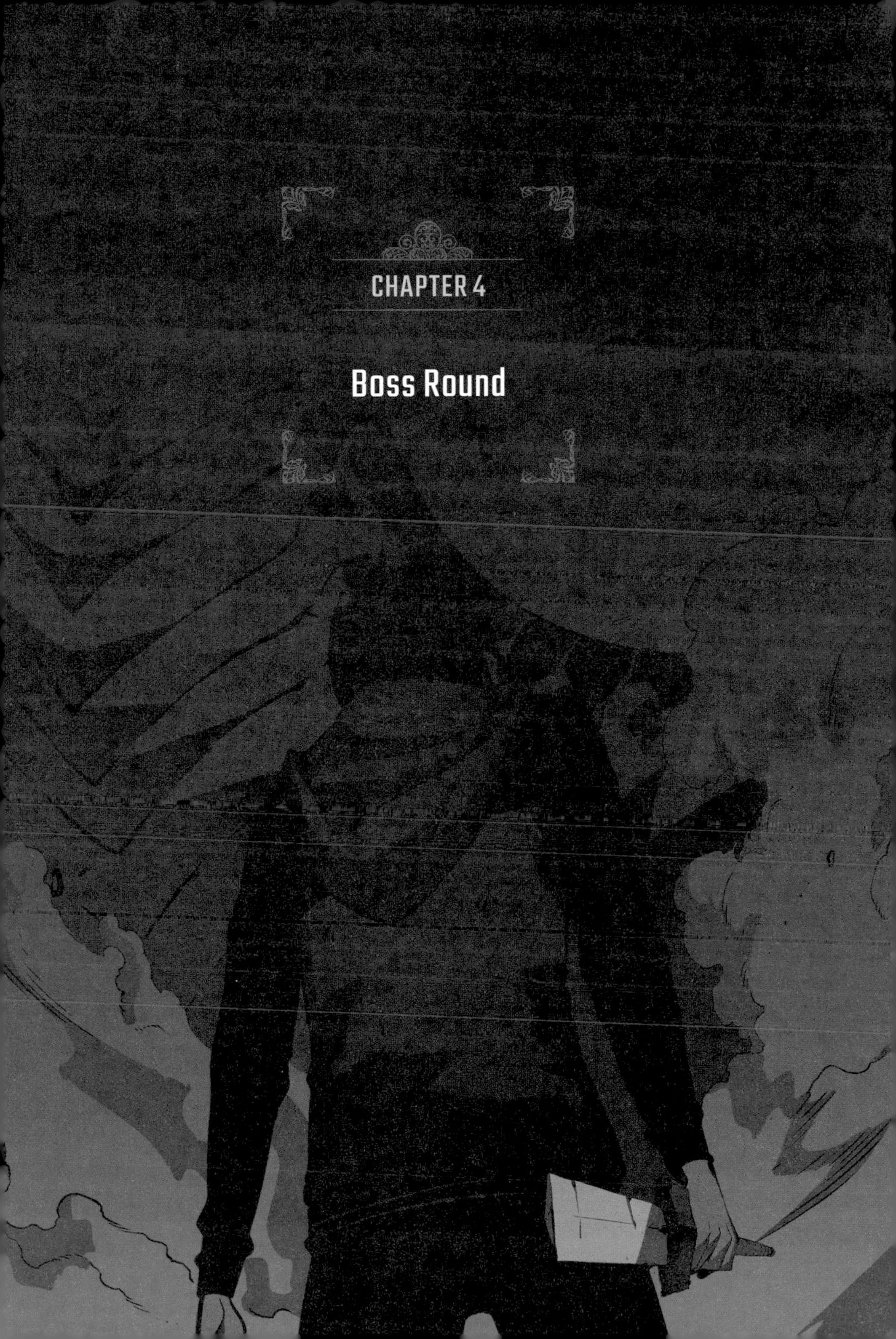

Solo
Leveling

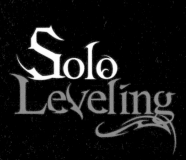

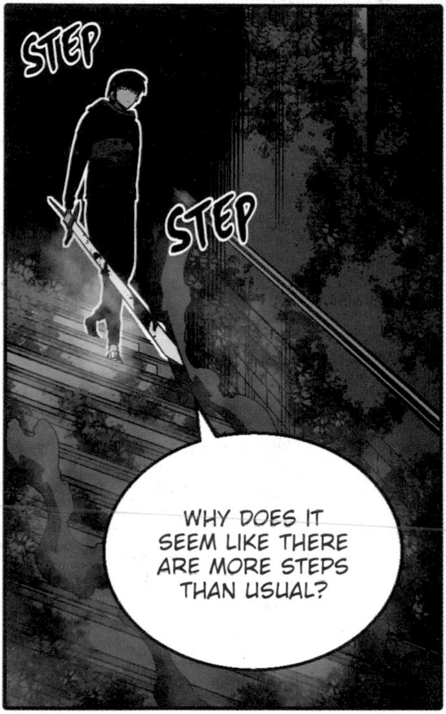
STEP
STEP
WHY DOES IT SEEM LIKE THERE ARE MORE STEPS THAN USUAL?

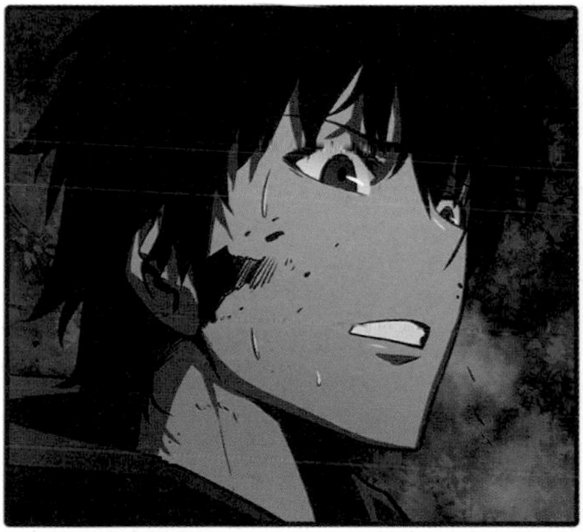

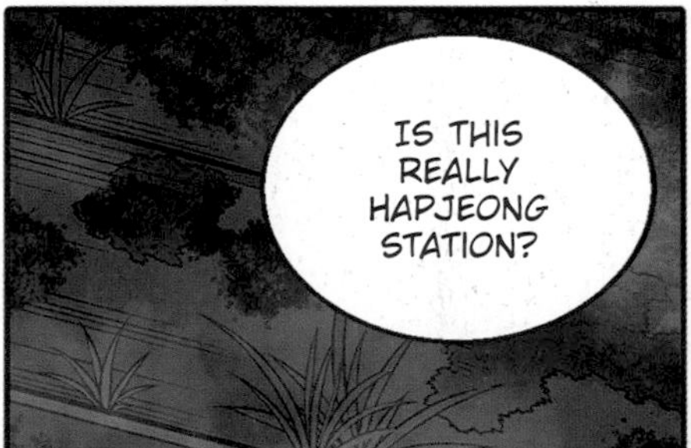
IS THIS REALLY HAPJEONG STATION?

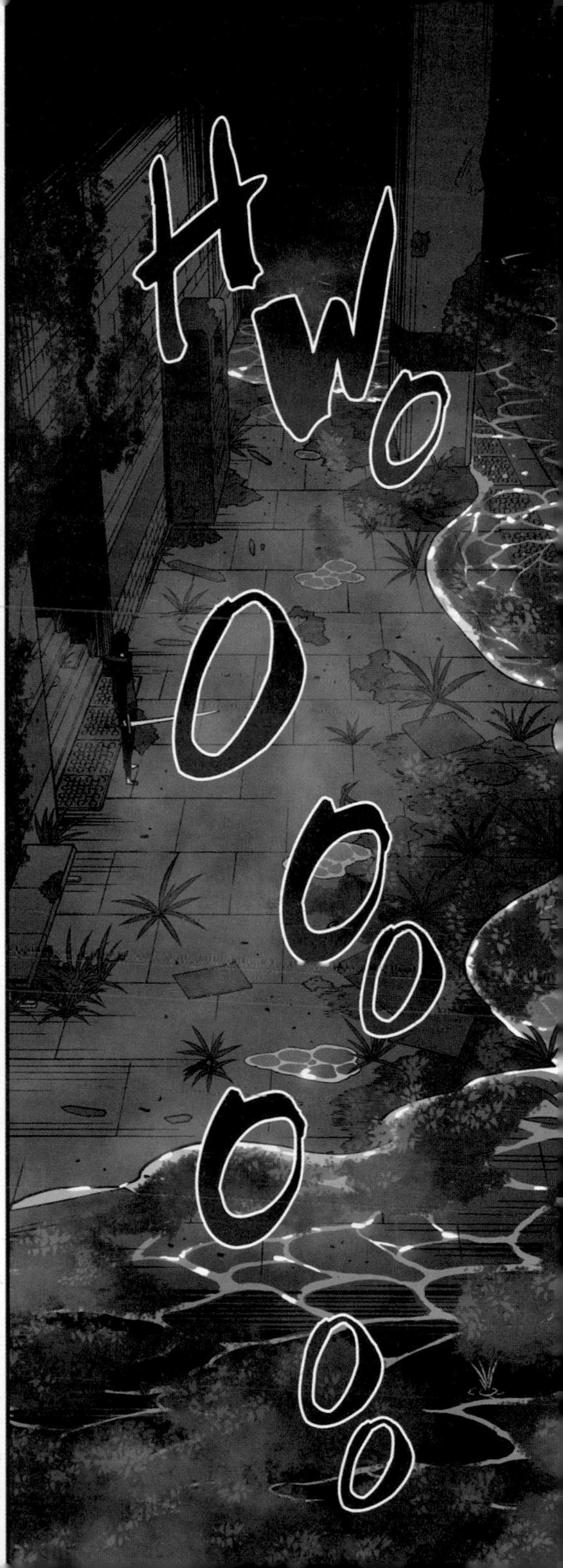
HWOOOOOOOO

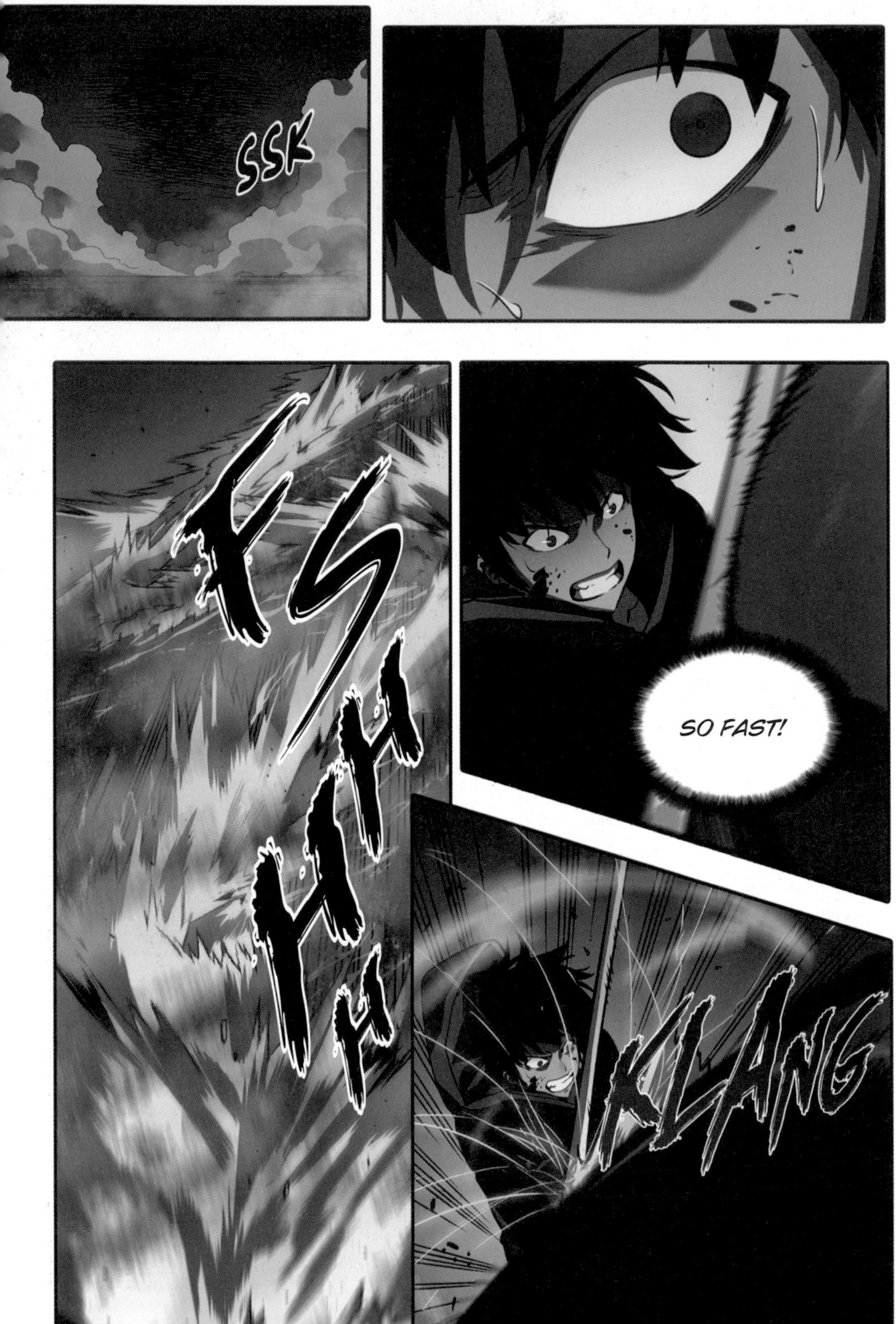
SSK
FSHHH
SO FAST!
KLANG

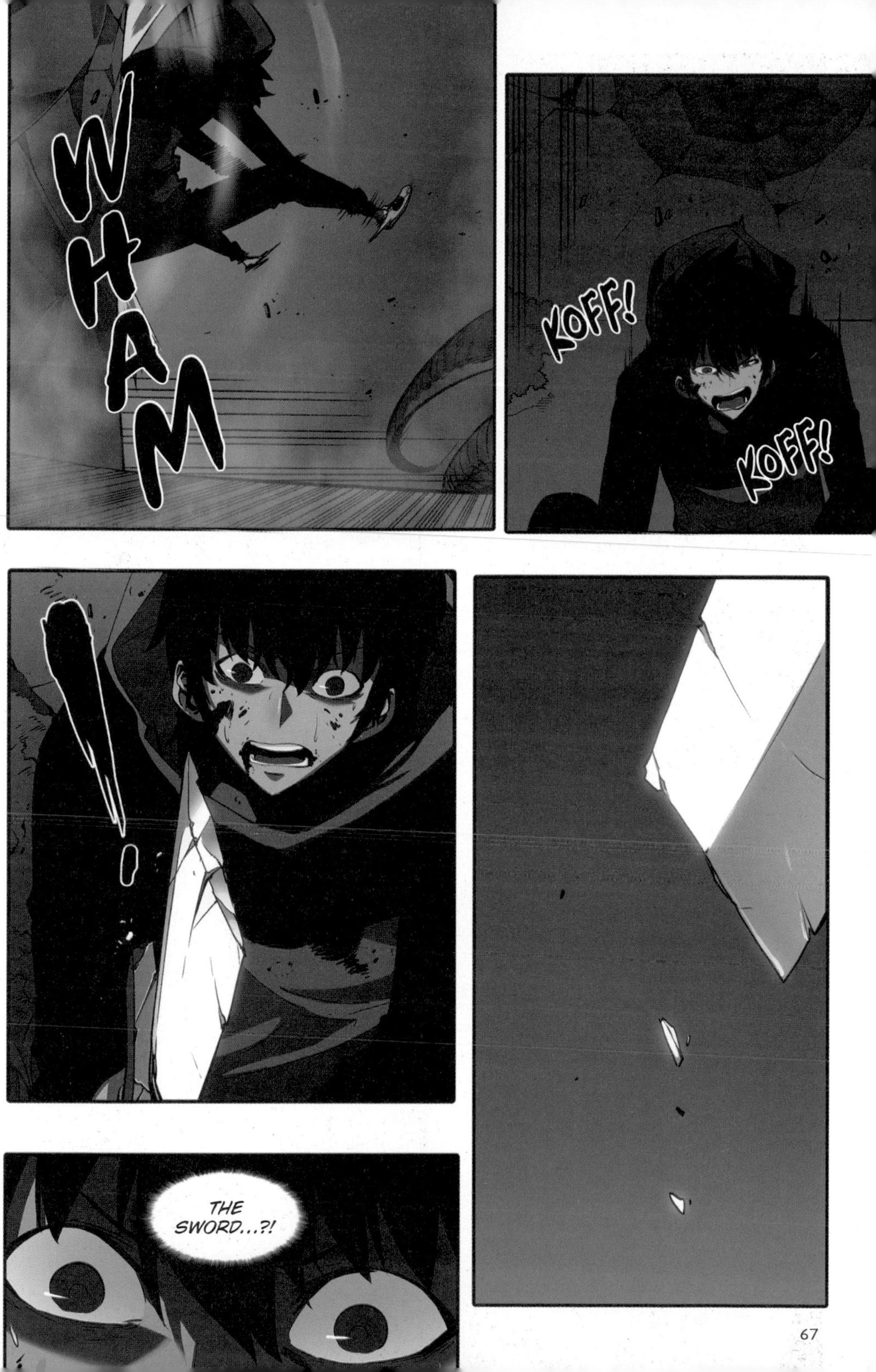
WHAM
KOFF!
KOFF!
!
THE SWORD...?!

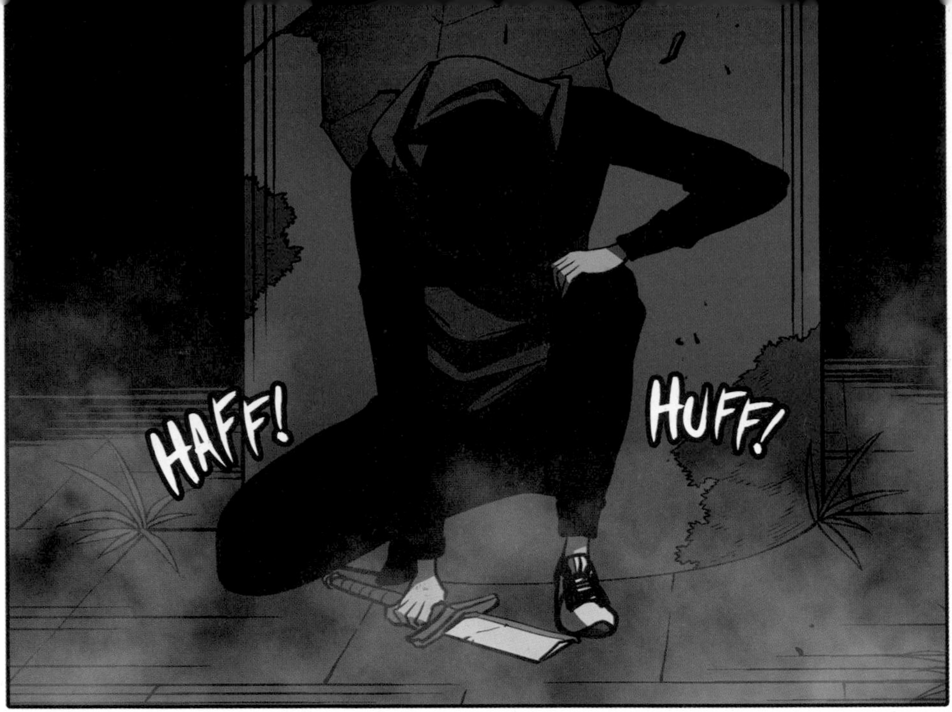
HAFF!
HUFF!
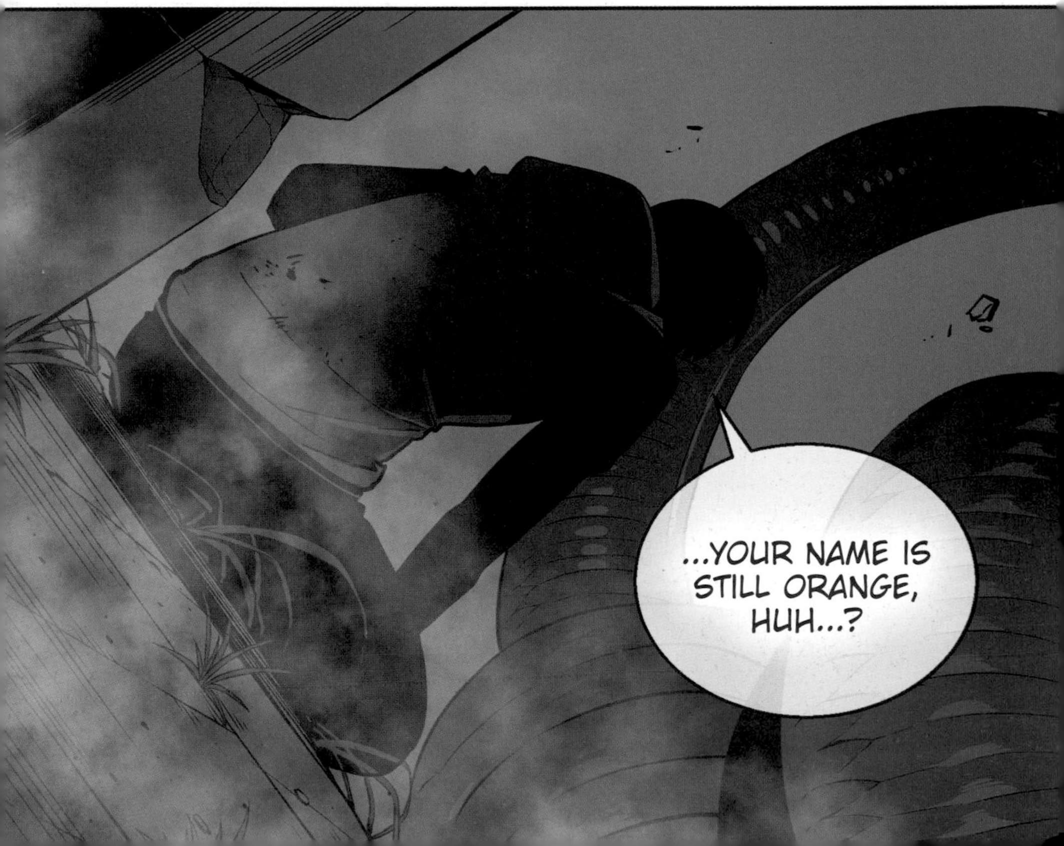
...YOUR NAME IS STILL ORANGE, HUH...?

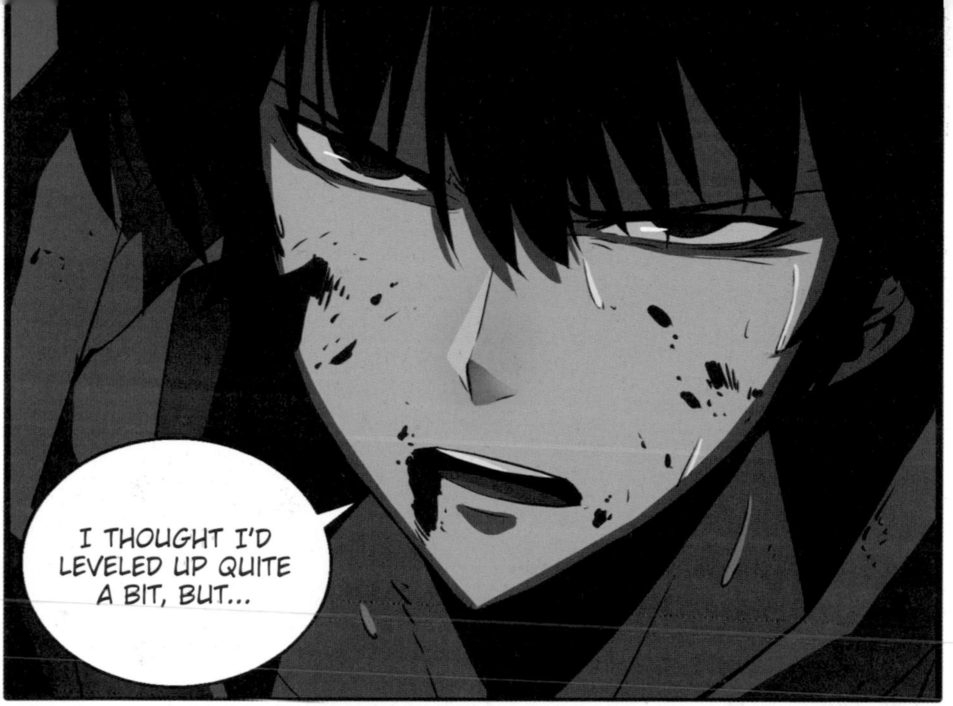
I THOUGHT I'D LEVELED UP QUITE A BIT, BUT...
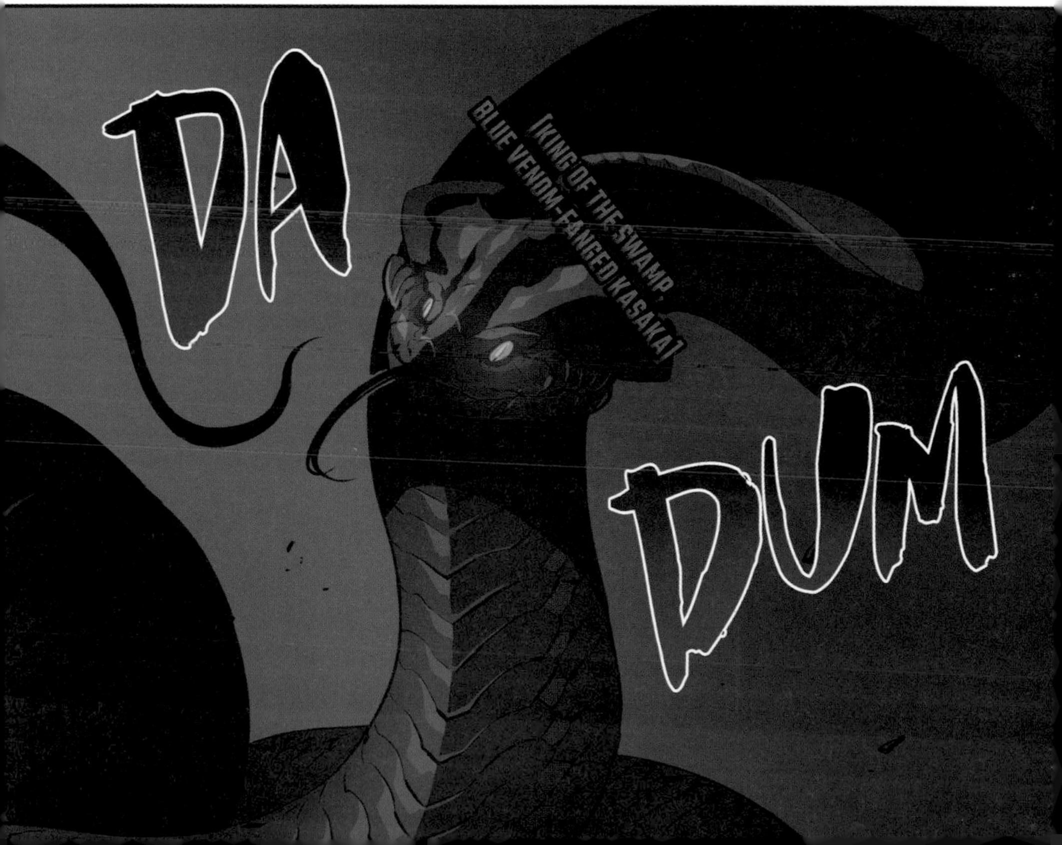
DA
[KING OF THE SWAMP, BLUE VENOM-FANGED KASAKA]
DUM

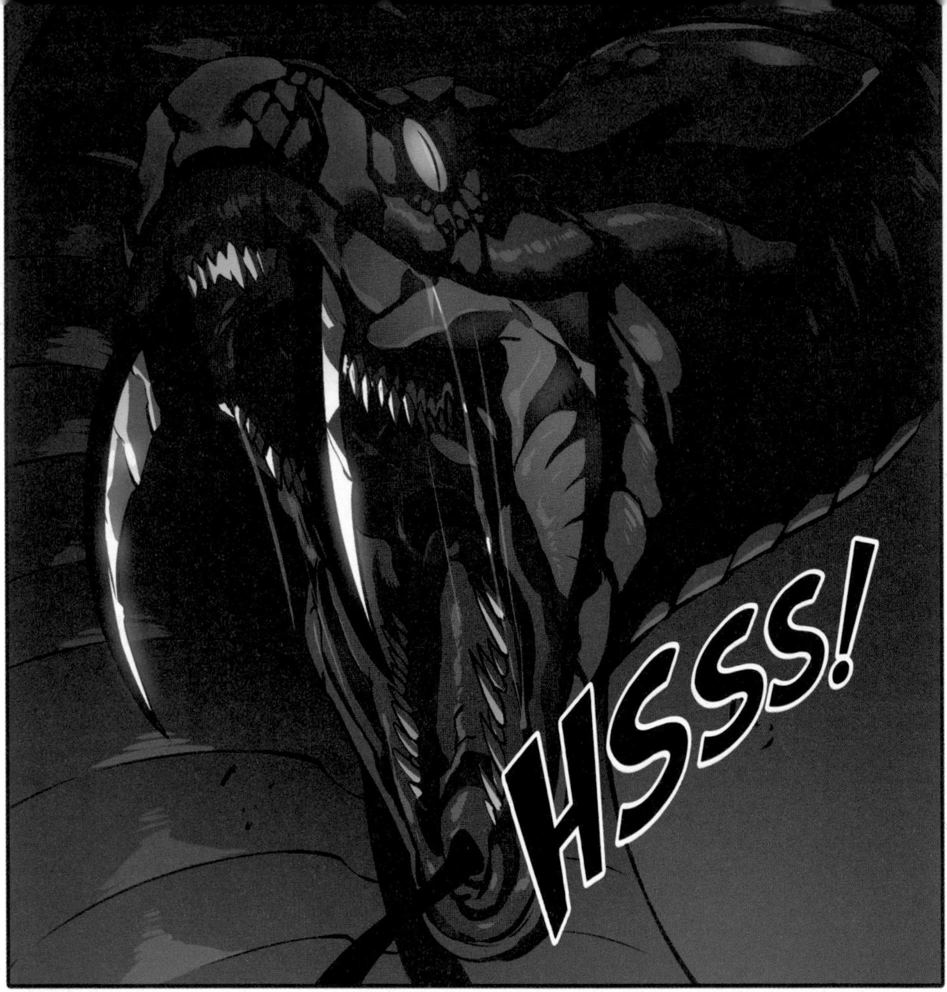
HSSS!

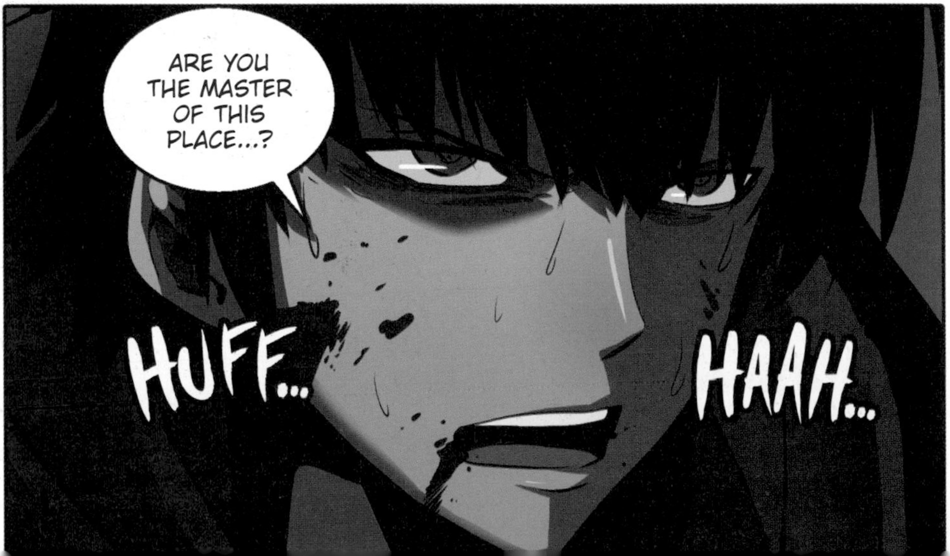
ARE YOU THE MASTER OF THIS PLACE...?
HUFF...
HAAH...

SPIN

GRIP

SWORD ATTACKS ARE USELESS ON THOSE SCALES.

ATTACKING WITH MY FISTS PROBABLY WOULDN'T DO A THING.

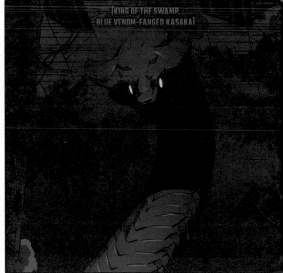

[KING OF THE SWAMP, BLUE VENOM-FANGED KASAKA]

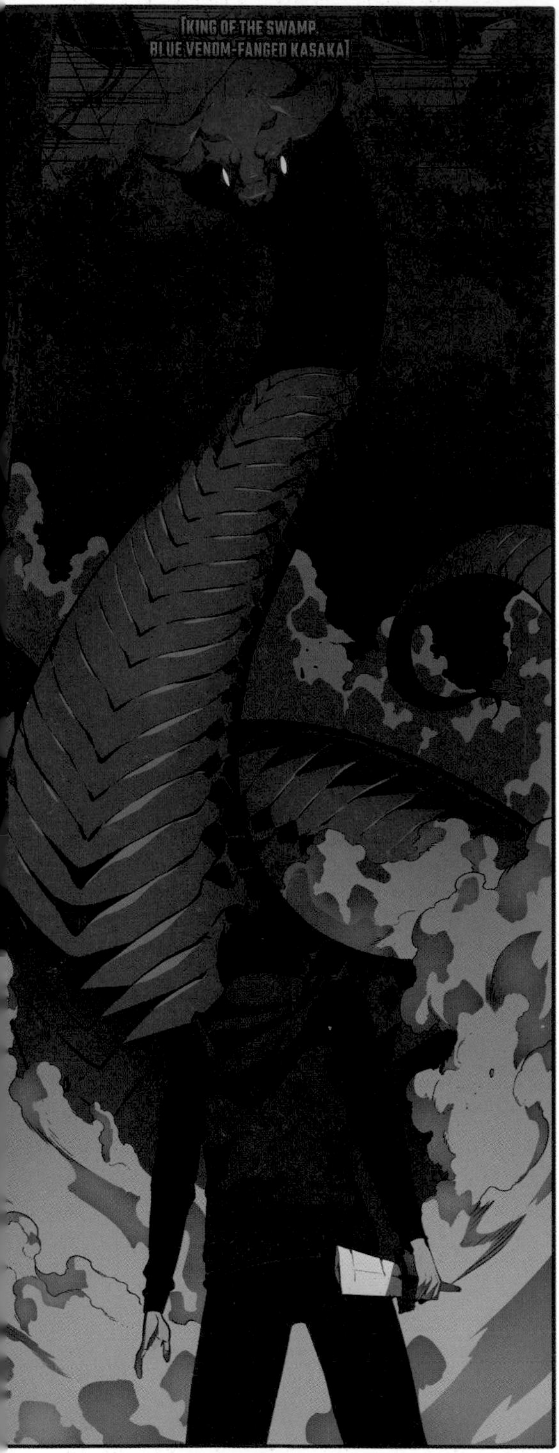
[KING OF THE SWAMP, BLUE VENOM-FANGED KASAKA]

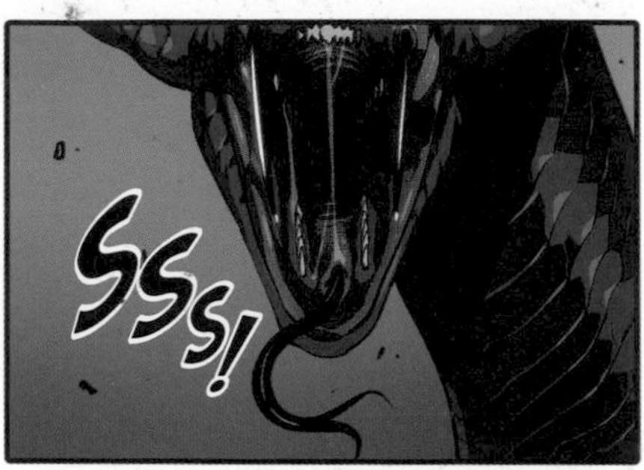
SSS!

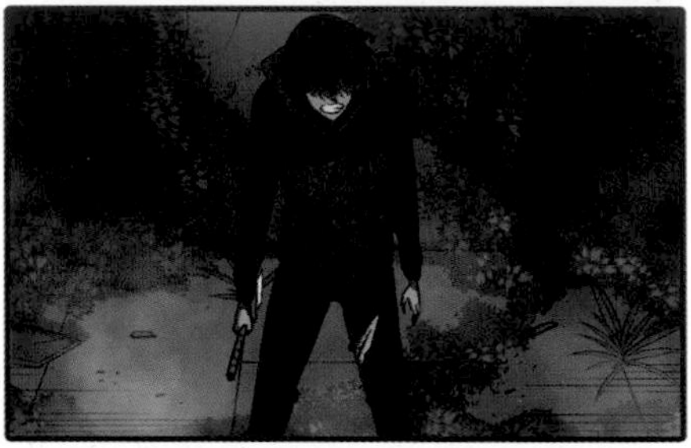

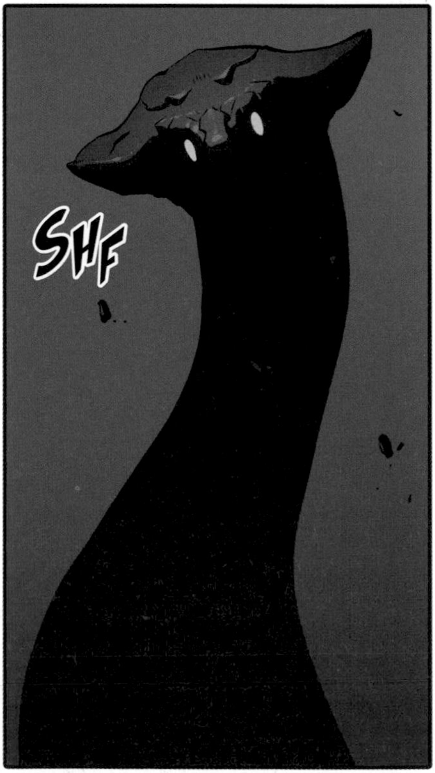
SHF

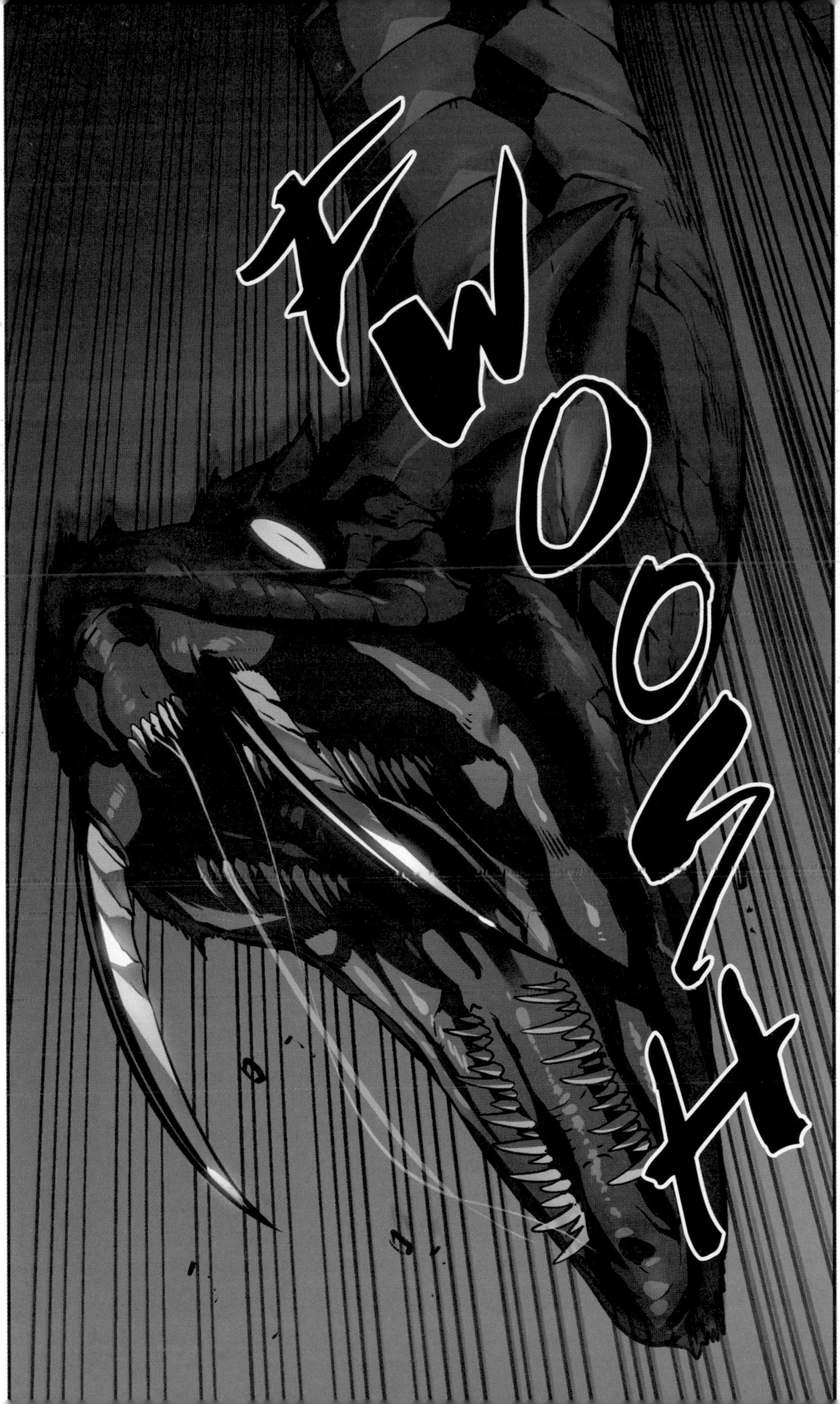
FWOOSH

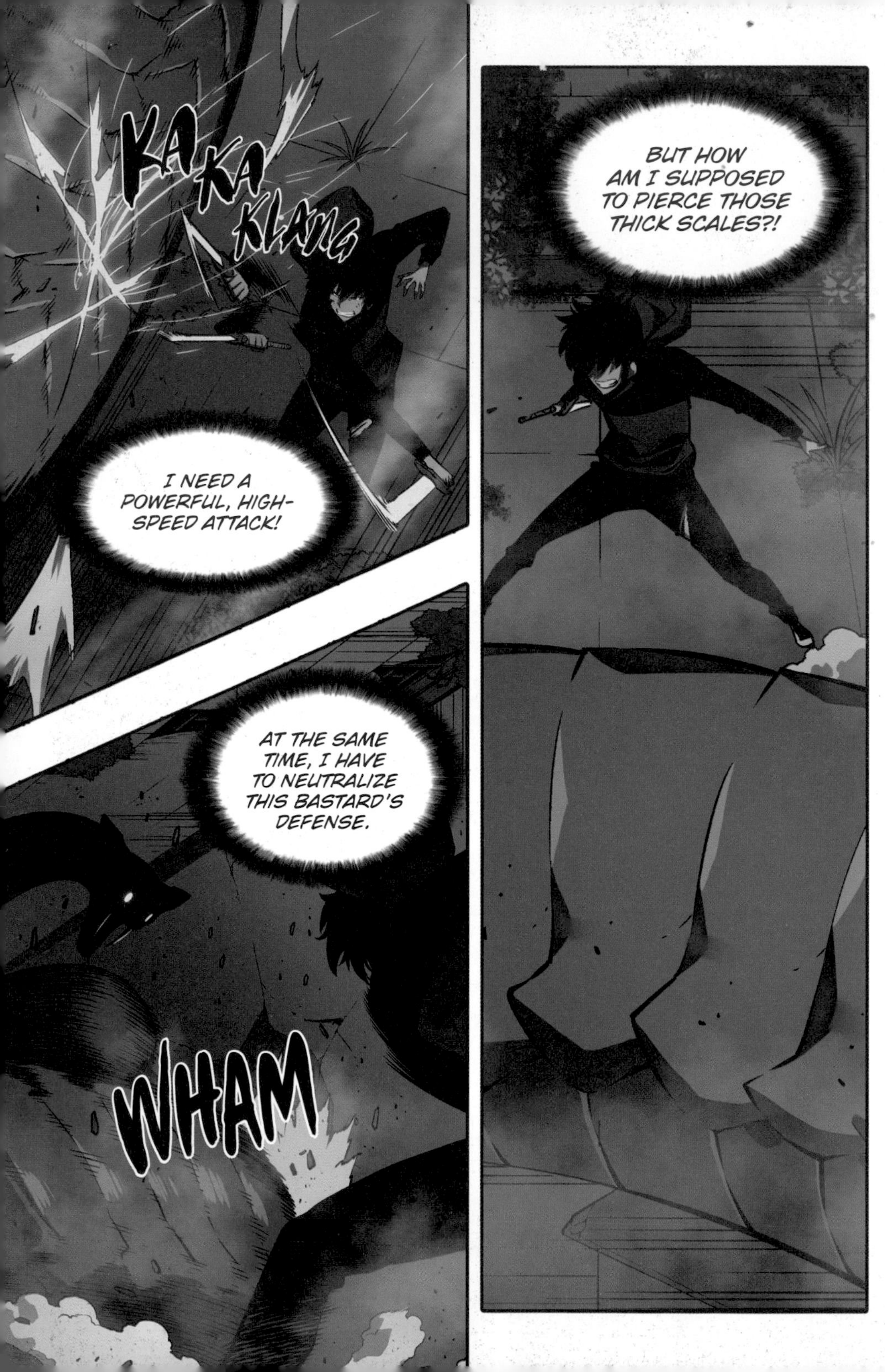
KA KA KLANG
I NEED A POWERFUL, HIGH-SPEED ATTACK!
AT THE SAME TIME, I HAVE TO NEUTRALIZE THIS BASTARD'S DEFENSE.
WHAM
BUT HOW AM I SUPPOSED TO PIERCE THOSE THICK SCALES?!

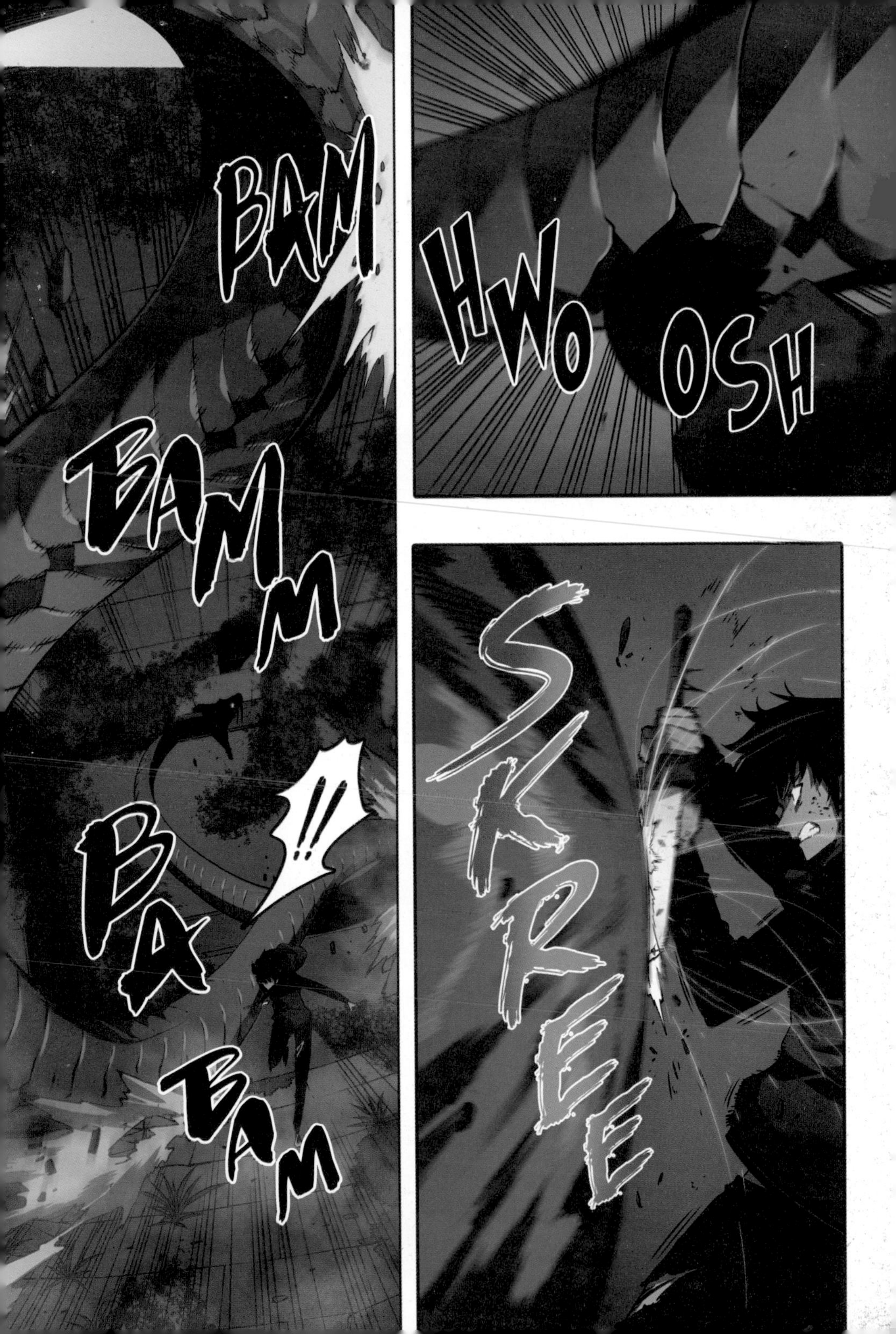
BAM
BAMMM
BA
!!
BAM
HWOOSH
SKREEE

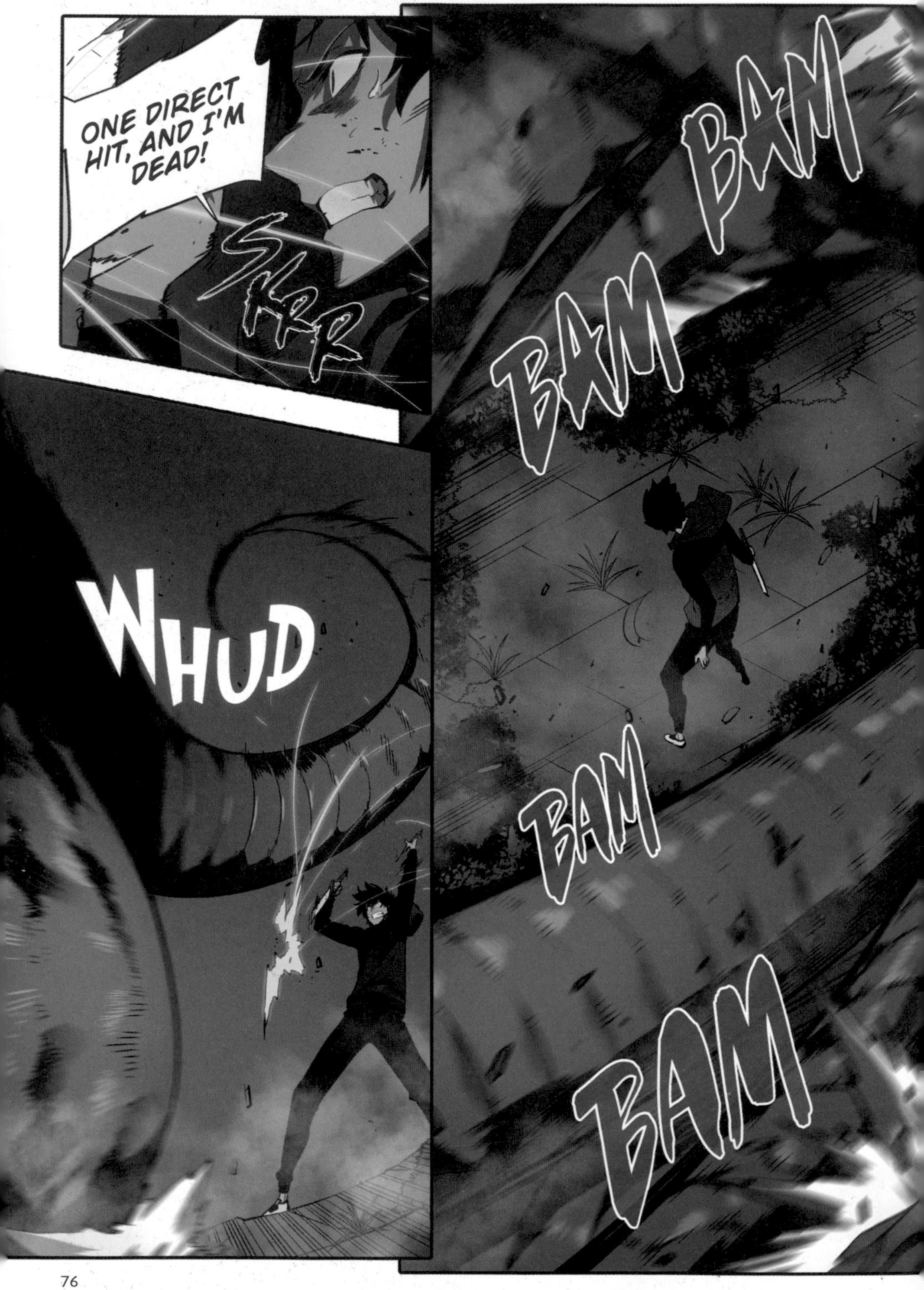
ONE DIRECT HIT, AND I'M DEAD!
SKRR
WHUD
BAM BAM
BAM
BAM
BAM

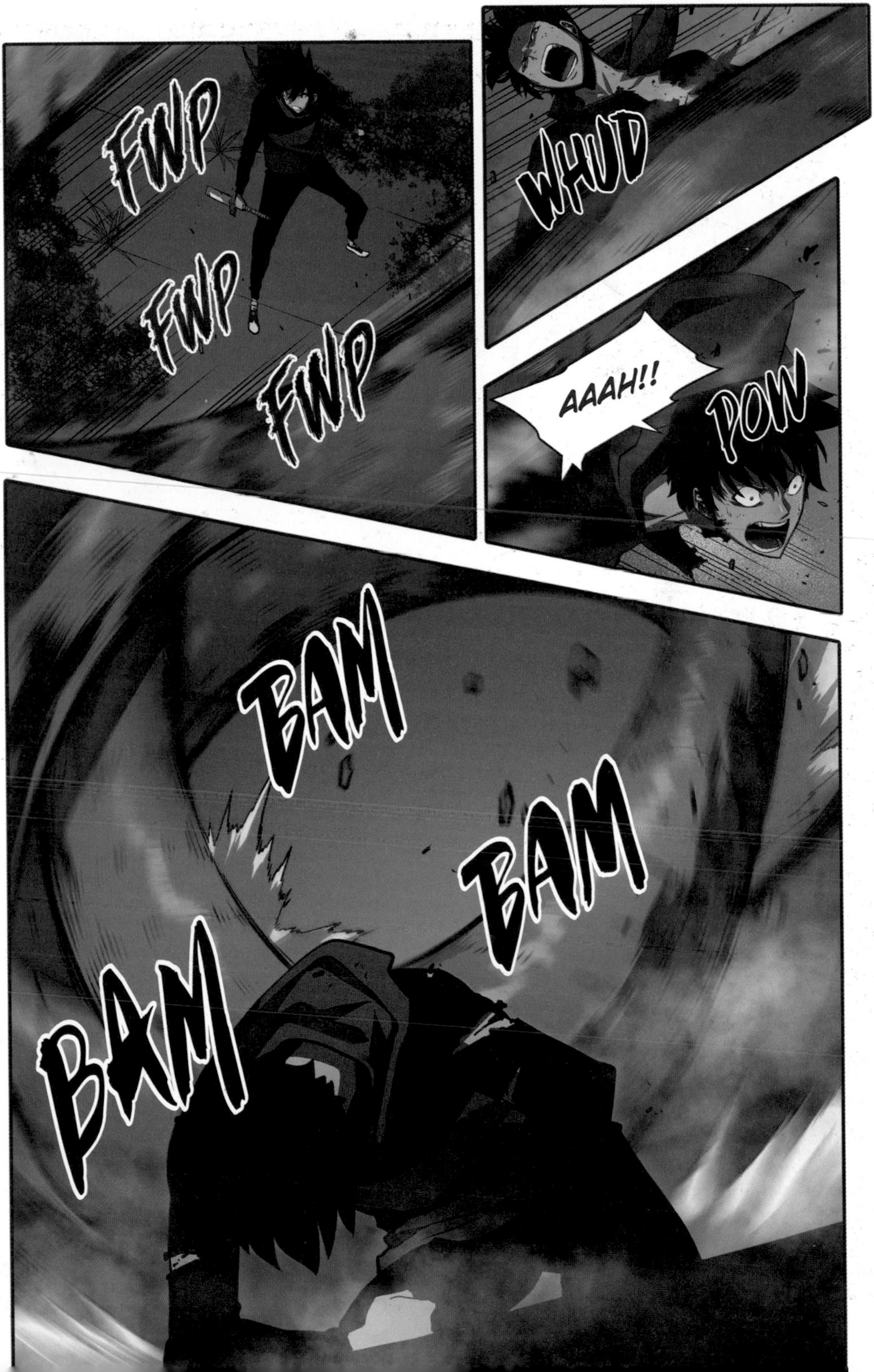
FWP
FWP
FWP
WHUD
AAAH!!
POW
BAM
BAM
BAM

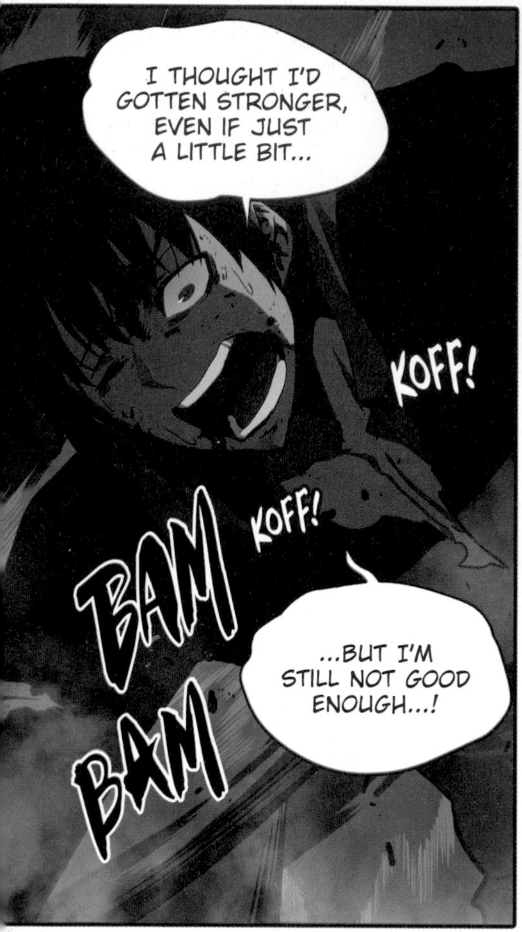
I THOUGHT I'D GOTTEN STRONGER, EVEN IF JUST A LITTLE BIT...
KOFF!
BAM
KOFF!
BAM
...BUT I'M STILL NOT GOOD ENOUGH...!
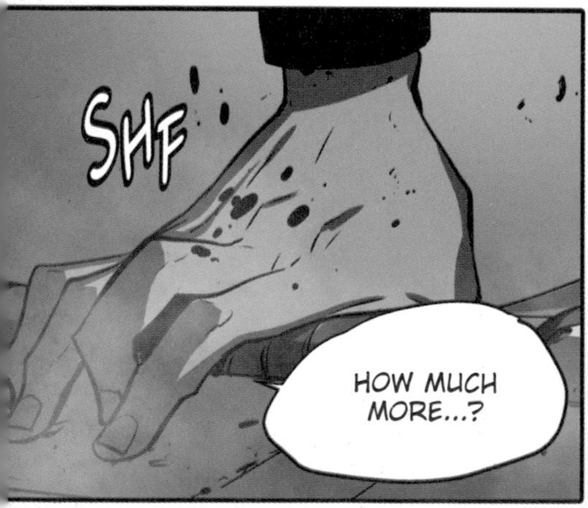
SHF
HOW MUCH MORE...?
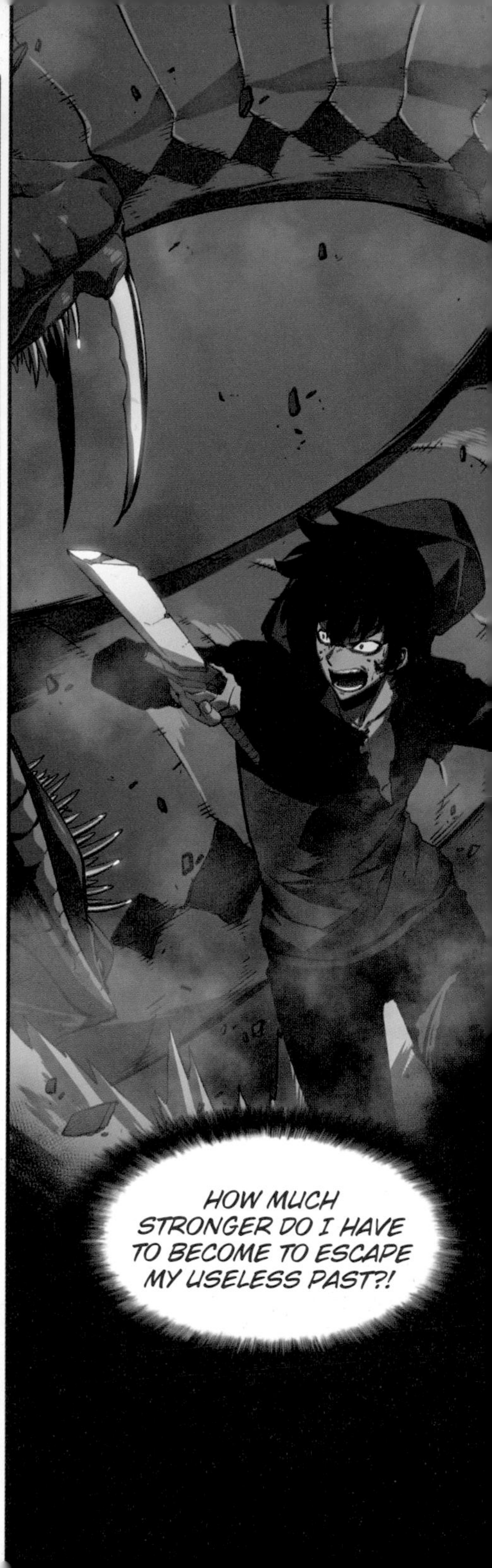
HOW MUCH STRONGER DO I HAVE TO BECOME TO ESCAPE MY USELESS PAST?!

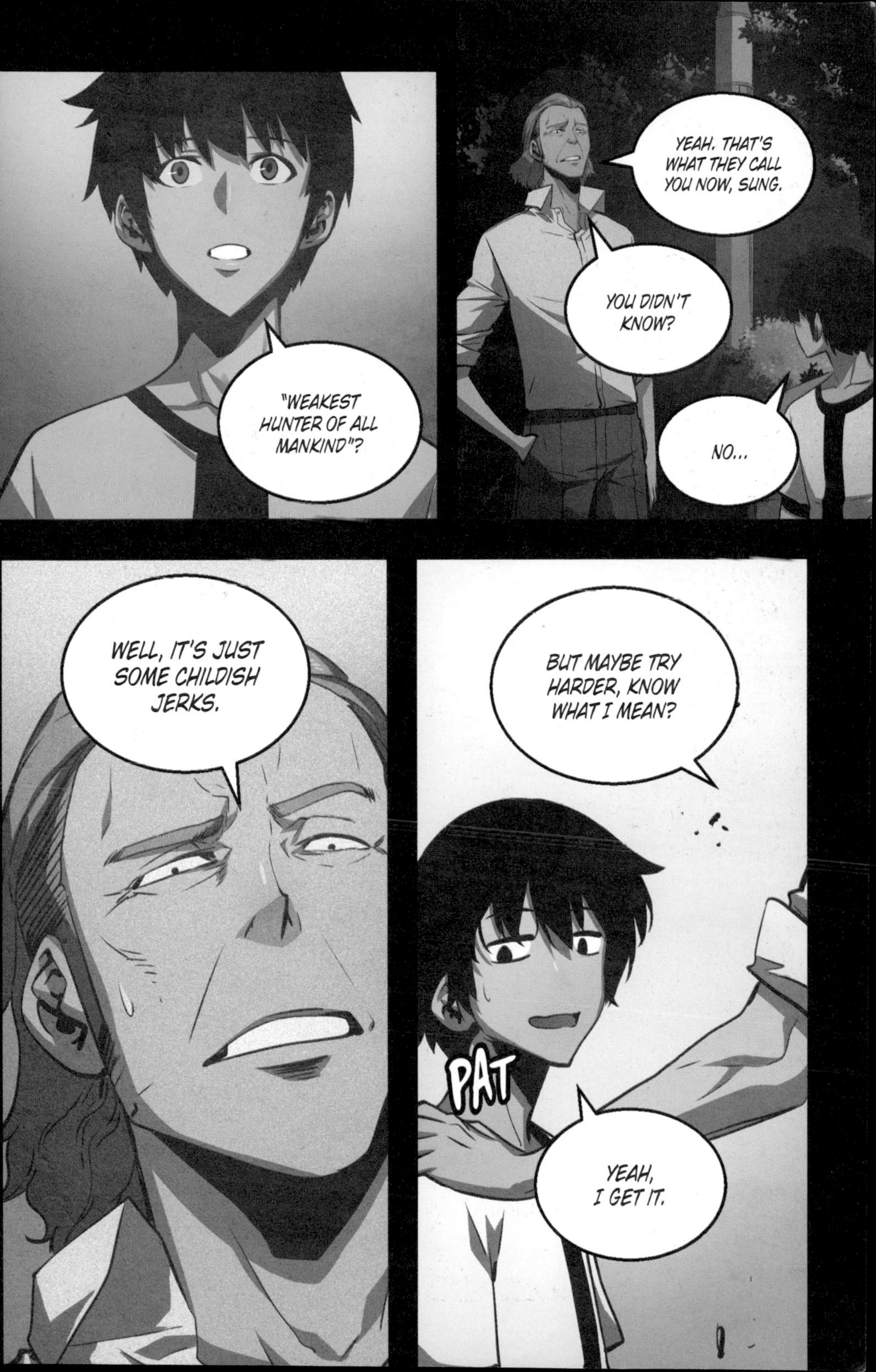
"WEAKEST HUNTER OF ALL MANKIND"?
YEAH. THAT'S WHAT THEY CALL YOU NOW, SUNG.
YOU DIDN'T KNOW?
NO...
WELL, IT'S JUST SOME CHILDISH JERKS.
BUT MAYBE TRY HARDER, KNOW WHAT I MEAN?
PAT
YEAH, I GET IT.

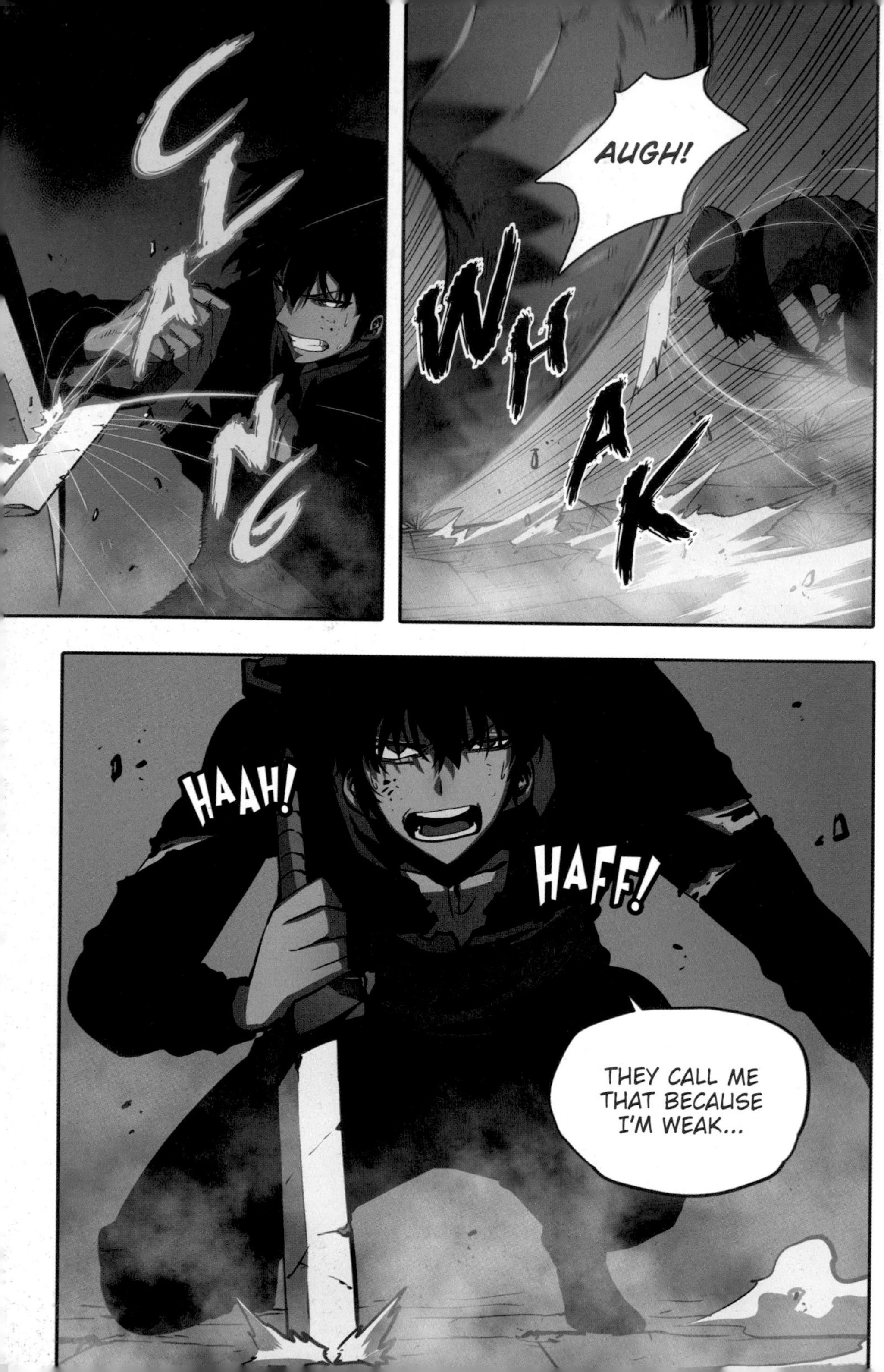
CLANG
AUGH!
WHAK
HAAH!
HAFF!
THEY CALL ME THAT BECAUSE I'M WEAK...

I'M NOT PROUD OF IT!

CLANG

I HATE HOW WORTHLESS I AM...!

POWER.

GREAT POWER BRINGS THEM TO THEIR KNEES.

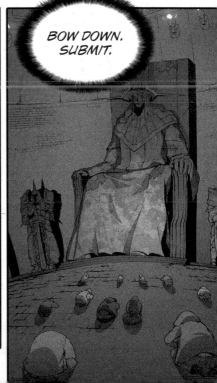

BOW DOWN. SUBMIT.

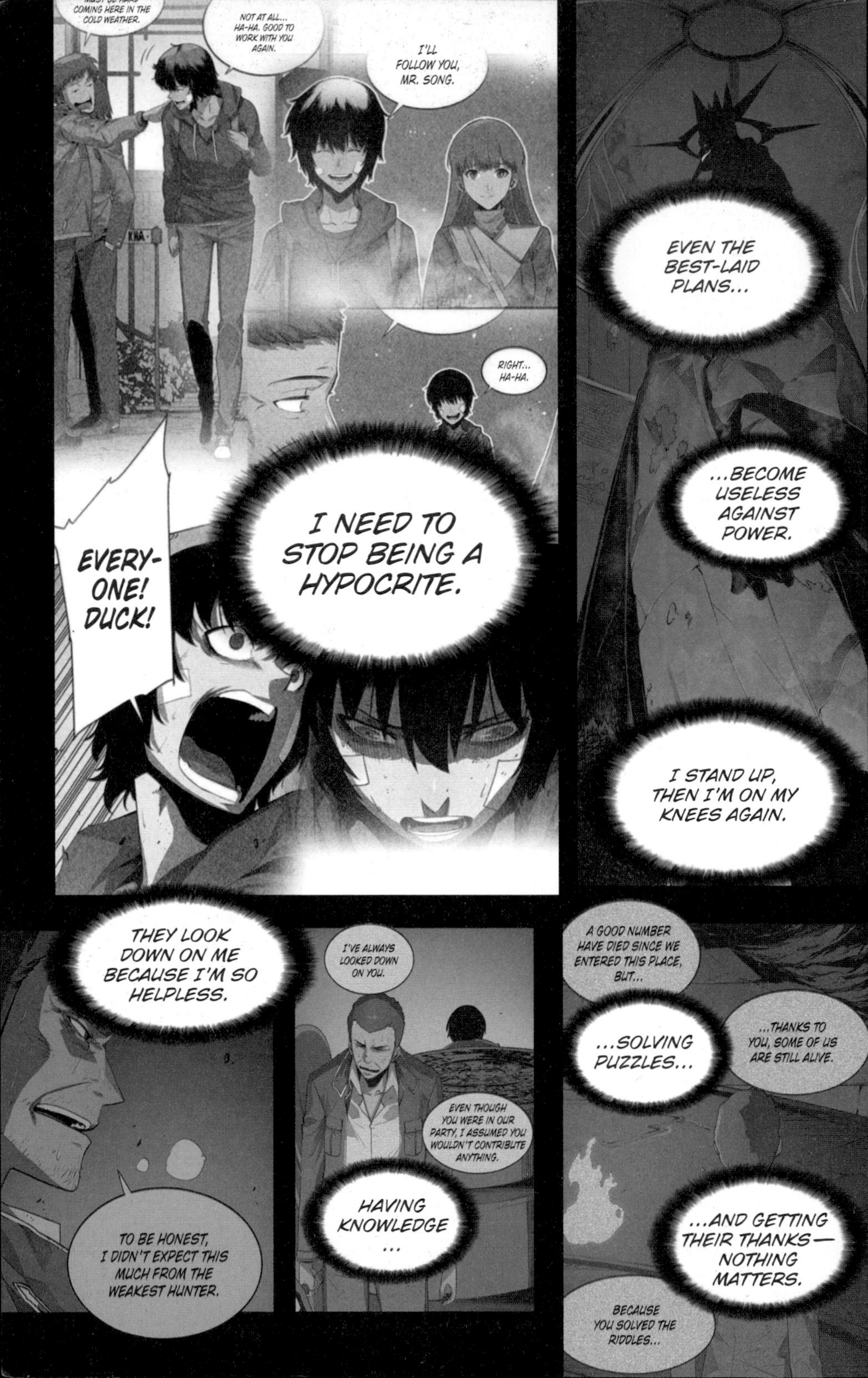
COMING HERE IN THE COLD WEATHER.
NOT AT ALL... HA-HA. GOOD TO WORK WITH YOU AGAIN.
I'LL FOLLOW YOU, MR. SONG.
RIGHT... HA-HA.
EVERY-ONE! DUCK!
I NEED TO STOP BEING A HYPOCRITE.
EVEN THE BEST-LAID PLANS...
...BECOME USELESS AGAINST POWER.
I STAND UP, THEN I'M ON MY KNEES AGAIN.
THEY LOOK DOWN ON ME BECAUSE I'M SO HELPLESS.
TO BE HONEST, I DIDN'T EXPECT THIS MUCH FROM THE WEAKEST HUNTER.
I'VE ALWAYS LOOKED DOWN ON YOU.
EVEN THOUGH YOU WERE IN OUR PARTY, I ASSUMED YOU WOULDN'T CONTRIBUTE ANYTHING.
HAVING KNOWLEDGE...
A GOOD NUMBER HAVE DIED SINCE WE ENTERED THIS PLACE, BUT...
...SOLVING PUZZLES...
...THANKS TO YOU, SOME OF US ARE STILL ALIVE.
...AND GETTING THEIR THANKS—NOTHING MATTERS.
BECAUSE YOU SOLVED THE RIDDLES...

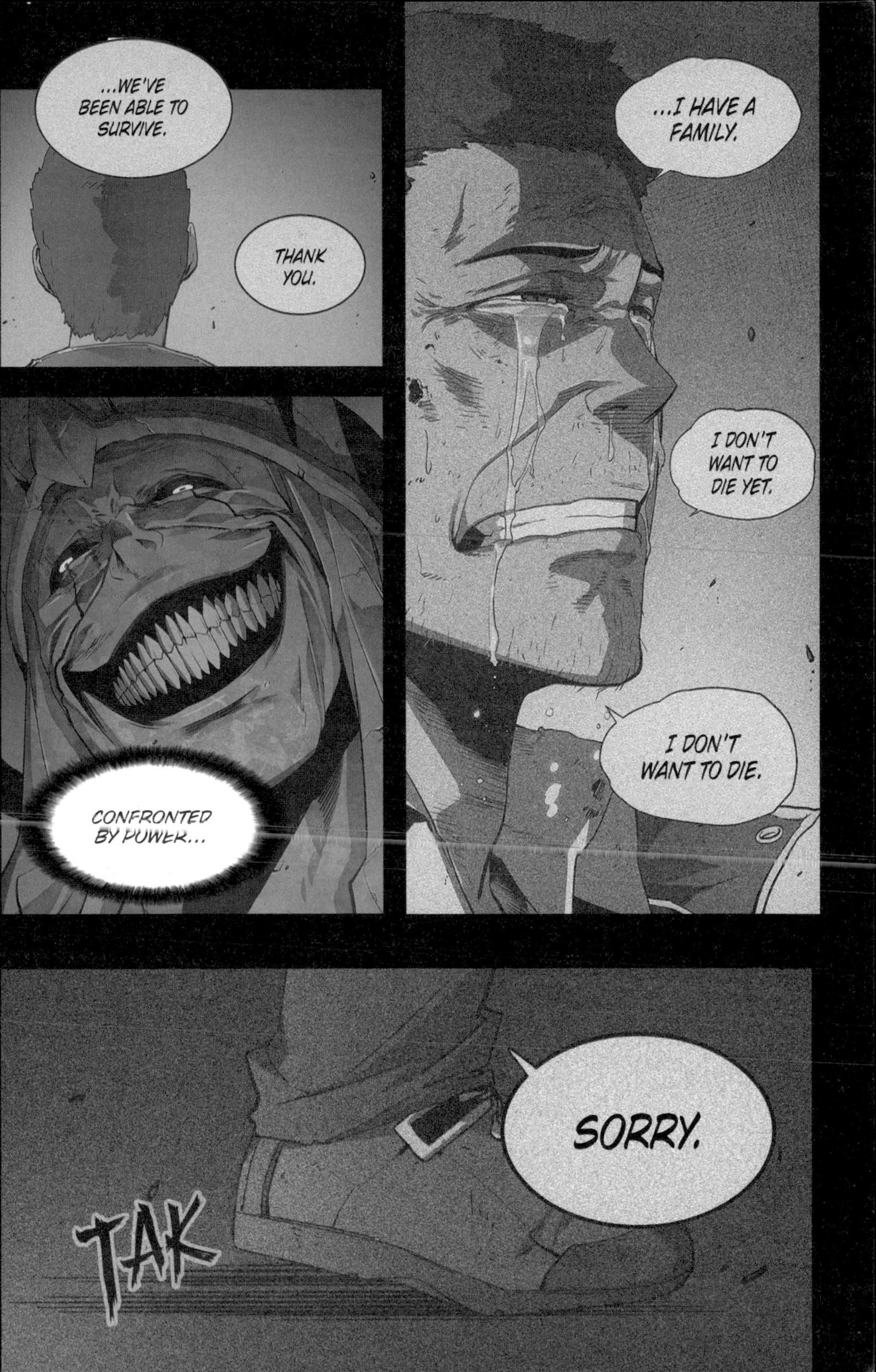
...WE'VE BEEN ABLE TO SURVIVE.
THANK YOU.
CONFRONTED BY POWER...
...I HAVE A FAMILY.
I DON'T WANT TO DIE YET.
I DON'T WANT TO DIE.
TAK
SORRY.

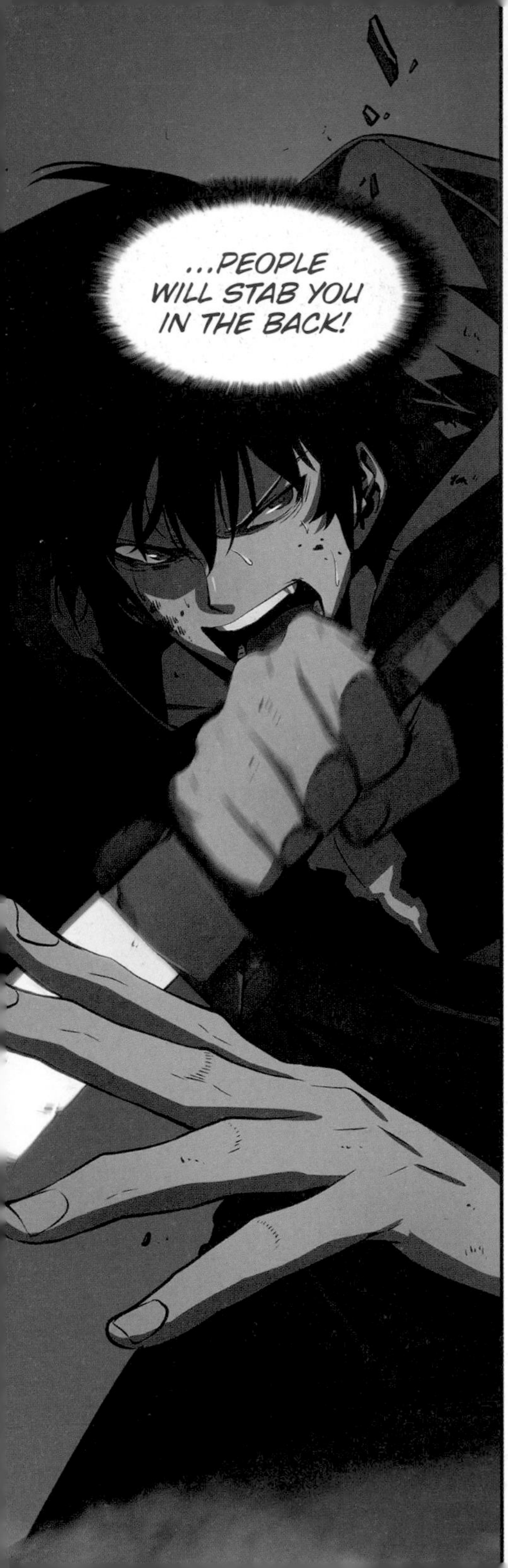
...PEOPLE WILL STAB YOU IN THE BACK!
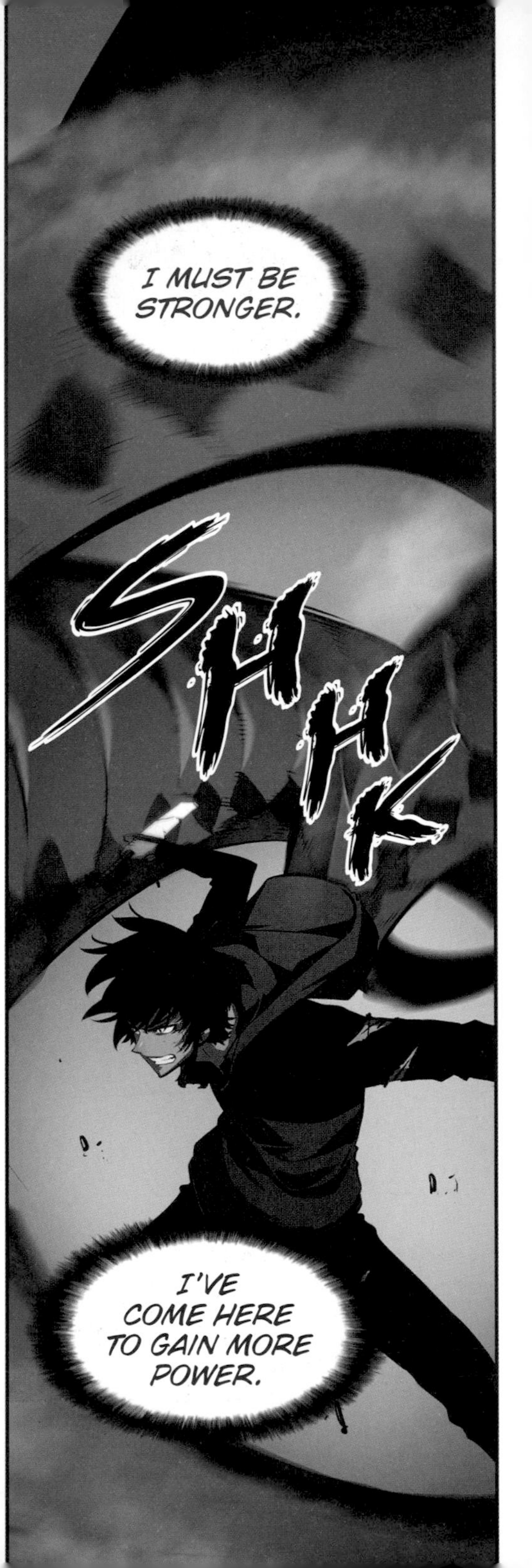
I MUST BE STRONGER.
SHHK
I'VE COME HERE TO GAIN MORE POWER.

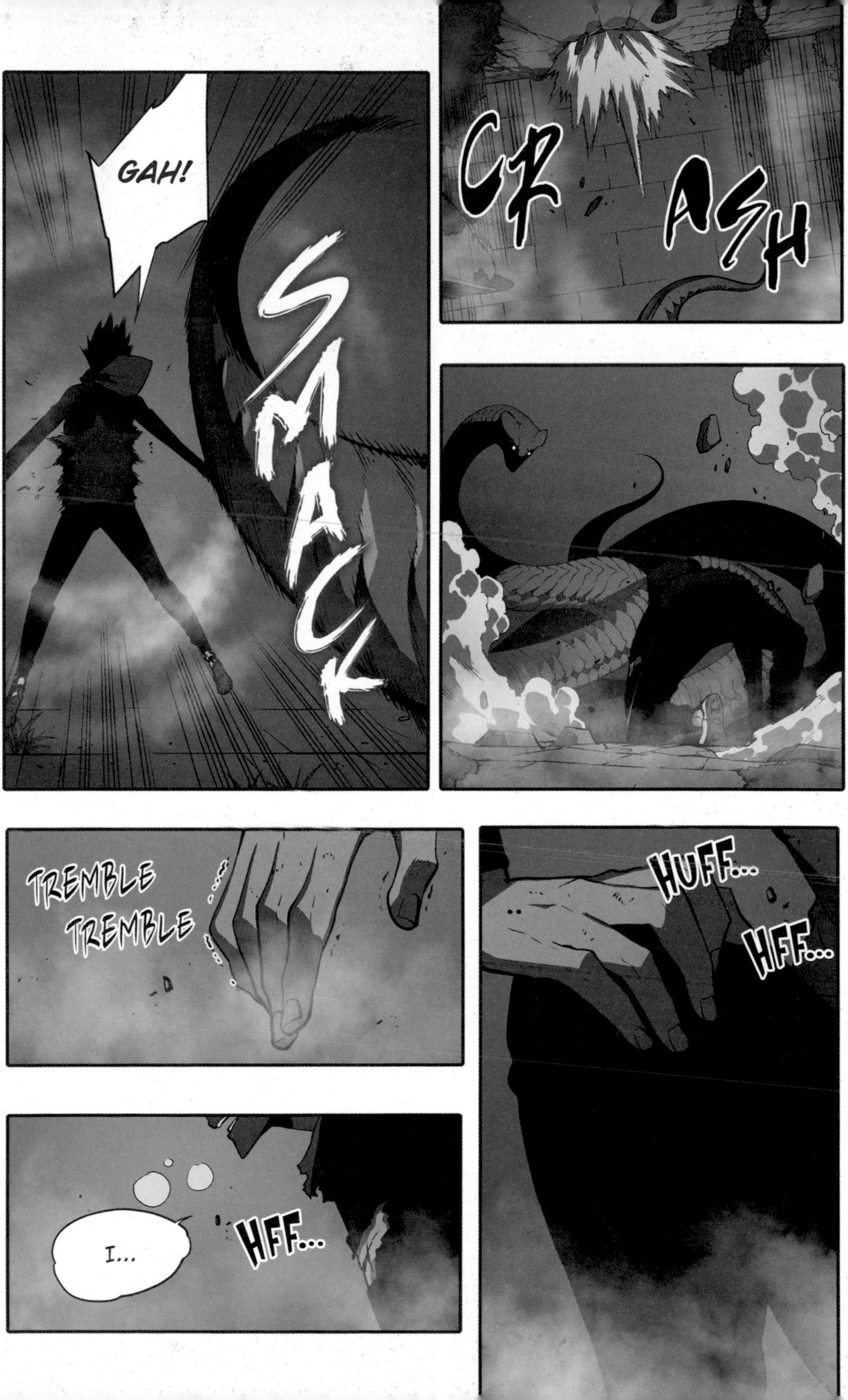
GAH!
SMACK
CRASH
TREMBLE TREMBLE
HUFF...
HFF...
I...
HFF...

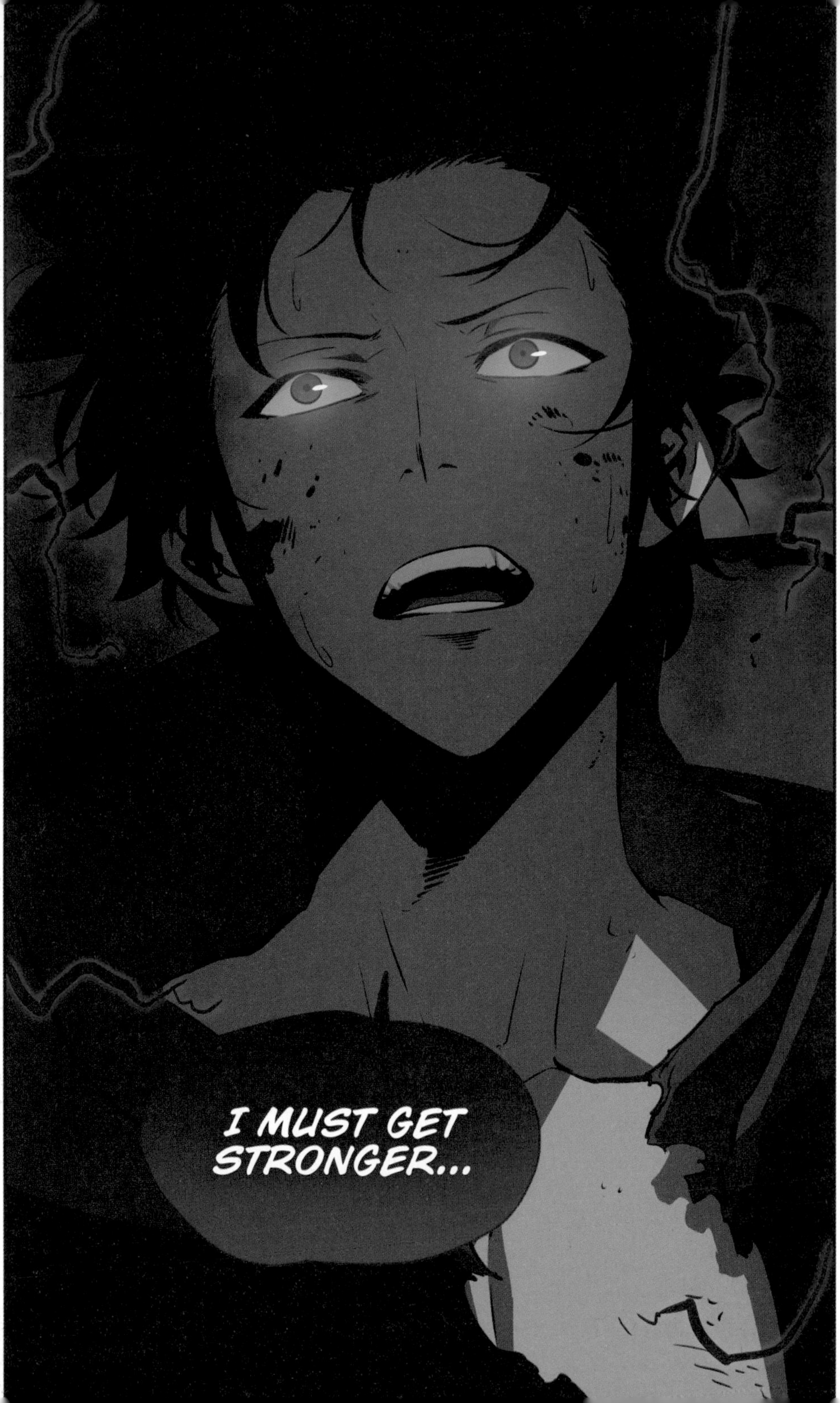
I MUST GET STRONGER...

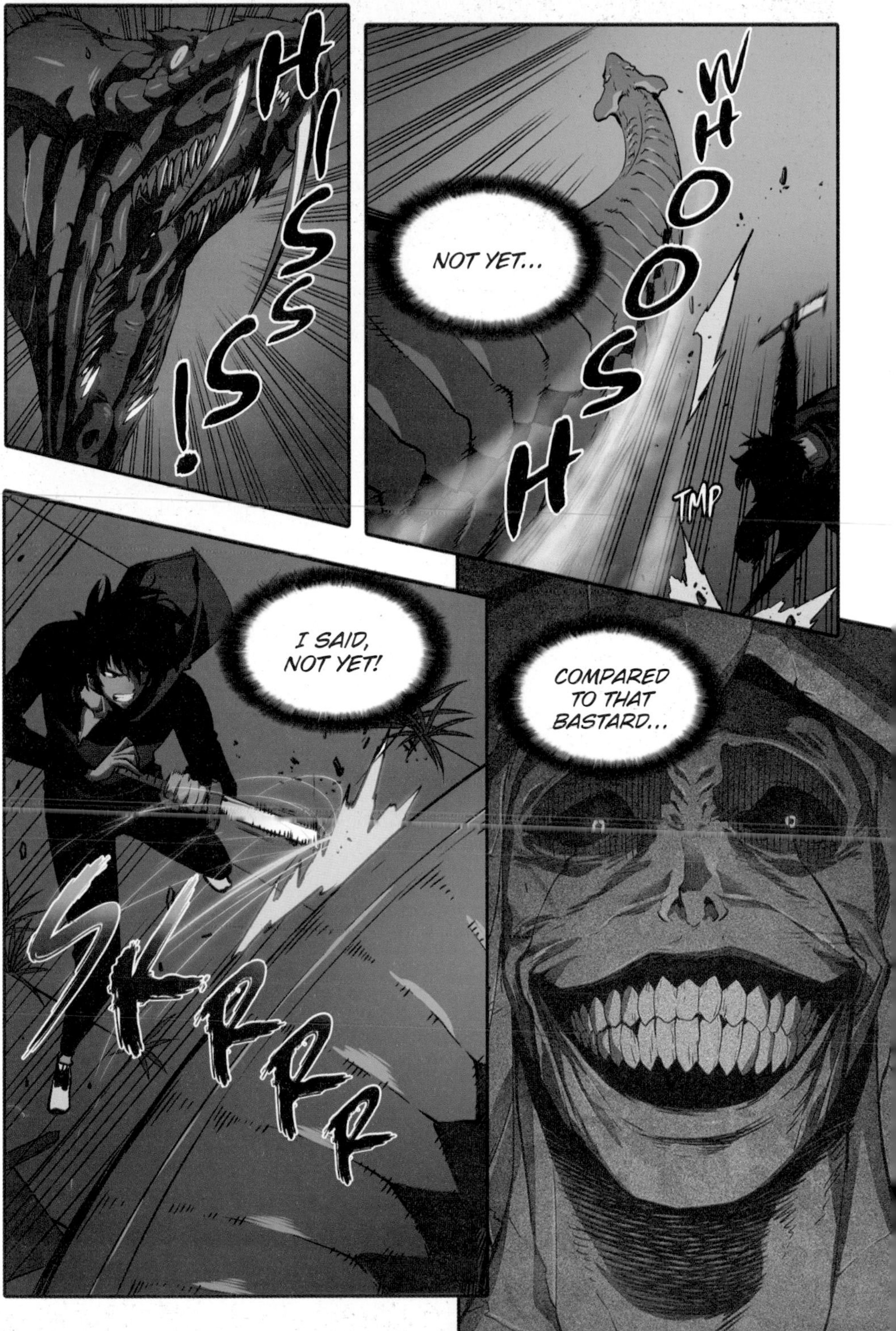
HISSS!
NOT YET...
WHOOSH
TMP
I SAID, NOT YET!
SKRRR
COMPARED TO THAT BASTARD...

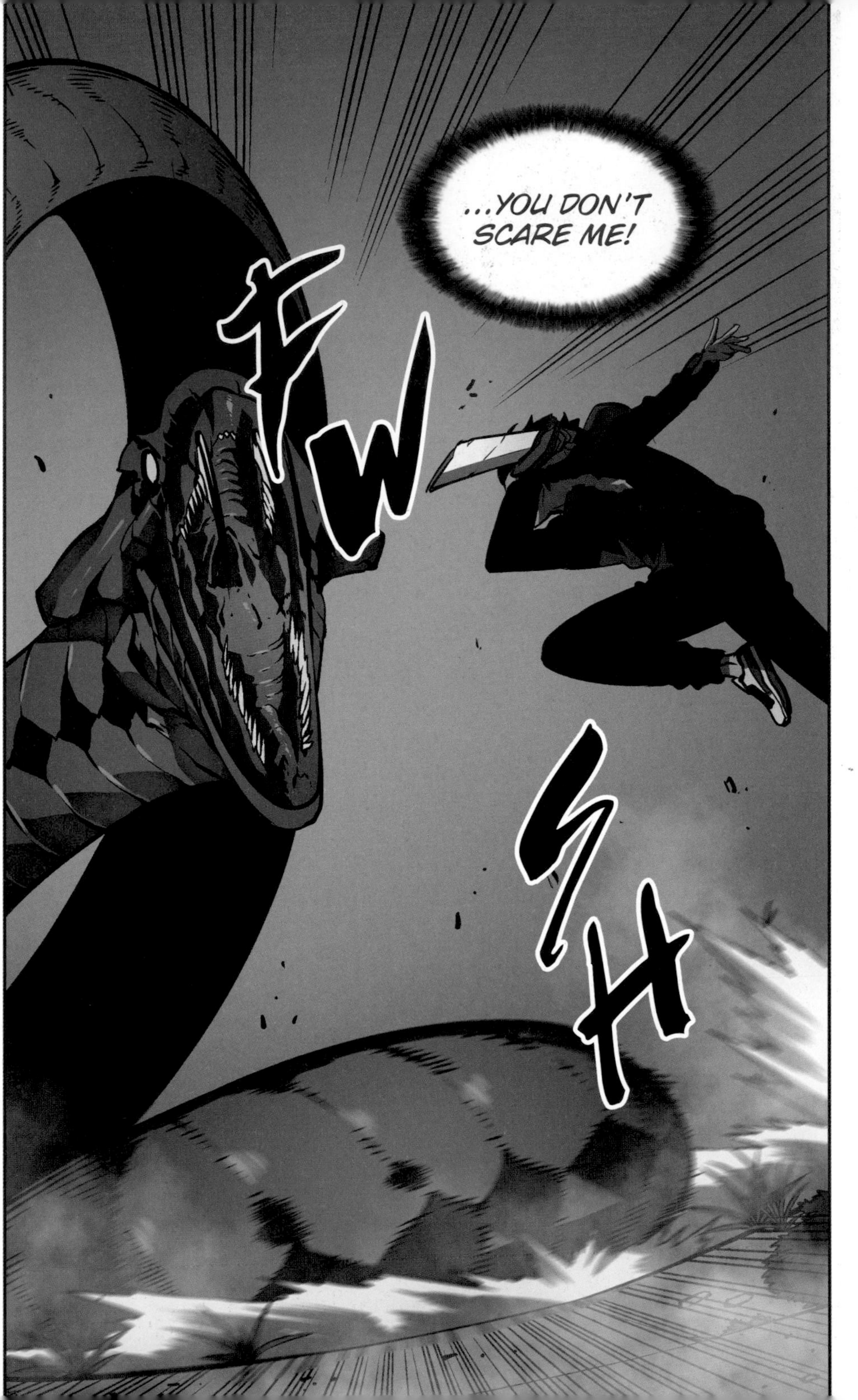
...YOU DON'T SCARE ME!
FWSH

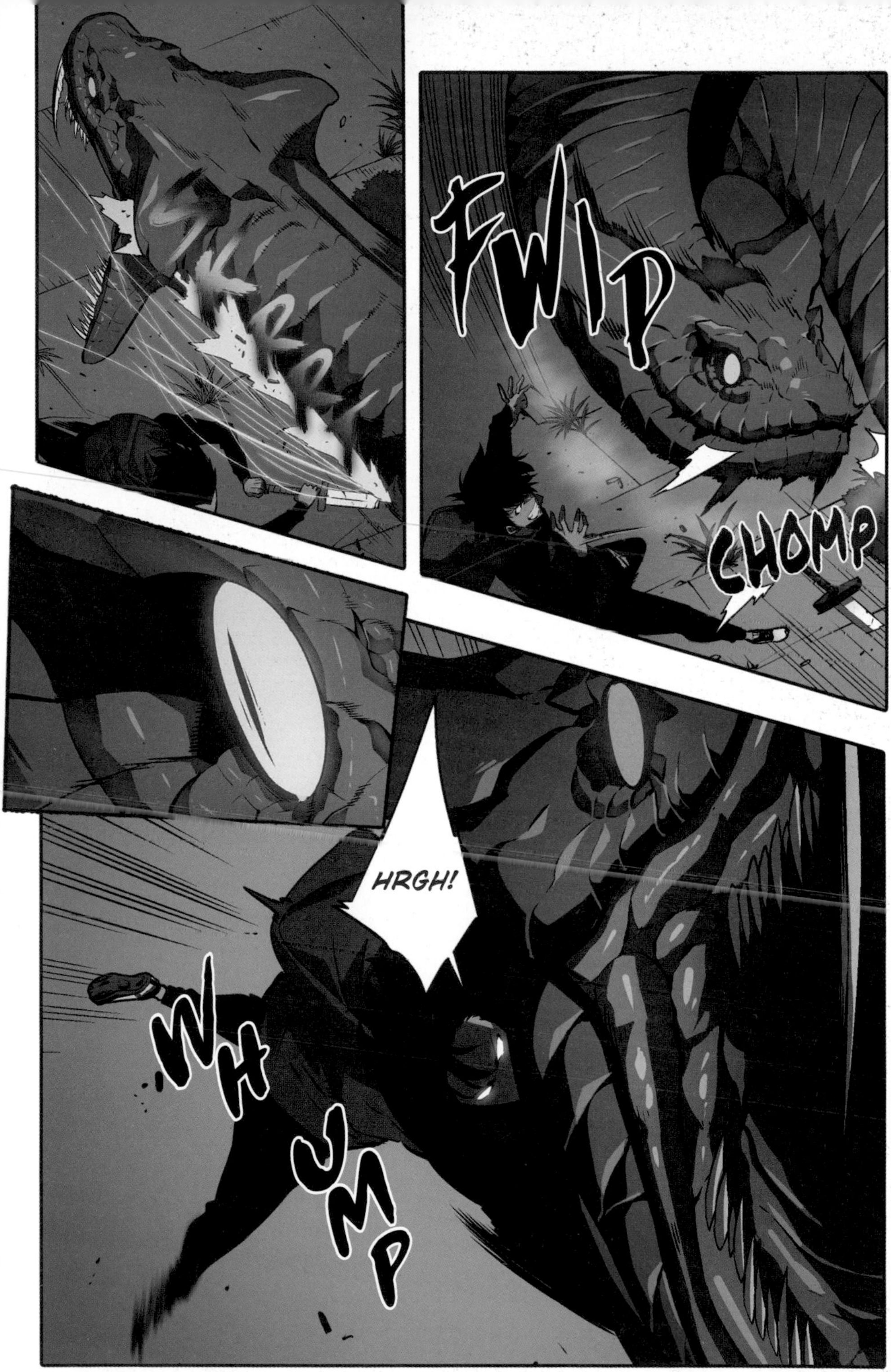
FWIP
CHOMP
HRGH!
WHUMP

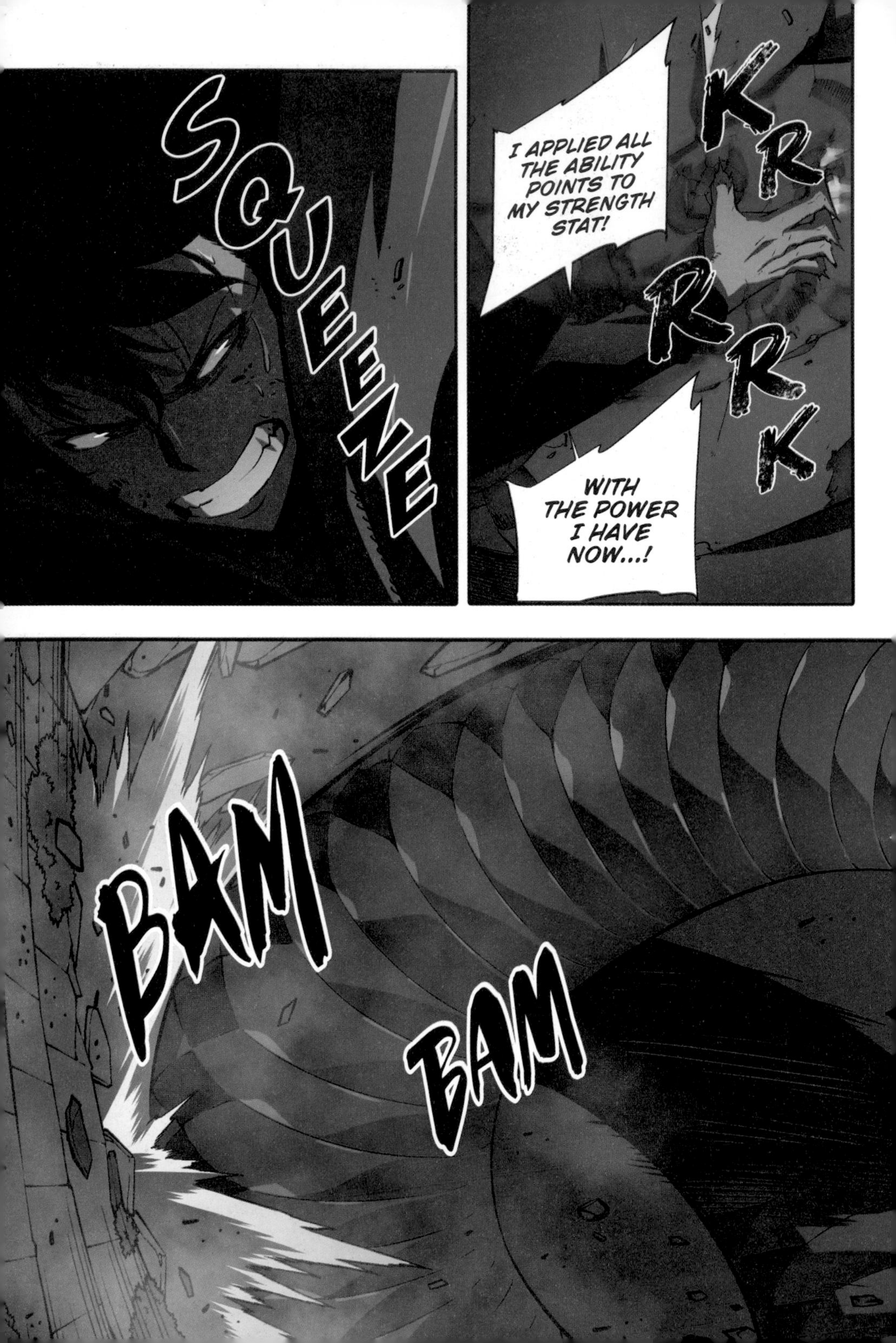
SQUEEZE
I APPLIED ALL THE ABILITY POINTS TO MY STRENGTH STAT!
KRRRRK
WITH THE POWER I HAVE NOW...!
BAM
BAM

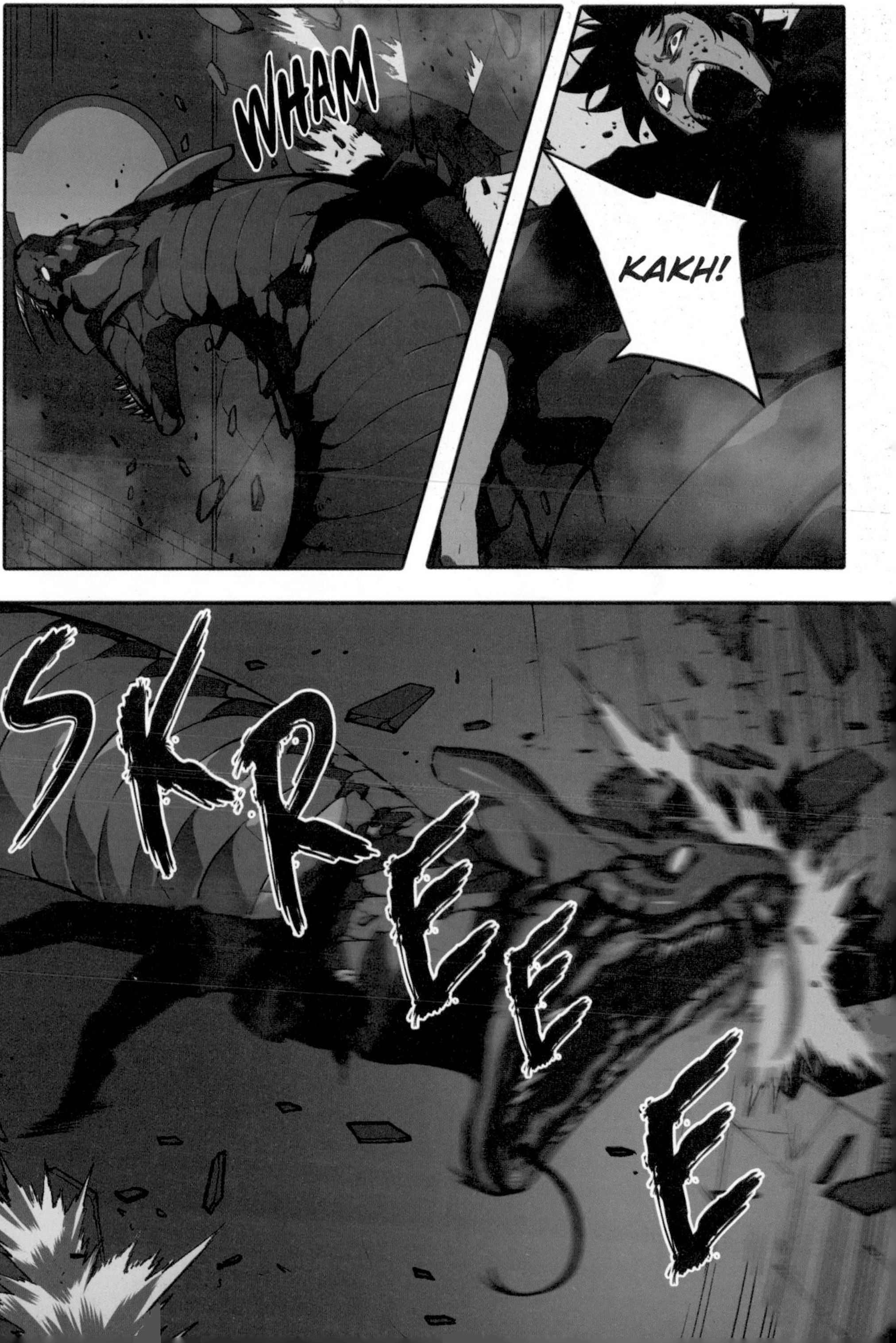
WHAM
KAKH!
SKREEEE

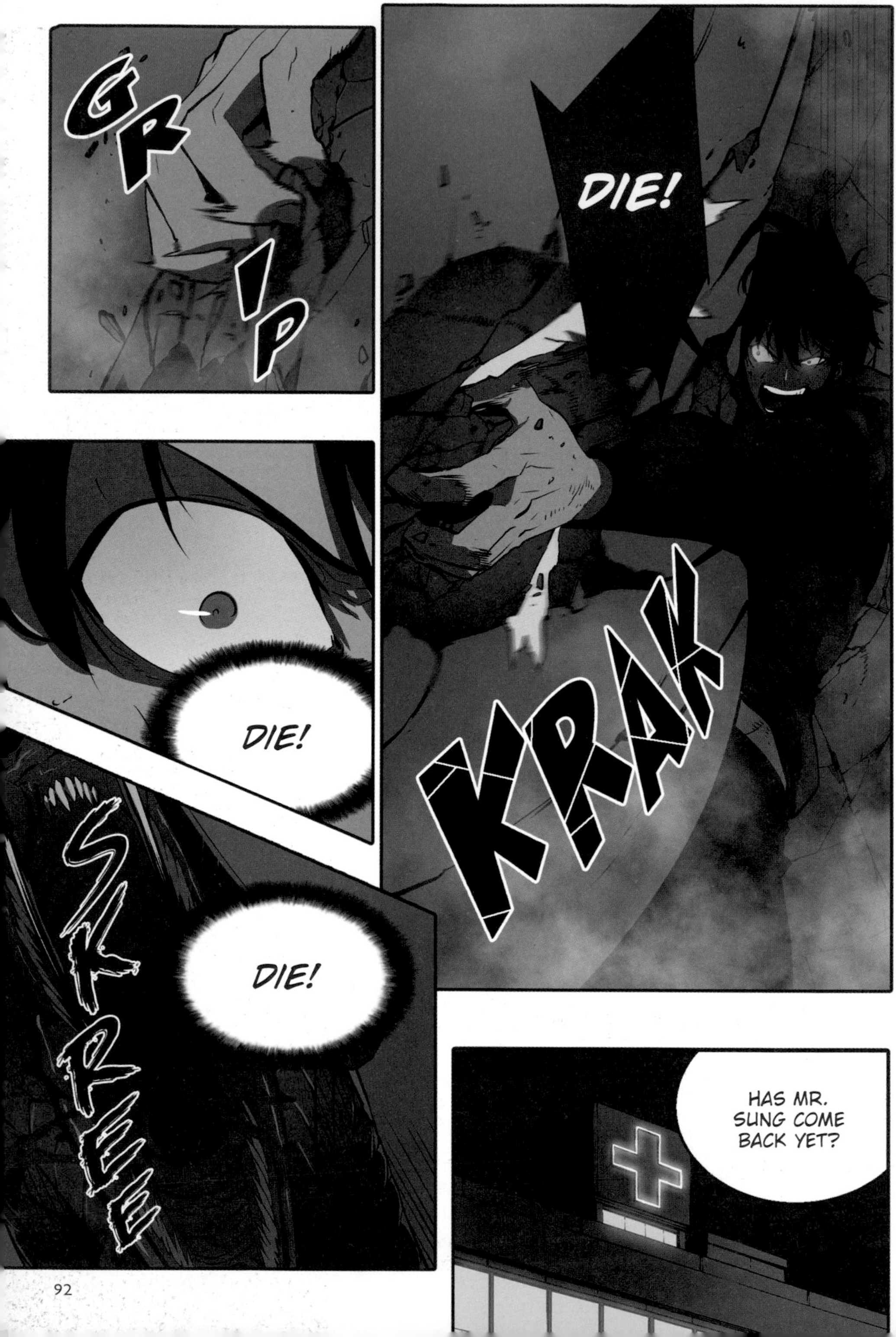
GRIP
DIE!
SKREE
DIE!
DIE!
KRAK
HAS MR. SUNG COME BACK YET?

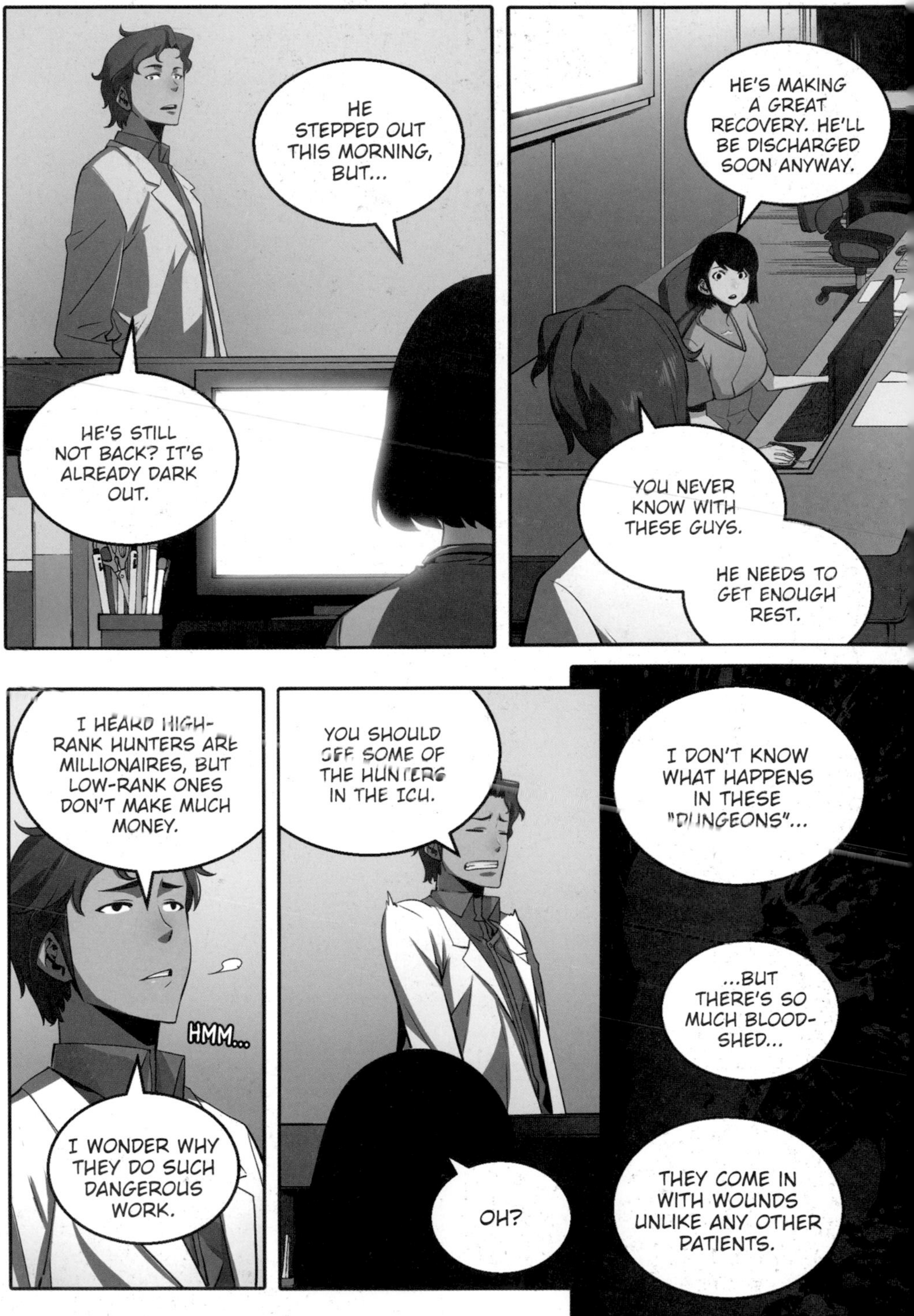
HE STEPPED OUT THIS MORNING, BUT...
HE'S STILL NOT BACK? IT'S ALREADY DARK OUT.
HE'S MAKING A GREAT RECOVERY. HE'LL BE DISCHARGED SOON ANYWAY.
YOU NEVER KNOW WITH THESE GUYS.
HE NEEDS TO GET ENOUGH REST.
I HEARD HIGH-RANK HUNTERS ARE MILLIONAIRES, BUT LOW-RANK ONES DON'T MAKE MUCH MONEY.
HMM...
I WONDER WHY THEY DO SUCH DANGEROUS WORK.
YOU SHOULD SEE SOME OF THE HUNTERS IN THE ICU.
OH?
I DON'T KNOW WHAT HAPPENS IN THESE "DUNGEONS"...
...BUT THERE'S SO MUCH BLOOD-SHED...
THEY COME IN WITH WOUNDS UNLIKE ANY OTHER PATIENTS.

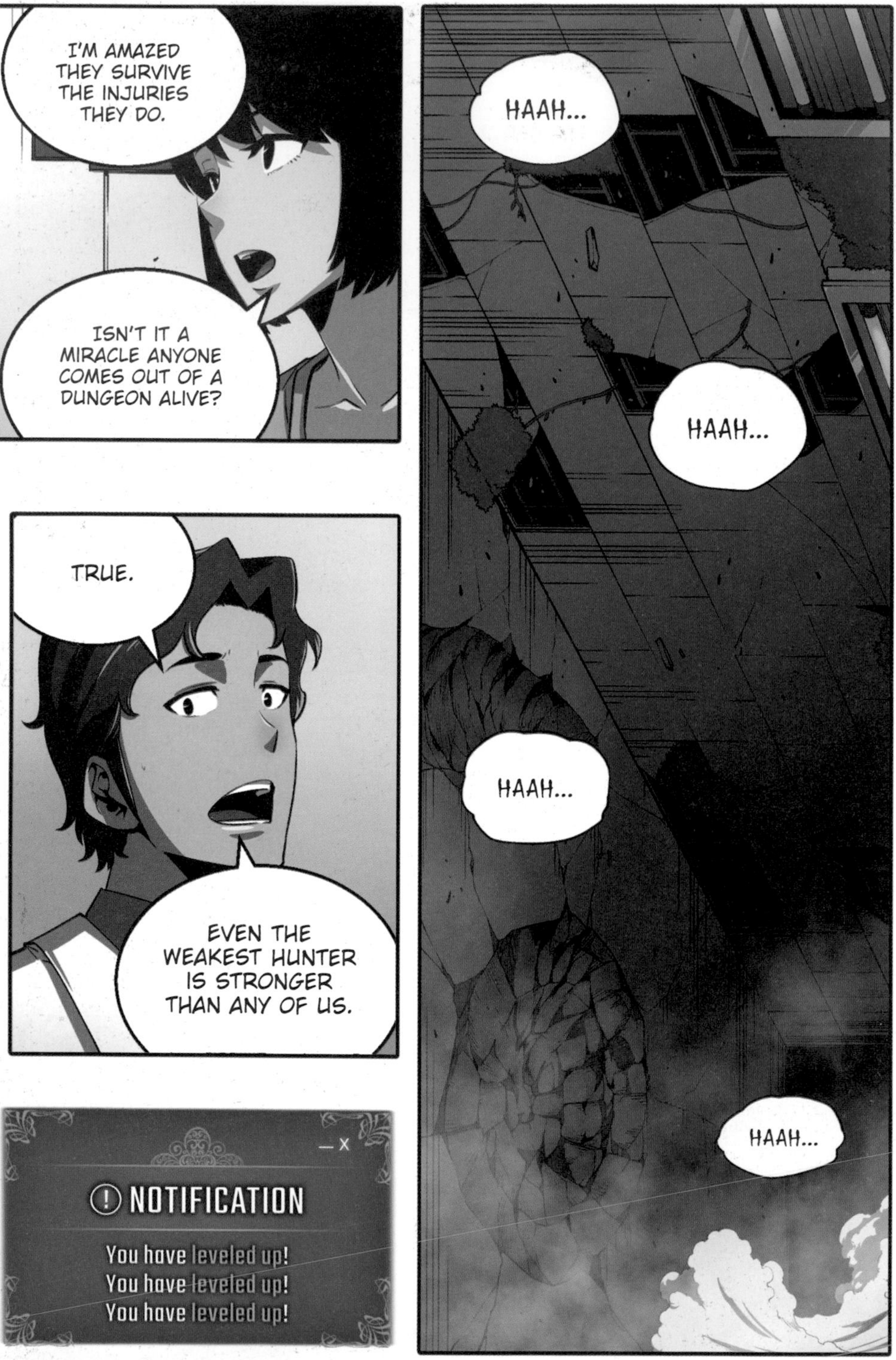
I'M AMAZED THEY SURVIVE THE INJURIES THEY DO.
ISN'T IT A MIRACLE ANYONE COMES OUT OF A DUNGEON ALIVE?
TRUE.
EVEN THE WEAKEST HUNTER IS STRONGER THAN ANY OF US.
— X
NOTIFICATION
You have leveled up!
You have leveled up!
You have leveled up!
HAAH...
HAAH...
HAAH...
HAAH...

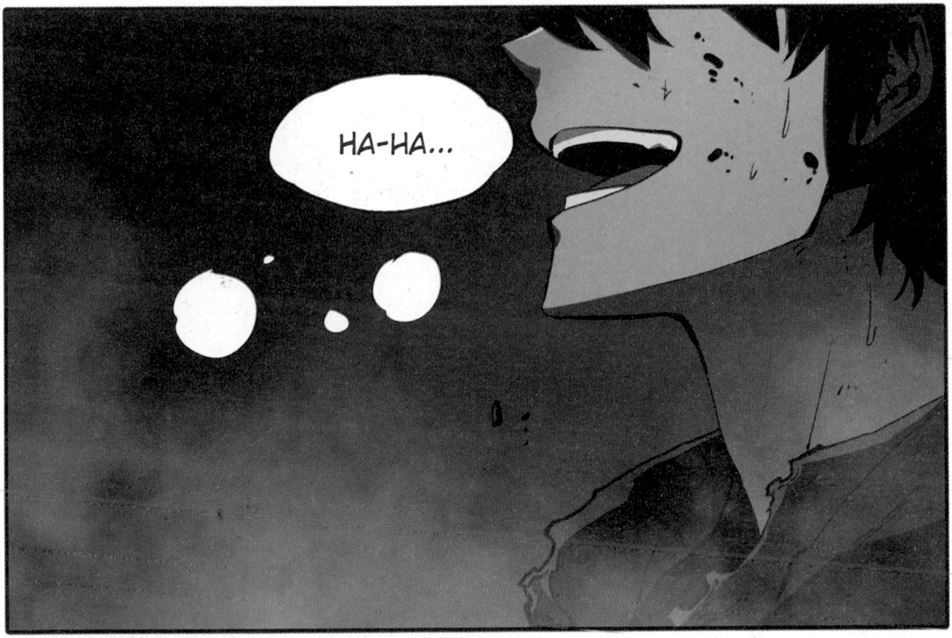
HA-HA...

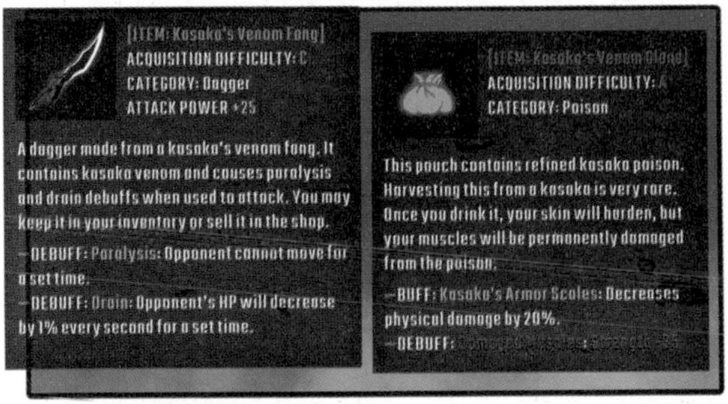
[ITEM: Kasaka's Venom Fang]
ACQUISITION DIFFICULTY: C
CATEGORY: Dagger
ATTACK POWER +25
A dagger made from a kasaka's venom fang. It contains kasaka venom and causes paralysis and drain debuffs when used to attack. You may keep it in your inventory or sell it in the shop.
—DEBUFF: Paralysis: Opponent cannot move for a set time.
—DEBUFF: Drain: Opponent's HP will decrease by 1% every second for a set time.
[ITEM: Kasaka's Venom Gland]
ACQUISITION DIFFICULTY: A
CATEGORY: Poison
This pouch contains refined kasaka poison. Harvesting this from a kasaka is very rare. Once you drink it, your skin will harden, but your muscles will be permanently damaged from the poison.
—BUFF: Kasaka's Armor Scales: Decreases physical damage by 20%.
—DEBUFF:

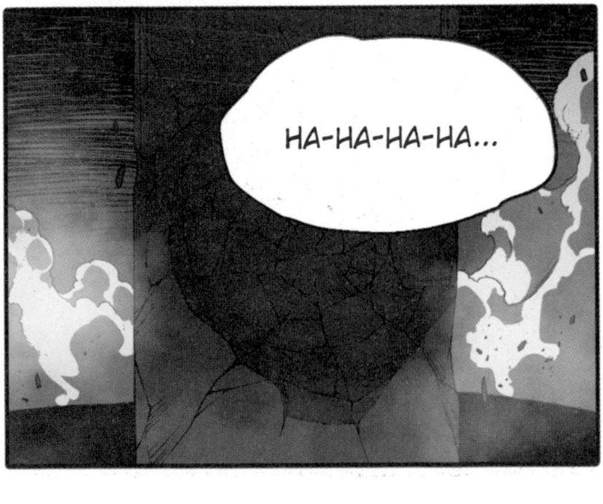
HA-HA-HA-HA...

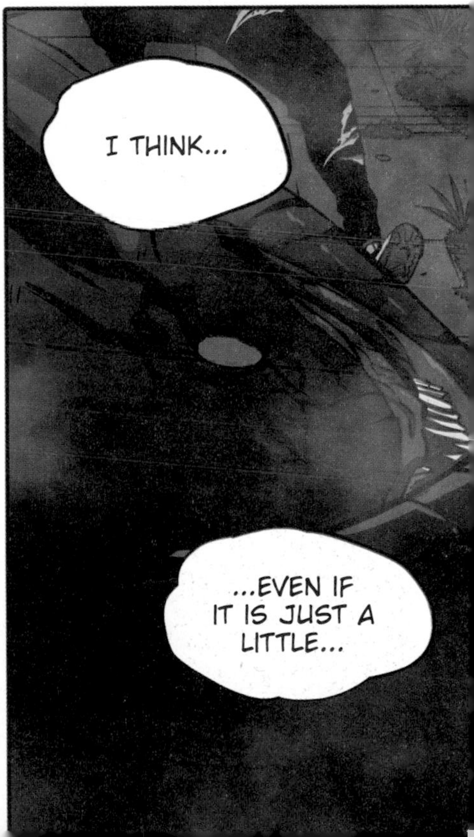
I THINK...
...EVEN IF IT IS JUST A LITTLE...

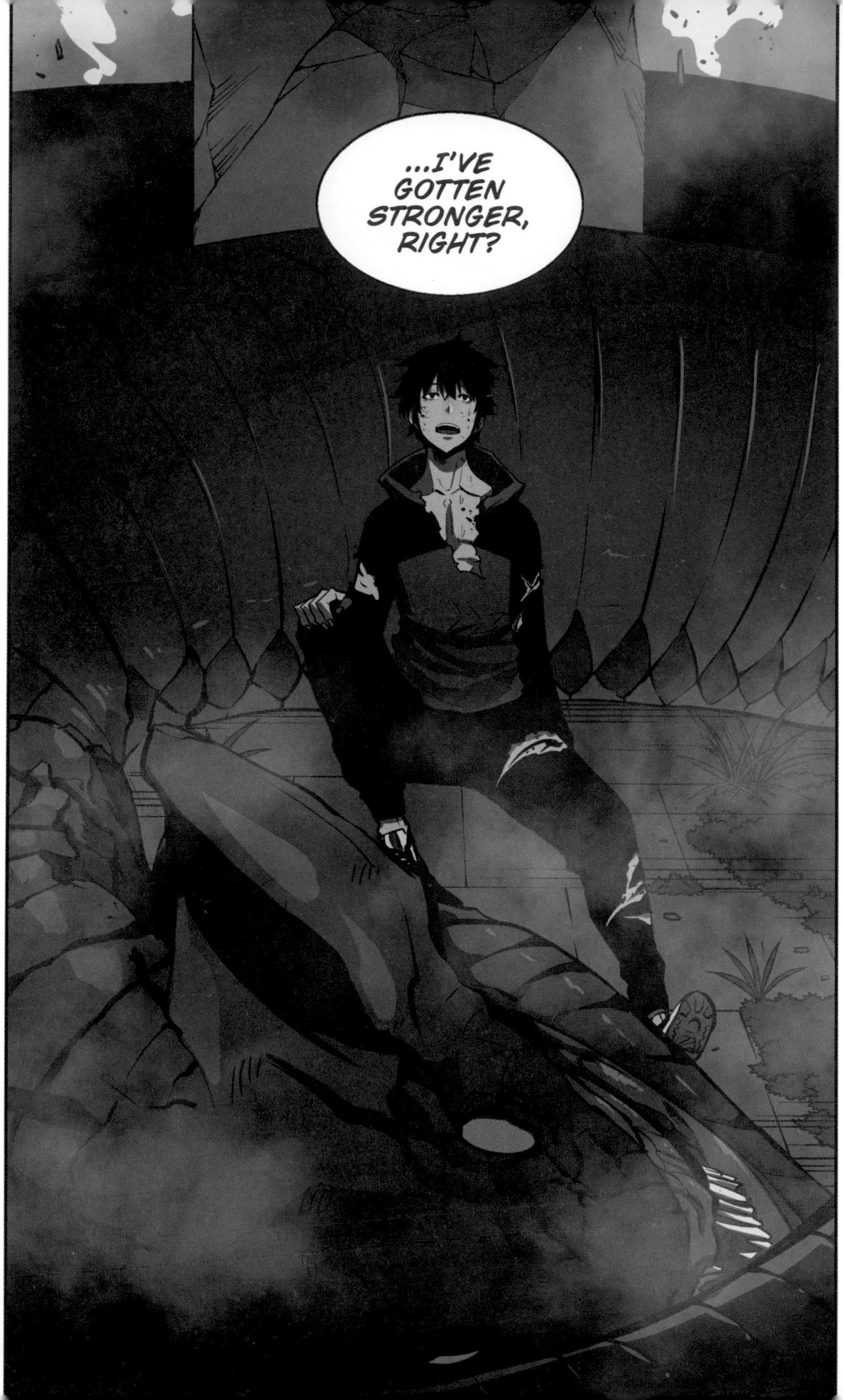
...I'VE GOTTEN STRONGER, RIGHT?

① NOTIFICATION

You have defeated King of the Swamp,
Blue Venom-Fanged Kasaka.

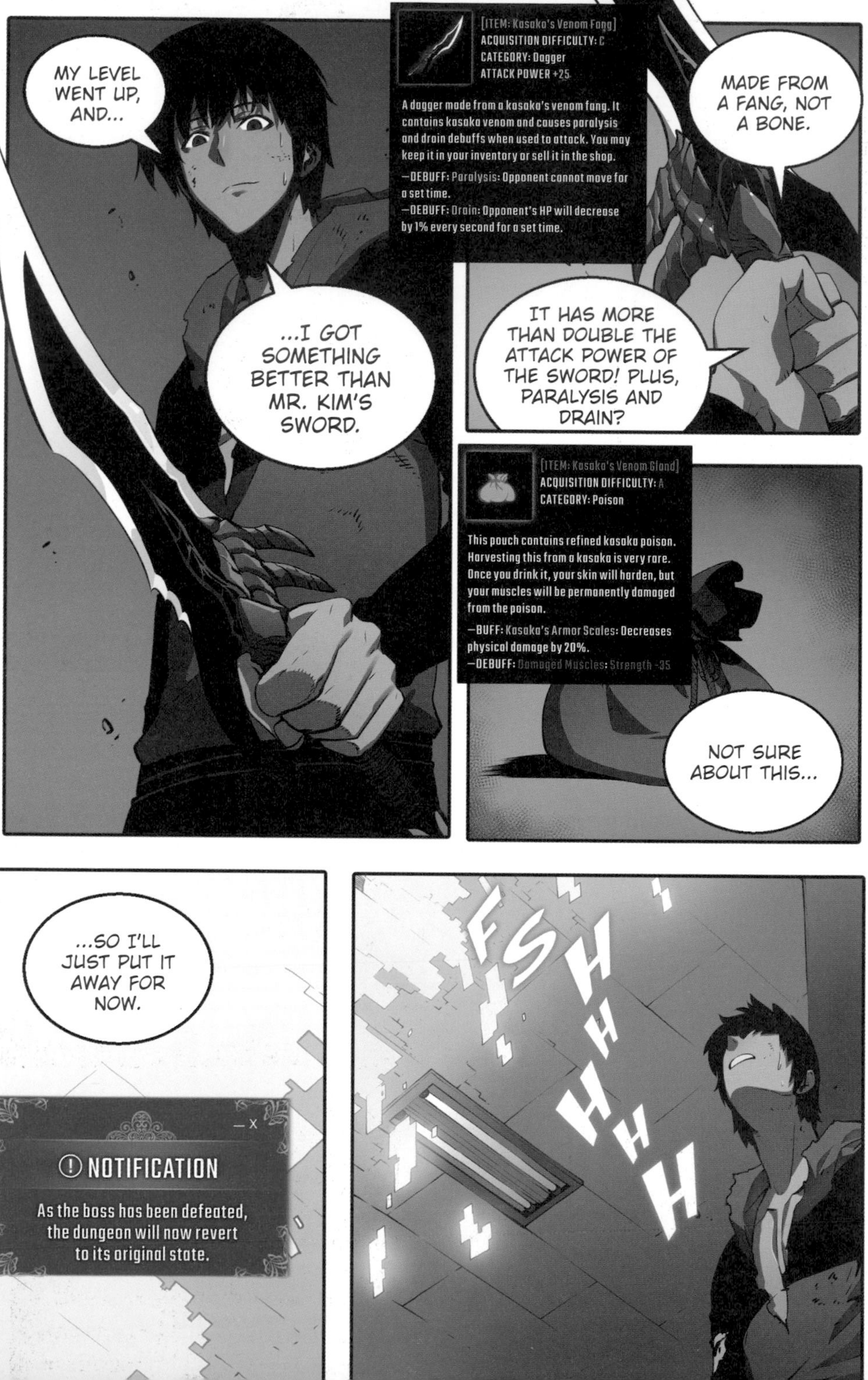
MY LEVEL WENT UP, AND...
...I GOT SOMETHING BETTER THAN MR. KIM'S SWORD.
[ITEM: Kasaka's Venom Fang]
ACQUISITION DIFFICULTY: C
CATEGORY: Dagger
ATTACK POWER +25
A dagger made from a kasaka's venom fang. It contains kasaka venom and causes paralysis and drain debuffs when used to attack. You may keep it in your inventory or sell it in the shop.
—DEBUFF: Paralysis: Opponent cannot move for a set time.
—DEBUFF: Drain: Opponent's HP will decrease by 1% every second for a set time.
MADE FROM A FANG, NOT A BONE.
IT HAS MORE THAN DOUBLE THE ATTACK POWER OF THE SWORD! PLUS, PARALYSIS AND DRAIN?
[ITEM: Kasaka's Venom Gland]
ACQUISITION DIFFICULTY: A
CATEGORY: Poison
This pouch contains refined kasaka poison. Harvesting this from a kasaka is very rare. Once you drink it, your skin will harden, but your muscles will be permanently damaged from the poison.
—BUFF: Kasaka's Armor Scales: Decreases physical damage by 20%.
—DEBUFF: Damaged Muscles: Strength -35
NOT SURE ABOUT THIS...
...SO I'LL JUST PUT IT AWAY FOR NOW.
— X
NOTIFICATION
As the boss has been defeated, the dungeon will now revert to its original state.
FSHHHHHH

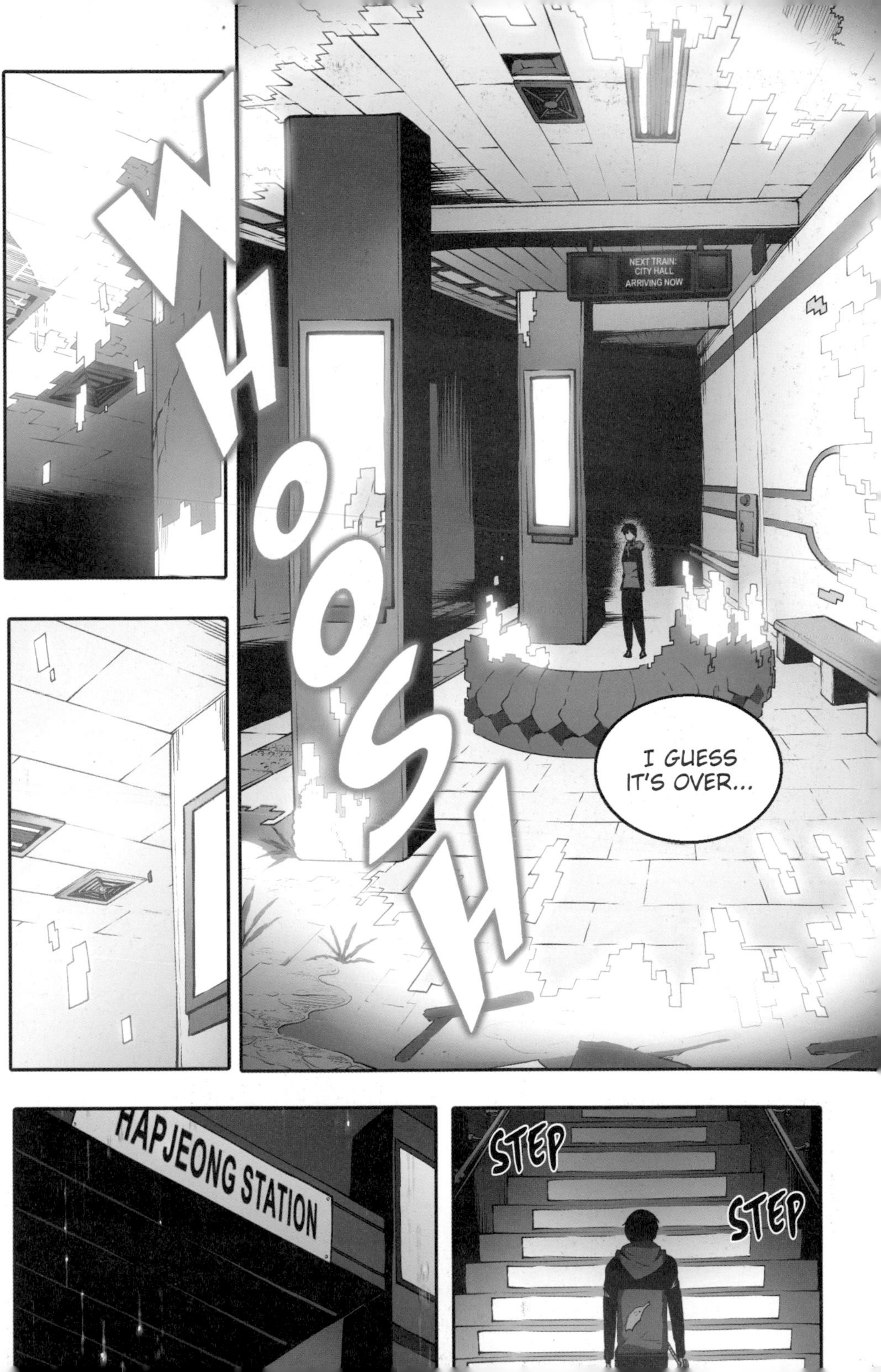
WHOOSH
NEXT TRAIN: CITY HALL ARRIVING NOW
I GUESS IT'S OVER...
HAPJEONG STATION
STEP
STEP

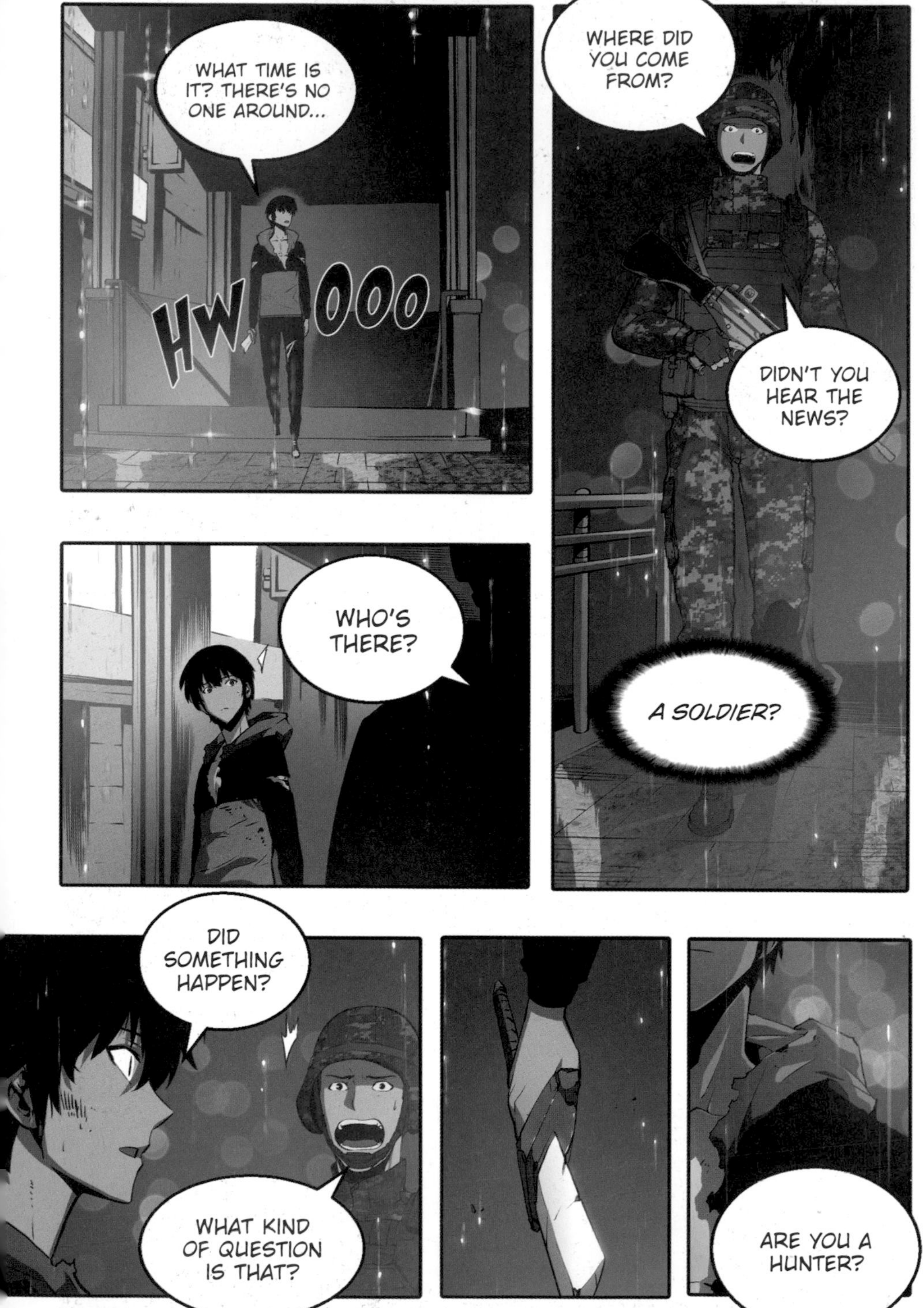
WHAT TIME IS IT? THERE'S NO ONE AROUND...
HWOOO
WHO'S THERE?
WHERE DID YOU COME FROM?
DIDN'T YOU HEAR THE NEWS?
A SOLDIER?
DID SOMETHING HAPPEN?
WHAT KIND OF QUESTION IS THAT?
ARE YOU A HUNTER?

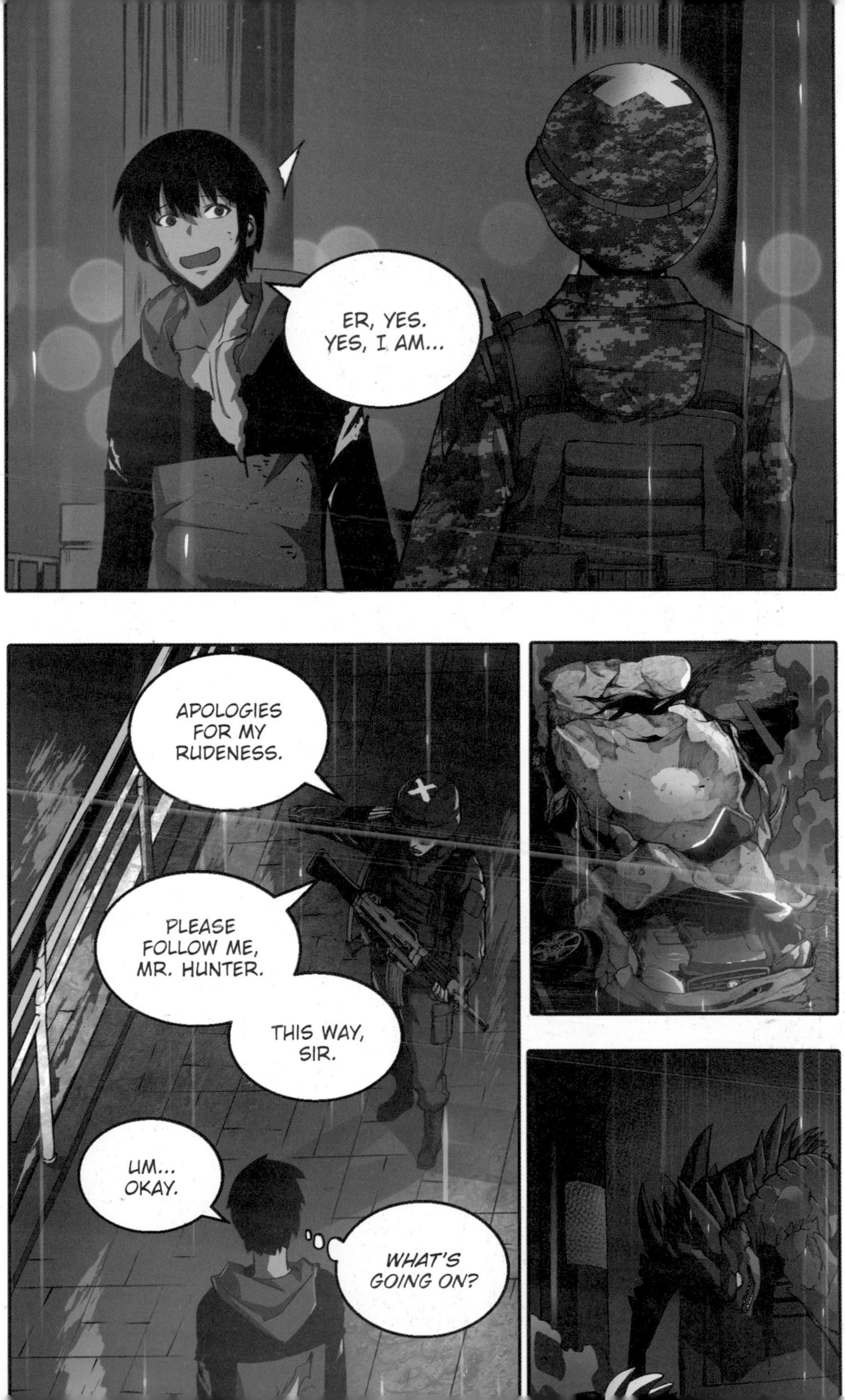
ER, YES. YES, I AM...
APOLOGIES FOR MY RUDENESS.
PLEASE FOLLOW ME, MR. HUNTER.
THIS WAY, SIR.
UM... OKAY.
WHAT'S GOING ON?

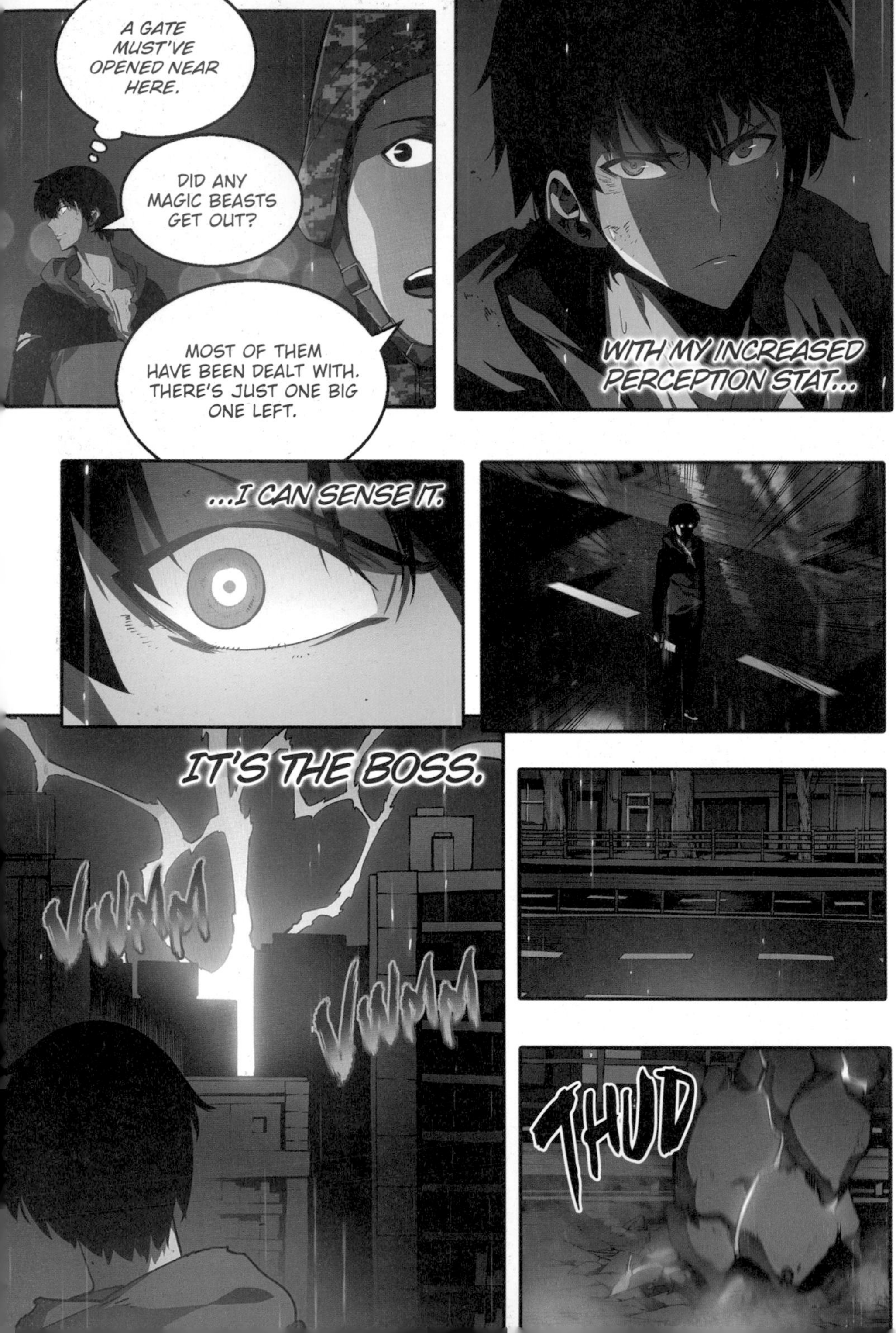
A GATE MUST'VE OPENED NEAR HERE.
DID ANY MAGIC BEASTS GET OUT?
MOST OF THEM HAVE BEEN DEALT WITH. THERE'S JUST ONE BIG ONE LEFT.
WITH MY INCREASED PERCEPTION STAT...
...I CAN SENSE IT.
IT'S THE BOSS.
VWMM
VWMM
THUD

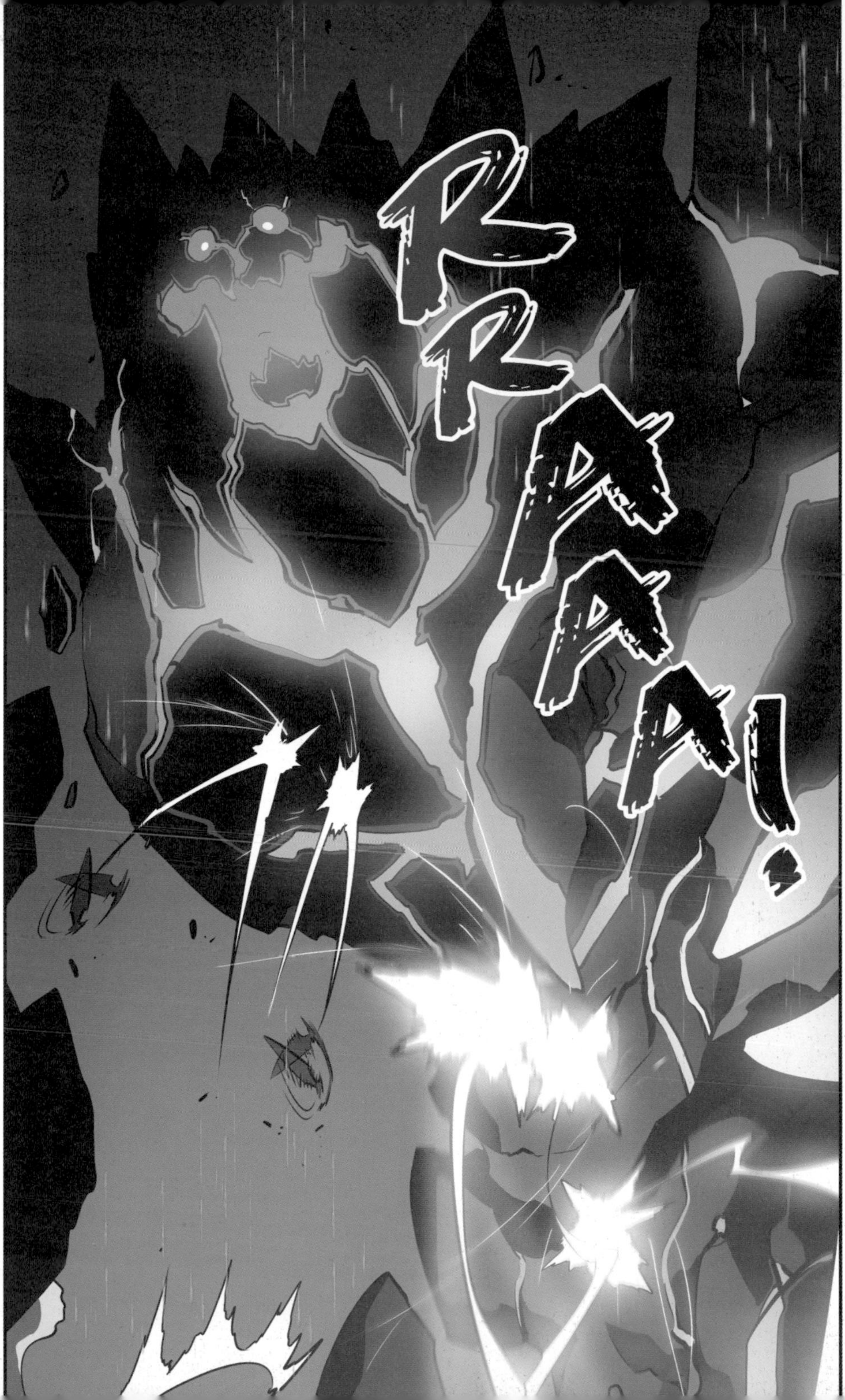
RRAAA!

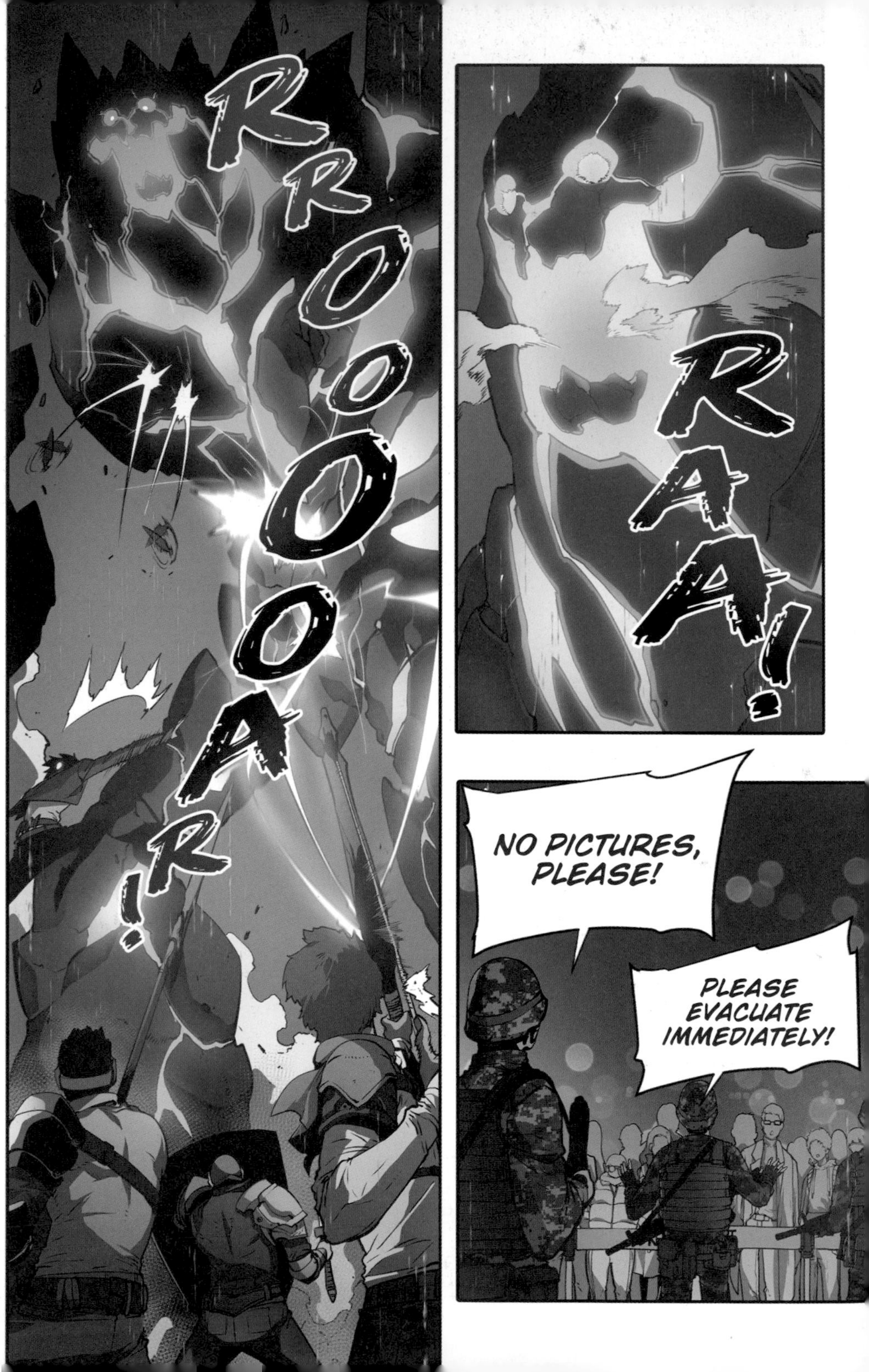
RROOOOAR!
RAA!
NO PICTURES, PLEASE!
PLEASE EVACUATE IMMEDIATELY!

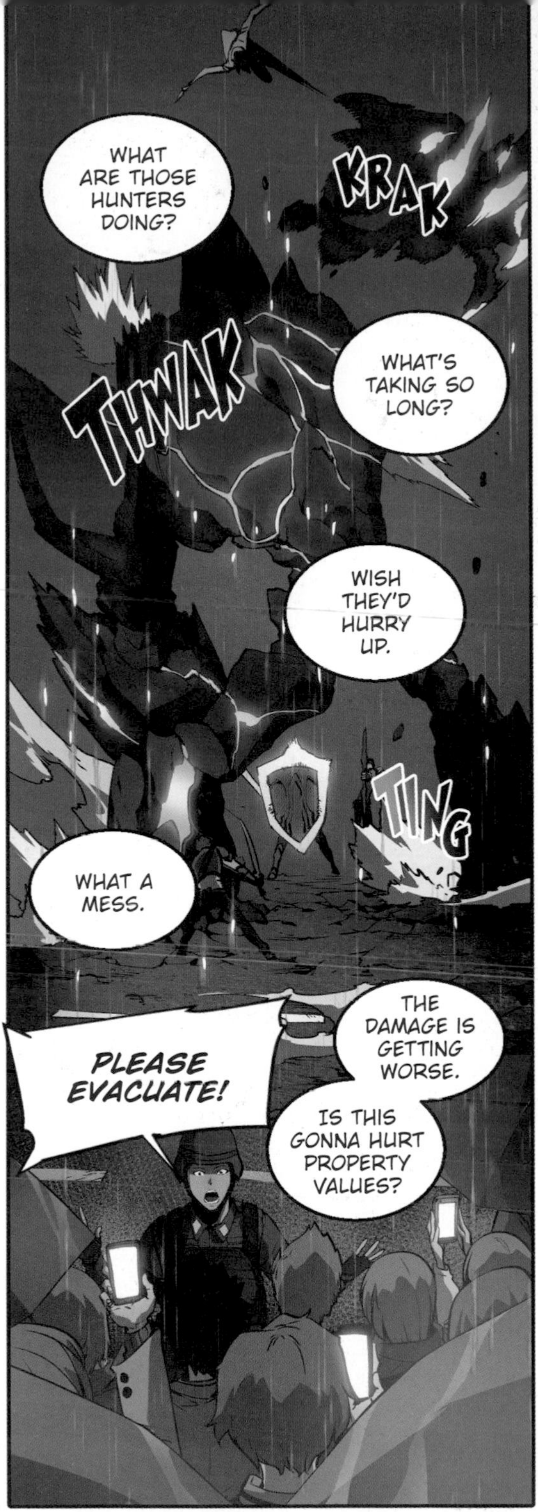
WHAT ARE THOSE HUNTERS DOING?
KRAK
THWAK
WHAT'S TAKING SO LONG?
WISH THEY'D HURRY UP.
TING
WHAT A MESS.
PLEASE EVACUATE!
THE DAMAGE IS GETTING WORSE.
IS THIS GONNA HURT PROPERTY VALUES?

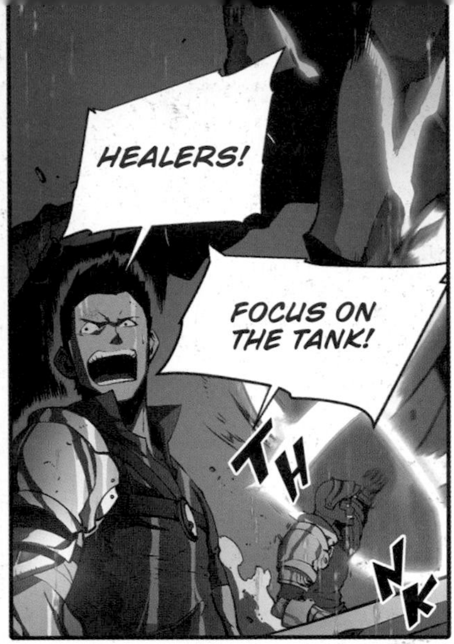
HEALERS!
FOCUS ON THE TANK!
THNK

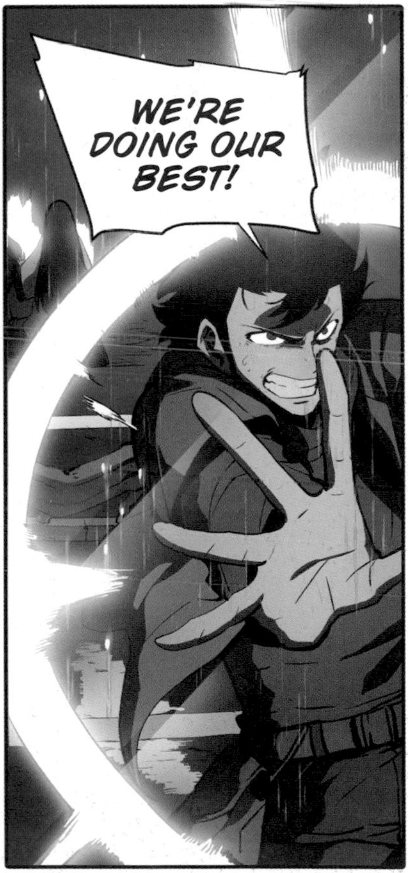
WE'RE DOING OUR BEST!

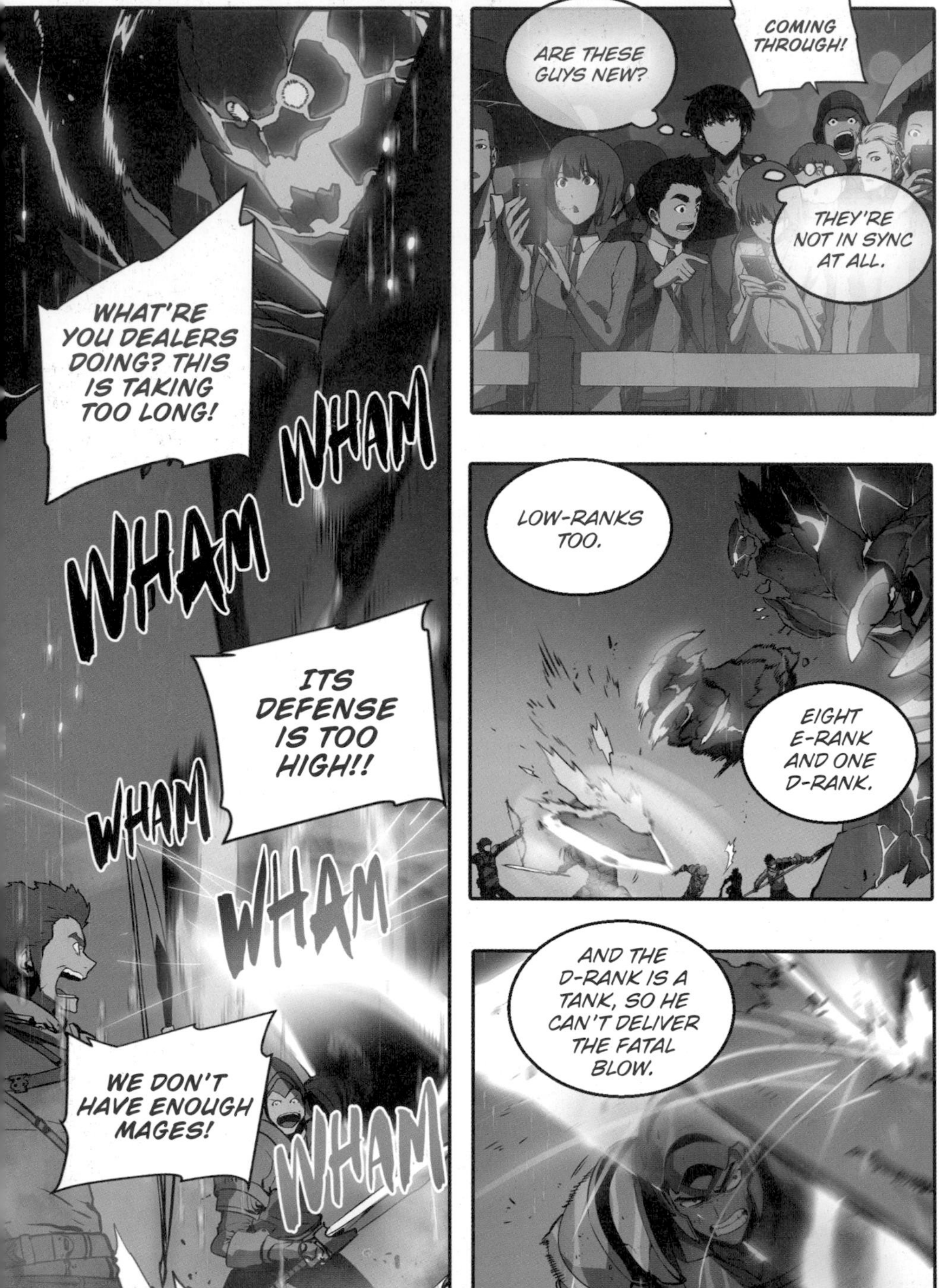
WHAT'RE YOU DEALERS DOING? THIS IS TAKING TOO LONG!
WHAM WHAM
ITS DEFENSE IS TOO HIGH!!
WHAM
WHAM
WE DON'T HAVE ENOUGH MAGES!
WHAM
ARE THESE GUYS NEW?
COMING THROUGH!
THEY'RE NOT IN SYNC AT ALL.
LOW-RANKS TOO.
EIGHT E-RANK AND ONE D-RANK.
AND THE D-RANK IS A TANK, SO HE CAN'T DELIVER THE FATAL BLOW.

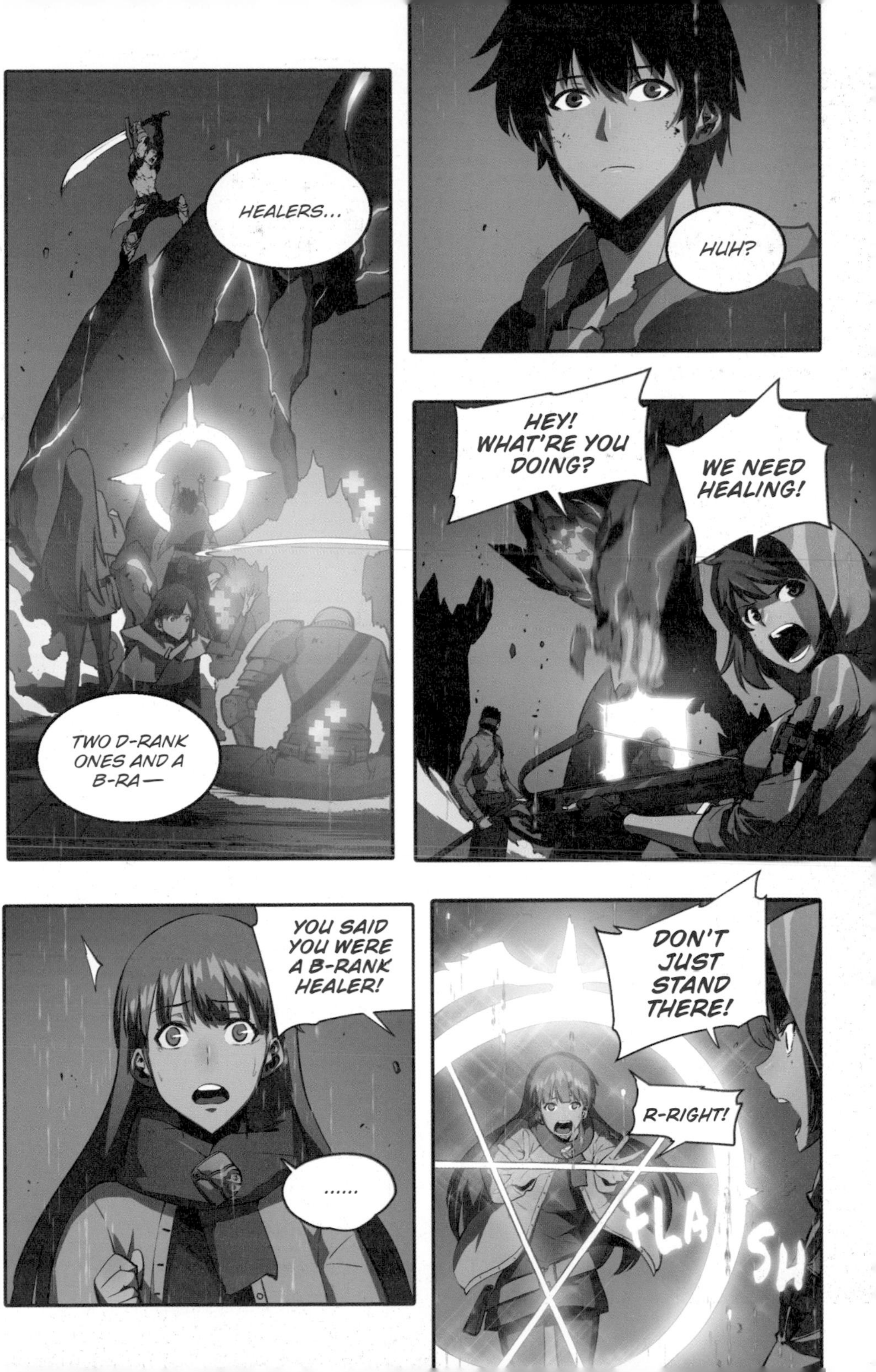
HEALERS...
TWO D-RANK ONES AND A B-RA—
HUH?
HEY! WHAT'RE YOU DOING?
WE NEED HEALING!
YOU SAID YOU WERE A B-RANK HEALER!
......
DON'T JUST STAND THERE!
R-RIGHT!
FLASH

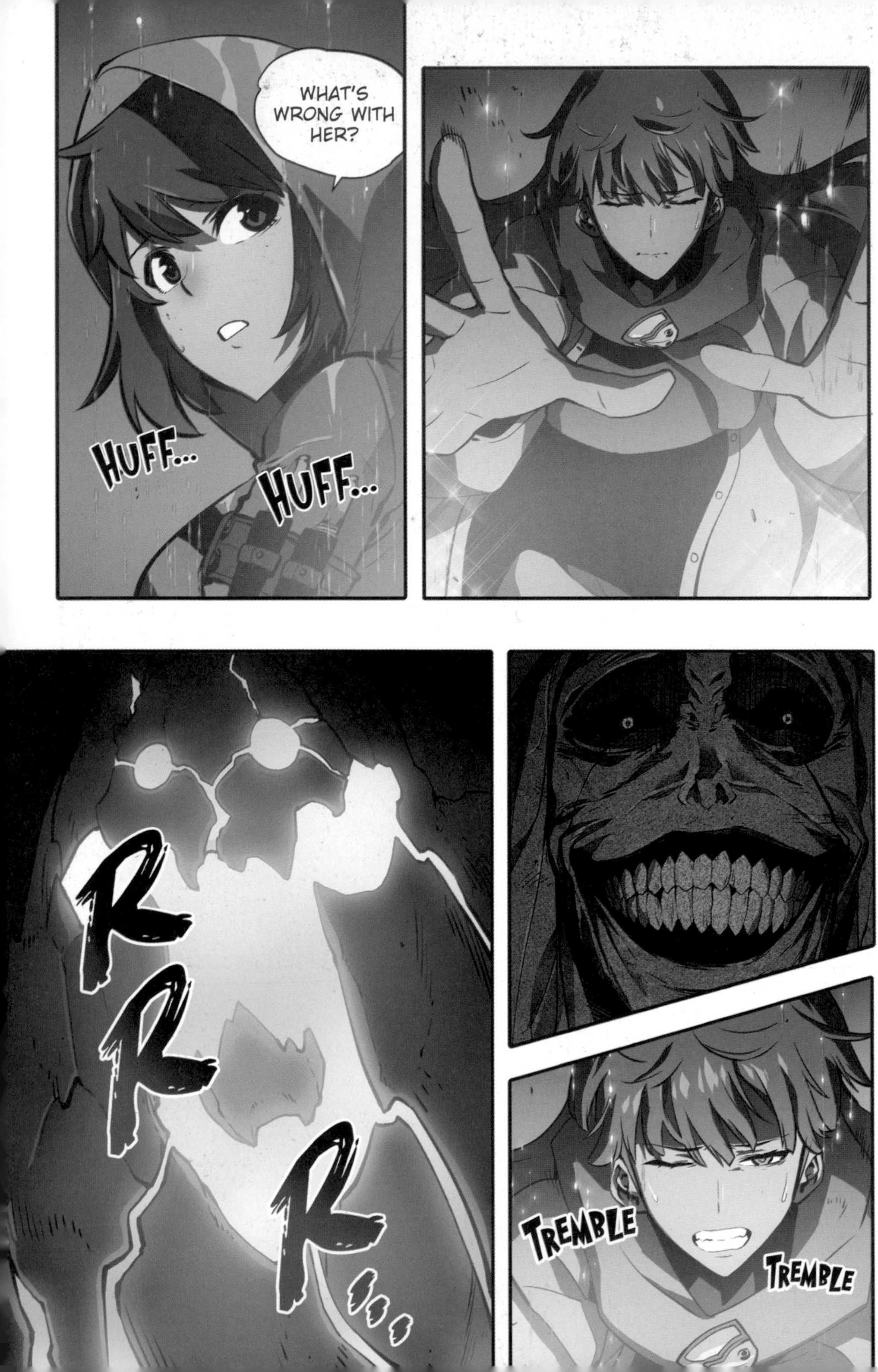
WHAT'S WRONG WITH HER?
HUFF...
HUFF...
RRR...
TREMBLE
TREMBLE

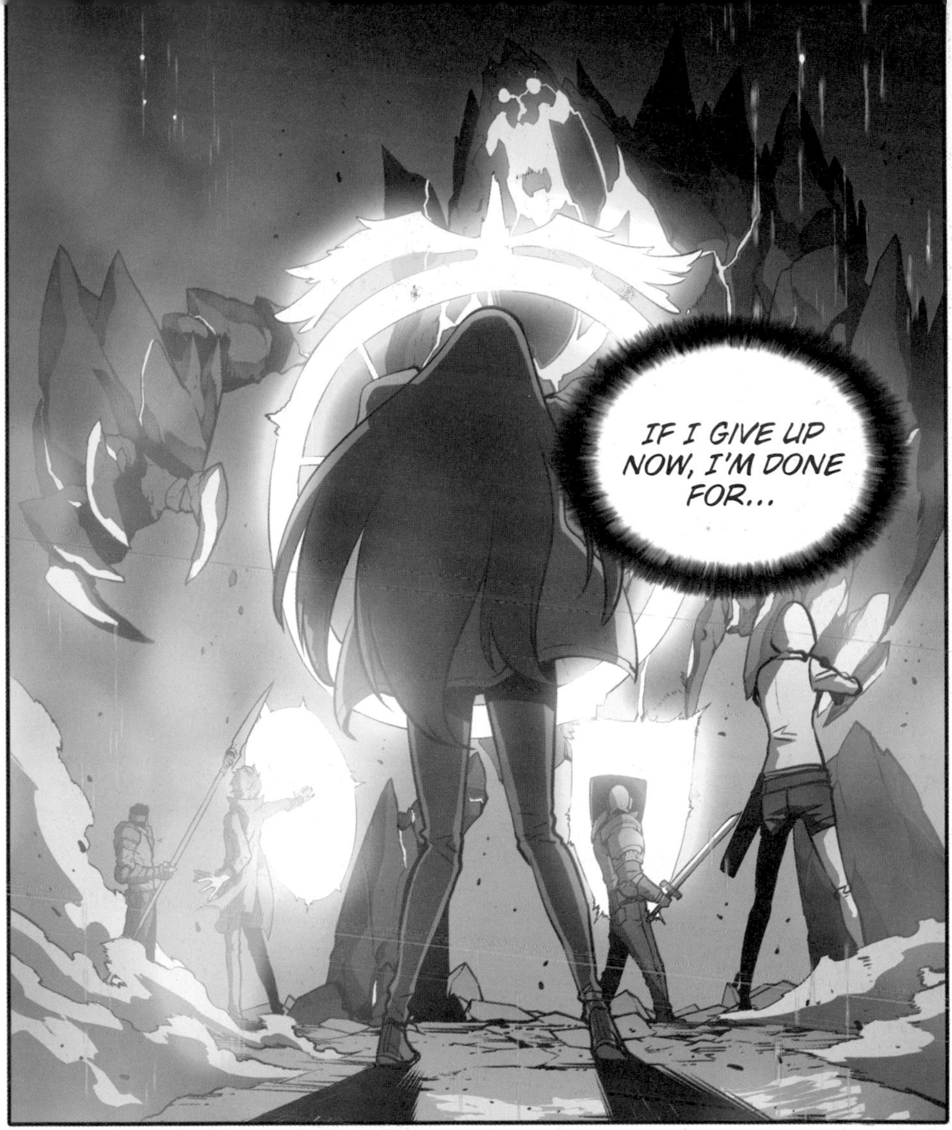
IF I GIVE UP NOW, I'M DONE FOR...

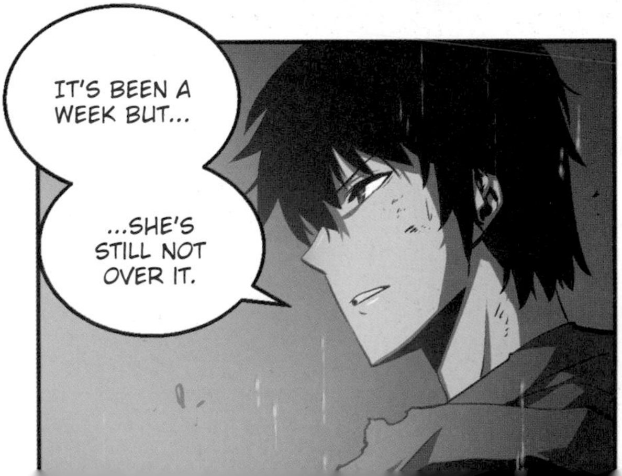
IT'S BEEN A WEEK BUT...
...SHE'S STILL NOT OVER IT.

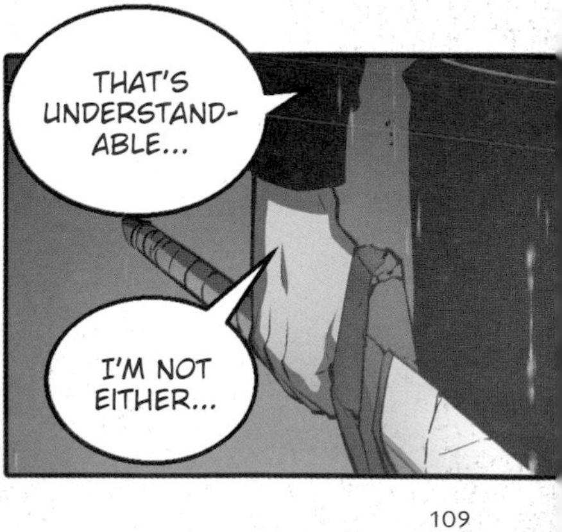
THAT'S UNDERSTAND-ABLE...
I'M NOT EITHER...

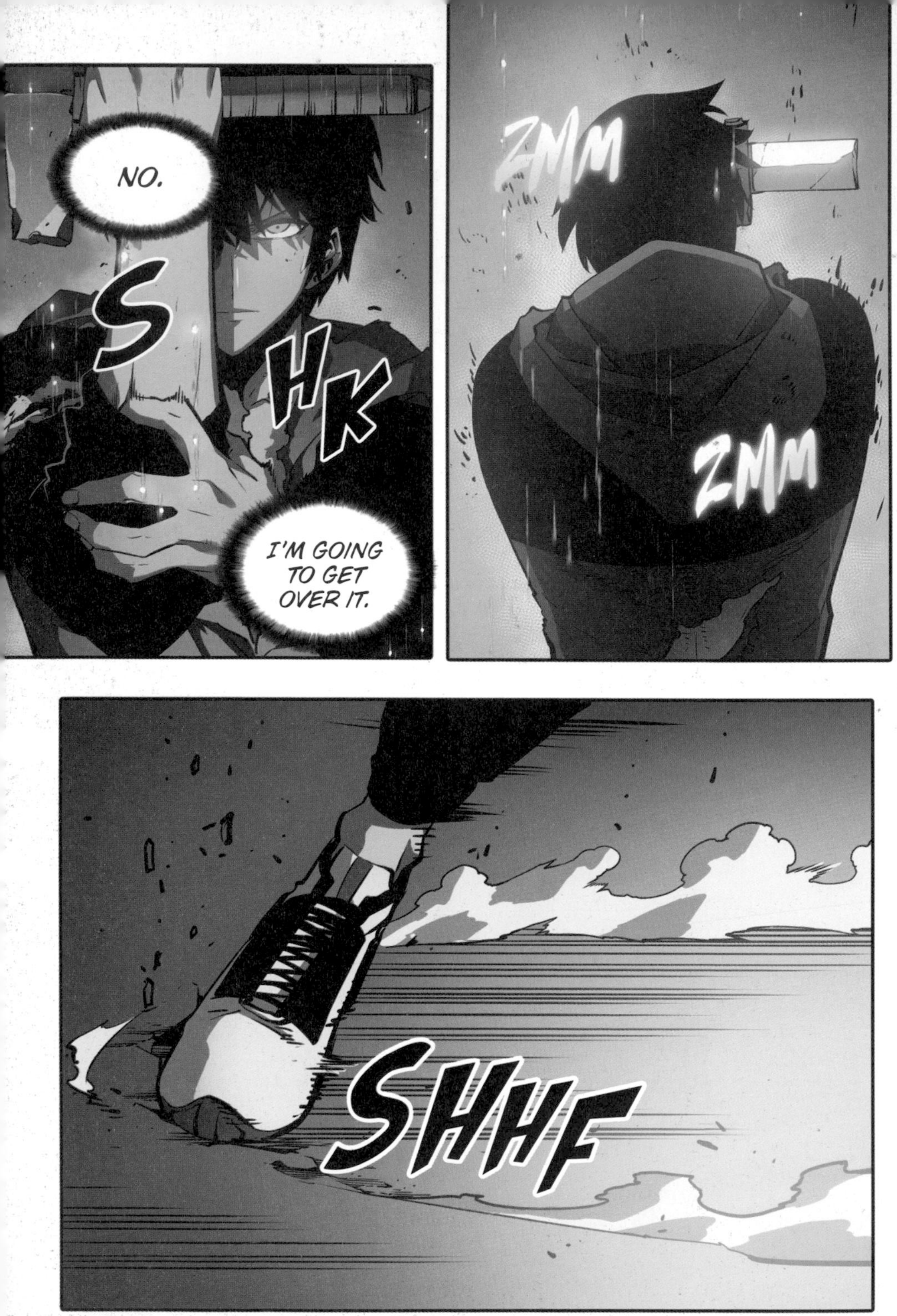
NO.
S
HK
I'M GOING TO GET OVER IT.
ZMM
ZMM
SHHF

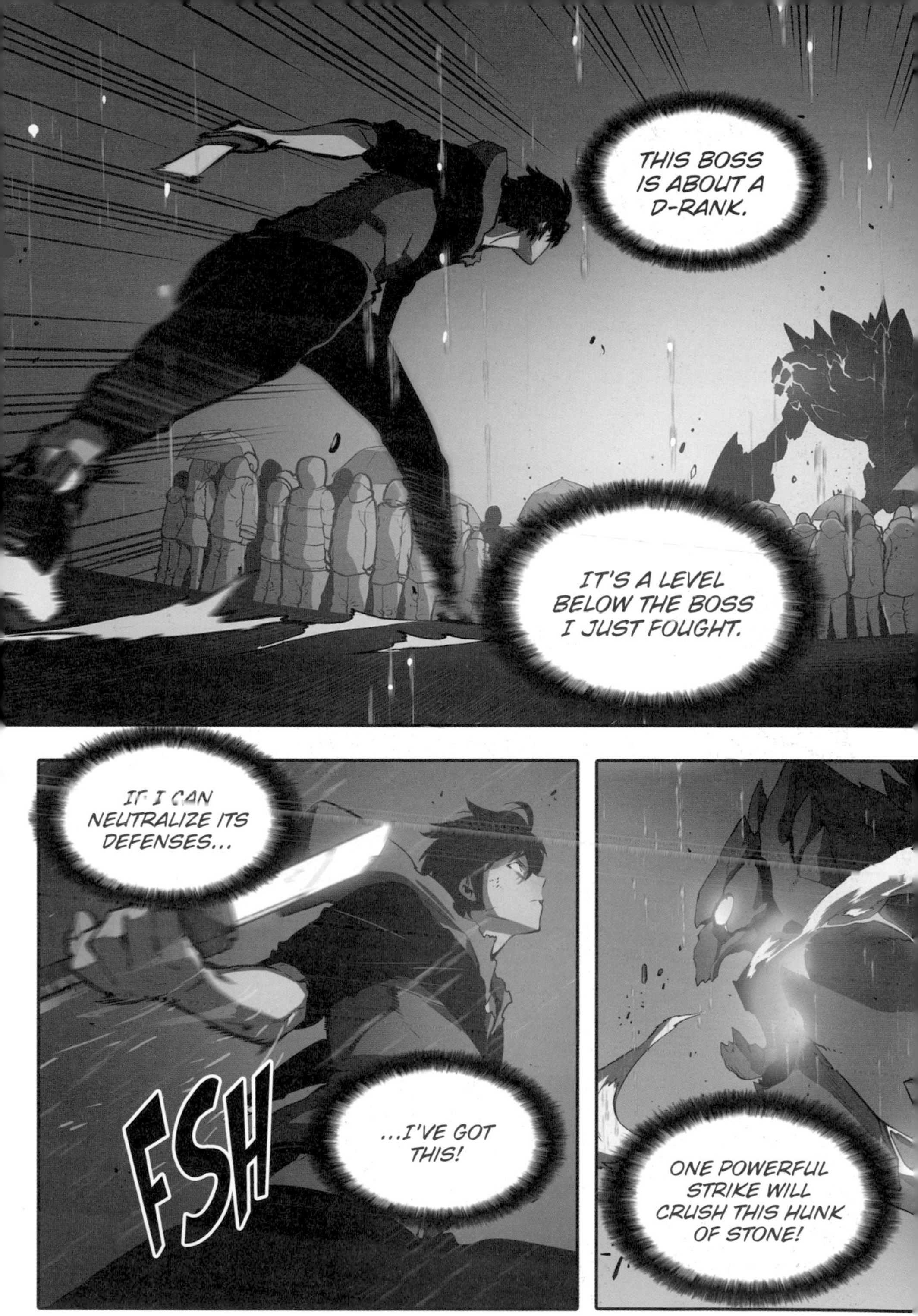
THIS BOSS IS ABOUT A D-RANK.
IT'S A LEVEL BELOW THE BOSS I JUST FOUGHT.
IF I CAN NEUTRALIZE ITS DEFENSES...
FSH
...I'VE GOT THIS!
ONE POWERFUL STRIKE WILL CRUSH THIS HUNK OF STONE!

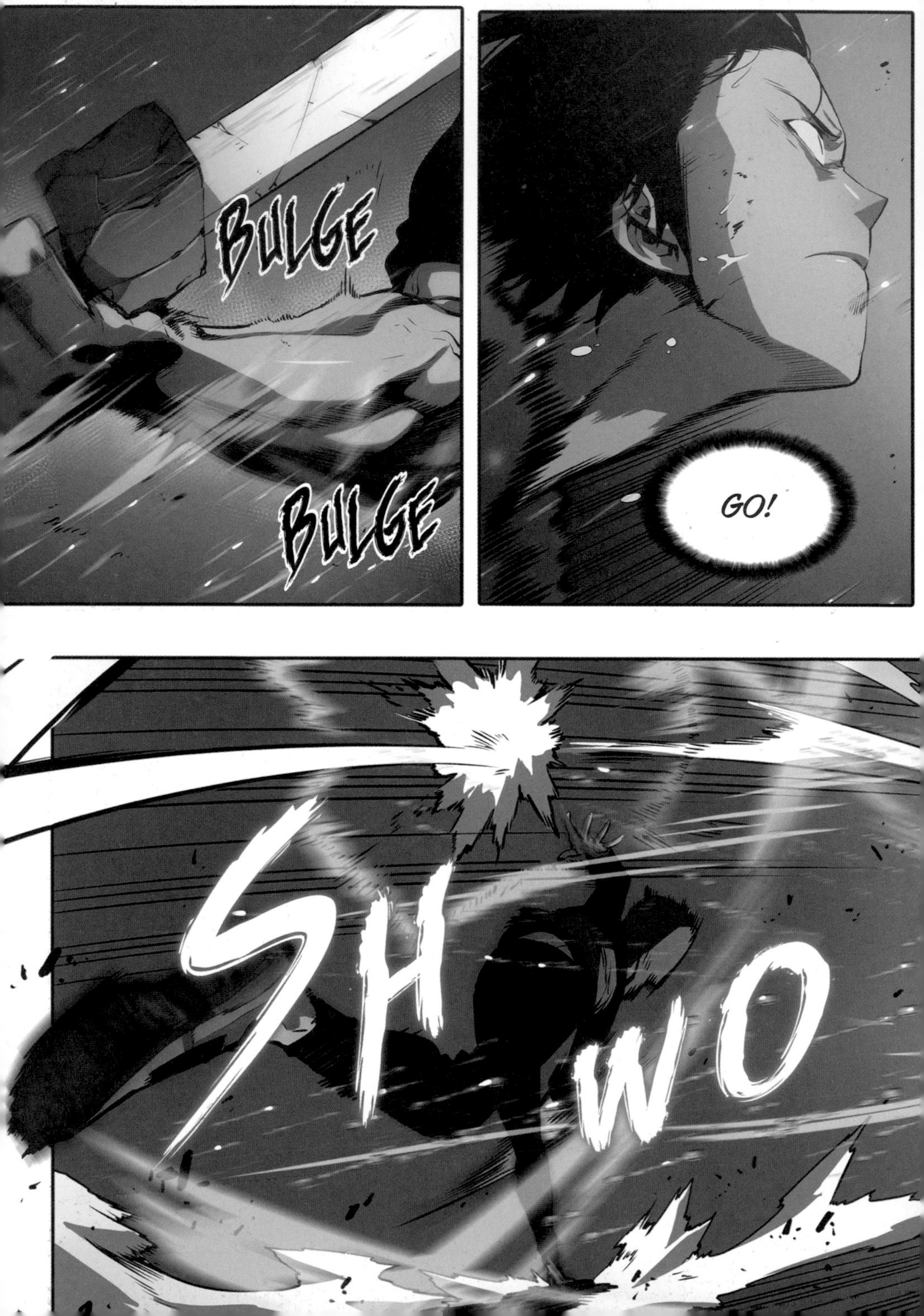
BULGE
BULGE
GO!
SHWO

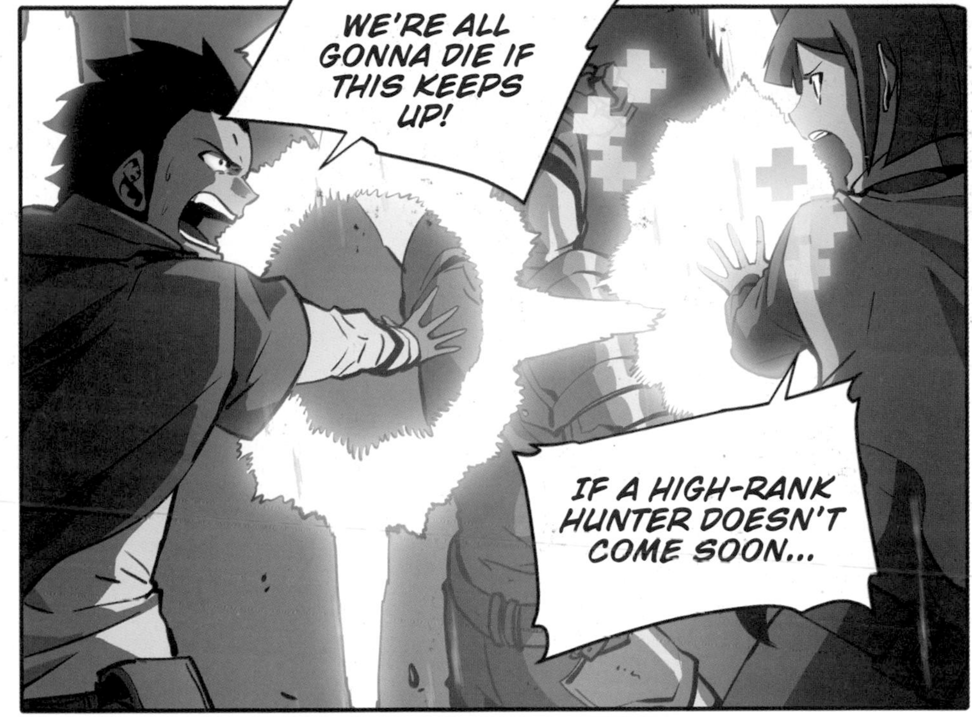
WE'RE ALL GONNA DIE IF THIS KEEPS UP!
IF A HIGH-RANK HUNTER DOESN'T COME SOON...

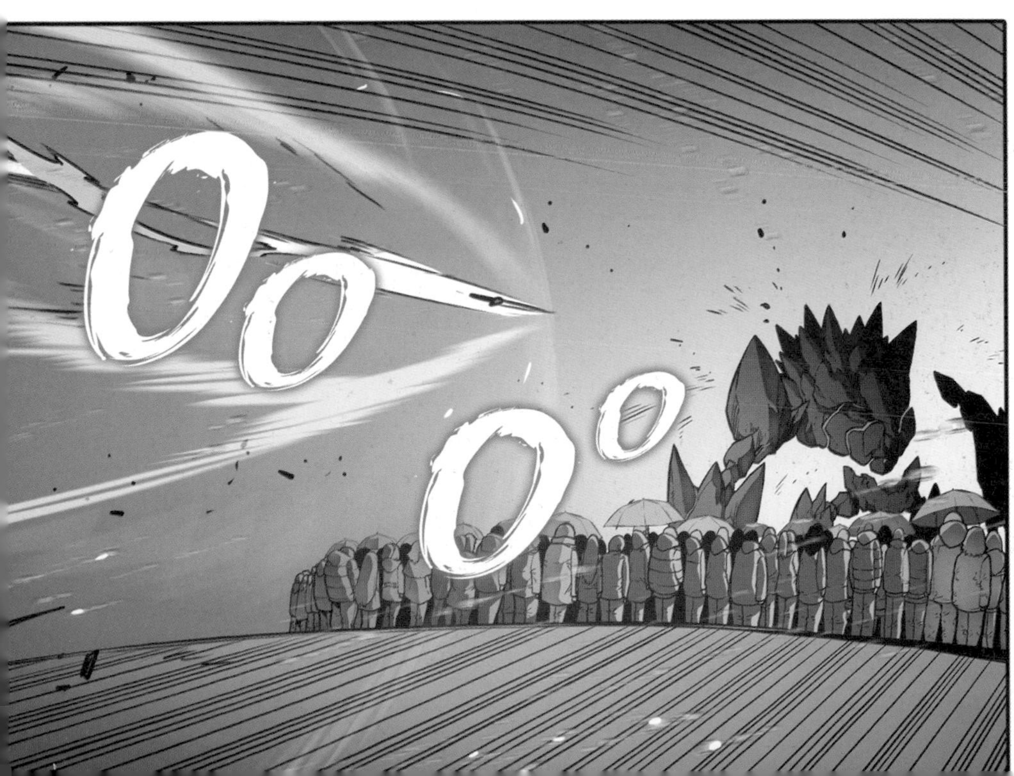
OOOO

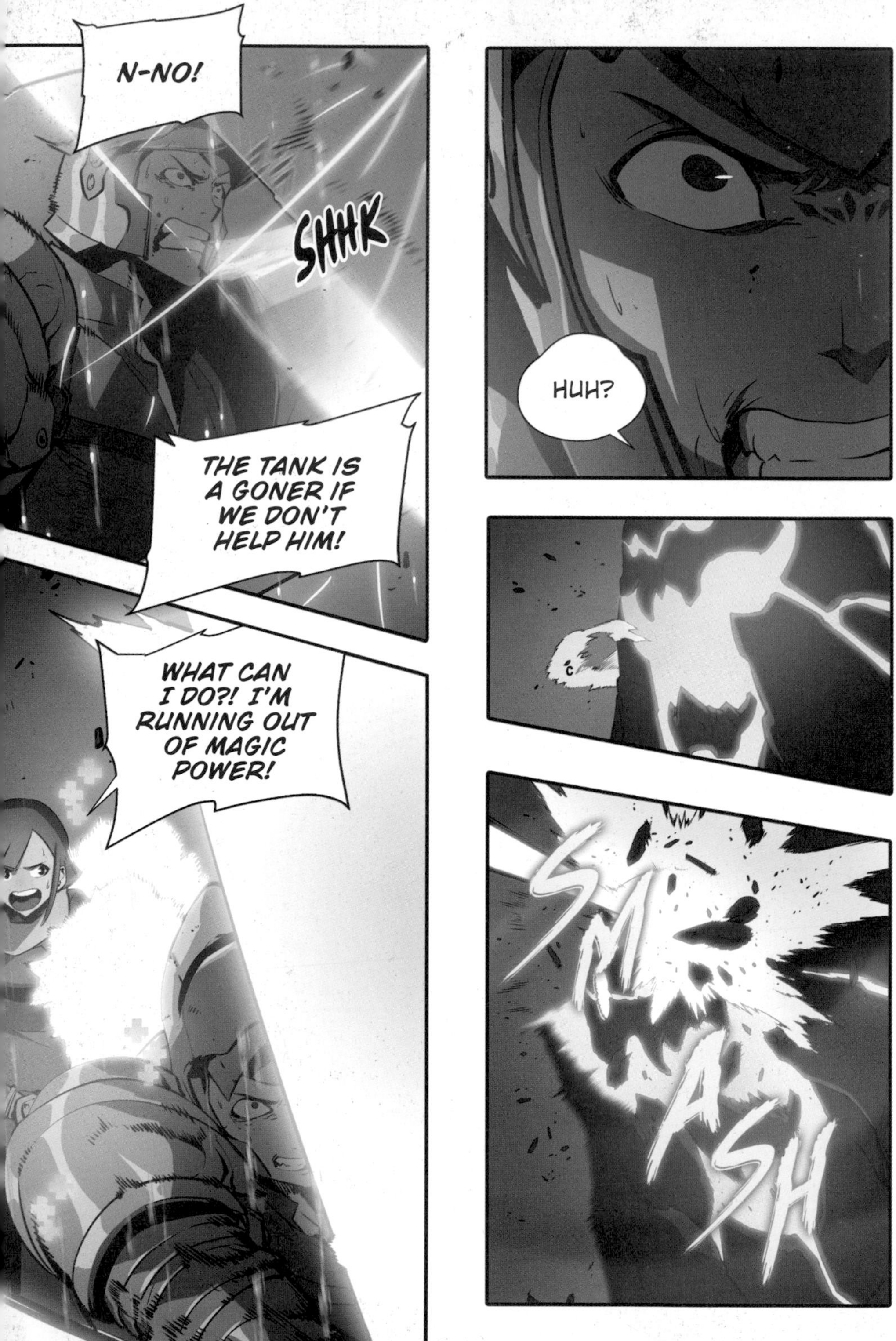
N-NO!
SHHK
THE TANK IS A GONER IF WE DON'T HELP HIM!
WHAT CAN I DO?! I'M RUNNING OUT OF MAGIC POWER!
HUH?
SMASH

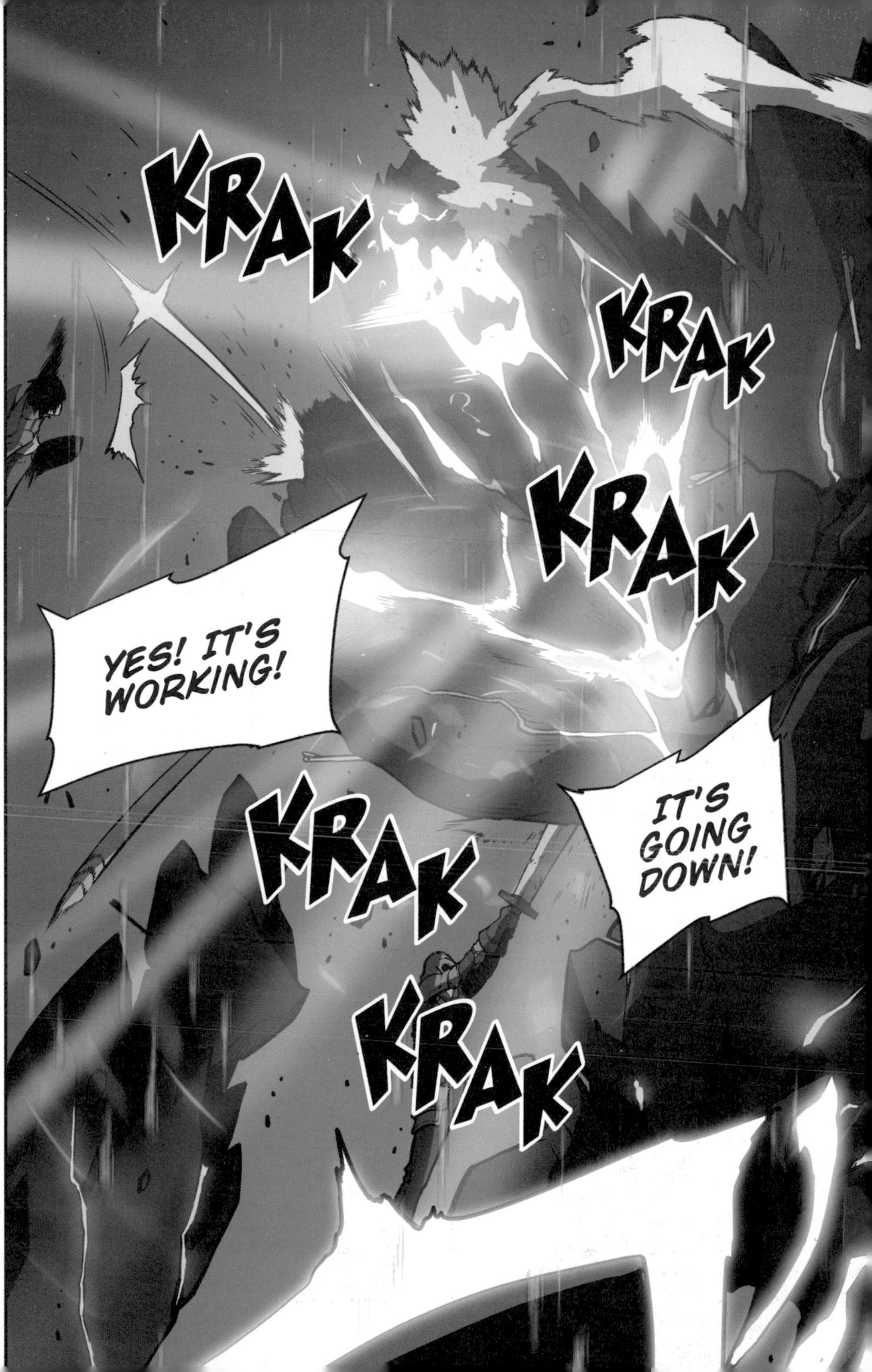
KRAK
KRAK
KRAK
YES! IT'S WORKING!
KRAK
IT'S GOING DOWN!
KRAK

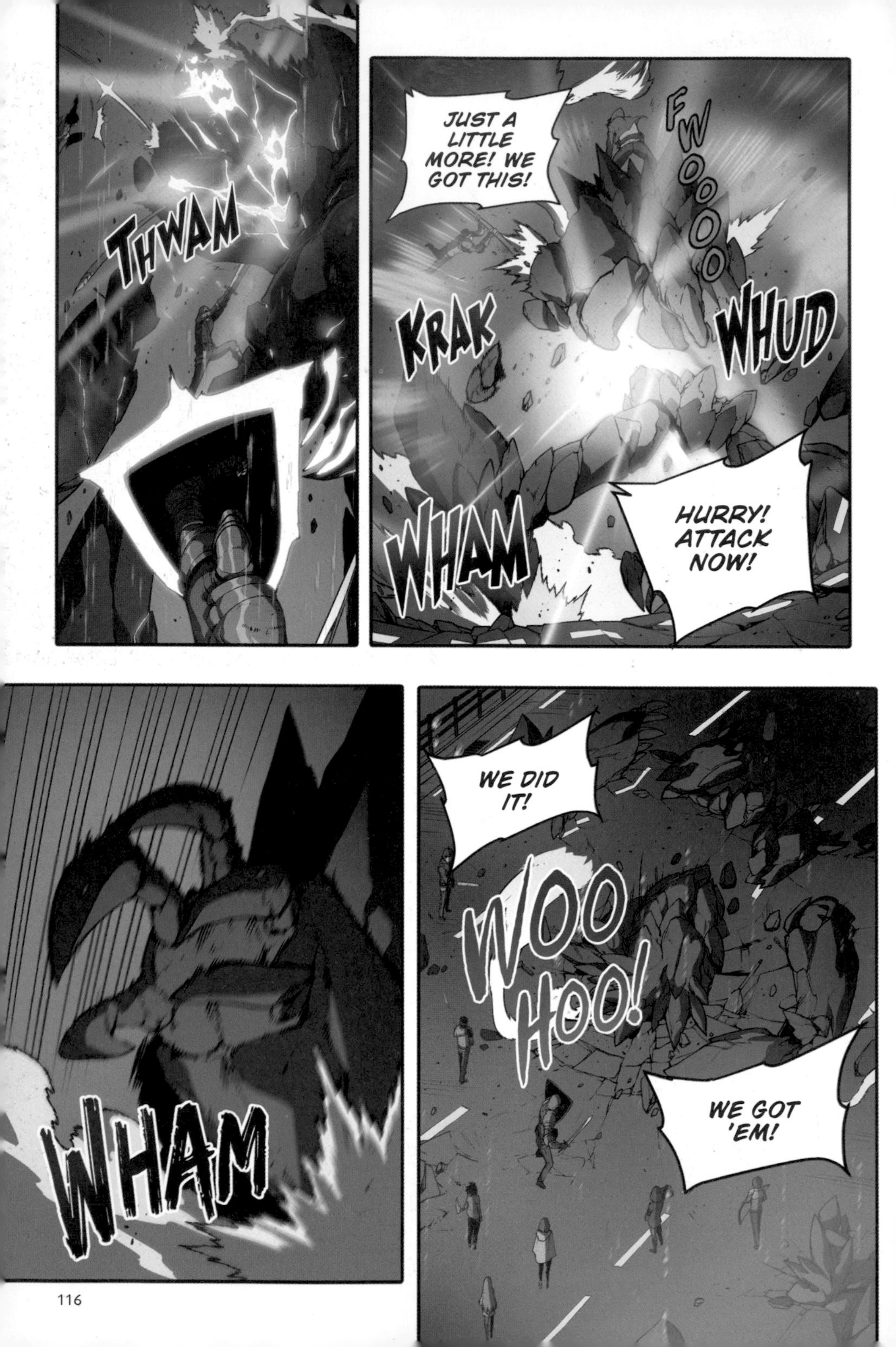
THWAM
JUST A LITTLE MORE! WE GOT THIS!
FWOOOO
KRAK
WHUD
WHAM
HURRY! ATTACK NOW!
WHAM
WE DID IT!
WOO HOO!
WE GOT 'EM!

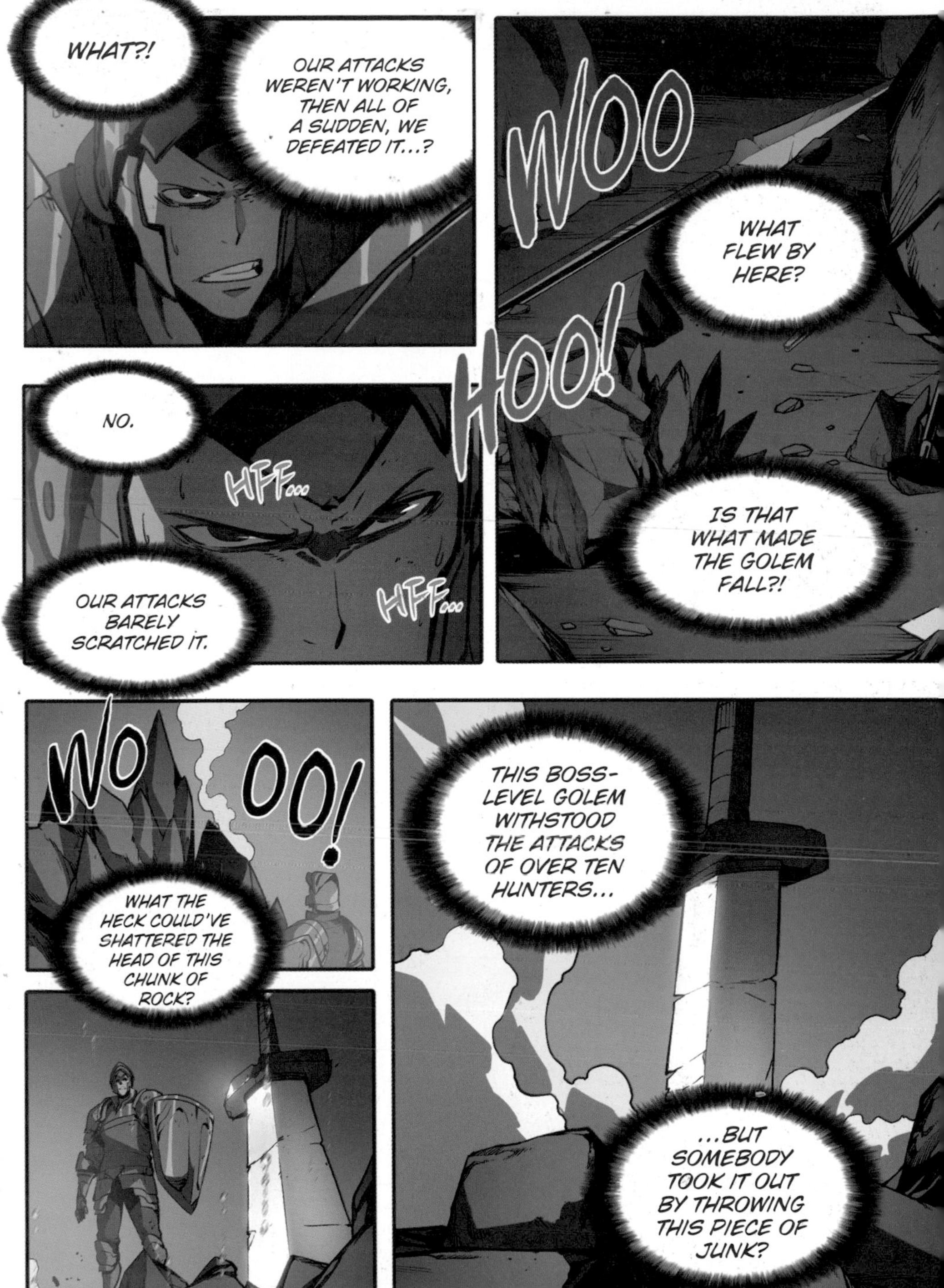
WHAT?!
OUR ATTACKS WEREN'T WORKING, THEN ALL OF A SUDDEN, WE DEFEATED IT...?
WOO
WHAT FLEW BY HERE?
HOO!
NO.
HFF...
OUR ATTACKS BARELY SCRATCHED IT.
HFF...
IS THAT WHAT MADE THE GOLEM FALL?!
WO OO!
WHAT THE HECK COULD'VE SHATTERED THE HEAD OF THIS CHUNK OF ROCK?
THIS BOSS-LEVEL GOLEM WITHSTOOD THE ATTACKS OF OVER TEN HUNTERS...
...BUT SOMEBODY TOOK IT OUT BY THROWING THIS PIECE OF JUNK?

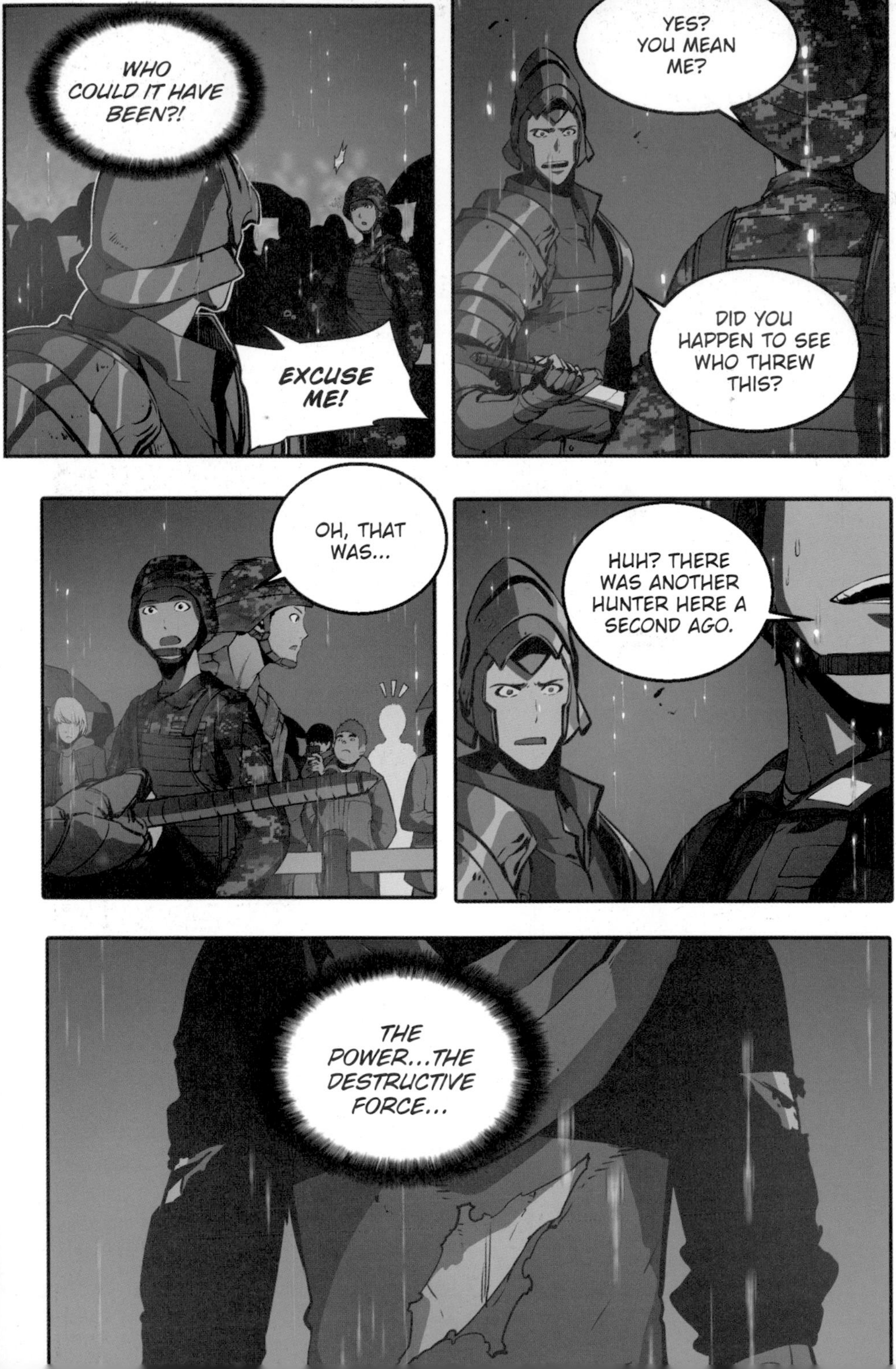
WHO COULD IT HAVE BEEN?!
EXCUSE ME!
YES? YOU MEAN ME?
DID YOU HAPPEN TO SEE WHO THREW THIS?
OH, THAT WAS...
HUH? THERE WAS ANOTHER HUNTER HERE A SECOND AGO.
THE POWER...THE DESTRUCTIVE FORCE...

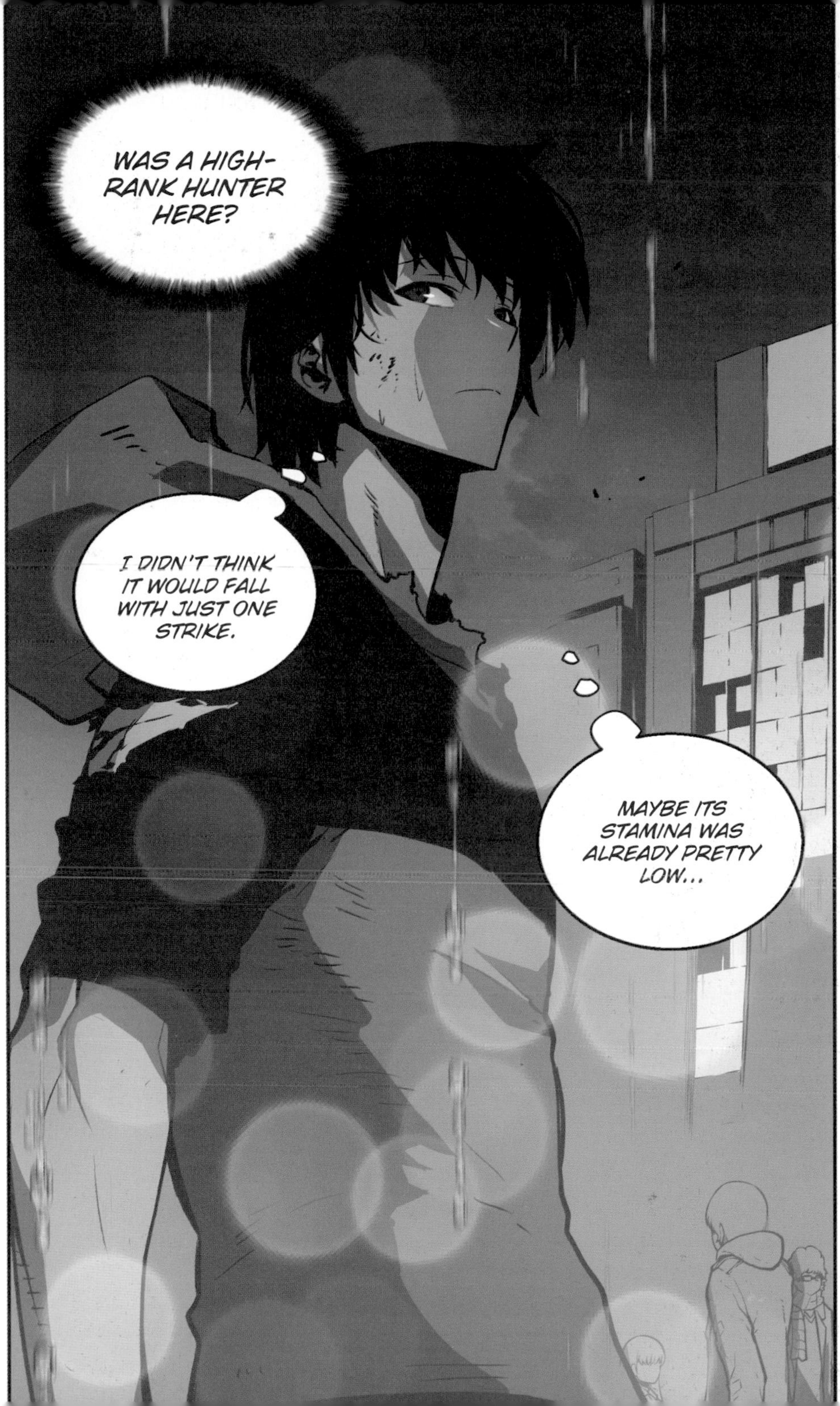
WAS A HIGH-RANK HUNTER HERE?
I DIDN'T THINK IT WOULD FALL WITH JUST ONE STRIKE.
MAYBE ITS STAMINA WAS ALREADY PRETTY LOW...

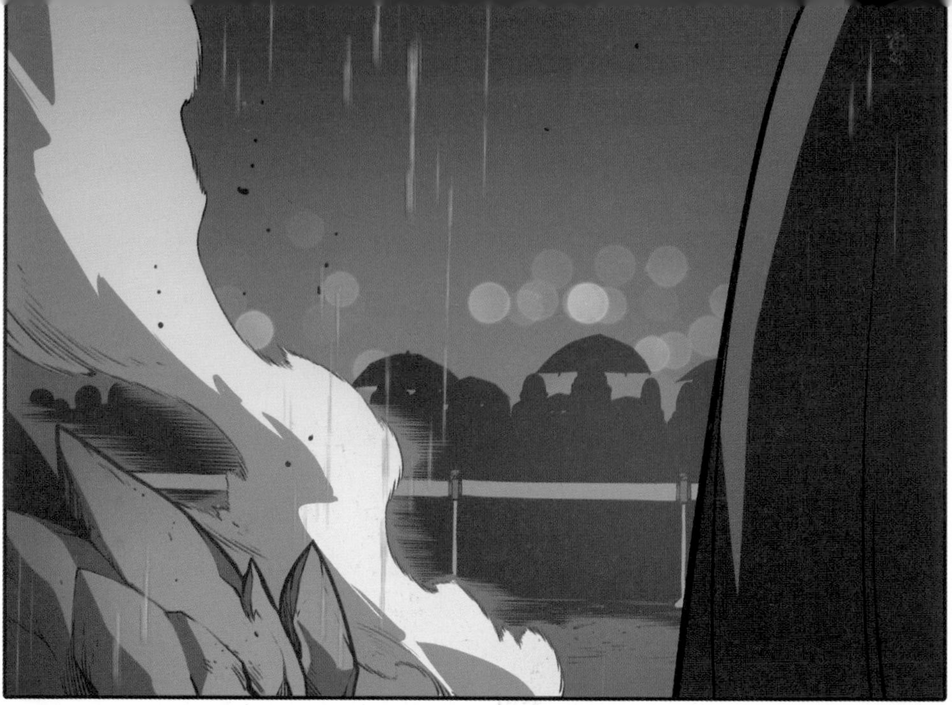

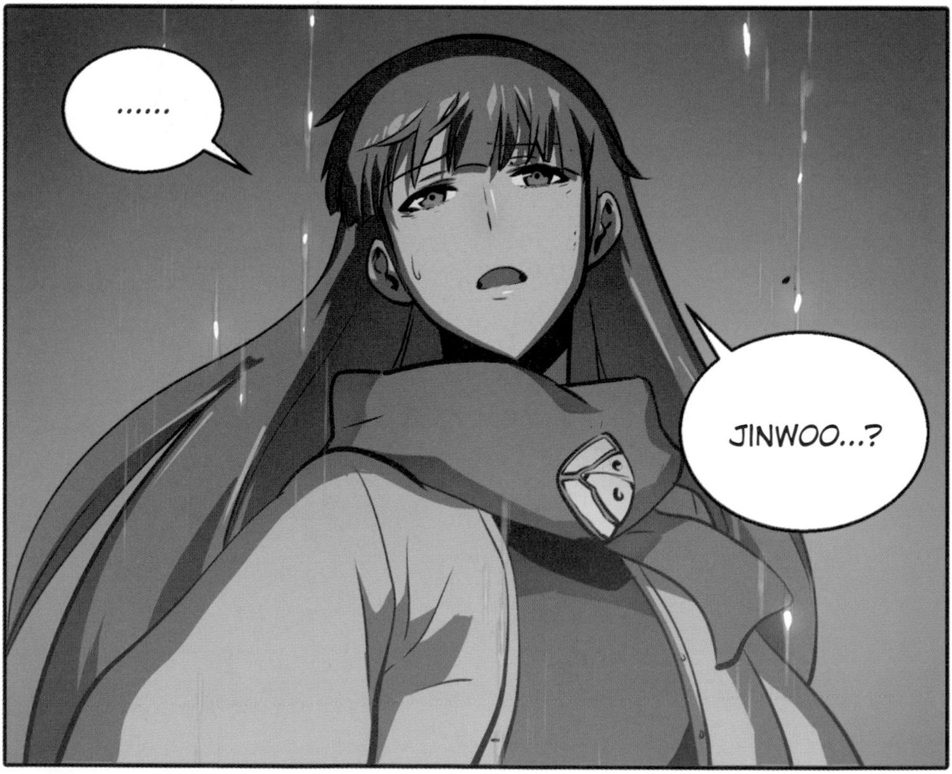
......
JINWOO...?

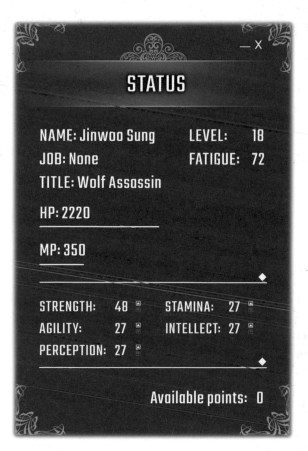

— X

STATUS

NAME: Jinwoo Sung   LEVEL: 18

JOB: None   FATIGUE: 72

TITLE: Wolf Assassin

HP: 2220

MP: 350

◆

STRENGTH: 48   STAMINA: 27

AGILITY: 27   INTELLECT: 27

PERCEPTION: 27

◆

Available points: 0

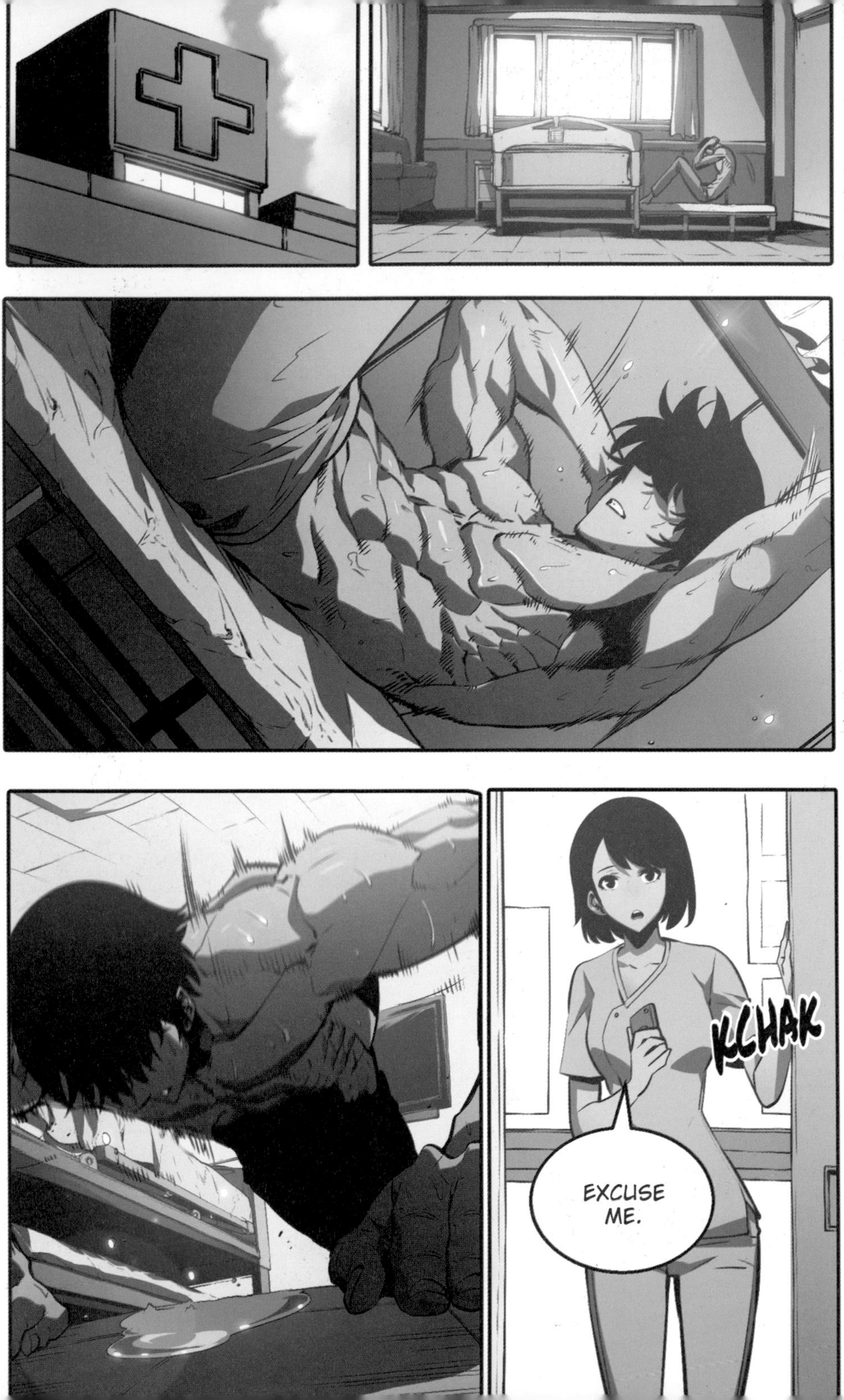
KCHAK
EXCUSE ME.

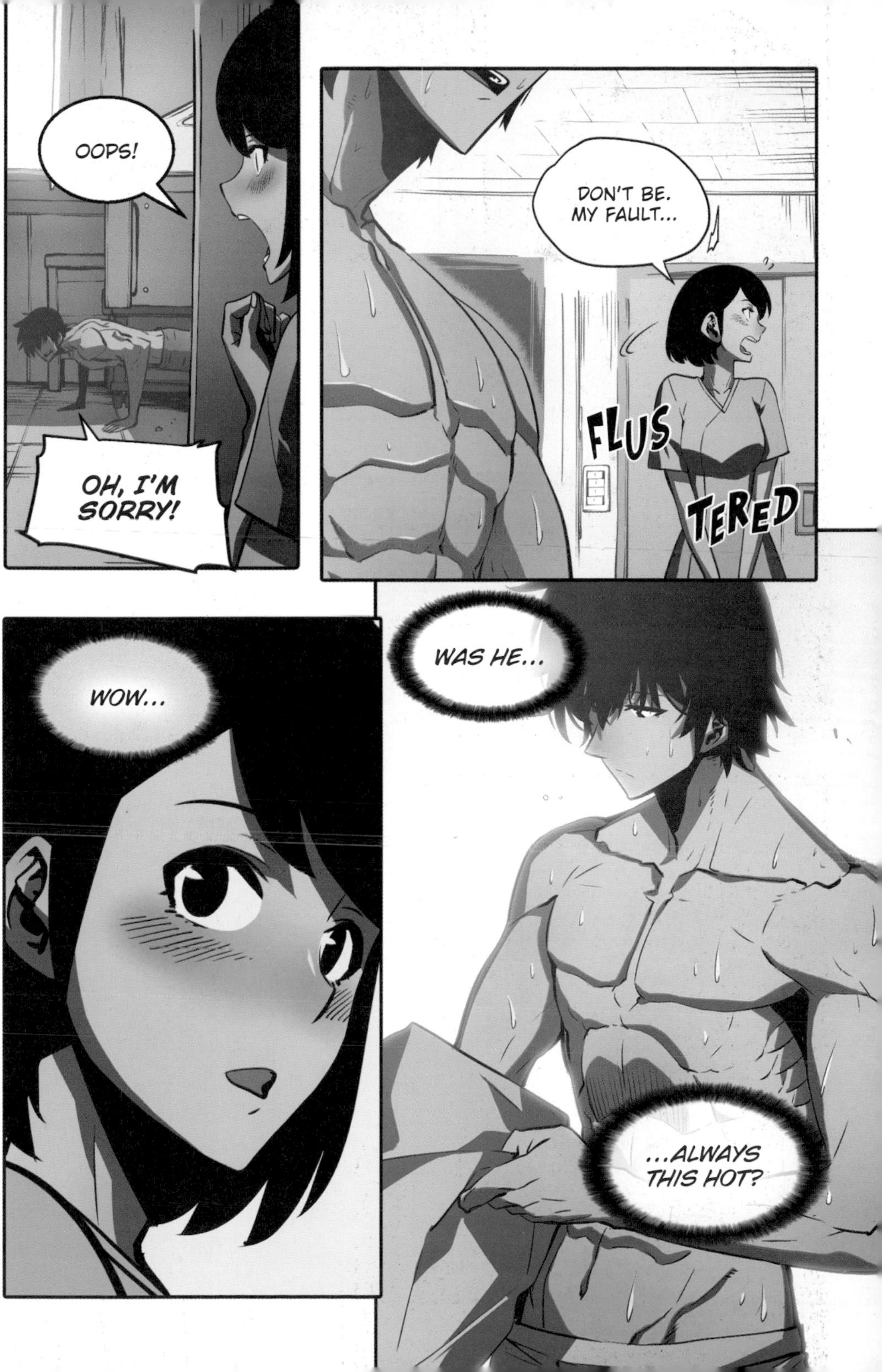
OOPS!
OH, I'M SORRY!
DON'T BE. MY FAULT...
FLUSTERED
WOW...
WAS HE...
...ALWAYS THIS HOT?

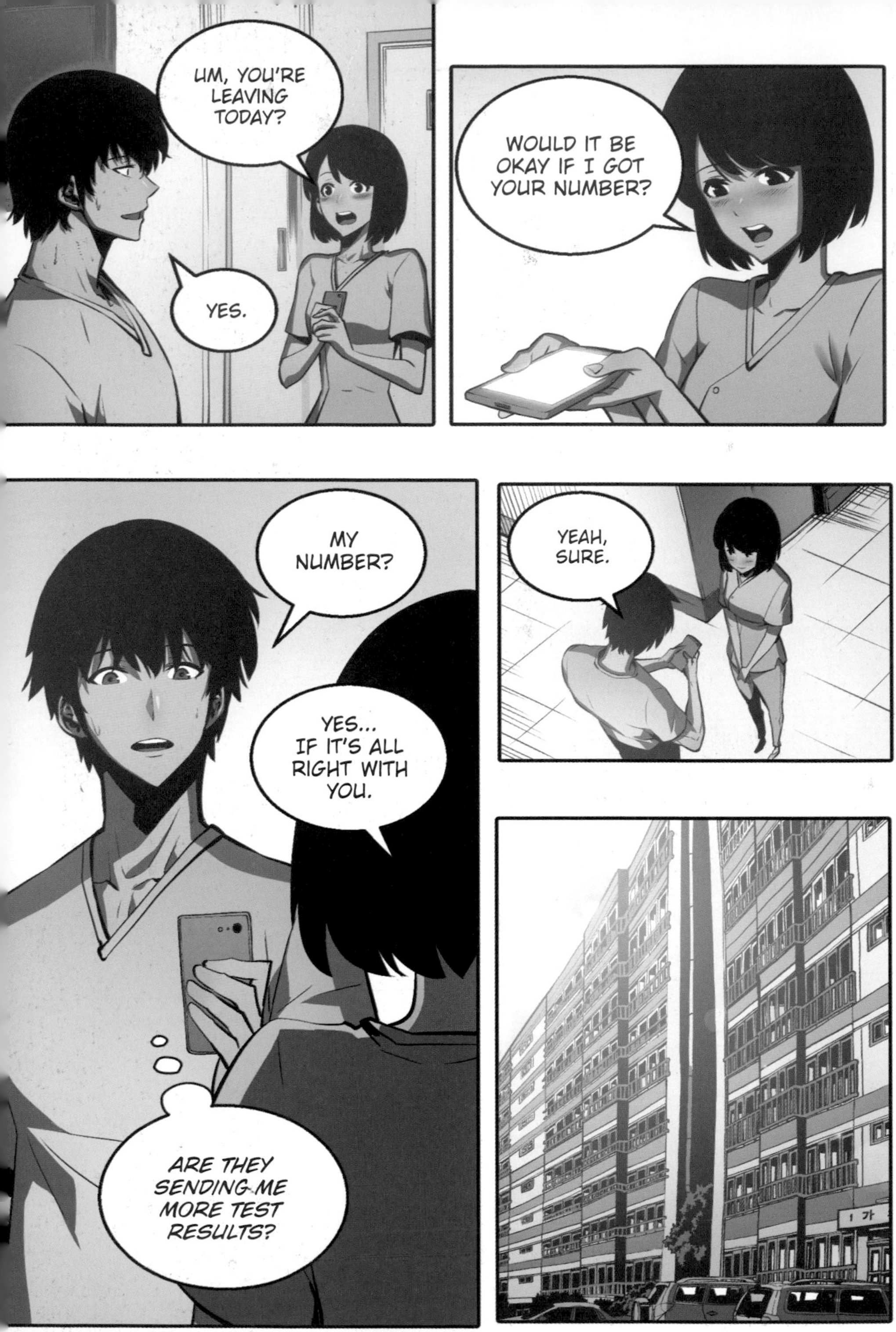
UM, YOU'RE LEAVING TODAY?
YES.
WOULD IT BE OKAY IF I GOT YOUR NUMBER?
MY NUMBER?
YES... IF IT'S ALL RIGHT WITH YOU.
ARE THEY SENDING ME MORE TEST RESULTS?
YEAH, SURE.

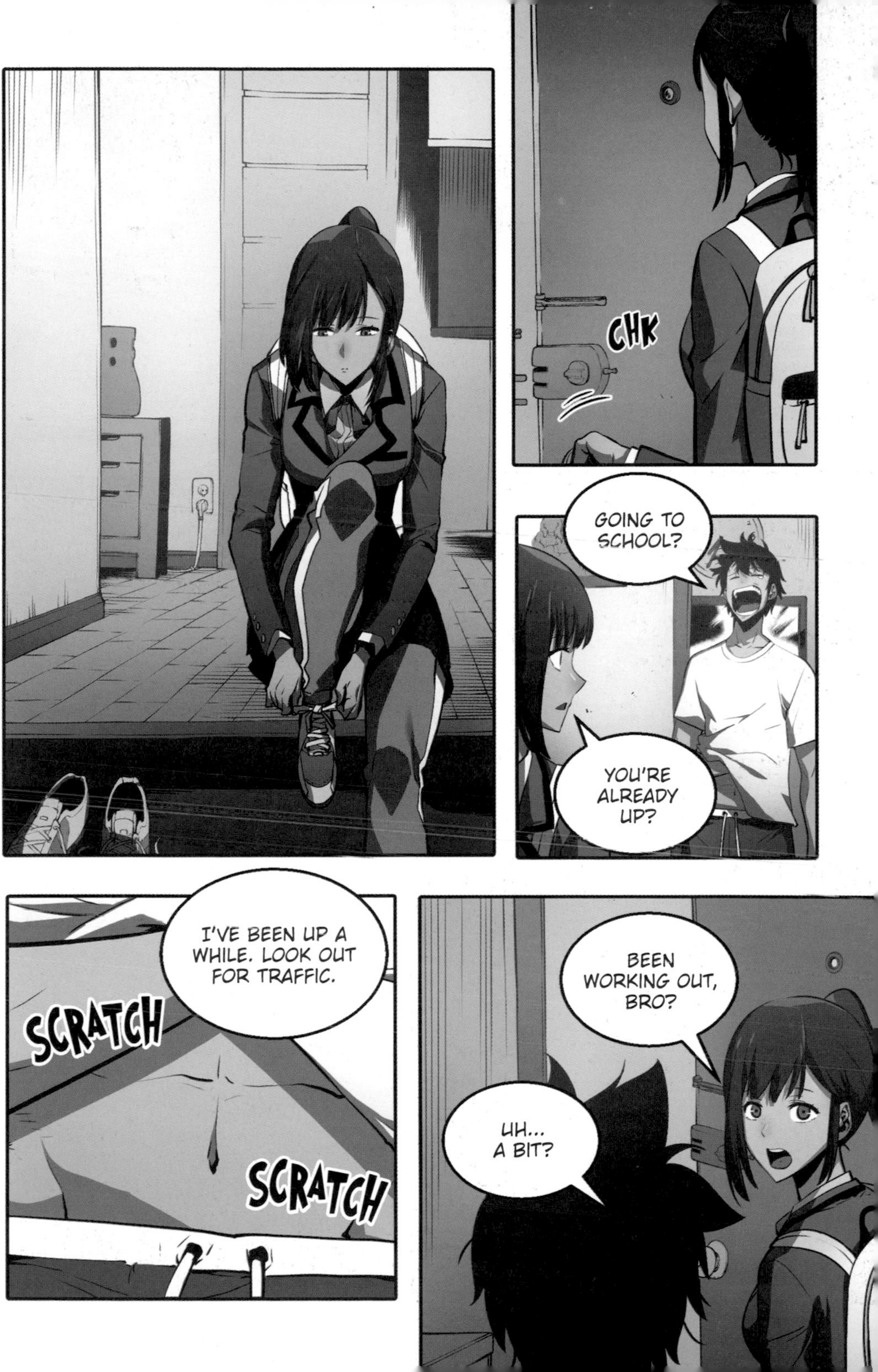
CHK
GOING TO SCHOOL?
YOU'RE ALREADY UP?
I'VE BEEN UP A WHILE. LOOK OUT FOR TRAFFIC.
SCRATCH
SCRATCH
BEEN WORKING OUT, BRO?
UH... A BIT?

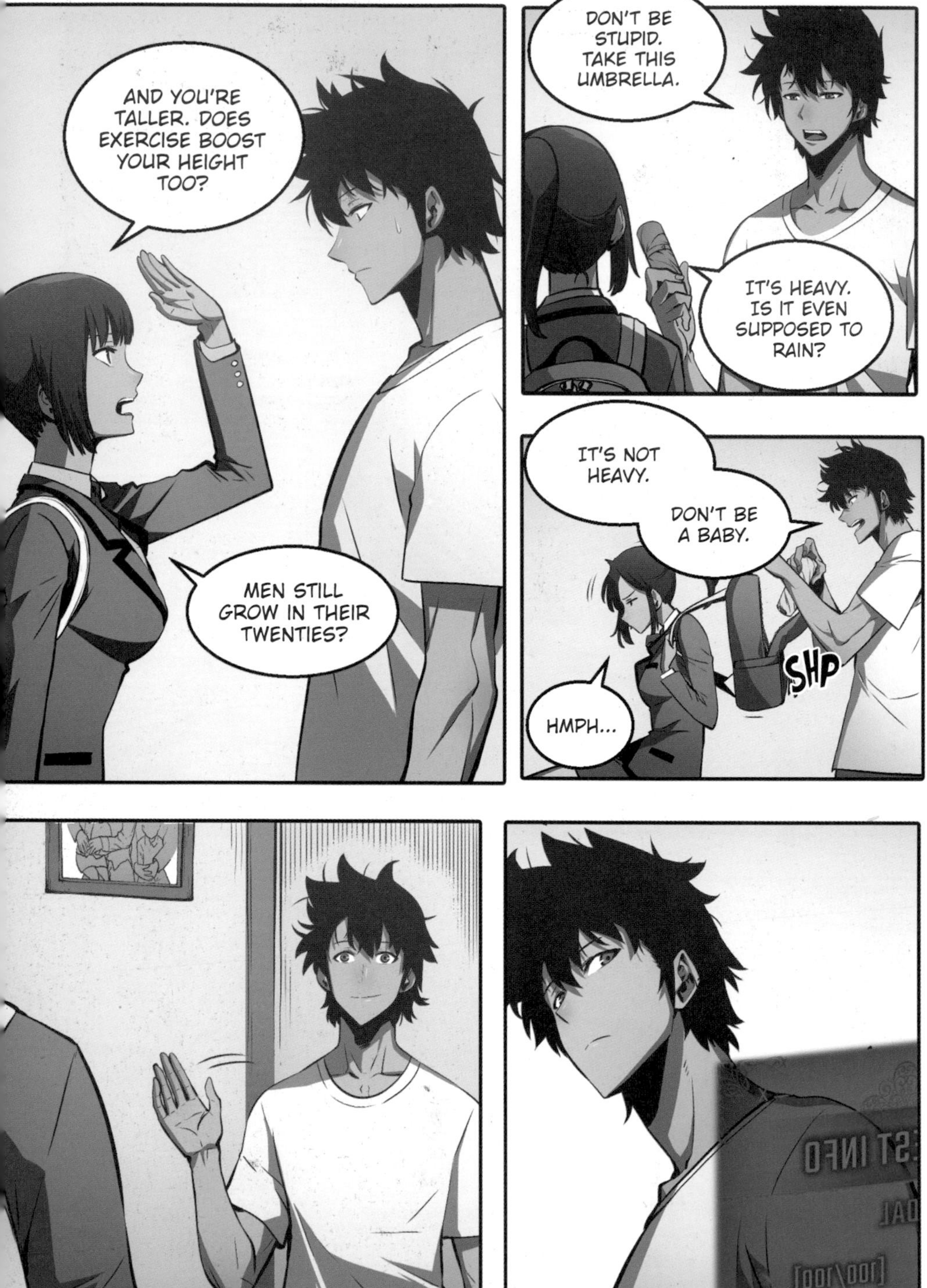
AND YOU'RE TALLER. DOES EXERCISE BOOST YOUR HEIGHT TOO?
MEN STILL GROW IN THEIR TWENTIES?
DON'T BE STUPID. TAKE THIS UMBRELLA.
IT'S HEAVY. IS IT EVEN SUPPOSED TO RAIN?
IT'S NOT HEAVY.
DON'T BE A BABY.
HMPH...
SHP

I'LL DO THE RUNNING LATER.
GOAL
Push-ups [100/100]
Sit-ups [100/100]
Squats [100/100]
Running [0/10km]
WARNING: Failure to complete the daily quest will result in an appropriate penalty.
I'VE BEEFED UP.
THAT DOESN'T HAPPEN AFTER ONLY TWO DAYS OF EXERCISE.
OBVIOUSLY THIS IS A RESULT OF THE STATS.
AS MY STRENGTH INCREASES, MY MUSCLES TRANSFORM FOR OPTIMUM EFFECT.
DID I INVEST TOO MUCH ON STRENGTH?
NAME: Jinwoo Sung
LEVEL:
JOB: None
FATIGUE: 0
TITLE: Wolf Assassin
HP: 2220
MP: 350
STRENGTH: 48
STAMINA: 27
AGILITY: 27
INTELLECT: 27
PERCEPTION: 27
Available points: 12

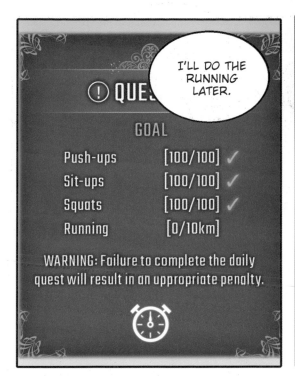

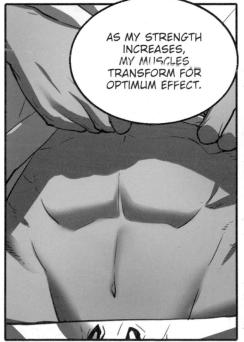

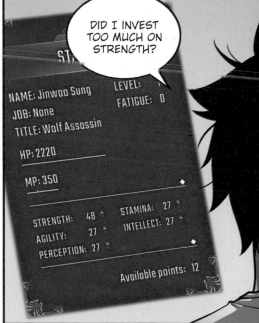

WHAT IF I KEEP INVESTING IN STRENGTH?

HA HA

I'M OVERFLOWING WITH POWER, DUDE!

HA HA!

WOULD THAT ACTUALLY HAPPEN?

BEING ABLE TO DEAL A LOT OF DAMAGE IS USELESS IF I CAN'T HIT A TARGET.

PING!

3

ENGTH: 48   STAMINA:

ITY: 27   INTELLECT:

CEPTION: 27

AND VICE VERSA.

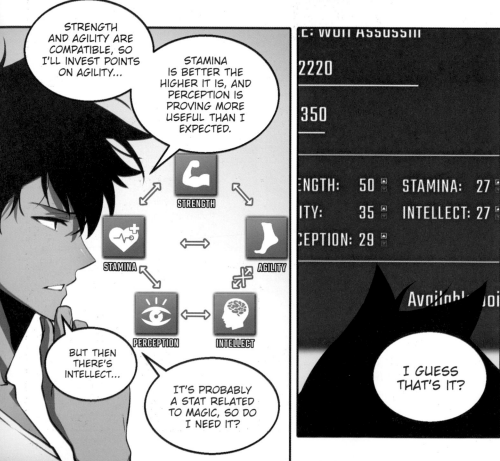

STRENGTH AND AGILITY ARE COMPATIBLE, SO I'LL INVEST POINTS ON AGILITY...

STAMINA IS BETTER THE HIGHER IT IS, AND PERCEPTION IS PROVING MORE USEFUL THAN I EXPECTED.

STRENGTH

STAMINA

AGILITY

PERCEPTION   INTELLECT

BUT THEN THERE'S INTELLECT...

IT'S PROBABLY A STAT RELATED TO MAGIC, SO DO I NEED IT?

E: Wolf Assassin

2220

350

ENGTH: 50   STAMINA: 27

ITY: 35   INTELLECT: 27

CEPTION: 29

Available oi

I GUESS THAT'S IT?

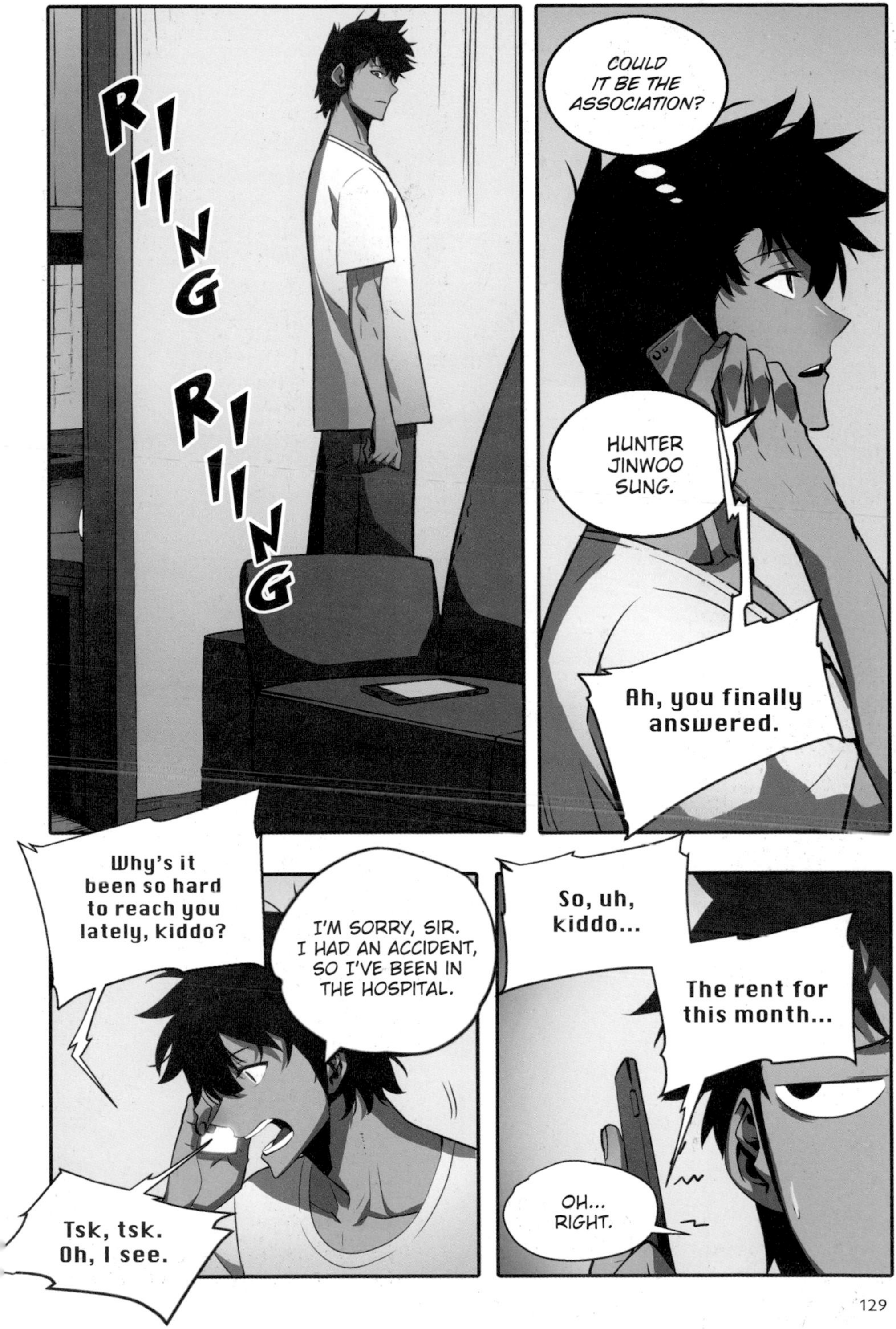
RIIING RIIING
COULD IT BE THE ASSOCIATION?
HUNTER JINWOO SUNG.
Ah, you finally answered.
Why's it been so hard to reach you lately, kiddo?
I'M SORRY, SIR. I HAD AN ACCIDENT, SO I'VE BEEN IN THE HOSPITAL.
Tsk, tsk. Oh, I see.
So, uh, kiddo...
The rent for this month...
OH... RIGHT.

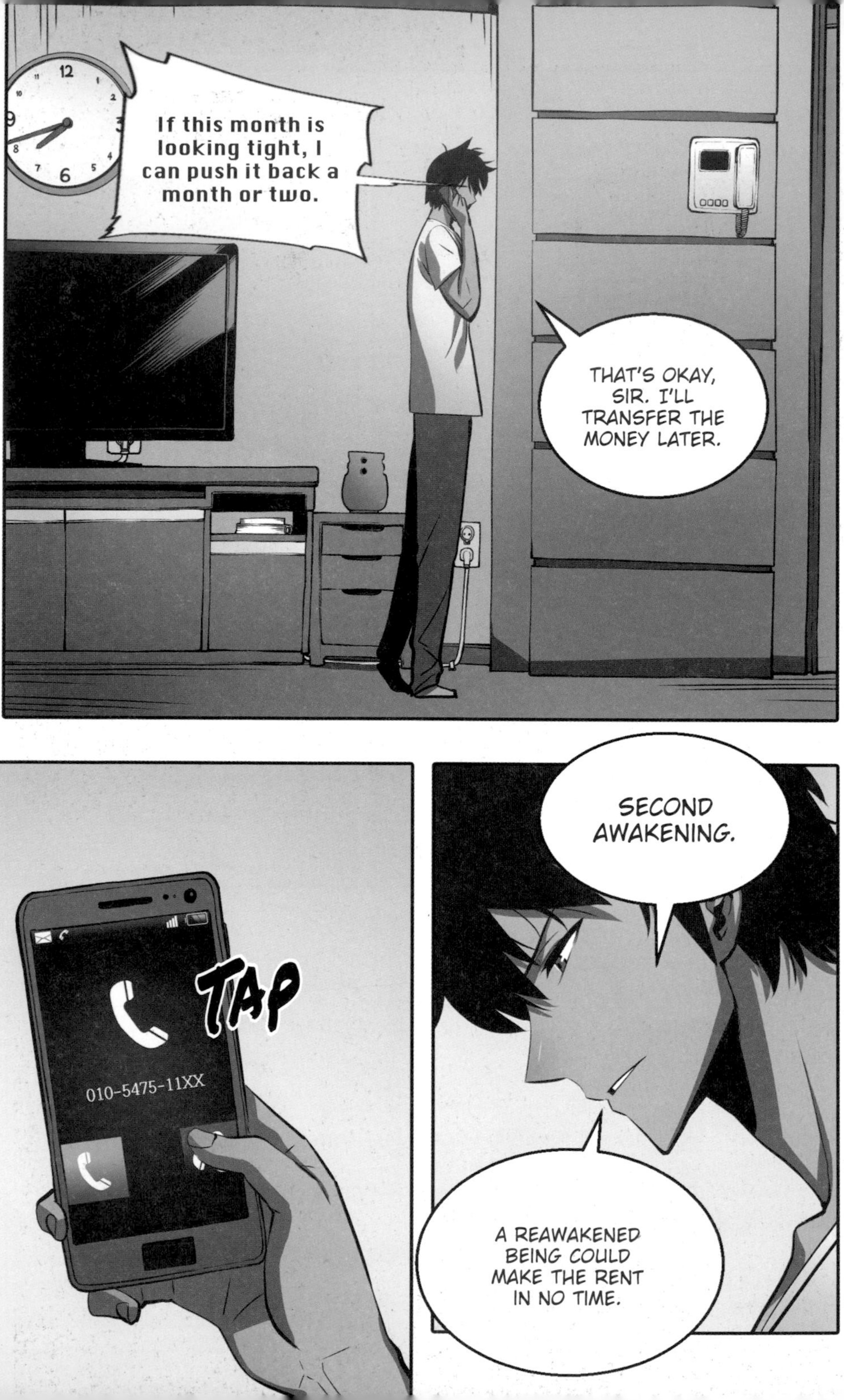
If this month is looking tight, I can push it back a month or two.
THAT'S OKAY, SIR. I'LL TRANSFER THE MONEY LATER.
010-5475-11XX
TAP
SECOND AWAKENING.
A REAWAKENED BEING COULD MAKE THE RENT IN NO TIME.

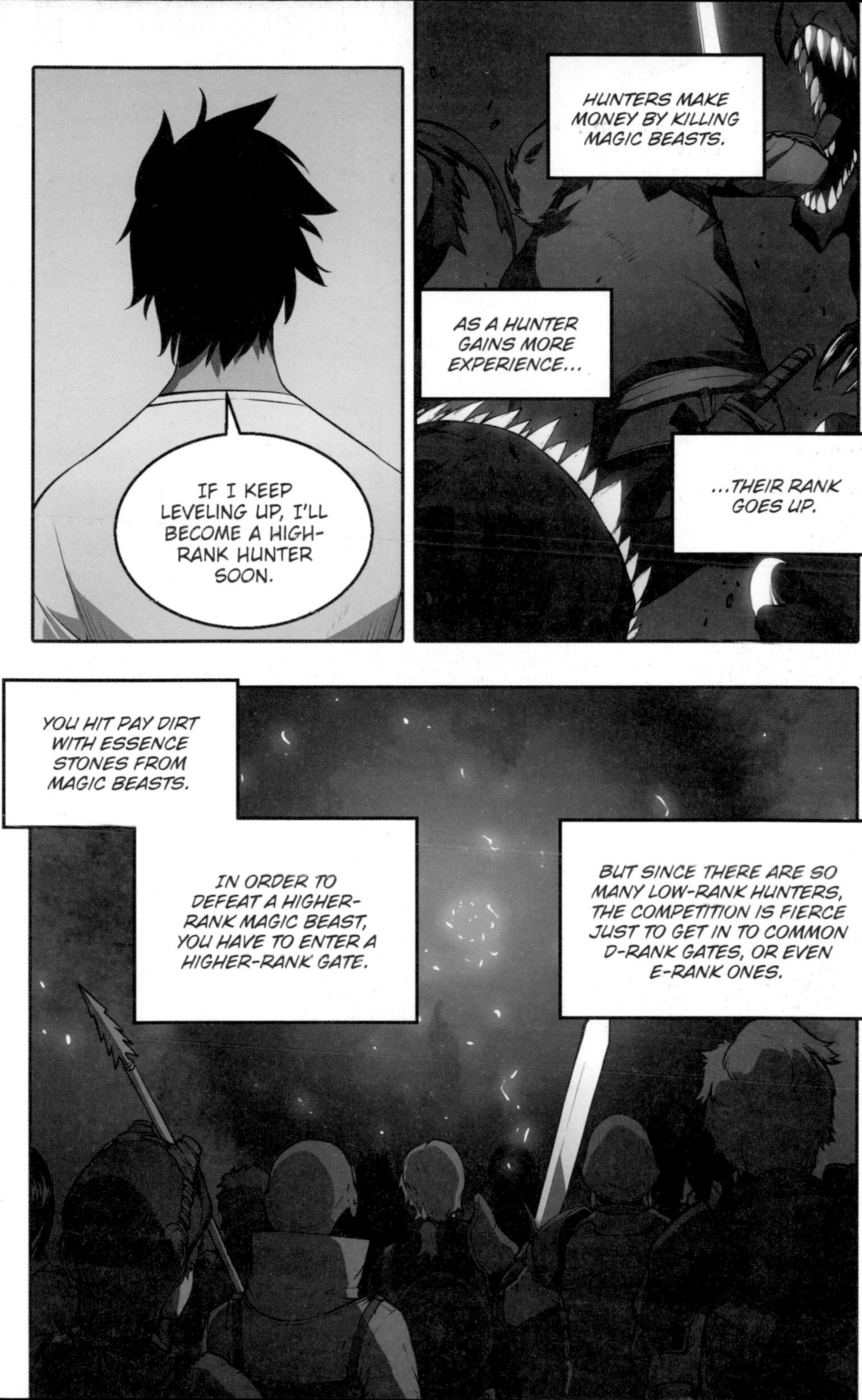
IF I KEEP LEVELING UP, I'LL BECOME A HIGH-RANK HUNTER SOON.
HUNTERS MAKE MONEY BY KILLING MAGIC BEASTS.
AS A HUNTER GAINS MORE EXPERIENCE...
...THEIR RANK GOES UP.
YOU HIT PAY DIRT WITH ESSENCE STONES FROM MAGIC BEASTS.
IN ORDER TO DEFEAT A HIGHER-RANK MAGIC BEAST, YOU HAVE TO ENTER A HIGHER-RANK GATE.
BUT SINCE THERE ARE SO MANY LOW-RANK HUNTERS, THE COMPETITION IS FIERCE JUST TO GET IN TO COMMON D-RANK GATES, OR EVEN E-RANK ONES.

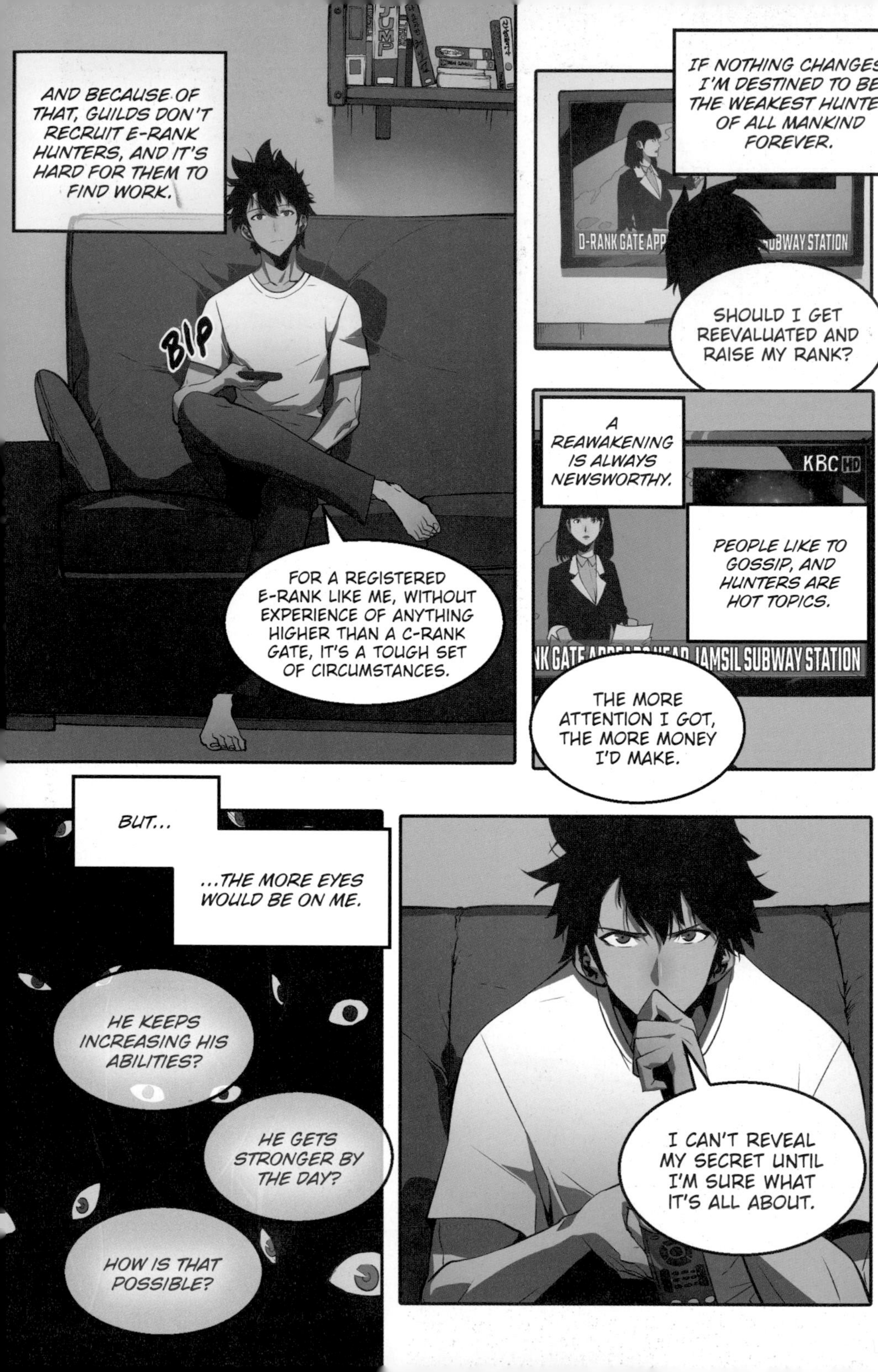
AND BECAUSE OF THAT, GUILDS DON'T RECRUIT E-RANK HUNTERS, AND IT'S HARD FOR THEM TO FIND WORK.
BIP
FOR A REGISTERED E-RANK LIKE ME, WITHOUT EXPERIENCE OF ANYTHING HIGHER THAN A C-RANK GATE, IT'S A TOUGH SET OF CIRCUMSTANCES.
IF NOTHING CHANGES, I'M DESTINED TO BE THE WEAKEST HUNTER OF ALL MANKIND FOREVER.
SHOULD I GET REEVALUATED AND RAISE MY RANK?
A REAWAKENING IS ALWAYS NEWSWORTHY.
PEOPLE LIKE TO GOSSIP, AND HUNTERS ARE HOT TOPICS.
THE MORE ATTENTION I GOT, THE MORE MONEY I'D MAKE.
BUT...
...THE MORE EYES WOULD BE ON ME.
HE KEEPS INCREASING HIS ABILITIES?
HE GETS STRONGER BY THE DAY?
HOW IS THAT POSSIBLE?
I CAN'T REVEAL MY SECRET UNTIL I'M SURE WHAT IT'S ALL ABOUT.

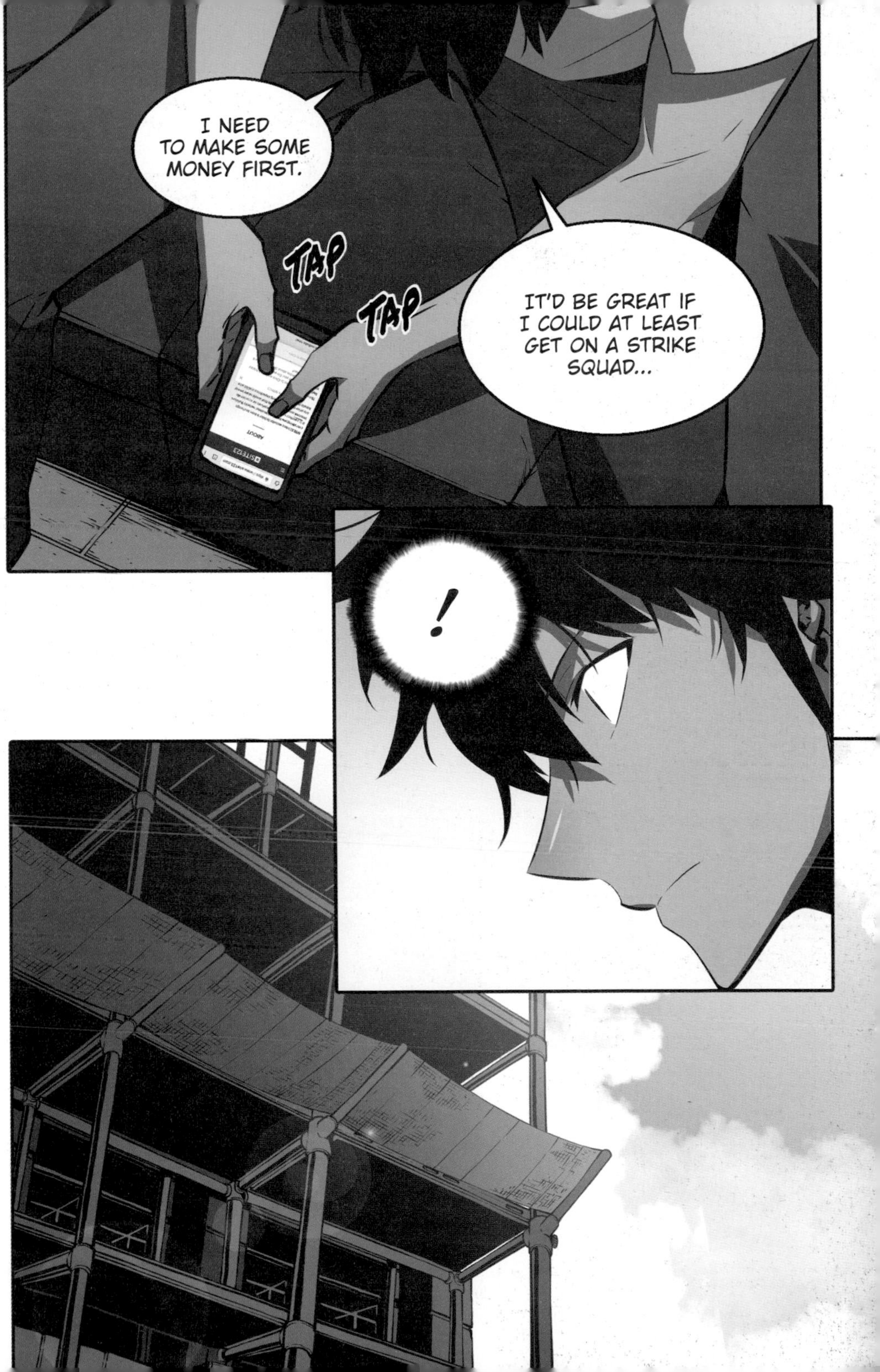
I NEED TO MAKE SOME MONEY FIRST.
TAP
TAP
IT'D BE GREAT IF I COULD AT LEAST GET ON A STRIKE SQUAD...
!

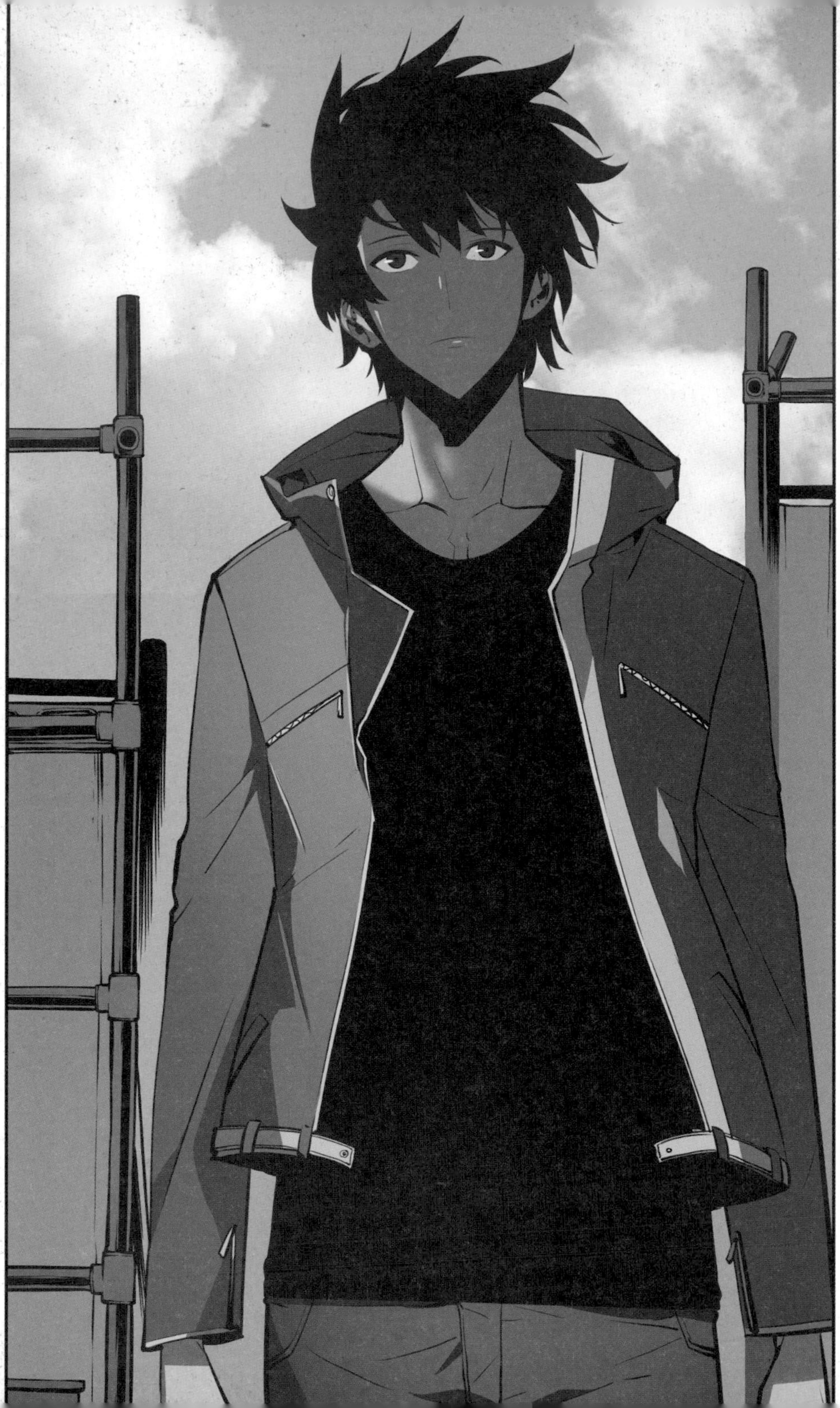

CHAPTER 5

The Lizards

Solo
Leveling

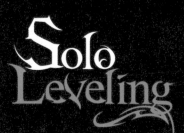

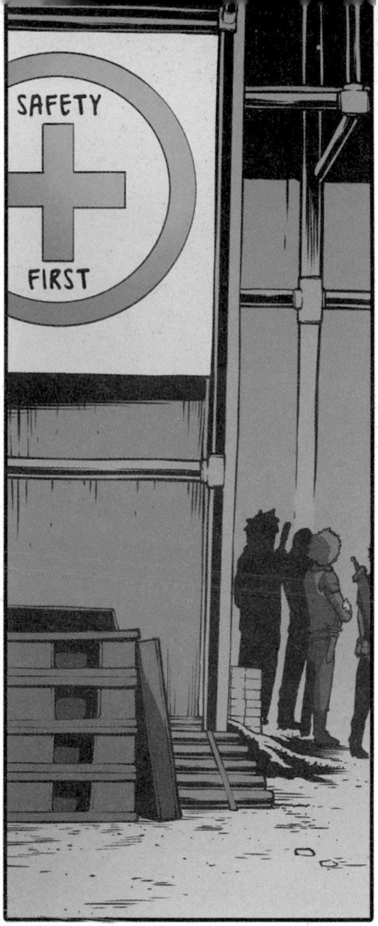
SAFETY
FIRST
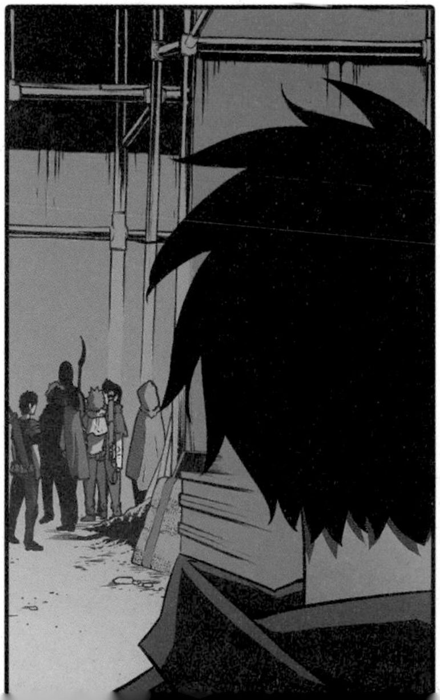
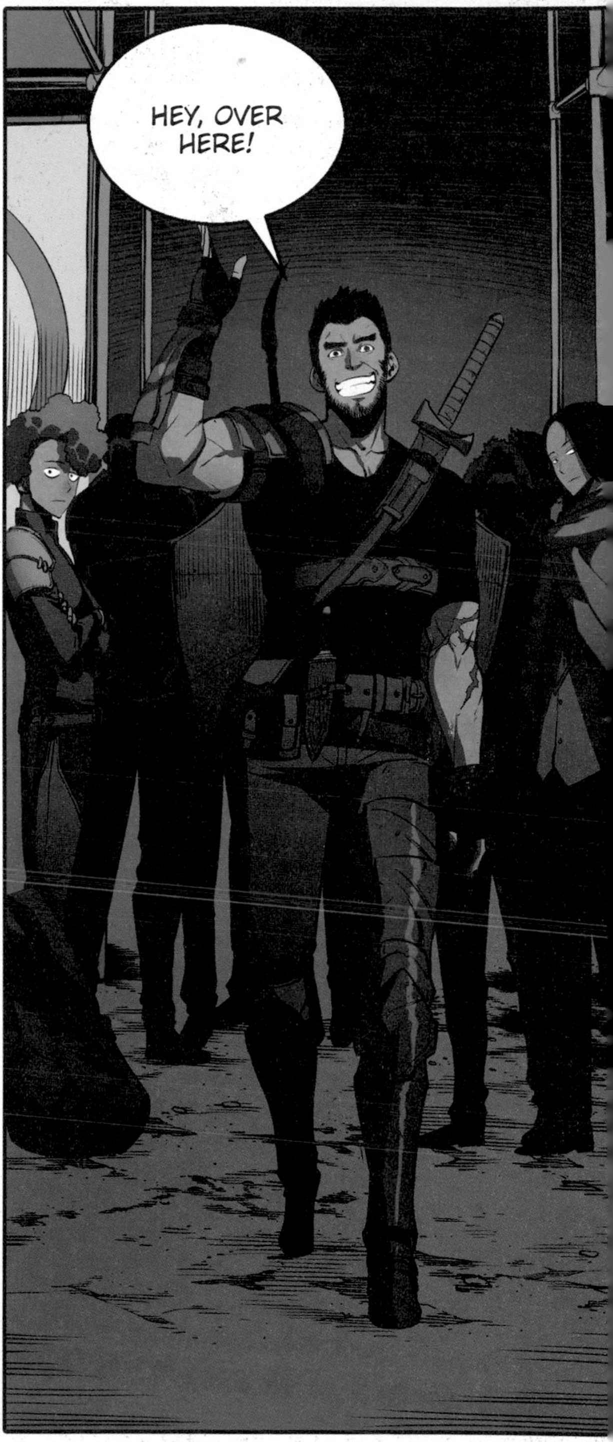
HEY, OVER HERE!

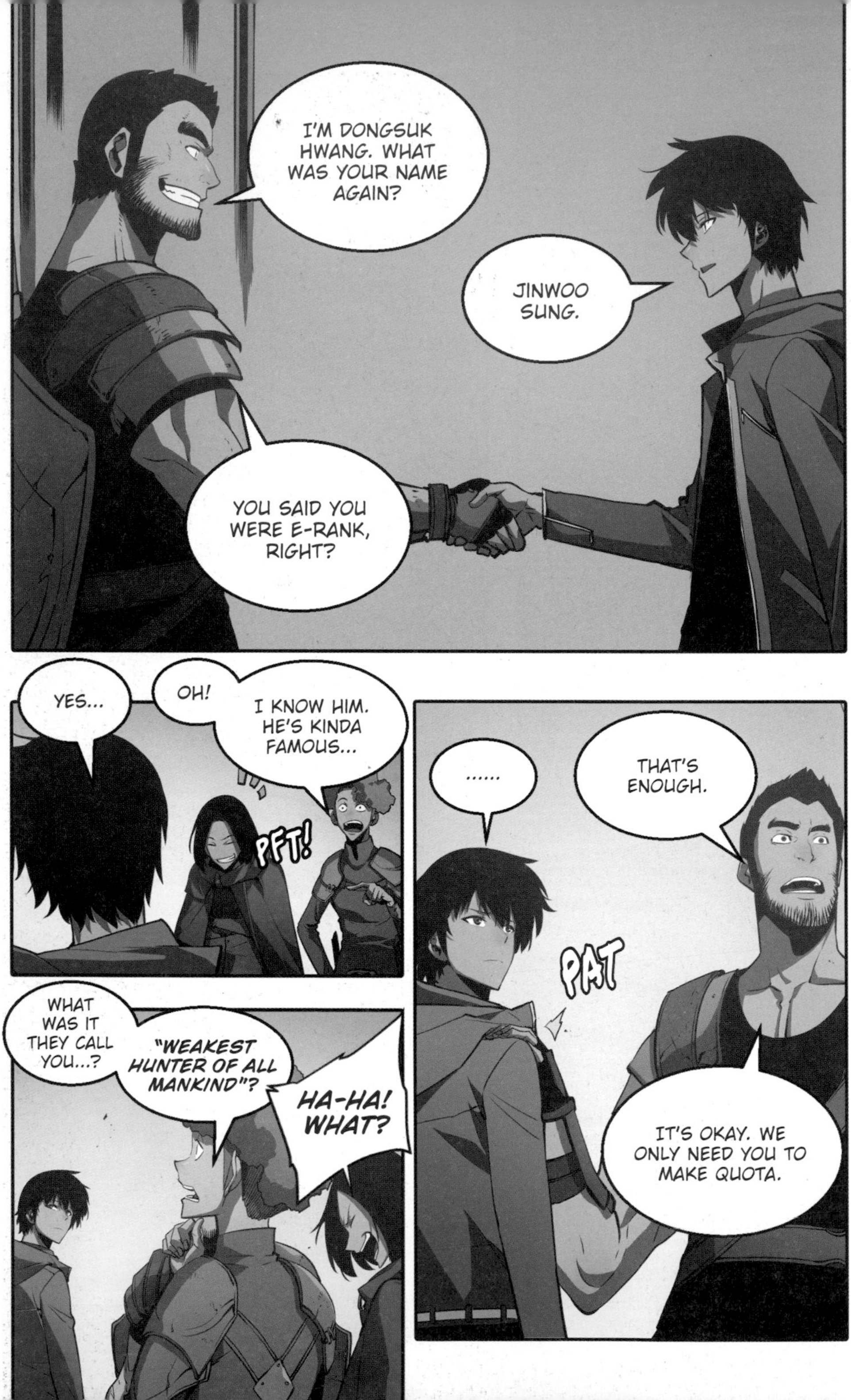
I'M DONGSUK HWANG. WHAT WAS YOUR NAME AGAIN?
JINWOO SUNG.
YOU SAID YOU WERE E-RANK, RIGHT?
YES...
OH!
I KNOW HIM. HE'S KINDA FAMOUS...
PFT!
WHAT WAS IT THEY CALL YOU...?
"WEAKEST HUNTER OF ALL MANKIND"?
HA-HA! WHAT?
......
THAT'S ENOUGH.
PAT
IT'S OKAY. WE ONLY NEED YOU TO MAKE QUOTA.

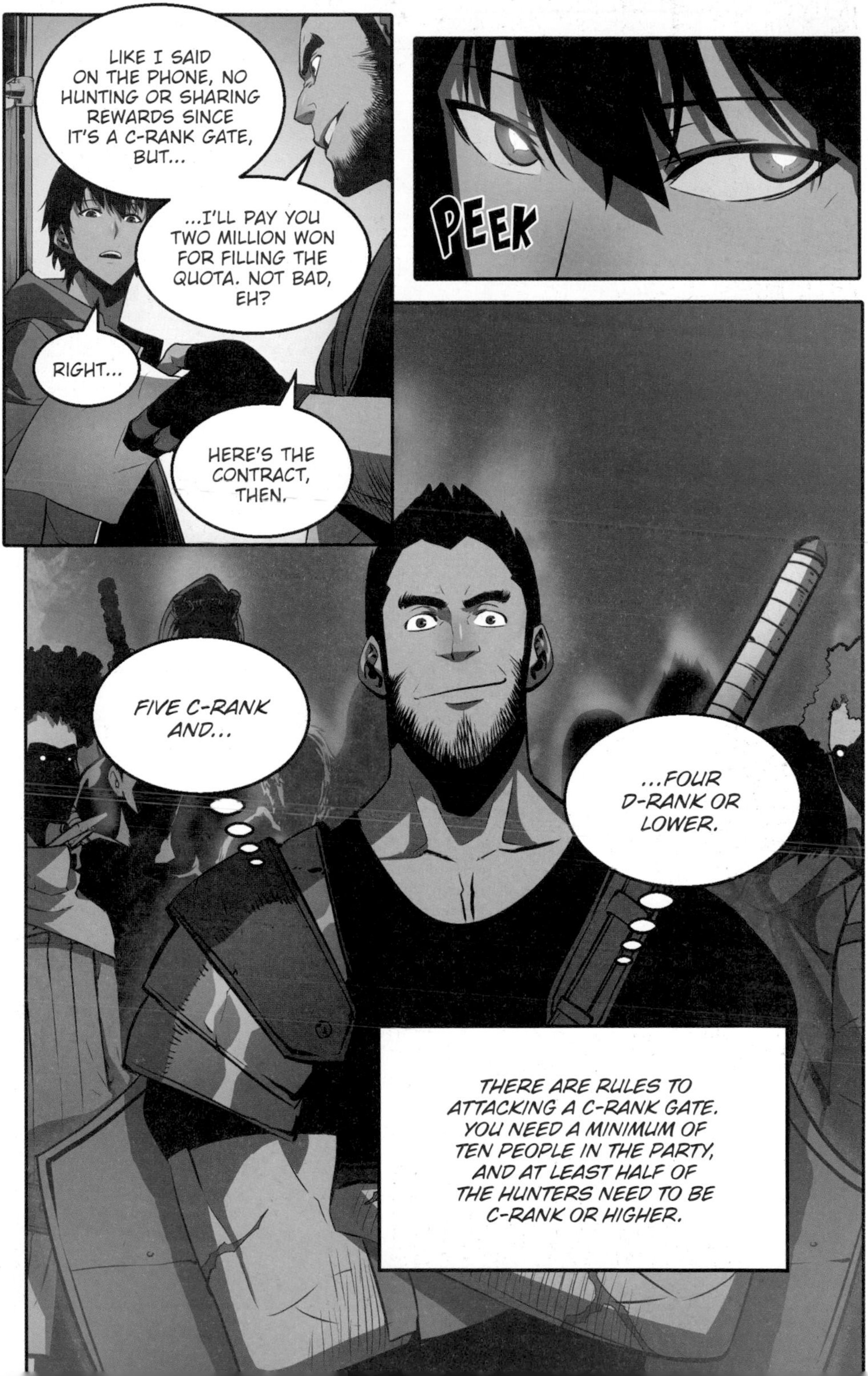
LIKE I SAID ON THE PHONE, NO HUNTING OR SHARING REWARDS SINCE IT'S A C-RANK GATE, BUT...
...I'LL PAY YOU TWO MILLION WON FOR FILLING THE QUOTA. NOT BAD, EH?
RIGHT...
HERE'S THE CONTRACT, THEN.
PEEK
FIVE C-RANK AND...
...FOUR D-RANK OR LOWER.
THERE ARE RULES TO ATTACKING A C-RANK GATE. YOU NEED A MINIMUM OF TEN PEOPLE IN THE PARTY, AND AT LEAST HALF OF THE HUNTERS NEED TO BE C-RANK OR HIGHER.

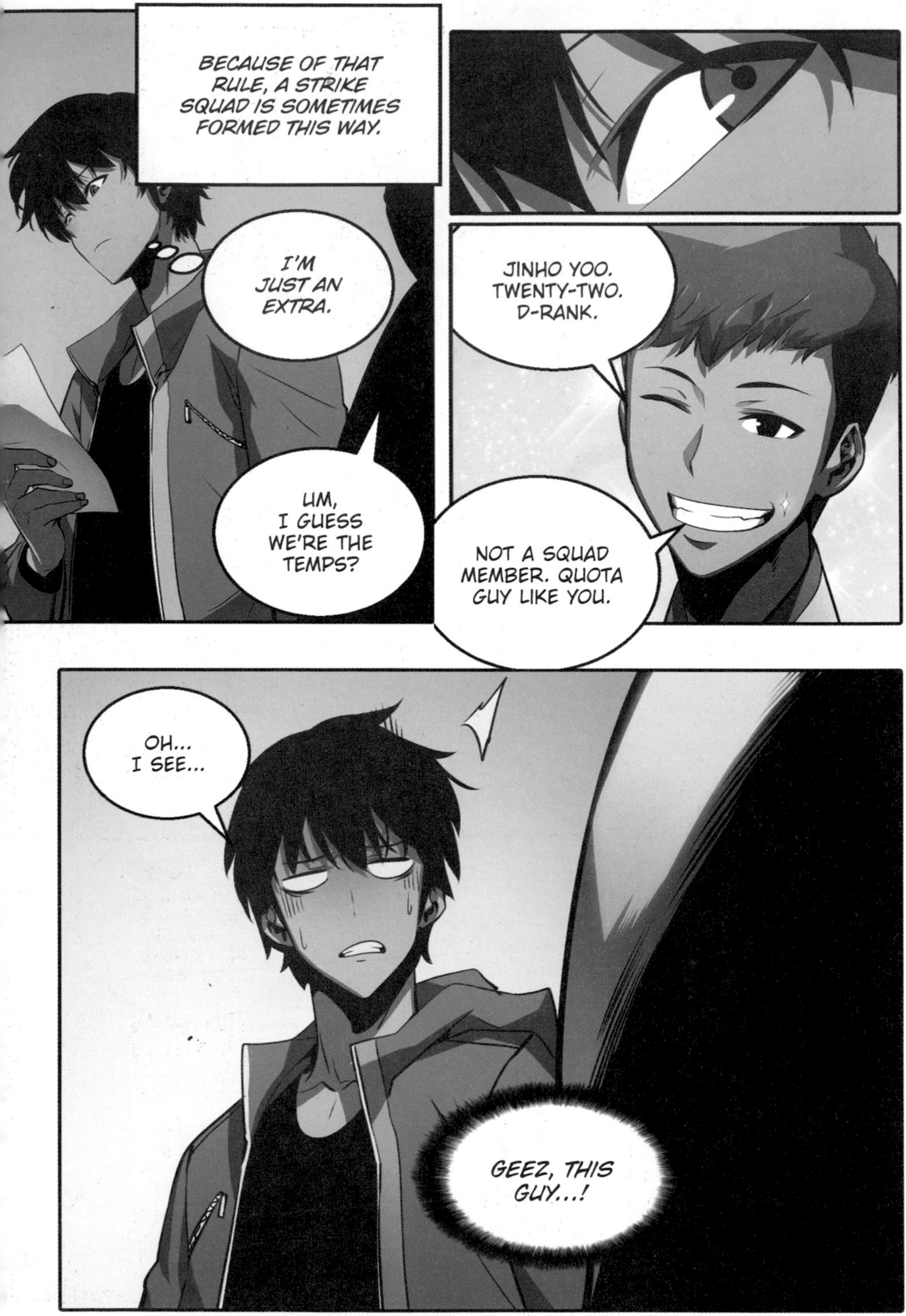
BECAUSE OF THAT RULE, A STRIKE SQUAD IS SOMETIMES FORMED THIS WAY.
I'M JUST AN EXTRA.
UM, I GUESS WE'RE THE TEMPS?
JINHO YOO. TWENTY-TWO. D-RANK.
NOT A SQUAD MEMBER. QUOTA GUY LIKE YOU.
OH... I SEE...
GEEZ, THIS GUY...!

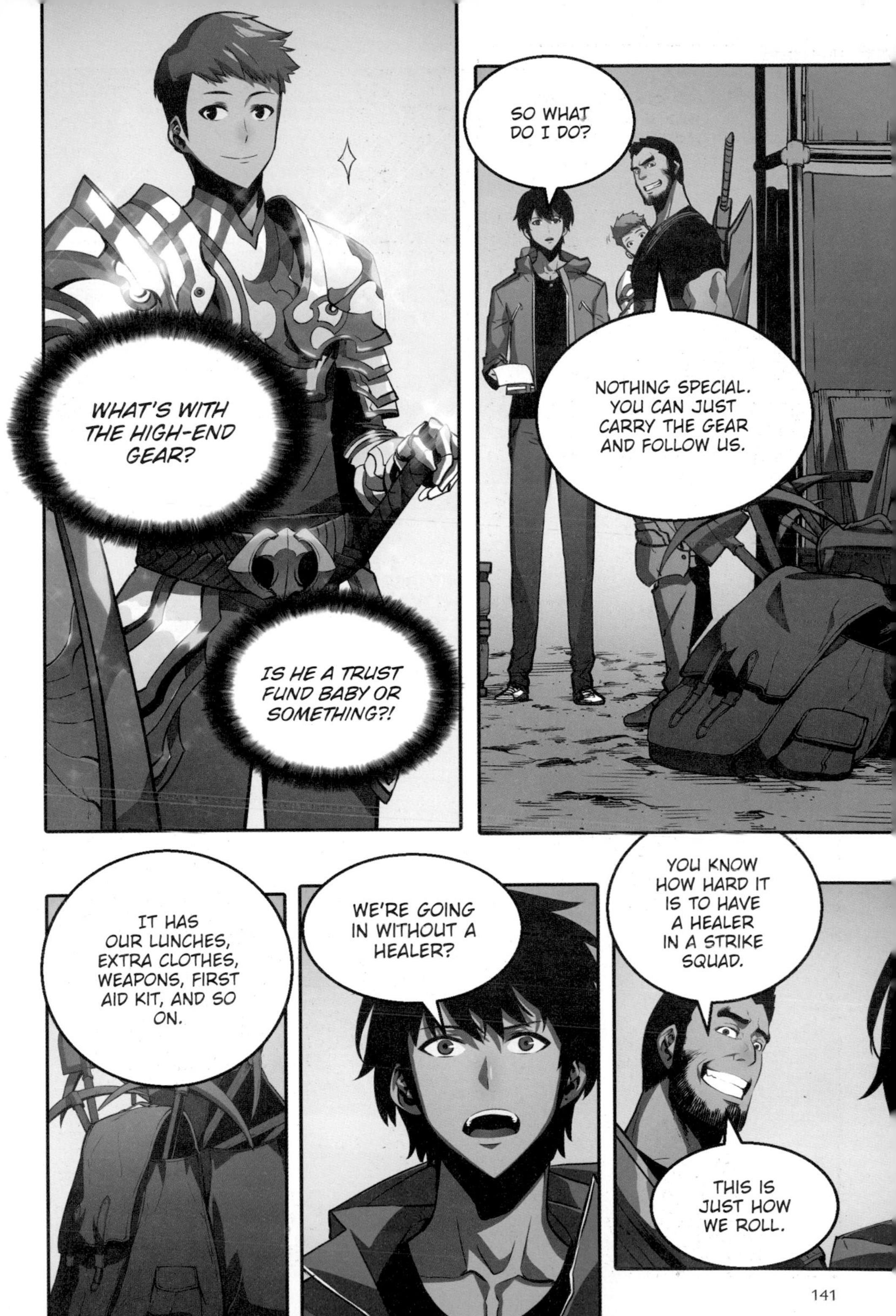
WHAT'S WITH THE HIGH-END GEAR?
IS HE A TRUST FUND BABY OR SOMETHING?!
SO WHAT DO I DO?
NOTHING SPECIAL. YOU CAN JUST CARRY THE GEAR AND FOLLOW US.
IT HAS OUR LUNCHES, EXTRA CLOTHES, WEAPONS, FIRST AID KIT, AND SO ON.
WE'RE GOING IN WITHOUT A HEALER?
YOU KNOW HOW HARD IT IS TO HAVE A HEALER IN A STRIKE SQUAD.
THIS IS JUST HOW WE ROLL.

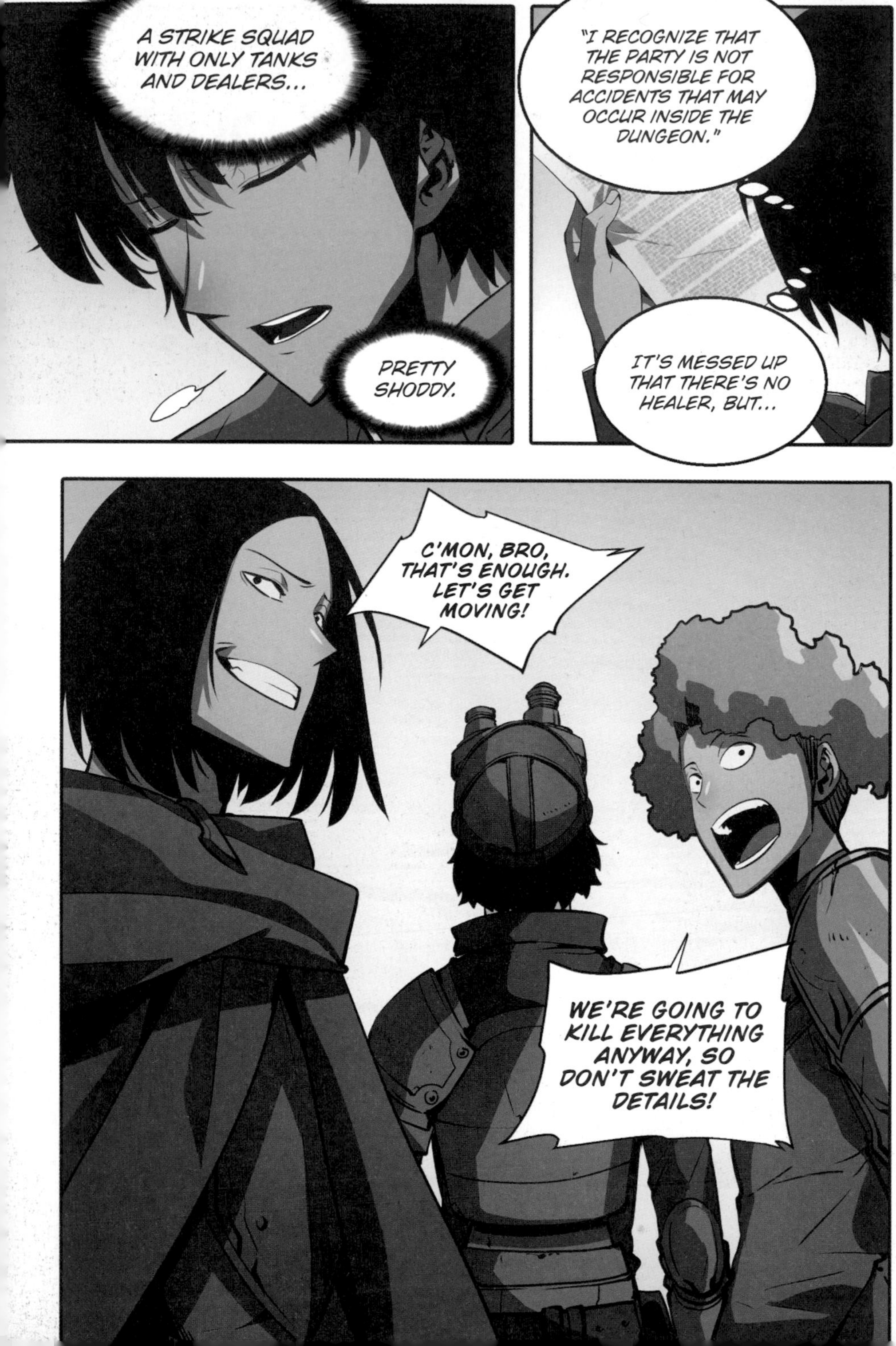
A STRIKE SQUAD WITH ONLY TANKS AND DEALERS...
PRETTY SHODDY.
"I RECOGNIZE THAT THE PARTY IS NOT RESPONSIBLE FOR ACCIDENTS THAT MAY OCCUR INSIDE THE DUNGEON."
IT'S MESSED UP THAT THERE'S NO HEALER, BUT...
C'MON, BRO, THAT'S ENOUGH. LET'S GET MOVING!
WE'RE GOING TO KILL EVERYTHING ANYWAY, SO DON'T SWEAT THE DETAILS!

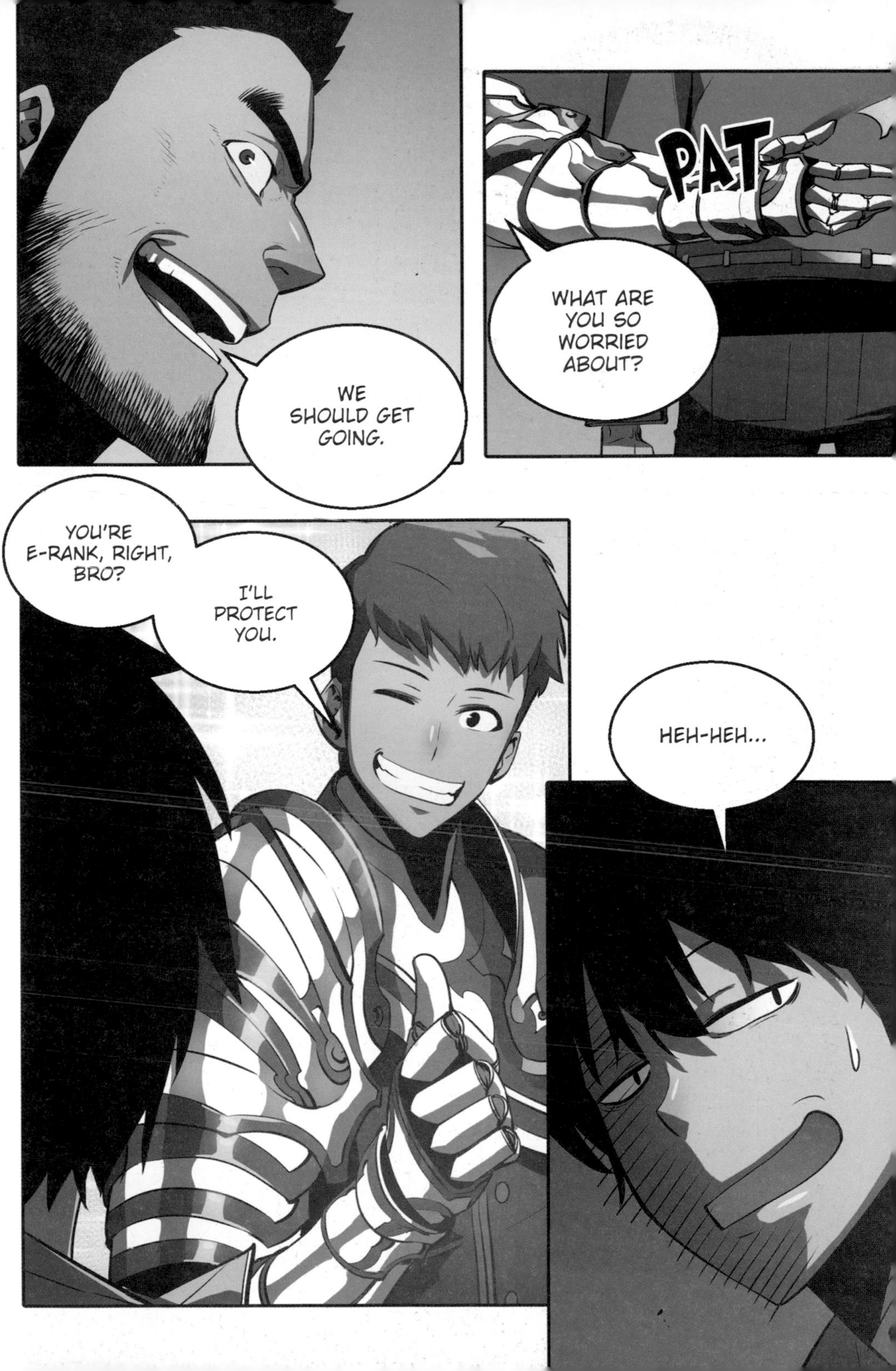
WE SHOULD GET GOING.
PAT
WHAT ARE YOU SO WORRIED ABOUT?
YOU'RE E-RANK, RIGHT, BRO?
I'LL PROTECT YOU.
HEH-HEH...

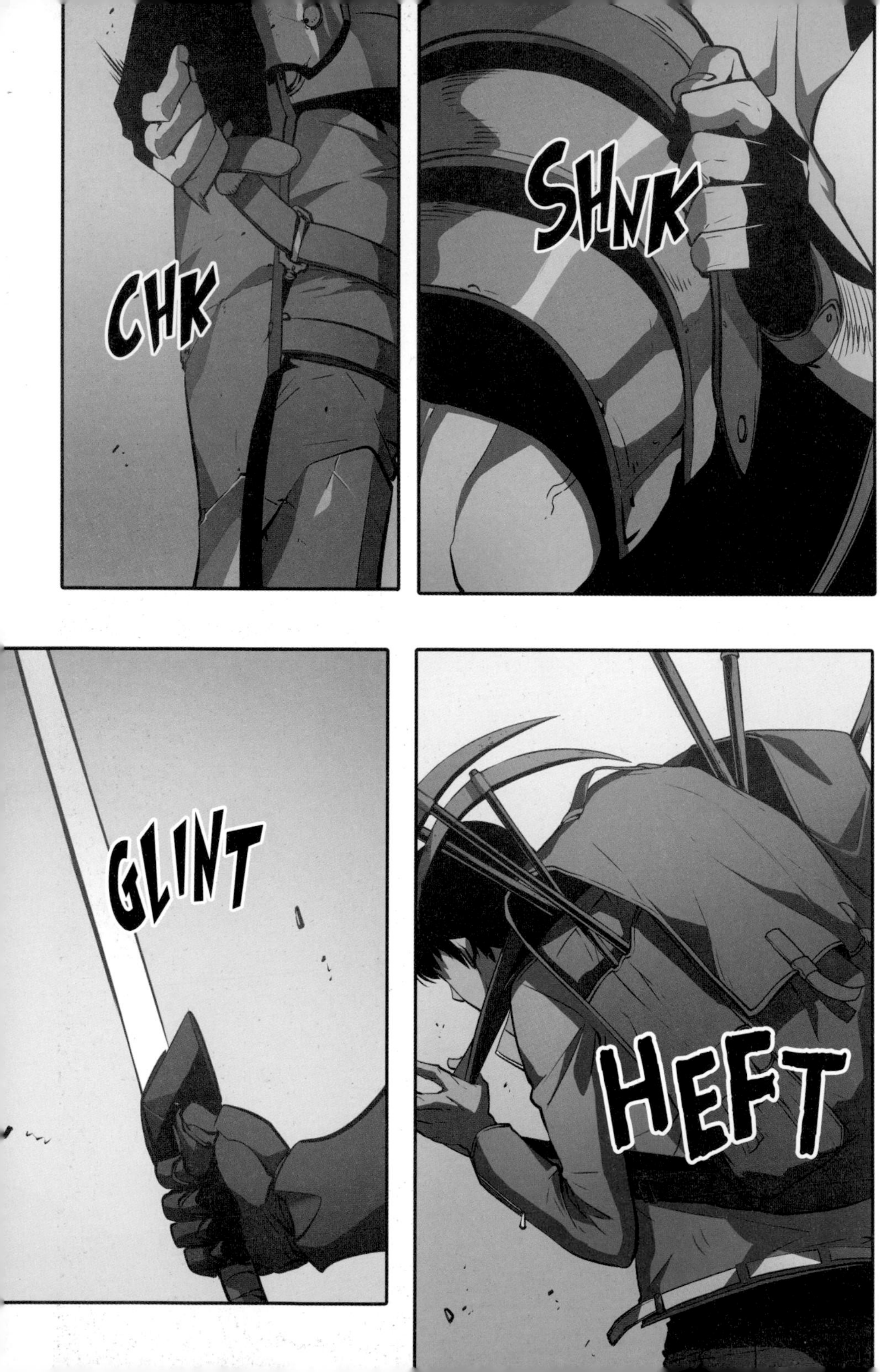
CHK
SHNK
GLINT
HEFT

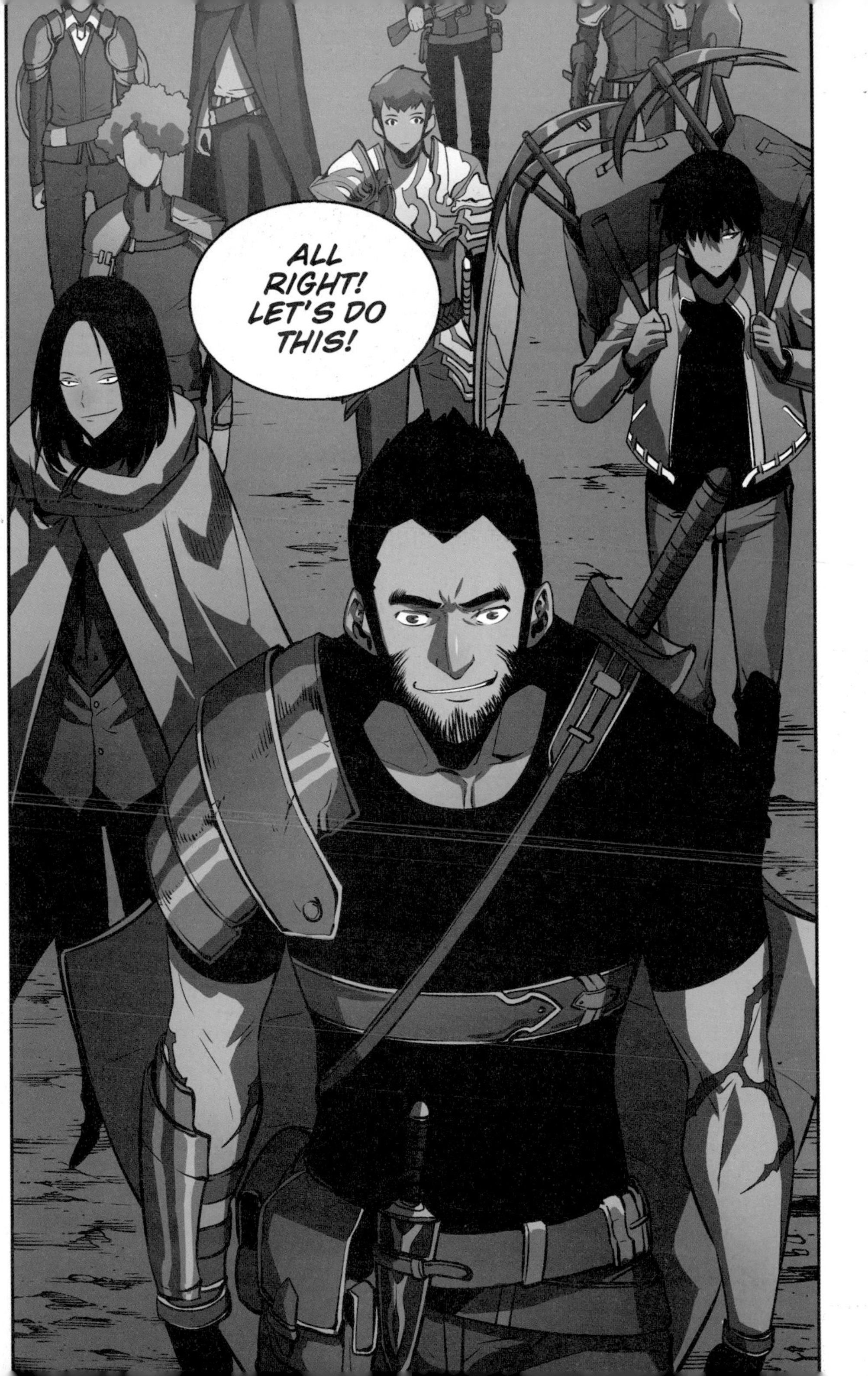
ALL RIGHT! LET'S DO THIS!

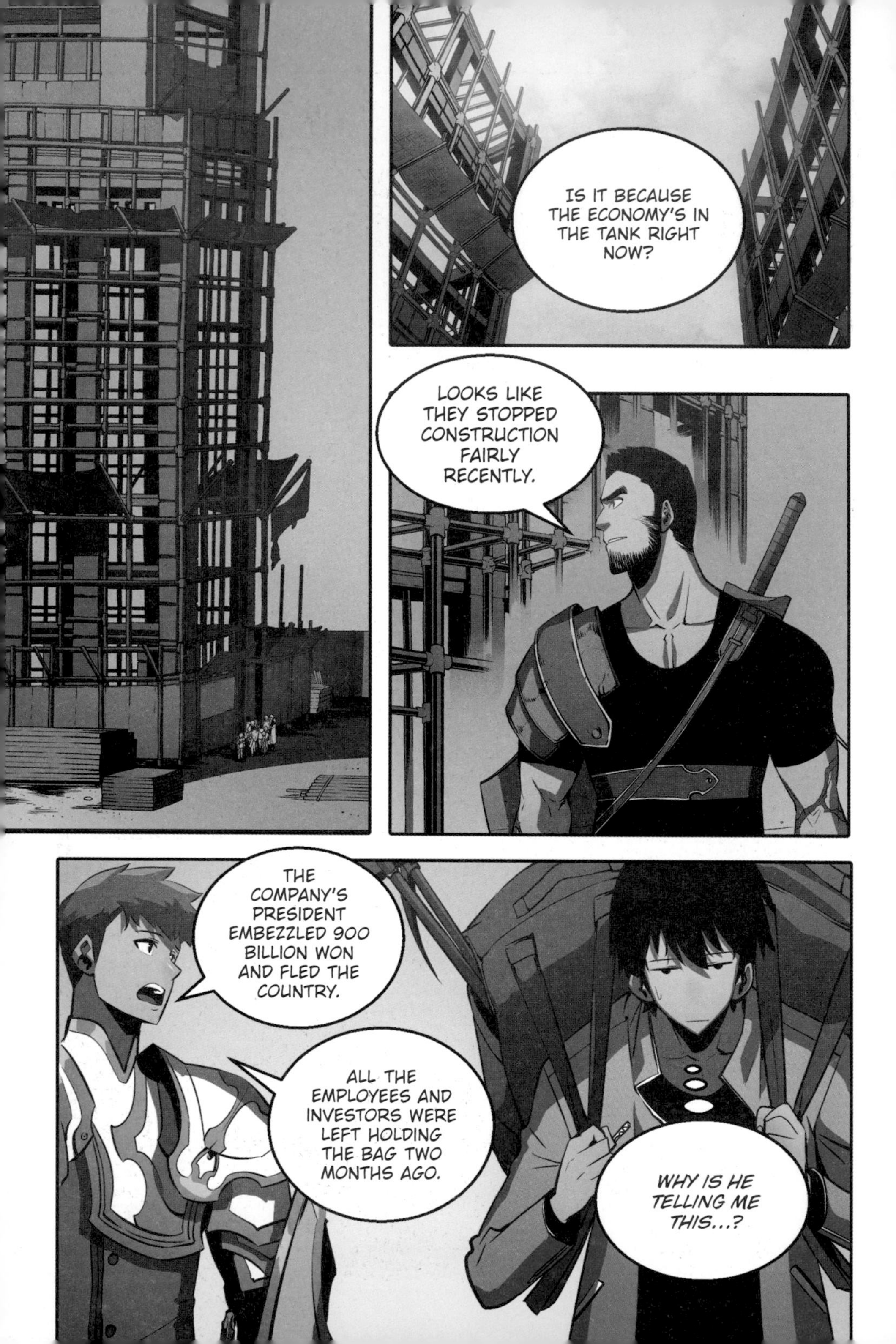
IS IT BECAUSE THE ECONOMY'S IN THE TANK RIGHT NOW?
LOOKS LIKE THEY STOPPED CONSTRUCTION FAIRLY RECENTLY.
THE COMPANY'S PRESIDENT EMBEZZLED 900 BILLION WON AND FLED THE COUNTRY.
ALL THE EMPLOYEES AND INVESTORS WERE LEFT HOLDING THE BAG TWO MONTHS AGO.
WHY IS HE TELLING ME THIS...?

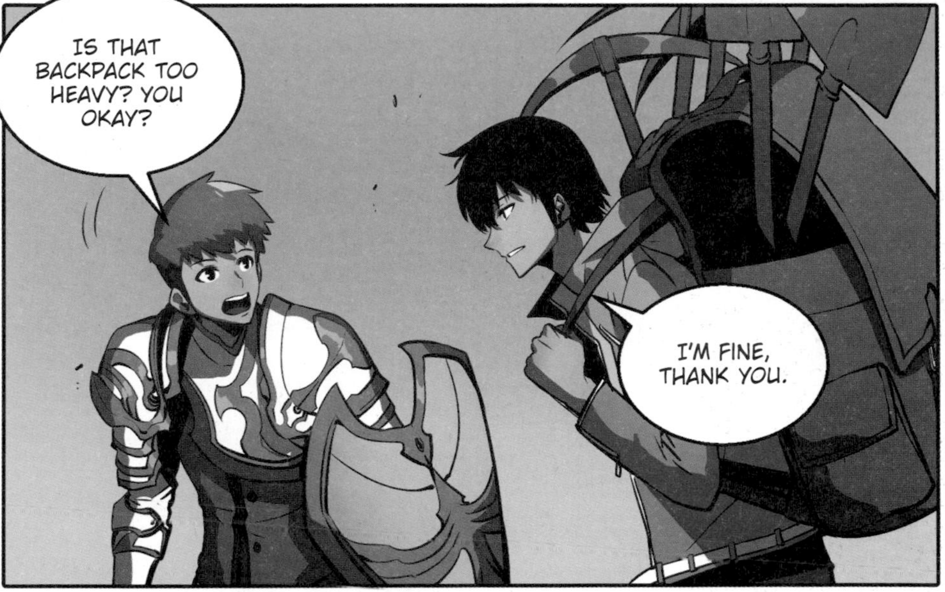
IS THAT BACKPACK TOO HEAVY? YOU OKAY?
I'M FINE, THANK YOU.

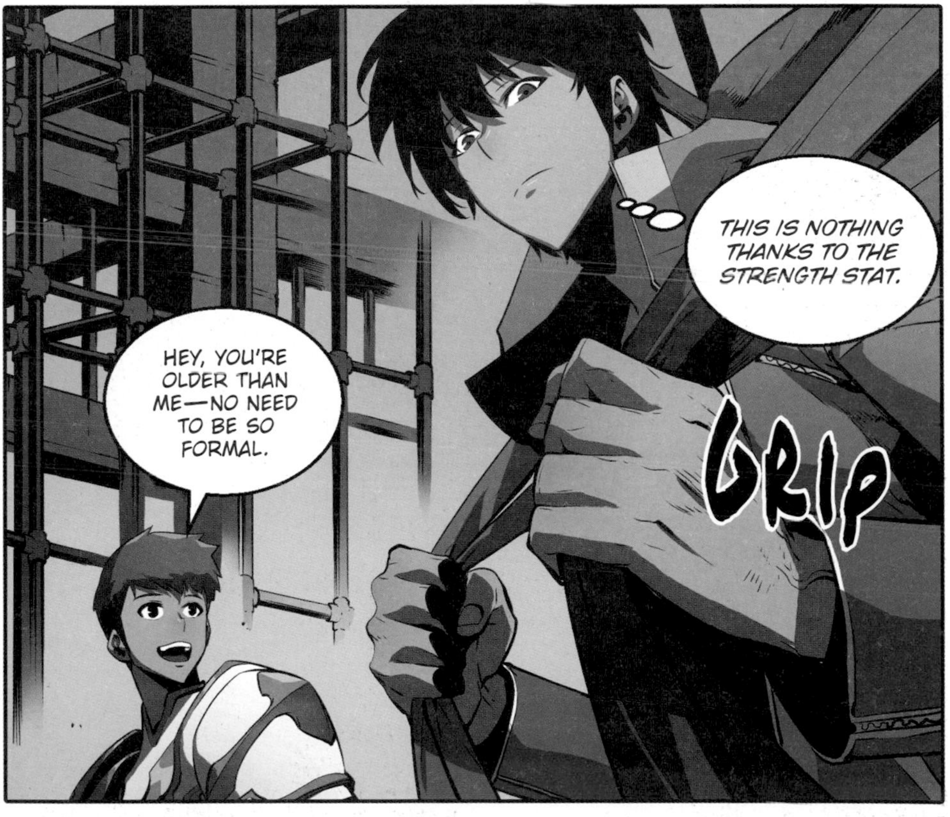
THIS IS NOTHING THANKS TO THE STRENGTH STAT.
HEY, YOU'RE OLDER THAN ME—NO NEED TO BE SO FORMAL.
GRIP

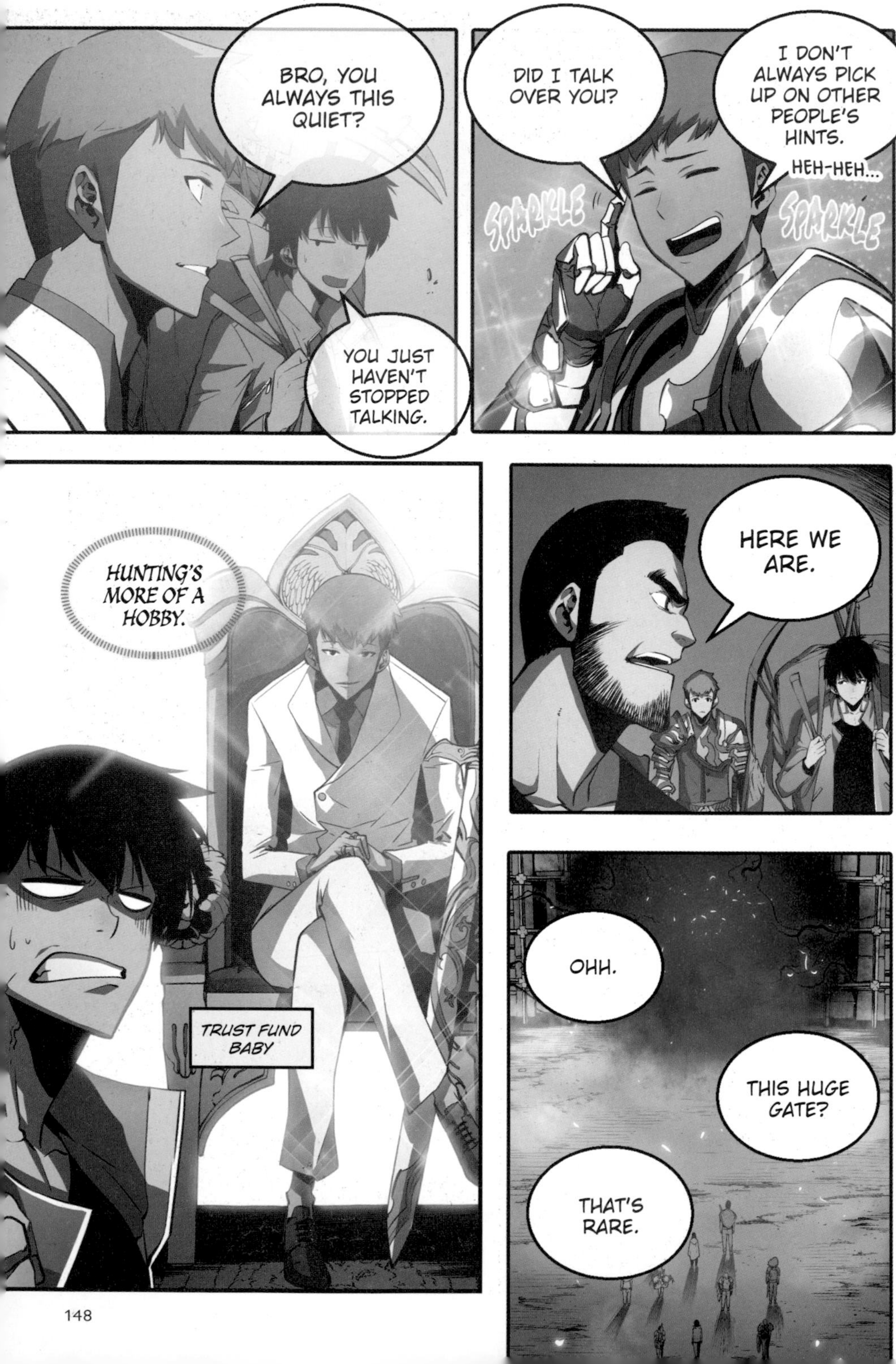
BRO, YOU ALWAYS THIS QUIET?
YOU JUST HAVEN'T STOPPED TALKING.
DID I TALK OVER YOU?
I DON'T ALWAYS PICK UP ON OTHER PEOPLE'S HINTS.
HEH-HEH...
SPARKLE
SPARKLE
HUNTING'S MORE OF A HOBBY.
TRUST FUND BABY
HERE WE ARE.
OHH.
THIS HUGE GATE?
THAT'S RARE.

DON'T YOU THINK IT'S AWFULLY BIG FOR A C-RANK GATE, BOSS?

WHY WOULD THE ASSOCIATION BULLSHIT US? INVESTIGATORS CHECKED IT TWICE.

BRO, THE GATE IS HUGE. WE'LL BE OKAY, RIGHT?

YOU'VE NEVER SEEN THIS?

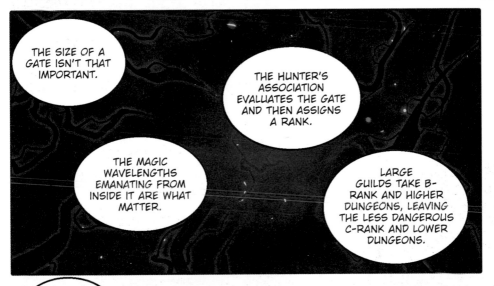

THE SIZE OF A GATE ISN'T THAT IMPORTANT.

THE HUNTER'S ASSOCIATION EVALUATES THE GATE AND THEN ASSIGNS A RANK.

THE MAGIC WAVELENGTHS EMANATING FROM INSIDE IT ARE WHAT MATTER.

LARGE GUILDS TAKE B-RANK AND HIGHER DUNGEONS, LEAVING THE LESS DANGEROUS C-RANK AND LOWER DUNGEONS.

TALKING LIKE I KNOW...

...WHEN THIS IS MY FIRST C-RANK DUNGEON.

OKAY, PEOPLE, I'LL HEAD IN FIRST. PLEASE STICK CLOSE.

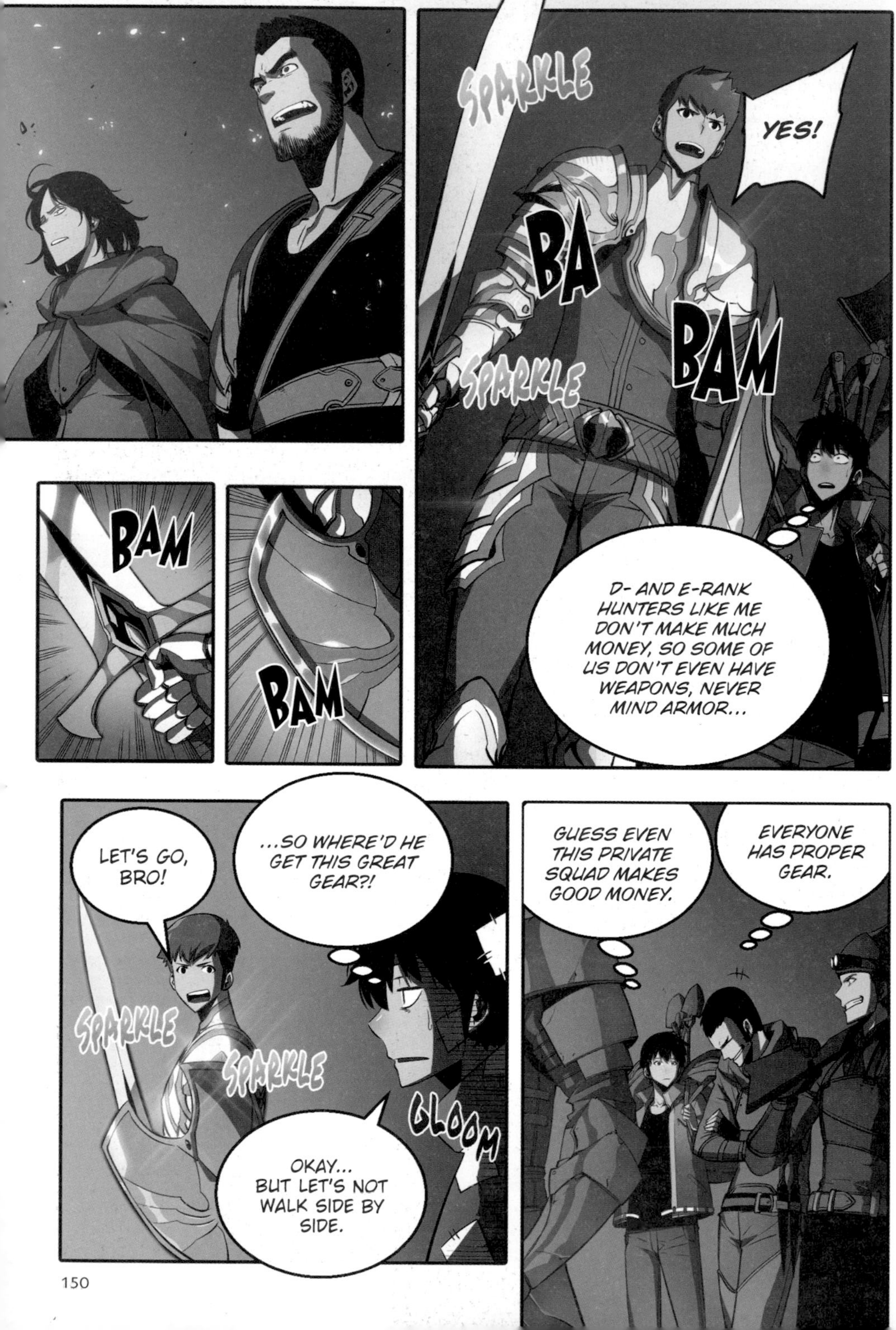
BAM
BAM
SPARKLE
YES!
BA
BAM
SPARKLE
D- AND E-RANK HUNTERS LIKE ME DON'T MAKE MUCH MONEY, SO SOME OF US DON'T EVEN HAVE WEAPONS, NEVER MIND ARMOR...
LET'S GO, BRO!
...SO WHERE'D HE GET THIS GREAT GEAR?!
SPARKLE
SPARKLE
GLOOM
OKAY... BUT LET'S NOT WALK SIDE BY SIDE.
GUESS EVEN THIS PRIVATE SQUAD MAKES GOOD MONEY.
EVERYONE HAS PROPER GEAR.

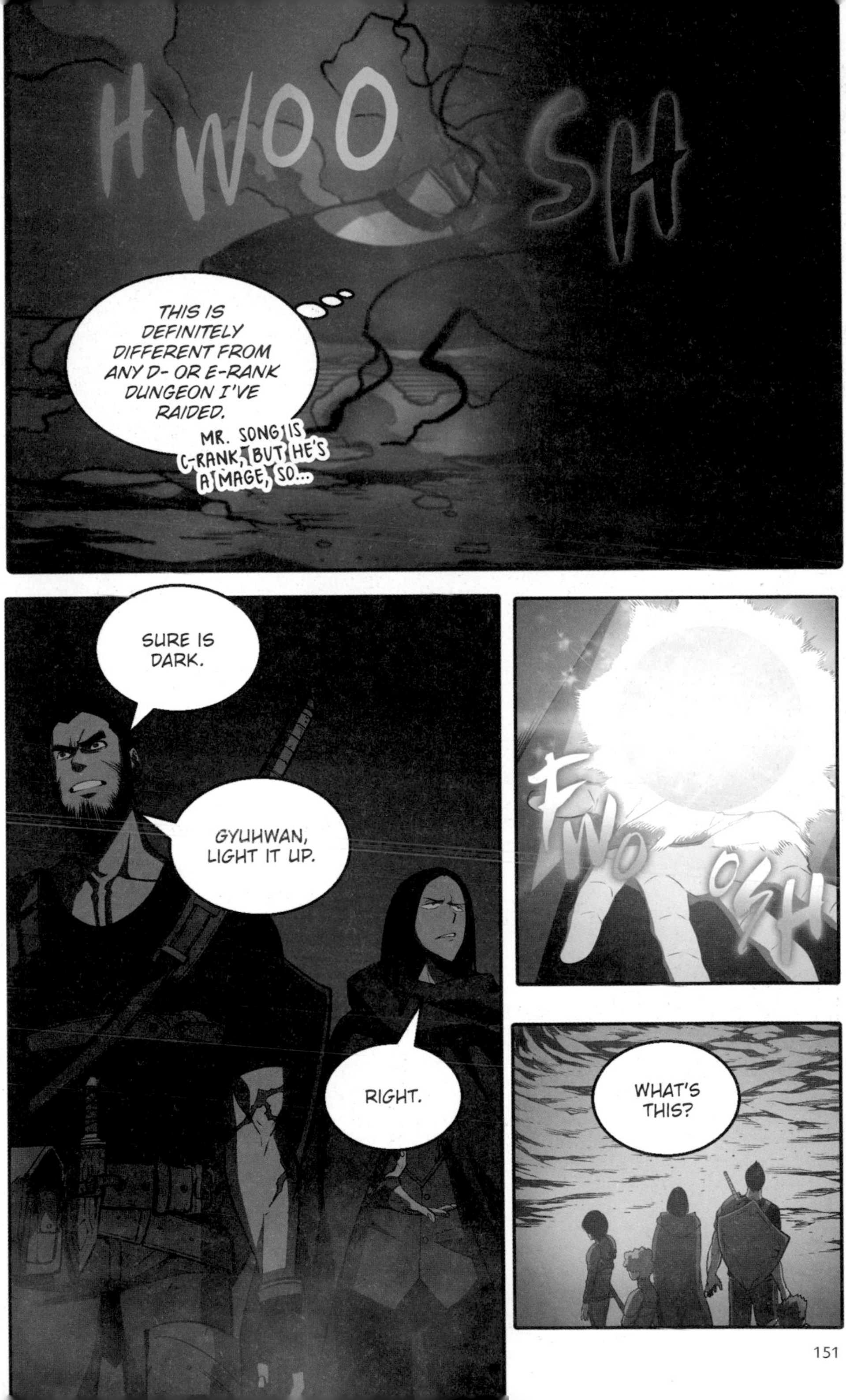

HWOOSH
THIS IS DEFINITELY DIFFERENT FROM ANY D- OR E-RANK DUNGEON I'VE RAIDED.
MR. SONG IS C-RANK, BUT HE'S A MAGE, SO...
SURE IS DARK.
GYUHWAN, LIGHT IT UP.
RIGHT.
FWOOSH
WHAT'S THIS?

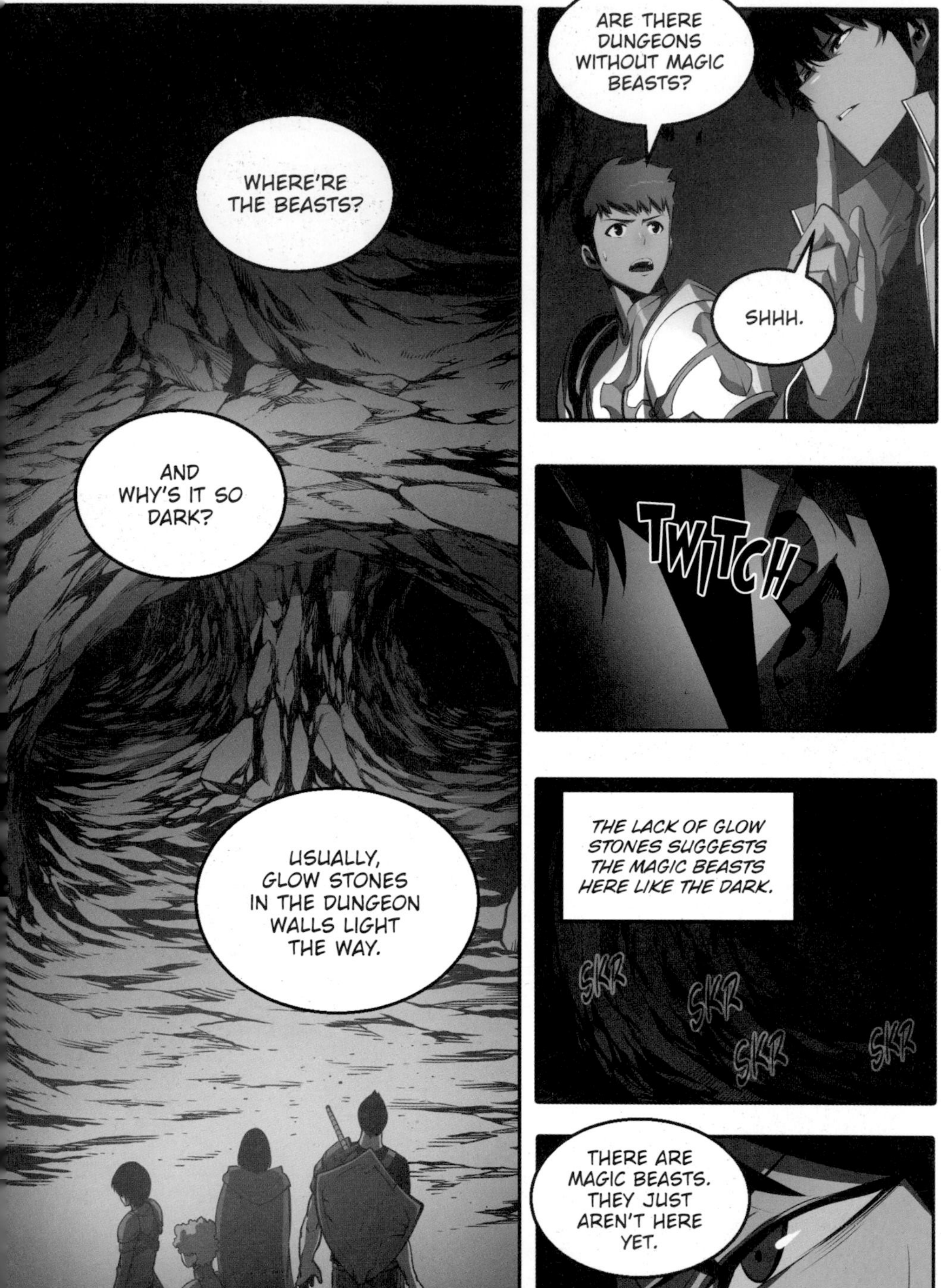
WHERE'RE THE BEASTS?
AND WHY'S IT SO DARK?
USUALLY, GLOW STONES IN THE DUNGEON WALLS LIGHT THE WAY.
ARE THERE DUNGEONS WITHOUT MAGIC BEASTS?
SHHH.
TWITCH
THE LACK OF GLOW STONES SUGGESTS THE MAGIC BEASTS HERE LIKE THE DARK.
SKR
SKR
SKR
SKR
THERE ARE MAGIC BEASTS. THEY JUST AREN'T HERE YET.

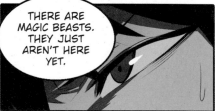

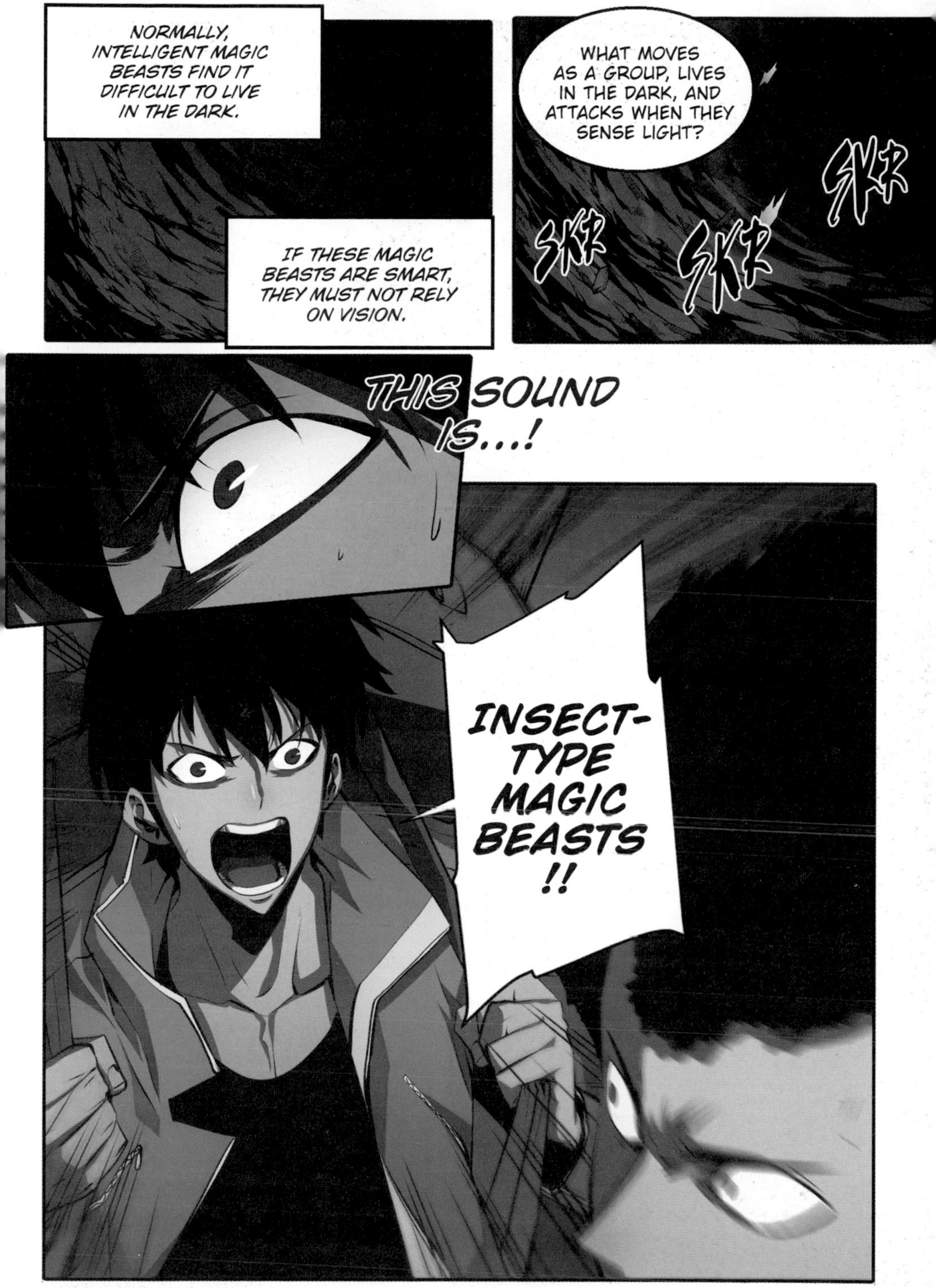
NORMALLY, INTELLIGENT MAGIC BEASTS FIND IT DIFFICULT TO LIVE IN THE DARK.
IF THESE MAGIC BEASTS ARE SMART, THEY MUST NOT RELY ON VISION.
WHAT MOVES AS A GROUP, LIVES IN THE DARK, AND ATTACKS WHEN THEY SENSE LIGHT?
SKR
SKR
SKR
THIS SOUND IS...!
INSECT-TYPE MAGIC BEASTS!!

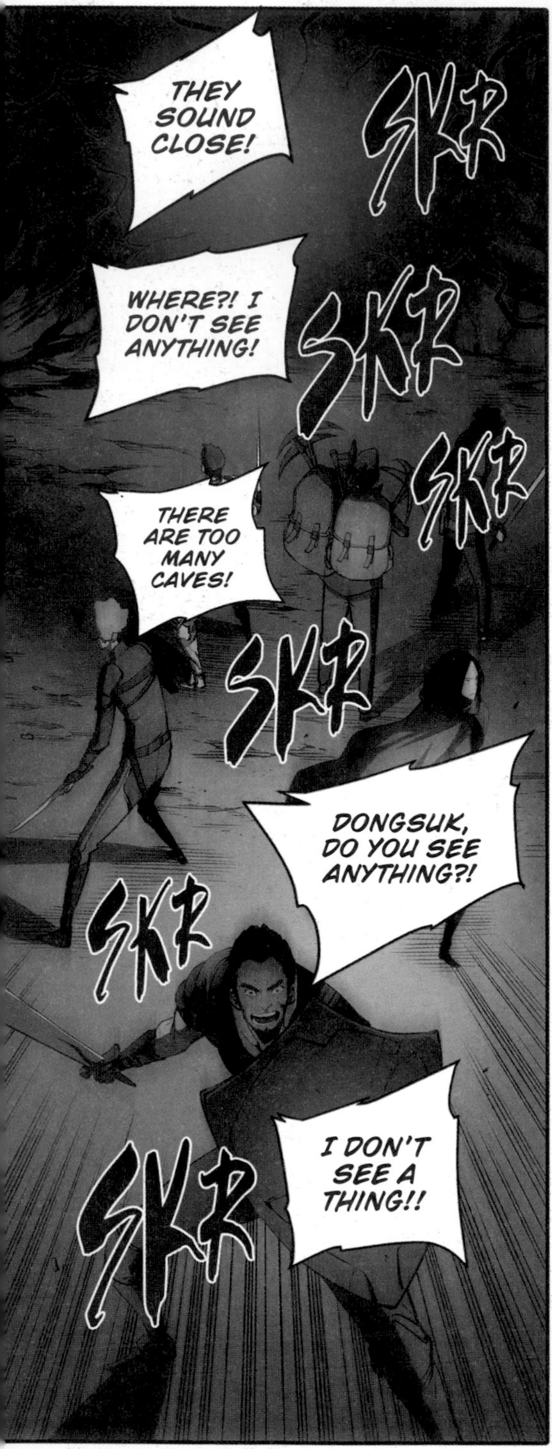
THEY SOUND CLOSE!
SKR
WHERE?! I DON'T SEE ANYTHING!
SKR
SKR
THERE ARE TOO MANY CAVES!
SKR
DONGSUK, DO YOU SEE ANYTHING?!
SKR
I DON'T SEE A THING!!
SKR

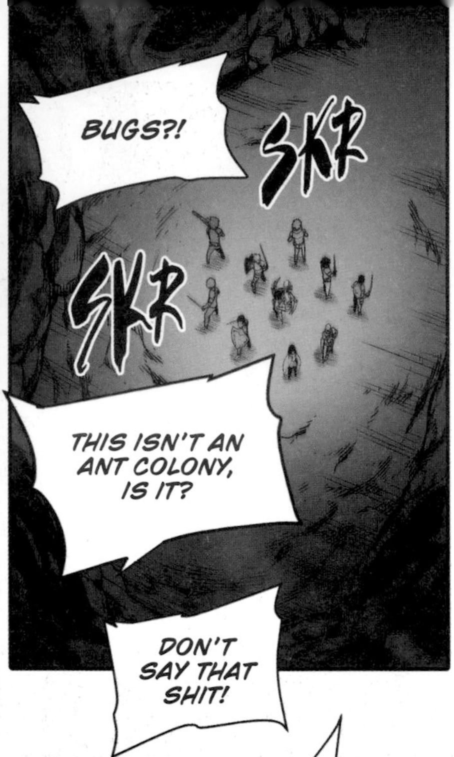
BUGS?!
SKR
SKR
THIS ISN'T AN ANT COLONY, IS IT?
DON'T SAY THAT SHIT!

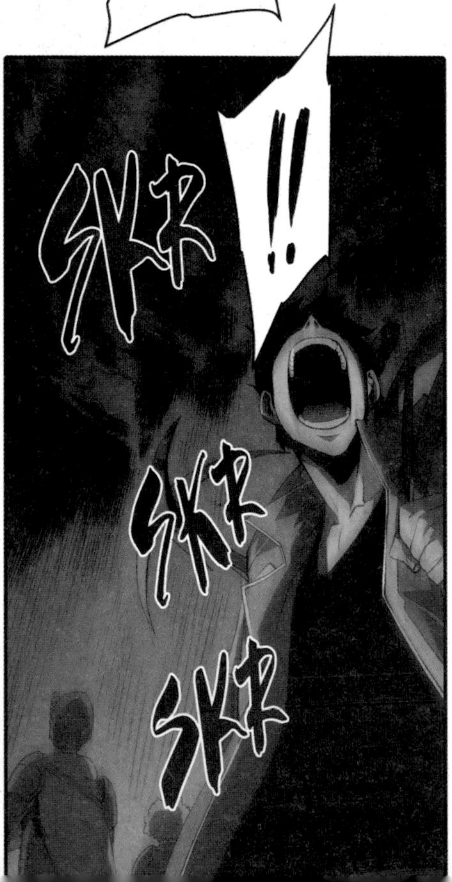
SKR
!!
SKR
SKR

UP!!

THEY'RE HERE!

SKR

OVER OUR HEADS!

SKR

SKR

LOOK! HOW MANY ARE THERE?!

USE MAGIC!

SKR

SKR

SKR

SHOOT THEM! MAKE 'EM DROP!

I'LL GO AGGRO ONCE THEY'RE DOWN!

SKR

SKR

THERE ARE TOO MANY!

DAMN IT! UP THERE?

BRO! STICK WITH ME!

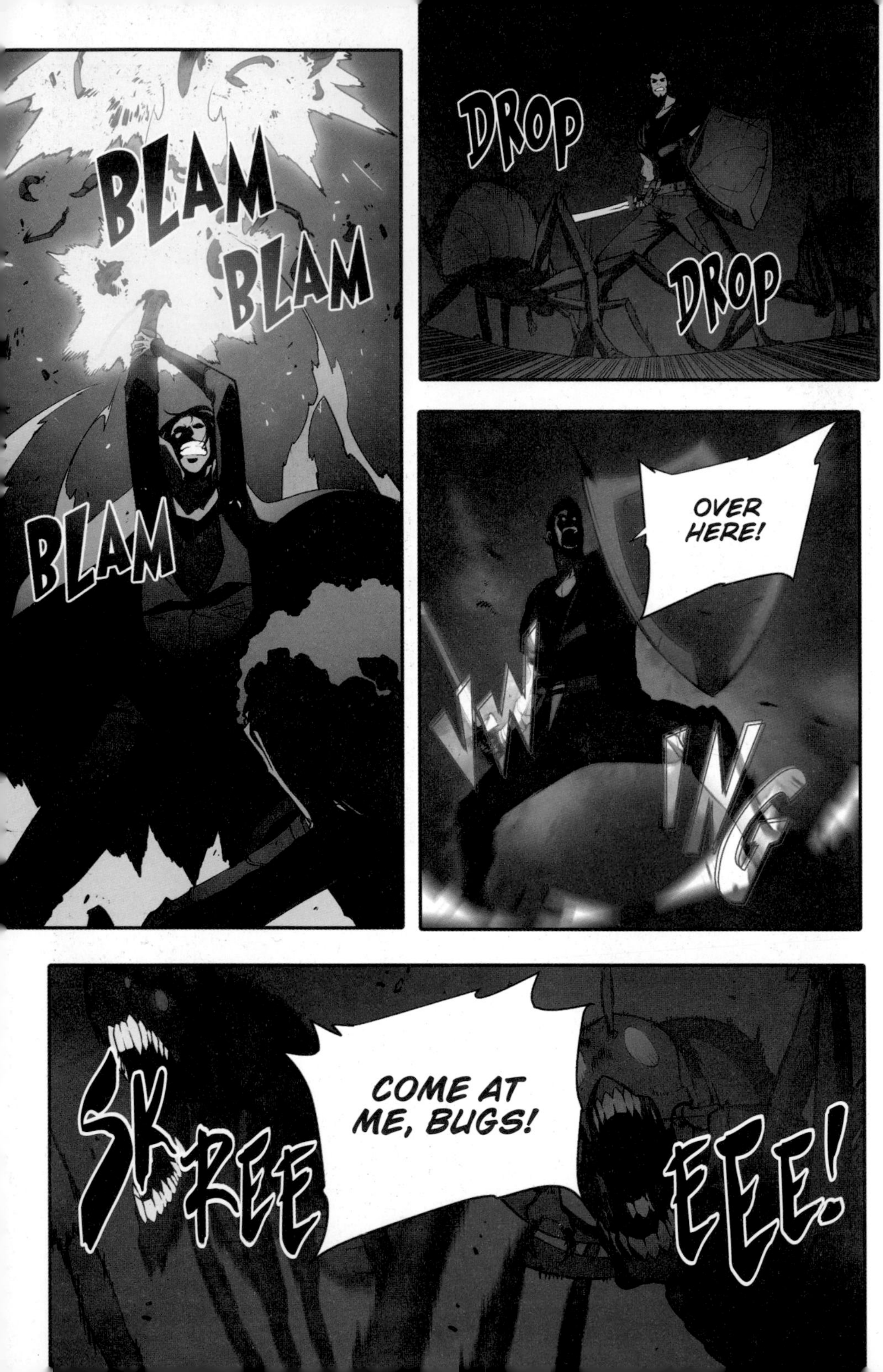
BLAM
BLAM
BLAM
DROP
DROP
OVER HERE!
VWING
SKREEEEE!
COME AT ME, BUGS!

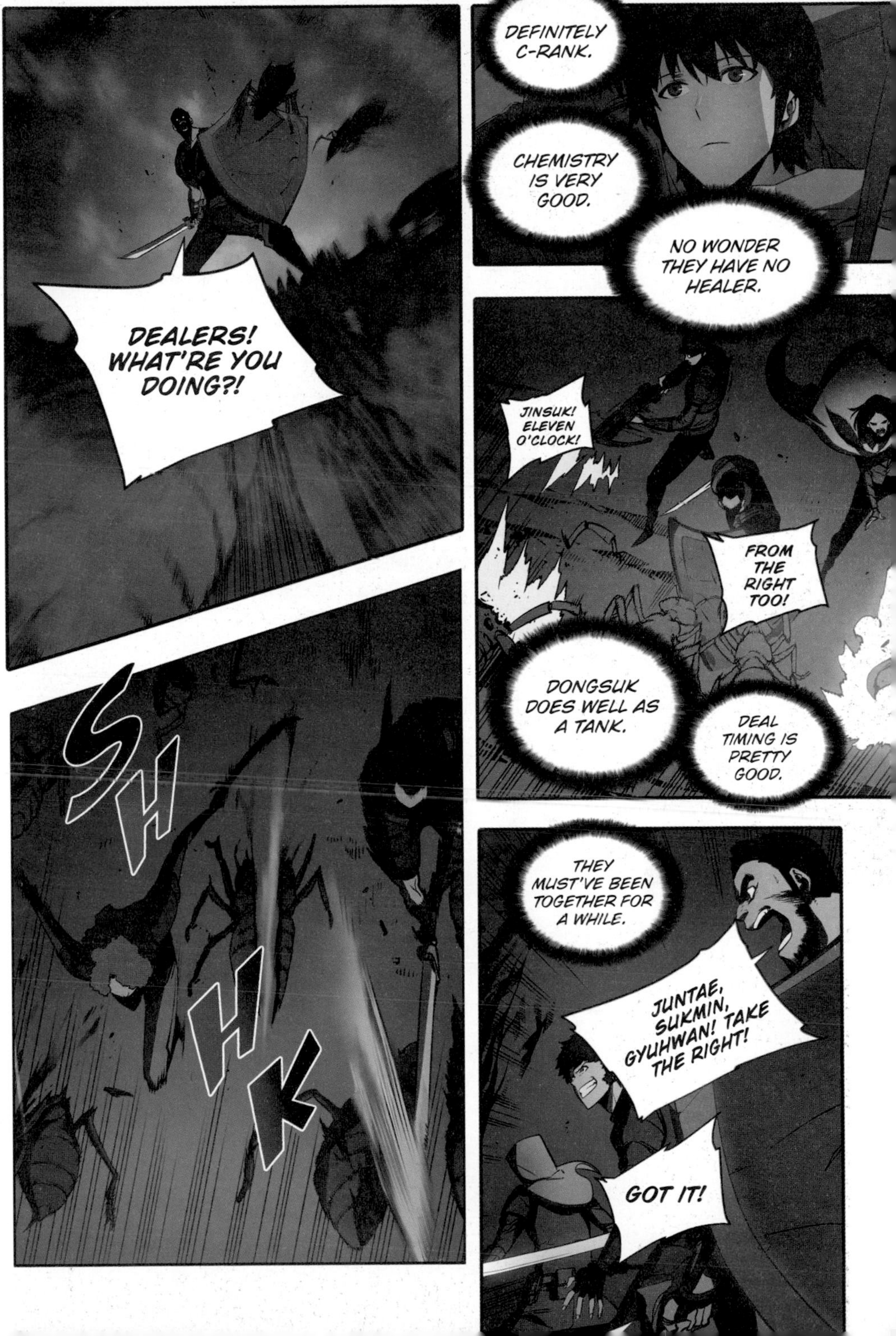
DEALERS! WHAT'RE YOU DOING?!
DEFINITELY C-RANK.
CHEMISTRY IS VERY GOOD.
NO WONDER THEY HAVE NO HEALER.
JINSUK! ELEVEN O'CLOCK!
FROM THE RIGHT TOO!
DONGSUK DOES WELL AS A TANK.
DEAL TIMING IS PRETTY GOOD.
SHHK
THEY MUST'VE BEEN TOGETHER FOR A WHILE.
JUNTAE, SUKMIN, GYUHWAN! TAKE THE RIGHT!
GOT IT!

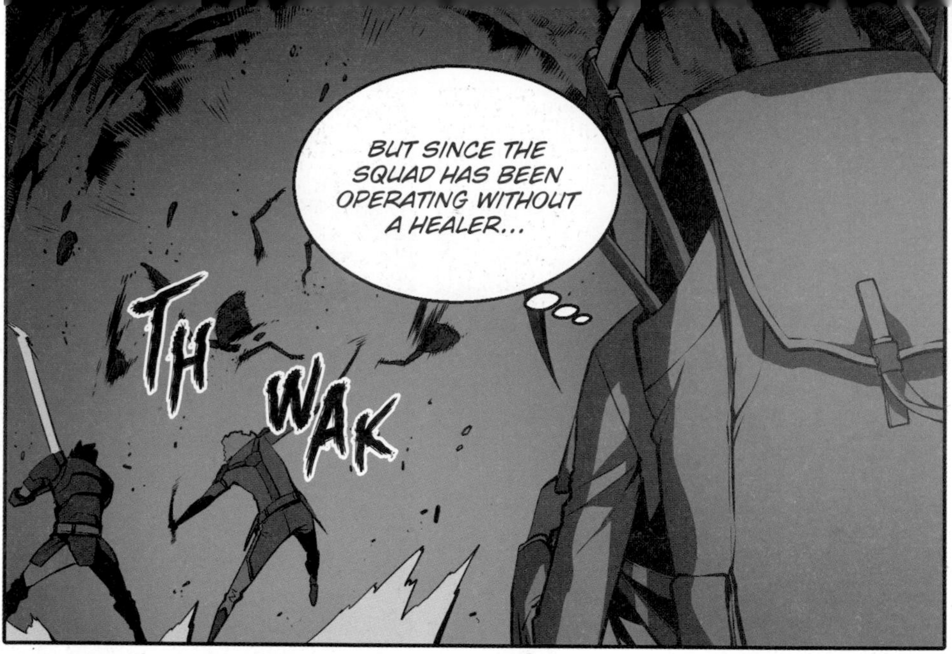
BUT SINCE THE SQUAD HAS BEEN OPERATING WITHOUT A HEALER...
THWAK
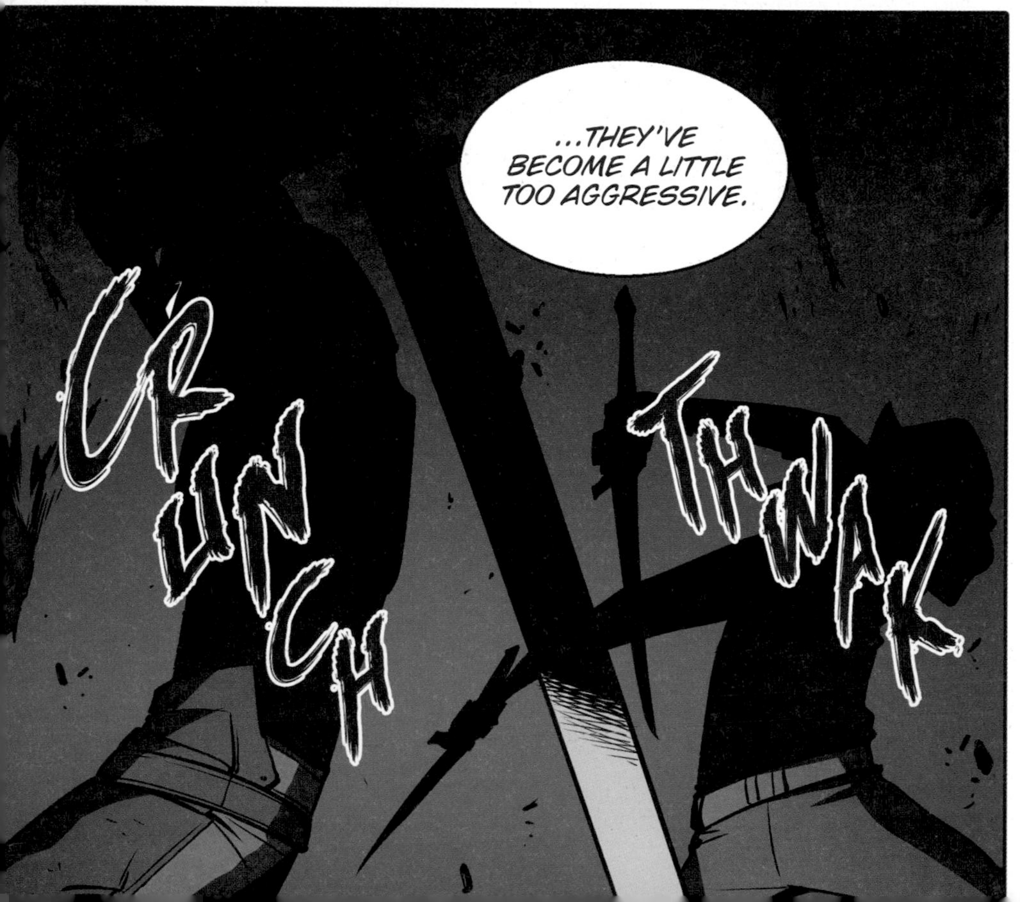
...THEY'VE BECOME A LITTLE TOO AGGRESSIVE.
CRUNCH
THWAK

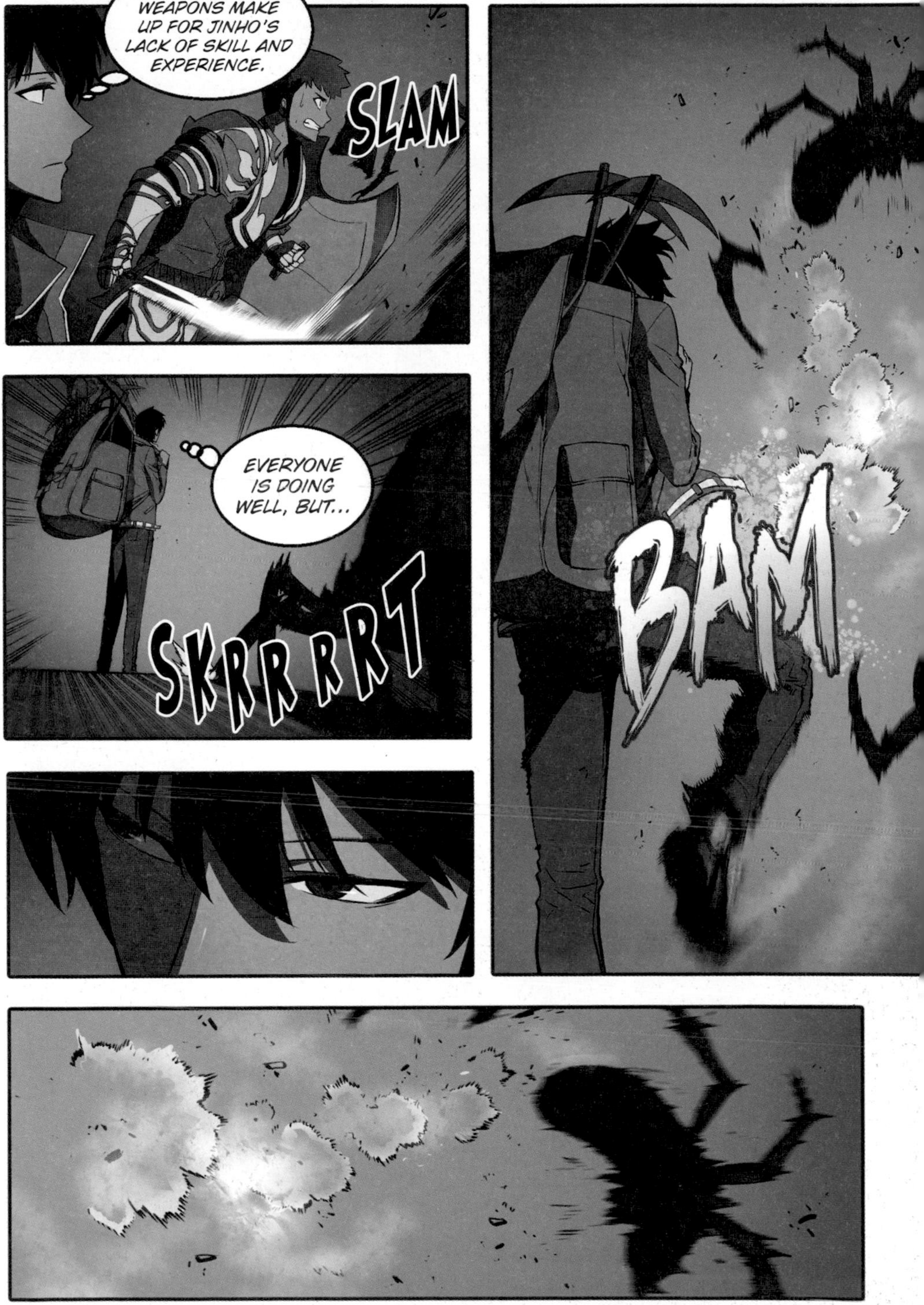
FANCY WEAPONS MAKE UP FOR JINHO'S LACK OF SKILL AND EXPERIENCE.
SLAM
EVERYONE IS DOING WELL, BUT...
SKRRRRT
BAM

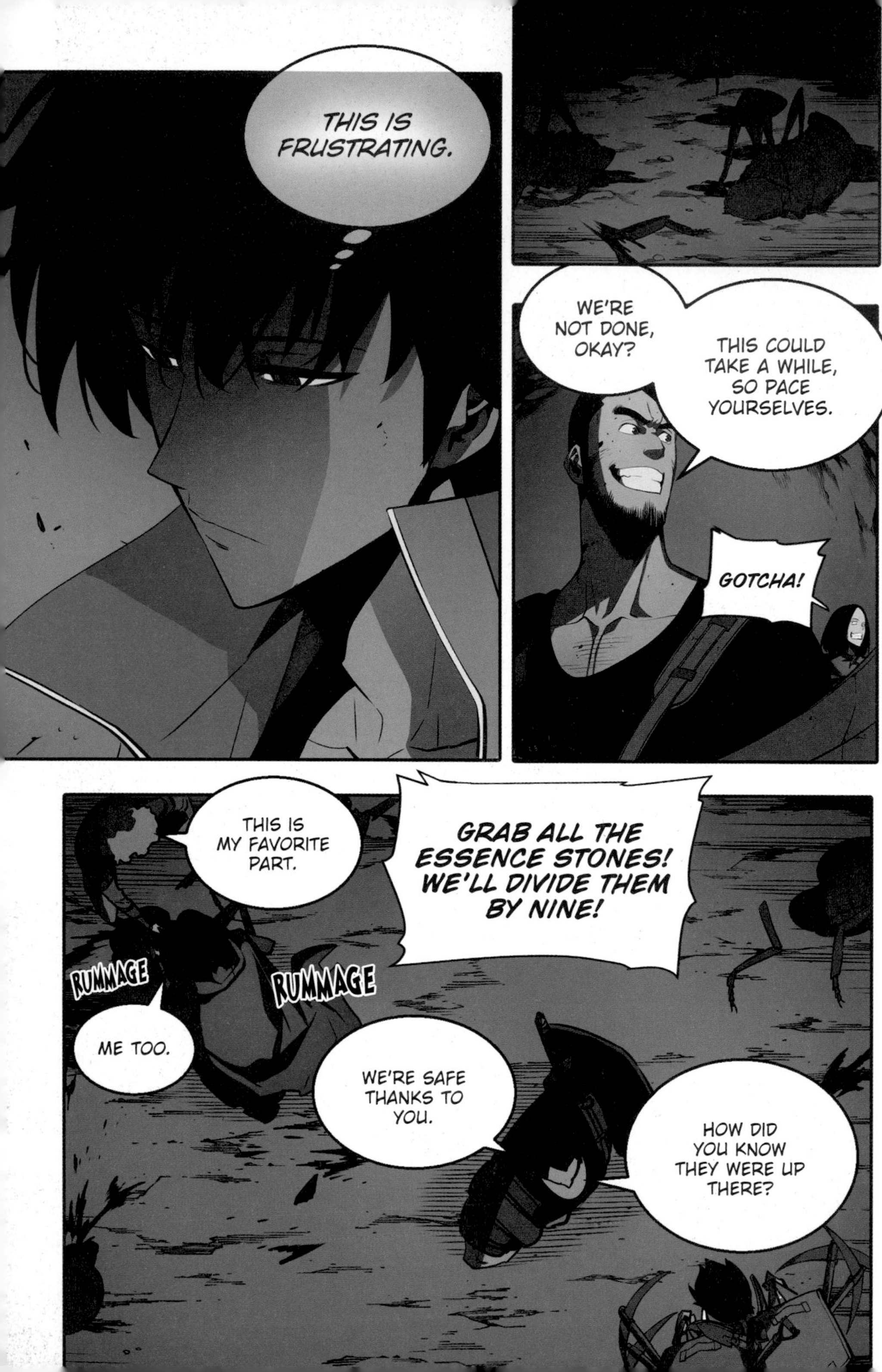
THIS IS FRUSTRATING.
WE'RE NOT DONE, OKAY?
THIS COULD TAKE A WHILE, SO PACE YOURSELVES.
GOTCHA!
THIS IS MY FAVORITE PART.
GRAB ALL THE ESSENCE STONES! WE'LL DIVIDE THEM BY NINE!
RUMMAGE
RUMMAGE
ME TOO.
WE'RE SAFE THANKS TO YOU.
HOW DID YOU KNOW THEY WERE UP THERE?

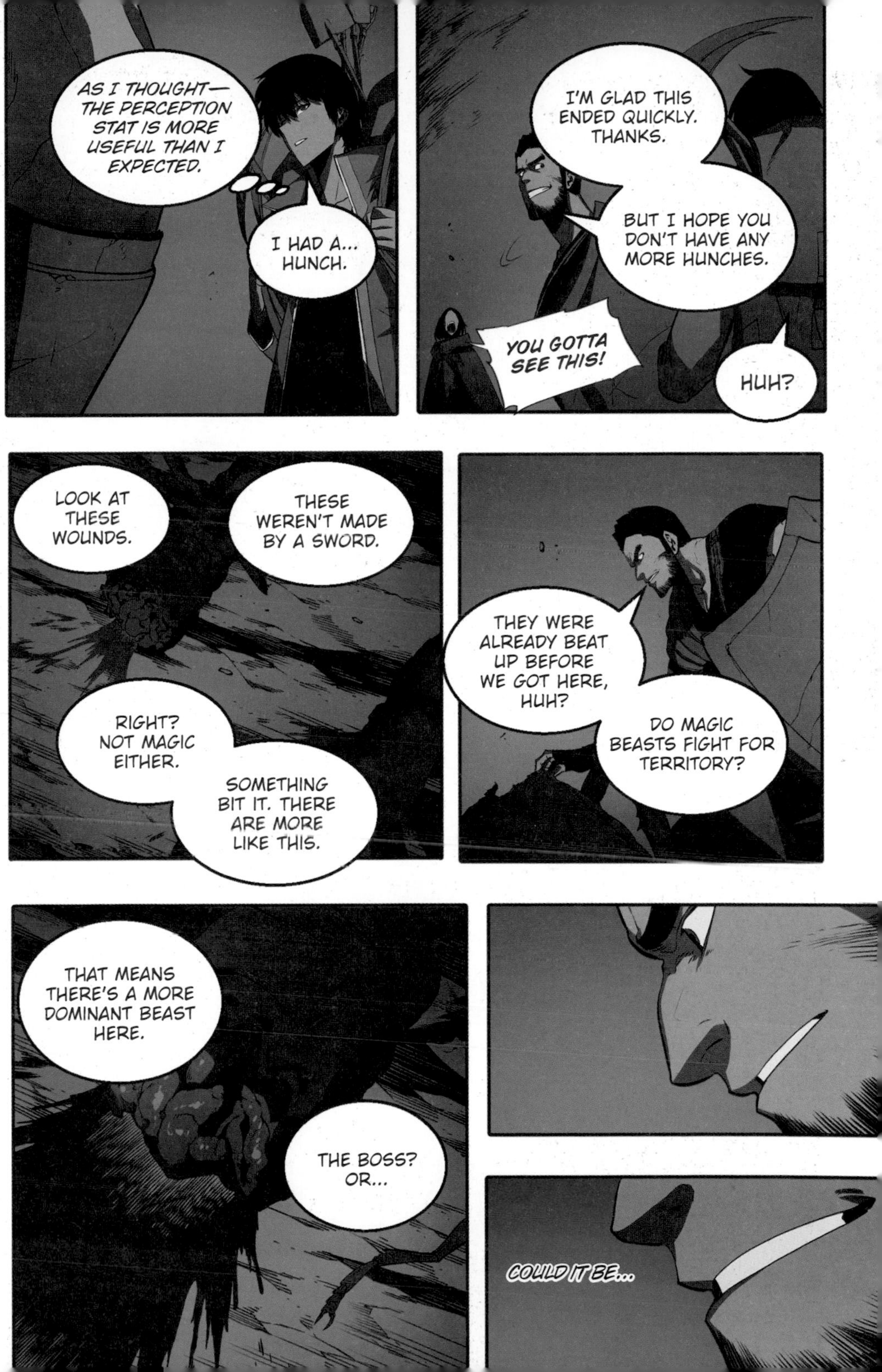
AS I THOUGHT— THE PERCEPTION STAT IS MORE USEFUL THAN I EXPECTED.
I HAD A... HUNCH.
I'M GLAD THIS ENDED QUICKLY. THANKS.
BUT I HOPE YOU DON'T HAVE ANY MORE HUNCHES.
YOU GOTTA SEE THIS!
HUH?
LOOK AT THESE WOUNDS.
THESE WEREN'T MADE BY A SWORD.
RIGHT? NOT MAGIC EITHER.
SOMETHING BIT IT. THERE ARE MORE LIKE THIS.
THEY WERE ALREADY BEAT UP BEFORE WE GOT HERE, HUH?
DO MAGIC BEASTS FIGHT FOR TERRITORY?
THAT MEANS THERE'S A MORE DOMINANT BEAST HERE.
THE BOSS? OR...
COULD IT BE...

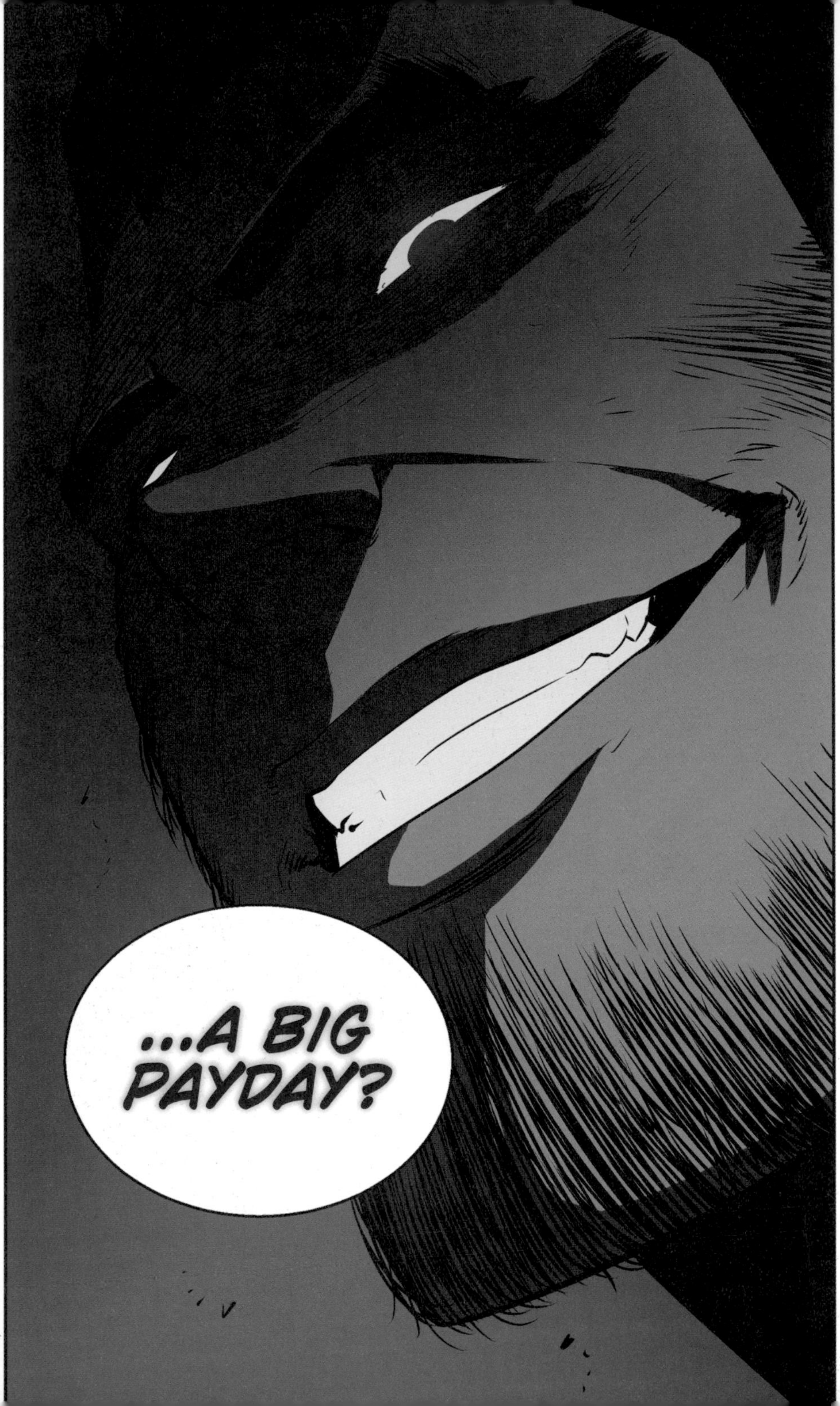
...A BIG PAYDAY?

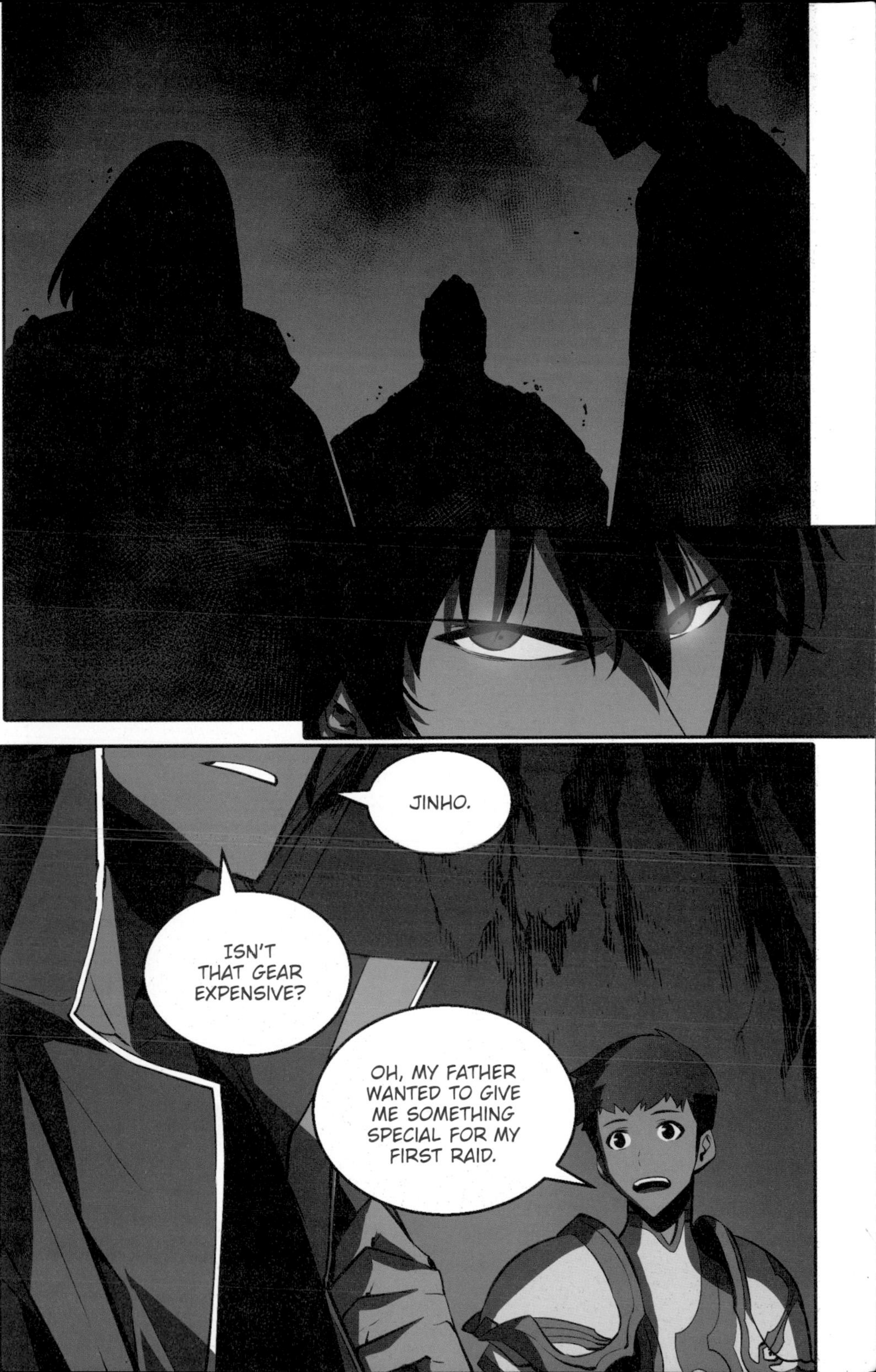
JINHO.
ISN'T THAT GEAR EXPENSIVE?
OH, MY FATHER WANTED TO GIVE ME SOMETHING SPECIAL FOR MY FIRST RAID.

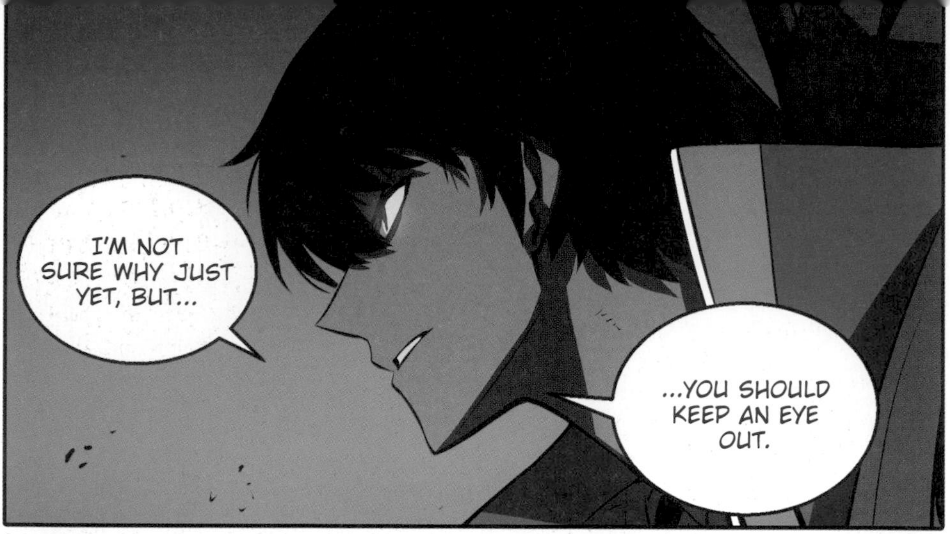
I'M NOT SURE WHY JUST YET, BUT...
...YOU SHOULD KEEP AN EYE OUT.
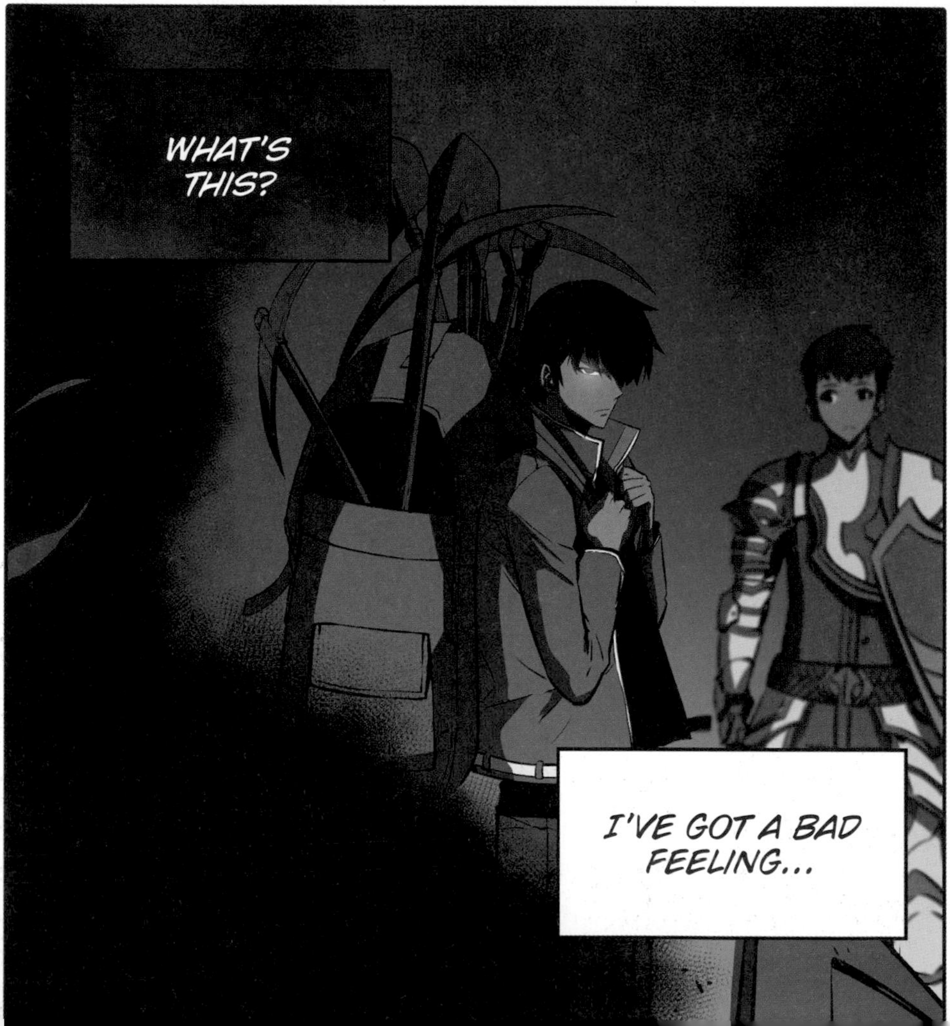
WHAT'S THIS?
I'VE GOT A BAD FEELING...

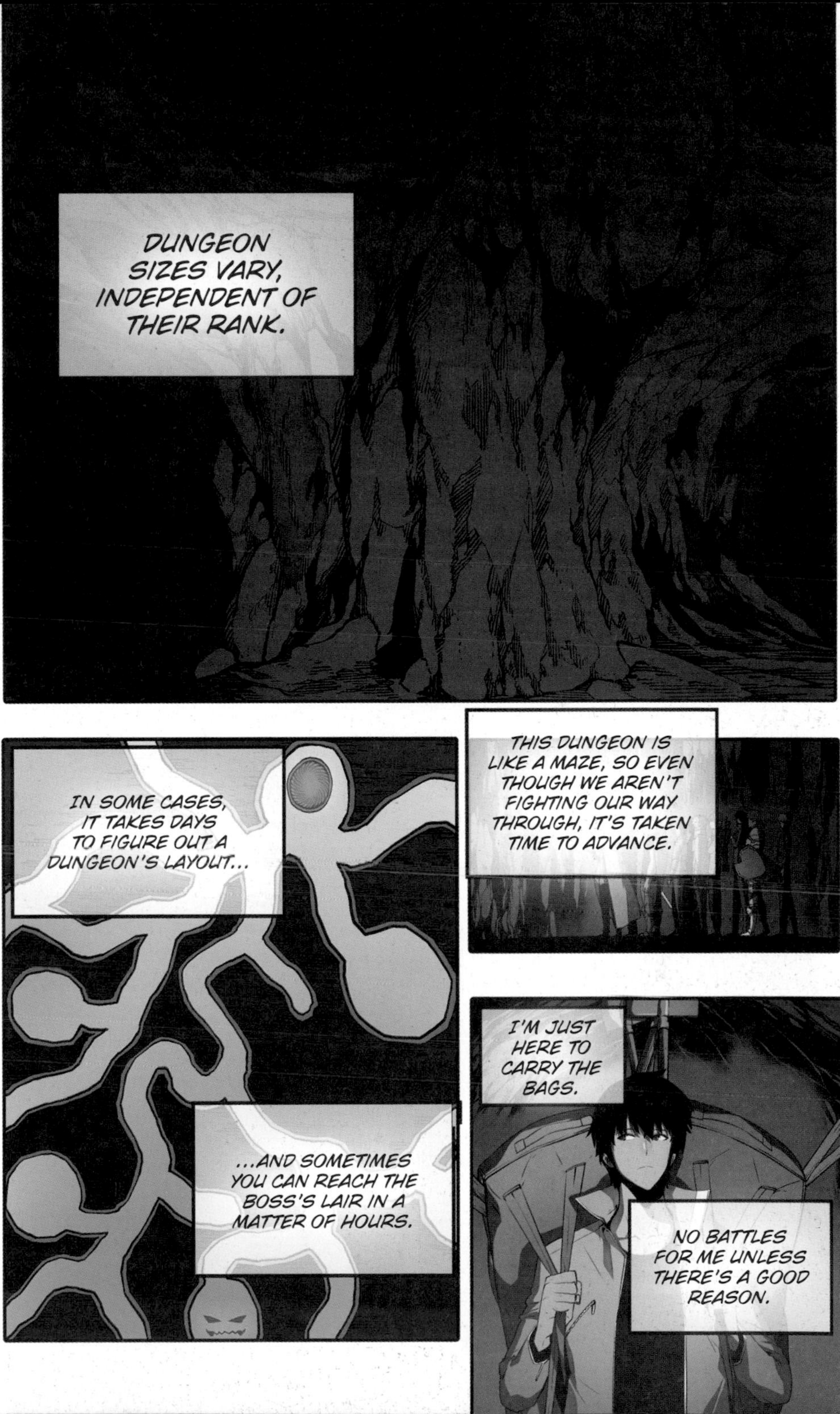
DUNGEON SIZES VARY, INDEPENDENT OF THEIR RANK.
IN SOME CASES, IT TAKES DAYS TO FIGURE OUT A DUNGEON'S LAYOUT...
...AND SOMETIMES YOU CAN REACH THE BOSS'S LAIR IN A MATTER OF HOURS.
THIS DUNGEON IS LIKE A MAZE, SO EVEN THOUGH WE AREN'T FIGHTING OUR WAY THROUGH, IT'S TAKEN TIME TO ADVANCE.
I'M JUST HERE TO CARRY THE BAGS.
NO BATTLES FOR ME UNLESS THERE'S A GOOD REASON.

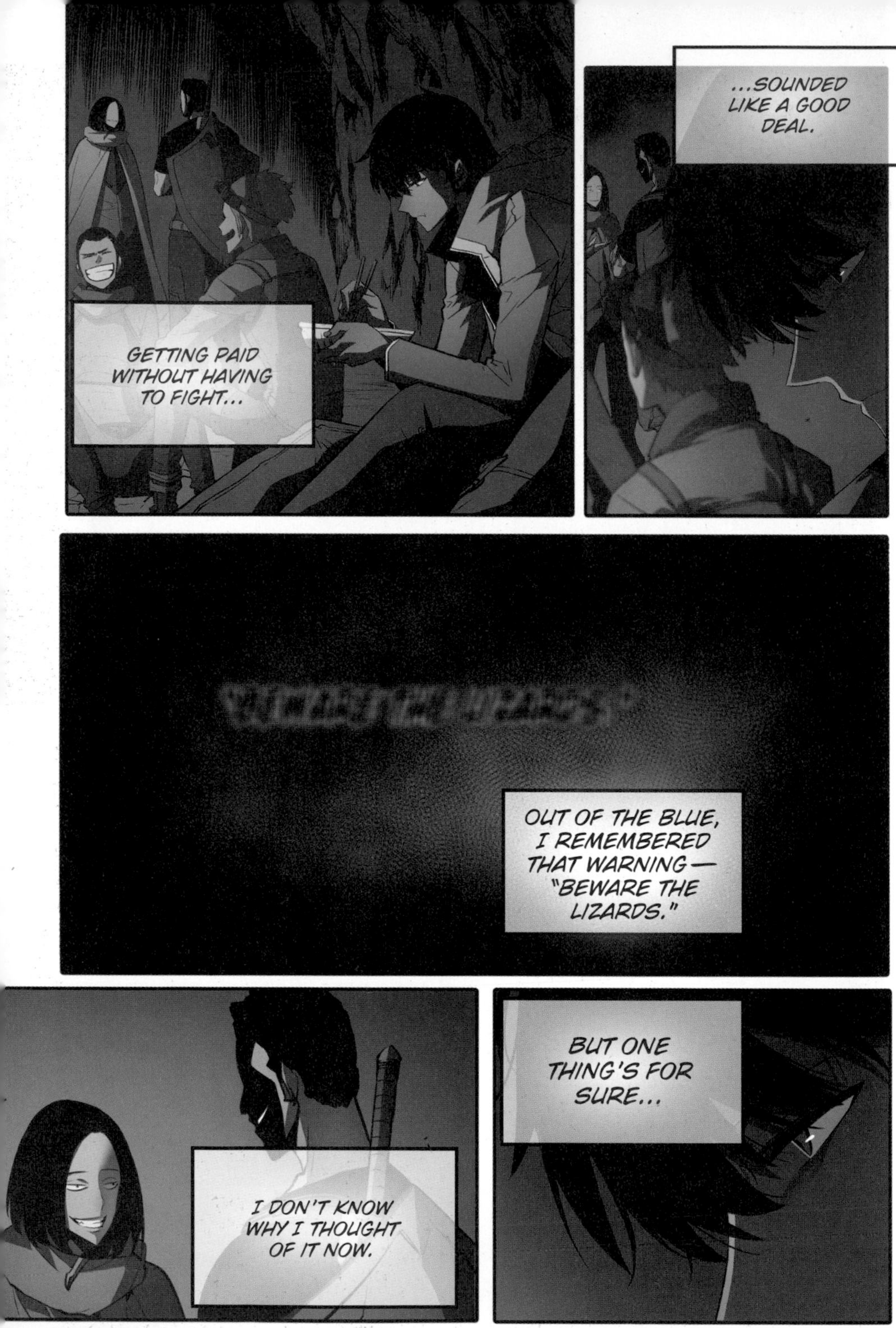
GETTING PAID WITHOUT HAVING TO FIGHT...
...SOUNDED LIKE A GOOD DEAL.
OUT OF THE BLUE, I REMEMBERED THAT WARNING— "BEWARE THE LIZARDS."
I DON'T KNOW WHY I THOUGHT OF IT NOW.
BUT ONE THING'S FOR SURE...

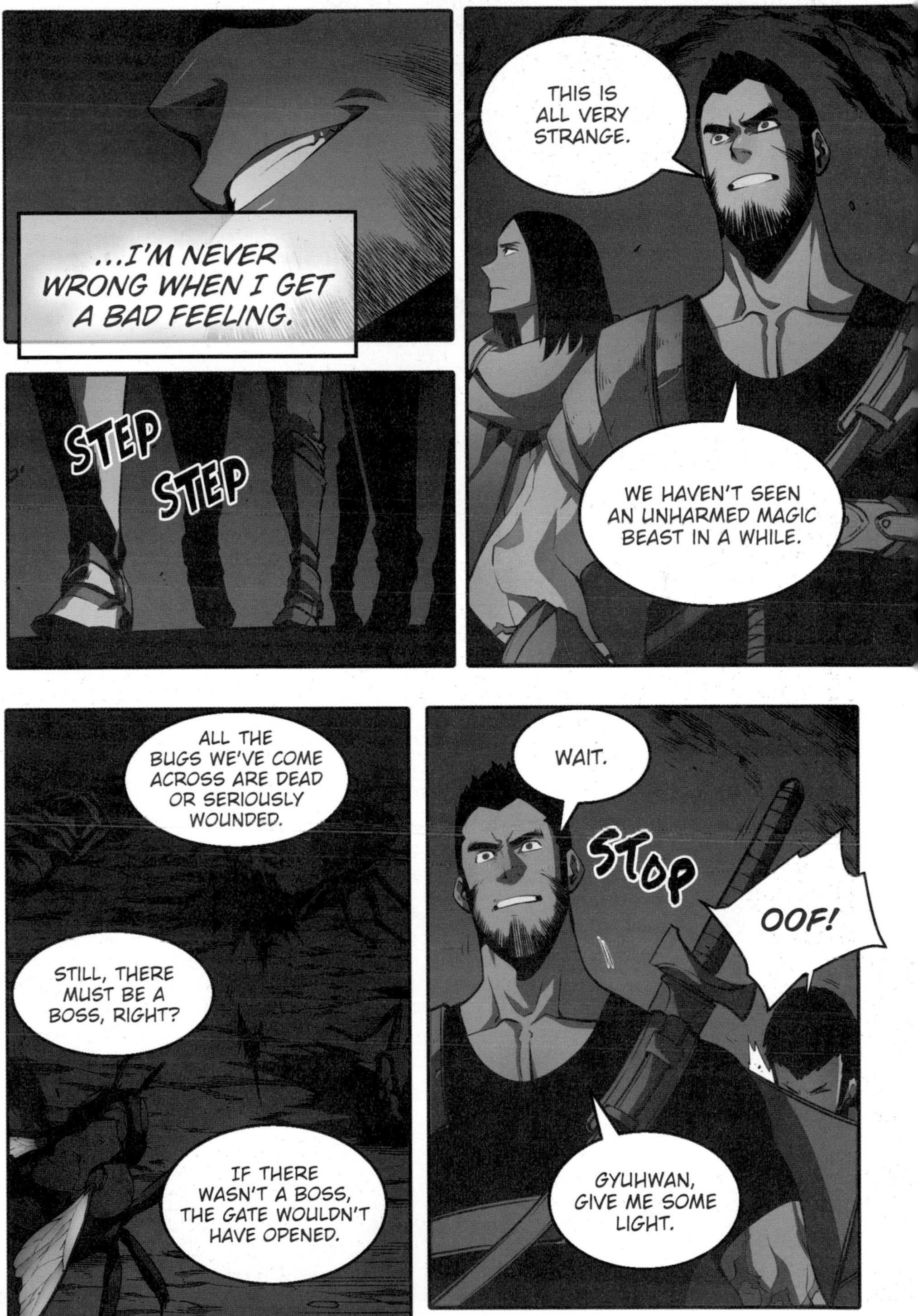
...I'M NEVER WRONG WHEN I GET A BAD FEELING.
STEP
STEP
THIS IS ALL VERY STRANGE.
WE HAVEN'T SEEN AN UNHARMED MAGIC BEAST IN A WHILE.
ALL THE BUGS WE'VE COME ACROSS ARE DEAD OR SERIOUSLY WOUNDED.
STILL, THERE MUST BE A BOSS, RIGHT?
IF THERE WASN'T A BOSS, THE GATE WOULDN'T HAVE OPENED.
WAIT.
STOP
OOF!
GYUHWAN, GIVE ME SOME LIGHT.

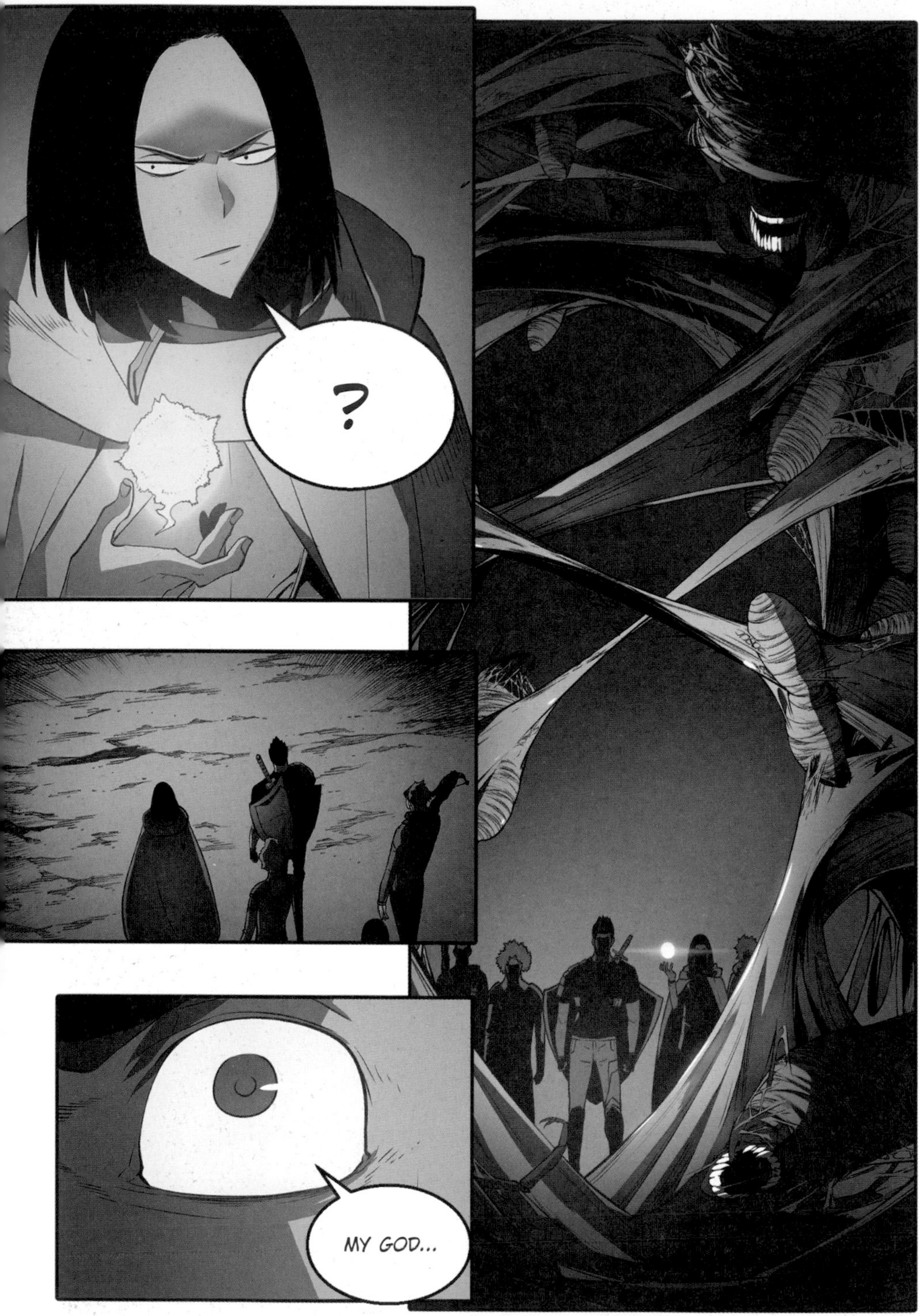
?
MY GOD...

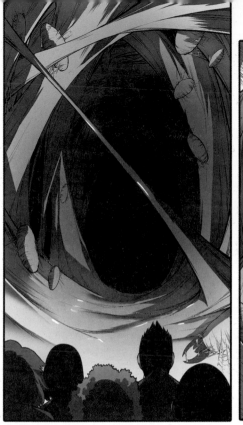

IT'S
THE BOSS'S
LAIR.

GET
READY.

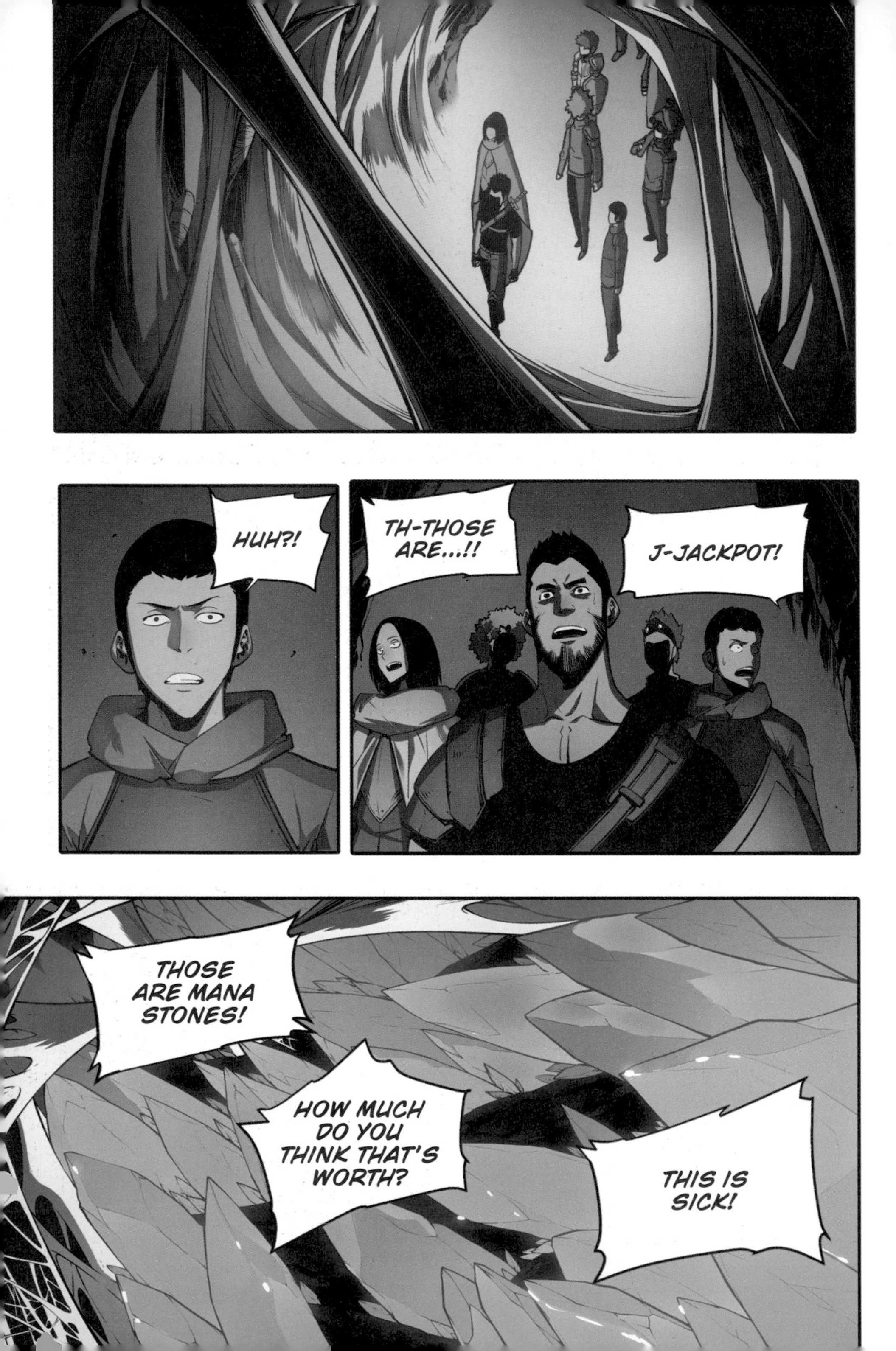
HUH?!
TH-THOSE ARE...!!
J-JACKPOT!
THOSE ARE MANA STONES!
HOW MUCH DO YOU THINK THAT'S WORTH?
THIS IS SICK!

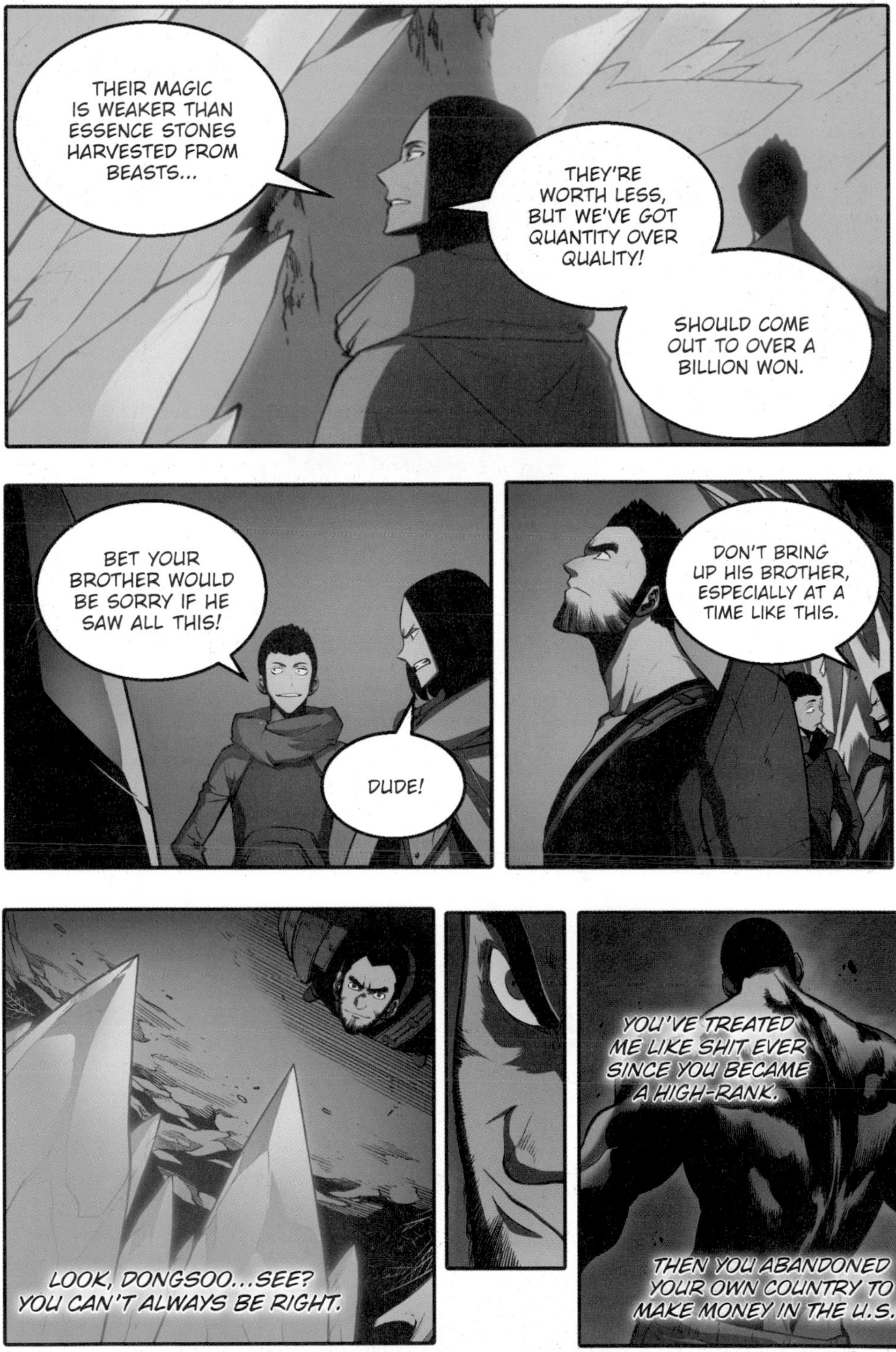
THEIR MAGIC IS WEAKER THAN ESSENCE STONES HARVESTED FROM BEASTS...
THEY'RE WORTH LESS, BUT WE'VE GOT QUANTITY OVER QUALITY!
SHOULD COME OUT TO OVER A BILLION WON.
BET YOUR BROTHER WOULD BE SORRY IF HE SAW ALL THIS!
DUDE!
DON'T BRING UP HIS BROTHER, ESPECIALLY AT A TIME LIKE THIS.
LOOK, DONGSOO...SEE? YOU CAN'T ALWAYS BE RIGHT.
YOU'VE TREATED ME LIKE SHIT EVER SINCE YOU BECAME A HIGH-RANK.
THEN YOU ABANDONED YOUR OWN COUNTRY TO MAKE MONEY IN THE U.S.?

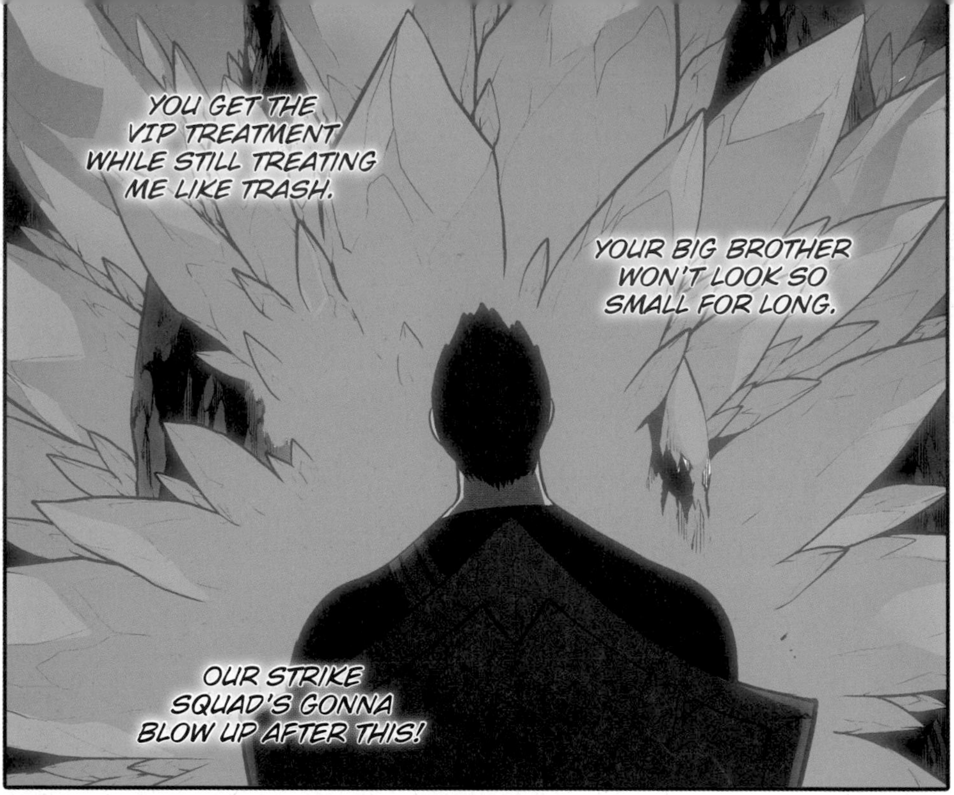
YOU GET THE VIP TREATMENT WHILE STILL TREATING ME LIKE TRASH.
YOUR BIG BROTHER WON'T LOOK SO SMALL FOR LONG.
OUR STRIKE SQUAD'S GONNA BLOW UP AFTER THIS!

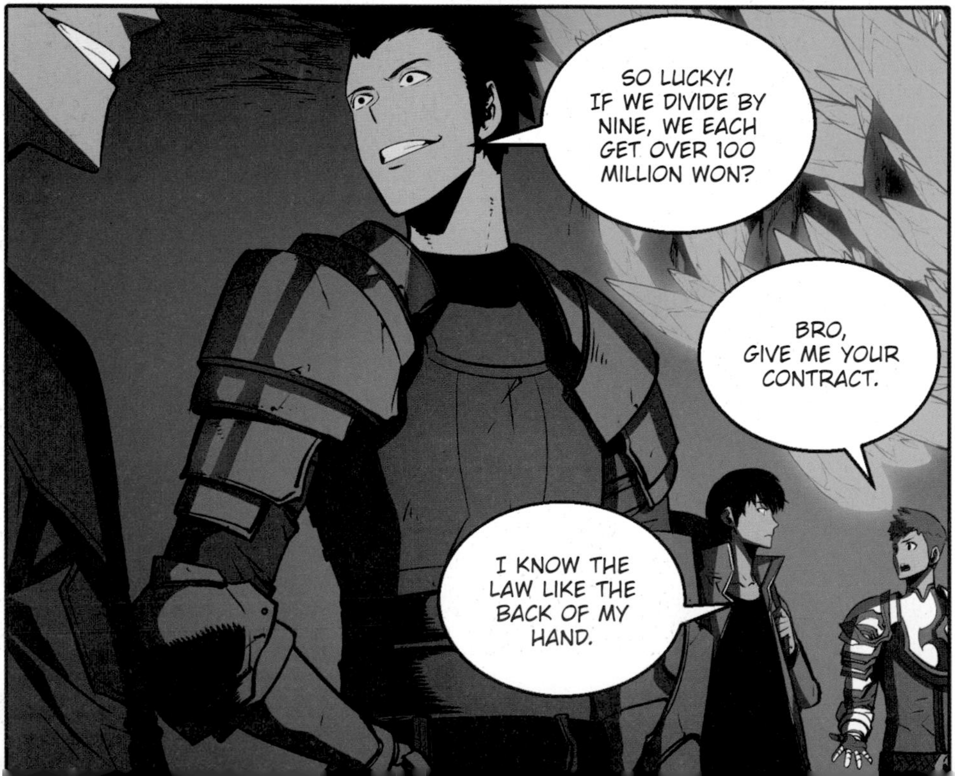
SO LUCKY! IF WE DIVIDE BY NINE, WE EACH GET OVER 100 MILLION WON?
BRO, GIVE ME YOUR CONTRACT.
I KNOW THE LAW LIKE THE BACK OF MY HAND.

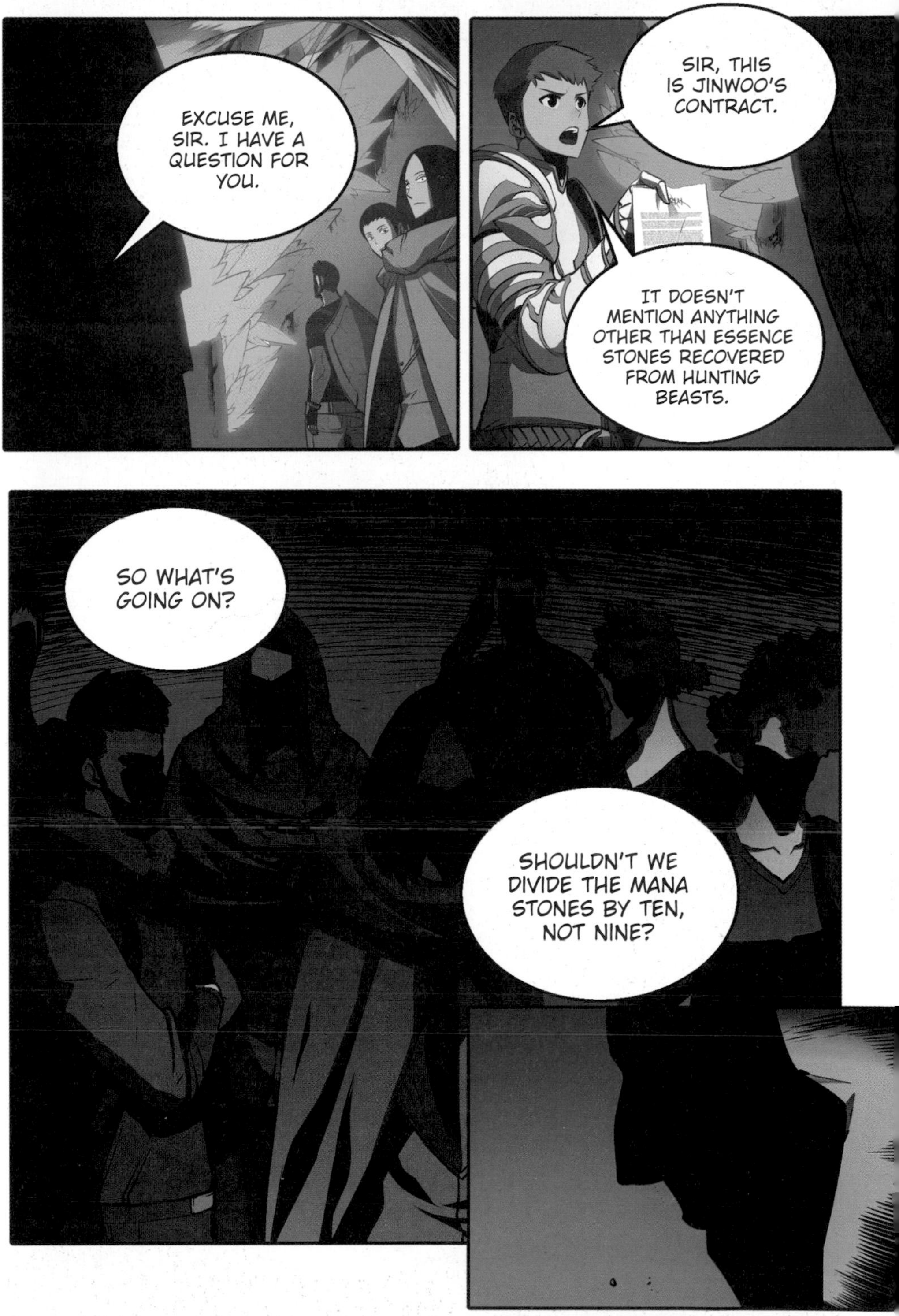
EXCUSE ME, SIR. I HAVE A QUESTION FOR YOU.
SIR, THIS IS JINWOO'S CONTRACT.
IT DOESN'T MENTION ANYTHING OTHER THAN ESSENCE STONES RECOVERED FROM HUNTING BEASTS.
SO WHAT'S GOING ON?
SHOULDN'T WE DIVIDE THE MANA STONES BY TEN, NOT NINE?

OF COURSE! WE'LL DIVIDE THESE EQUALLY.

DON'T WORRY, WE KNOW.

WE JUST HAVE SOMETHING TO TAKE CARE OF FIRST.

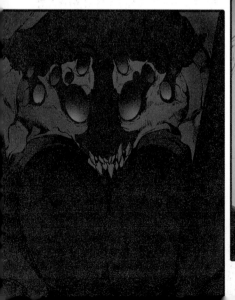

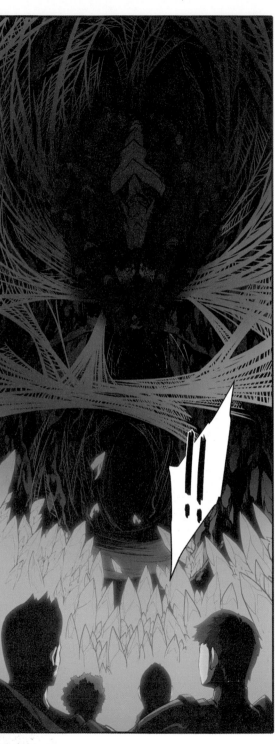

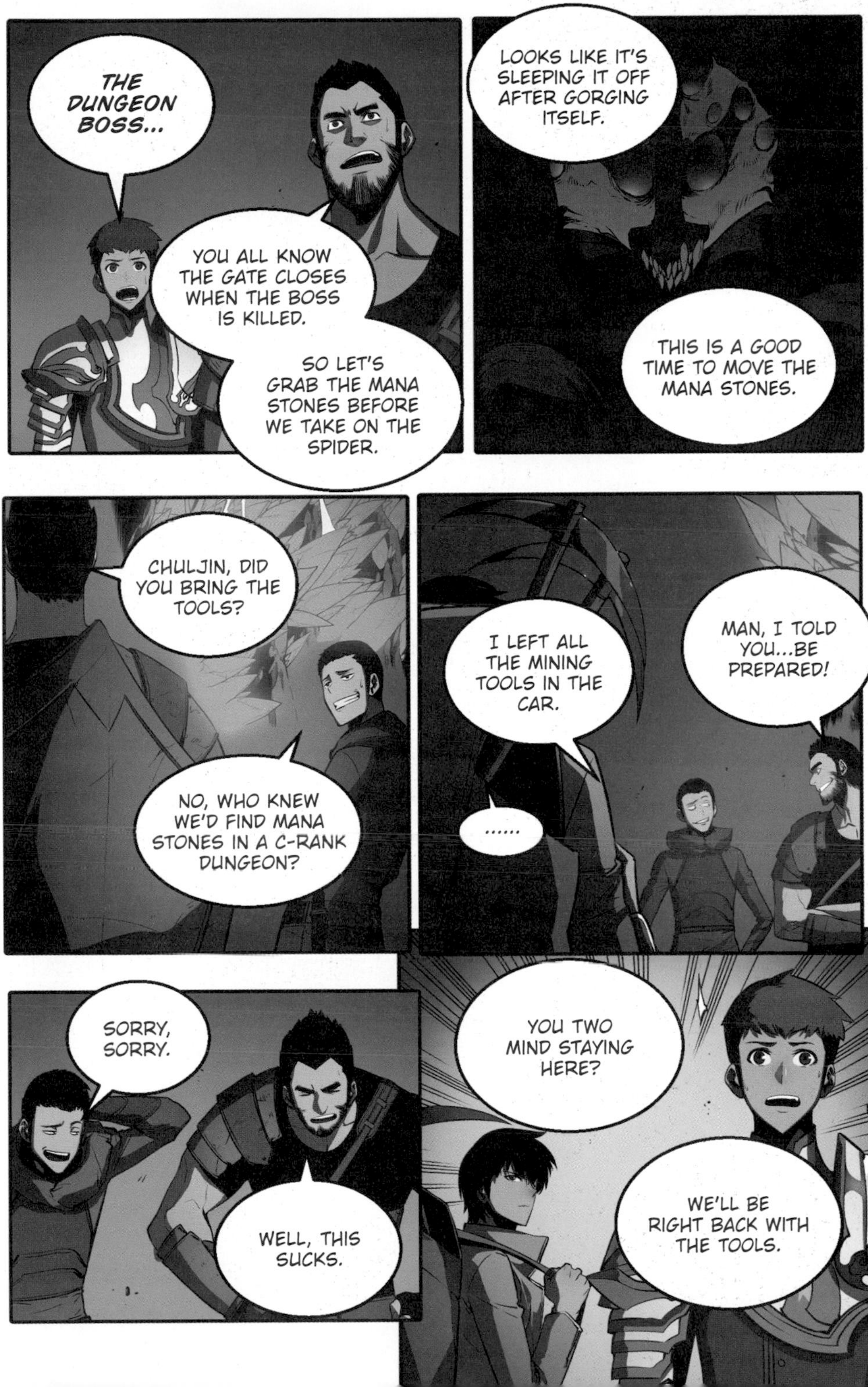
THE DUNGEON BOSS...
YOU ALL KNOW THE GATE CLOSES WHEN THE BOSS IS KILLED.
SO LET'S GRAB THE MANA STONES BEFORE WE TAKE ON THE SPIDER.
LOOKS LIKE IT'S SLEEPING IT OFF AFTER GORGING ITSELF.
THIS IS A GOOD TIME TO MOVE THE MANA STONES.
CHULJIN, DID YOU BRING THE TOOLS?
NO, WHO KNEW WE'D FIND MANA STONES IN A C-RANK DUNGEON?
I LEFT ALL THE MINING TOOLS IN THE CAR.
MAN, I TOLD YOU...BE PREPARED!
......
SORRY, SORRY.
WELL, THIS SUCKS.
YOU TWO MIND STAYING HERE?
WE'LL BE RIGHT BACK WITH THE TOOLS.

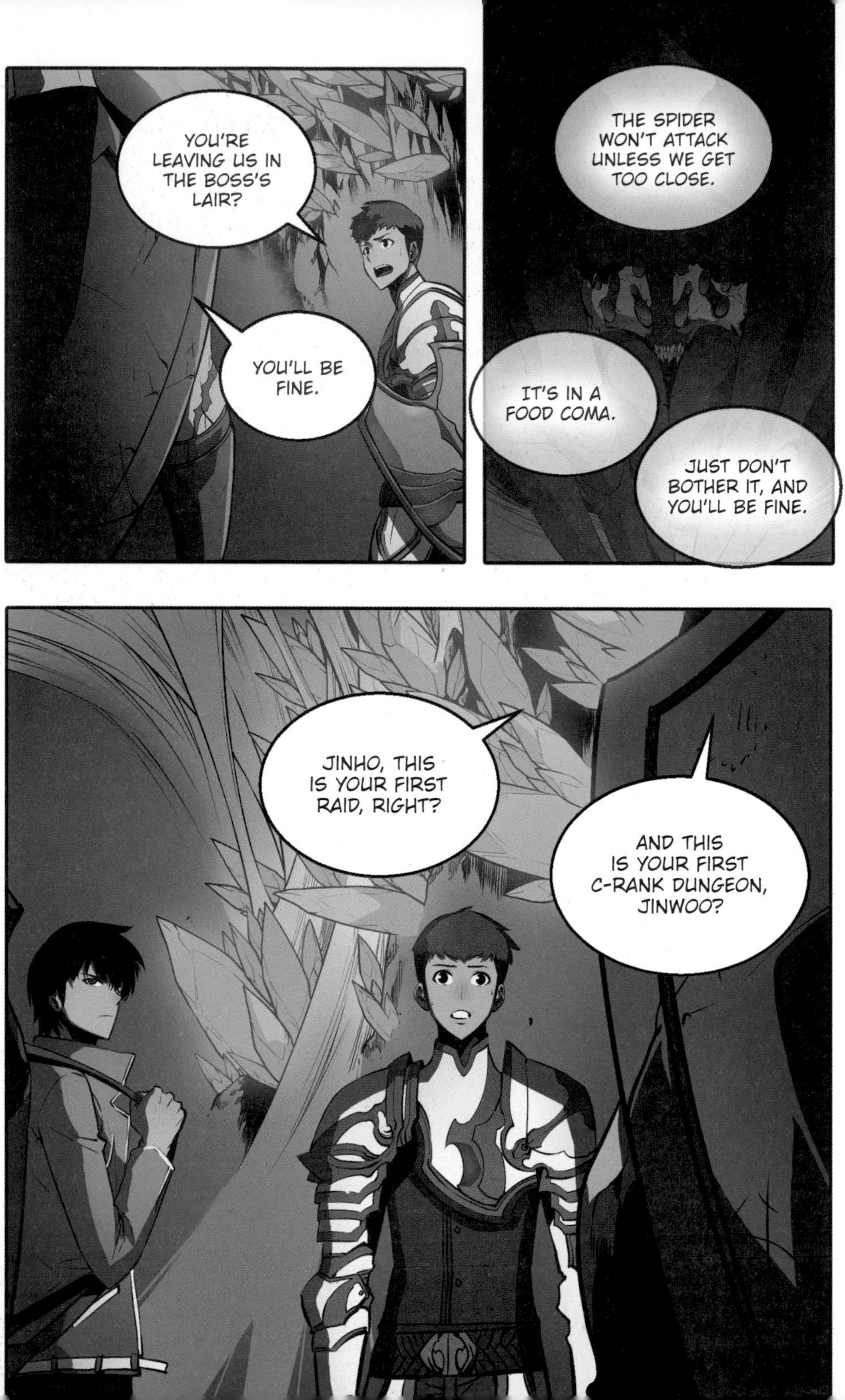
YOU'RE LEAVING US IN THE BOSS'S LAIR?
YOU'LL BE FINE.
THE SPIDER WON'T ATTACK UNLESS WE GET TOO CLOSE.
IT'S IN A FOOD COMA.
JUST DON'T BOTHER IT, AND YOU'LL BE FINE.
JINHO, THIS IS YOUR FIRST RAID, RIGHT?
AND THIS IS YOUR FIRST C-RANK DUNGEON, JINWOO?

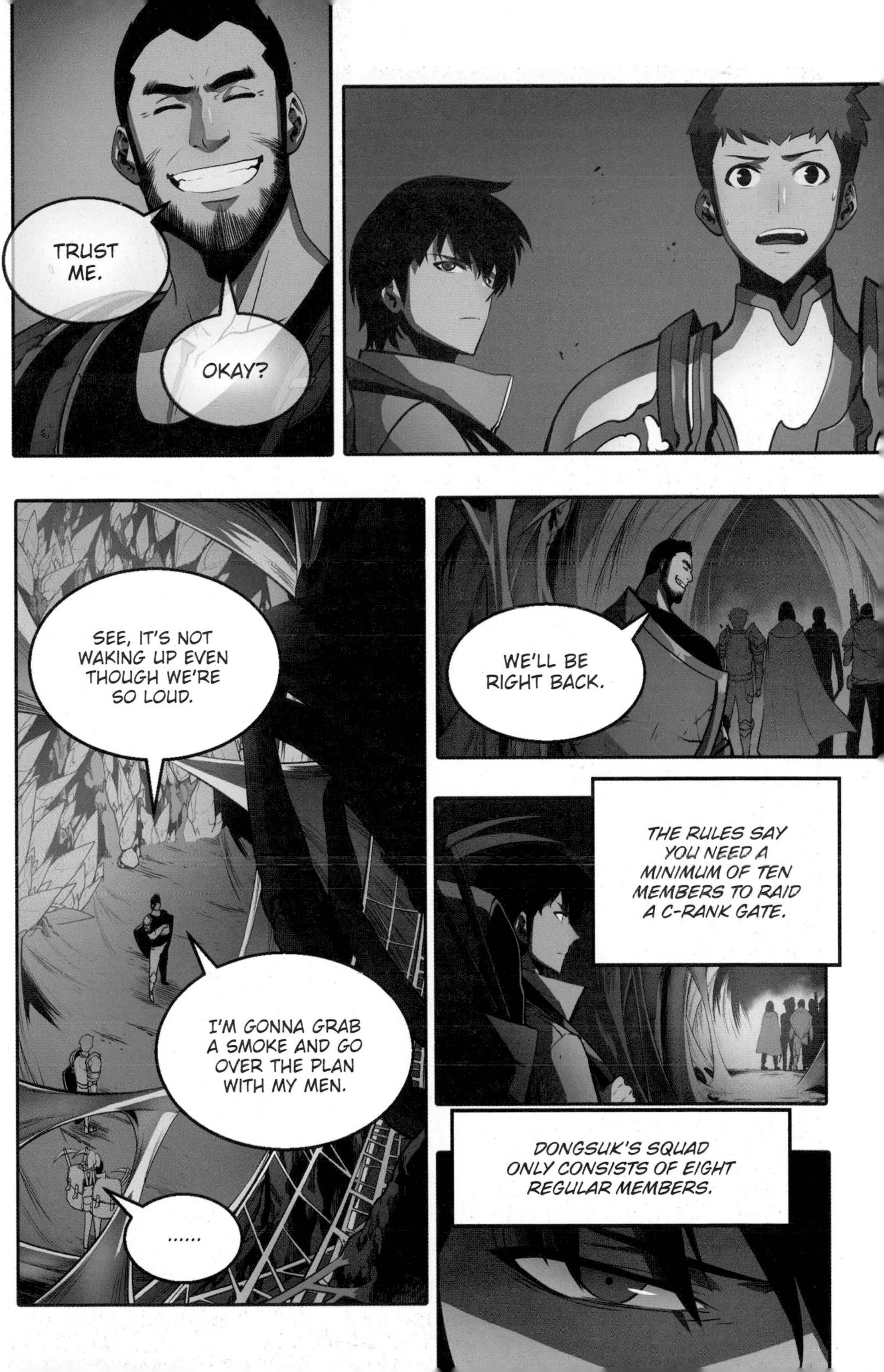
TRUST ME.
OKAY?
SEE, IT'S NOT WAKING UP EVEN THOUGH WE'RE SO LOUD.
I'M GONNA GRAB A SMOKE AND GO OVER THE PLAN WITH MY MEN.
......
WE'LL BE RIGHT BACK.
THE RULES SAY YOU NEED A MINIMUM OF TEN MEMBERS TO RAID A C-RANK GATE.
DONGSUK'S SQUAD ONLY CONSISTS OF EIGHT REGULAR MEMBERS.

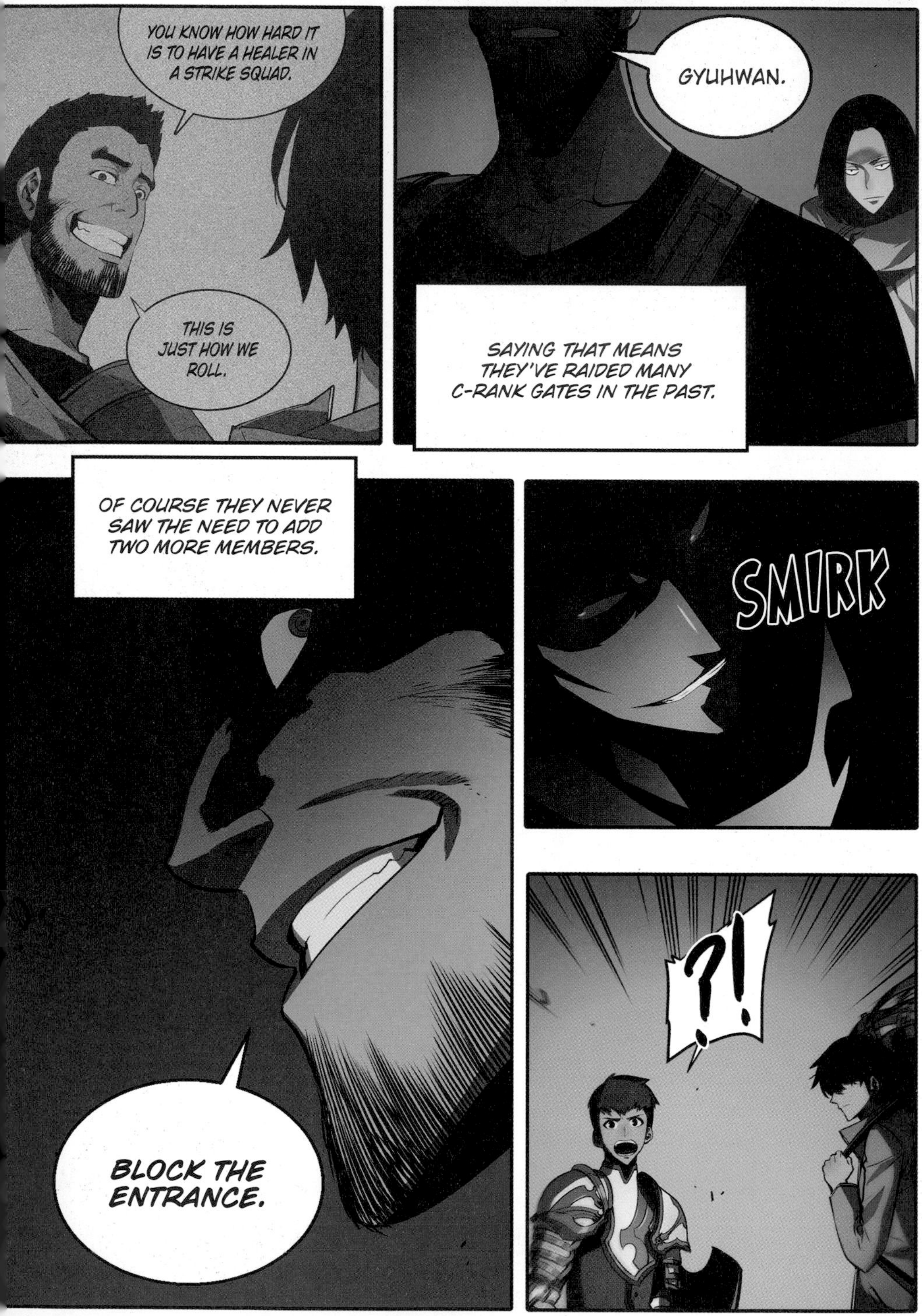
YOU KNOW HOW HARD IT IS TO HAVE A HEALER IN A STRIKE SQUAD.
THIS IS JUST HOW WE ROLL.
GYUHWAN.
SAYING THAT MEANS THEY'VE RAIDED MANY C-RANK GATES IN THE PAST.
OF COURSE THEY NEVER SAW THE NEED TO ADD TWO MORE MEMBERS.
BLOCK THE ENTRANCE.
SMIRK
?!

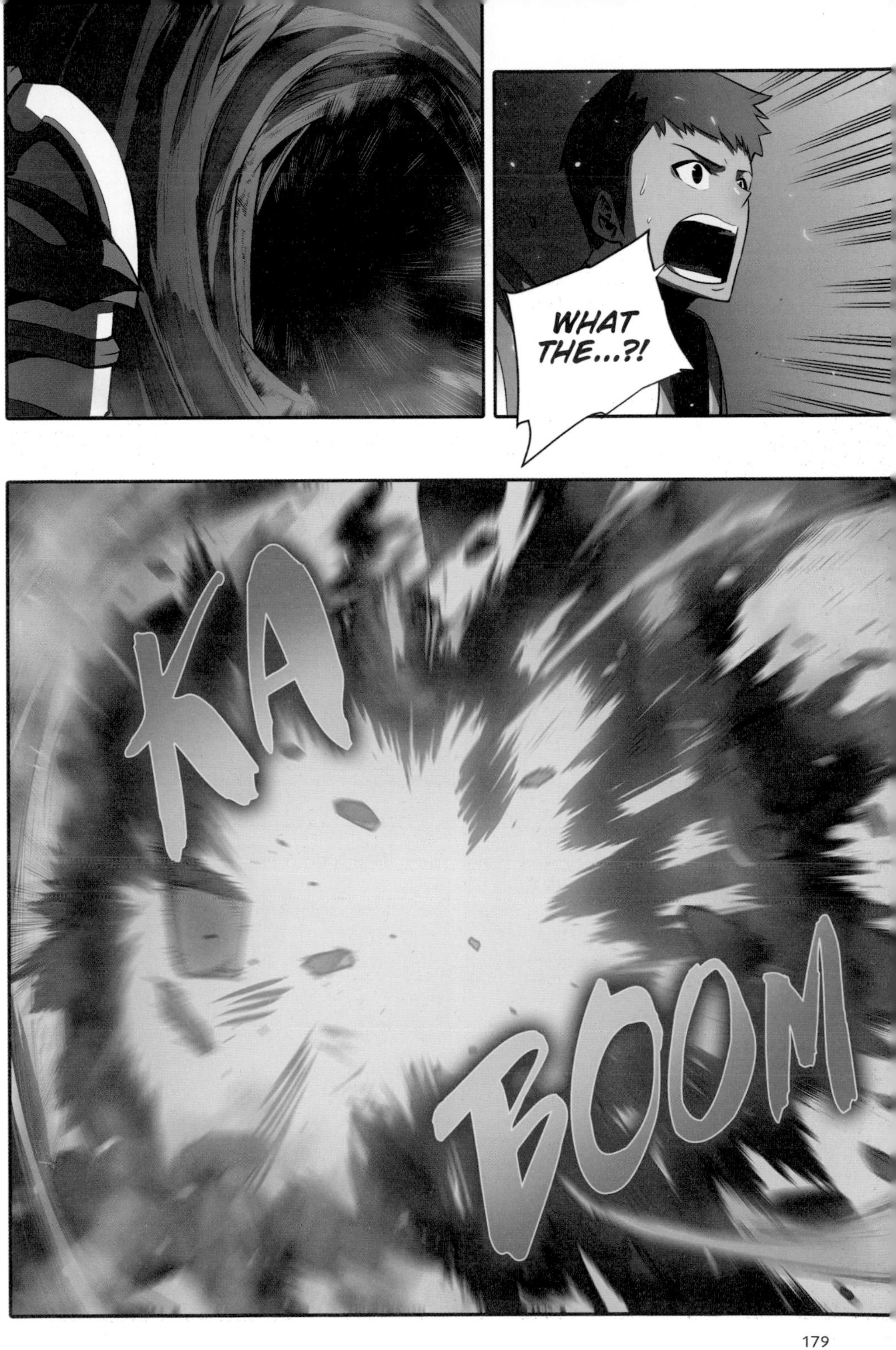
WHAT THE...?!
KA
BOOM

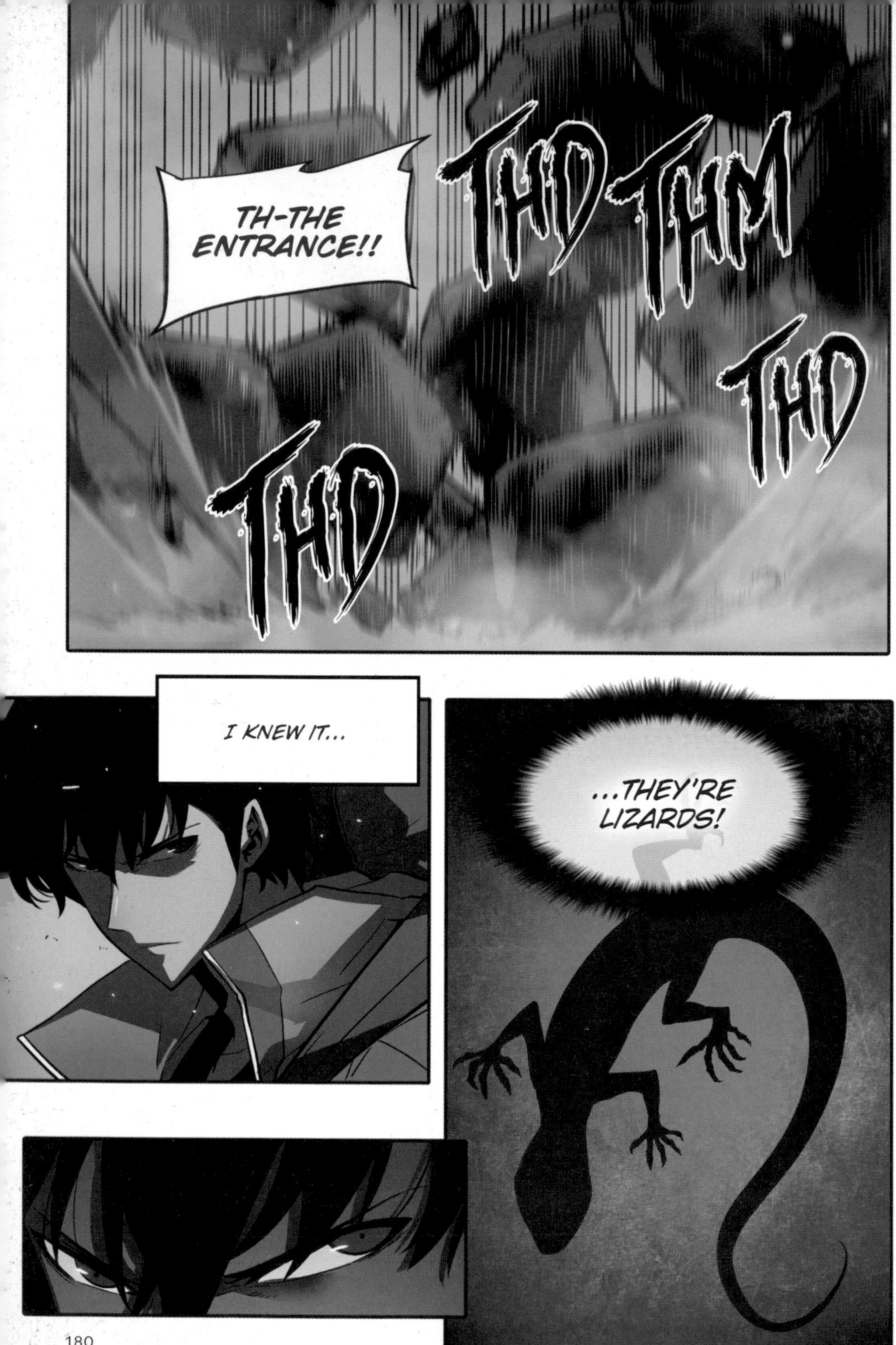
TH-THE ENTRANCE!!
THD THM
THD
THD
I KNEW IT...
...THEY'RE LIZARDS!

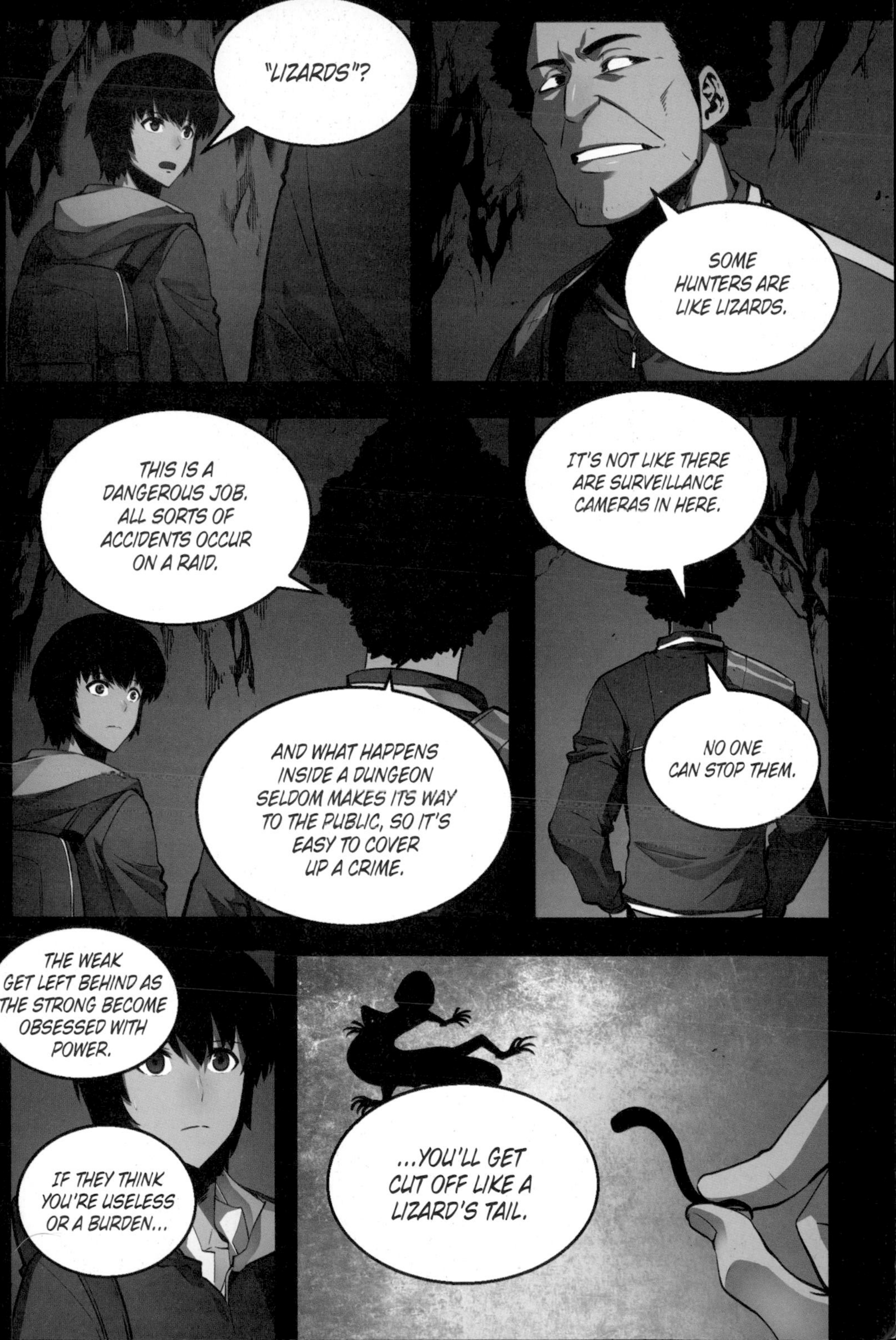
"LIZARDS"?
SOME HUNTERS ARE LIKE LIZARDS.
THIS IS A DANGEROUS JOB. ALL SORTS OF ACCIDENTS OCCUR ON A RAID.
AND WHAT HAPPENS INSIDE A DUNGEON SELDOM MAKES ITS WAY TO THE PUBLIC, SO IT'S EASY TO COVER UP A CRIME.
IT'S NOT LIKE THERE ARE SURVEILLANCE CAMERAS IN HERE.
NO ONE CAN STOP THEM.
THE WEAK GET LEFT BEHIND AS THE STRONG BECOME OBSESSED WITH POWER.
IF THEY THINK YOU'RE USELESS OR A BURDEN...
...YOU'LL GET CUT OFF LIKE A LIZARD'S TAIL.

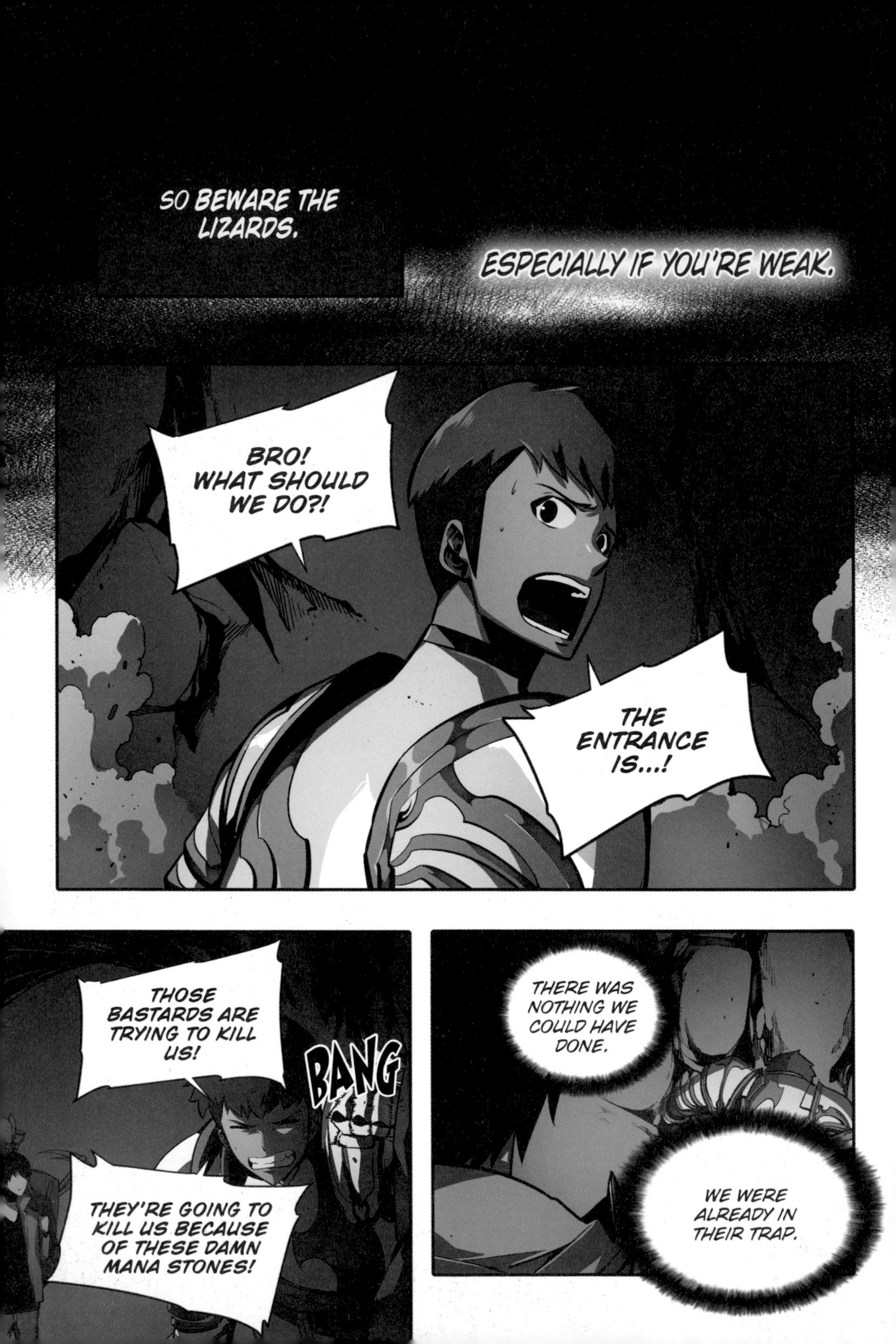
SO BEWARE THE LIZARDS.
ESPECIALLY IF YOU'RE WEAK.
BRO! WHAT SHOULD WE DO?!
THE ENTRANCE IS...!
THOSE BASTARDS ARE TRYING TO KILL US!
BANG
THEY'RE GOING TO KILL US BECAUSE OF THESE DAMN MANA STONES!
THERE WAS NOTHING WE COULD HAVE DONE.
WE WERE ALREADY IN THEIR TRAP.

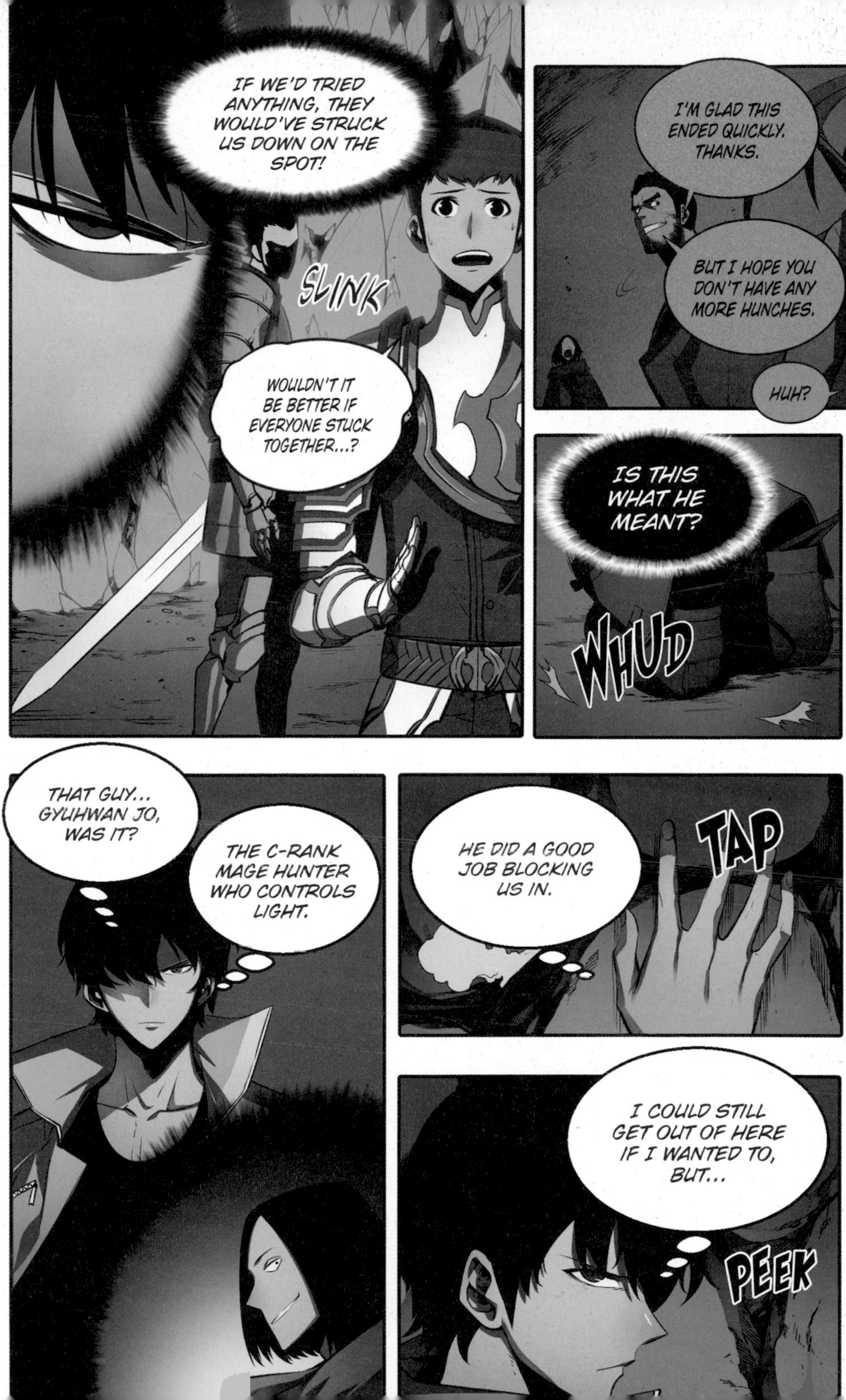
IF WE'D TRIED ANYTHING, THEY WOULD'VE STRUCK US DOWN ON THE SPOT!
SLINK
WOULDN'T IT BE BETTER IF EVERYONE STUCK TOGETHER...?
I'M GLAD THIS ENDED QUICKLY. THANKS.
BUT I HOPE YOU DON'T HAVE ANY MORE HUNCHES.
HUH?
IS THIS WHAT HE MEANT?
WHUD
THAT GUY... GYUHWAN JO, WAS IT?
THE C-RANK MAGE HUNTER WHO CONTROLS LIGHT.
HE DID A GOOD JOB BLOCKING US IN.
TAP
I COULD STILL GET OUT OF HERE IF I WANTED TO, BUT...
PEEK

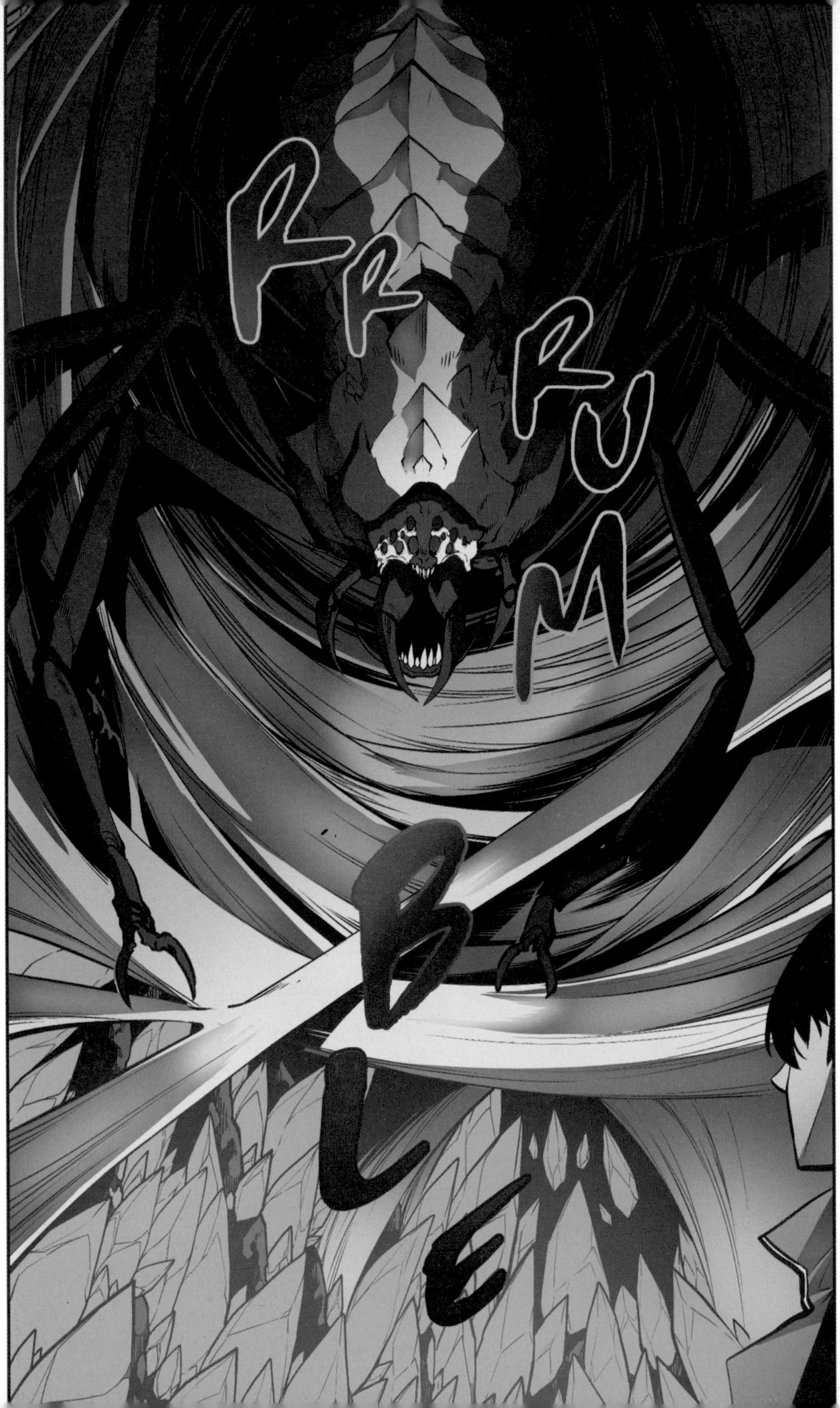
RRRUMBLE

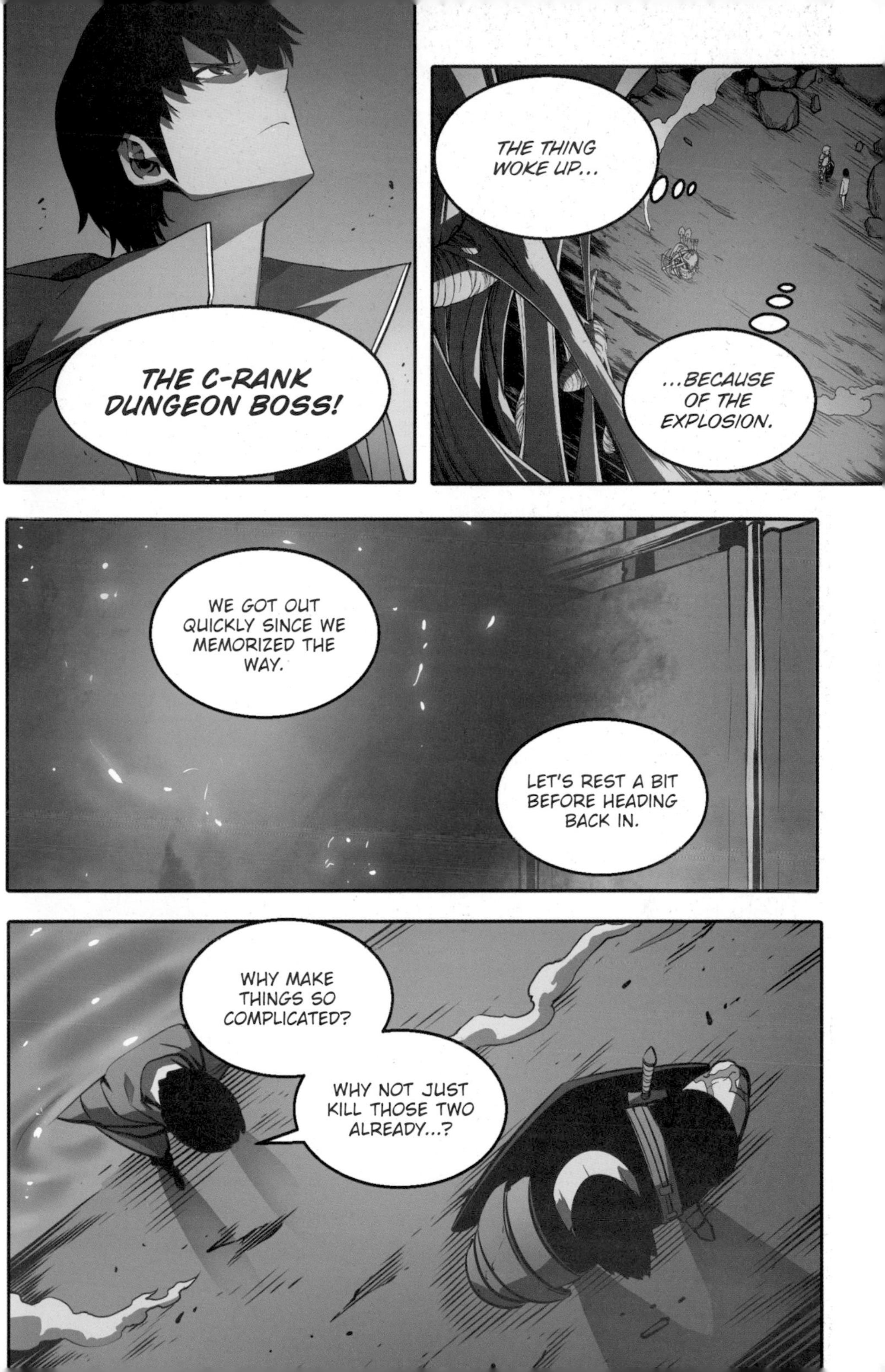
THE C-RANK DUNGEON BOSS!
THE THING WOKE UP...
...BECAUSE OF THE EXPLOSION.
WE GOT OUT QUICKLY SINCE WE MEMORIZED THE WAY.
LET'S REST A BIT BEFORE HEADING BACK IN.
WHY MAKE THINGS SO COMPLICATED?
WHY NOT JUST KILL THOSE TWO ALREADY...?

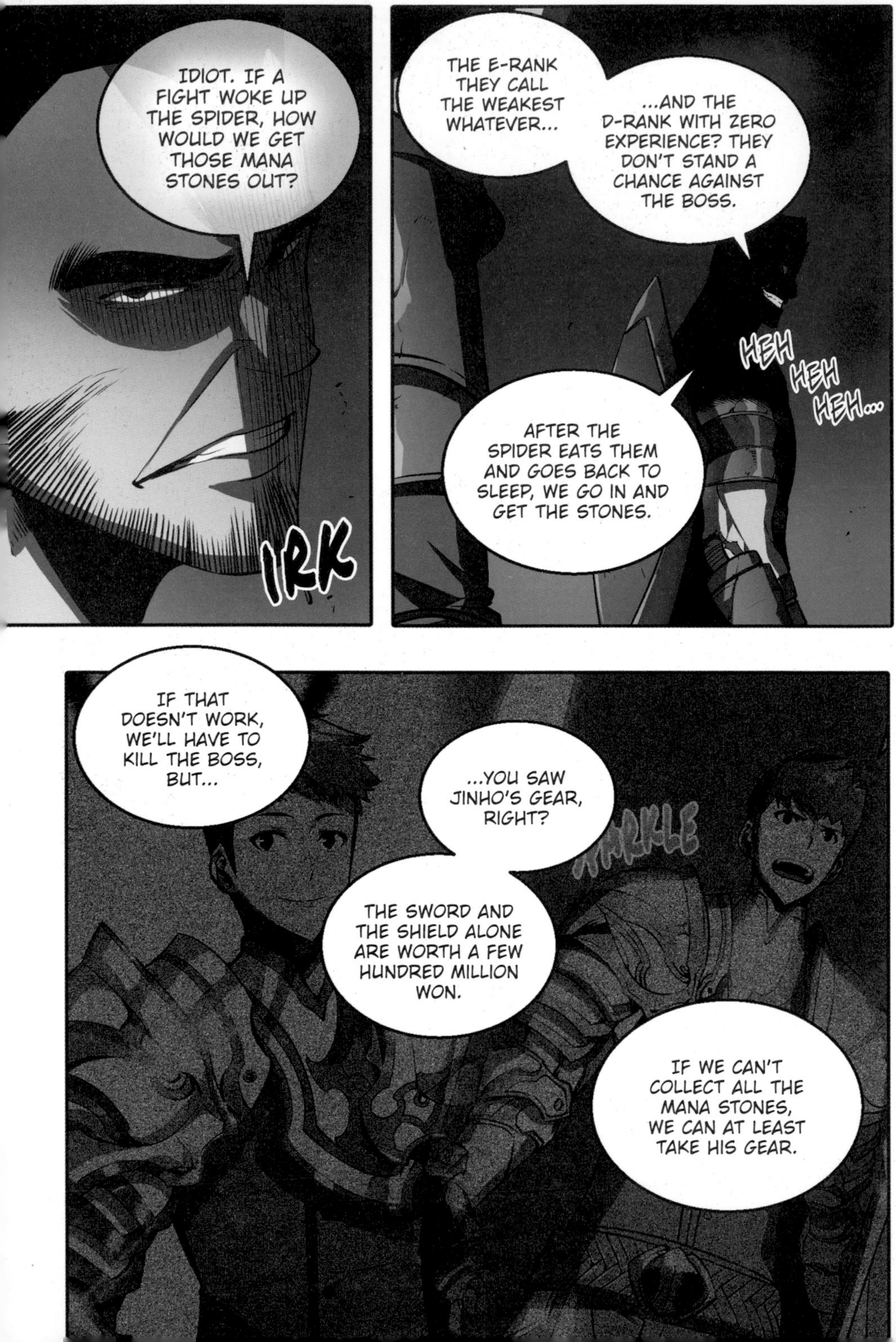
IDIOT. IF A FIGHT WOKE UP THE SPIDER, HOW WOULD WE GET THOSE MANA STONES OUT?
IRK
THE E-RANK THEY CALL THE WEAKEST WHATEVER...
...AND THE D-RANK WITH ZERO EXPERIENCE? THEY DON'T STAND A CHANCE AGAINST THE BOSS.
HEH HEH HEH...
AFTER THE SPIDER EATS THEM AND GOES BACK TO SLEEP, WE GO IN AND GET THE STONES.
IF THAT DOESN'T WORK, WE'LL HAVE TO KILL THE BOSS, BUT...
...YOU SAW JINHO'S GEAR, RIGHT?
THE SWORD AND THE SHIELD ALONE ARE WORTH A FEW HUNDRED MILLION WON.
IF WE CAN'T COLLECT ALL THE MANA STONES, WE CAN AT LEAST TAKE HIS GEAR.

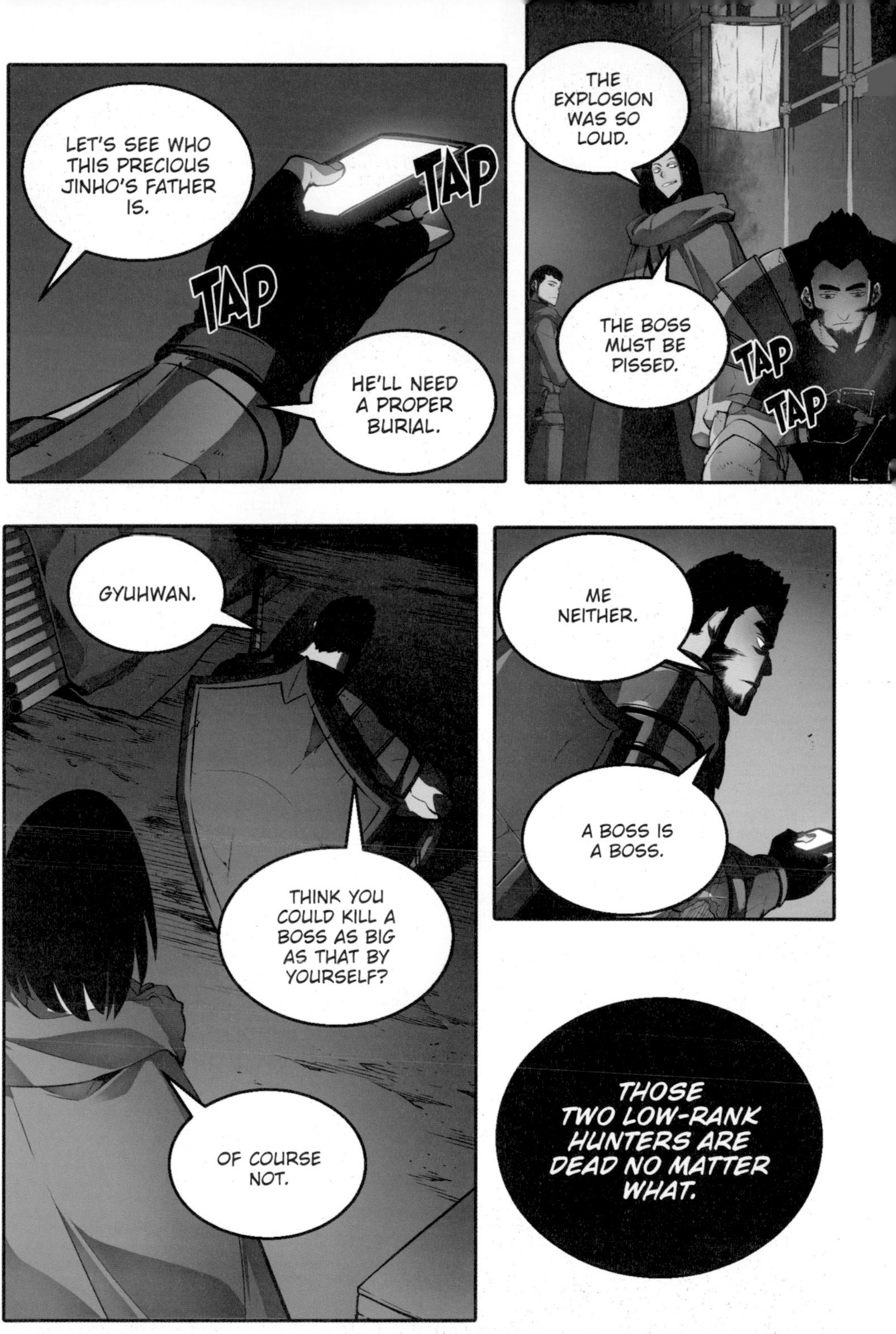
LET'S SEE WHO THIS PRECIOUS JINHO'S FATHER IS.
TAP
TAP
HE'LL NEED A PROPER BURIAL.
THE EXPLOSION WAS SO LOUD.
THE BOSS MUST BE PISSED.
TAP
TAP
GYUHWAN.
THINK YOU COULD KILL A BOSS AS BIG AS THAT BY YOURSELF?
OF COURSE NOT.
ME NEITHER.
A BOSS IS A BOSS.
THOSE TWO LOW-RANK HUNTERS ARE DEAD NO MATTER WHAT.

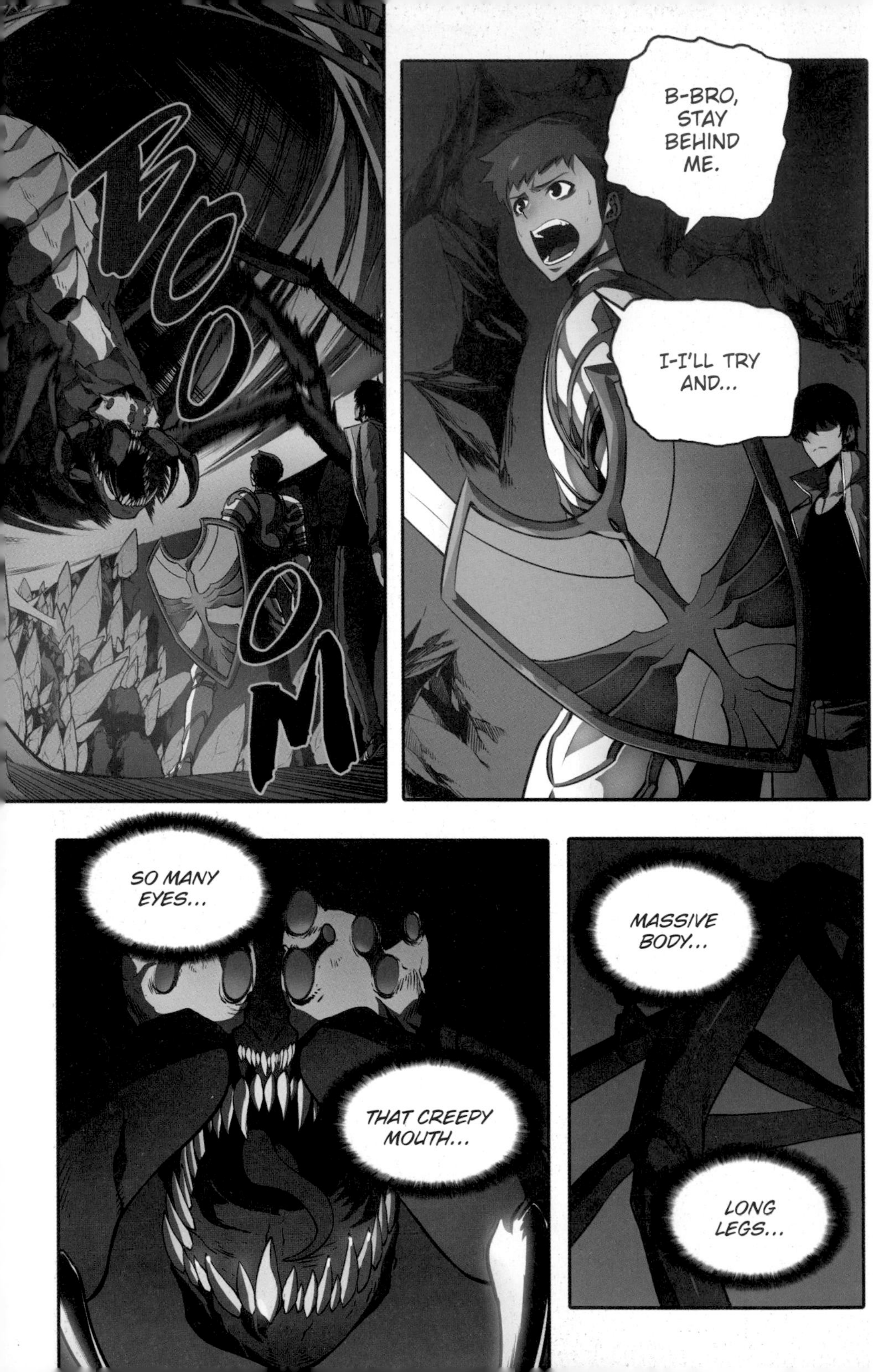
BOOOOM
B-BRO, STAY BEHIND ME.
I-I'LL TRY AND...
SO MANY EYES...
THAT CREEPY MOUTH...
MASSIVE BODY...
LONG LEGS...

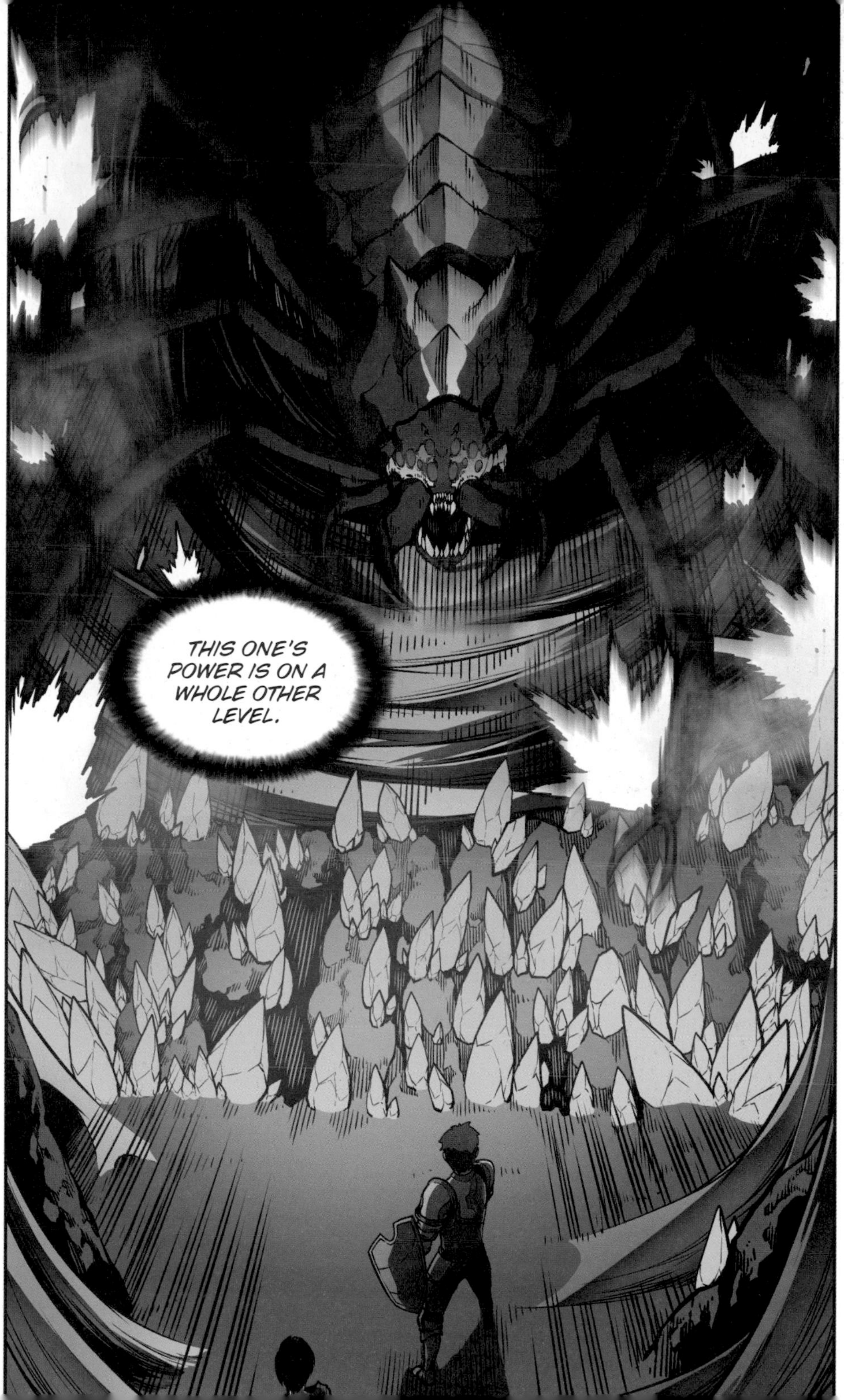
THIS ONE'S POWER IS ON A WHOLE OTHER LEVEL.

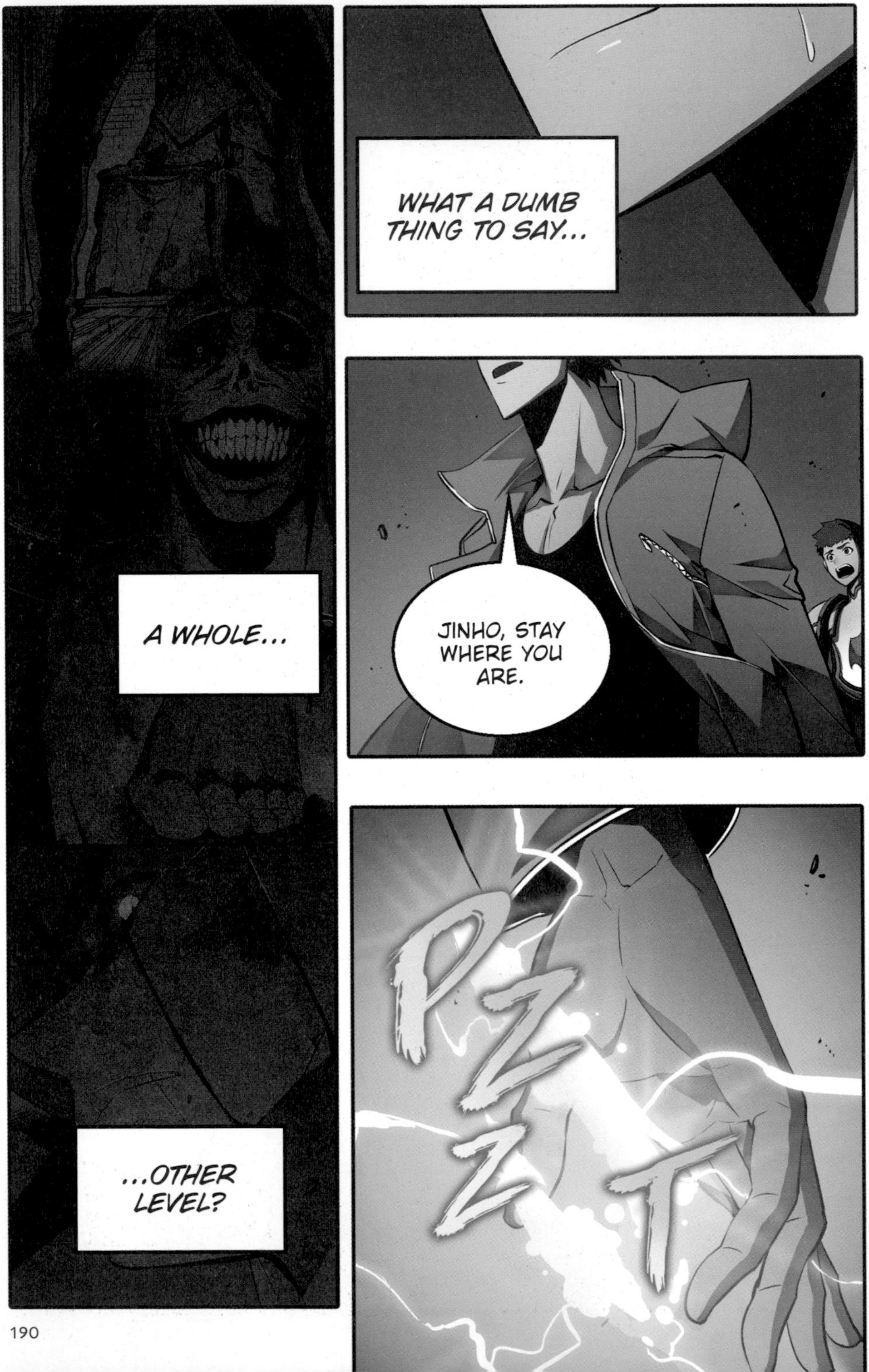
A WHOLE...
...OTHER LEVEL?
WHAT A DUMB THING TO SAY...
JINHO, STAY WHERE YOU ARE.
PZZT

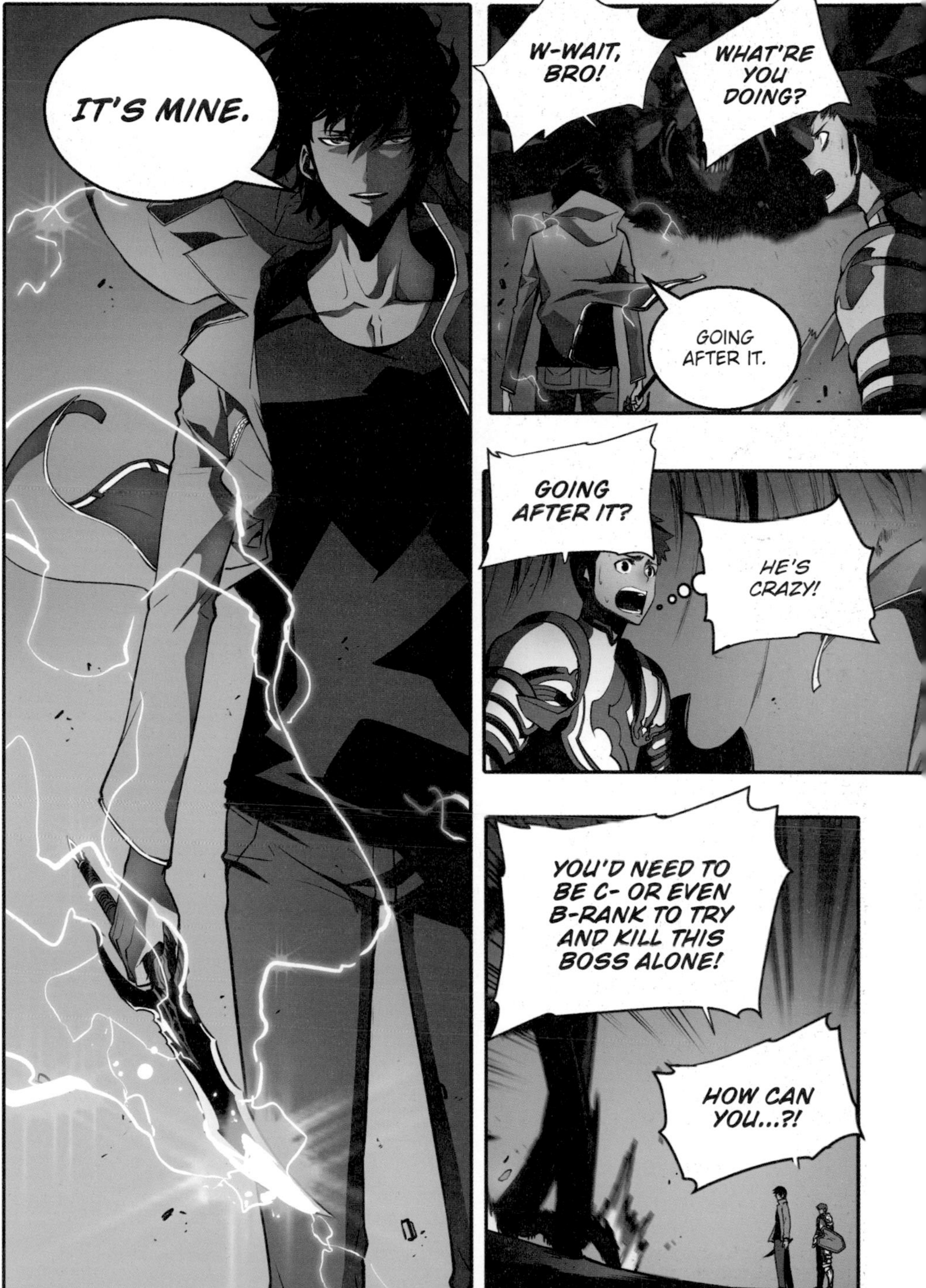
IT'S MINE.
W-WAIT, BRO!
WHAT'RE YOU DOING?
GOING AFTER IT.
GOING AFTER IT?
HE'S CRAZY!
YOU'D NEED TO BE C- OR EVEN B-RANK TO TRY AND KILL THIS BOSS ALONE!
HOW CAN YOU...?!

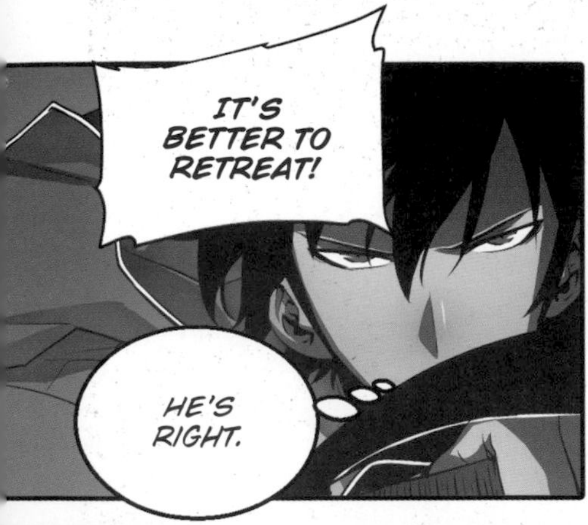
IT'S BETTER TO RETREAT!
HE'S RIGHT.
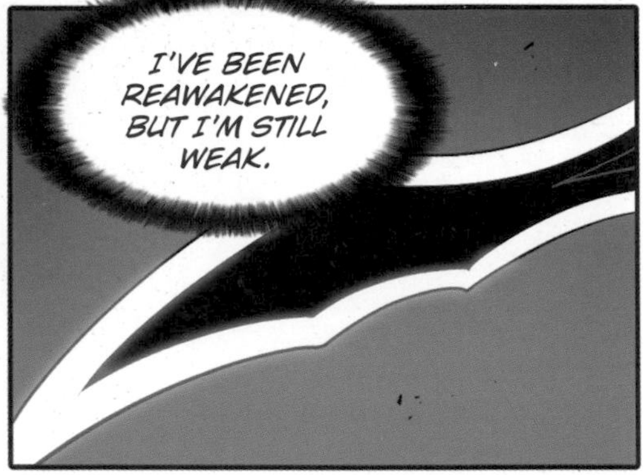
I'VE BEEN REAWAKENED, BUT I'M STILL WEAK.
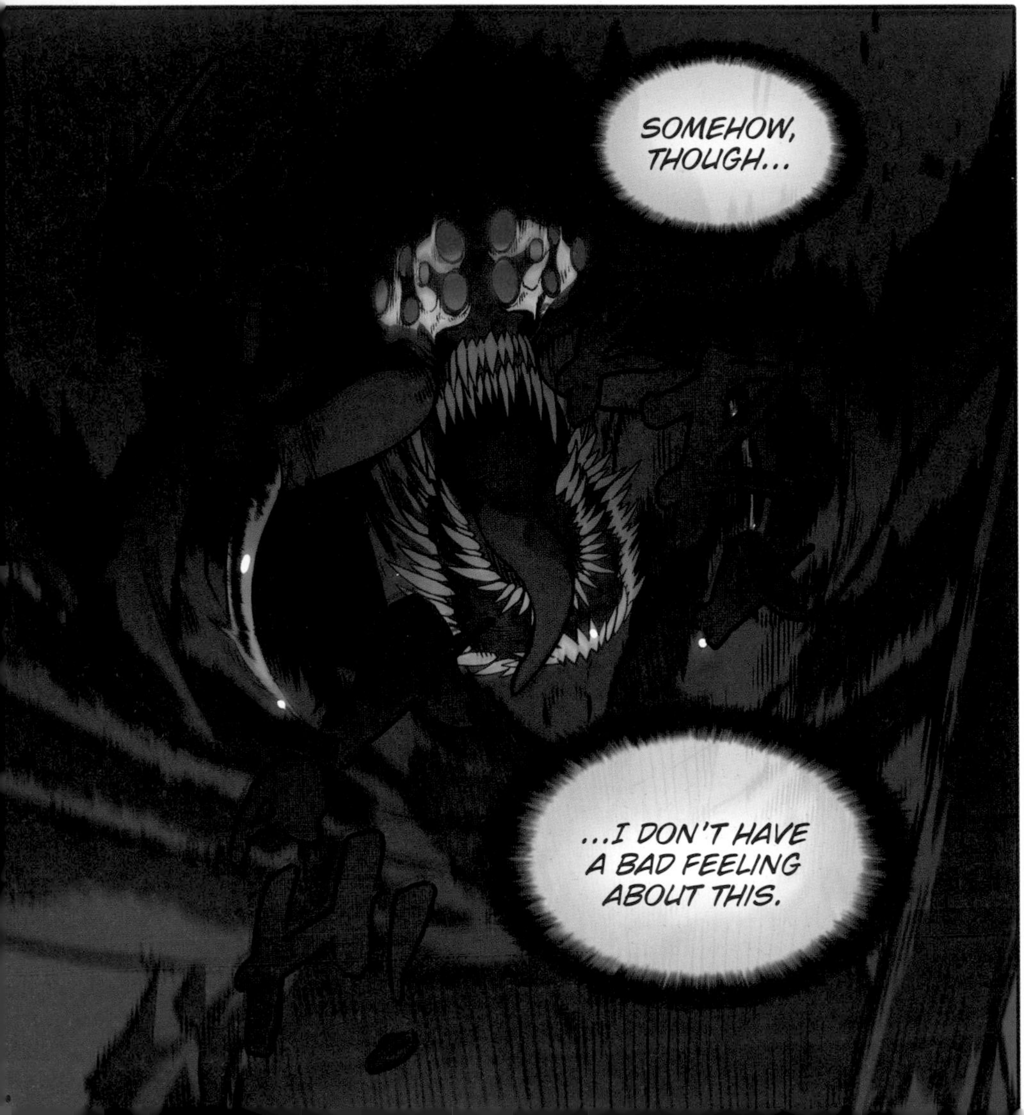
SOMEHOW, THOUGH...
...I DON'T HAVE A BAD FEELING ABOUT THIS.

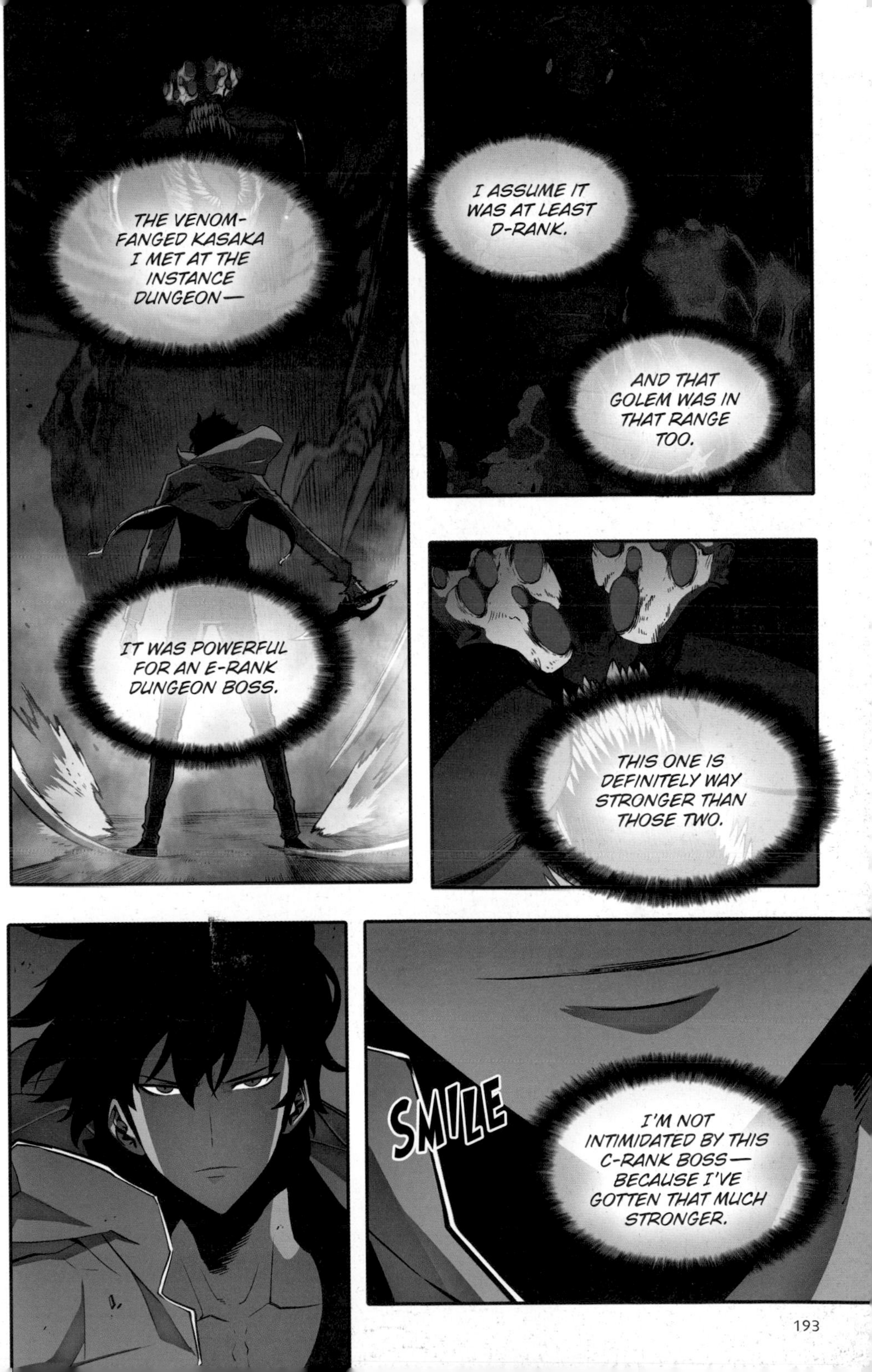
THE VENOM-FANGED KASAKA I MET AT THE INSTANCE DUNGEON—
IT WAS POWERFUL FOR AN E-RANK DUNGEON BOSS.
I ASSUME IT WAS AT LEAST D-RANK.
AND THAT GOLEM WAS IN THAT RANGE TOO.
THIS ONE IS DEFINITELY WAY STRONGER THAN THOSE TWO.
SMILE
I'M NOT INTIMIDATED BY THIS C-RANK BOSS—BECAUSE I'VE GOTTEN THAT MUCH STRONGER.

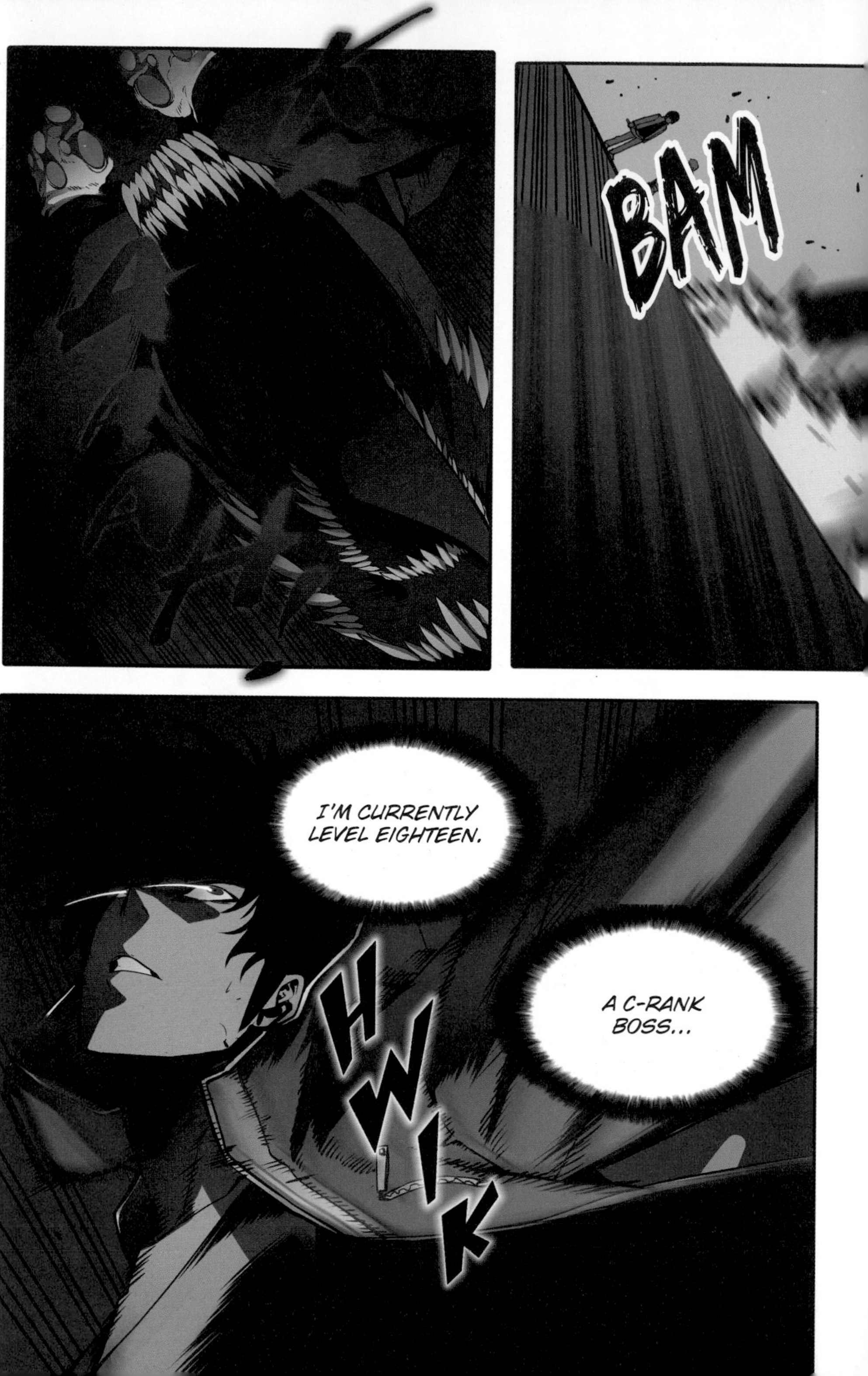
BAM
I'M CURRENTLY LEVEL EIGHTEEN.
HWIK
A C-RANK BOSS...

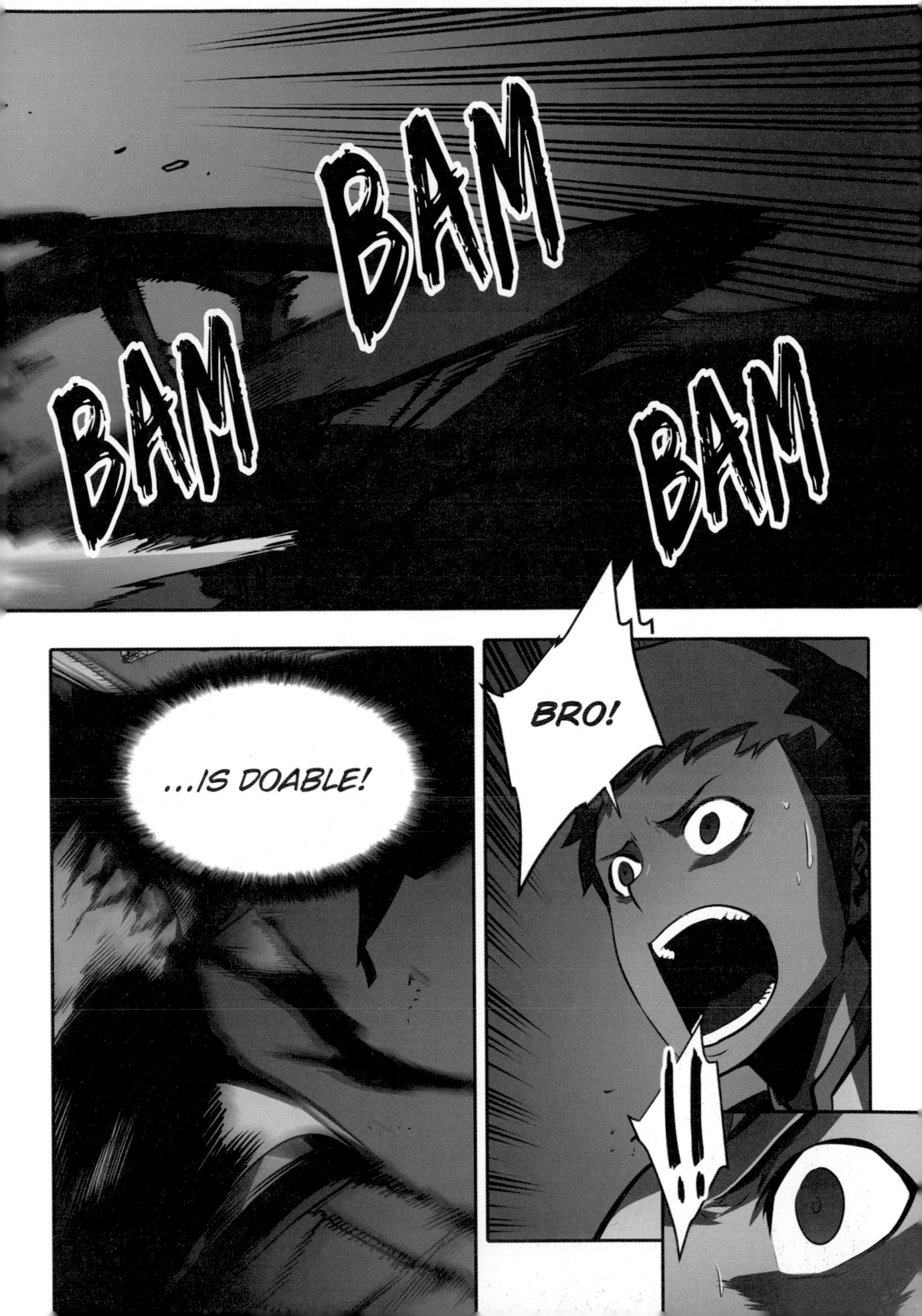
BAM
BAM
BAM
...IS DOABLE!
BRO!
!!

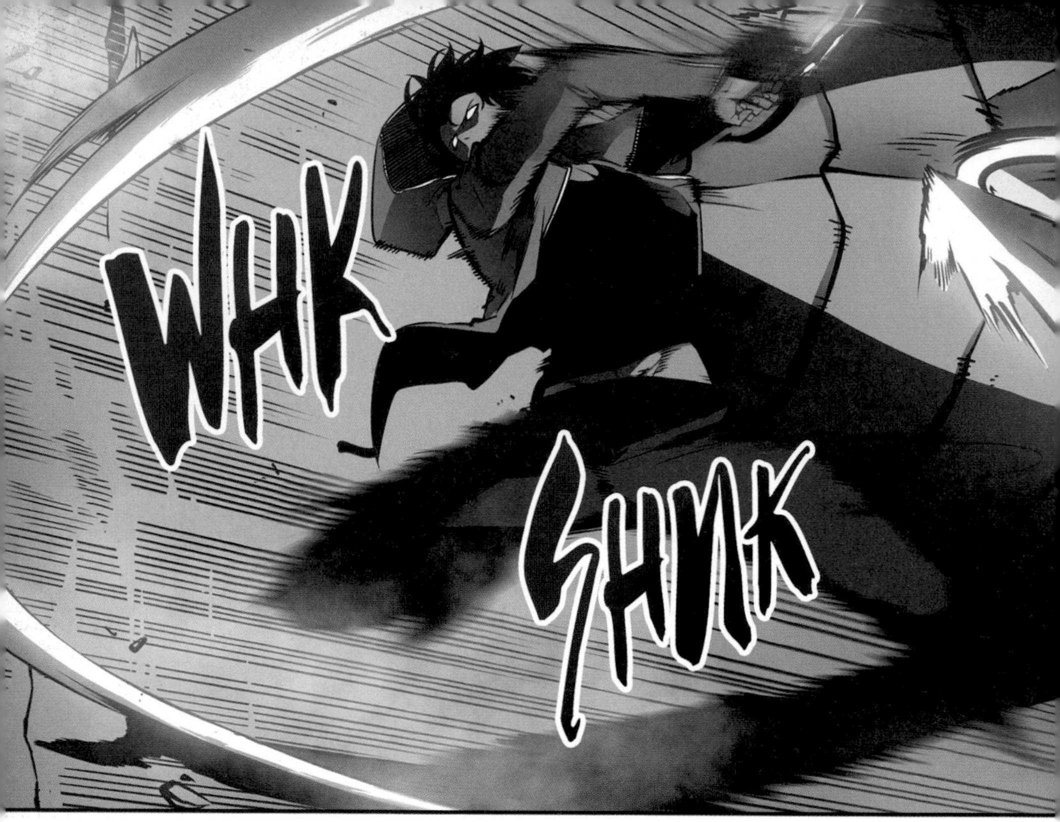
WHK
SHNK
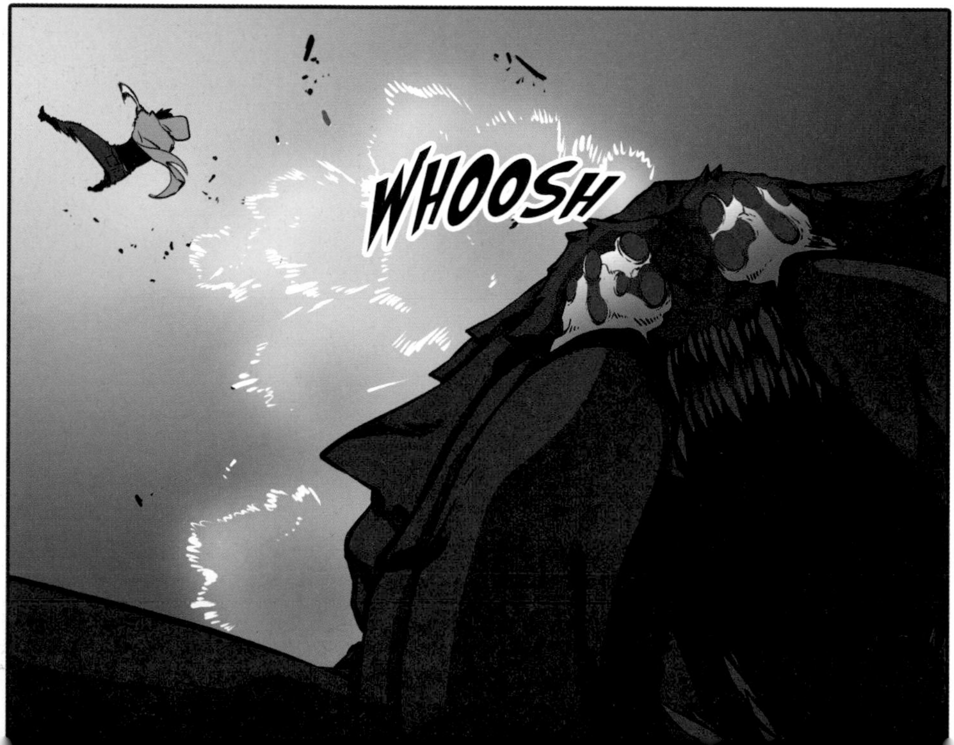
WHOOSH

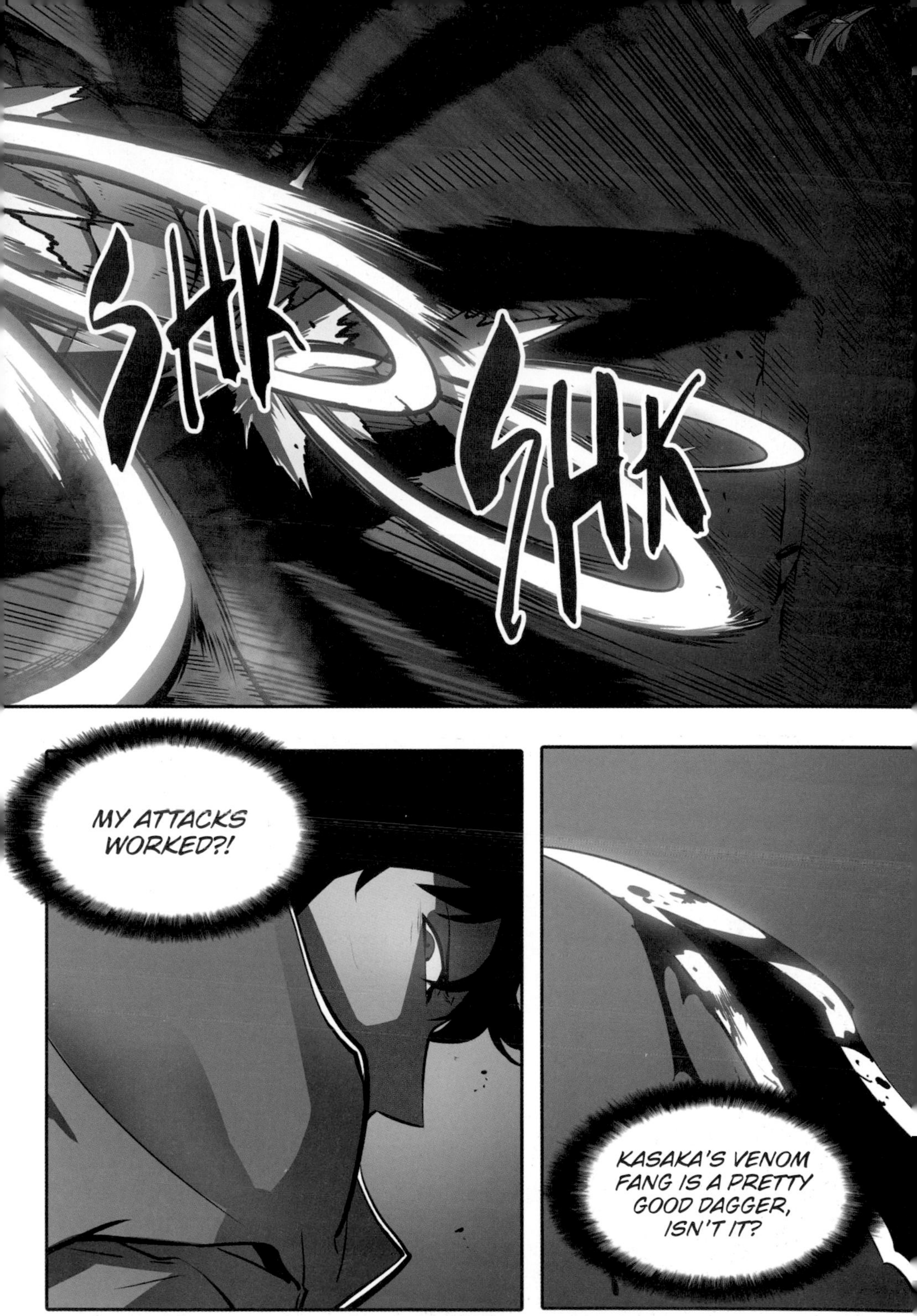
SHK
SHK
MY ATTACKS WORKED?!
KASAKA'S VENOM FANG IS A PRETTY GOOD DAGGER, ISN'T IT?

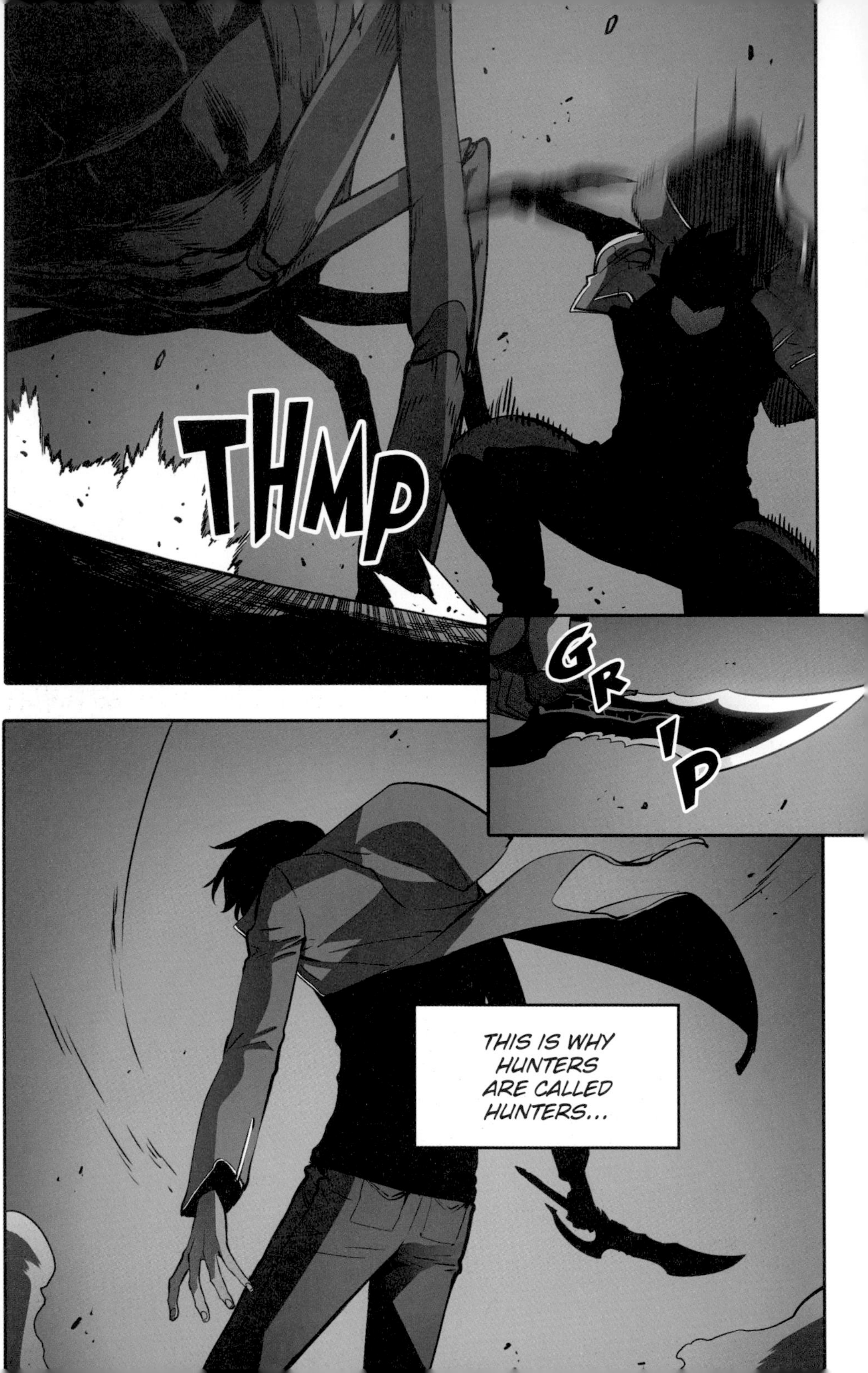
THMP
GRIP
THIS IS WHY HUNTERS ARE CALLED HUNTERS...

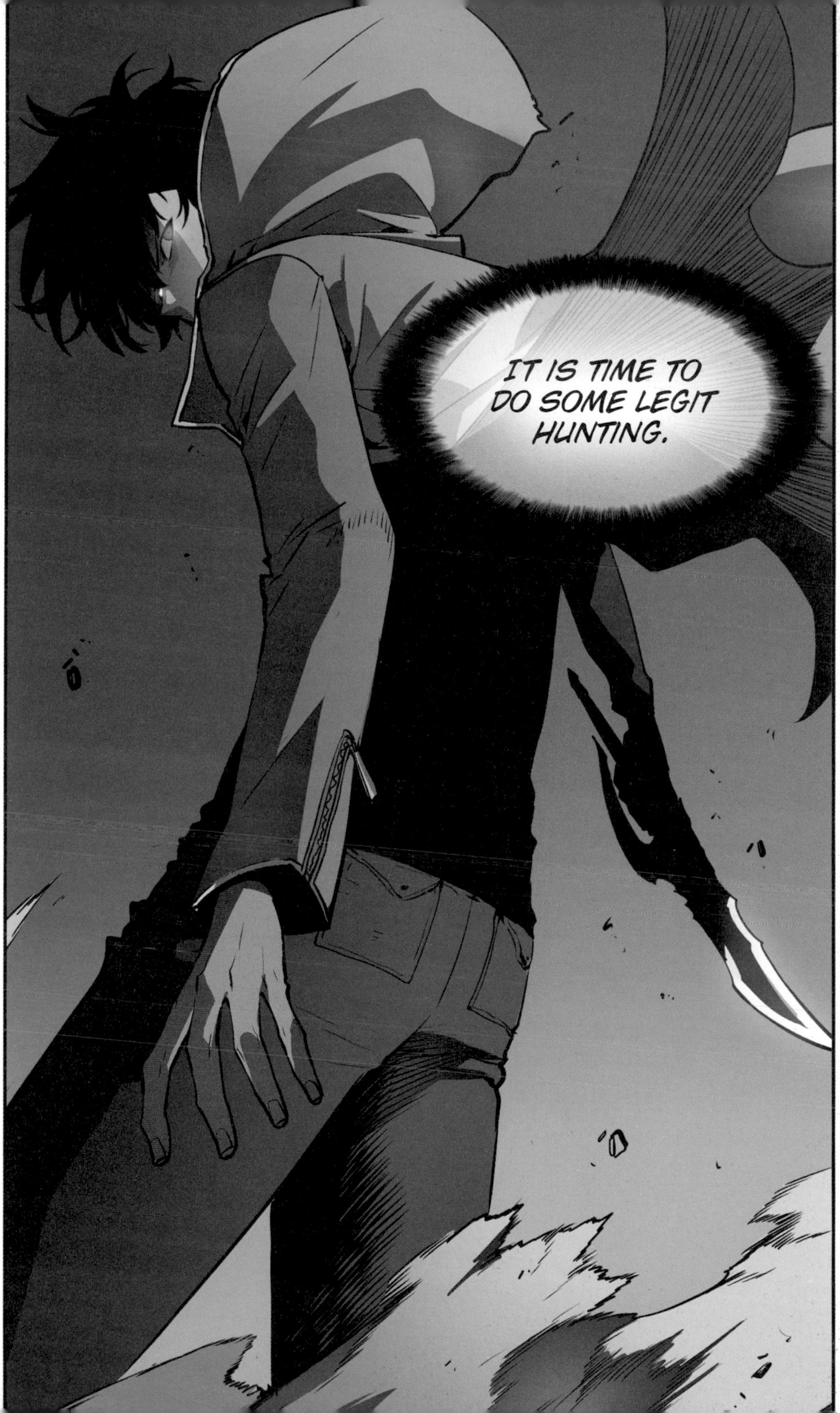
IT IS TIME TO DO SOME LEGIT HUNTING.

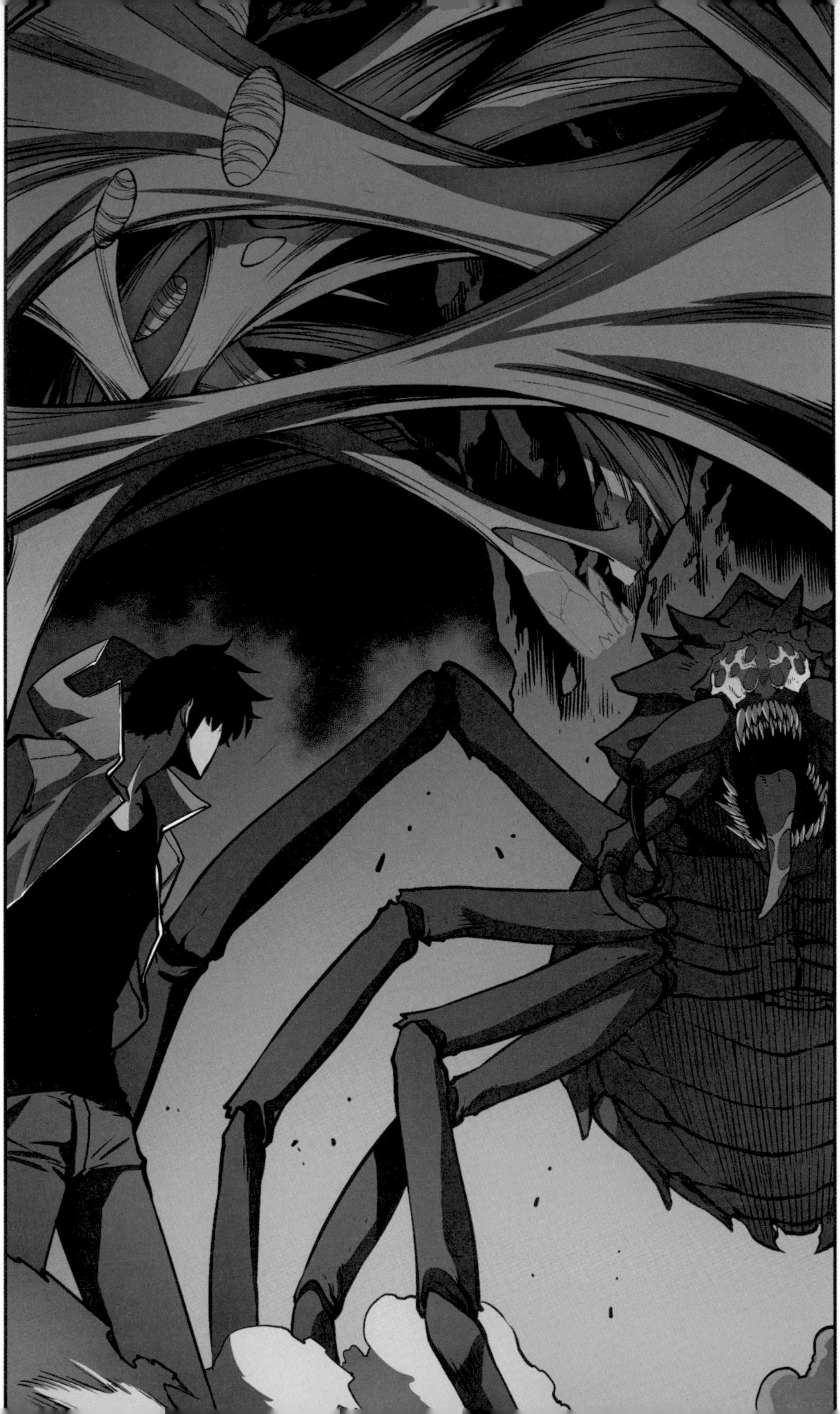

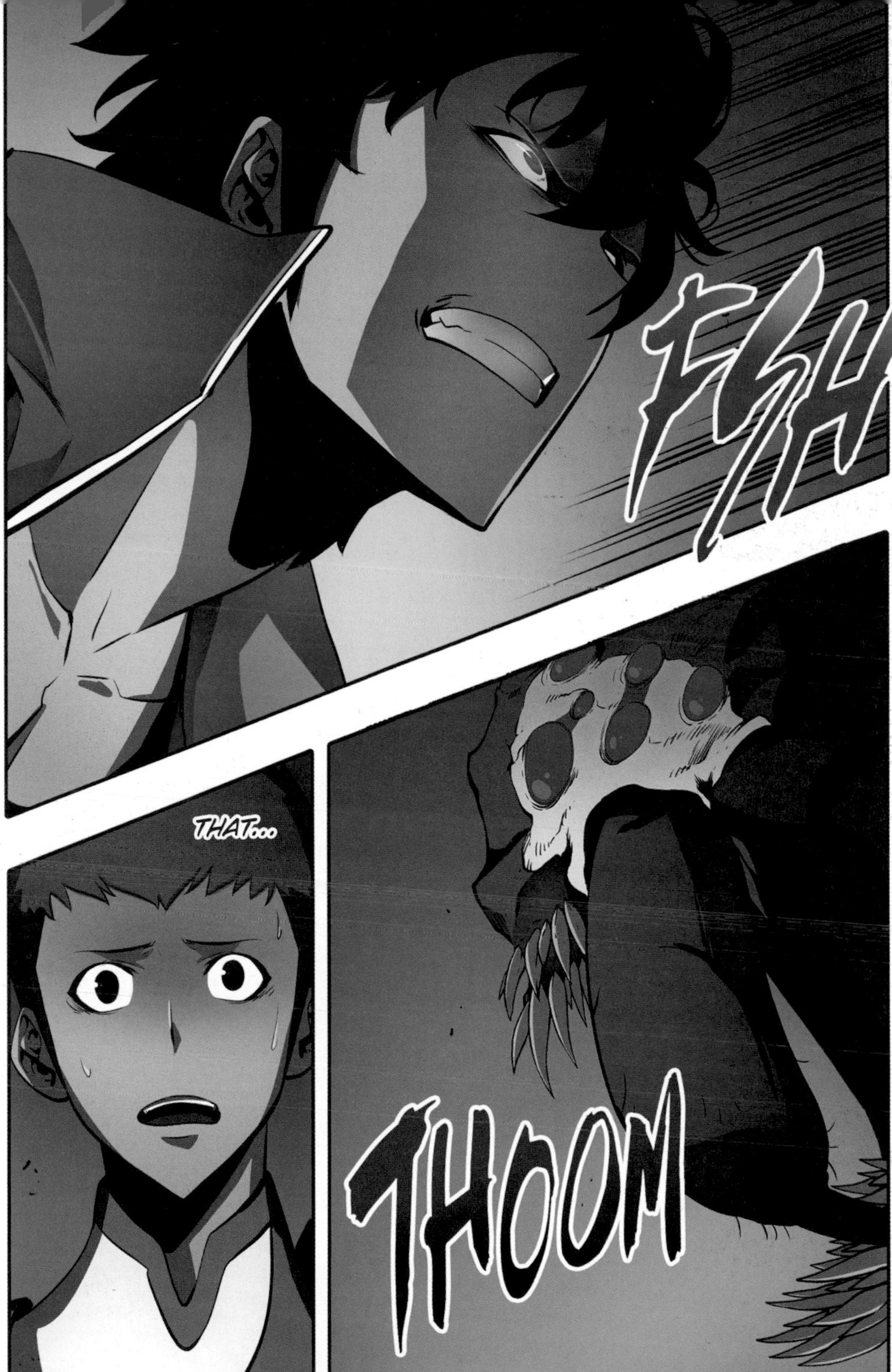
FSH
THAT...
THOOM

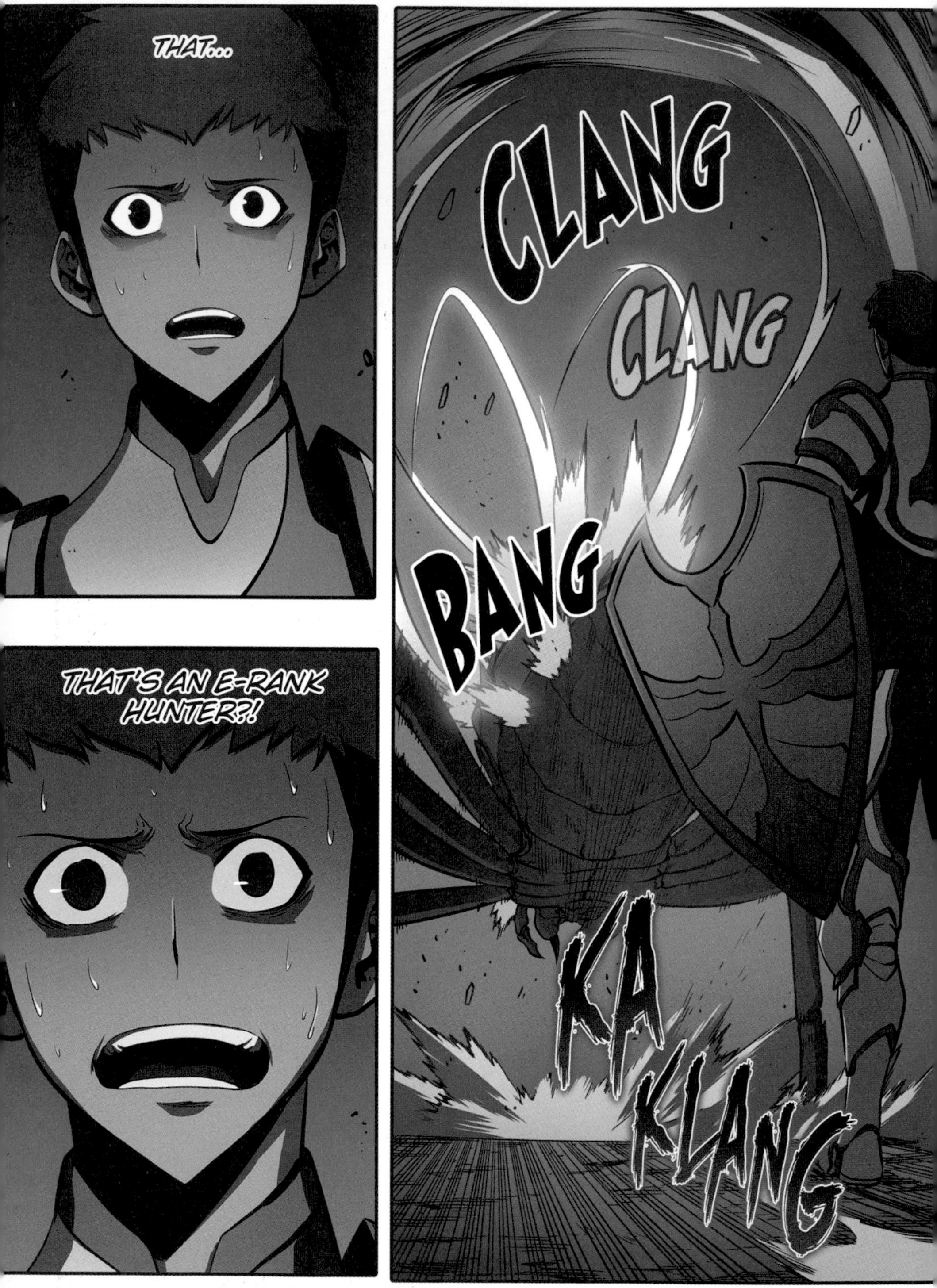
THAT...
THAT'S AN E-RANK HUNTER?!
CLANG
CLANG
BANG
KA KLANG

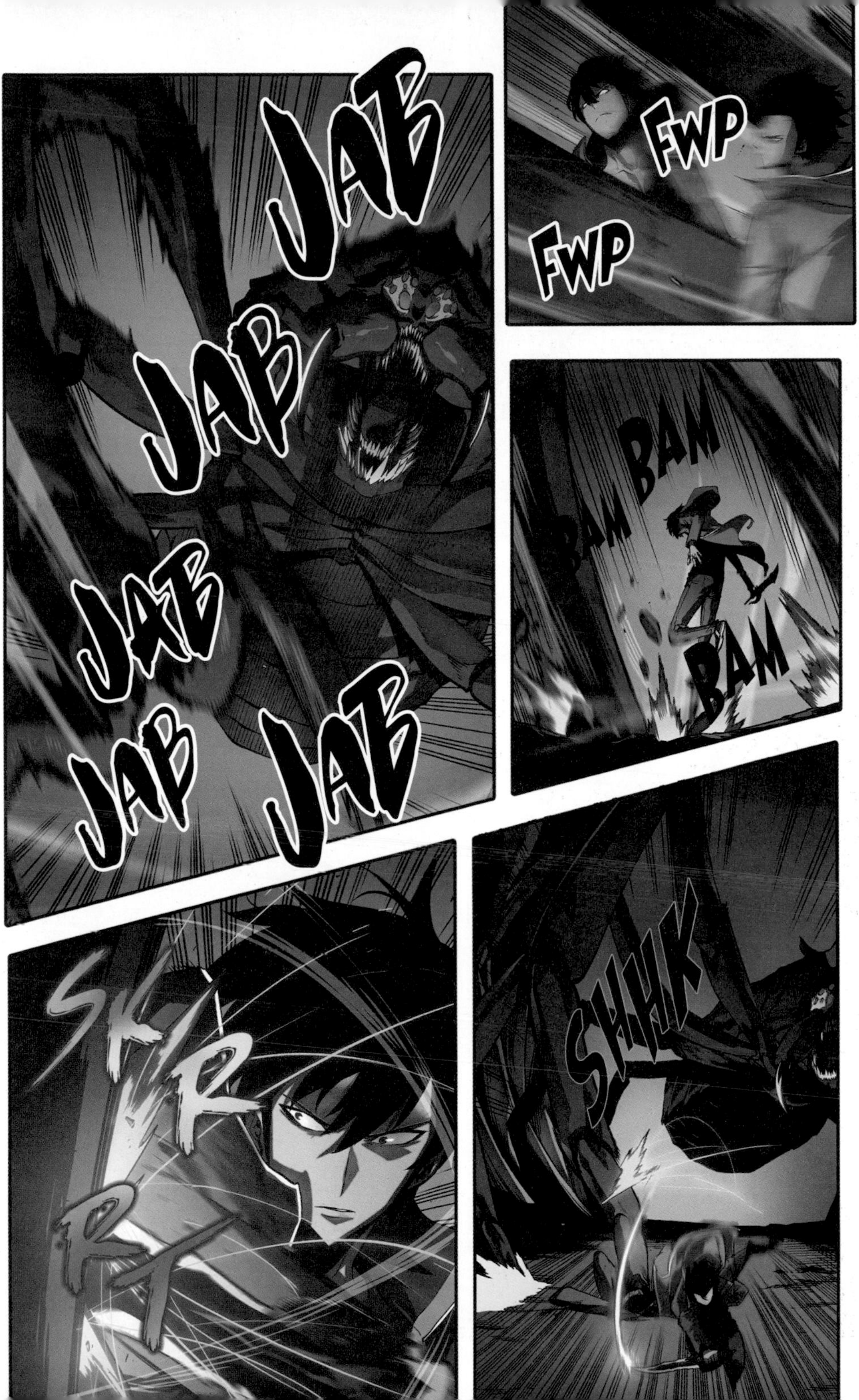
JAB
JAB
JAB
JAB
JAB
FWP
FWP
BAM
BAM
BAM
BAM
SKRRT
SHHK

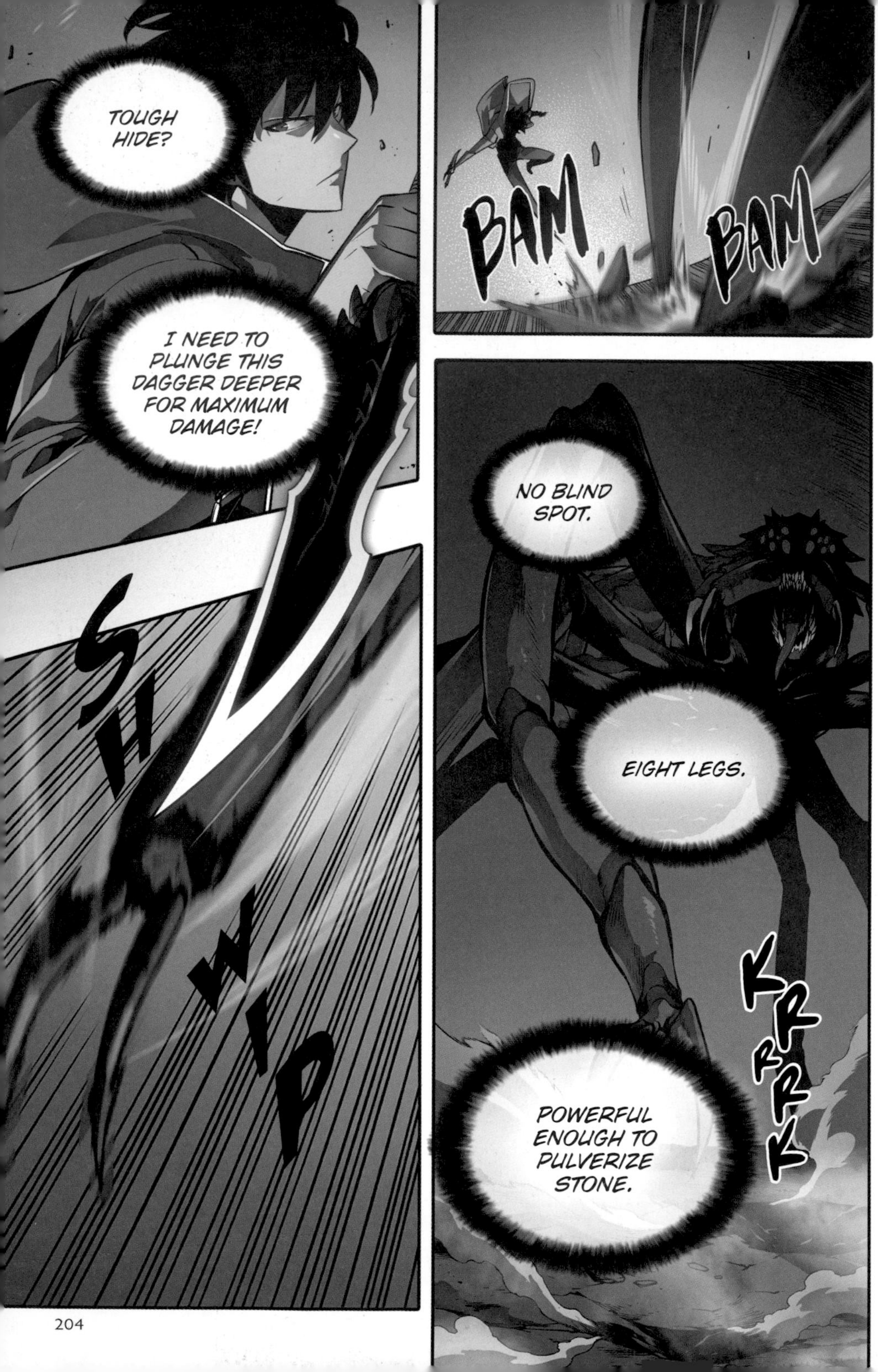
TOUGH HIDE?
I NEED TO PLUNGE THIS DAGGER DEEPER FOR MAXIMUM DAMAGE!
BAM
BAM
SHWIP
NO BLIND SPOT.
EIGHT LEGS.
POWERFUL ENOUGH TO PULVERIZE STONE.
KRRRK

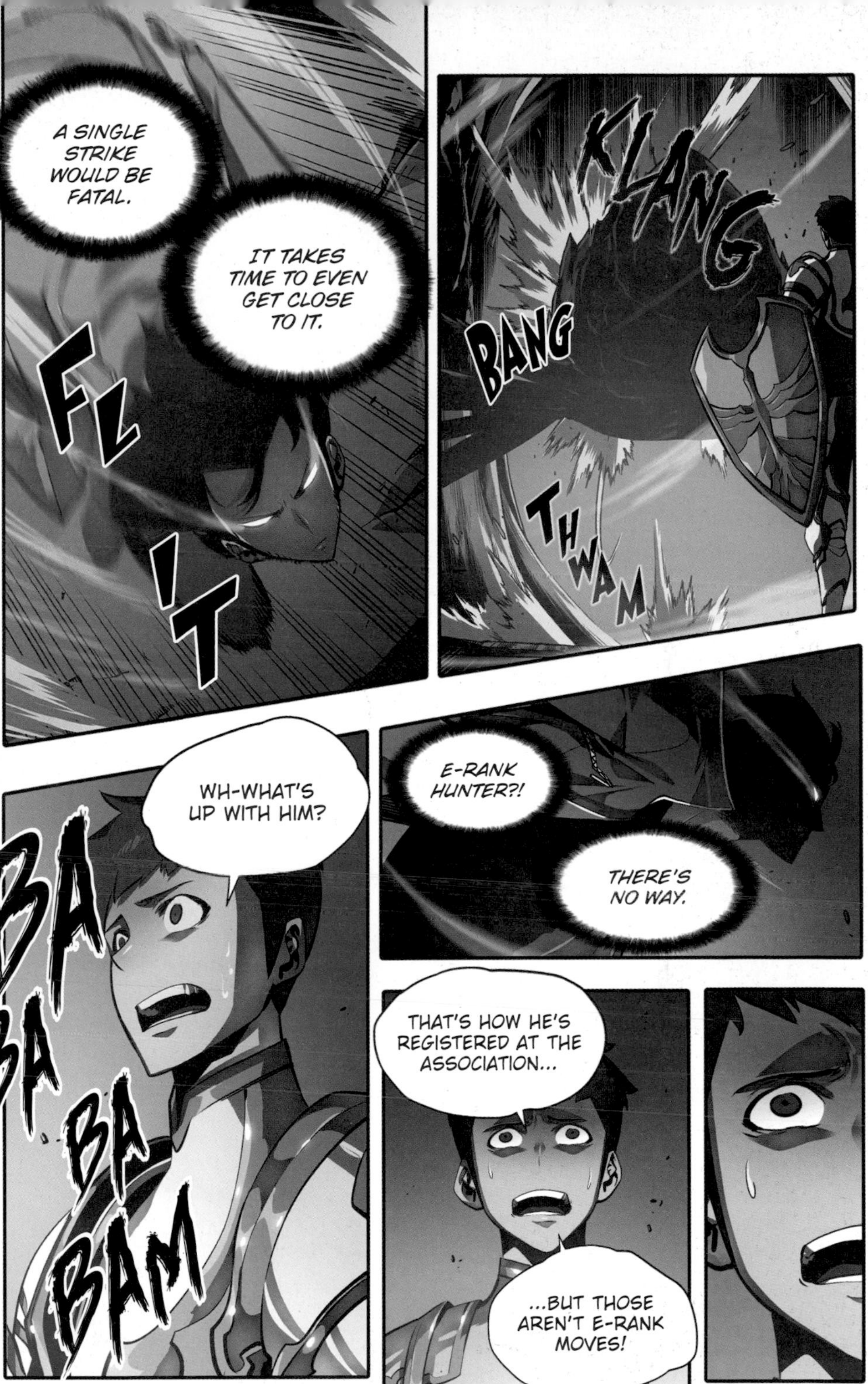
A SINGLE STRIKE WOULD BE FATAL.
IT TAKES TIME TO EVEN GET CLOSE TO IT.
FLIT
KLANG
BANG
THWAM
WH-WHAT'S UP WITH HIM?
BA BA BA BAM
E-RANK HUNTER?!
THERE'S NO WAY.
THAT'S HOW HE'S REGISTERED AT THE ASSOCIATION...
...BUT THOSE AREN'T E-RANK MOVES!

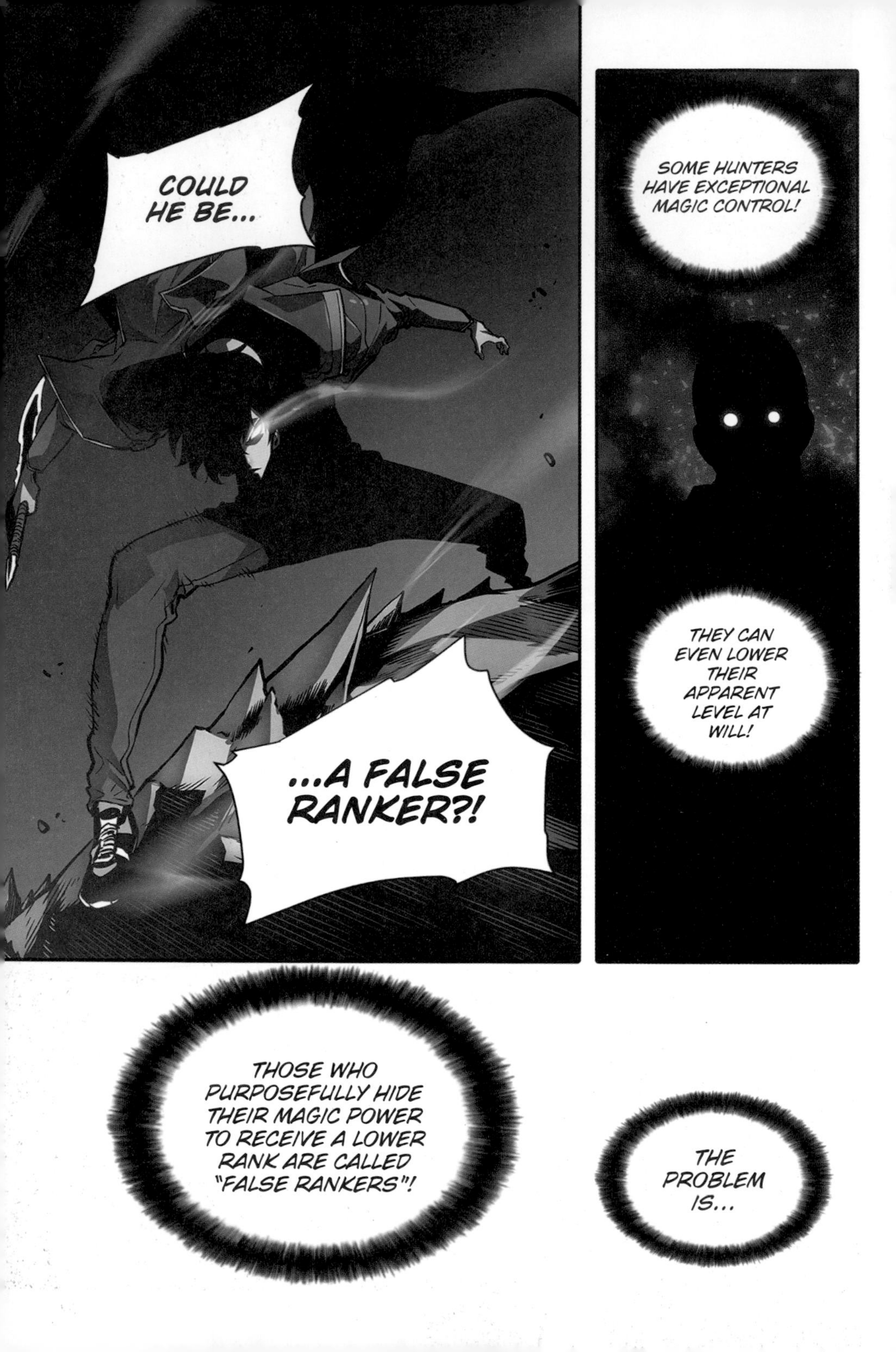
COULD HE BE...
...A FALSE RANKER?!
SOME HUNTERS HAVE EXCEPTIONAL MAGIC CONTROL!
THEY CAN EVEN LOWER THEIR APPARENT LEVEL AT WILL!
THOSE WHO PURPOSEFULLY HIDE THEIR MAGIC POWER TO RECEIVE A LOWER RANK ARE CALLED "FALSE RANKERS"!
THE PROBLEM IS...

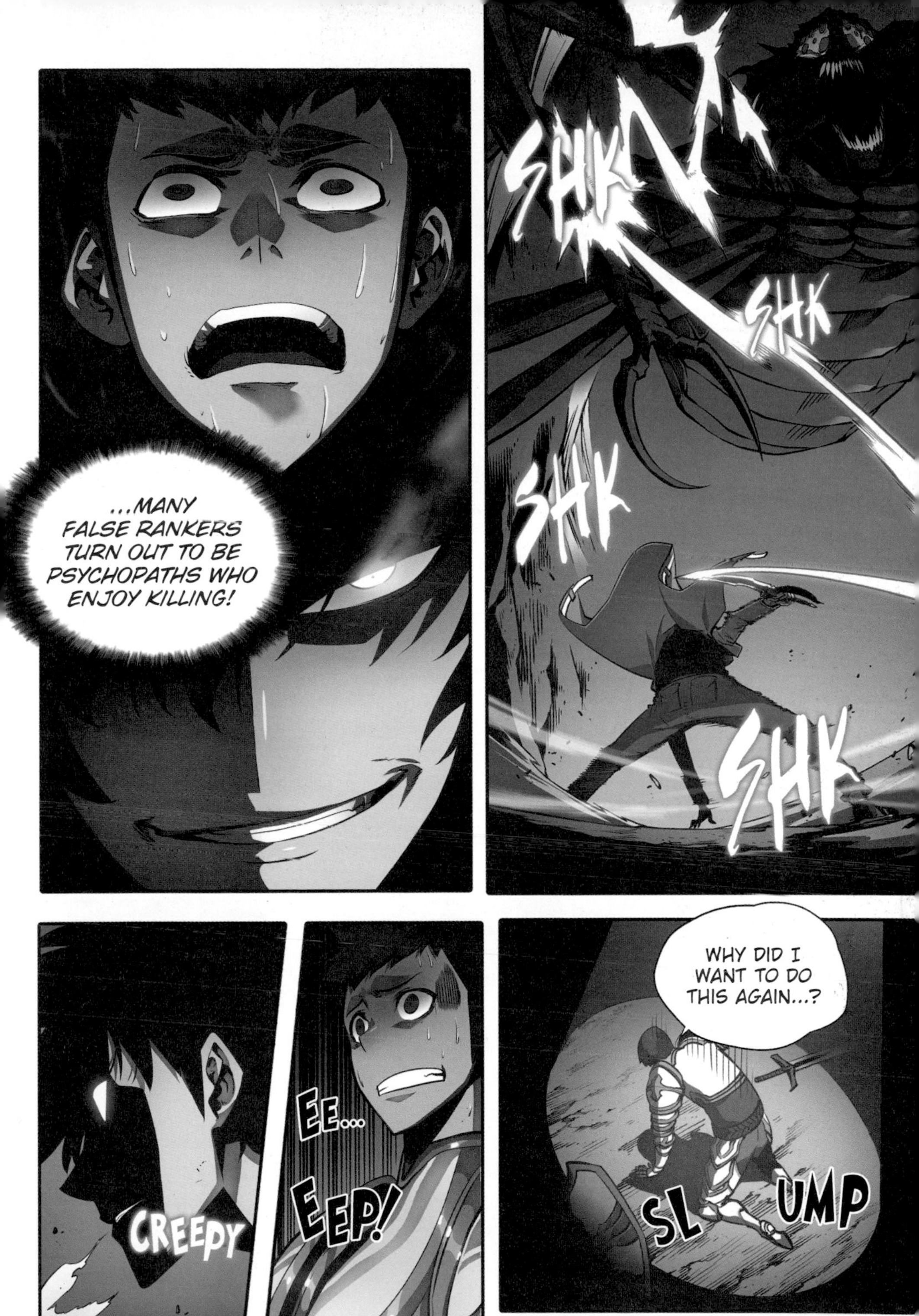
...MANY FALSE RANKERS TURN OUT TO BE PSYCHOPATHS WHO ENJOY KILLING!
SHK
SHK
SHK
SHK
CREEPY
EE...
EEP!
WHY DID I WANT TO DO THIS AGAIN...?
SL UMP

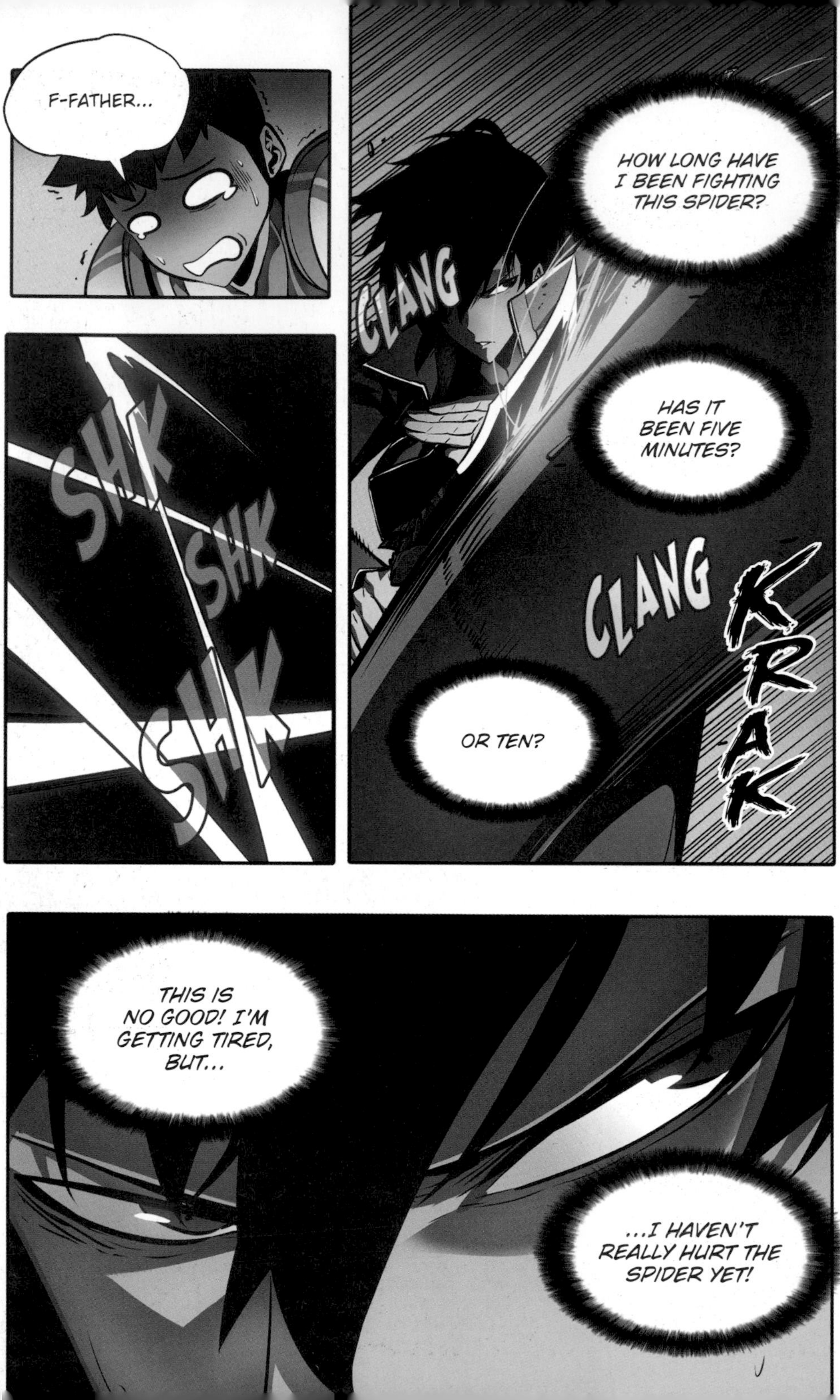
F-FATHER...
SHK
SHK
SHK
HOW LONG HAVE I BEEN FIGHTING THIS SPIDER?
CLANG
HAS IT BEEN FIVE MINUTES?
CLANG
KRAK
OR TEN?
THIS IS NO GOOD! I'M GETTING TIRED, BUT...
...I HAVEN'T REALLY HURT THE SPIDER YET!

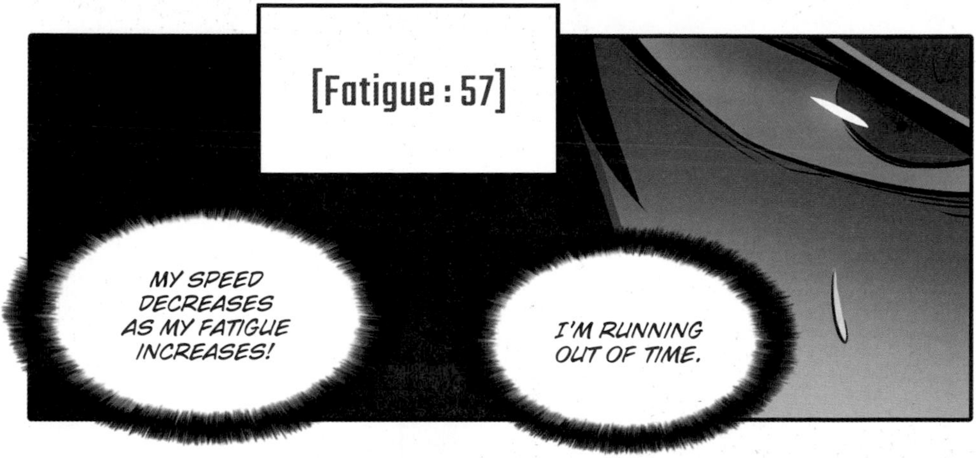
[Fatigue : 57]
MY SPEED DECREASES AS MY FATIGUE INCREASES!
I'M RUNNING OUT OF TIME.

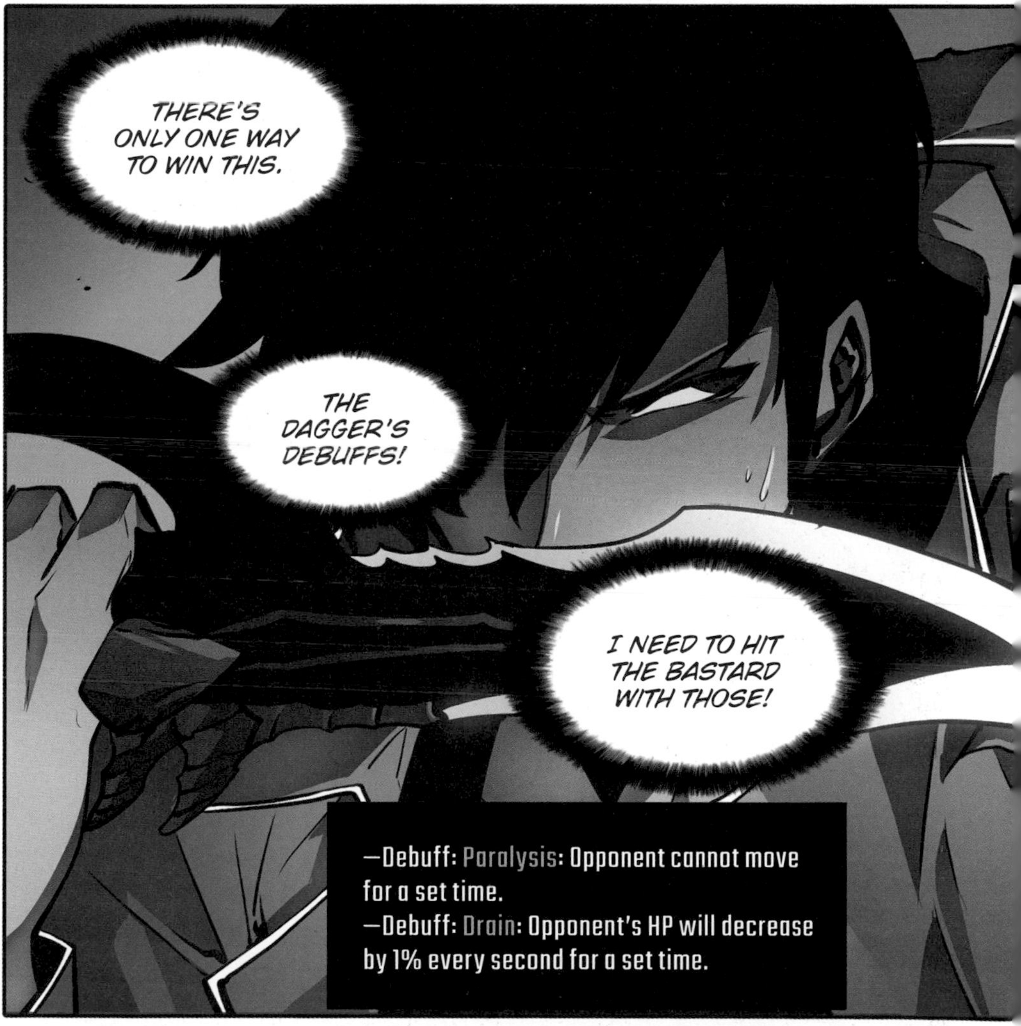
THERE'S ONLY ONE WAY TO WIN THIS.
THE DAGGER'S DEBUFFS!
I NEED TO HIT THE BASTARD WITH THOSE!
—Debuff: Paralysis: Opponent cannot move for a set time.
—Debuff: Drain: Opponent's HP will decrease by 1% every second for a set time.

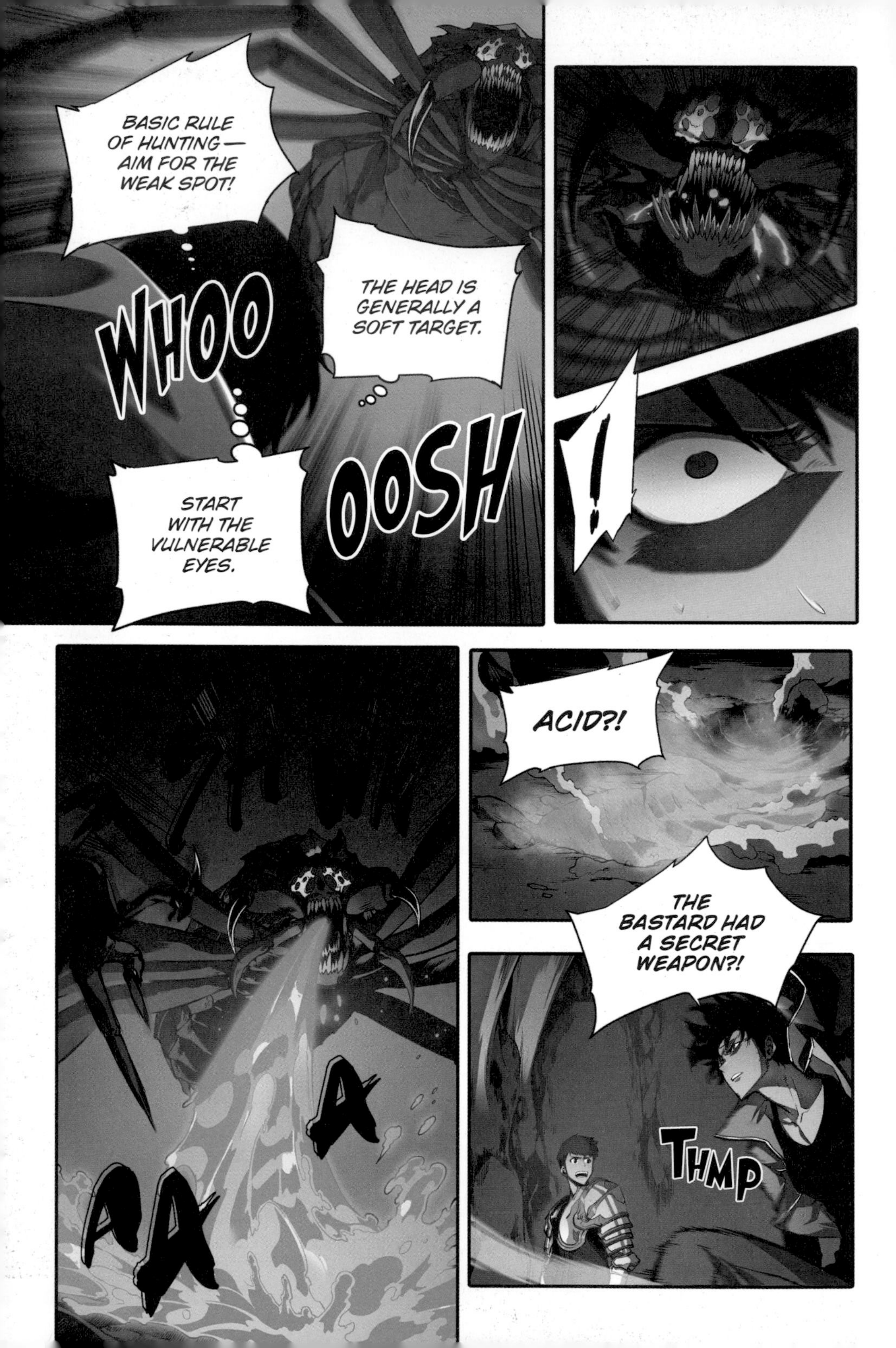
BASIC RULE OF HUNTING— AIM FOR THE WEAK SPOT!
WHOO
THE HEAD IS GENERALLY A SOFT TARGET.
START WITH THE VULNERABLE EYES.
OOSH
!
AA
A
ACID?!
THE BASTARD HAD A SECRET WEAPON?!
THMP

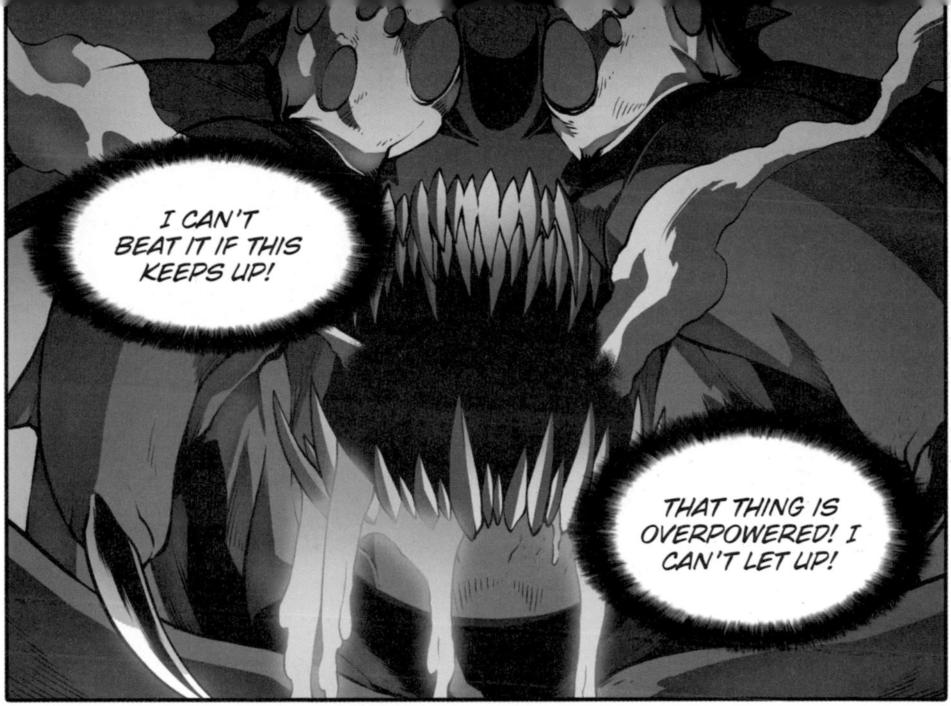
I CAN'T BEAT IT IF THIS KEEPS UP!
THAT THING IS OVERPOWERED! I CAN'T LET UP!

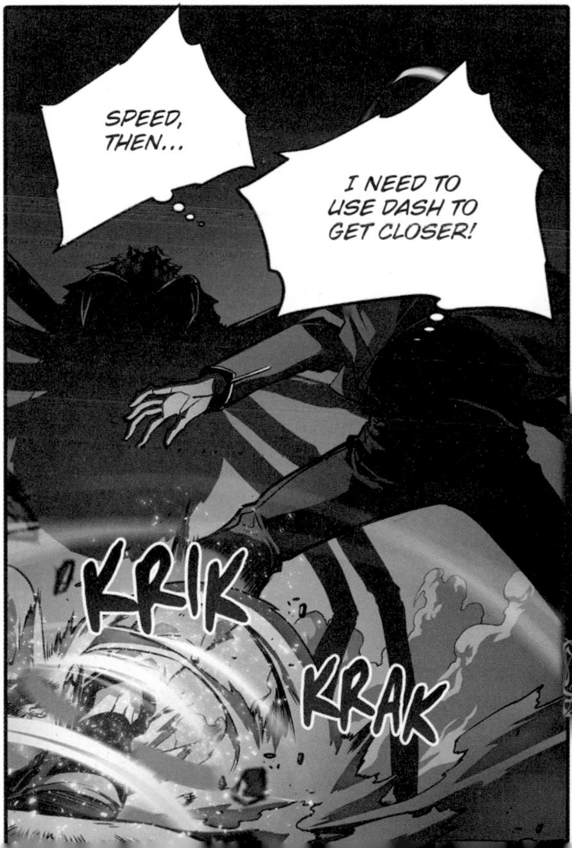
SPEED, THEN...
I NEED TO USE DASH TO GET CLOSER!
KRIK
KRAK

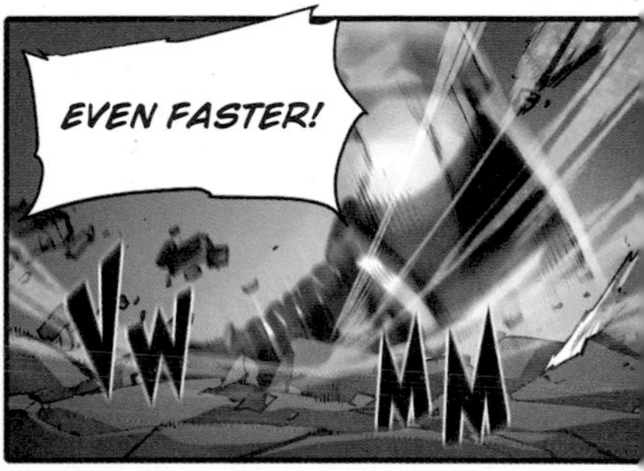
EVEN FASTER!
VW
MM

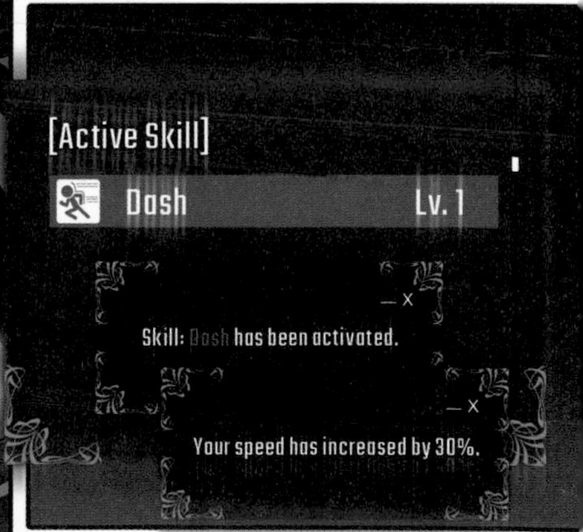
[Active Skill]
Dash Lv. 1
Skill: Dash has been activated.
Your speed has increased by 30%.

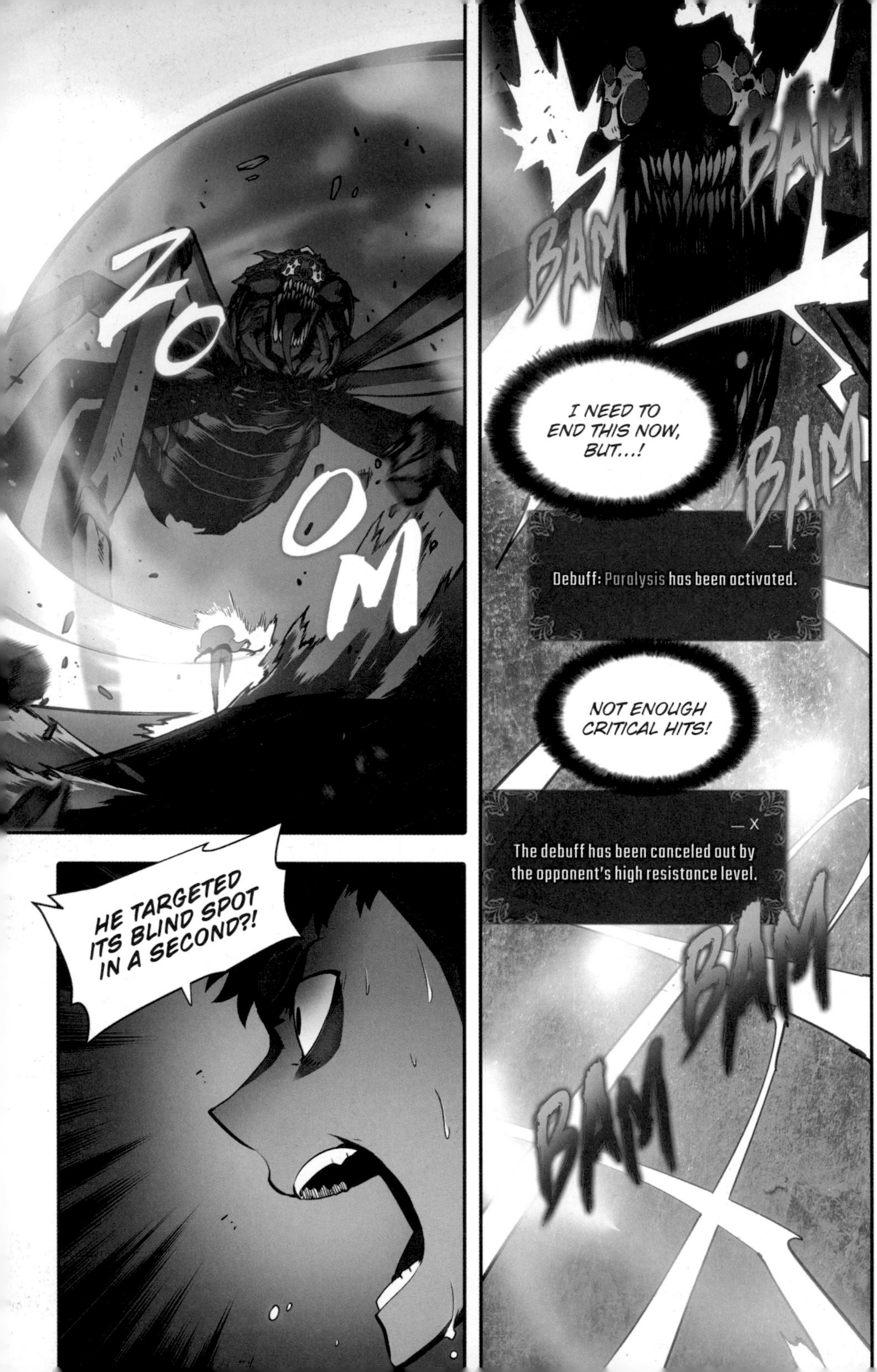
ZOOOM
HE TARGETED ITS BLIND SPOT IN A SECOND?!
BAM BAM
BAM
I NEED TO END THIS NOW, BUT...!
BAM
Debuff: Paralysis has been activated.
NOT ENOUGH CRITICAL HITS!
The debuff has been canceled out by the opponent's high resistance level.
BAM BAM
BAM

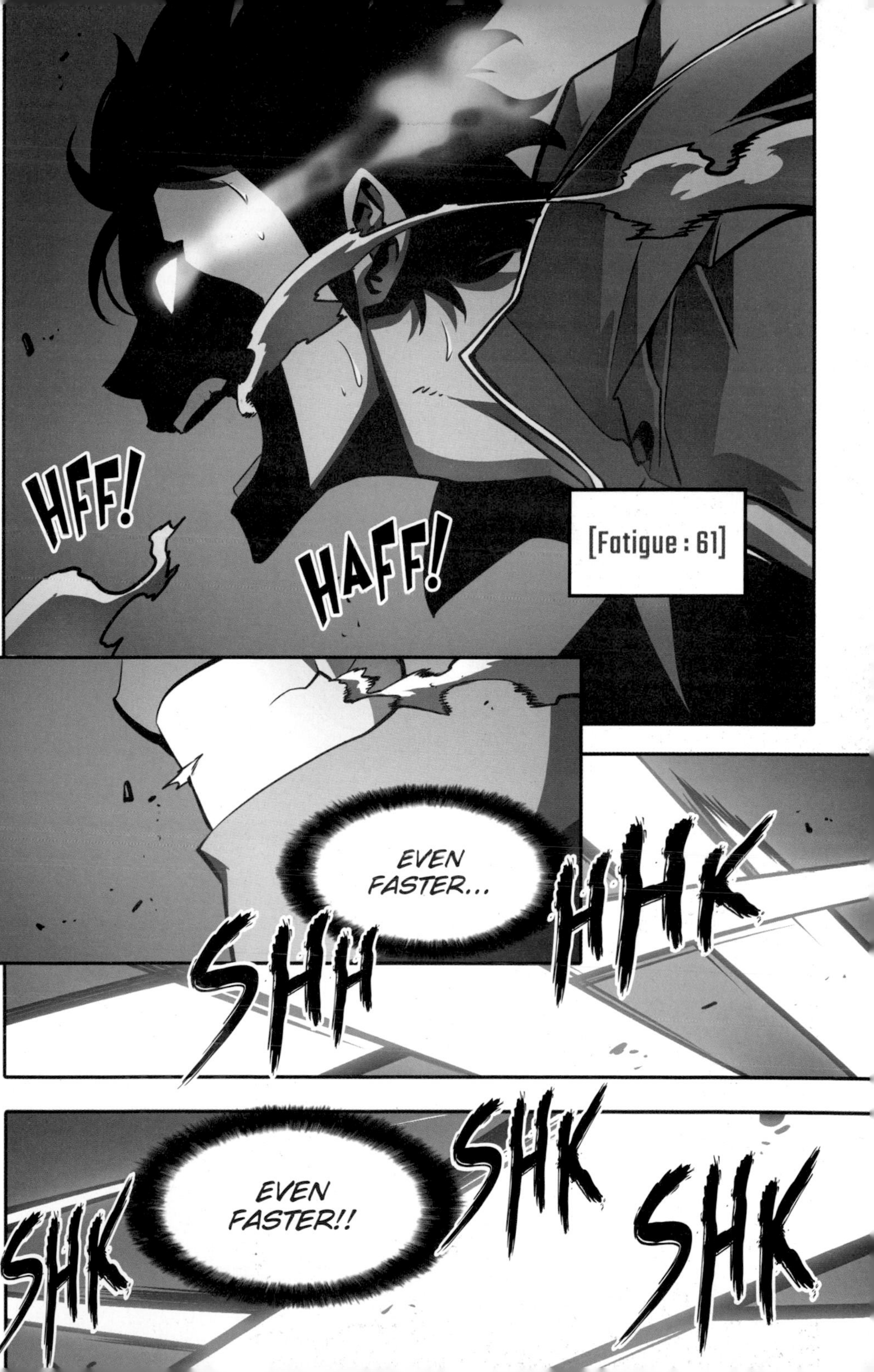
HFF!
HAFF!
[Fatigue : 61]
EVEN FASTER...
SHH
HHK
SHK
EVEN FASTER!!
SHK
SHK

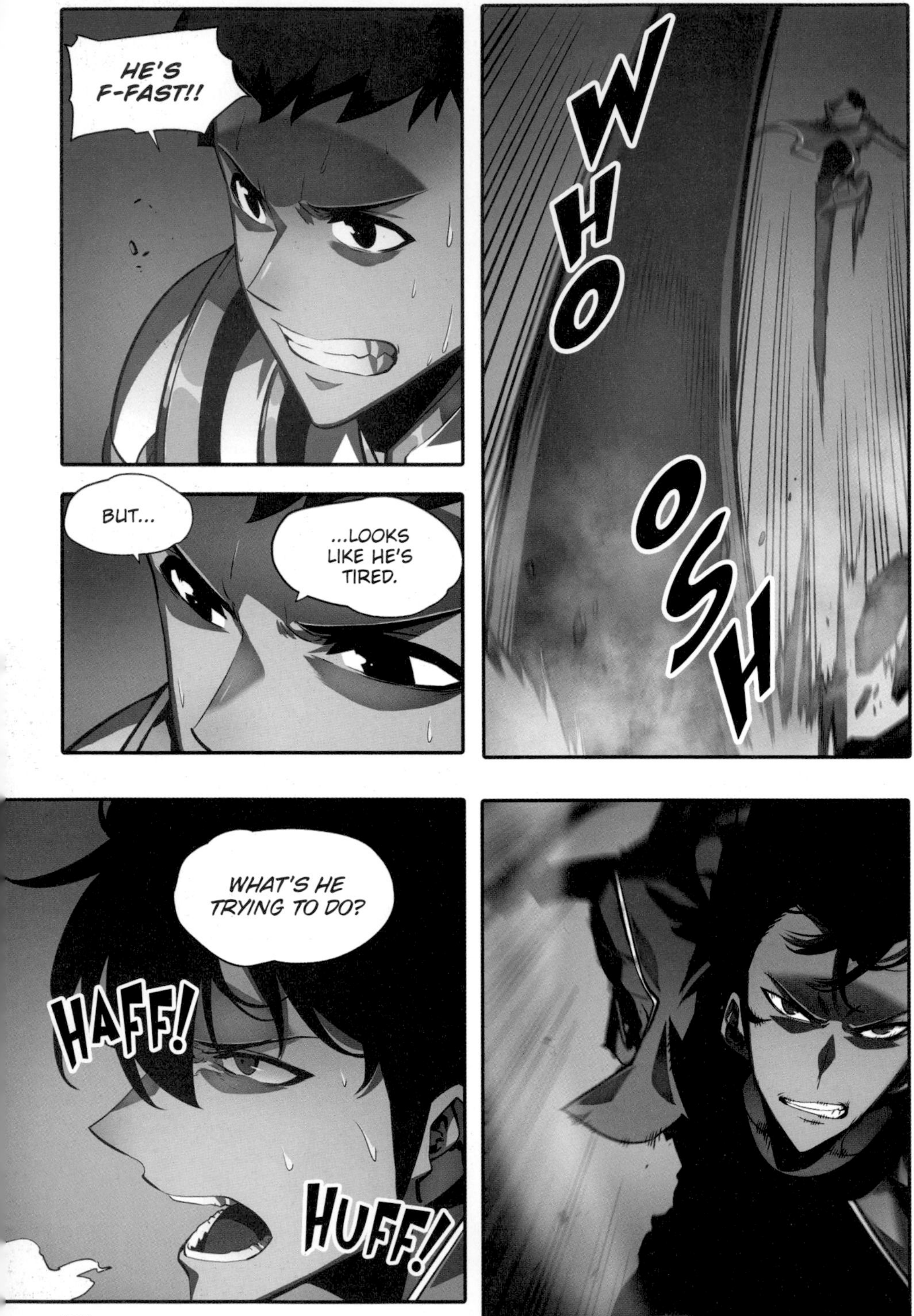
HE'S F-FAST!!
BUT...
...LOOKS LIKE HE'S TIRED.
WHOOOSH
WHAT'S HE TRYING TO DO?
HAFF!
HUFF!

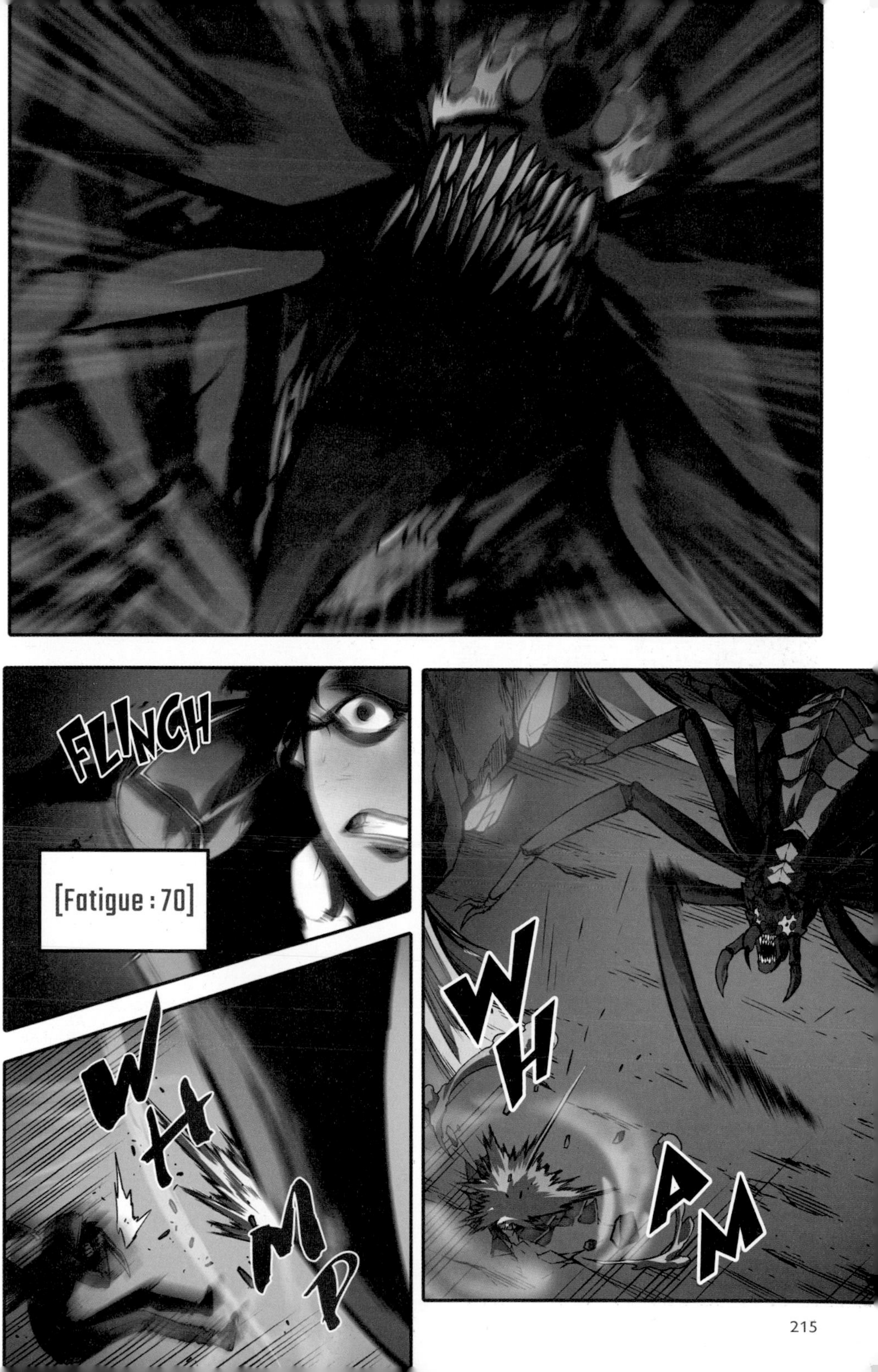
FLINCH
[Fatigue : 70]
WHMP
WHAM

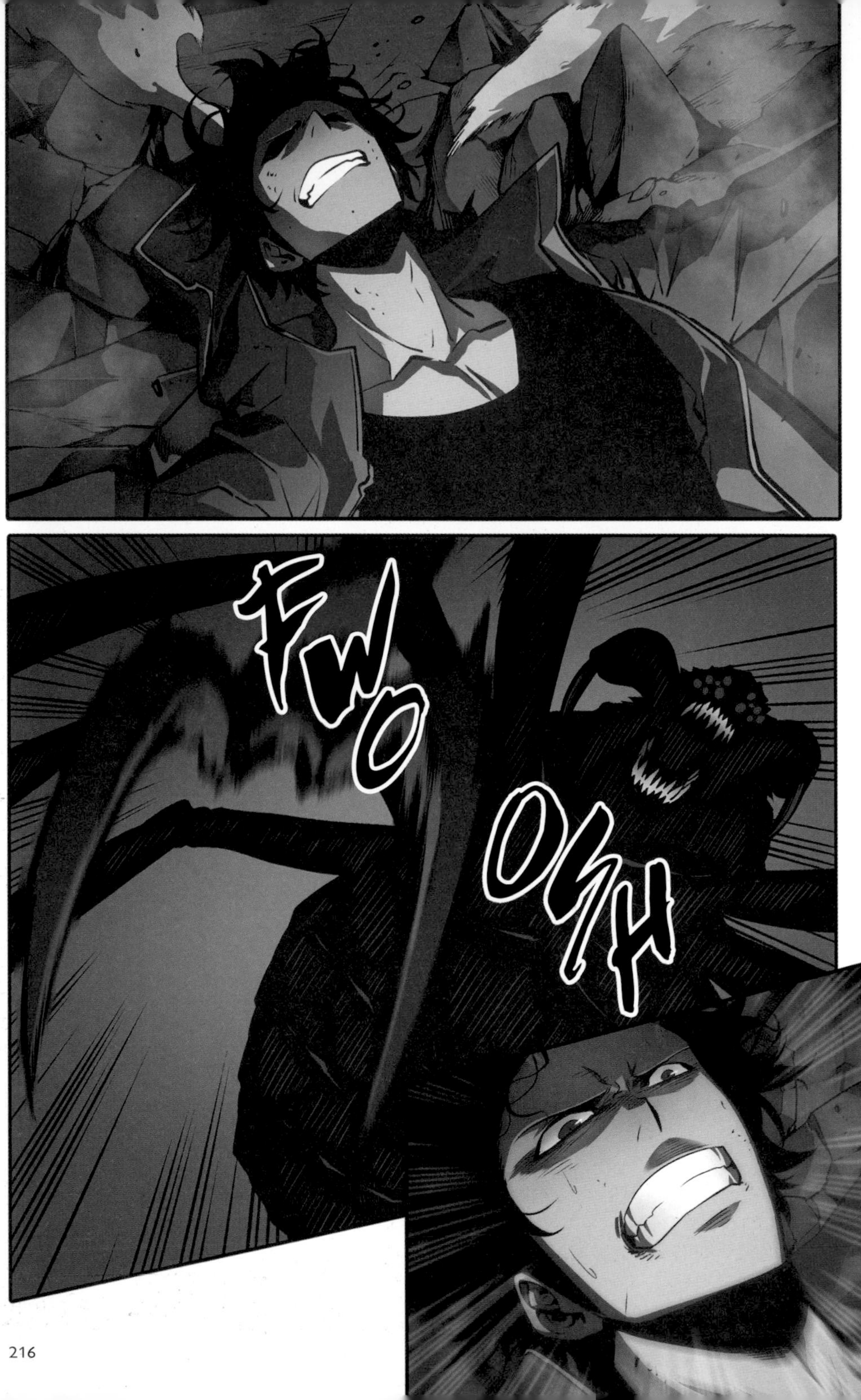
FWOOSH

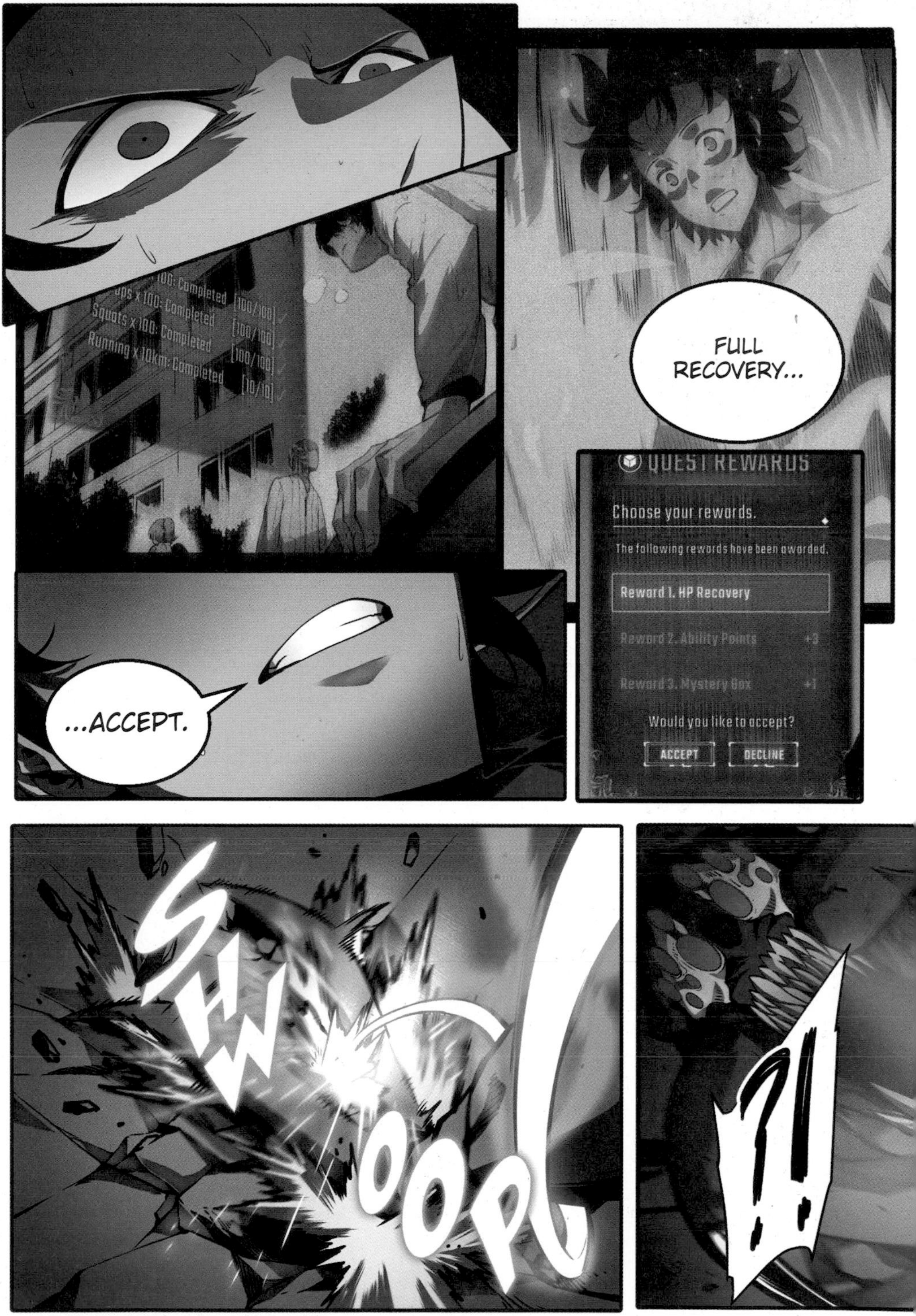
100: Completed [100/100]
ups x 100: Completed [100/100]
Squats x 100: Completed [100/100]
Running x 10km: Completed [10/10]
FULL RECOVERY...
QUEST REWARDS
Choose your rewards.
The following rewards have been awarded.
Reward 1. HP Recovery
Reward 2. Ability Points +3
Reward 3. Mystery Box +1
Would you like to accept?
ACCEPT
DECLINE
...ACCEPT.
SHWOOP
?!

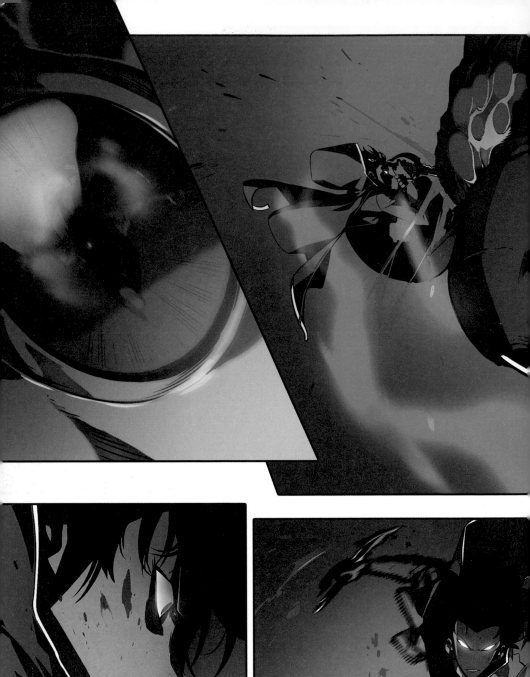

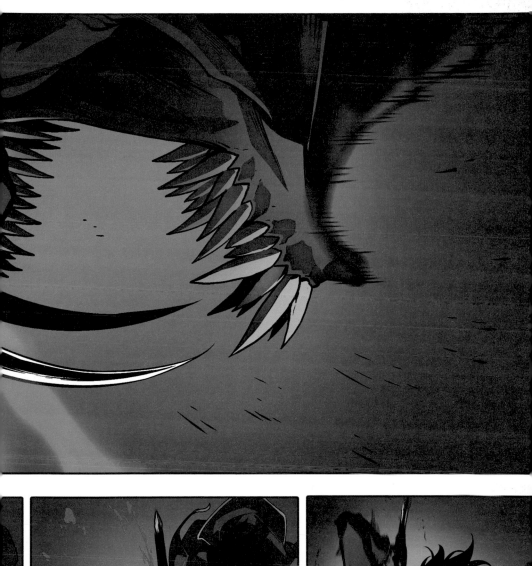

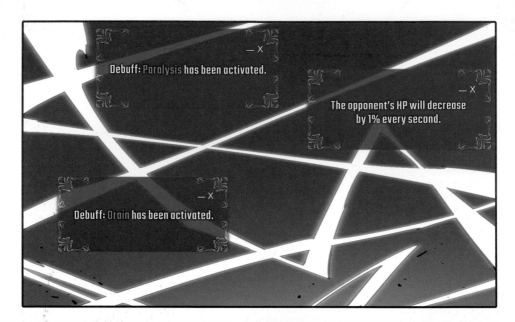

Debuff: Paralysis has been activated.

— X

The opponent's HP will decrease
by 1% every second.

— X

Debuff: Drain has been activated.

— X

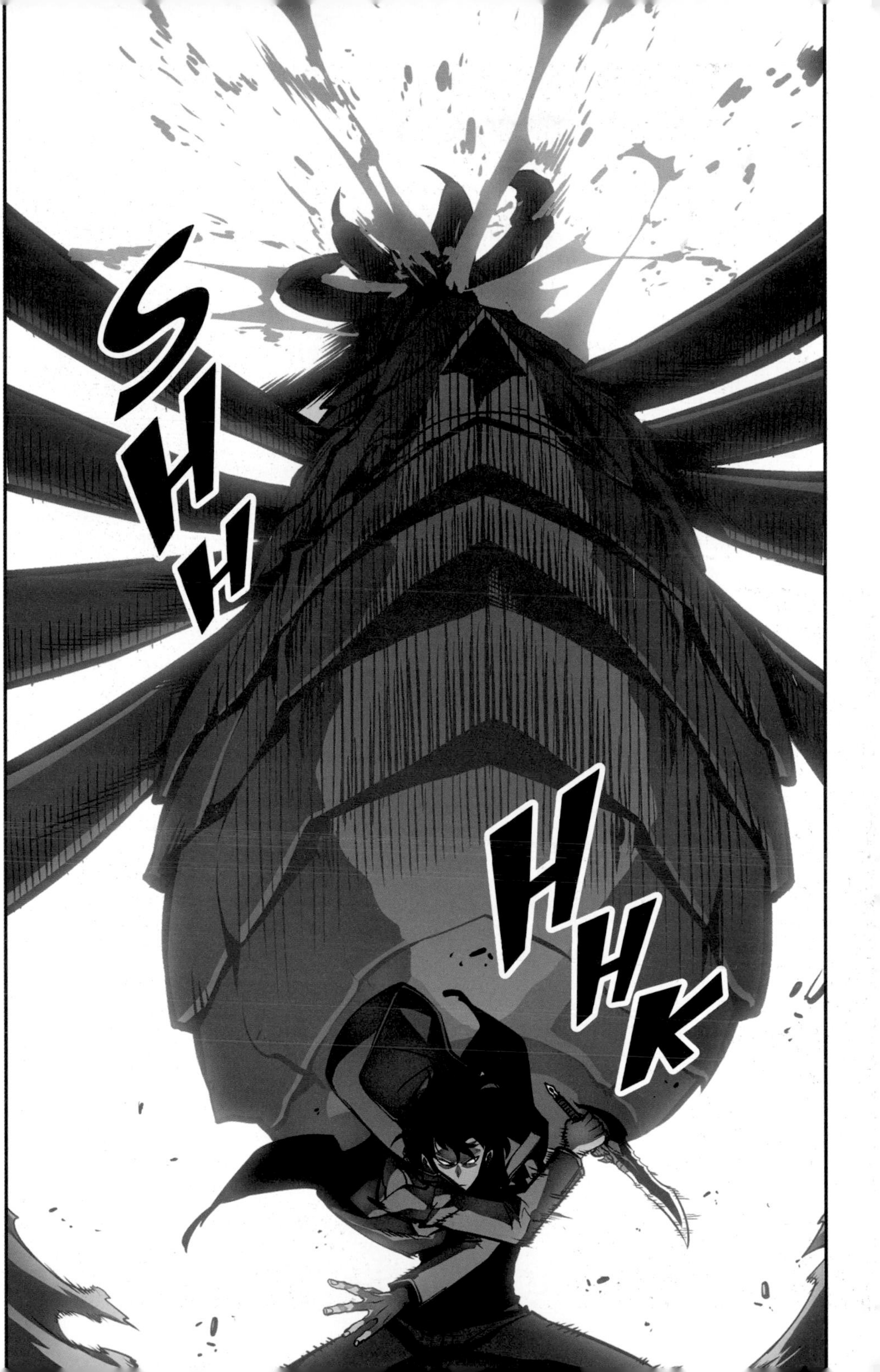
SHH
HHK

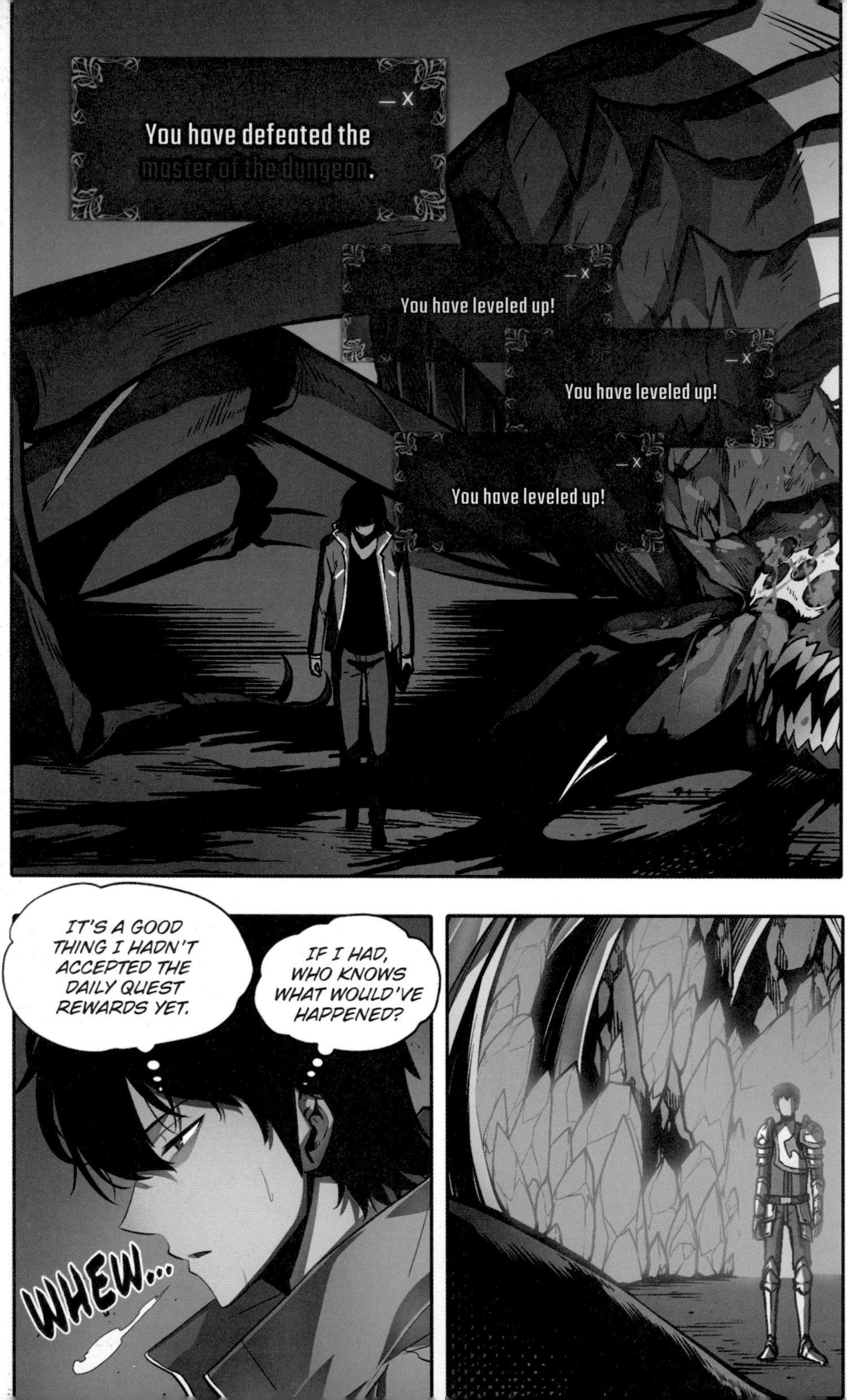
You have defeated the master of the dungeon.
You have leveled up!
You have leveled up!
You have leveled up!
IT'S A GOOD THING I HADN'T ACCEPTED THE DAILY QUEST REWARDS YET.
IF I HAD, WHO KNOWS WHAT WOULD'VE HAPPENED?
WHEW...

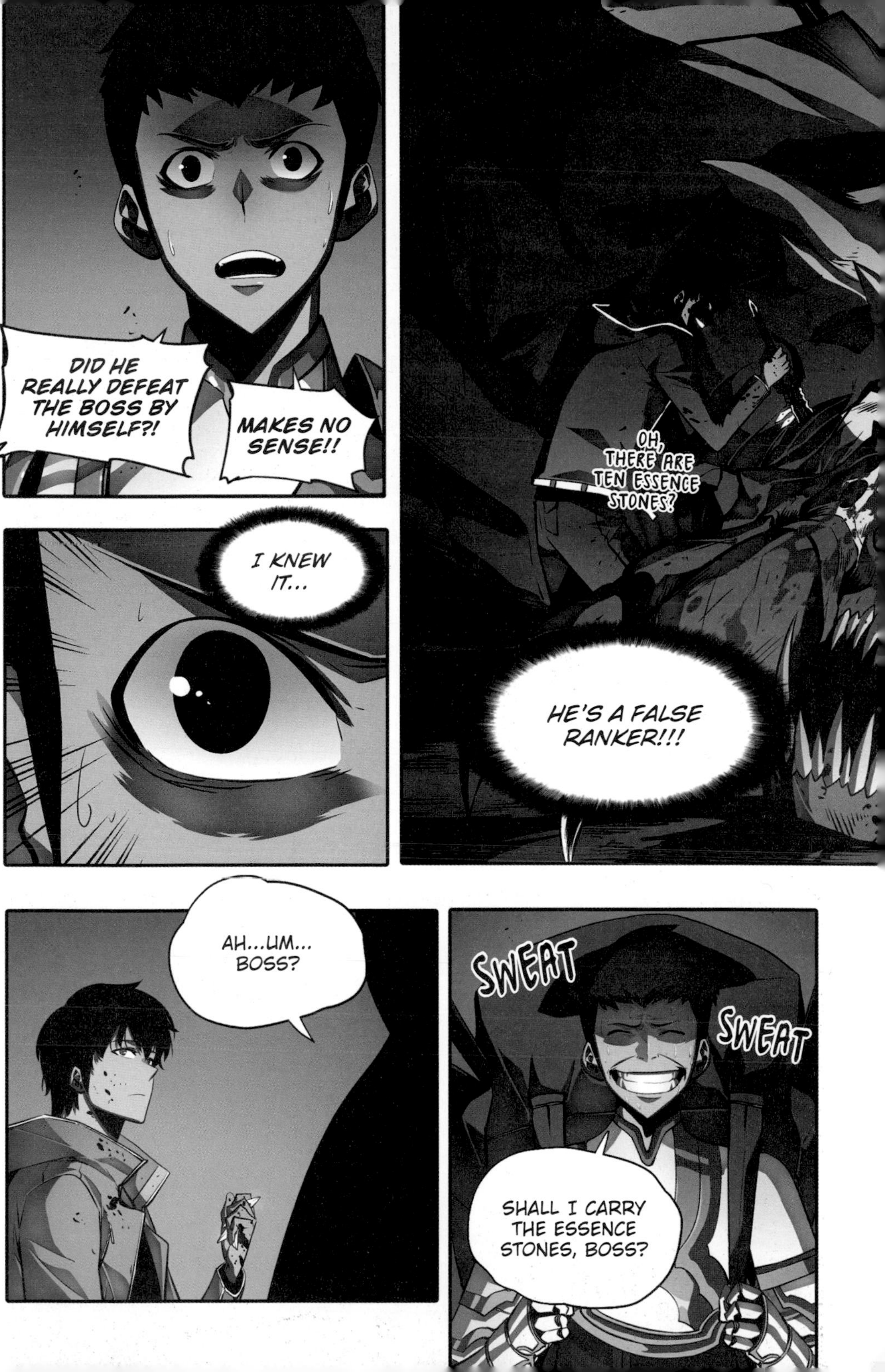
DID HE REALLY DEFEAT THE BOSS BY HIMSELF?!
MAKES NO SENSE!!
I KNEW IT...
OH, THERE ARE TEN ESSENCE STONES?
HE'S A FALSE RANKER!!!
AH...UM... BOSS?
SWEAT
SWEAT
SHALL I CARRY THE ESSENCE STONES, BOSS?

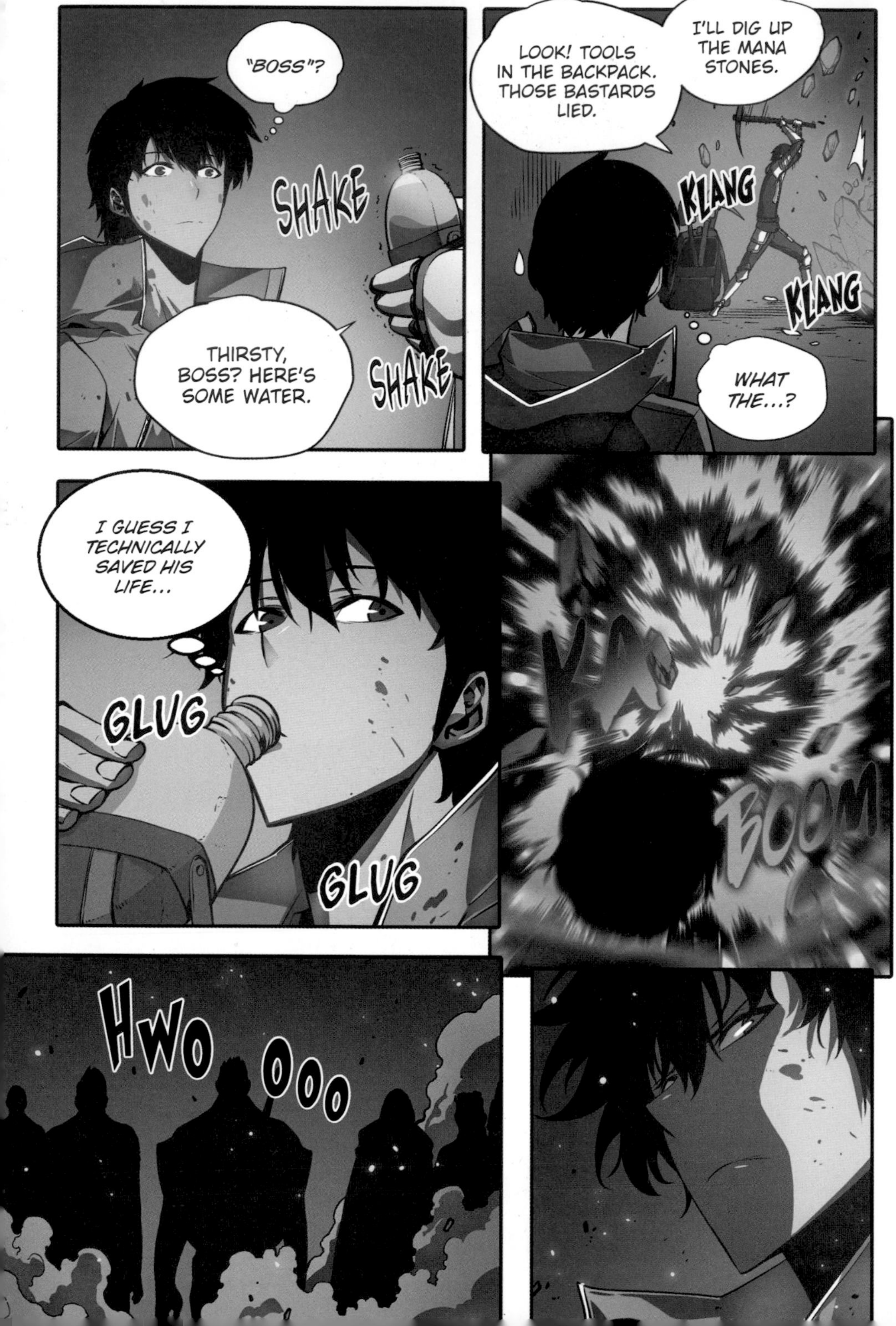
"BOSS"?
SHAKE
THIRSTY, BOSS? HERE'S SOME WATER.
SHAKE
LOOK! TOOLS IN THE BACKPACK. THOSE BASTARDS LIED.
I'LL DIG UP THE MANA STONES.
KLANG
KLANG
WHAT THE...?
I GUESS I TECHNICALLY SAVED HIS LIFE...
GLUG
GLUG
BOOM
HWO OOO

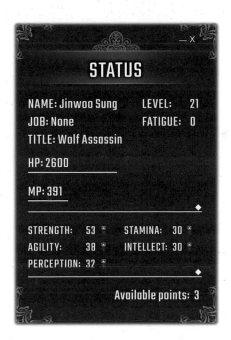

STATUS

NAME: Jinwoo Sung   LEVEL: 21
JOB: None   FATIGUE: 0
TITLE: Wolf Assassin

HP: 2600

MP: 391

◆

STRENGTH: 53   STAMINA: 30
AGILITY: 38   INTELLECT: 30
PERCEPTION: 32

◆

Available points: 3

ⓘ SKILL

[Passive Skill]

? (Unknown)   MAX

🧍 Willpower   Lv. 1

[Active Skill]

🏃 Dash   Lv. 1

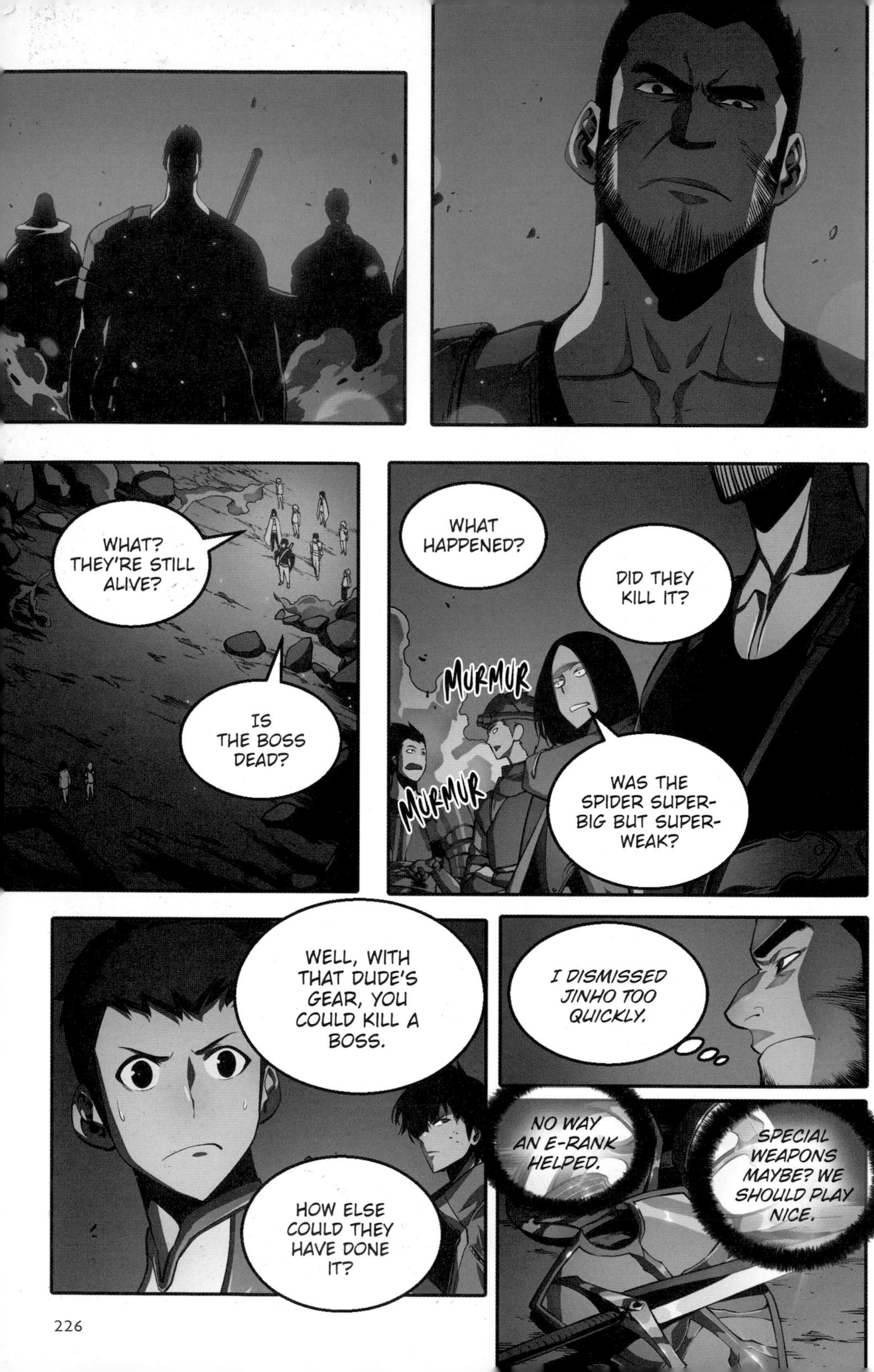
WHAT? THEY'RE STILL ALIVE?
IS THE BOSS DEAD?
WHAT HAPPENED?
DID THEY KILL IT?
MURMUR
MURMUR
WAS THE SPIDER SUPER-BIG BUT SUPER-WEAK?
WELL, WITH THAT DUDE'S GEAR, YOU COULD KILL A BOSS.
HOW ELSE COULD THEY HAVE DONE IT?
I DISMISSED JINHO TOO QUICKLY.
NO WAY AN E-RANK HELPED.
SPECIAL WEAPONS MAYBE? WE SHOULD PLAY NICE.

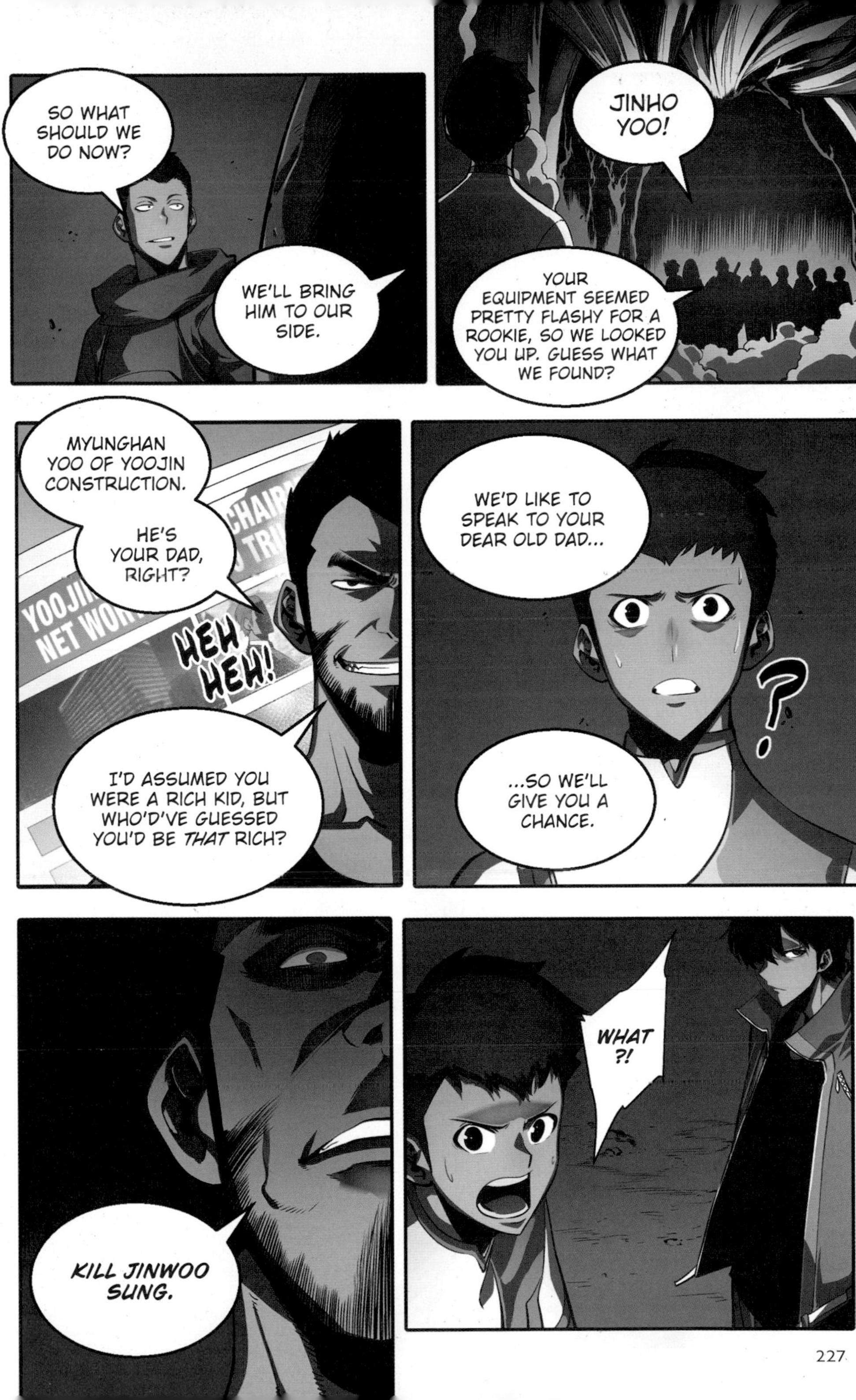
SO WHAT SHOULD WE DO NOW?
WE'LL BRING HIM TO OUR SIDE.
JINHO YOO!
YOUR EQUIPMENT SEEMED PRETTY FLASHY FOR A ROOKIE, SO WE LOOKED YOU UP. GUESS WHAT WE FOUND?
MYUNGHAN YOO OF YOOJIN CONSTRUCTION.
HE'S YOUR DAD, RIGHT?
HEH HEH!
I'D ASSUMED YOU WERE A RICH KID, BUT WHO'D'VE GUESSED YOU'D BE *THAT* RICH?
WE'D LIKE TO SPEAK TO YOUR DEAR OLD DAD...
?
...SO WE'LL GIVE YOU A CHANCE.
KILL JINWOO SUNG.
WHAT ?!

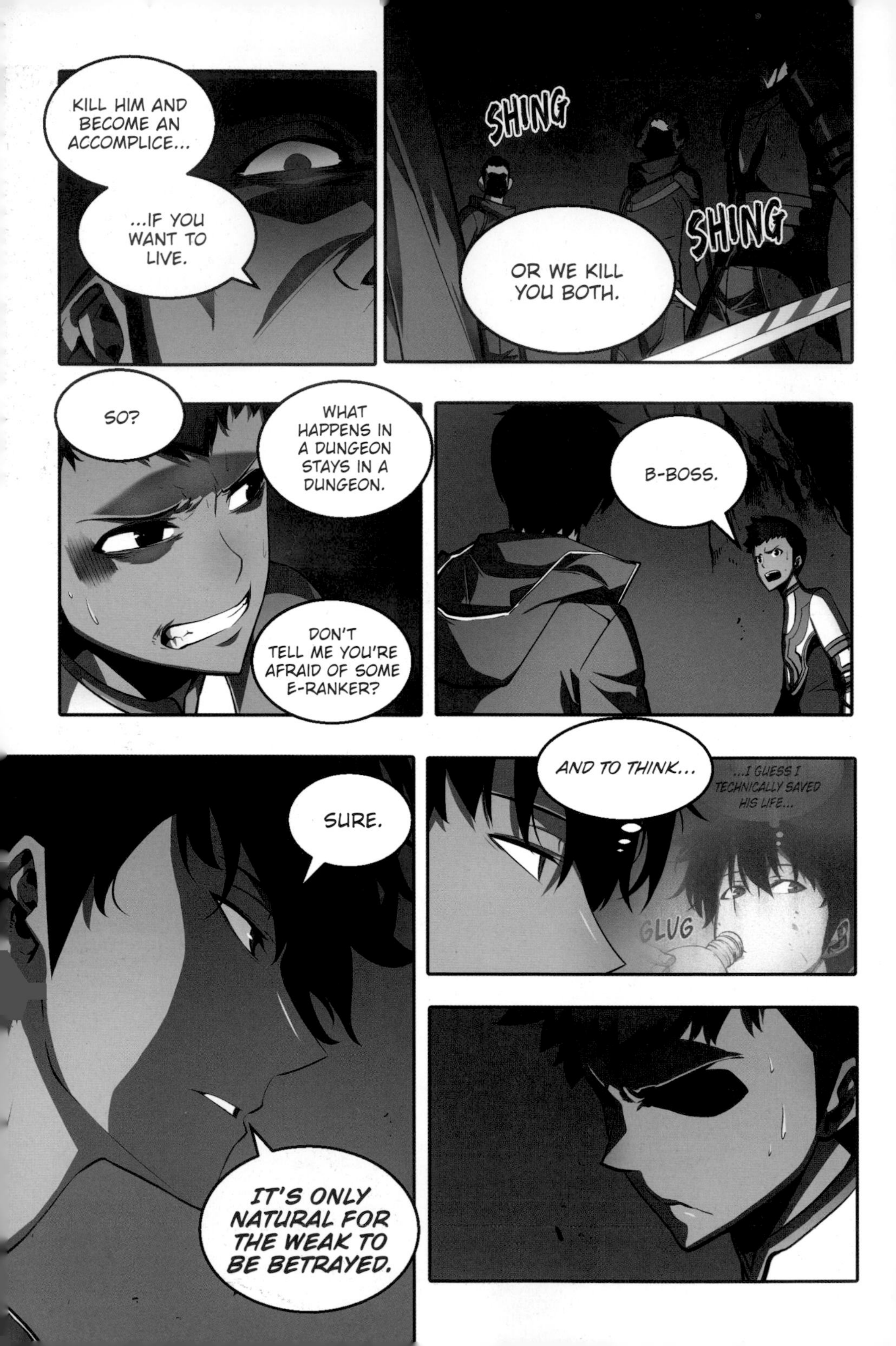
KILL HIM AND BECOME AN ACCOMPLICE...
...IF YOU WANT TO LIVE.
SHING
SHING
OR WE KILL YOU BOTH.
SO?
WHAT HAPPENS IN A DUNGEON STAYS IN A DUNGEON.
DON'T TELL ME YOU'RE AFRAID OF SOME E-RANKER?
B-BOSS.
SURE.
IT'S ONLY NATURAL FOR THE WEAK TO BE BETRAYED.
AND TO THINK...
...I GUESS I TECHNICALLY SAVED HIS LIFE...
GLUG

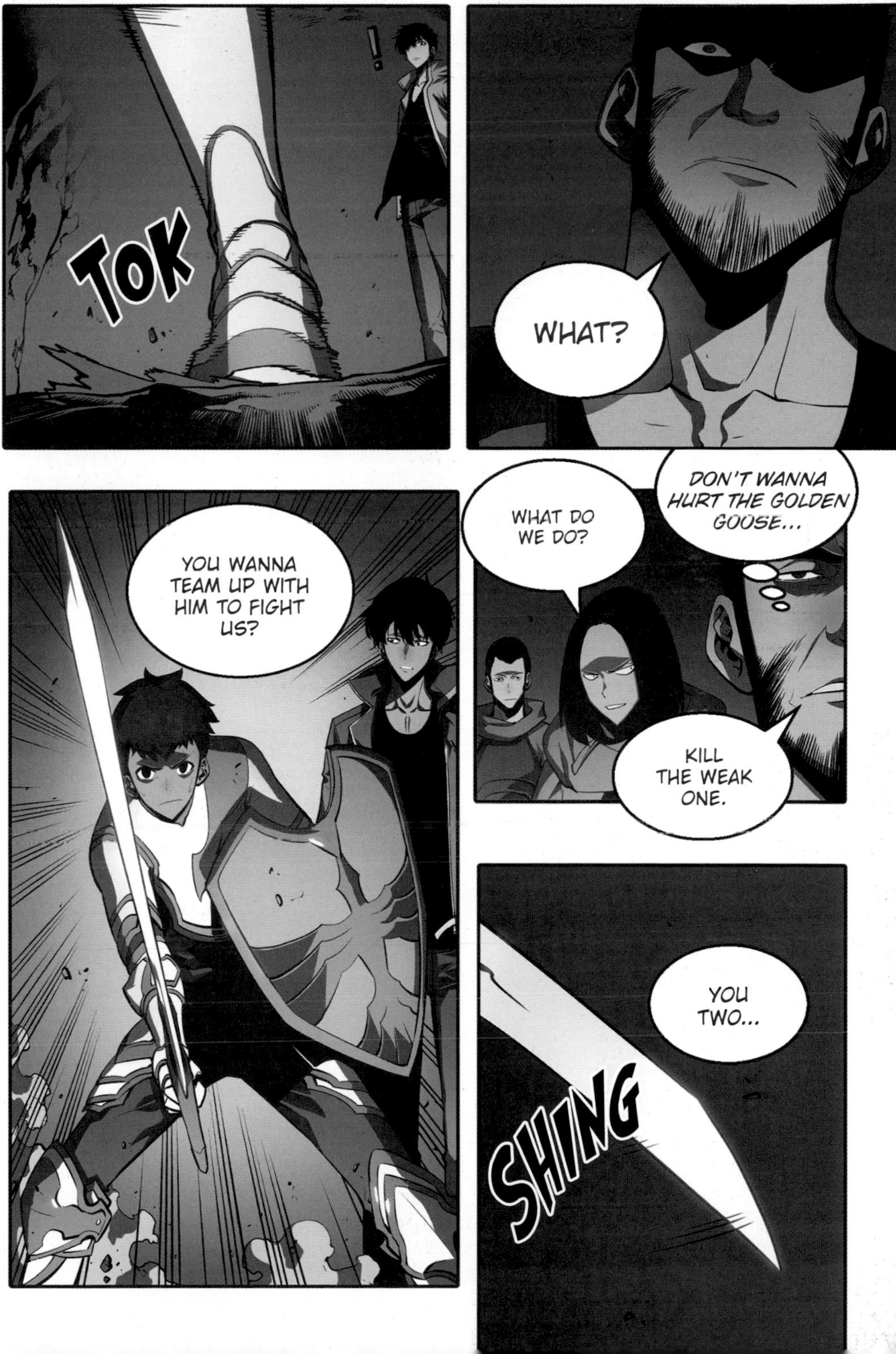
TOK
!
WHAT?
YOU WANNA TEAM UP WITH HIM TO FIGHT US?
WHAT DO WE DO?
DON'T WANNA HURT THE GOLDEN GOOSE...
KILL THE WEAK ONE.
YOU TWO...
SHING

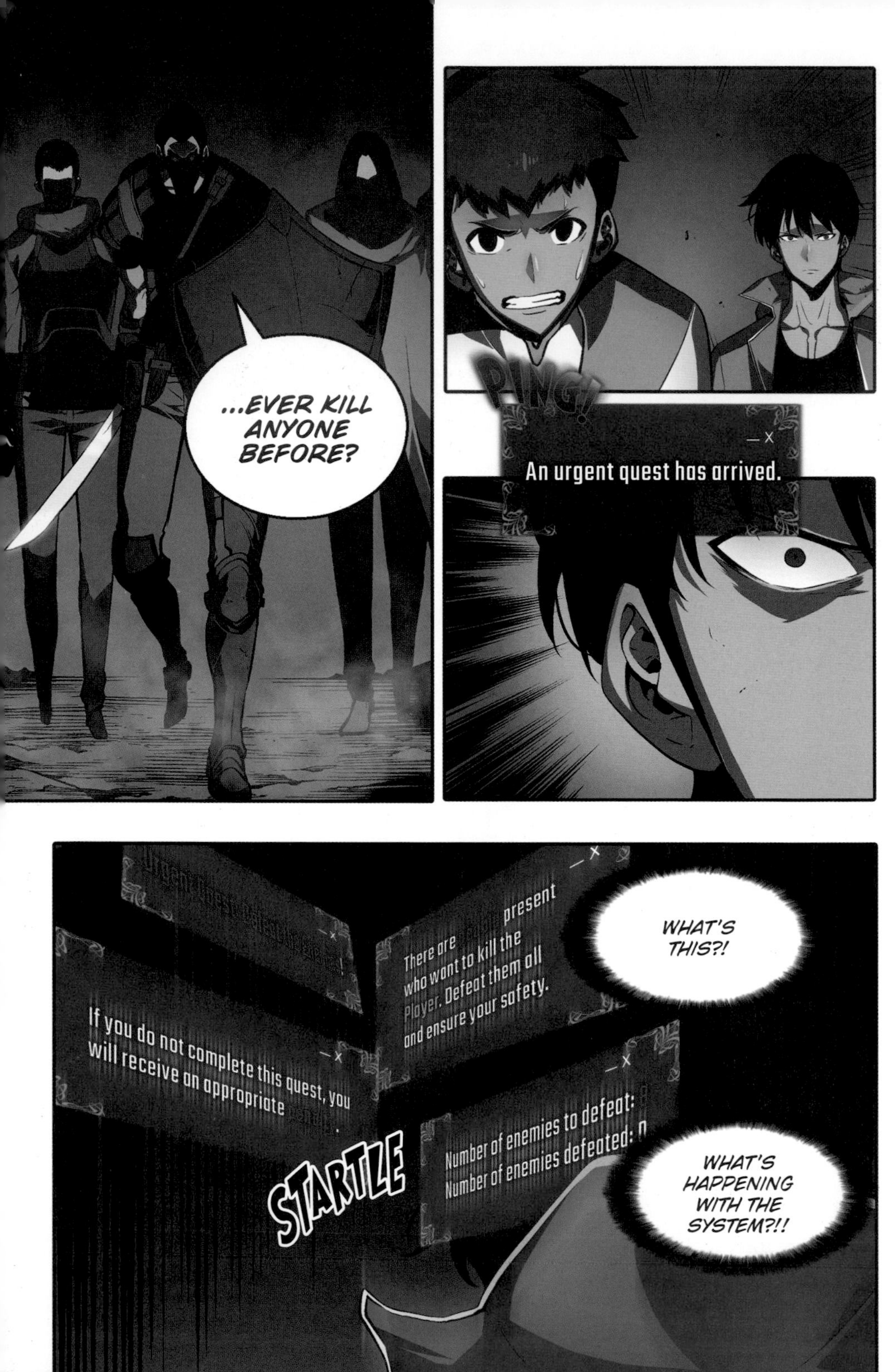
...EVER KILL ANYONE BEFORE?
PING!
An urgent quest has arrived.
There are present who want to kill the Player. Defeat them all and ensure your safety.
If you do not complete this quest, you will receive an appropriate .
WHAT'S THIS?!
STARTLE
Number of enemies to defeat:
Number of enemies defeated: 0
WHAT'S HAPPENING WITH THE SYSTEM?!!

! QUEST INFO

Urgent Quest: Defeat the Enemies!

There are people present who want to kill the Player.
Defeat them all and ensure your safety.
If you do not complete this quest, your heart will stop.
Number of enemies to defeat: 8
Number of enemies defeated: 0

KABOOM

WHAM

BOSS!

JINHO!
HE'S ALREADY
DEAD. COME
WITH US.

231

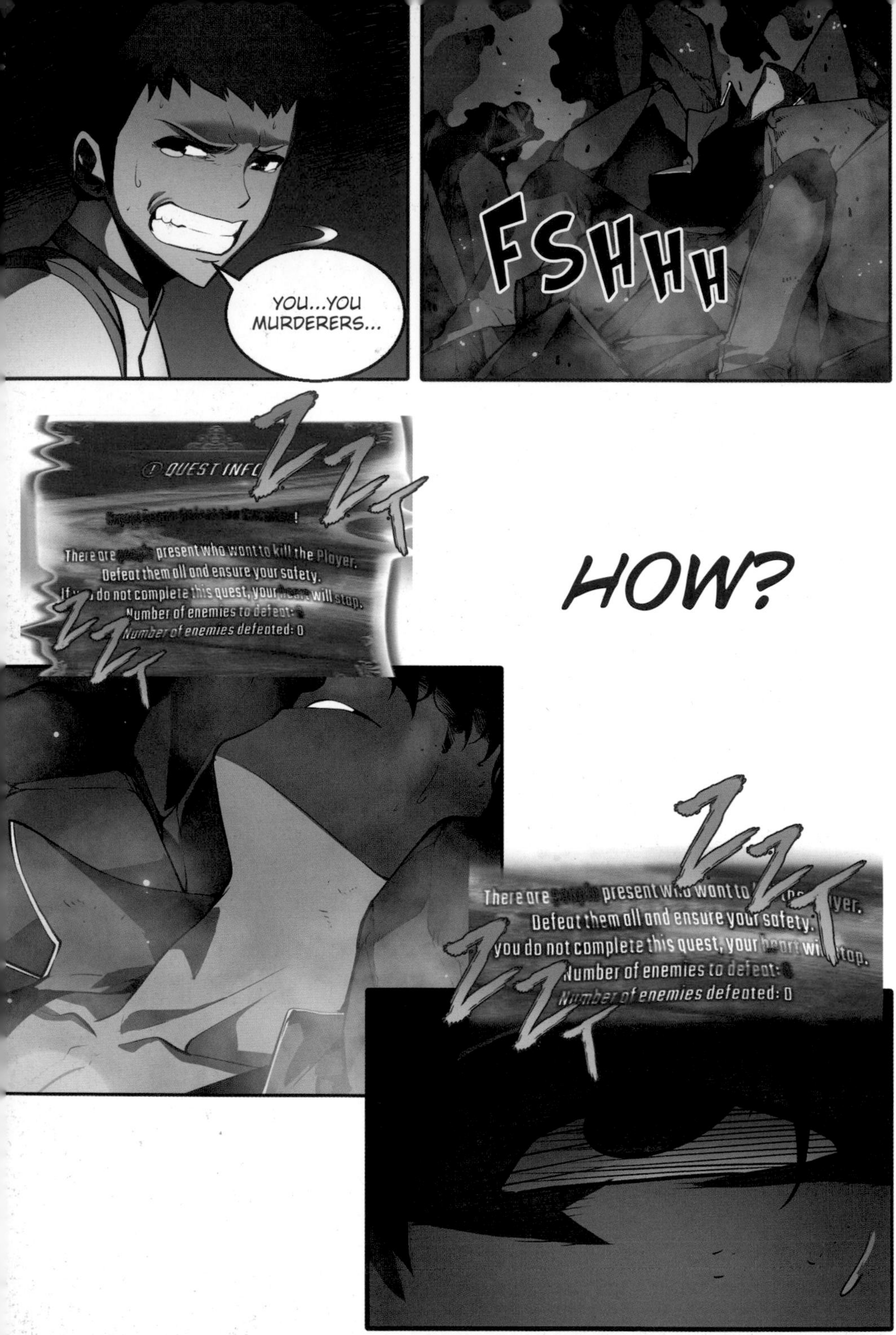
YOU...YOU MURDERERS...
FSHHHH
QUEST INF
ZZZT
There are present who want to kill the Player.
Defeat them all and ensure your safety.
do not complete this quest, your will stop.
Number of enemies to defeat:
Number of enemies defeated: 0
ZZZT
HOW?
ZZZT
There are present w want to yer.
Defeat them all and ensure your safety.
you do not complete this quest, your wi stop.
Number of enemies to defeat:
of enemies defeated: 0
ZZZT

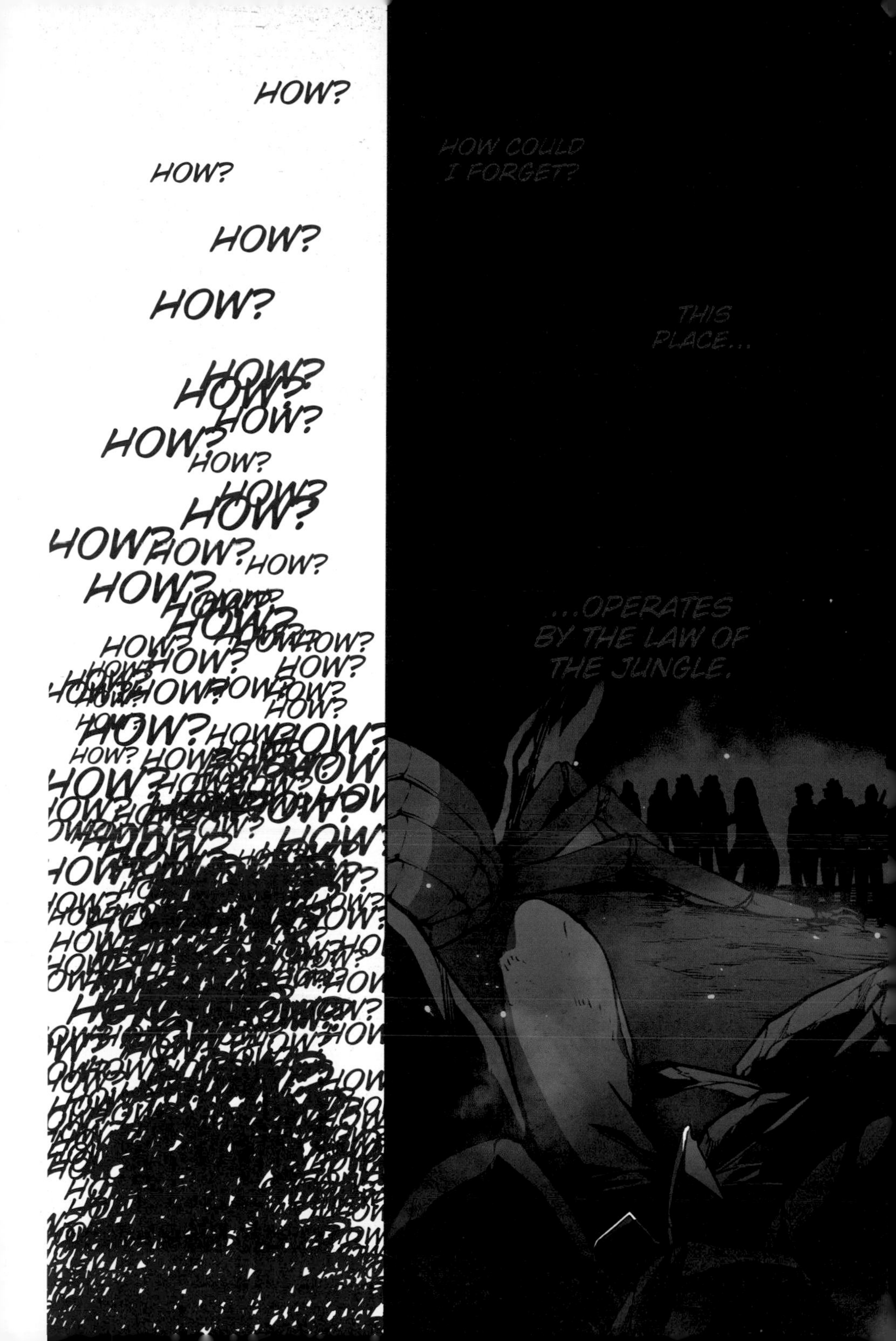
HOW COULD I FORGET?
THIS PLACE...
...OPERATES BY THE LAW OF THE JUNGLE.
HOW?
HOW?
HOW?
HOW?

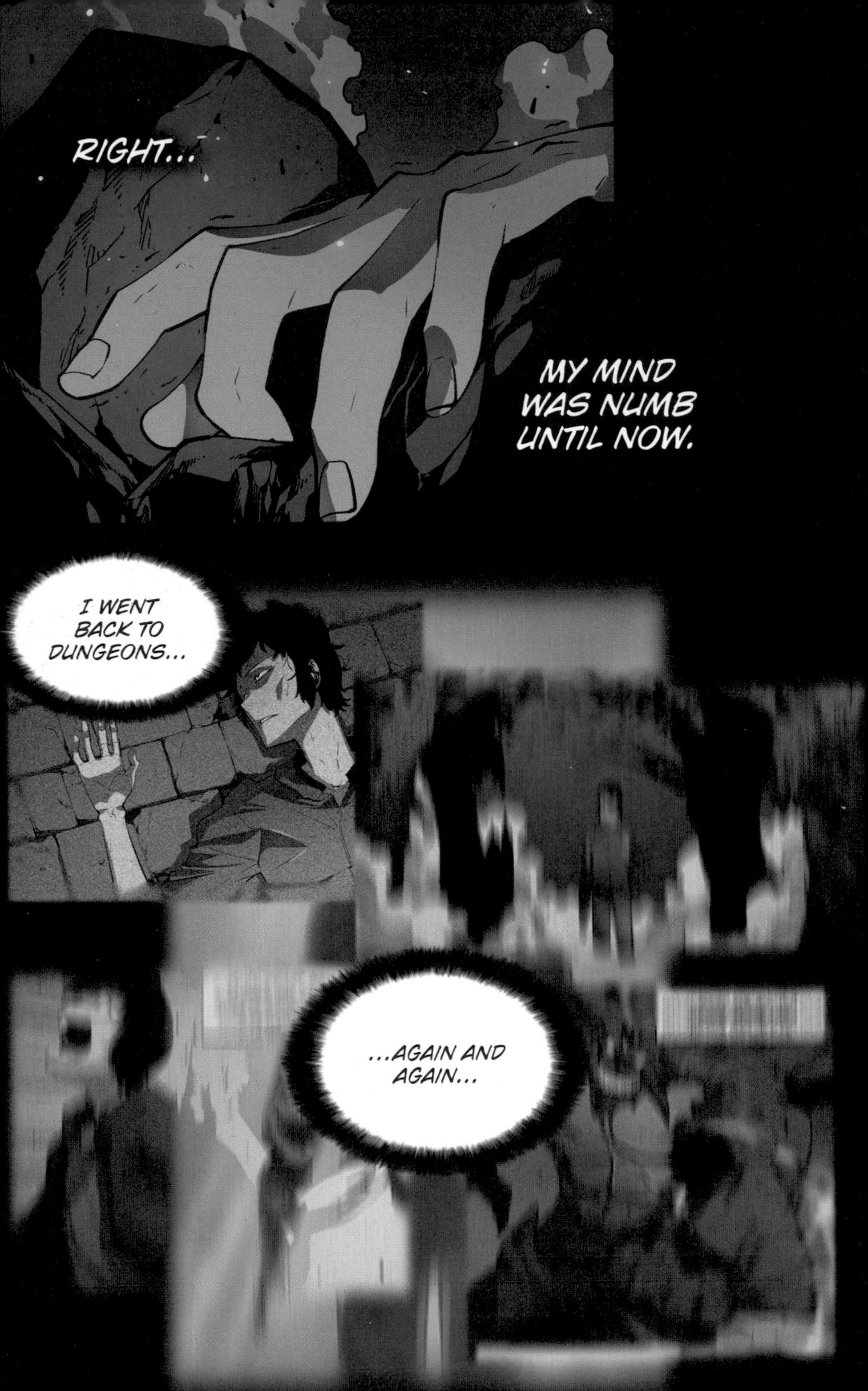
RIGHT...
MY MIND WAS NUMB UNTIL NOW.
I WENT BACK TO DUNGEONS...
...AGAIN AND AGAIN...

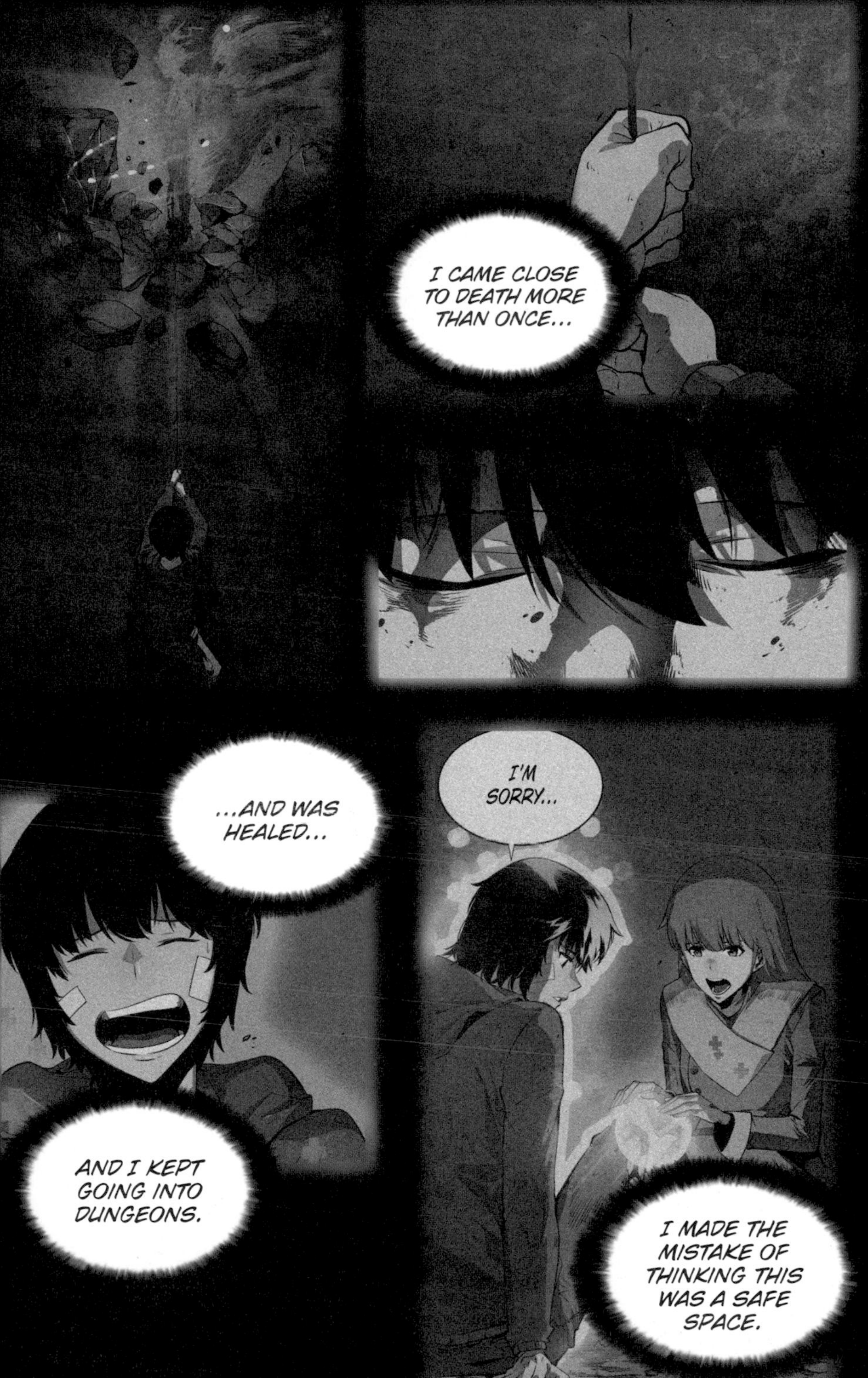
I CAME CLOSE TO DEATH MORE THAN ONCE…
…AND WAS HEALED…
AND I KEPT GOING INTO DUNGEONS.
I'M SORRY…
I MADE THE MISTAKE OF THINKING THIS WAS A SAFE SPACE.

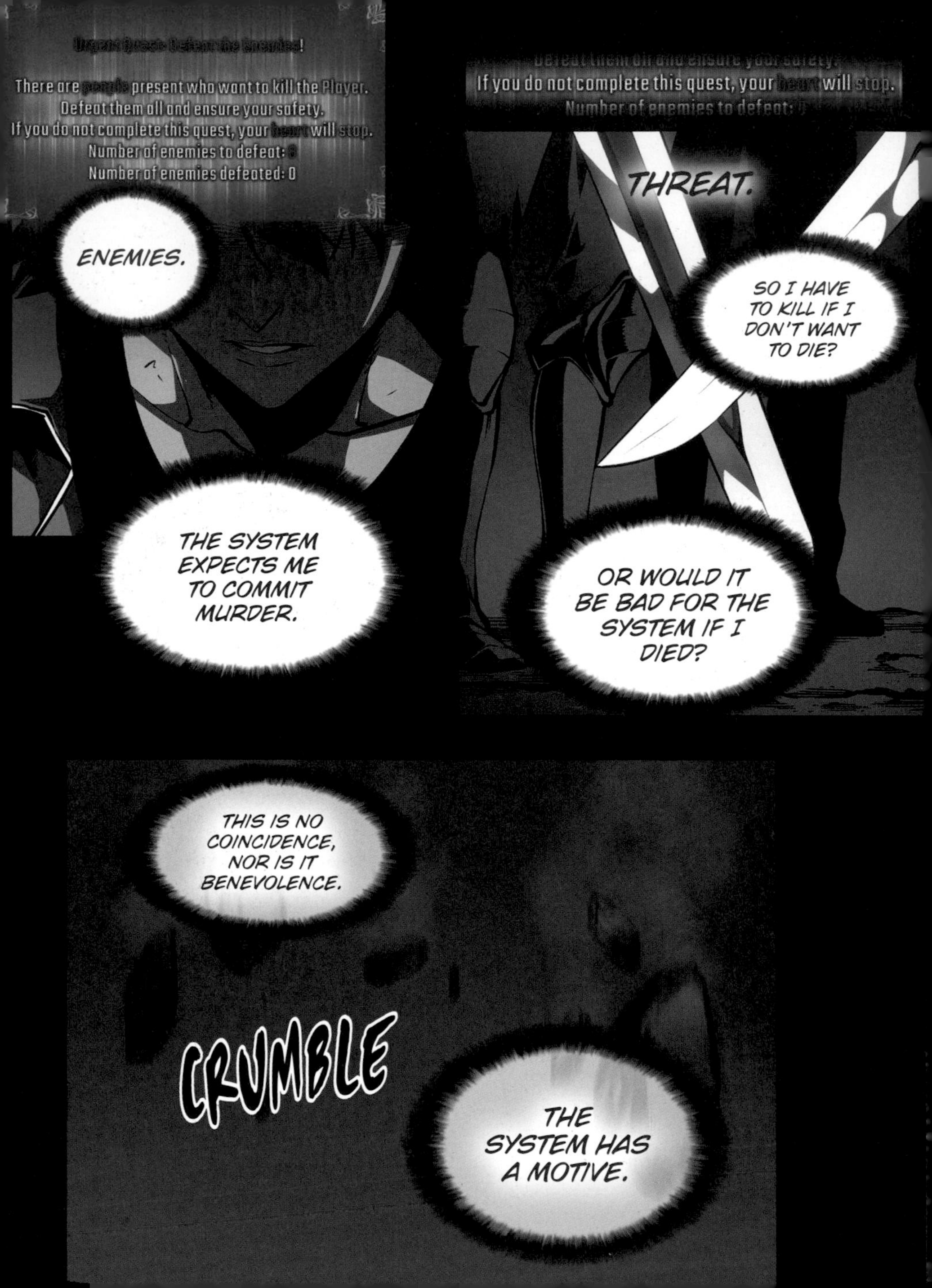
Urgent Quest: Defeat the Enemies!
There are people present who want to kill the Player.
Defeat them all and ensure your safety.
If you do not complete this quest, your heart will stop.
Number of enemies to defeat:
Number of enemies defeated: 0
ENEMIES.
THE SYSTEM EXPECTS ME TO COMMIT MURDER.
If you do not complete this quest, your heart will stop.
Number of enemies to defeat:
THREAT.
SO I HAVE TO KILL IF I DON'T WANT TO DIE?
OR WOULD IT BE BAD FOR THE SYSTEM IF I DIED?
THIS IS NO COINCIDENCE, NOR IS IT BENEVOLENCE.
CRUMBLE
THE SYSTEM HAS A MOTIVE.

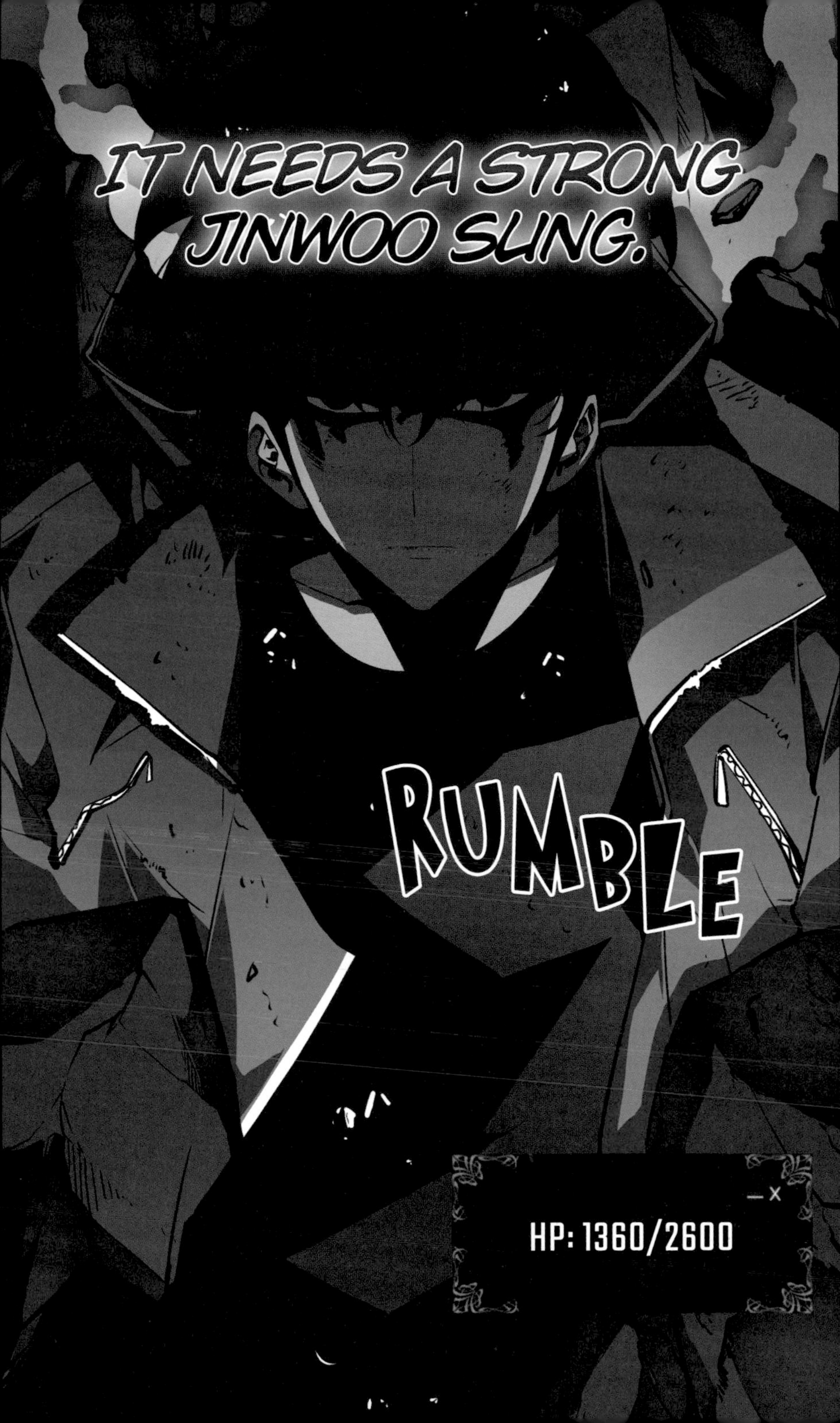
IT NEEDS A STRONG JINWOO SUNG.
RUMBLE
HP: 1360/2600

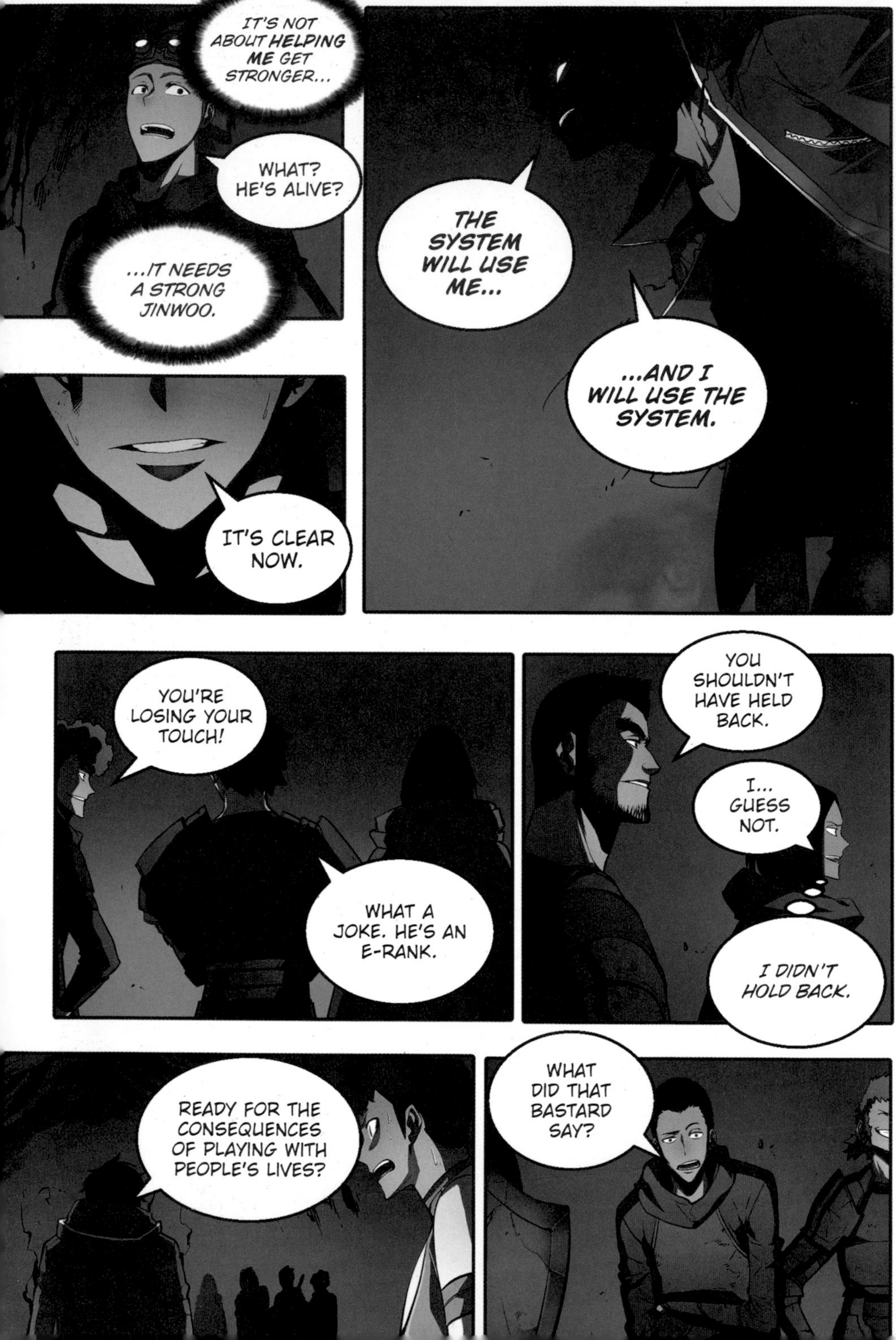
IT'S NOT ABOUT HELPING ME GET STRONGER...
WHAT? HE'S ALIVE?
...IT NEEDS A STRONG JINWOO.
IT'S CLEAR NOW.
THE SYSTEM WILL USE ME...
...AND I WILL USE THE SYSTEM.
YOU'RE LOSING YOUR TOUCH!
WHAT A JOKE. HE'S AN E-RANK.
YOU SHOULDN'T HAVE HELD BACK.
I... GUESS NOT.
I DIDN'T HOLD BACK.
READY FOR THE CONSEQUENCES OF PLAYING WITH PEOPLE'S LIVES?
WHAT DID THAT BASTARD SAY?

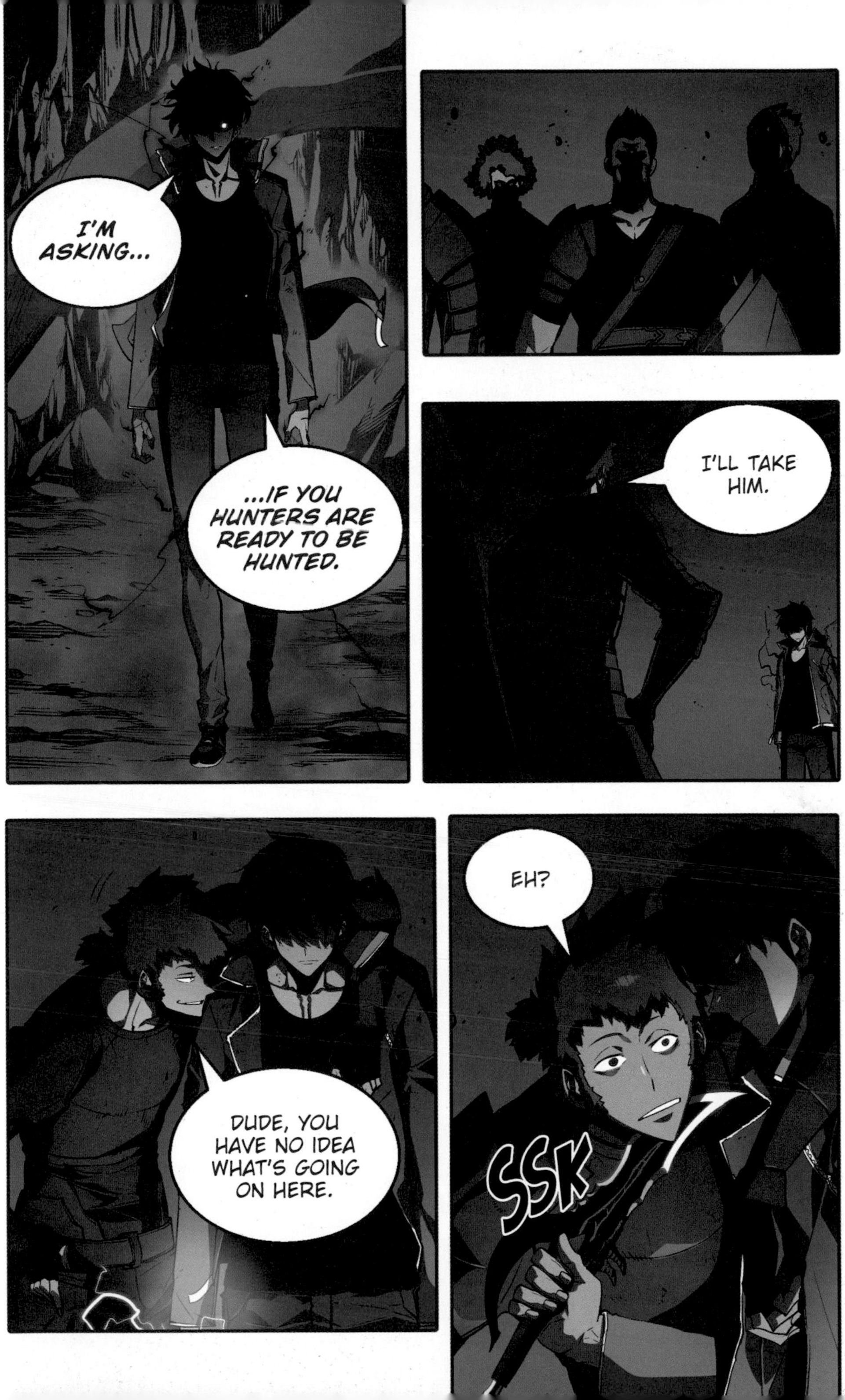
I'M ASKING...
...IF YOU HUNTERS ARE READY TO BE HUNTED.
I'LL TAKE HIM.
DUDE, YOU HAVE NO IDEA WHAT'S GOING ON HERE.
EH?
SSK

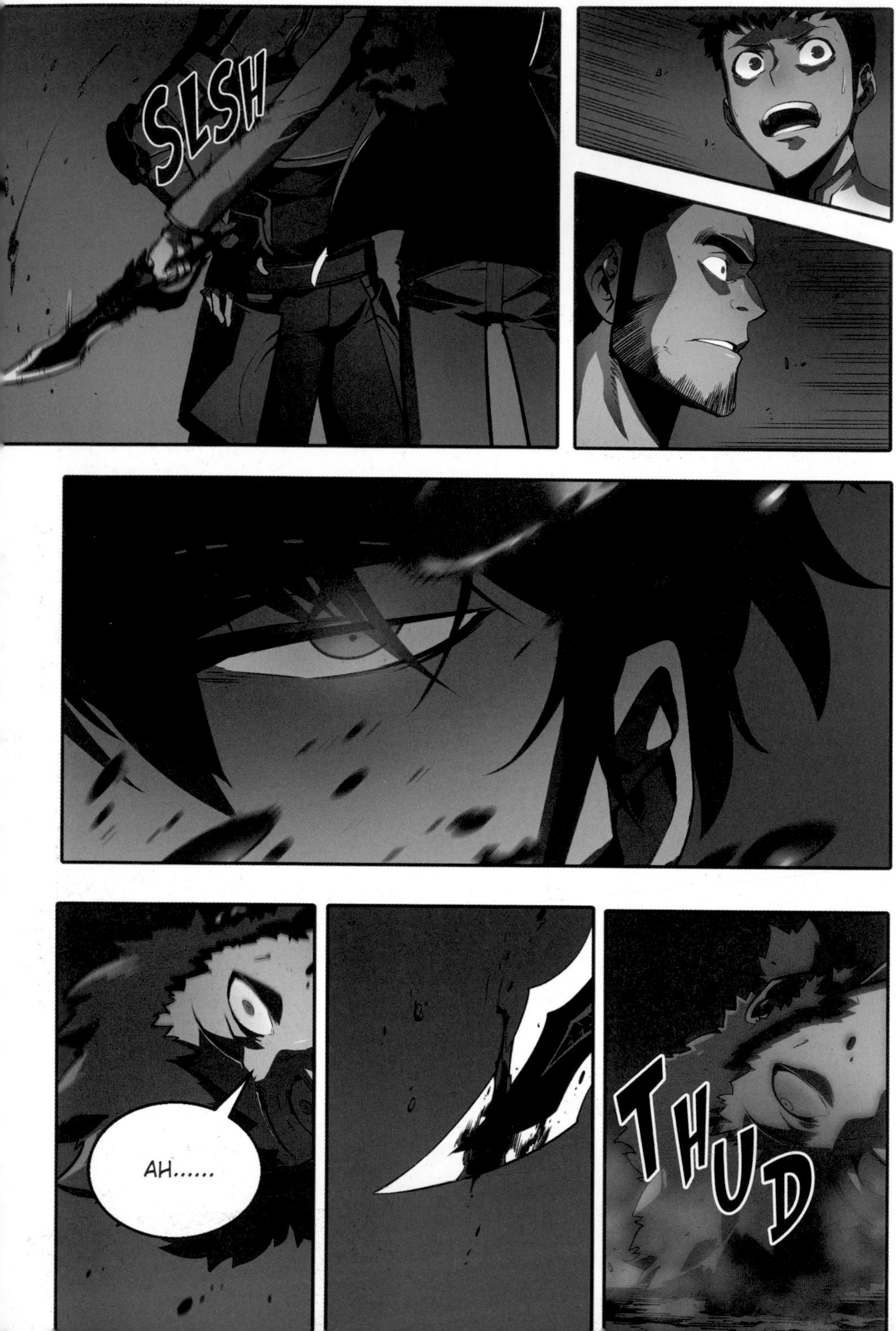
SLSH
AH......
THUD

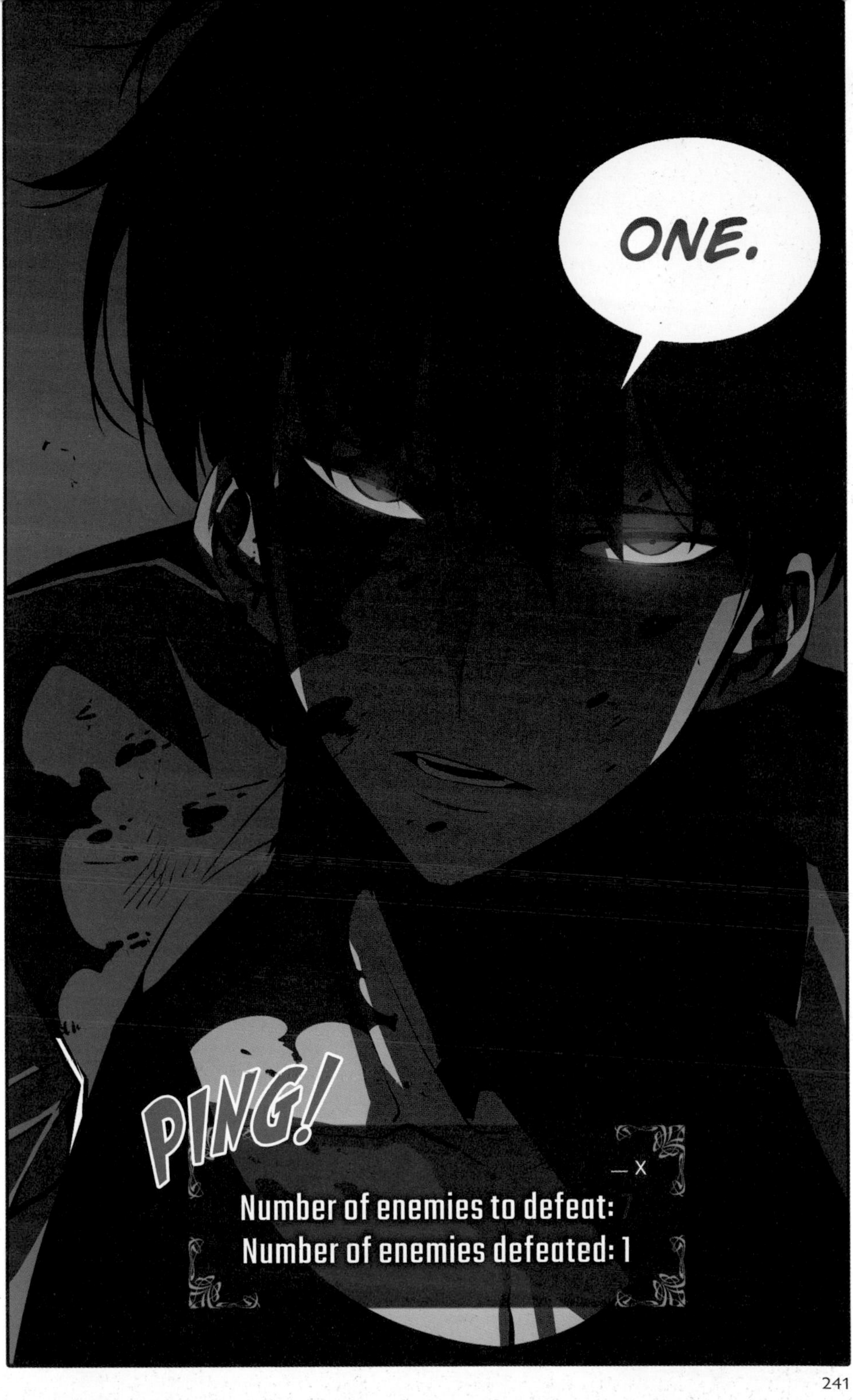
ONE.
PING!
— X
Number of enemies to defeat: 7
Number of enemies defeated: 1

J-JUNTAE!

WH-WHAT?

HOW DID HE GET A DAGGER?!

WHERE'D IT COME FROM?!

EVEN IF JUNTAE WAS CAUGHT OFF GUARD...

...HE WAS A D-RANK!

STATUS

NAME: Jinwoo Sung   LEVEL: 21
JOB: None   FATIGUE: 0
TITLE: Wolf Assassin

HP: 1360

MP: 391

STRENGTH: 53   STAMINA: 30
AGILITY: 38   INTELLECT: 30
PERCEPTION: 32

Available points: 3

I'VE KILLED A MAN...

A PERSON...

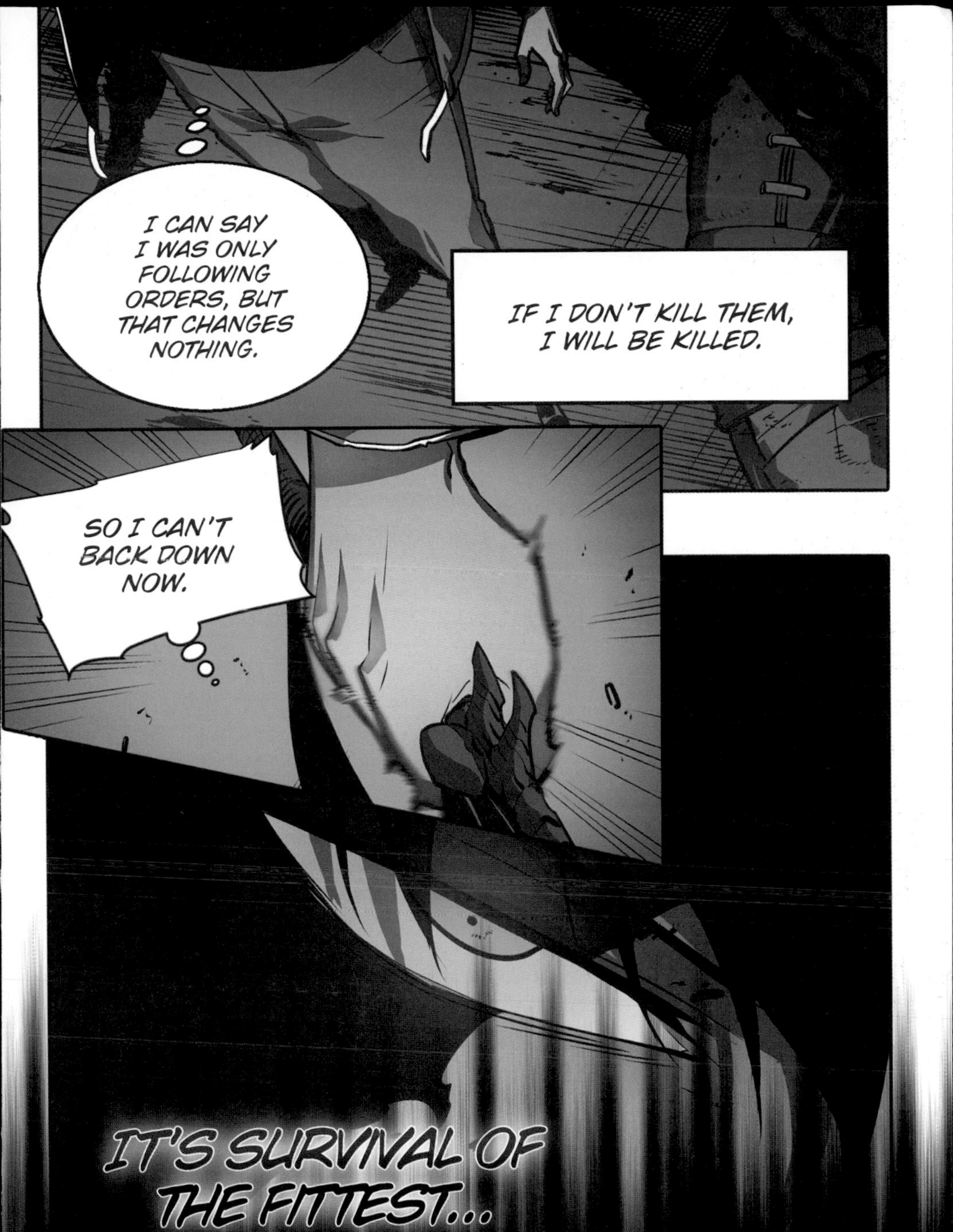
I CAN SAY I WAS ONLY FOLLOWING ORDERS, BUT THAT CHANGES NOTHING.
IF I DON'T KILL THEM, I WILL BE KILLED.
SO I CAN'T BACK DOWN NOW.
IT'S SURVIVAL OF THE FITTEST...

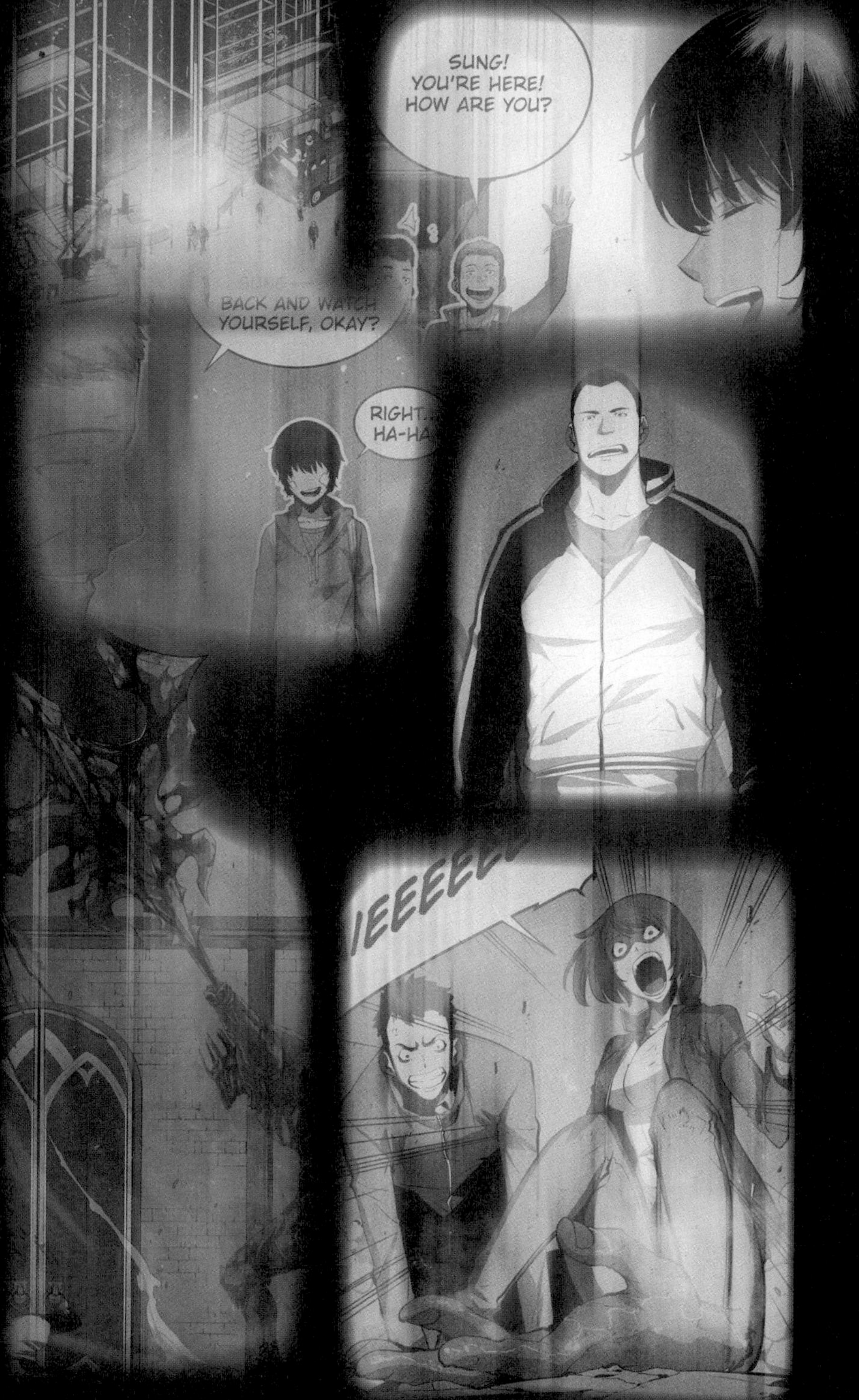
SUNG! YOU'RE HERE! HOW ARE YOU?
BACK AND WATCH YOURSELF, OKAY?
RIGHT. HA-HA
IEEEEE

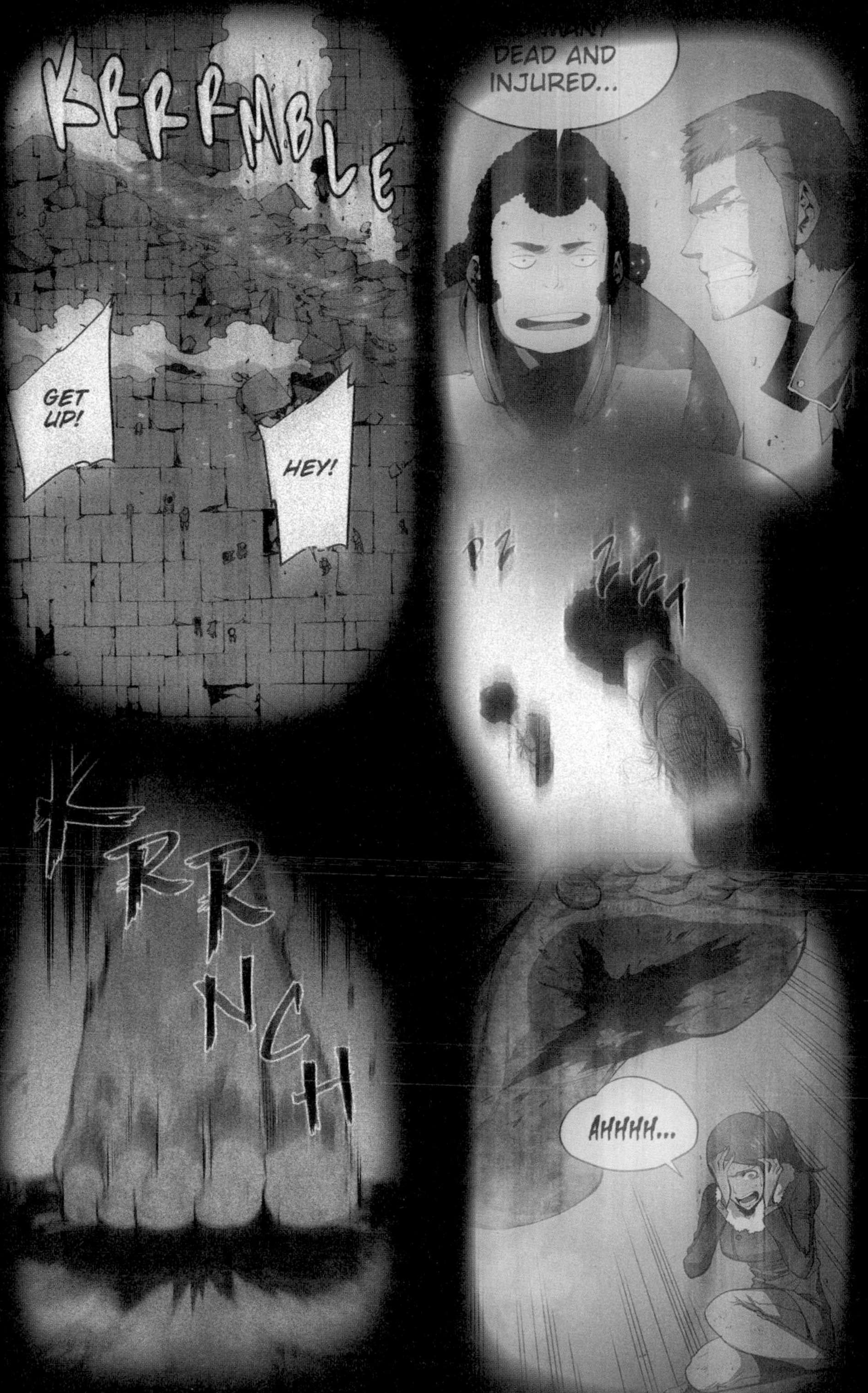
DEAD AND INJURED...
KRRRMBLE
HEY!
GET UP!
AHHHH...
KRRRNCH

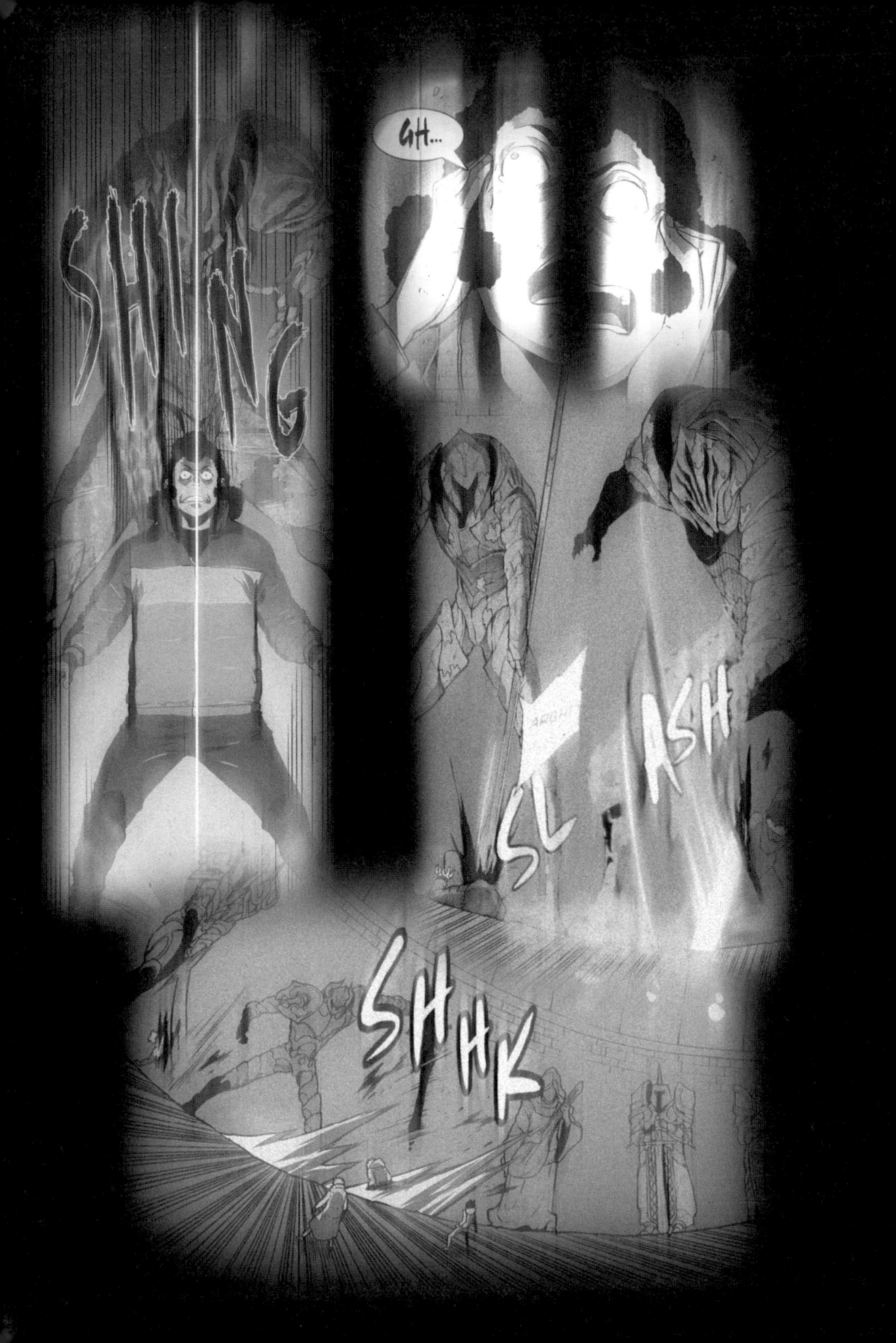
SHING
GH...
SLASH
SHHK

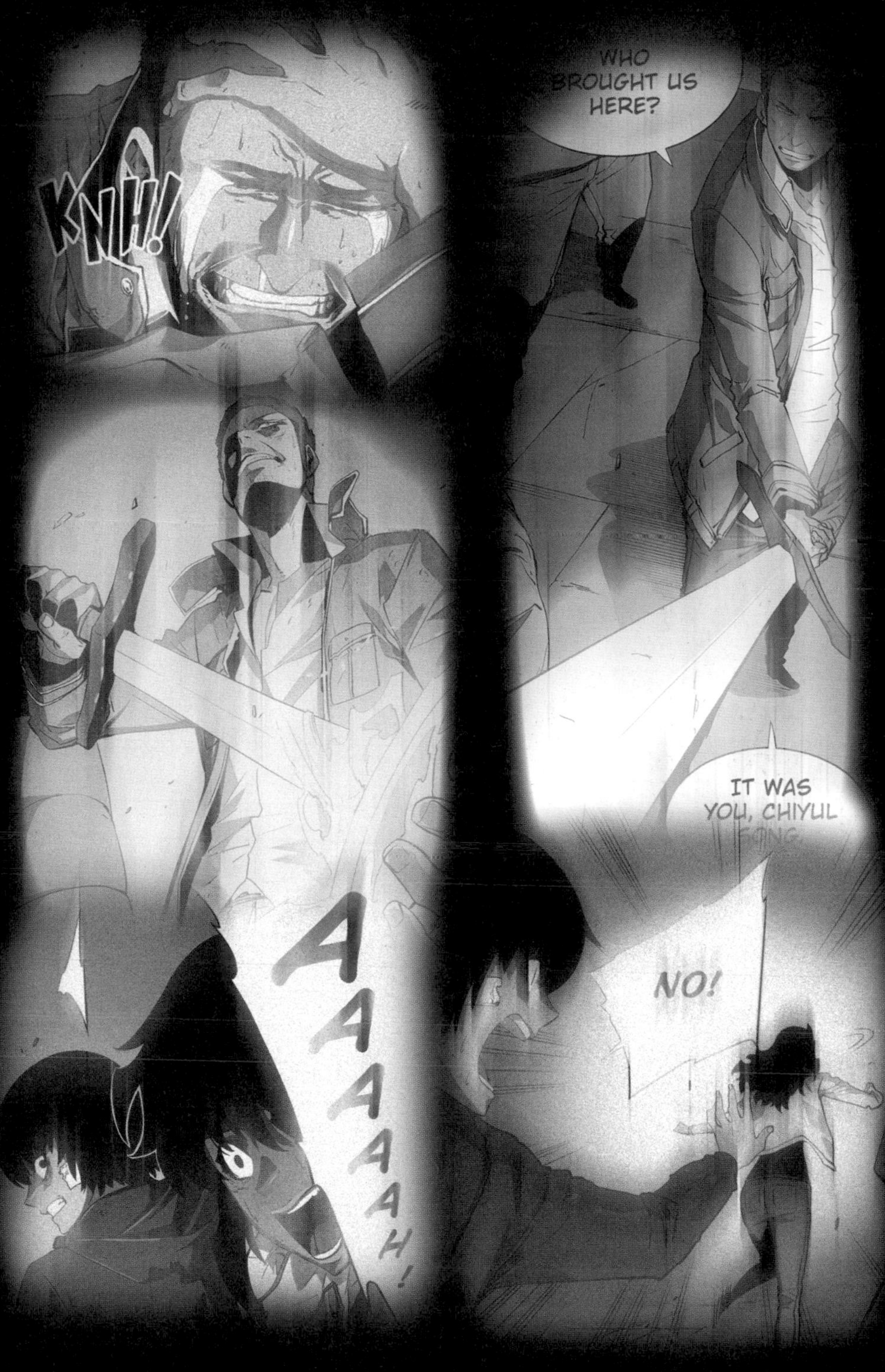
KNH!!
WHO BROUGHT US HERE?
IT WAS YOU, CHIYUL
AAAAAAH!
NO!

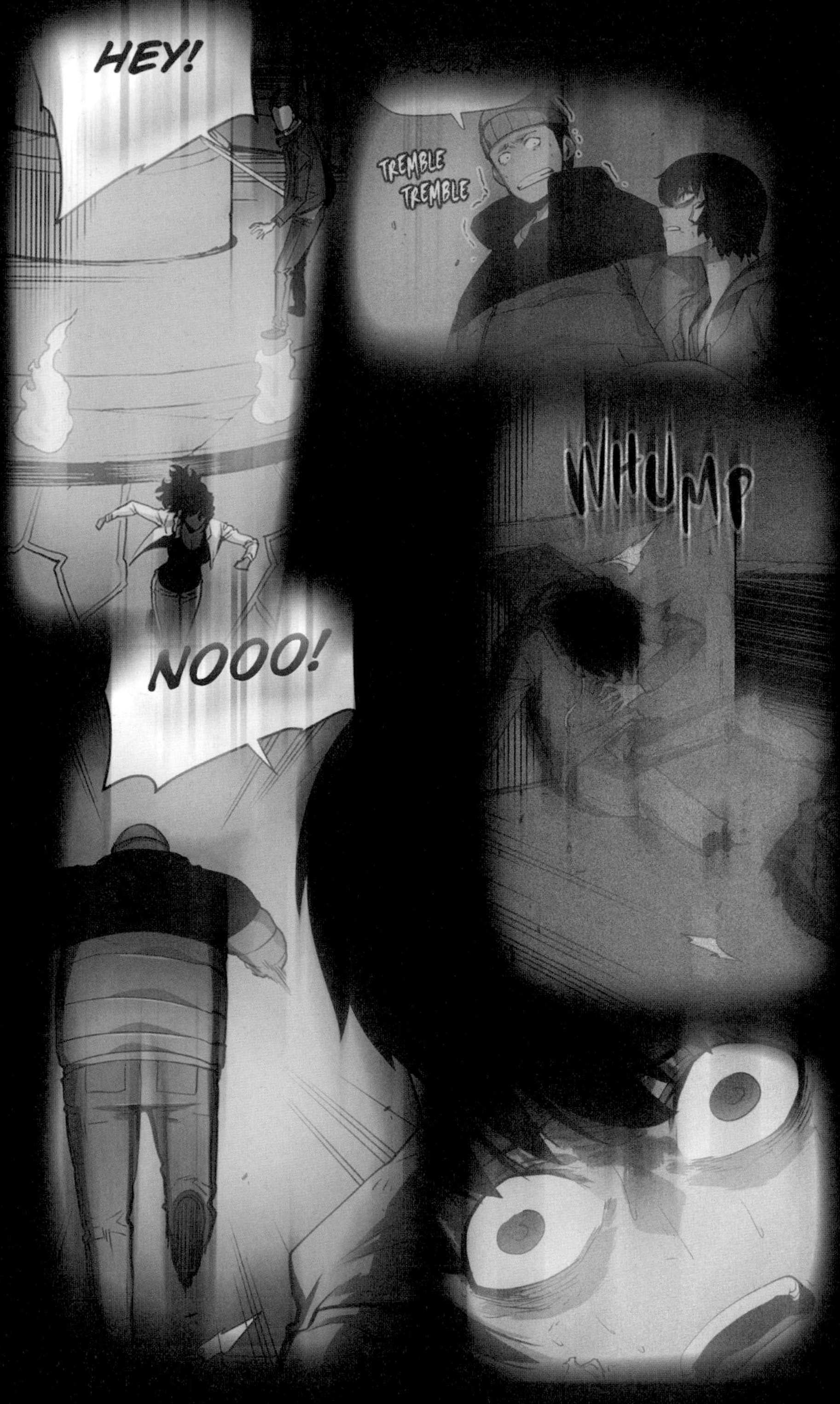
HEY!
TREMBLE TREMBLE
WHUMP
NOOO!

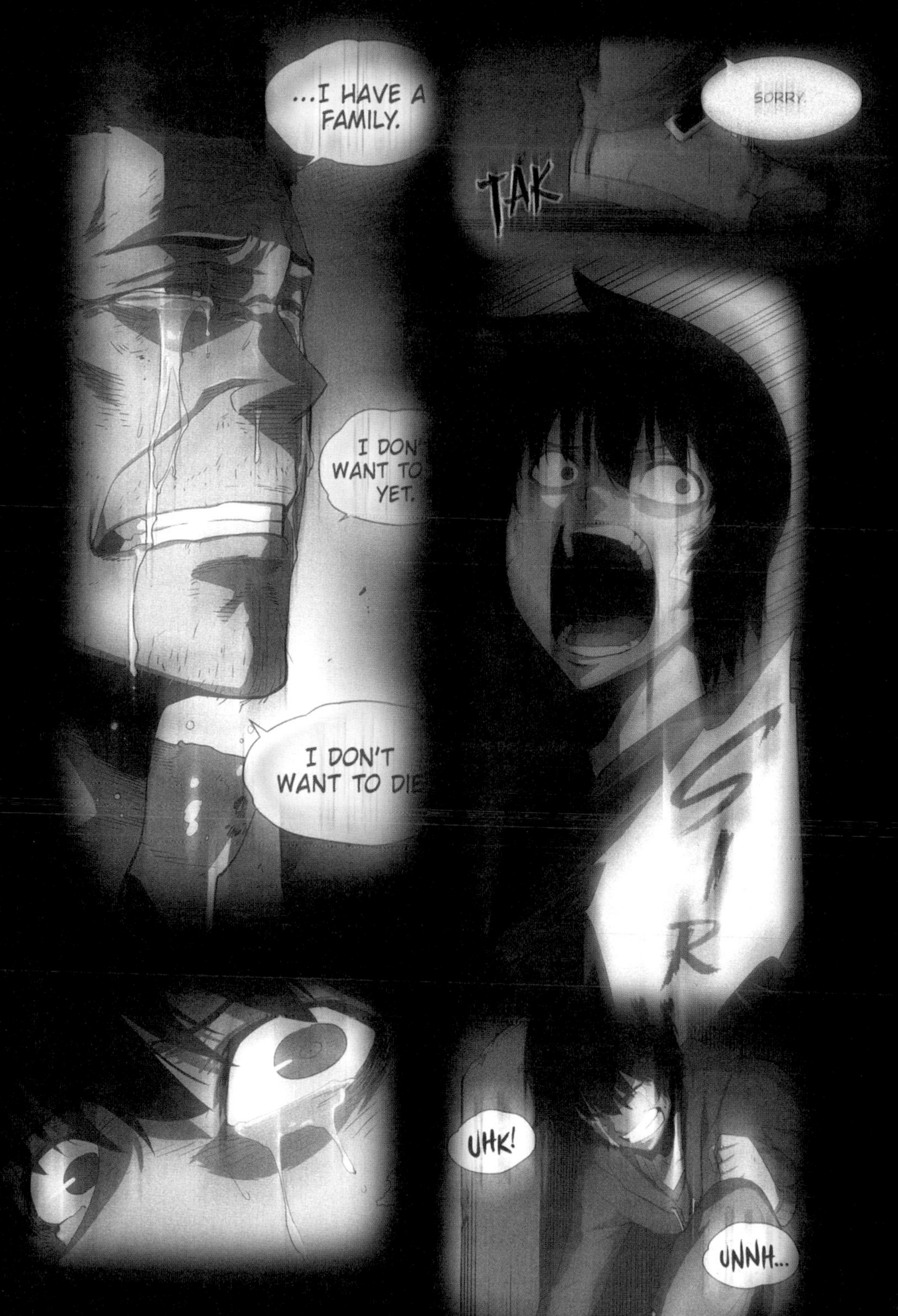
...I HAVE A FAMILY.
SORRY.
TAK
I DON WANT TO YET.
I DON'T WANT TO DIE
SIR
UHK!
UNNH...

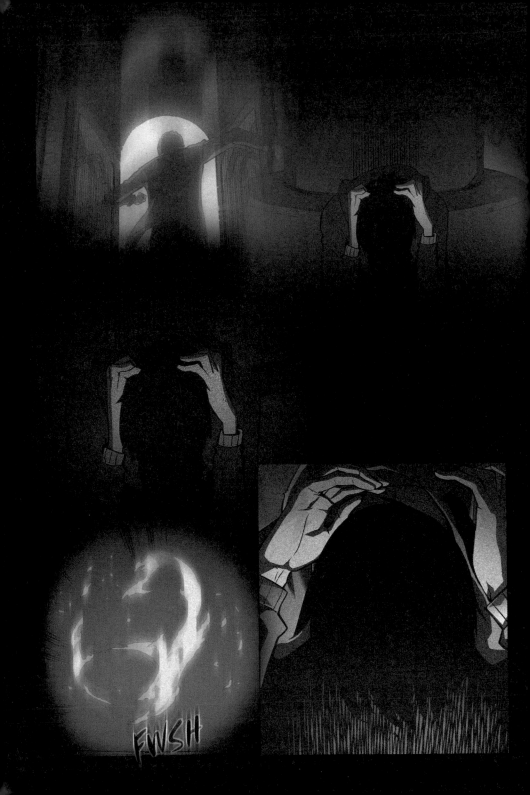

FWSH

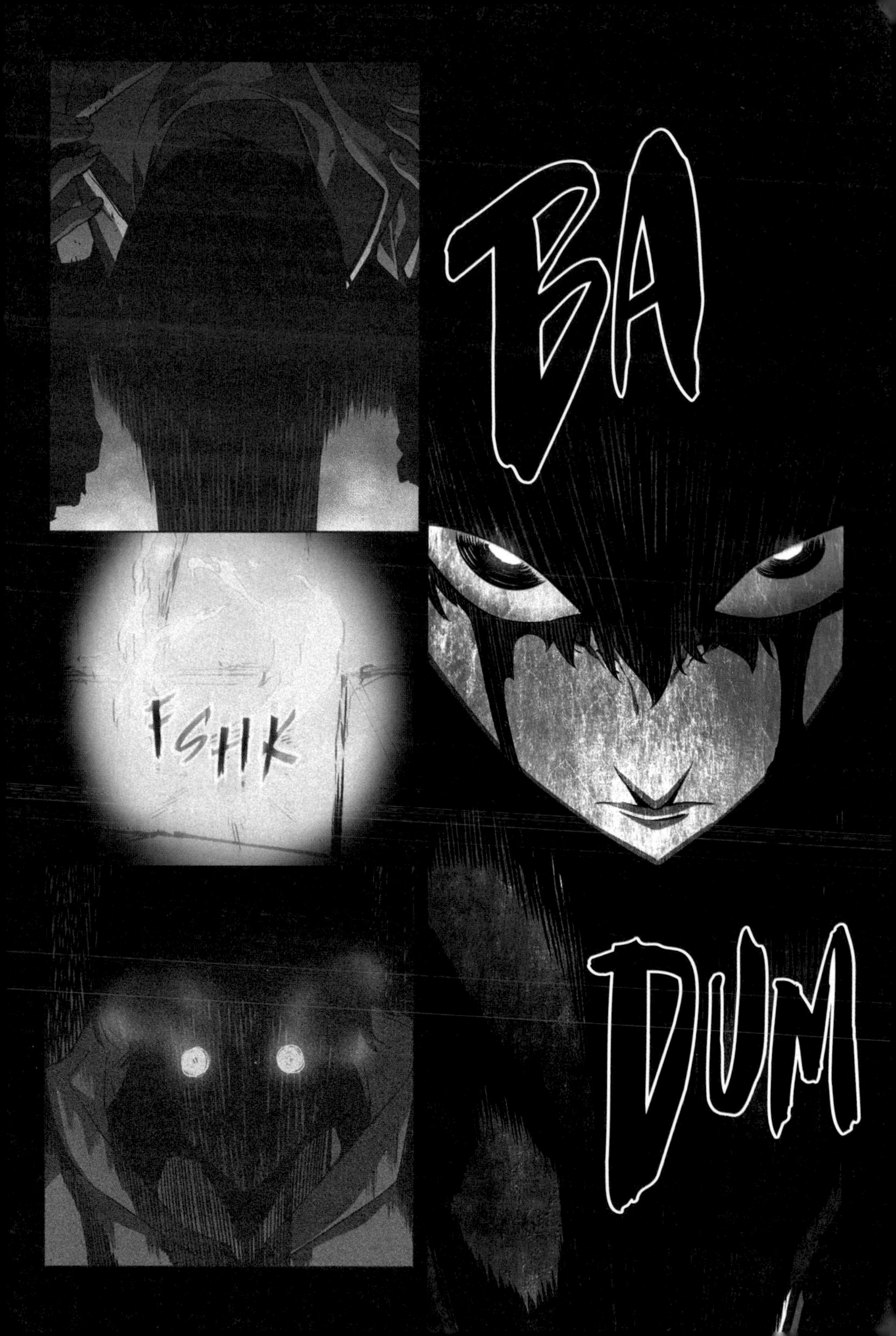
FSHK
BA
DUM

I DON'T KNOW WHAT HE'S UP TO. WATCH YOURSELF.

HIT HIM AGAIN.

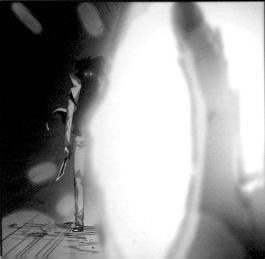

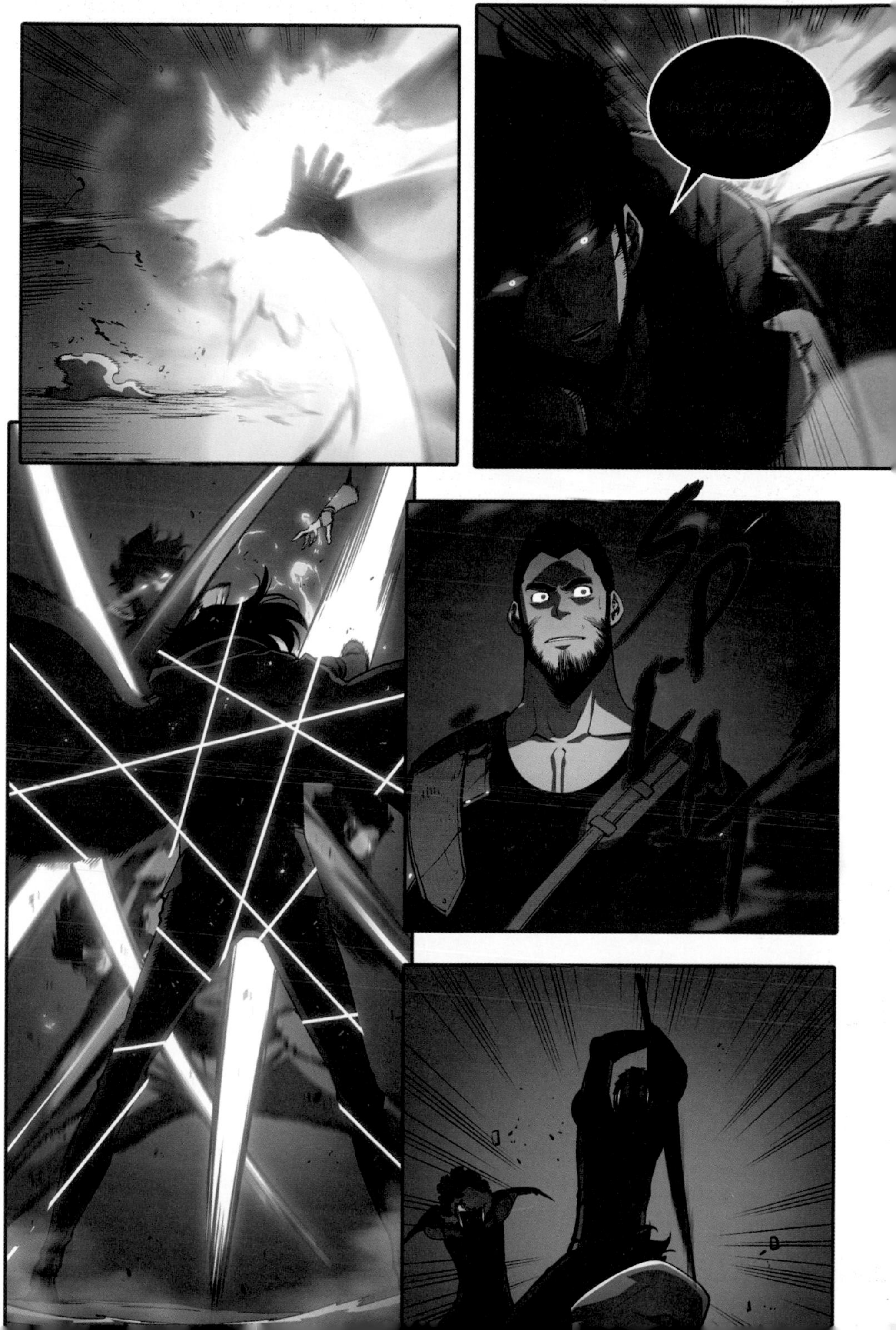

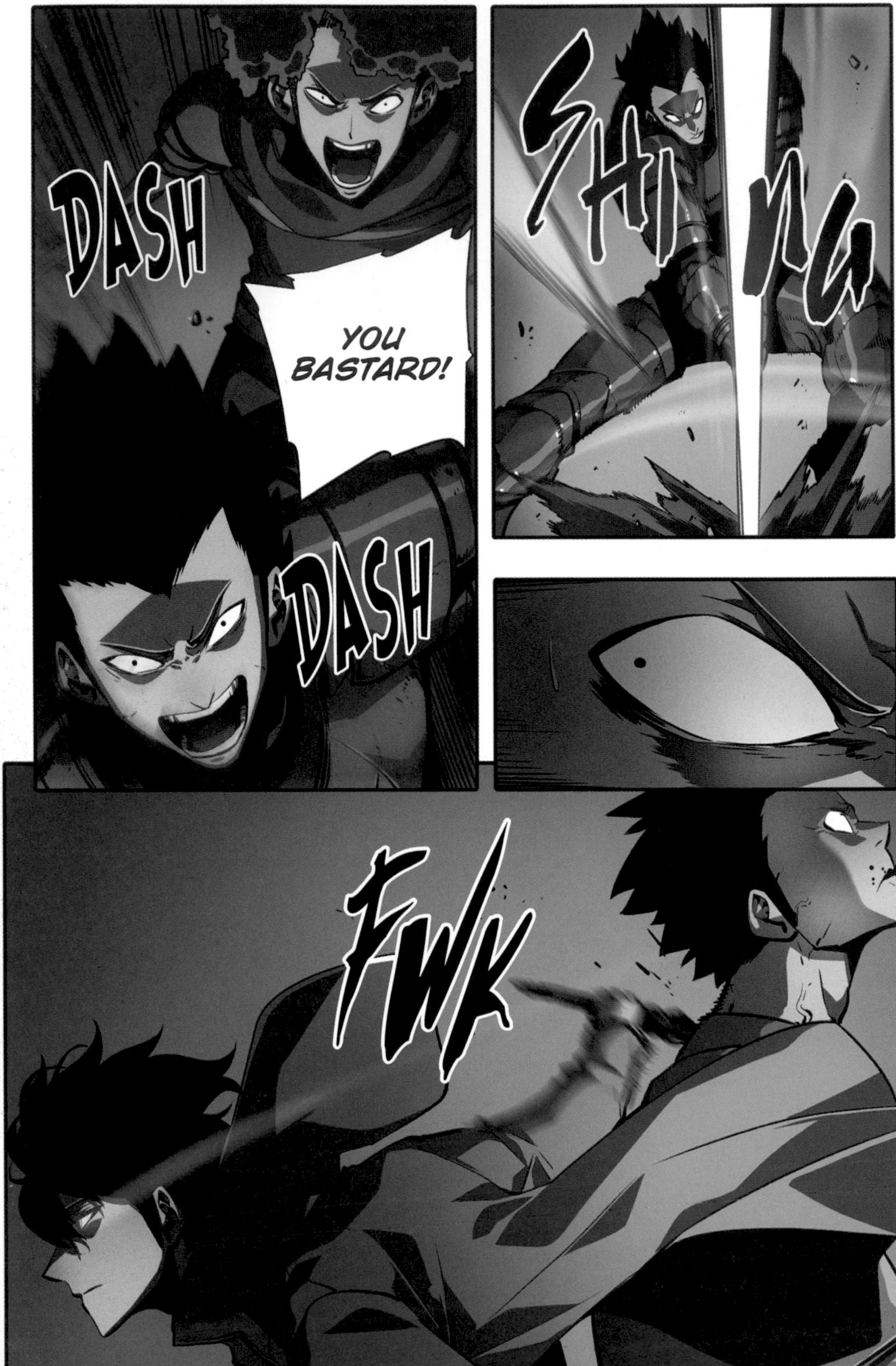
DASH
YOU BASTARD!
DASH
SHING
FWK

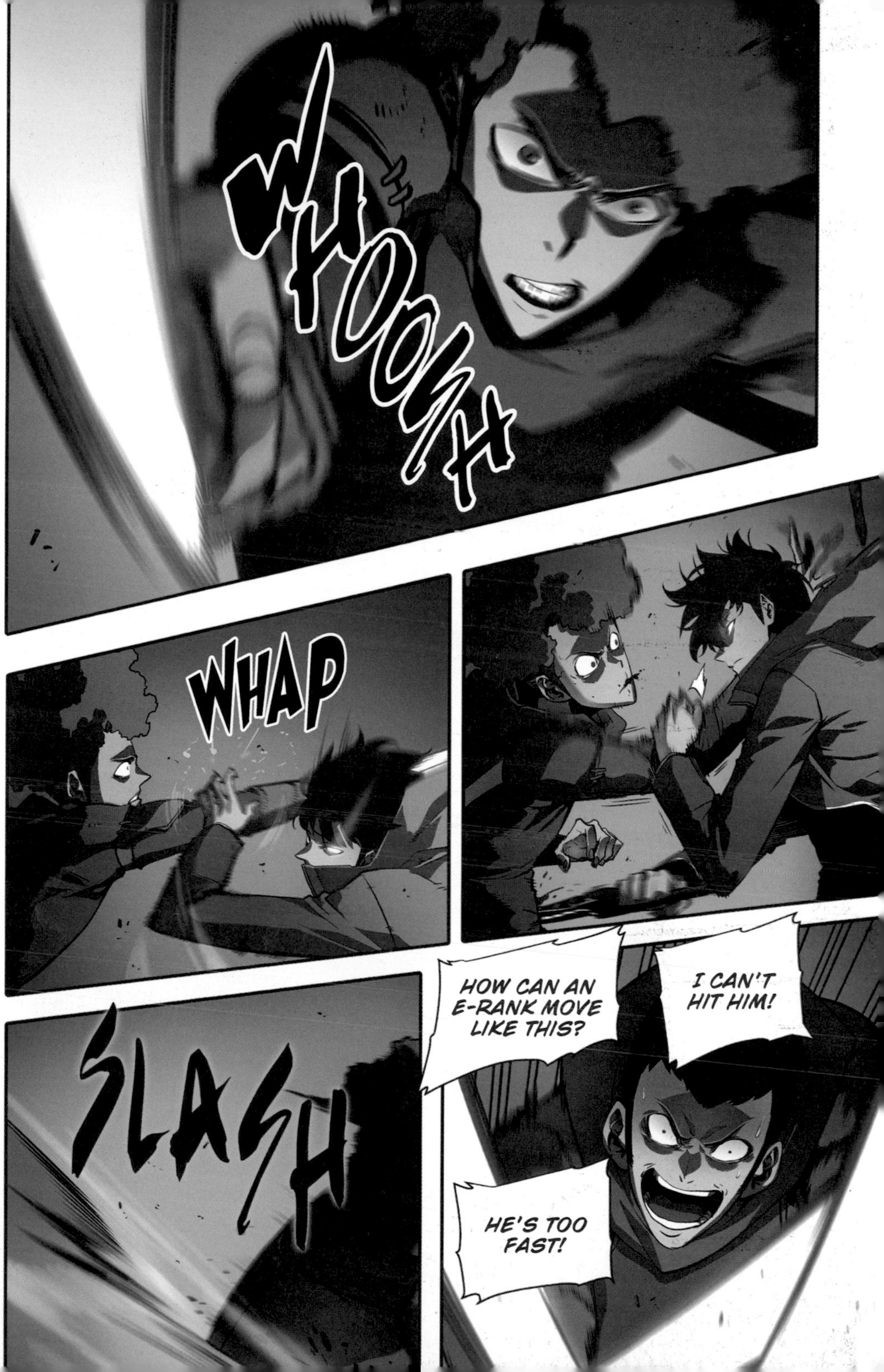
WHOOOSH
WHAP
SLASH
HOW CAN AN E-RANK MOVE LIKE THIS?
I CAN'T HIT HIM!
HE'S TOO FAST!

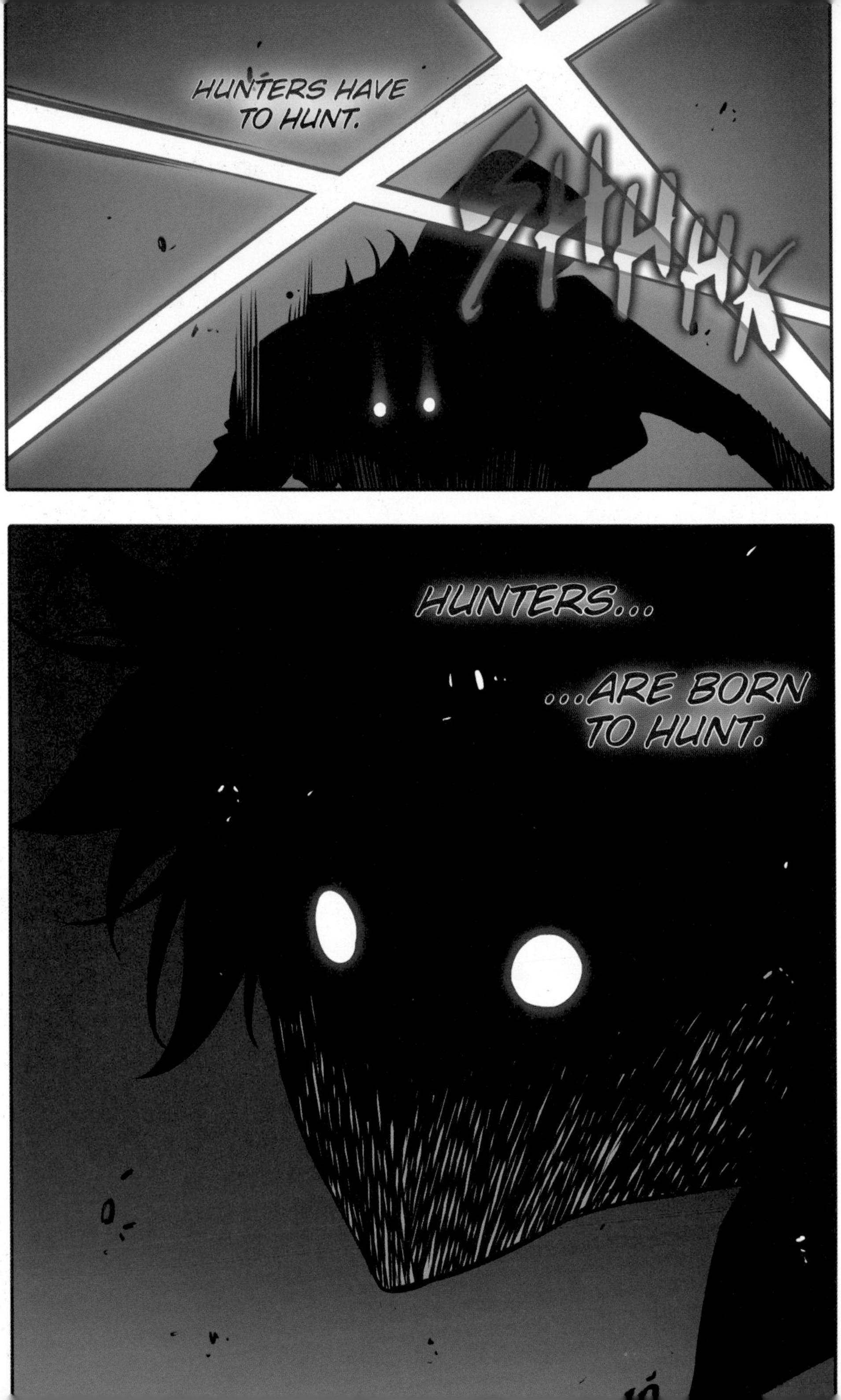
HUNTERS HAVE TO HUNT.
SHUNK
HUNTERS...
...ARE BORN TO HUNT.

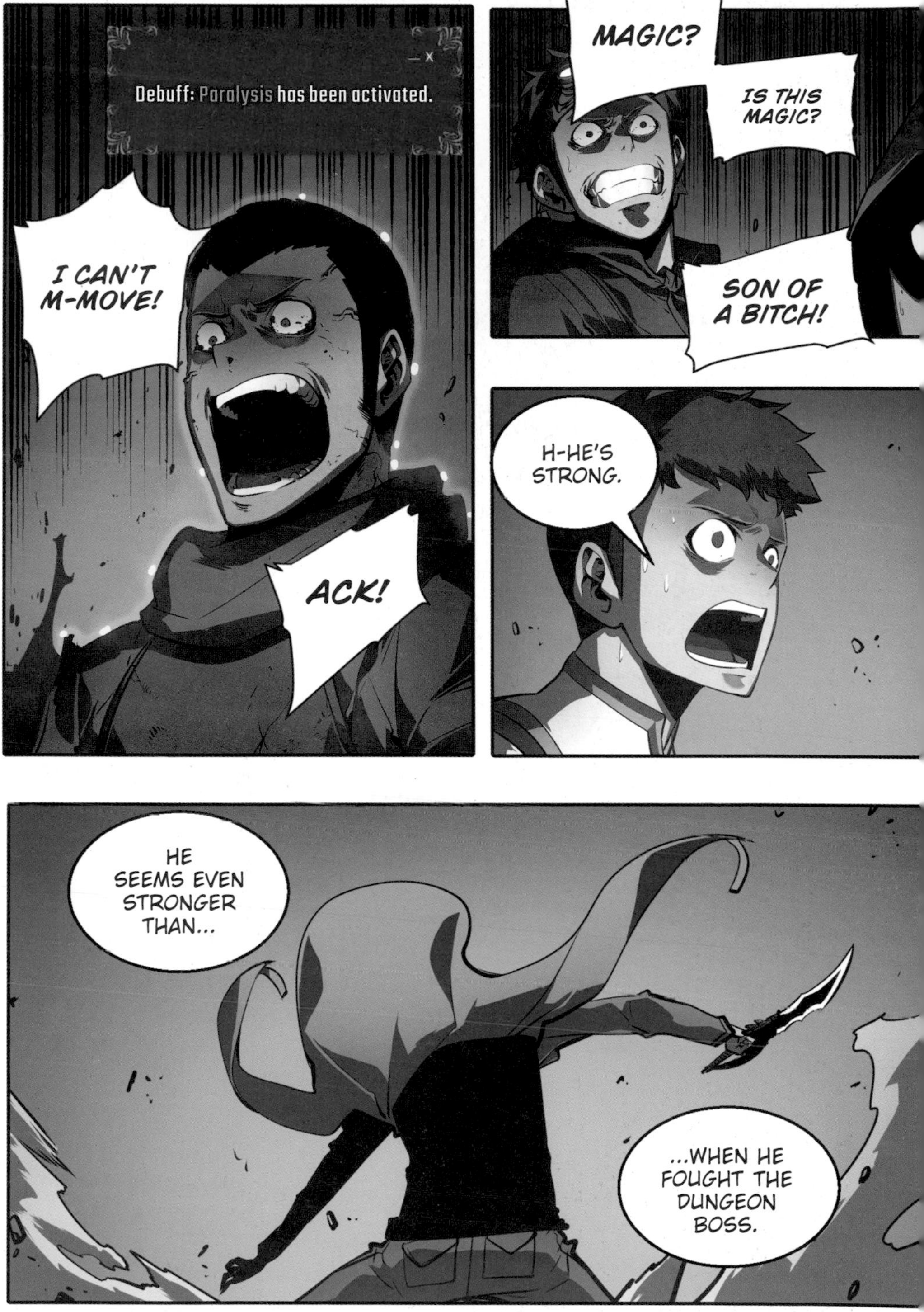

Debuff: Paralysis has been activated.
I CAN'T M-MOVE!
ACK!
MAGIC?
IS THIS MAGIC?
SON OF A BITCH!
H-HE'S STRONG.
HE SEEMS EVEN STRONGER THAN...
...WHEN HE FOUGHT THE DUNGEON BOSS.

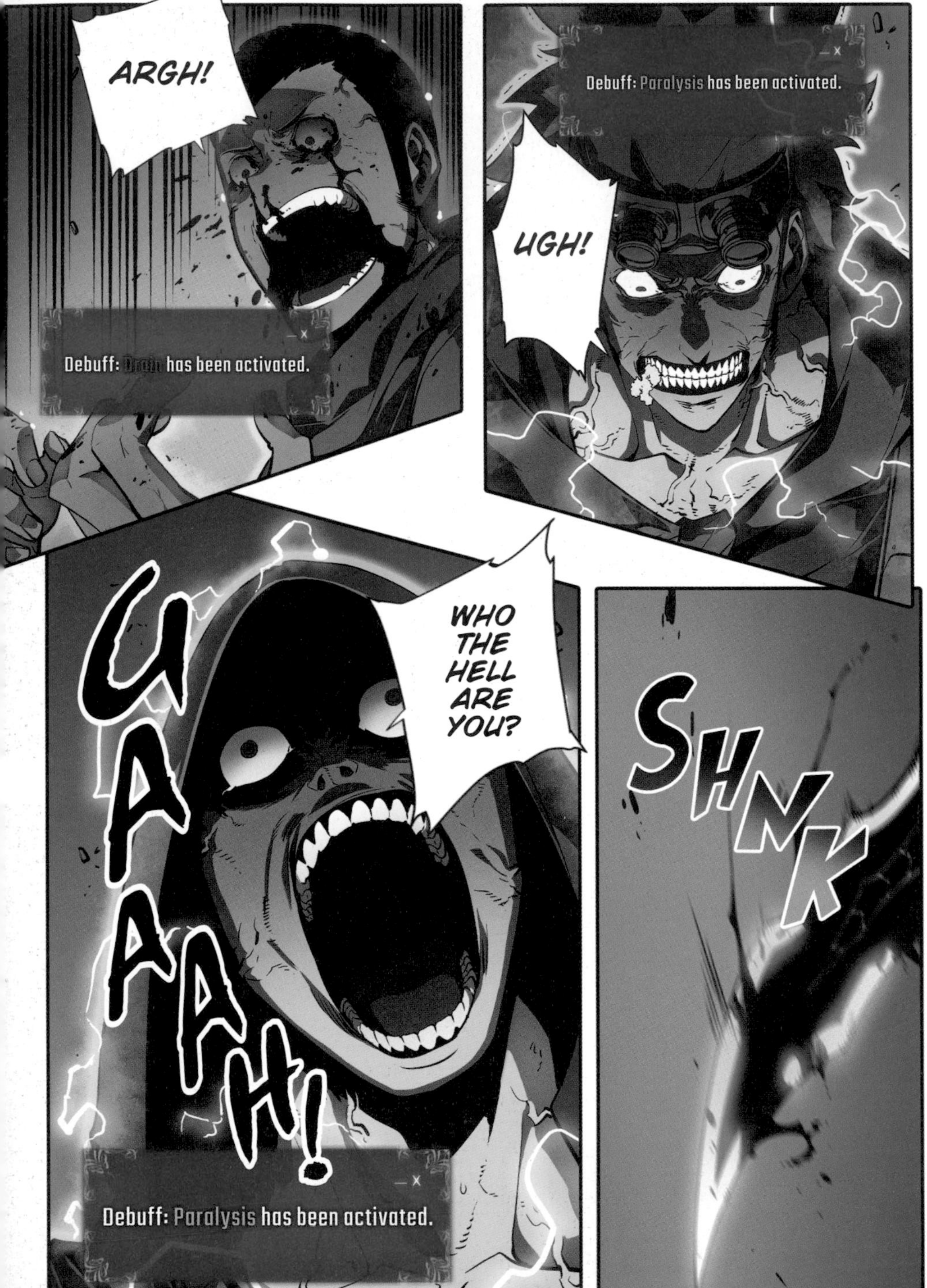
ARGH!
Debuff: Drain has been activated.
Debuff: Paralysis has been activated.
UGH!
UAAAH!
WHO THE HELL ARE YOU?
Debuff: Paralysis has been activated.
SHNK

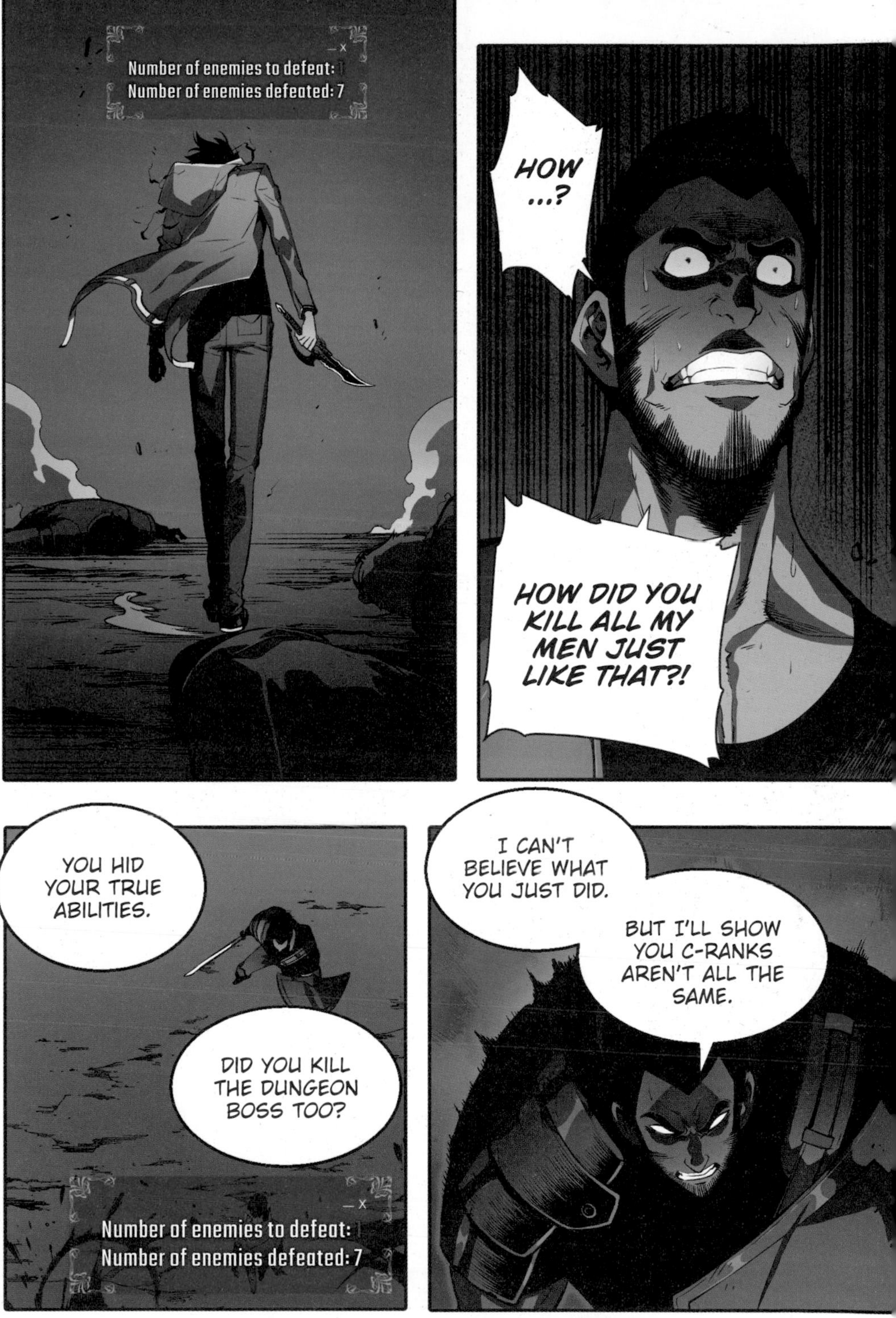
Number of enemies to defeat: 1
Number of enemies defeated: 7
HOW ...?
HOW DID YOU KILL ALL MY MEN JUST LIKE THAT?!
YOU HID YOUR TRUE ABILITIES.
DID YOU KILL THE DUNGEON BOSS TOO?
Number of enemies to defeat: 1
Number of enemies defeated: 7
I CAN'T BELIEVE WHAT YOU JUST DID.
BUT I'LL SHOW YOU C-RANKS AREN'T ALL THE SAME.

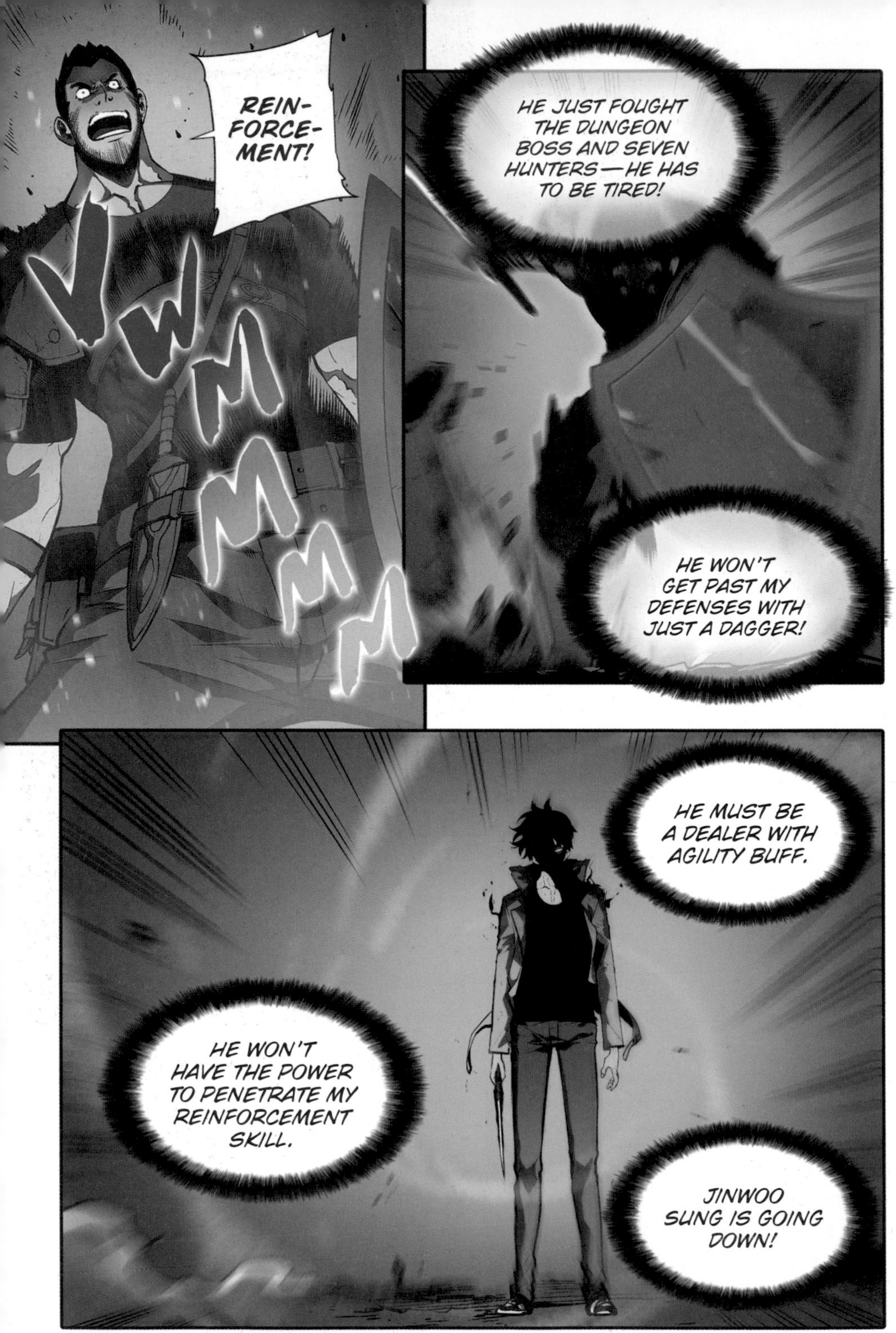
REIN-FORCE-MENT!
VWMMMM
HE JUST FOUGHT THE DUNGEON BOSS AND SEVEN HUNTERS—HE HAS TO BE TIRED!
HE WON'T GET PAST MY DEFENSES WITH JUST A DAGGER!
HE MUST BE A DEALER WITH AGILITY BUFF.
HE WON'T HAVE THE POWER TO PENETRATE MY REINFORCEMENT SKILL.
JINWOO SUNG IS GOING DOWN!

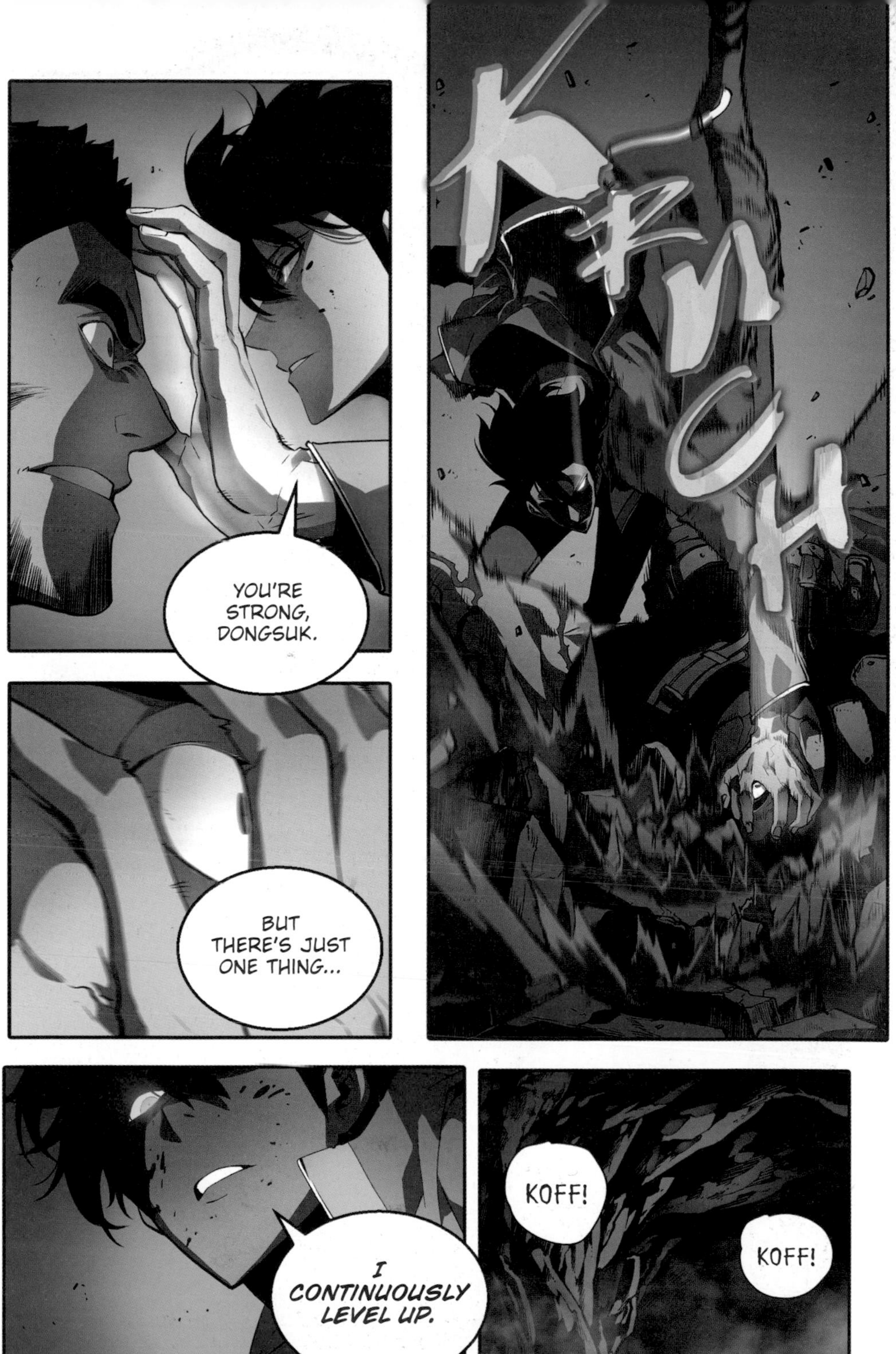
YOU'RE STRONG, DONGSUK.
BUT THERE'S JUST ONE THING...
I CONTINUOUSLY LEVEL UP.
KOFF!
KOFF!

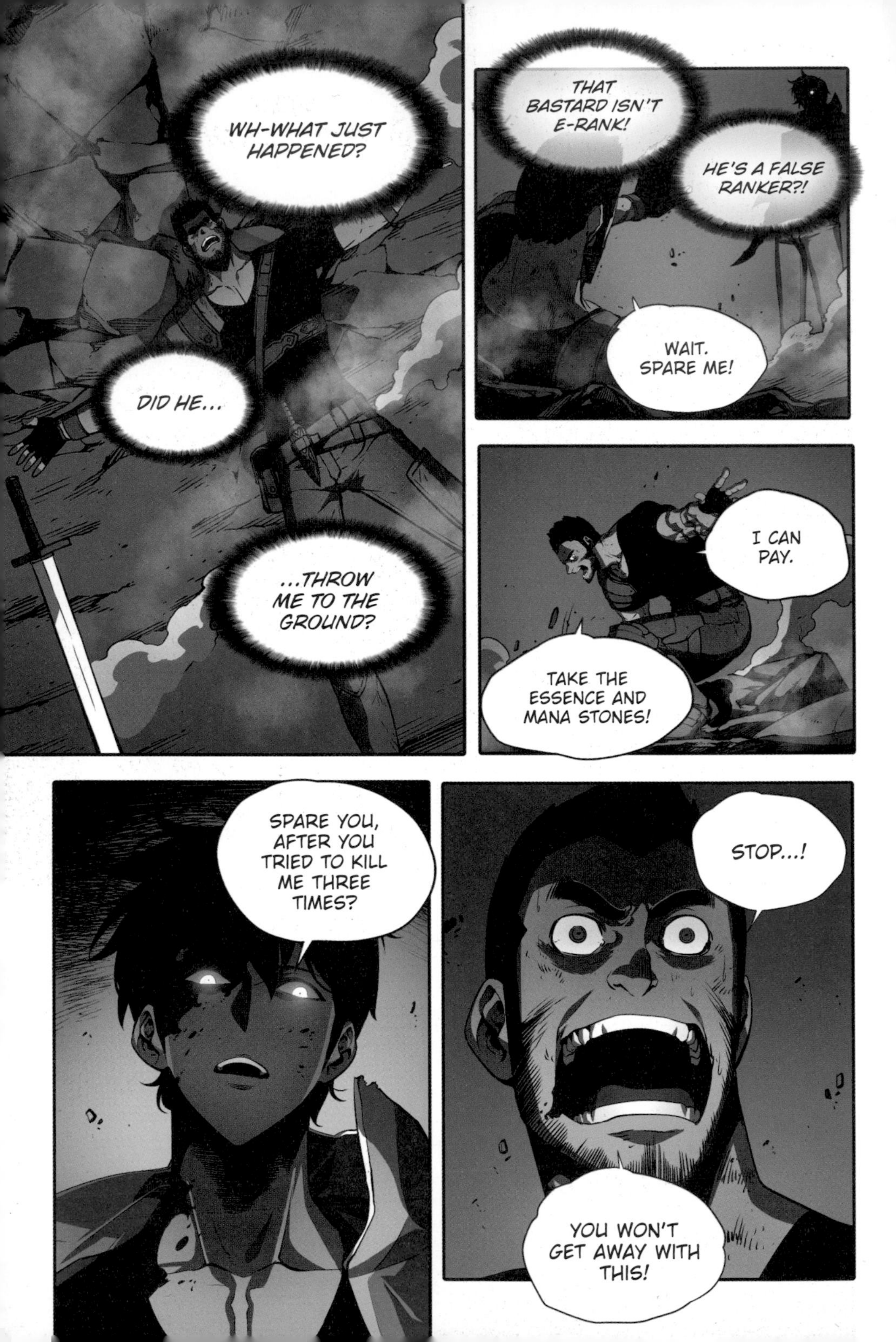
WH-WHAT JUST HAPPENED?
DID HE...
...THROW ME TO THE GROUND?
THAT BASTARD ISN'T E-RANK!
HE'S A FALSE RANKER?!
WAIT. SPARE ME!
I CAN PAY.
TAKE THE ESSENCE AND MANA STONES!
SPARE YOU, AFTER YOU TRIED TO KILL ME THREE TIMES?
STOP...!
YOU WON'T GET AWAY WITH THIS!

WHAT HAPPENS IN A DUNGEON...

...STAYS IN A DUNGEON, RIGHT?

SHUDDER

YOU BASTARD!

DO YOU HAVE ANY IDEA WHO MY YOUNGER BROTHE—

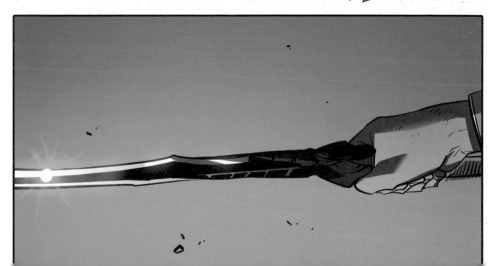

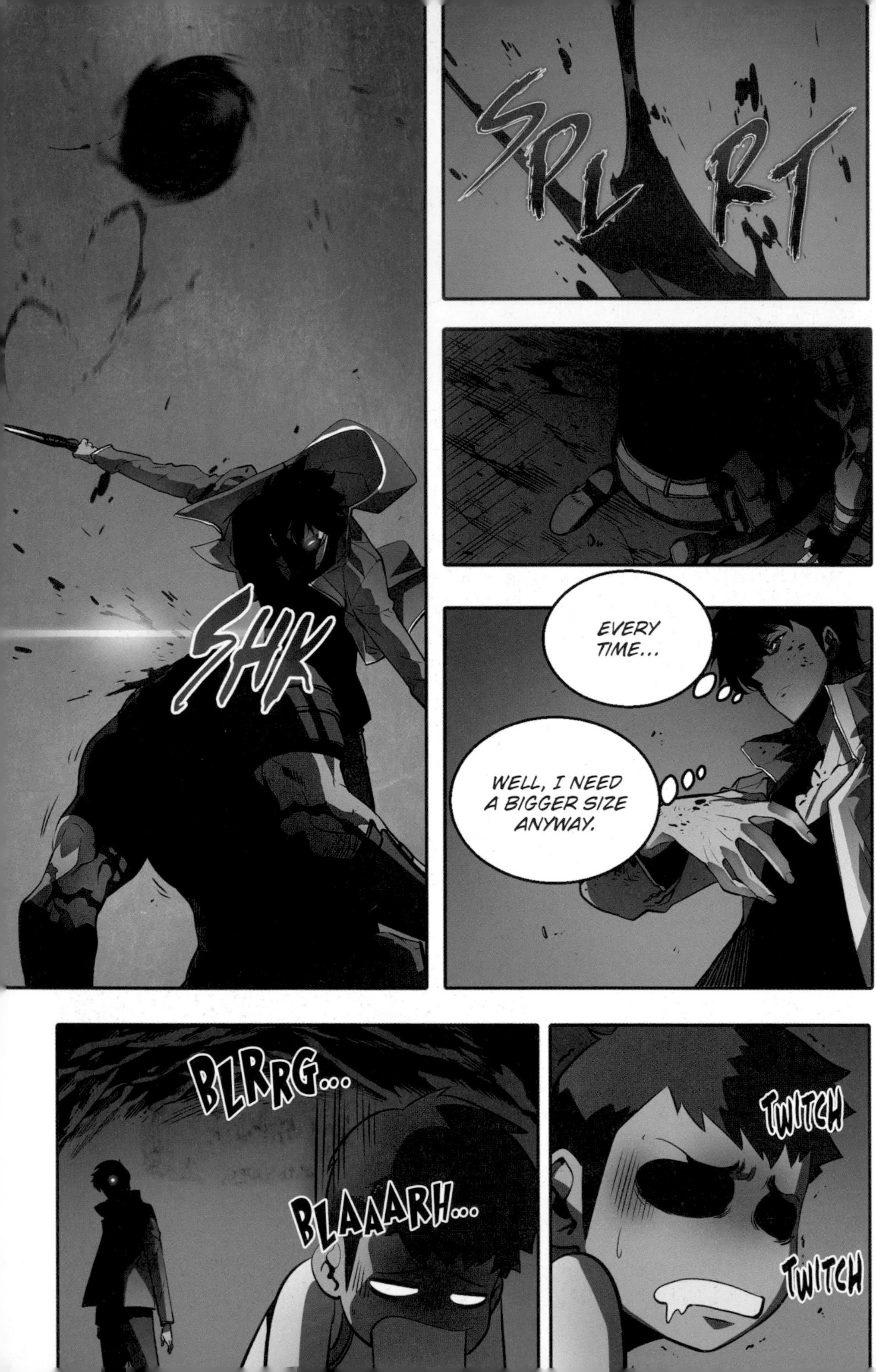
SHK
SPLRT
EVERY TIME...
WELL, I NEED A BIGGER SIZE ANYWAY.
BLRRG...
BLAAARH...
TWITCH
TWITCH

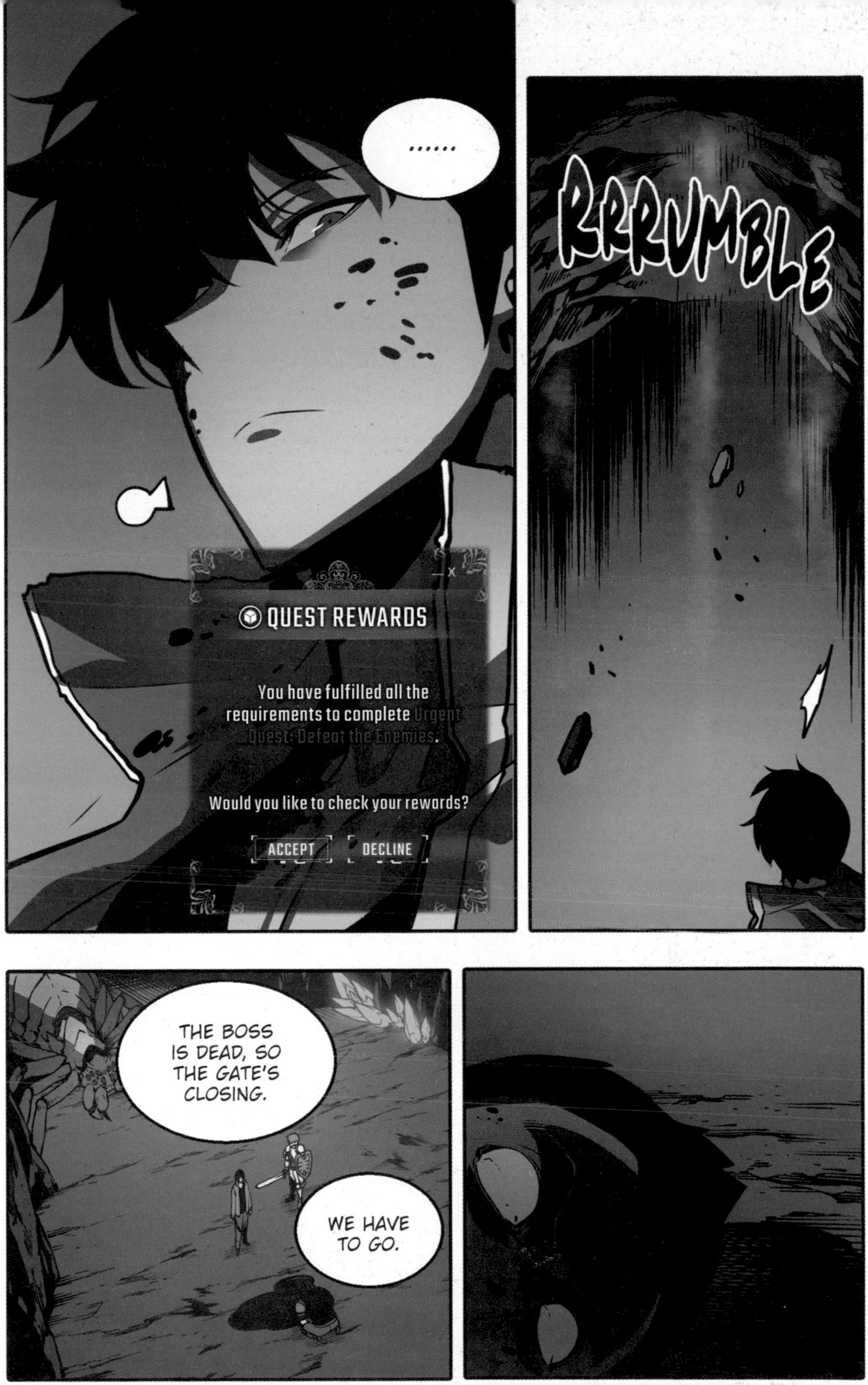
......
QUEST REWARDS
You have fulfilled all the requirements to complete Urgent Quest: Defeat the Enemies.
Would you like to check your rewards?
ACCEPT
DECLINE
RRRUMBLE
THE BOSS IS DEAD, SO THE GATE'S CLOSING.
WE HAVE TO GO.

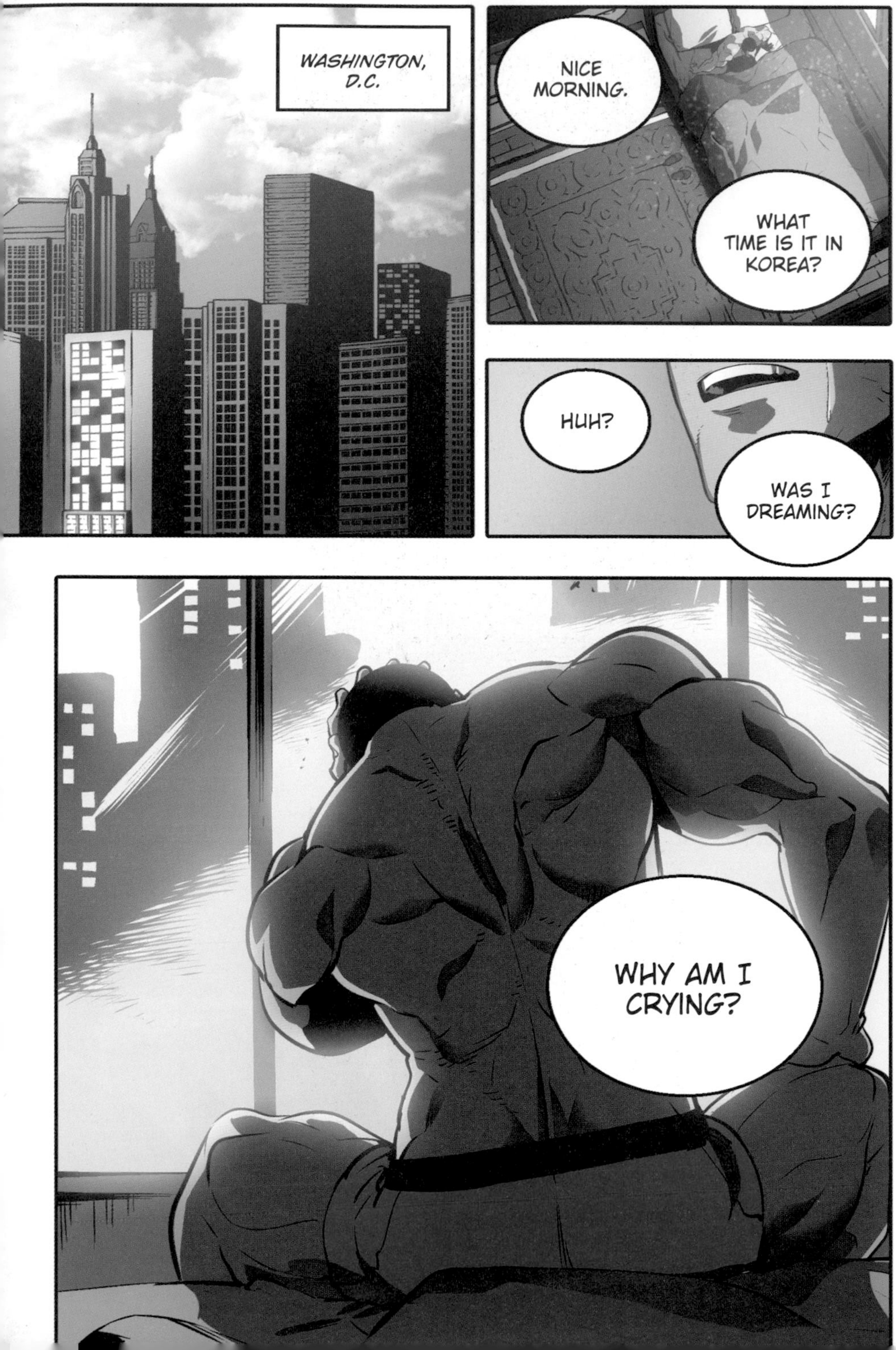
WASHINGTON, D.C.
NICE MORNING.
WHAT TIME IS IT IN KOREA?
HUH?
WAS I DREAMING?
WHY AM I CRYING?

⬢ QUEST REWARDS

Choose your rewards.

The following rewards have been delivered.

Reward 1. Full Recovery	
Reward 2. Ability Points	+10
Reward 3. Skill: Murderous Intent	

Would you like to accept?

ACCEPT   DECLINE

⏺ SKILL

[Active Skill]

🧟 Murderous Intent	Lv. 1

100 mana required.
Emits strong pressure on the chosen target to
put them in an extreme panic for 1 minute.
You may select several targets at once.
—Debuff: Panic: All abilities -50%

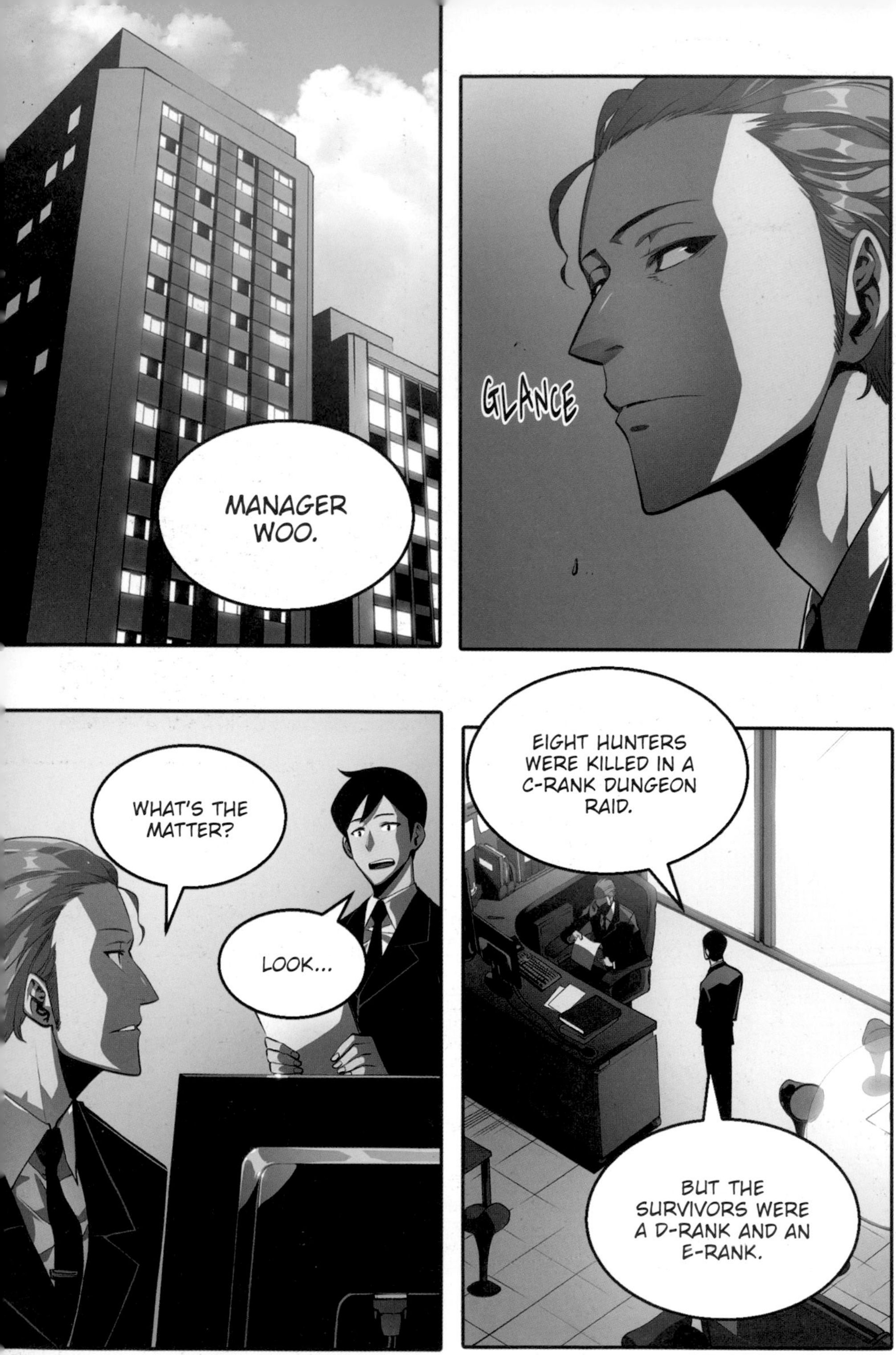
MANAGER WOO.
GLANCE
WHAT'S THE MATTER?
LOOK...
EIGHT HUNTERS WERE KILLED IN A C-RANK DUNGEON RAID.
BUT THE SURVIVORS WERE A D-RANK AND AN E-RANK.

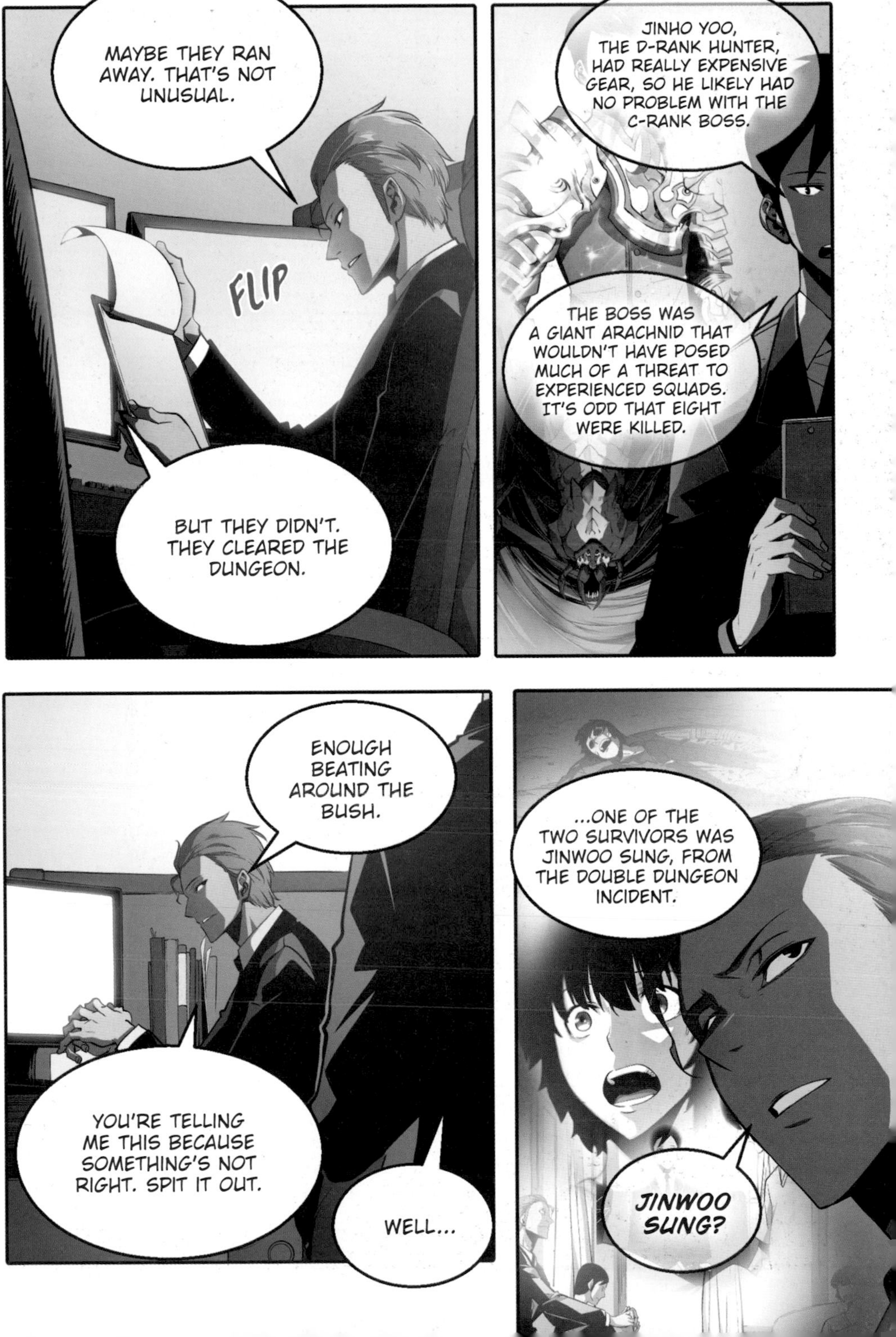
MAYBE THEY RAN AWAY. THAT'S NOT UNUSUAL.
FLIP
BUT THEY DIDN'T. THEY CLEARED THE DUNGEON.
JINHO YOO, THE D-RANK HUNTER, HAD REALLY EXPENSIVE GEAR, SO HE LIKELY HAD NO PROBLEM WITH THE C-RANK BOSS.
THE BOSS WAS A GIANT ARACHNID THAT WOULDN'T HAVE POSED MUCH OF A THREAT TO EXPERIENCED SQUADS. IT'S ODD THAT EIGHT WERE KILLED.
ENOUGH BEATING AROUND THE BUSH.
YOU'RE TELLING ME THIS BECAUSE SOMETHING'S NOT RIGHT. SPIT IT OUT.
WELL...
...ONE OF THE TWO SURVIVORS WAS JINWOO SUNG, FROM THE DOUBLE DUNGEON INCIDENT.
JINWOO SUNG?

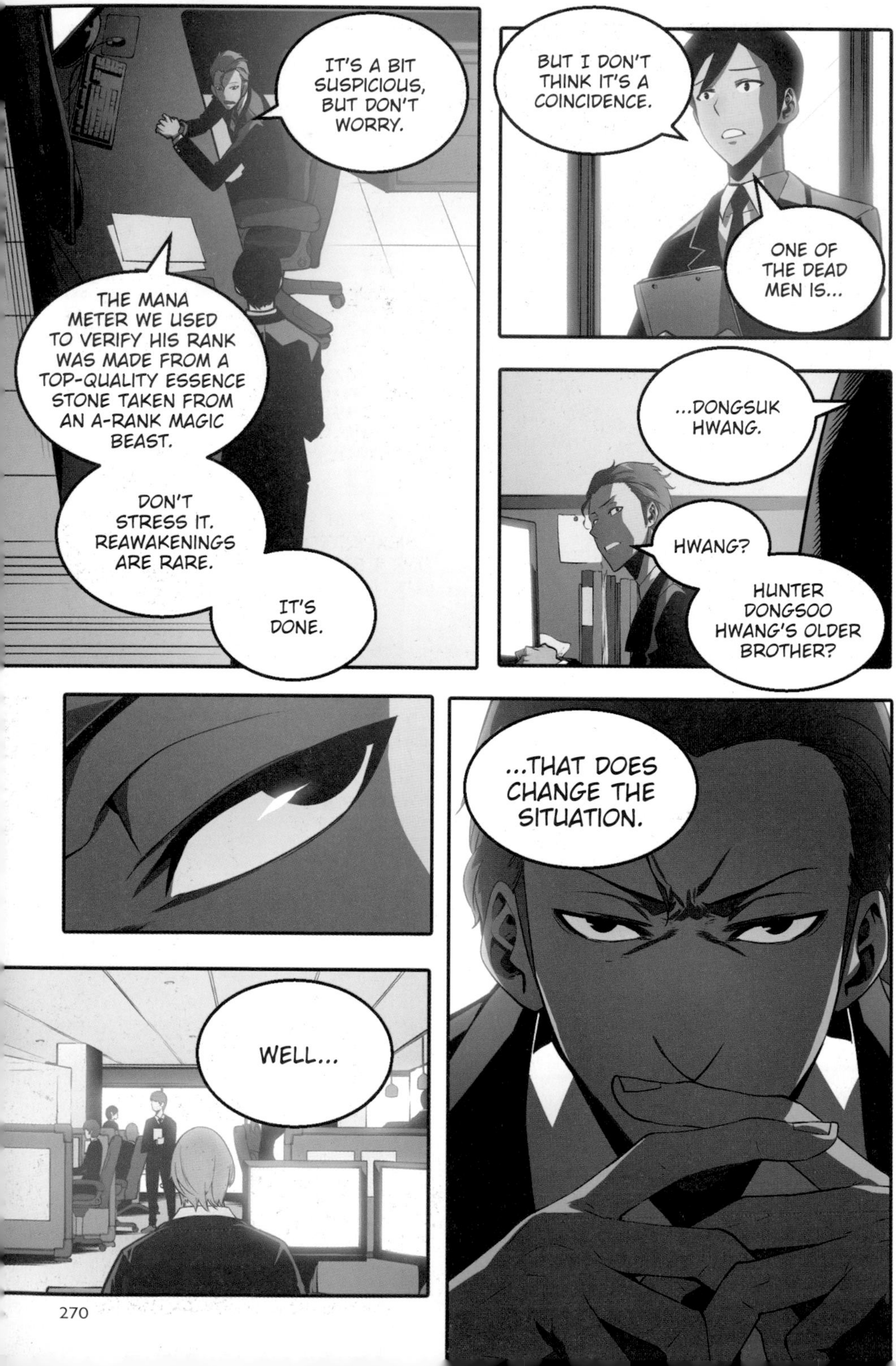
IT'S A BIT SUSPICIOUS, BUT DON'T WORRY.
THE MANA METER WE USED TO VERIFY HIS RANK WAS MADE FROM A TOP-QUALITY ESSENCE STONE TAKEN FROM AN A-RANK MAGIC BEAST.
DON'T STRESS IT. REAWAKENINGS ARE RARE.
IT'S DONE.
BUT I DON'T THINK IT'S A COINCIDENCE.
ONE OF THE DEAD MEN IS...
...DONGSUK HWANG.
HWANG?
HUNTER DONGSOO HWANG'S OLDER BROTHER?
WELL...
...THAT DOES CHANGE THE SITUATION.

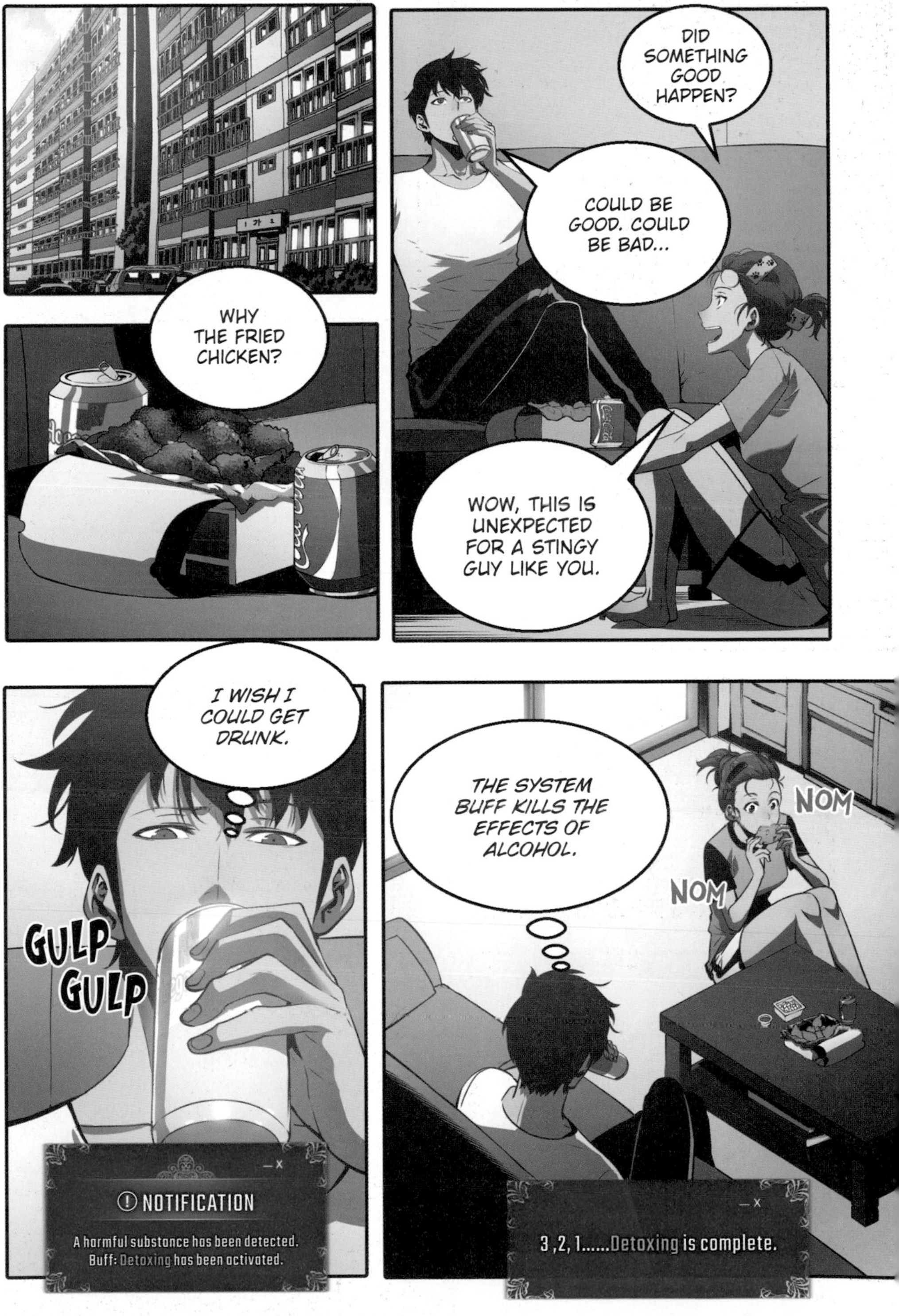
WHY THE FRIED CHICKEN?
DID SOMETHING GOOD HAPPEN?
COULD BE GOOD. COULD BE BAD...
WOW, THIS IS UNEXPECTED FOR A STINGY GUY LIKE YOU.
I WISH I COULD GET DRUNK.
GULP GULP
NOTIFICATION
A harmful substance has been detected.
Buff: Detoxing has been activated.
THE SYSTEM BUFF KILLS THE EFFECTS OF ALCOHOL.
NOM
NOM
3 ,2, 1......Detoxing is complete.

THE REWARD I GOT AFTER I WAS REVIVED FROM THE DOUBLE DUNGEON.

!NOTIFICATION

You have satisfied all the conditions to complete Secret Quest: Courage of the Weak.

SO MUCH HAPPENED BACK THEN THAT I DIDN'T REALIZE...

You have unread message

...THIS WAS A "GIFT" THAT KEEPS ON GIVING.

The system is designed to assist the development of the Player.

!NOTIFICATION

Failure to comply with the system may result in a penalty.

!NOTIFICATION

The rewards have been delivered.

REGENERATION OF MY SEVERED LEG WAS ALSO A REWARD FROM THE SYSTEM.

QUEST REWARD

Secret Quest: Courage of the Weak

The Great Spell Caster Kandiaru's Blessing:
The Great Spell Caster Kandiaru has gifted you with this special blessing.
With Kandiaru's blessing, you may enjoy a strong and healthy life.

QUEST REWARDS

—Temporary Buff:
Spirit of Rehabilitation: All injuries will be healed.

—Long-lasting Buff:
Health and Longevity: You are immunized against all diseases, poisons, and any other debuffs, and your healing ability increases exponentially when you are asleep.

WAIT...

IMMUNE TO ALL POISONS...

SSK

CAN I EAT ALL OF THIS IF YOU'RE DONE?

IF YOU WANT TO GET FAT.

I'M NOT SO SURE ABOUT THIS "BUFF BRO."

LICK

YOU USED TO BE NICER.

HE DOES LOOK GOOD, THOUGH.

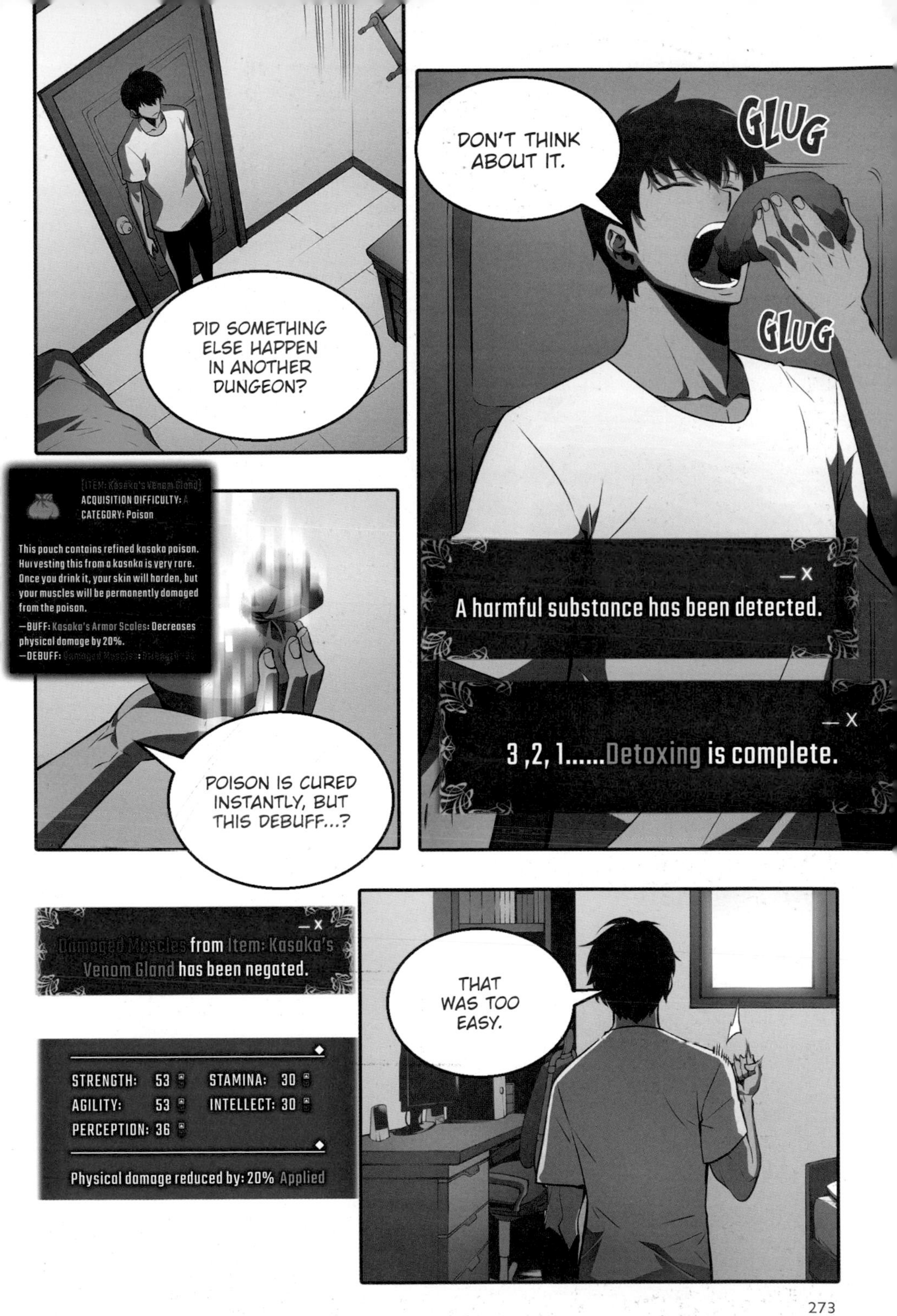

DID SOMETHING ELSE HAPPEN IN ANOTHER DUNGEON?
[ITEM: Kasaka's Venom Gland]
ACQUISITION DIFFICULTY: A
CATEGORY: Poison
This pouch contains refined kasaka poison. Hurvesting this from a kasaka is very rare. Once you drink it, your skin will harden, but your muscles will be permanently damaged from the poison.
—BUFF: Kasaka's Armor Scales: Decreases physical damage by 20%.
—DEBUFF:
POISON IS CURED INSTANTLY, BUT THIS DEBUFF...?
DON'T THINK ABOUT IT.
GLUG
GLUG
— X
A harmful substance has been detected.
— X
3 ,2, 1......Detoxing is complete.
— X
Damaged Muscles from Item: Kasaka's Venom Gland has been negated.
STRENGTH: 53 STAMINA: 30
AGILITY: 53 INTELLECT: 30
PERCEPTION: 36
Physical damage reduced by: 20% Applied
THAT WAS TOO EASY.

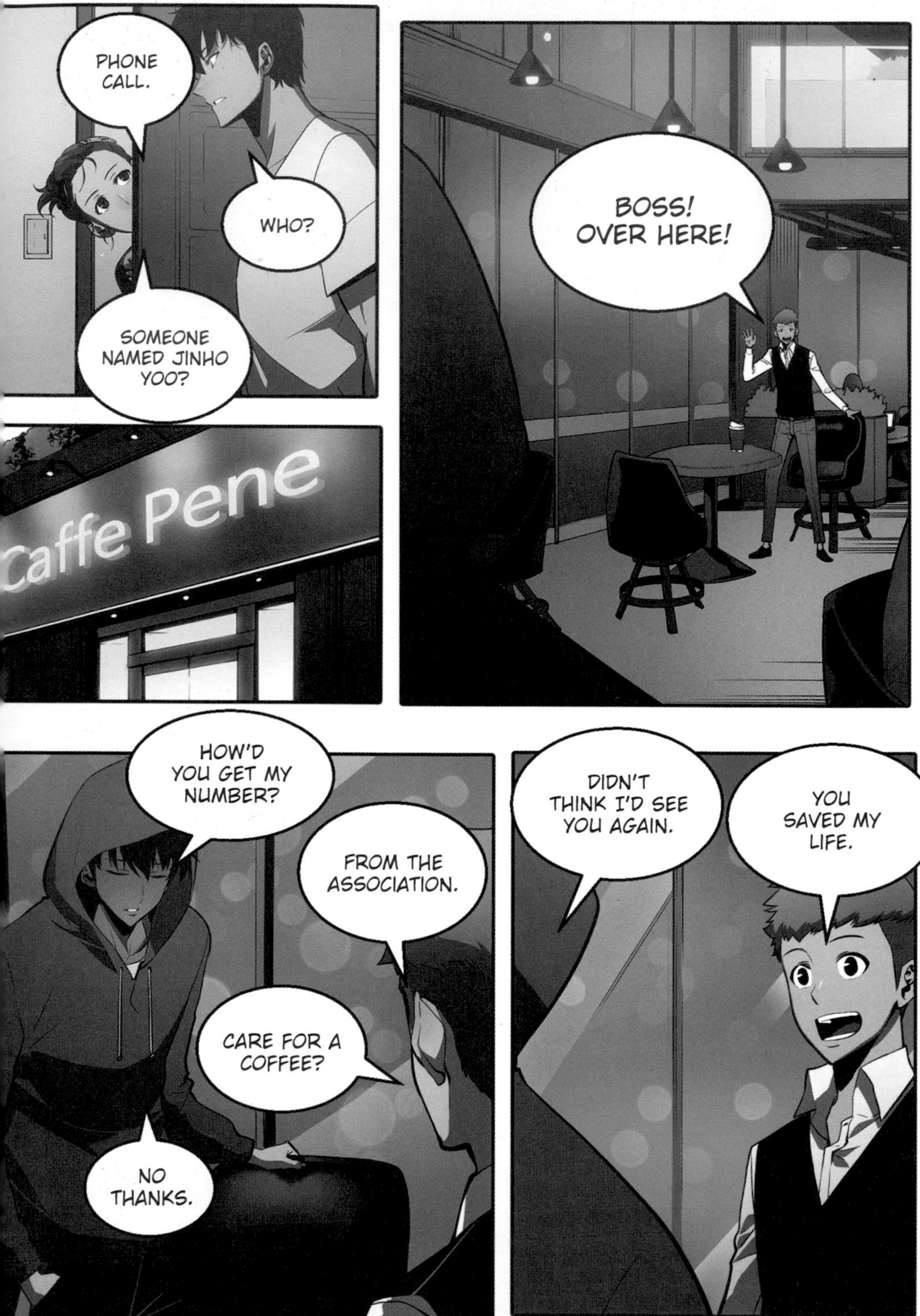
PHONE CALL.
WHO?
SOMEONE NAMED JINHO YOO?
Caffe Pene
BOSS! OVER HERE!
HOW'D YOU GET MY NUMBER?
FROM THE ASSOCIATION.
CARE FOR A COFFEE?
NO THANKS.
DIDN'T THINK I'D SEE YOU AGAIN.
YOU SAVED MY LIFE.

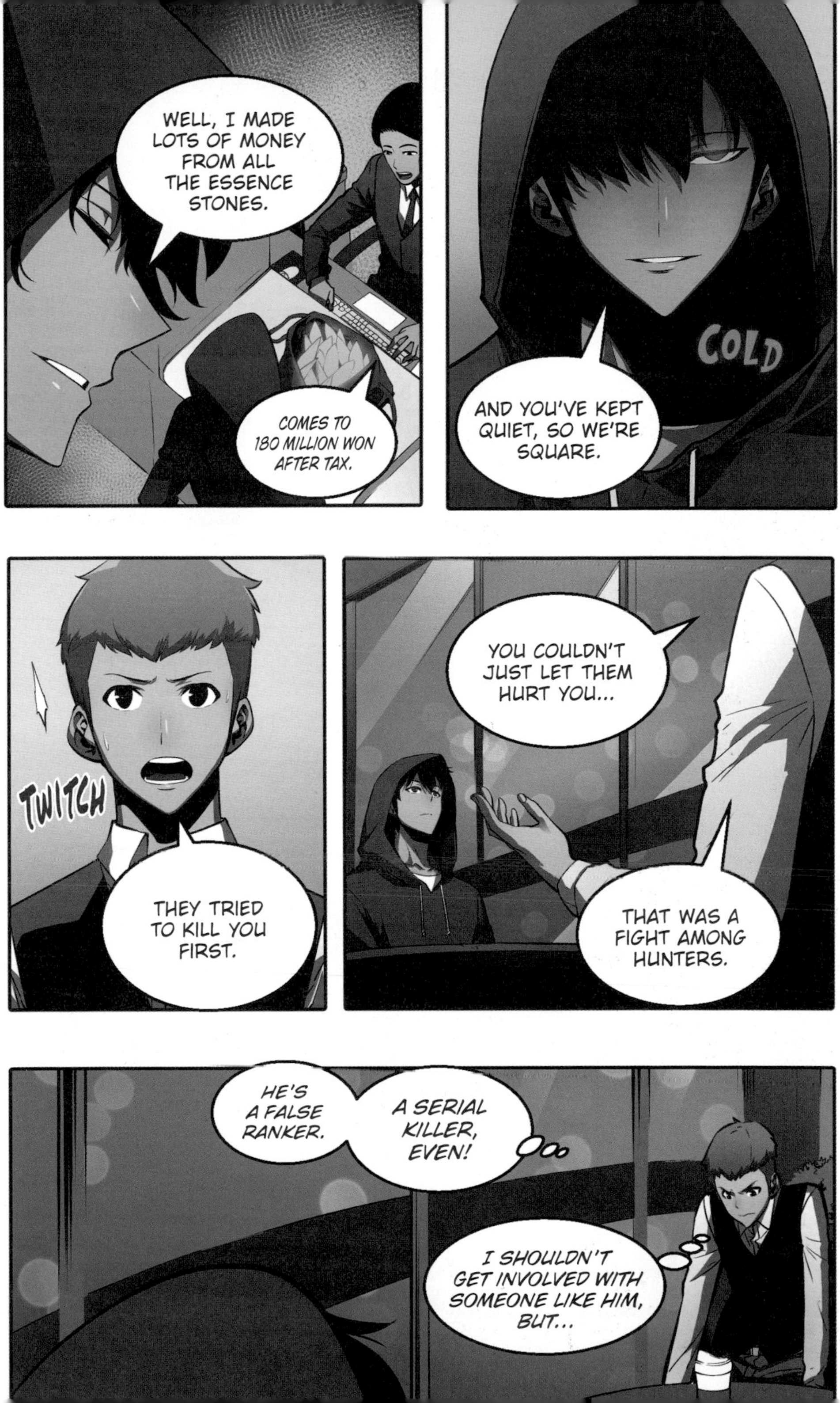
WELL, I MADE LOTS OF MONEY FROM ALL THE ESSENCE STONES.
COMES TO 180 MILLION WON AFTER TAX.
COLD
AND YOU'VE KEPT QUIET, SO WE'RE SQUARE.
TWITCH
THEY TRIED TO KILL YOU FIRST.
YOU COULDN'T JUST LET THEM HURT YOU...
THAT WAS A FIGHT AMONG HUNTERS.
HE'S A FALSE RANKER.
A SERIAL KILLER, EVEN!
I SHOULDN'T GET INVOLVED WITH SOMEONE LIKE HIM, BUT...

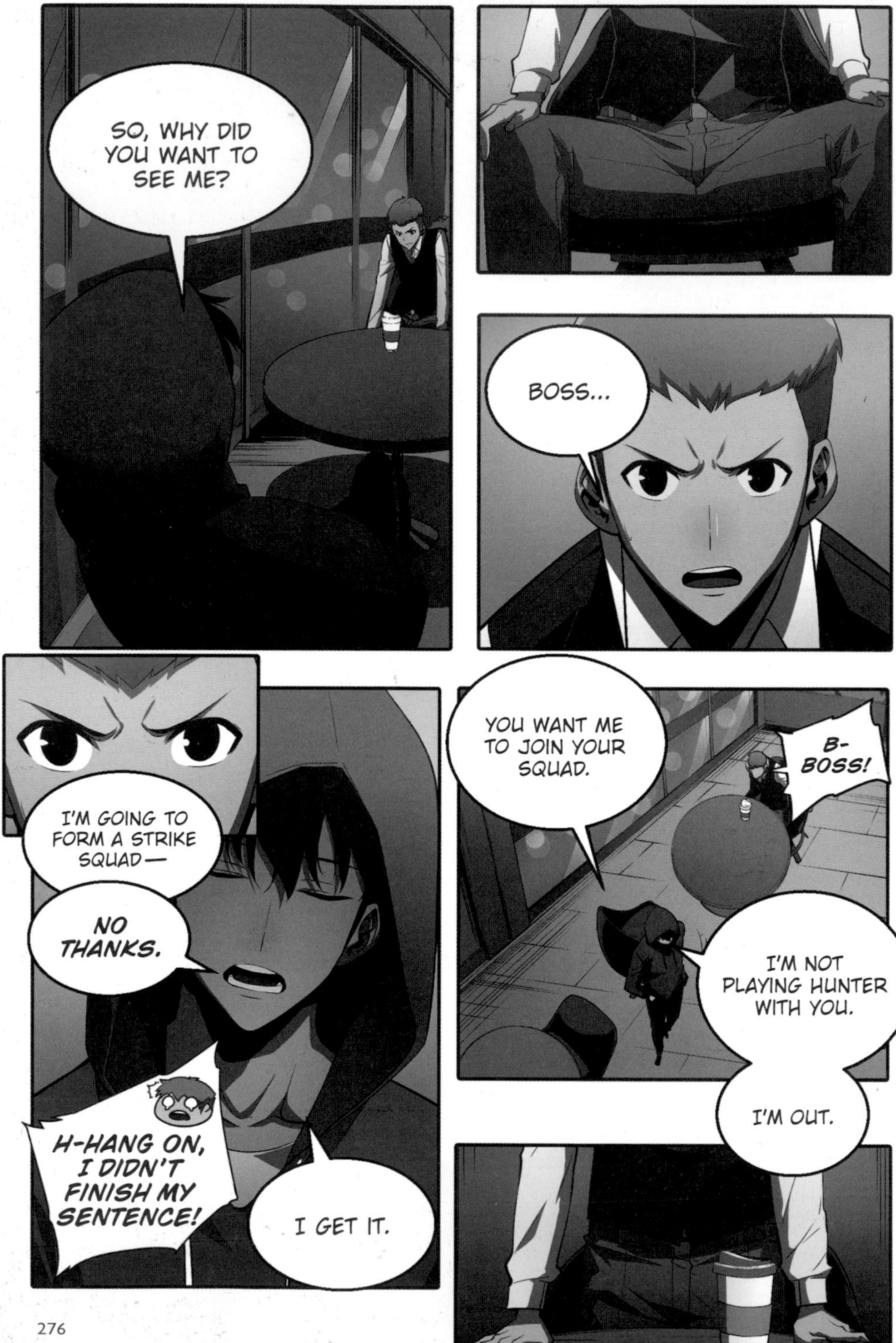
SO, WHY DID YOU WANT TO SEE ME?
BOSS...
I'M GOING TO FORM A STRIKE SQUAD—
NO THANKS.
H-HANG ON, I DIDN'T FINISH MY SENTENCE!
I GET IT.
YOU WANT ME TO JOIN YOUR SQUAD.
B-BOSS!
I'M NOT PLAYING HUNTER WITH YOU.
I'M OUT.

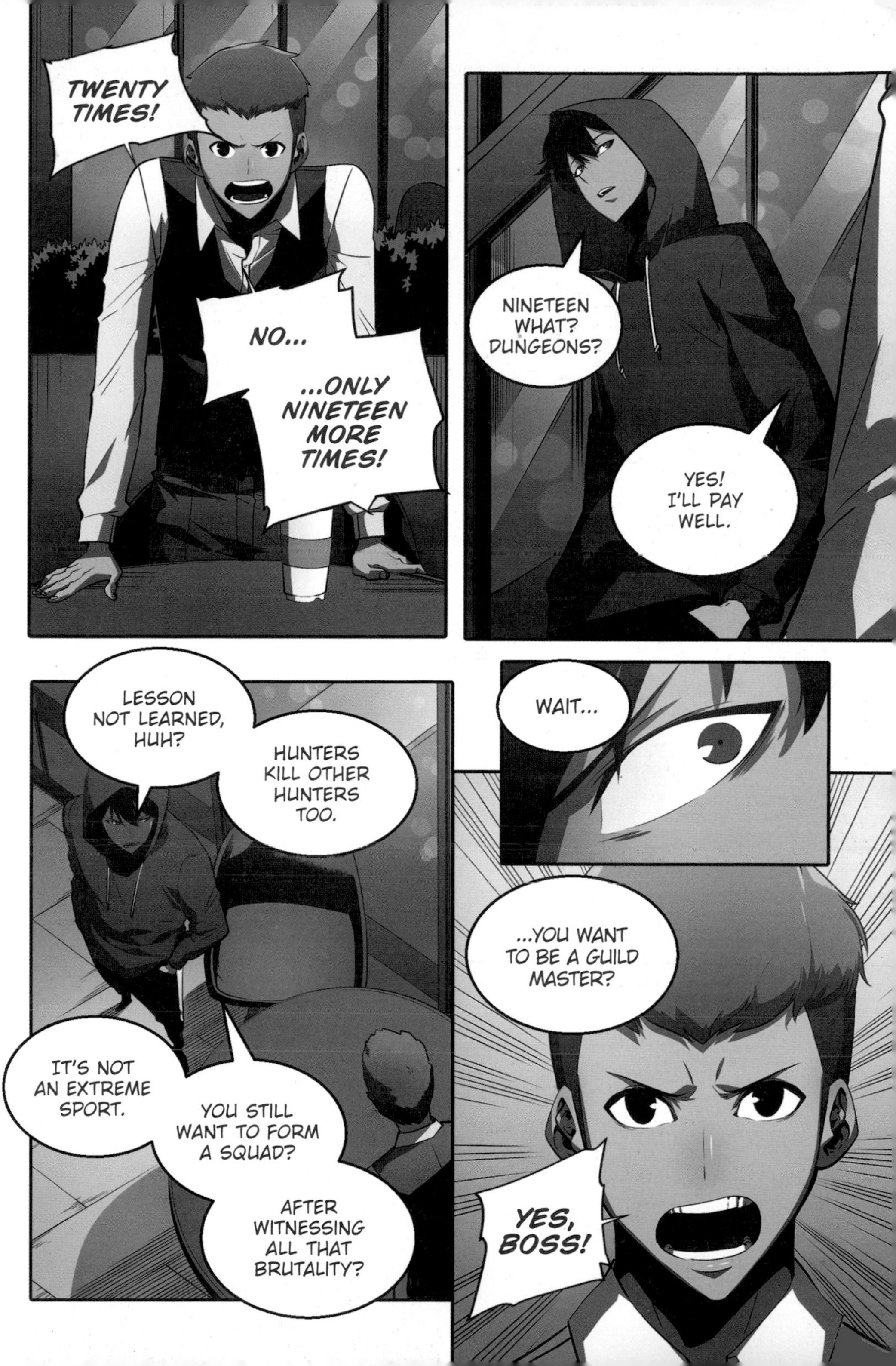
TWENTY TIMES!
NO...
...ONLY NINETEEN MORE TIMES!
NINETEEN WHAT? DUNGEONS?
YES! I'LL PAY WELL.
LESSON NOT LEARNED, HUH?
HUNTERS KILL OTHER HUNTERS TOO.
IT'S NOT AN EXTREME SPORT.
YOU STILL WANT TO FORM A SQUAD?
AFTER WITNESSING ALL THAT BRUTALITY?
WAIT...
...YOU WANT TO BE A GUILD MASTER?
YES, BOSS!

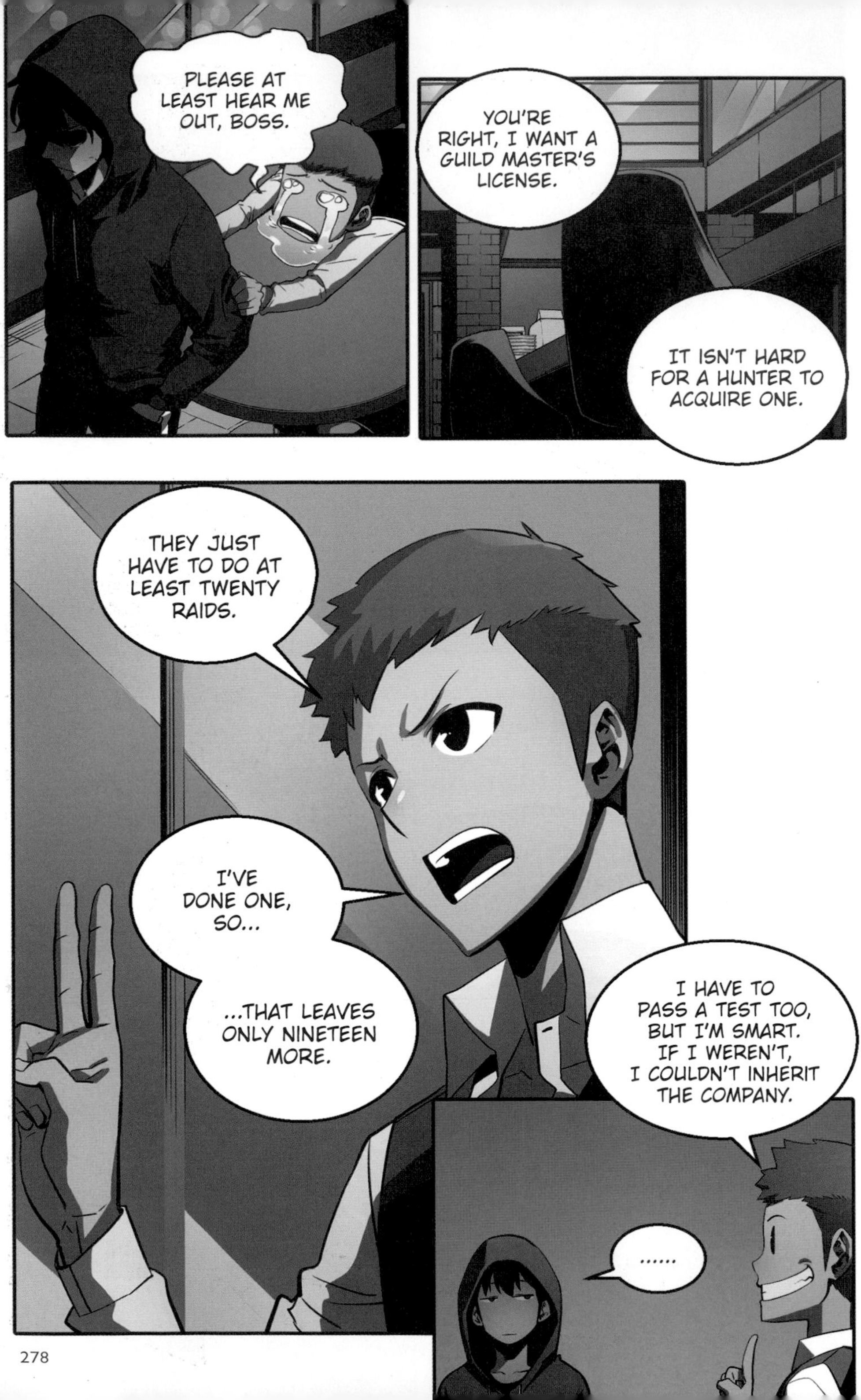
PLEASE AT LEAST HEAR ME OUT, BOSS.
YOU'RE RIGHT, I WANT A GUILD MASTER'S LICENSE.
IT ISN'T HARD FOR A HUNTER TO ACQUIRE ONE.
THEY JUST HAVE TO DO AT LEAST TWENTY RAIDS.
I'VE DONE ONE, SO...
...THAT LEAVES ONLY NINETEEN MORE.
I HAVE TO PASS A TEST TOO, BUT I'M SMART. IF I WEREN'T, I COULDN'T INHERIT THE COMPANY.
......

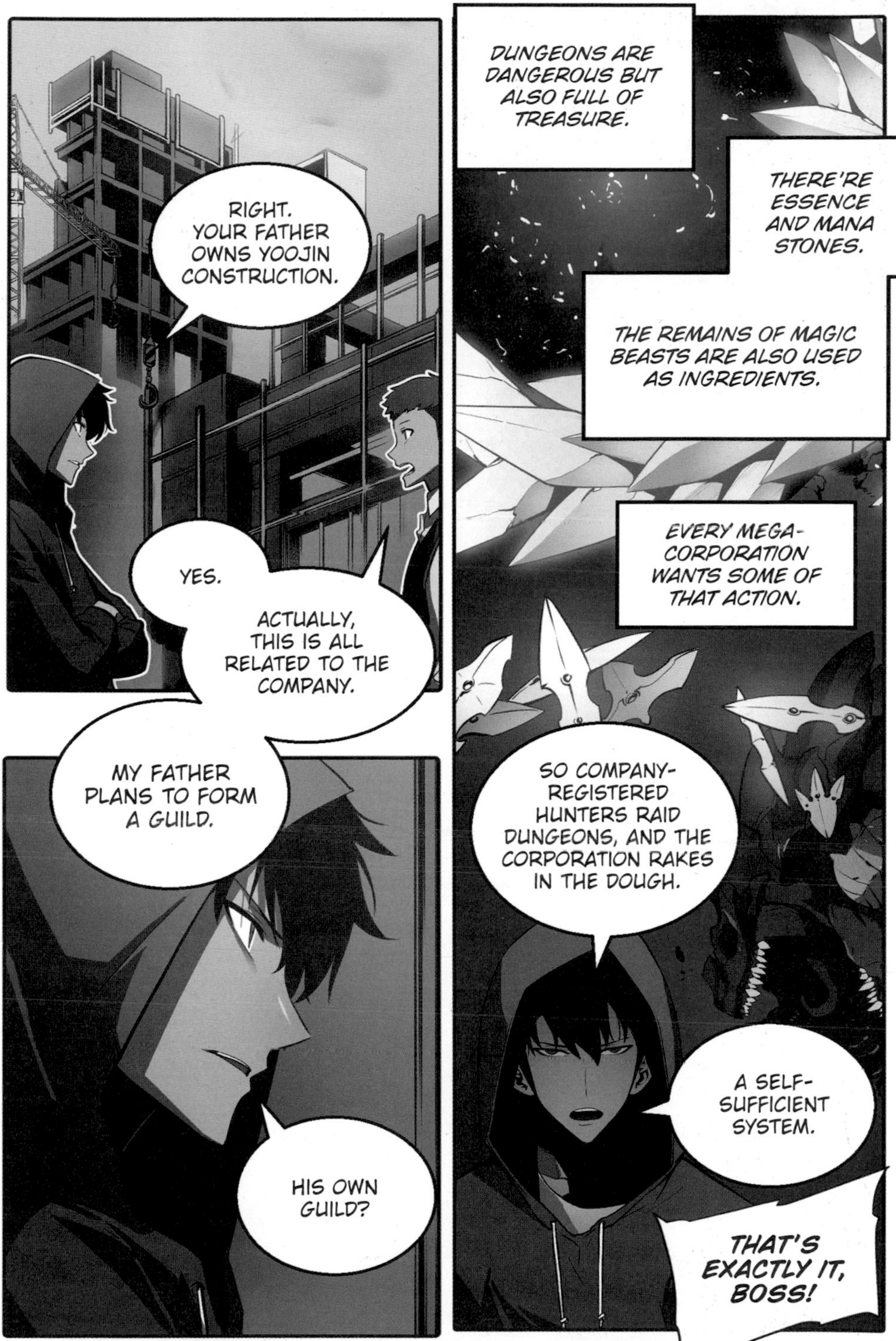
RIGHT. YOUR FATHER OWNS YOOJIN CONSTRUCTION.
YES.
ACTUALLY, THIS IS ALL RELATED TO THE COMPANY.
MY FATHER PLANS TO FORM A GUILD.
HIS OWN GUILD?
DUNGEONS ARE DANGEROUS BUT ALSO FULL OF TREASURE.
THERE'RE ESSENCE AND MANA STONES.
THE REMAINS OF MAGIC BEASTS ARE ALSO USED AS INGREDIENTS.
EVERY MEGA-CORPORATION WANTS SOME OF THAT ACTION.
SO COMPANY-REGISTERED HUNTERS RAID DUNGEONS, AND THE CORPORATION RAKES IN THE DOUGH.
A SELF-SUFFICIENT SYSTEM.
THAT'S EXACTLY IT, BOSS!

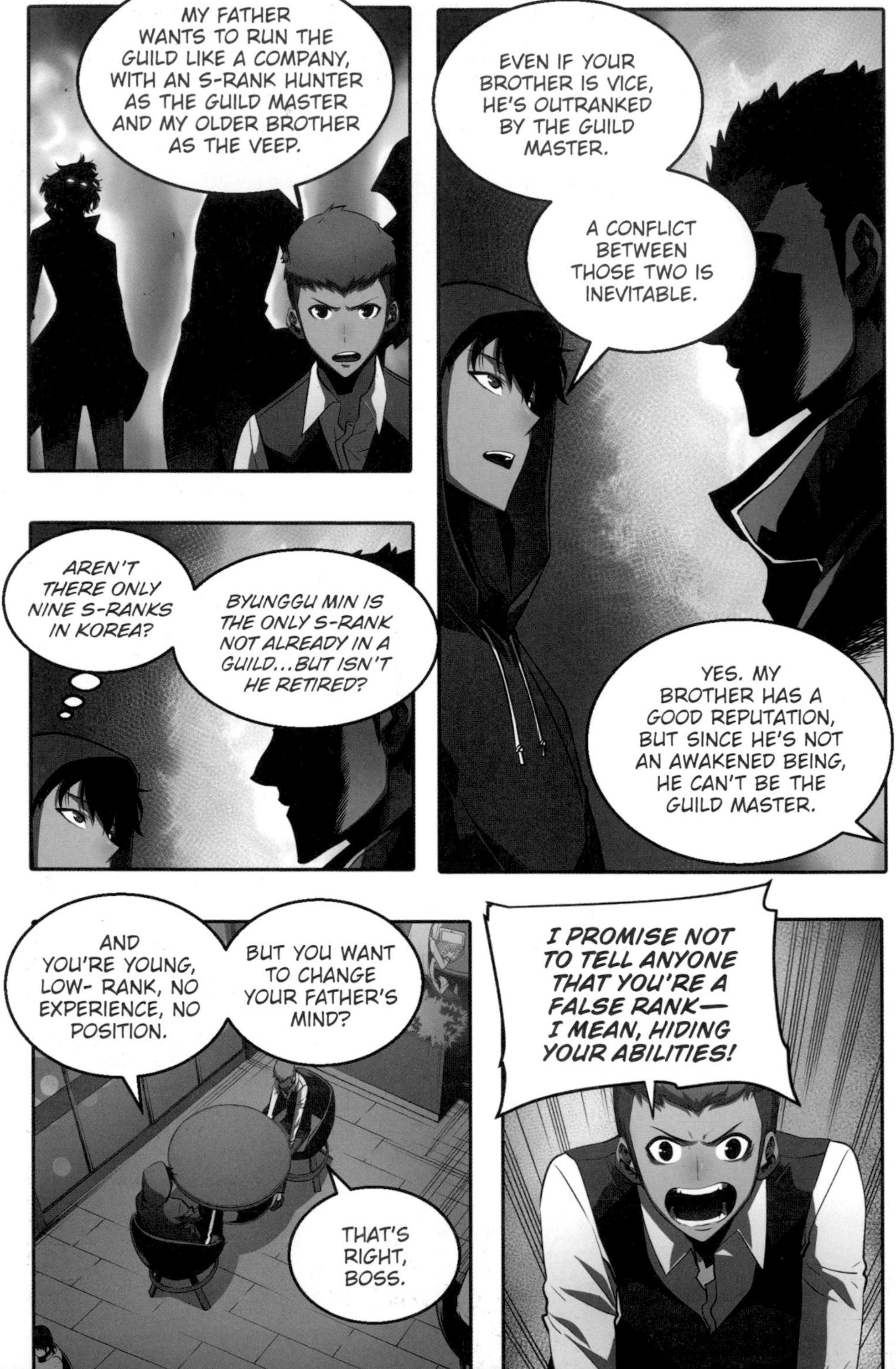
MY FATHER WANTS TO RUN THE GUILD LIKE A COMPANY, WITH AN S-RANK HUNTER AS THE GUILD MASTER AND MY OLDER BROTHER AS THE VEEP.
AREN'T THERE ONLY NINE S-RANKS IN KOREA?
BYUNGGU MIN IS THE ONLY S-RANK NOT ALREADY IN A GUILD...BUT ISN'T HE RETIRED?
EVEN IF YOUR BROTHER IS VICE, HE'S OUTRANKED BY THE GUILD MASTER.
A CONFLICT BETWEEN THOSE TWO IS INEVITABLE.
YES. MY BROTHER HAS A GOOD REPUTATION, BUT SINCE HE'S NOT AN AWAKENED BEING, HE CAN'T BE THE GUILD MASTER.
AND YOU'RE YOUNG, LOW- RANK, NO EXPERIENCE, NO POSITION.
BUT YOU WANT TO CHANGE YOUR FATHER'S MIND?
THAT'S RIGHT, BOSS.
I PROMISE NOT TO TELL ANYONE THAT YOU'RE A FALSE RANK— I MEAN, HIDING YOUR ABILITIES!

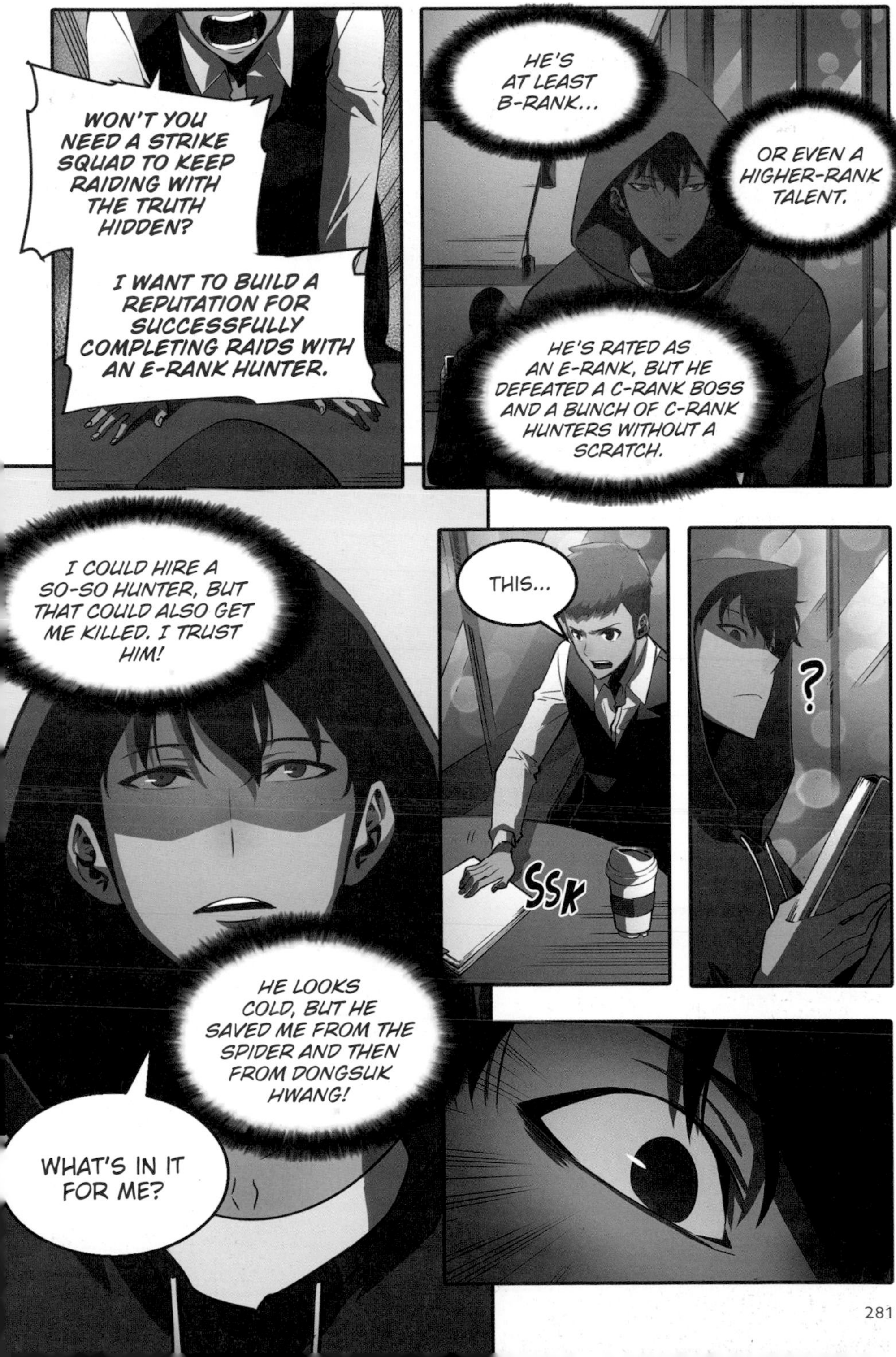

WON'T YOU NEED A STRIKE SQUAD TO KEEP RAIDING WITH THE TRUTH HIDDEN?
I WANT TO BUILD A REPUTATION FOR SUCCESSFULLY COMPLETING RAIDS WITH AN E-RANK HUNTER.
HE'S AT LEAST B-RANK...
OR EVEN A HIGHER-RANK TALENT.
HE'S RATED AS AN E-RANK, BUT HE DEFEATED A C-RANK BOSS AND A BUNCH OF C-RANK HUNTERS WITHOUT A SCRATCH.
I COULD HIRE A SO-SO HUNTER, BUT THAT COULD ALSO GET ME KILLED. I TRUST HIM!
HE LOOKS COLD, BUT HE SAVED ME FROM THE SPIDER AND THEN FROM DONGSUK HWANG!
WHAT'S IN IT FOR ME?
THIS...
SSK
?

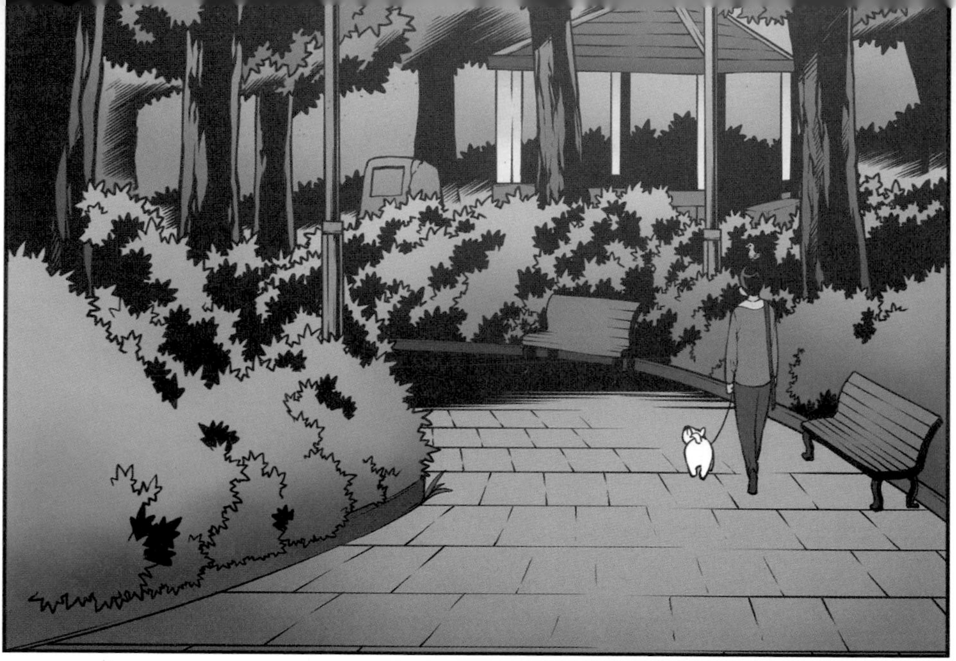

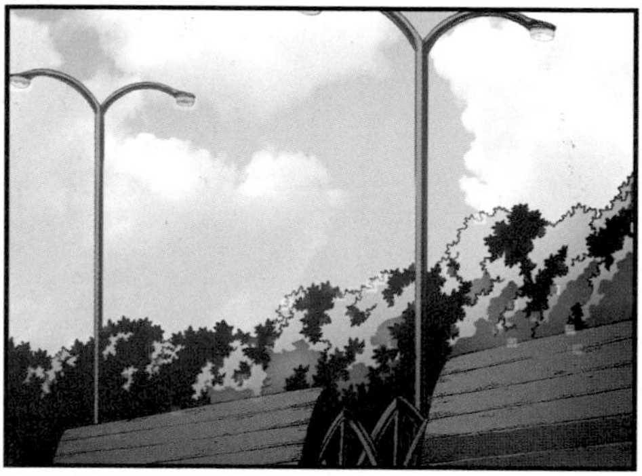

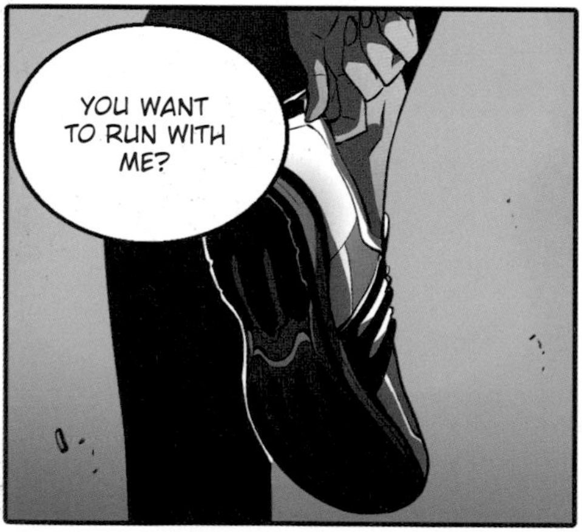
YOU WANT TO RUN WITH ME?

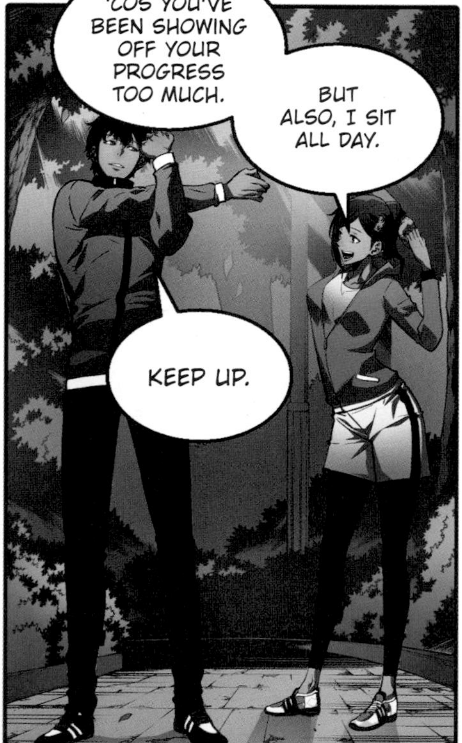
'COS YOU'VE BEEN SHOWING OFF YOUR PROGRESS TOO MUCH.
BUT ALSO, I SIT ALL DAY.
KEEP UP.

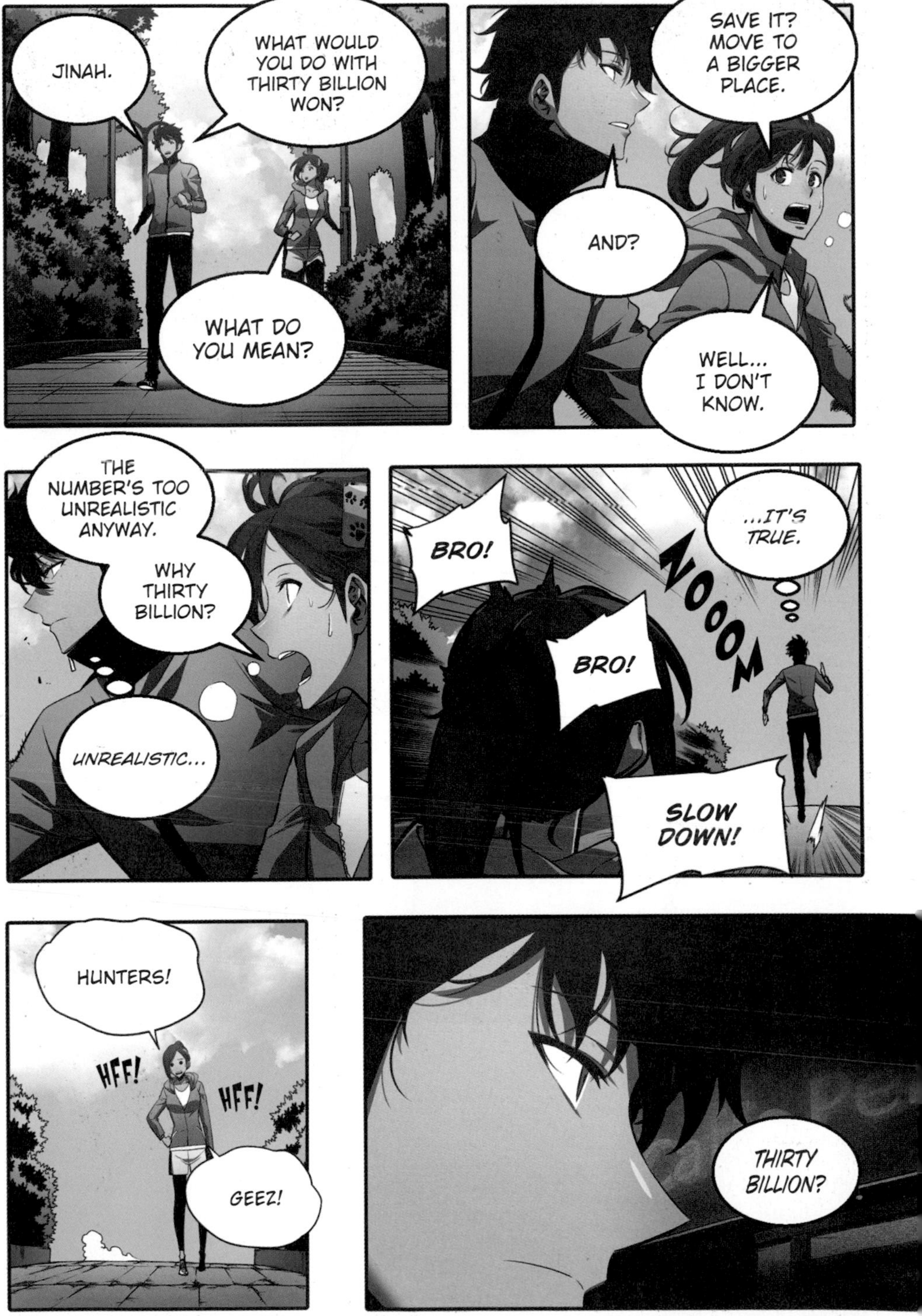
JINAH.
WHAT WOULD YOU DO WITH THIRTY BILLION WON?
WHAT DO YOU MEAN?
SAVE IT? MOVE TO A BIGGER PLACE.
AND?
WELL... I DON'T KNOW.
THE NUMBER'S TOO UNREALISTIC ANYWAY.
WHY THIRTY BILLION?
UNREALISTIC...
BRO!
BRO!
VOOOM
...IT'S TRUE.
SLOW DOWN!
HUNTERS!
HFF!
HFF!
GEEZ!
THIRTY BILLION?

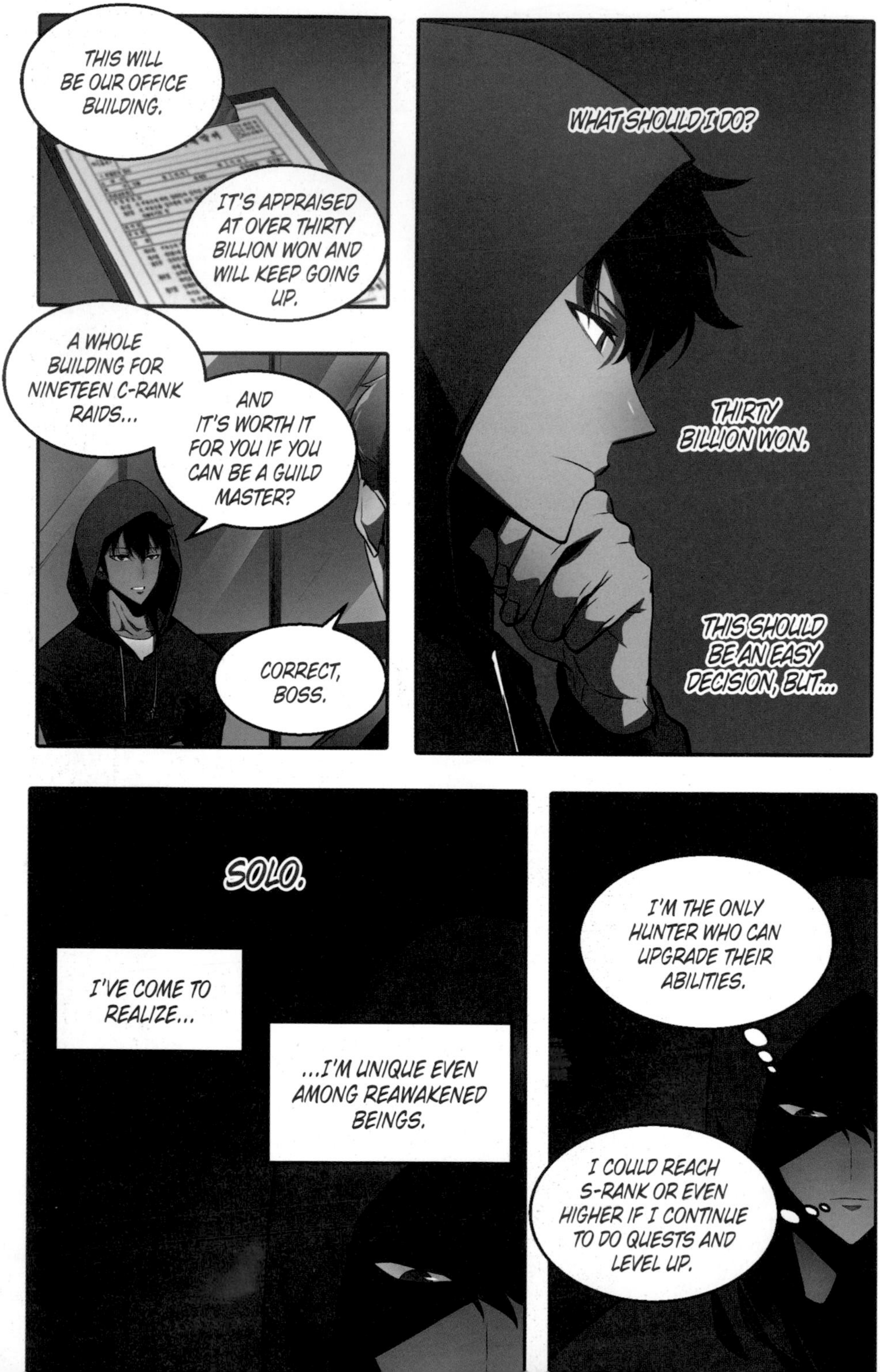
THIS WILL BE OUR OFFICE BUILDING.
IT'S APPRAISED AT OVER THIRTY BILLION WON AND WILL KEEP GOING UP.
A WHOLE BUILDING FOR NINETEEN C-RANK RAIDS...
AND IT'S WORTH IT FOR YOU IF YOU CAN BE A GUILD MASTER?
CORRECT, BOSS.
WHAT SHOULD I DO?
THIRTY BILLION WON.
THIS SHOULD BE AN EASY DECISION, BUT...
SOLO.
I'VE COME TO REALIZE...
...I'M UNIQUE EVEN AMONG REAWAKENED BEINGS.
I'M THE ONLY HUNTER WHO CAN UPGRADE THEIR ABILITIES.
I COULD REACH S-RANK OR EVEN HIGHER IF I CONTINUE TO DO QUESTS AND LEVEL UP.

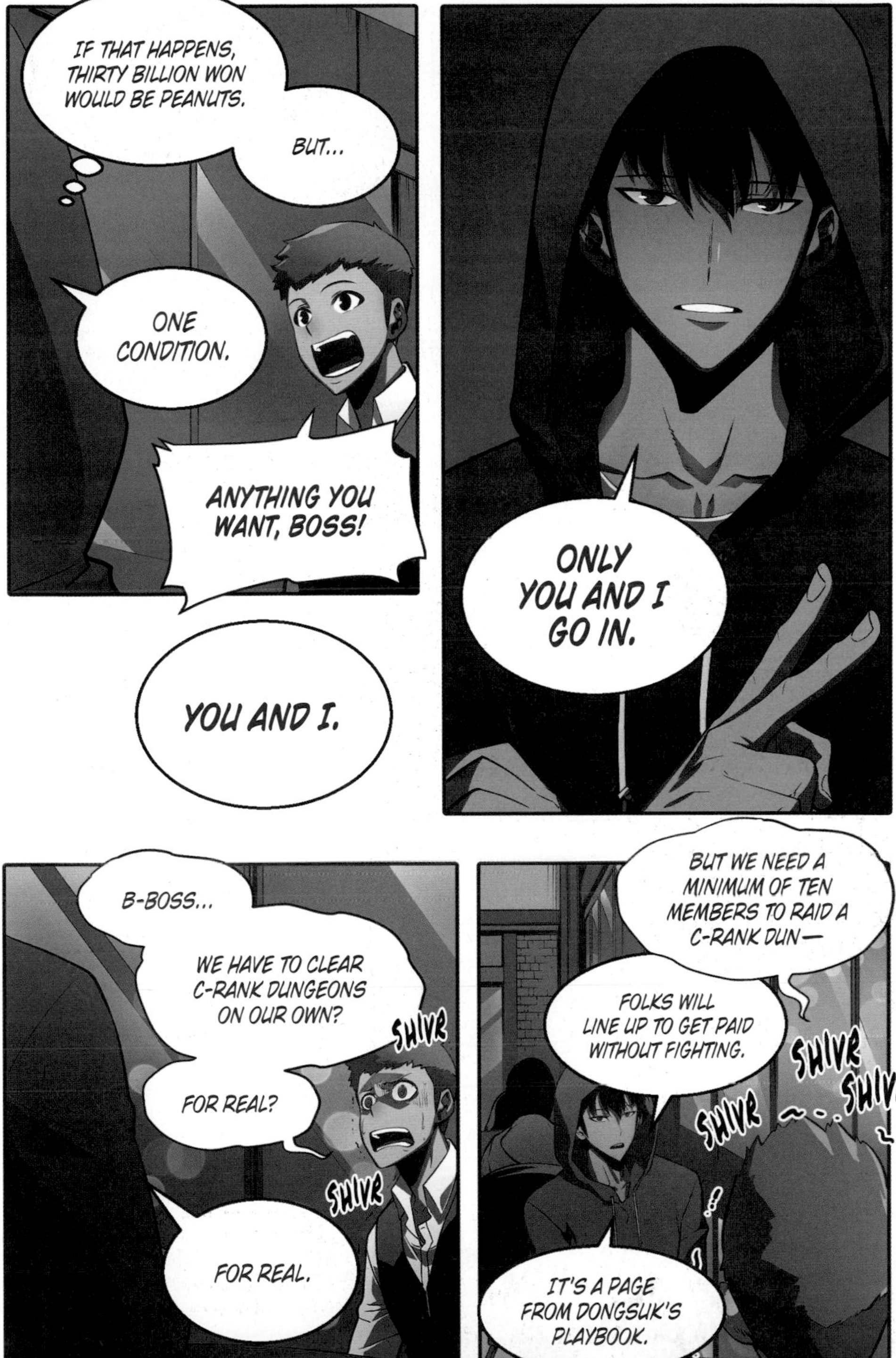
IF THAT HAPPENS, THIRTY BILLION WON WOULD BE PEANUTS.
BUT...
ONE CONDITION.
ANYTHING YOU WANT, BOSS!
ONLY YOU AND I GO IN.
YOU AND I.
B-BOSS...
WE HAVE TO CLEAR C-RANK DUNGEONS ON OUR OWN?
SHIVR
FOR REAL?
SHIVR
FOR REAL.
BUT WE NEED A MINIMUM OF TEN MEMBERS TO RAID A C-RANK DUN—
FOLKS WILL LINE UP TO GET PAID WITHOUT FIGHTING.
SHIVR
SHIVR
SHIVR
!!
IT'S A PAGE FROM DONGSUK'S PLAYBOOK.

WOULDN'T THAT BE TOO DANGEROUS, BOSS?

LOOK AT IT THIS WAY.

NOBODY GETS HURT AS LONG AS NEITHER OF US DOES.

YOU'LL BE KNOWN AS THE "ACCIDENT-FREE SQUAD."

NINETEEN RAIDS WITHOUT ANYONE GETTING HURT.

WON'T THAT MAKE IT EASIER TO PERSUADE YOUR FATHER?

RIGHT...!

LET'S DO THIS, BOSS! I'LL RECRUIT SOME MEMBERS!

PING!

① NOTIFICATION

You have completed
Daily Quest: Strength Training.

OOPS, I GOT LOST IN THOUGHT AND OVERDID IT!

SCRE ECH

Push-ups	[100/100]
Sit-ups	[100/100]
Squats	[100/100]
Running	[11/10km]

WHERE'S JINAH...?

HWOOO

OH WELL.

IT KEEPS COUNTING AFTER I HIT THE GOAL?

Push-ups	[100/100] ✓
Sit-ups	[100/100] ✓
Squats	[100/100] ✓
Running	[11/10km]

WARNING: Failure to complete the daily quest will result in an appropriate penalty.

SHOULD I KEEP GOING UNTIL I MAX OUT?

HUP!

TWENTY MINUTES LATER

Push-ups	[200/100]
Sit-ups	[200/100]
Squats	[200/100]
Running	[11/10km]

IT WON'T GO OVER TWO HUNDRED.

PHEW!

WILL IT BE THE SAME FOR RUNNING TOO?

I CAN'T RUN TWO HUNDRED KILOMETERS, SO LET'S TRY TWENTY.

HFF!

HFF!

UH, BRO?

BRO!!

ZOOOM!

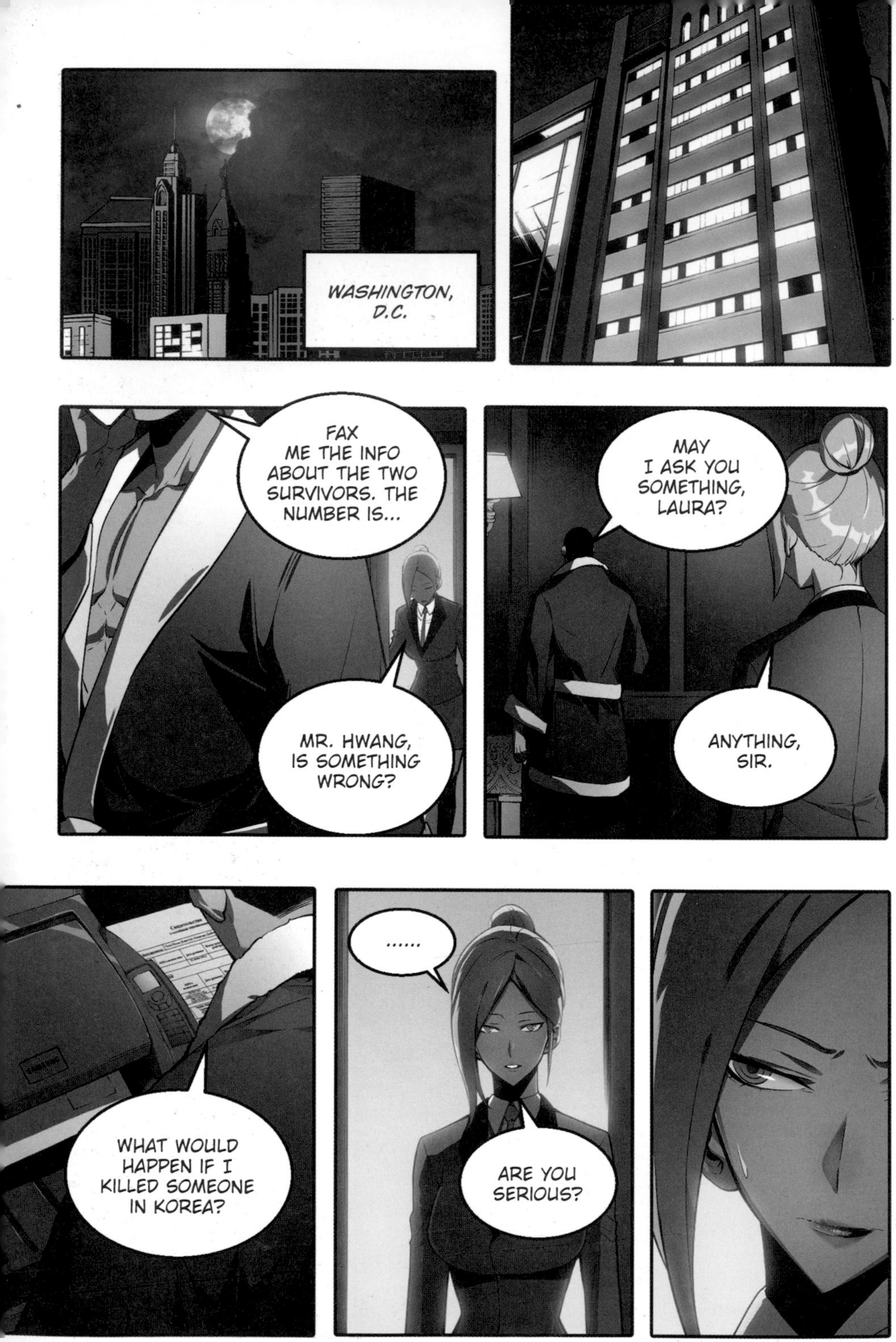
WASHINGTON, D.C.
FAX ME THE INFO ABOUT THE TWO SURVIVORS. THE NUMBER IS...
MR. HWANG, IS SOMETHING WRONG?
MAY I ASK YOU SOMETHING, LAURA?
ANYTHING, SIR.
WHAT WOULD HAPPEN IF I KILLED SOMEONE IN KOREA?
......
ARE YOU SERIOUS?

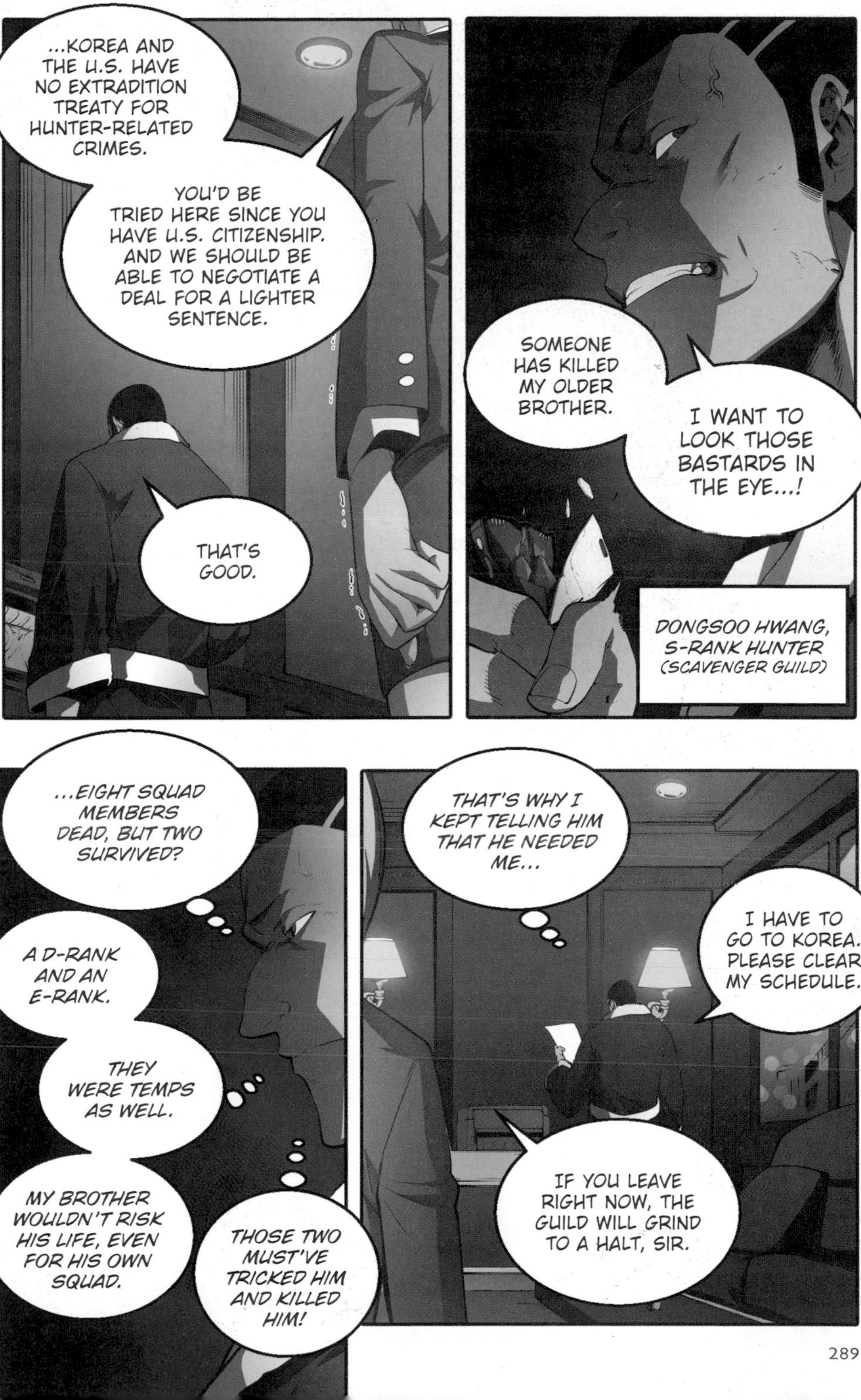
...KOREA AND THE U.S. HAVE NO EXTRADITION TREATY FOR HUNTER-RELATED CRIMES.
YOU'D BE TRIED HERE SINCE YOU HAVE U.S. CITIZENSHIP. AND WE SHOULD BE ABLE TO NEGOTIATE A DEAL FOR A LIGHTER SENTENCE.
THAT'S GOOD.
SOMEONE HAS KILLED MY OLDER BROTHER.
I WANT TO LOOK THOSE BASTARDS IN THE EYE...!
DONGSOO HWANG, S-RANK HUNTER (SCAVENGER GUILD)
...EIGHT SQUAD MEMBERS DEAD, BUT TWO SURVIVED?
A D-RANK AND AN E-RANK.
THEY WERE TEMPS AS WELL.
MY BROTHER WOULDN'T RISK HIS LIFE, EVEN FOR HIS OWN SQUAD.
THOSE TWO MUST'VE TRICKED HIM AND KILLED HIM!
THAT'S WHY I KEPT TELLING HIM THAT HE NEEDED ME...
I HAVE TO GO TO KOREA. PLEASE CLEAR MY SCHEDULE.
IF YOU LEAVE RIGHT NOW, THE GUILD WILL GRIND TO A HALT, SIR.

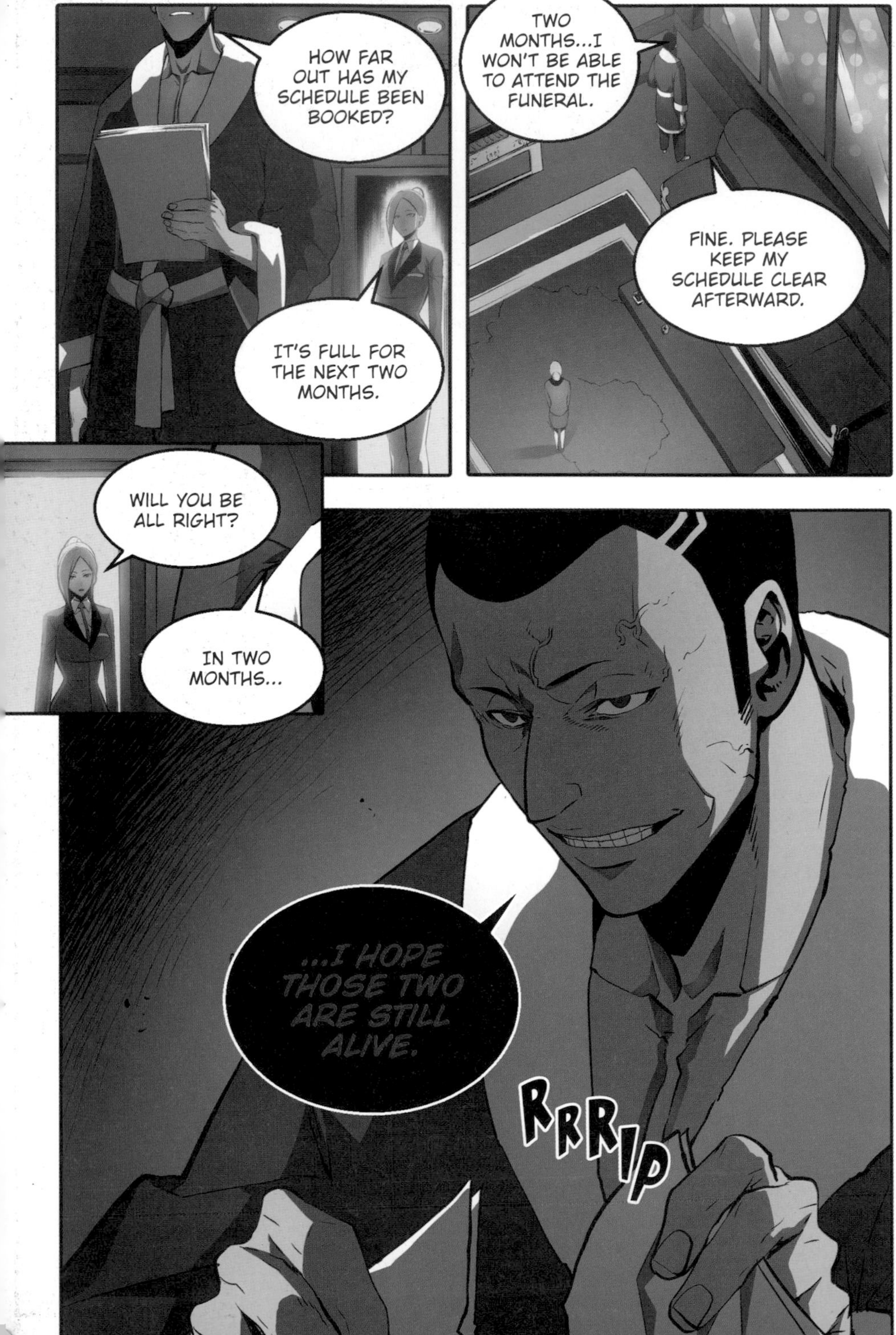
HOW FAR OUT HAS MY SCHEDULE BEEN BOOKED?
IT'S FULL FOR THE NEXT TWO MONTHS.
TWO MONTHS...I WON'T BE ABLE TO ATTEND THE FUNERAL.
FINE. PLEASE KEEP MY SCHEDULE CLEAR AFTERWARD.
WILL YOU BE ALL RIGHT?
IN TWO MONTHS...
...I HOPE THOSE TWO ARE STILL ALIVE.
RRRIP

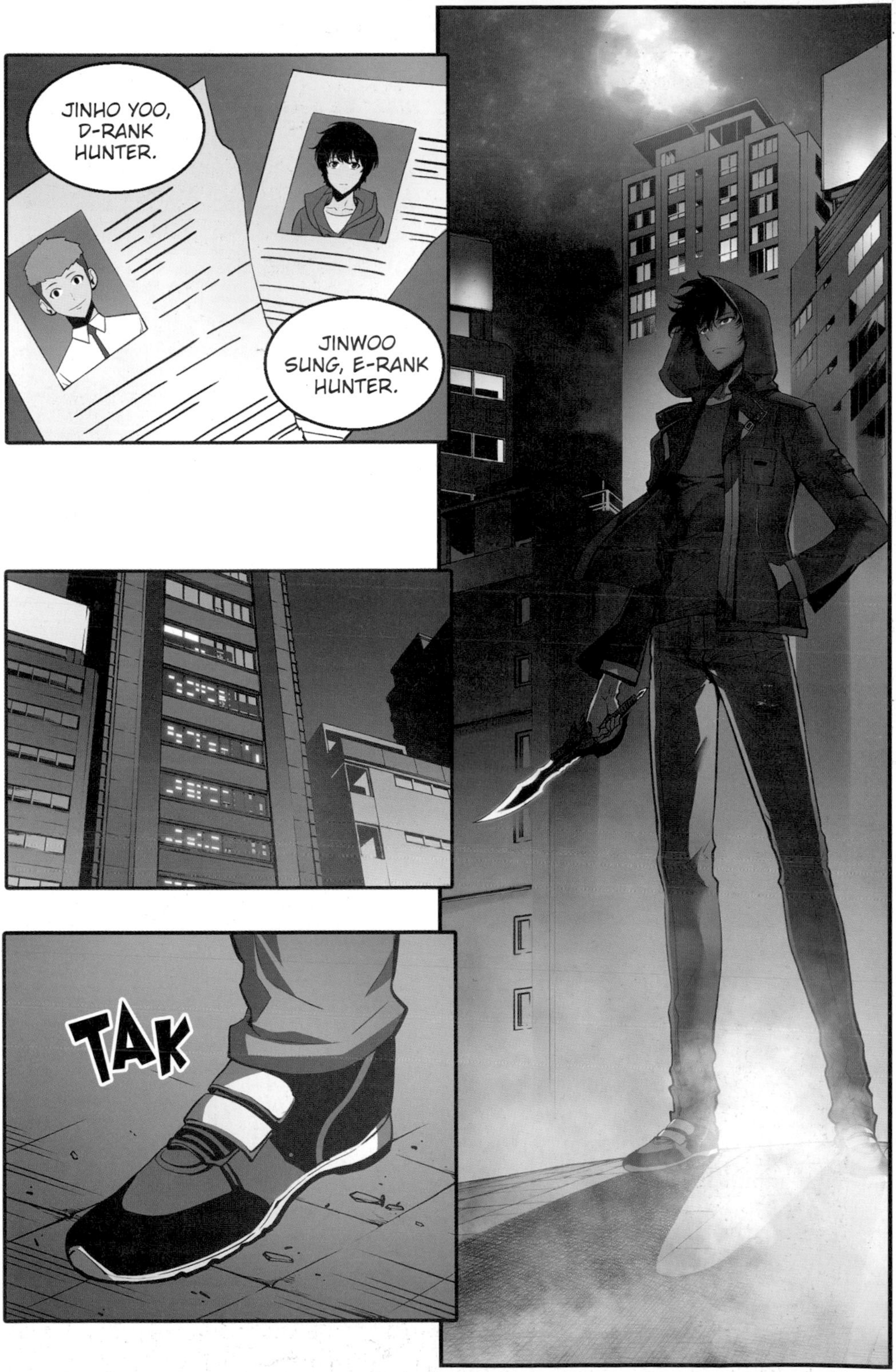
JINHO YOO, D-RANK HUNTER.
JINWOO SUNG, E-RANK HUNTER.
TAK

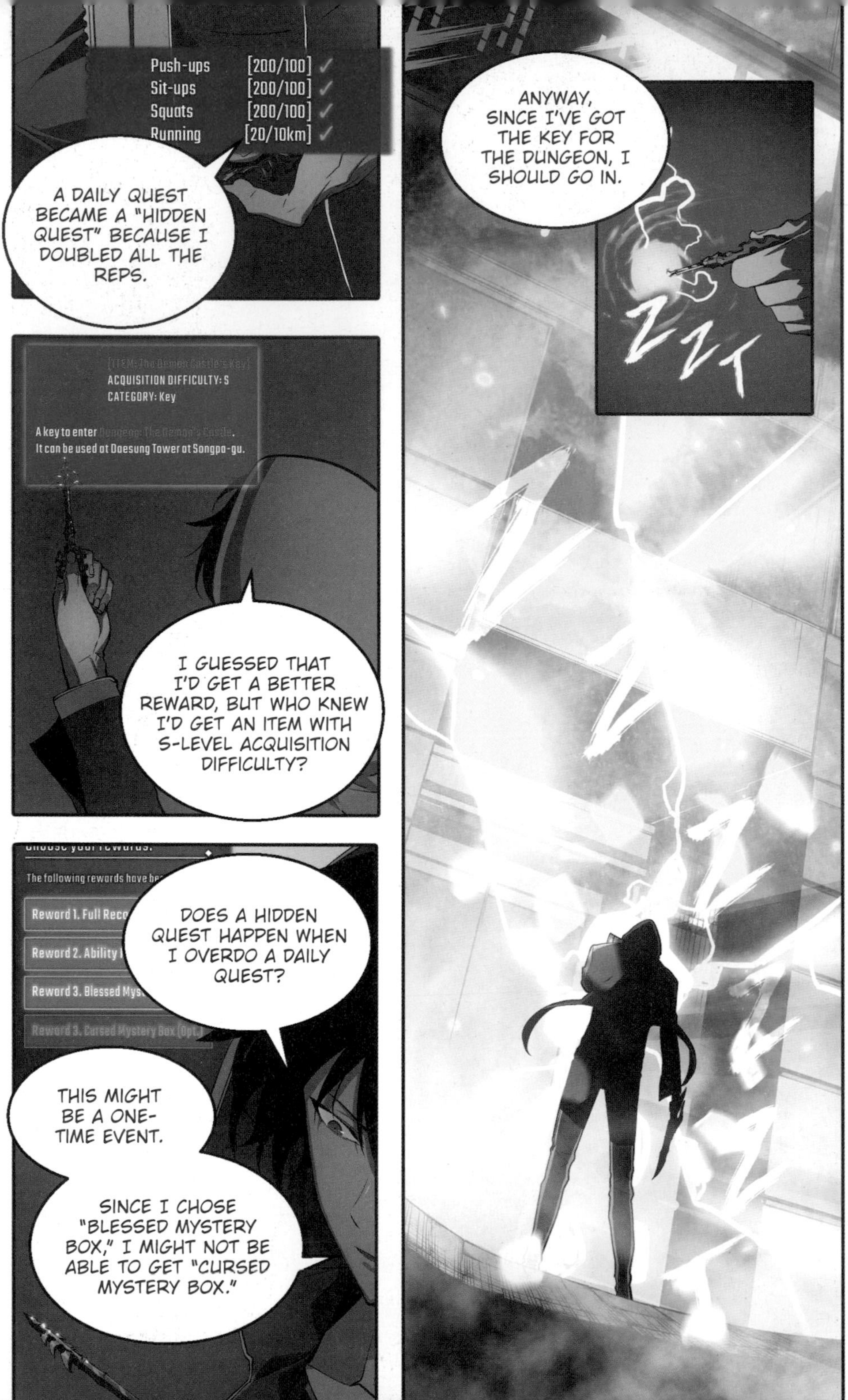

Push-ups [200/100]
Sit-ups [200/100]
Squats [200/100]
Running [20/10km]
A DAILY QUEST BECAME A "HIDDEN QUEST" BECAUSE I DOUBLED ALL THE REPS.
[ITEM: The Demon Castle's Key]
ACQUISITION DIFFICULTY: S
CATEGORY: Key
A key to enter Dungeon: The Demon's Castle.
It can be used at Daesung Tower at Songpa-gu.
I GUESSED THAT I'D GET A BETTER REWARD, BUT WHO KNEW I'D GET AN ITEM WITH S-LEVEL ACQUISITION DIFFICULTY?
The following rewards have be
Reward 1. Full Reco
Reward 2. Ability
Reward 3. Blessed Mys
Reward 3. Cursed Mystery Box (Opt.)
DOES A HIDDEN QUEST HAPPEN WHEN I OVERDO A DAILY QUEST?
THIS MIGHT BE A ONE-TIME EVENT.
SINCE I CHOSE "BLESSED MYSTERY BOX," I MIGHT NOT BE ABLE TO GET "CURSED MYSTERY BOX."
ANYWAY, SINCE I'VE GOT THE KEY FOR THE DUNGEON, I SHOULD GO IN.
ZZZT

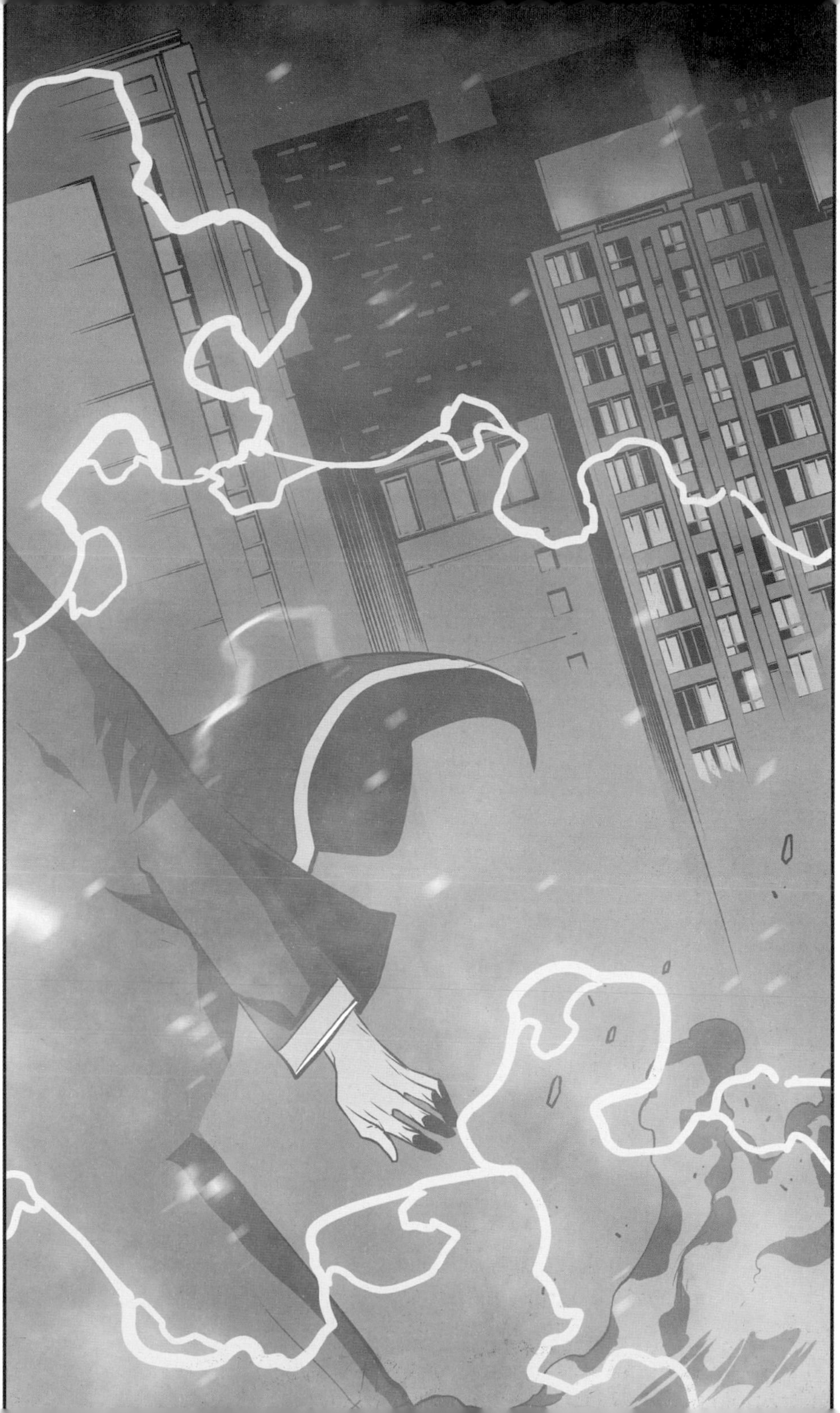

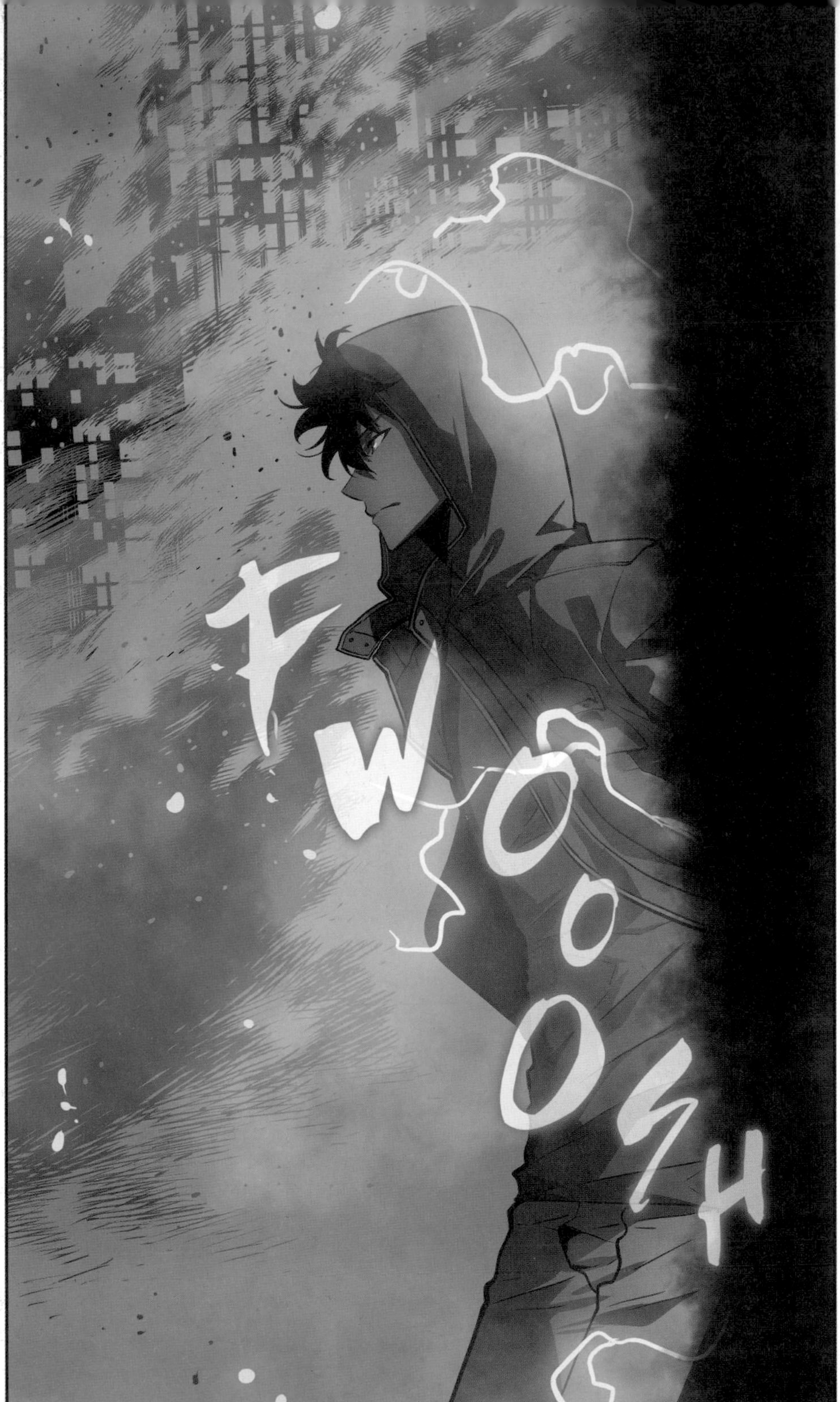
FWOOOSH

IF THE ACQUISITION DIFFICULTY LEVEL MATCHES THE DIFFICULTY LEVEL OF A DUNGEON...

FSHH

FSHH

...THIS DUNGEON IS AN S-RANK!

THERE'S NO WAY I'LL SURVIVE!

FZH

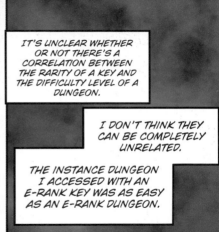

IT'S UNCLEAR WHETHER OR NOT THERE'S A CORRELATION BETWEEN THE RARITY OF A KEY AND THE DIFFICULTY LEVEL OF A DUNGEON.

I DON'T THINK THEY CAN BE COMPLETELY UNRELATED.

THE INSTANCE DUNGEON I ACCESSED WITH AN E-RANK KEY WAS AS EASY AS AN E-RANK DUNGEON.

IF I'M IN DANGER, I CAN USE THE TELEPORTATION STONE I GOT FROM THE LAST INSTANCE DUNGEON.

ALL I CAN DO NOW IS MY BEST.

FROM NOW ON, IT'S ONLY ME AND JINHO CLEARING C-RANK DUNGEONS.

TAK

TAK

IN ORDER TO DO THAT, I NEED TO KNOW WHAT I'M CAPABLE OF.

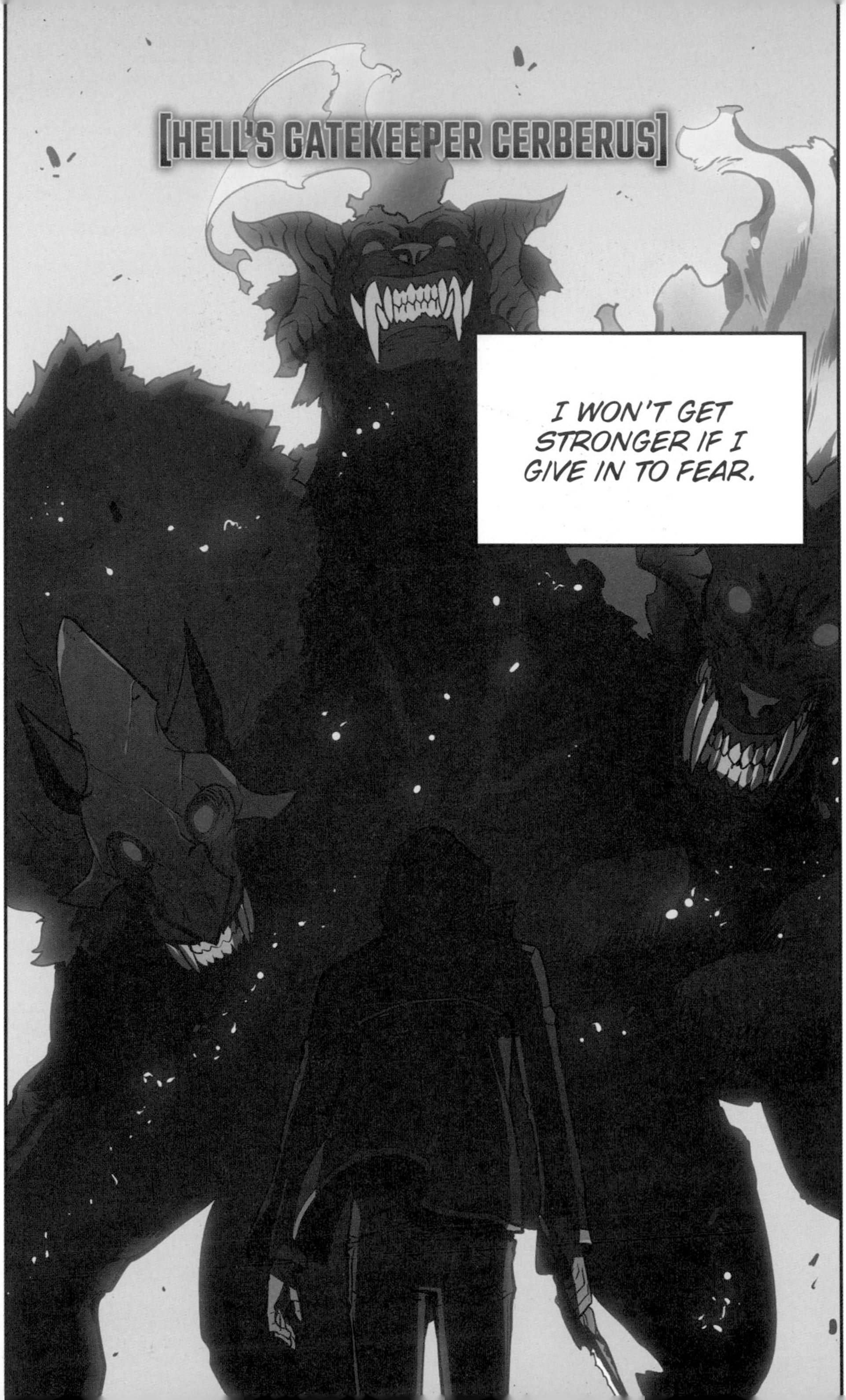
[HELL'S GATEKEEPER CERBERUS]
I WON'T GET STRONGER IF I GIVE IN TO FEAR.

GET STRONGER AND...

NOPE. I'M NOT DYING HERE.

...LEVEL UP!

TO BE CONTINUED IN VOLUME 3...

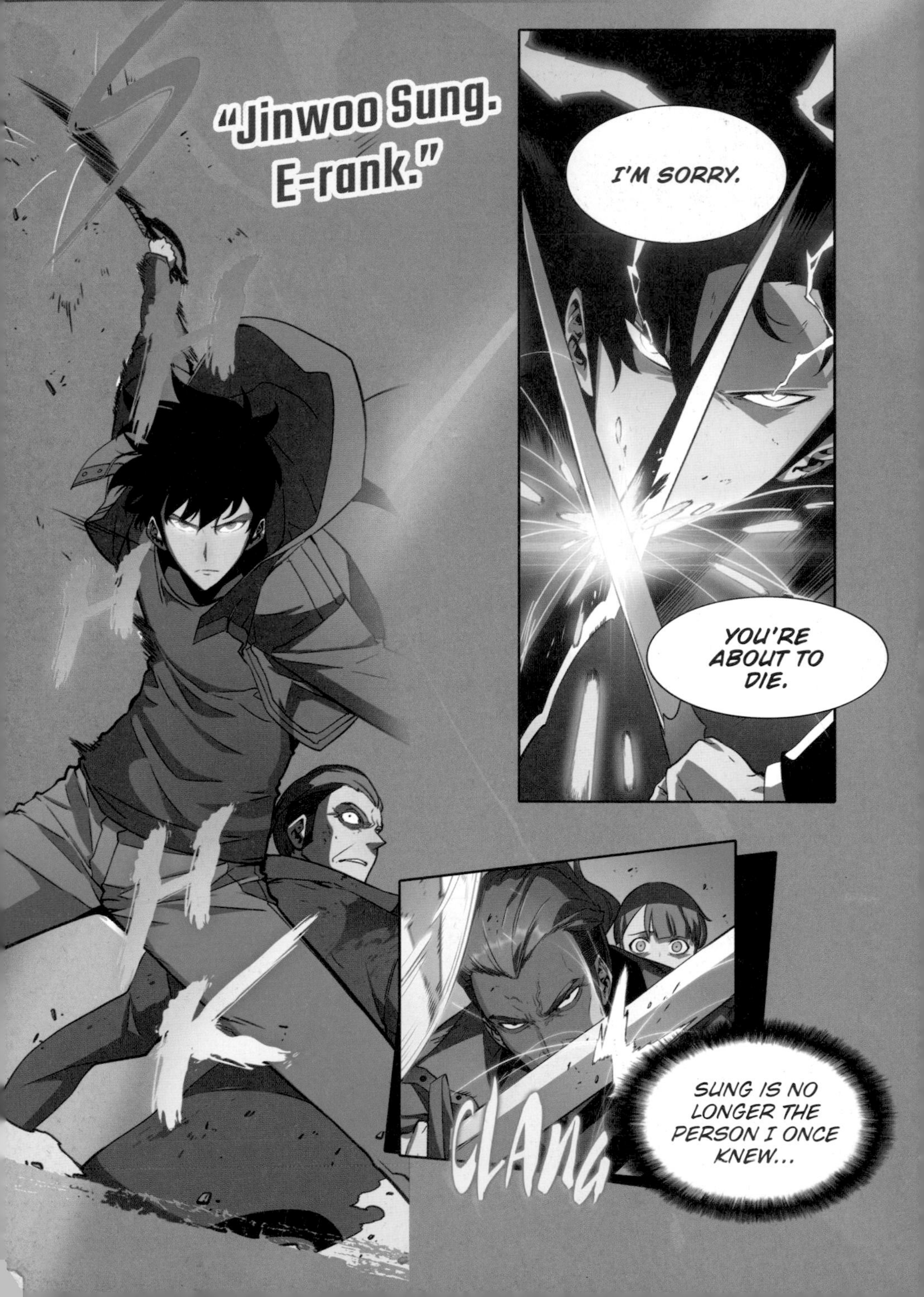
"Jinwoo Sung. E-rank."
I'M SORRY.
YOU'RE ABOUT TO DIE.
CLANG
SUNG IS NO LONGER THE PERSON I ONCE KNEW...

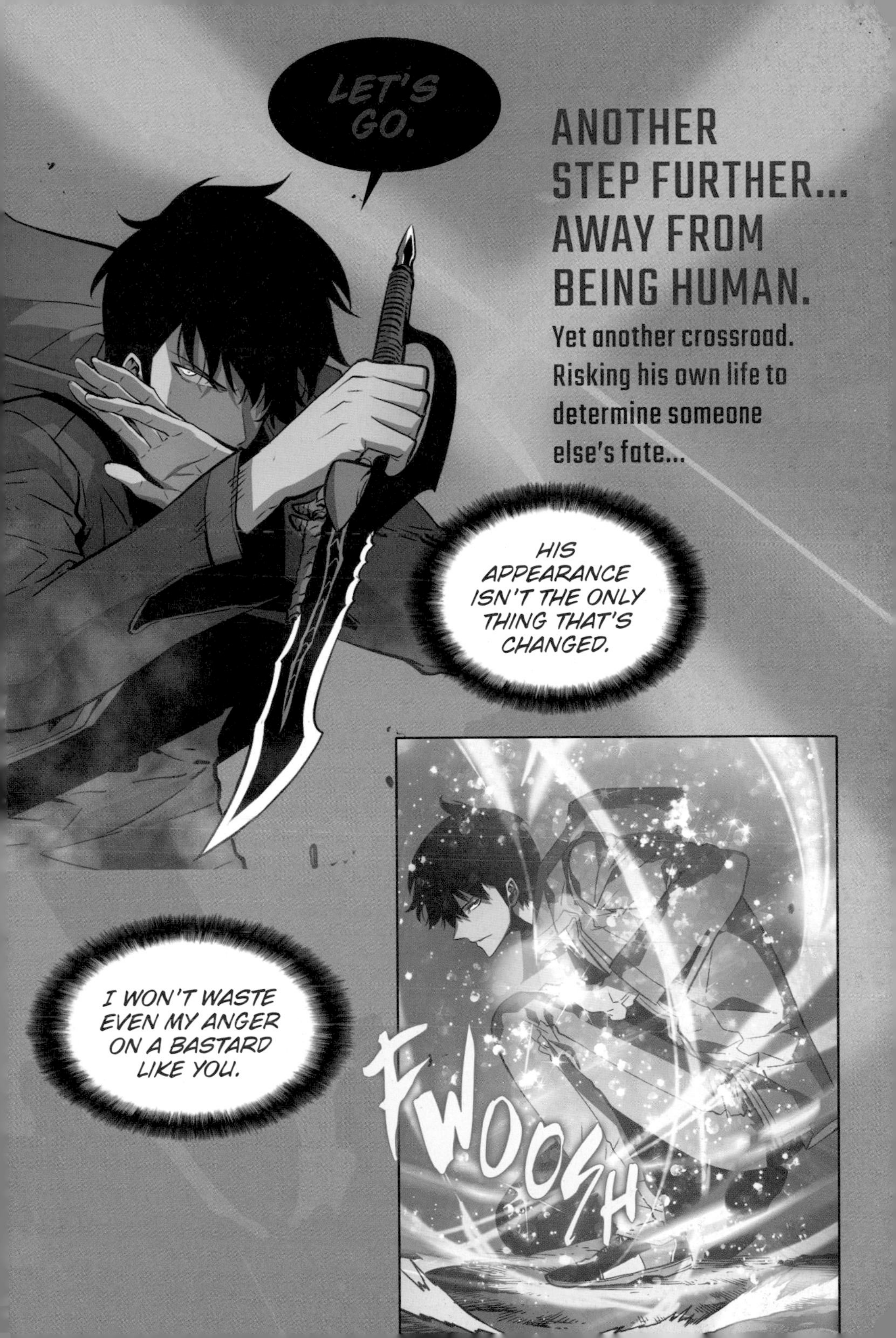
LET'S GO.
ANOTHER STEP FURTHER... AWAY FROM BEING HUMAN.
Yet another crossroad. Risking his own life to determine someone else's fate...
HIS APPEARANCE ISN'T THE ONLY THING THAT'S CHANGED.
I WON'T WASTE EVEN MY ANGER ON A BASTARD LIKE YOU.
FWOOSH

READ THE NOVEL WHERE IT ALL BEGAN!

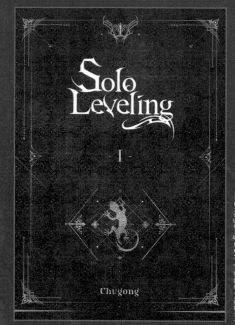

© Chugong 2017 / D&C MEDIA

SOLO LEVELING

E-rank hunter Jinwoo Sung has no money, no talent, and no prospects to speak of—and apparently, no luck, either! When he enters a hidden double dungeon one fateful day, he's abandoned by his party and left to die at the hands of some of the most horrific monsters he's ever encountered. But just before the last, fatal blow...

PING!
[CONGRATULATIONS ON BECOMING A PLAYER.]

VOLUME 1 AVAILABLE WHEREVER BOOKS ARE SOLD!

Solo
Leveling

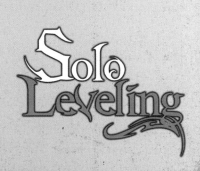

SOLO LEVELING

DUBU
(REDICE STUDIO)

2

ORIGINAL STORY
CHUGONG

Translation: Hye Young Im ◆ Rewrite: J. Torres ◆ Lettering: Abigail Blackman

SOLO LEVELING Volume 2
© DUBU(REDICE STUDIO), Chugong 2018 / D&C WEBTOON Biz
All rights reserved.
First published in Korea in 2018 by D&C WEBTOON Biz Co., Ltd.

English translation © 2021 by Yen Press, LLC

Yen Press
150 West 30th Street, 19th Floor
New York, NY 10001

Visit us at yenpress.com
facebook.com/yenpress
twitter.com/yenpress
yenpress.tumblr.com
instagram.com/yenpress

First Yen Press Edition: June 2021

Yen Press is an imprint of Yen Press, LLC.
The Yen Press name and logo are trademarks of Yen Press, LLC.

The publisher is not responsible for websites (or their content) that are not owned by the publisher.

Library of Congress Control Number: 2020950228

ISBNs: 978-1-9753-1945-8 (paperback)
978-1-9753-1946-5 (ebook)

10 9 8 7 6 5

TPA

Printed in South Korea